Change of State

Change of State

Information, Policy, and Power

Sandra Braman

The MIT Press
Cambridge, Massachusetts
London, England

First MIT Press paperback edition, 2009

This book was set in Sabon on 3B2 by Asco Typesetters, Hong Kong.

Library of Congress Cataloging-in-Publication Data

Braman, Sandra.
Change of state : information, policy, and power / Sandra Braman.
p. cm.
Includes bibliographical references and index.
ISBN-13: 978-0-262-02597-3 (hc. : alk. paper)—978-0-262-51324-1 (pb. : alk. paper)
1. Information policy—United States. I. Title.

JK468.S4B73 2006
303.48′330973—dc22 2006043344

In memoriam
Donald W. Braman
1917–2005

The fast runner
runs ever faster
into the future
in search of
present records

—Douglas Woolf, *John-Juan*

Contents

Detailed Contents

Tables

Tables

Preface

Digital technologies—meta-technologies—are qualitatively different from industrial technologies because they vastly multiply the degrees of freedom with which we can interact with each other and with the material world. This increase in flexibility and capacity has altered the nature of power, the economy, knowledge, and how we come together in groups and communities in order to act. As we try to understand the nature of our political lives in this environment, we face three sets of questions.

The first to have appeared chronologically, and still the first in terms of the amount of attention it is receiving, is how to interpret, adapt, amend, or replace existing laws and regulations so that we can achieve enduring social and political goals under these new, and still changing, conditions. These are important issues, but the law is not of interest for its own sake; we care about the law because it shapes the world in which we live, creating the conditions under which we speak with each other and live together. A second set of questions, therefore, deals with what changes in the law mean for the conditions of our daily lives. Since the law is no more autonomously deterministic of society than are technologies, this question can be phrased as follows: What are we doing to ourselves?

Efforts to address each of these two sets of questions show such marked changes in the ways laws and regulations are being used and the effects of those uses that a third set of questions comes into view. What is the nature of government in the deeply informatized world of the twenty-first century?

Information policy—law and policy for information creation, processing, flows, and use—is at the conjuncture of all three sets of questions. It is the subject of a great deal of debate, experimentation, litigation, and legislation within the legal system. Information policy fundamentally shapes the conditions within which we undertake all other political, social, cultural, and economic activity. And it is information policy that is the legal domain through which the government wields the most important form of power in today's world, informational power.

This book offers a theoretical and conceptual framework for thinking about the world within which information policy operates and toward which it is directed. It then populates that framework, bringing together under a common analytical lens laws and regulations from across the entire terrain of government. Looking at commonalities in these trends as they appear in places otherwise conceptually distant makes it possible to understand transformations in individual and state identity, social structures, system borders, and relationships with change processes themselves.

Evidence that comes to light in pursuit of these three sets of questions makes clear that the state itself has undergone parametric change. The bureaucratic welfare state has been succeeded by a new form of government, the informational state.

Note on Text

It is both the curse and the pleasure of interdisciplinary work that it requires immersion in multiple different literatures. Of course one hopes the final product does not betray the conceptual, empirical, and logistical complexities along the way. The goal here is to maximize the readability of the text, while simultaneously referencing the diverse literatures that provide support for the arguments presented. Thus the structure of the book is threefold. The narrative itself does not include references, though it does from time to time name specific individuals whose work has been so overwhelmingly influential that I believe everyone should be familiar with these authors. The narrative is followed by extensive bibliographic essays, organized by chapter and topic within chapter, discussing the literatures upon which I depended and including citations to many more specific works. Finally, there is a complete reference list in standard format with every author included in both the text and the bibliographic essays.

Acknowledgments

In 1969, Larry Miller, the Harvard minister who performed my older brother's wedding, asked at the reception what I was interested in pursuing. When I answered, "how traditional cultural forms might survive under today's technological conditions," he suggested I might be interested in reading Jacques Ellul. I would give the same answer to that question today, though perhaps more elaborately: to "cultural forms" I would add "and the unique relations with the human and natural environment that they enable." And to the definition of "traditional," in the early twenty-first century, I would add the life practices and freedoms that seemed so familiar and enduring in our own lifetimes, just a short time ago, that today appear to be threatened or are already unavailable. The minister was right. Ellul was indeed useful, as were other philosophers of technology to whom his work led. But while I started my reading in this area at that time, other paths were also followed en route to addressing the problem. It has been a long ride.

Knowing that poetry embodies our deepest forms of knowledge, I turned there first. "Embodies," not "codifies" and not "embeds," for the job of poetry is to offer the affordances for the paths along which both tacit and codified knowledge might ultimately go. Our richest stores of knowledge come from the most ancient of stories; reading and listening ultimately led to praxis as first a storyteller and then a performance artist. Here Homer and Rav Nachman of Bratslav must be acknowledged, along with Albert B. Lord for his *The Singer of Tales*, which helped me understand how and why the oldest stories are constantly told anew in ever-changing, and ever-the-same, form, and Bob Dylan for demonstrating the same.

On the other hand, it meant turning to contemporary writers and poetic practice. While Douglas Woolf was not the first encountered among those to have an enduring influence, certainly his was the deepest and most expansive; it was Doug with whom I experienced the real wildernesses of the mind, of society, and of the natural world ("out and out, out and out"). Others whose impact was profound, some in person and some in print, include William Carlos Williams ("No ideas but in things"), Charles Olson ("I have had to learn the simplest things last"), Ed Dorn ("apparently, we wobble"), Robert Creeley ("for love"), and Denise Levertov for demonstrating how to climb Jacob's ladder. Some of my own stories and poems remain littered about, though most of the oral performances were, upon insistence, not recorded.

The driving question, and the general task—large-scale pattern recognition—remained the same when I entered academia, though the modes of argument and of investigation changed. The question did, however, become more focused, on the problem of how to conceptualize the information policy environment in such a way that it might be possible to continue to protect traditional values under contemporary conditions. Now the acknowledgments become more familiar: to Ted Glasser, Jerry Kline, and Don Gillmor, for encouraging me to pursue my research interest despite its unfamiliarity. To Anne Wells Branscomb, for early and sustained support from someone who understood very well the nature of the problem. To Harlan Cleveland, for increasing my sophistication regarding just how the question looked to those with political power. To John Nerone, for appreciation of the vertigo of history and company along the way. To Loy Singleton, for graciousness and constancy of support, and to Rob Potter for the joys of discovery. To Steve Wildman, for acting on the belief that wherever my mind took me, it was worth going. To those whose conversations—whether singular or many, brief or sustained—provided the food: Michele Jackson, Fred Wasser, Thomas Malaby, Marwan Kraidy, Paul Gandel, Kandice Salomone, Linda Garcia, James Carey, Mark Levy, Terhi Rantanen, David Levy, Colin Sparks, Yacov Shamir, Michal Shamir, Brian Kahin, Robin Mansell, Eli Noam, Geoffrey Bowker, Christo van Staden, Pat Aufderheide, Michael Joyce, Johanna Drucker, Arthur Norberg, Akiba Cohen, Ellen Wartella, and many more. To my colleagues at the University of Wisconsin-Milwaukee, welcome and welcoming during the concluding stages of this project.

Enduring appreciation must go to my editor at MIT Press, Bob Prior, for his eye, his wisdom, and his patience. Even when in the midst of the academic world, of course, it remains only one among many. Thanks to the many personal friends who also live a life in which working with ideas is a normal part of daily practice. The most intimate relations are, of course, the most important. Thanks yet again to my parents, Sally and the late Donald Braman, for unending support and the confidence that even the most complex of projects could be brought to fruition. And to my husband, Guy Milford, who taught me how to fly.

Change of State brings together into one framework the work I have undertaken since entering academia over twenty years ago. Answering the pragmatic questions of how to resolve the myriad specific information policy issues in such a way that the entire range of human values can be taken into account irrespective of changing social and technological conditions will take more than another twenty years of effort, by myself and many others. But it is hoped that the first step, a way of seeing, at the very least has been achieved.

I am reminded, oddly, of a dinner party held by Steve Clay, of Granary Books. I was seated to Steve's right, on the same side of an ordinary rectangular table. As the meal wore on, however, it became more and more difficult to converse with him because he kept pushing his chair further and further back until, finally, I would have had to turn my back to the table altogether in order to speak with him tête-à-tête. When asked why he was doing such a thing, he responded that he wanted to hold the entire dining group together as a whole. While it didn't work as a dinner party maneuver, the motive does make sense in one's intellectual life. Thus the final acknowledgment goes to the process itself.

1
An Introduction to Information Policy

It may seem late in the day to speak of an introduction to information policy but it is only now, with the transformation of the bureaucratic welfare state into the informational state, that the subject fully appears. We have passed the tipping point: While information policy is among the most ancient forms of governance, there has been a phase change—a change of state—in the extent to which governments deliberately, explicitly, and consistently control information creation, processing, flows, and use to exercise power.

The processes by which we got from there to here began over a century and a half ago. Step by step, through the stages of the history of the information society, industrial technologies were replaced by informational meta-technologies, organizations changed their form, new architectures of knowledge developed, and the information, or network, economy replaced industrial and agricultural economies. By the 1960s, we had become aware that these transformations were taking place. Those who saw the bureaucratic welfare state as the ultimate political form began to see information-induced changes in the nature of government as vulnerabilities and the overall effect as a weakening of the state. From a longer view, though, this particular form of the nation-state is only one among several that have appeared over the course of the several-hundred-year history of modern forms of government, and even within the general category of the bureaucratic welfare state there has always been variance. Ultimately it became clear that, whatever was happening to the nation-state, it was not going away. Rather, contemporary governments were using information, and information technologies, in new ways; these practices, in turn, led to shifts in the nature of power and its exercise via information policy.

This is not the first time the content and practice of the law have responded to changing empirical conditions. Earlier technological innovations, such as the railroad and electricity, stimulated legal developments, as have social trends such as urbanization, demographic shifts, alterations in political mood, economic developments, the appearance of new political ideas, and experience with laws and regulations already in place. The legal environment for information and communication has thus been under constant reconsideration ever since it was recognized as fundamental to the new forms of democratic governance of the late eighteenth century; both medium and message were repeatedly reproblematized beginning with the introduction of the telegraph in the mid-nineteenth century.

The duration and constancy of stress in the area of information policy is reflected in the ways we have talked about our use of information and communication technologies. The word "new" was first used in this context in the nineteenth century to refer to changes in journalism practices made possible because of technological innovation. The word "media" was coined in the 1920s to talk about the growing number of entries in this category. Only in the 1930s were separate broadcasting and telecommunications regulatory systems developed to deal with then-new, and then-distinct, electronic media. The first Supreme Court case using the phrase "new media" dealt with a bullhorn carried through streets on a truck in the early 1940s. The first scholarly article using that phrase appeared in 1948 in a discussion of the regulation of television, FM radio, and facsimile. And by 1954—only two decades after the Communications Act of 1934—the Federal Communications Commission (FCC) was forced to confront the need to break down the barriers between the two regulatory systems it managed. By the 1970s, Congress was dealing with issues raised by new information and communication technologies regularly.

Many of today's information policy problems are enduring in nature, but others are not. Traditional issues continue to appear in traditional forms, such as direct censorship of reporting from a battlefront during wartime. In some cases traditional issues appear in new forms, as when privacy is invaded via technologies that can be used at a distance in ways imperceptible to the surveillance subject. There are areas in which long-standing policy principles need reinterpretation in order to be applied in a qualitatively changed environment; the question of how to think about a public forum on the Internet falls into this category. And some completely new types of information policy issues are emerging because of technological capacities never before available, as with the question of liability for processes launched by intelligent agent software.

The ways in which we think about policy have also changed. New theories develop as thinkers elaborate on ideas, respond to critique, incorporate new information, or achieve original conceptualizations. Empirical change yields new policy subjects, such as the Internet. Traditional policy subjects (e.g., television) and constituencies (e.g., communities and ethnic groups) exhibit new behaviors in the electronic environment. New specializations appear, such as geographic information systems. Interest in familiar topics, such as archives and data structures, revives because of their functions in the exercise of informational power. Previously unconnected lines of thinking come together into new fields, as has happened with the economics of information.

Changes in the law, in the subject of the law, and in how we think about the law can result in a change in the very nature of the state itself because the institutions, processes, and policies of any given political form are but a moment of stability within a much wider, more diffuse, and constantly shifting policy field. The broad field within which particular legal systems appear, change, and disappear includes ethical and behavioral norms, discourse habits, cultural practices, knowledge structures, organizational forms, private sector and individual decision-making, and technologies themselves as well as the formal laws and regulations of officially recognized governments. The information policy field therefore includes

- *government* (formal institutions of the law);
- *governance* (decision-making with constitutive [structural] effect whether it takes place within the public or private sectors, and formally or informally; and
- *governmentality* (cultural predispositions and practices that produce and reproduce the conditions that make particular forms of governance and government possible).

The common saying that "the law is a moving target" captures only a part of the processes by which legal systems change; with a longer and wider view it is possible to see a specific law developing out cultural practice, becoming a form of discourse, and ultimately being translated into a technology. Laws and regulations left behind can take on new functions—what architects call "spandrels" when they are talking about building elements that are no longer needed for their original purpose but remain in use, stimulating new ways of using space. Whether deliberate or accidental, intended or not, the law thus triggers social change as well as responds to it. As a result, the very ways in which we conceptualize information policy is itself a form of agency.

In complex adaptive systems theory, and in its cousins such as theories of chaos, punctuated equilibrium, and second-order cybernetics, a system emerges when it has characteristics as a whole that cannot be predicted by any of its parts or the relationships among those parts. Systems differ from each other in kind, even though they share some constituent parts and relationships, when their emergent properties are qualitatively distinct. It is this that has happened with the appearance of the informational state: Many of the structures of U.S. law with which we are long familiar remain in place, and traditional processes such as elections and the passage of legislation continue. Because informational power has altered the materials, rules, institutions, ideas, and symbols that are the means by which other forms of power are exercised, a new type of system, the informational state, has emerged. Information policy is thus key both to understanding just how this change of state has come about and to analyzing how the informational state exercises power domestically and around the world. Information policy is the proprioceptive organ of the nation-state, the means by which it senses itself and, therefore, the medium through which all other decision-making, public or private, takes place. As Laurence Tribe comments, all such legal questions are of constitutional stature because they define social categories and the processes to be permitted within and between them, while other areas of the law deal with existing categories and processes.

Just as has happened with the many streams of economic thought that have now come together in the economics of information, so laws and regulations from diverse areas of the law are now understood to commonly populate the domain of information policy. Examining together all policy dealing with information creation, processing, flows, and use makes it possible to see relationships between policies not historically related, bringing to light lacunae, contradictions, and conflicts. Doing so also addresses an even larger problem: There is plenty of grand theory and broad-brush discussion of macrolevel social trends regarding the nature of the information society, and a seemingly infinite amount of detailed analysis of the specific laws and regulations dealing with information creation, processing, flows, and use that need tinkering. The first of these is useful as a frame but despite endless refutation of the notion of technological determinism (the idea that technologies inevitably affect society in specific ways), the macrolevel analysis on its own generates a sense that we are the subjects of history rather than its agents. The second of these certainly involves agency, but while adapting, reinterpreting, or replacing specific laws or regulations at the microlevel "makes something happen," it is difficult to link just what that is back to the larger picture. The study of information policy as a coherent body of law and regulation introduces the meso-level and lets us answer the real question: What are we doing to ourselves?

For the purposes of this book, U.S. law is taken as the case. To make the argument, and the analysis, it is necessary to focus on one government in the first instance. Both argument and analysis, however, are valuable for studying other political systems, whether at the state level or supra or infra to it. The U.S. case has value to those in other political systems, and for those seeking to understand international and global decision-making, because in some areas (not all) it is an innovator and because U.S. regulatory approaches have been doing relatively well in the global market for the law. Both of these features, of course, also mark the limits of the case. And while the focus of this book is on policy at the national level, it must also be emphasized that it was often *not* the United States that led the way among countries in policy innovations designed to adapt to changes in the information environment, and international and private sector decision-making have also been important.

It is a classical analytical error, however, to believe that it is possible to understand what is happening to society via the use of information policy to exercise power by looking at only laws and regulations. Rather, three types of knowledge must necessarily be brought together. Research on the empirical world provides evidence about the policy subject, the world for which information policy is made. Social theory provides a context within which to understand the empirical detail. Knowledge of current law and of its history provides a necessary foundation for those who seek to adapt, extend, reinterpret, or replace that law for the contemporary world. Historically, these diverse domains of knowledge were pursued within different disciplines that only rarely interacted, and unfortunately a number of barriers make it difficult to ensure that policy-makers are fully informed by what is known about the empirical environment for which they are making law. Still, failure to bring these different types of knowledge together cripples policy-making, creating the risk that legacy law and what develops from it will be inadequate at best or dysfunctional at worst.

Bringing these types of knowledge together, however, makes visible trends in U.S. society as they are manifested in the identities of the state and of its citizens, structures internal to society, the borders that determine relationships with other societies, and the very rules by which transformation—change—takes place. Since information policy also appears at the intersection of informational, technological, and social structures, these distinctions provide another analytical axis.

What do we see, when we address the question of what we are doing to ourselves, in this way? In very broad brushstroke:

- *Identity* In the area of identity, the mutual transparency between the individual and the state has been destroyed, with the state knowing ever more about the individual and the individual knowing ever less about the state. The identity relation between the individual and the state via citizenship, historically determined by relatively clear rules, has become a political tool with shifting, ambiguous, and at times hidden criteria for whether one is in or out.
- *Structure* The period of turbulence in social, technological, and informational structure has resolved into a new orientation that is more centralized and rigid than was the case in the past. The story isn't completely over: Some experimentation continues, particularly in the area of information architectures. It is not yet known just which regulatory tools will be feasible, effective, and constitutionally acceptable. And there is still a great deal of resistance to many aspects of the informational state as it is being experienced in the first decade of the twenty-first century.
- *Borders* While the notion of the borders of the state seems clear, in historical reality this has never quite so simple. In the U.S. case, for example, relaxation of border parameters in order to assert cultural identity and ease the lives of those who manage the technological infrastructure have long histories. Today, however, geopolitical borders retain only a rhetorical function used to justify a much more expansive sense of U.S. political territory globally. Within the United States, various means are being used to define the border as a condition as likely to be experienced internally as at the geopolitical edge, allowing exceptions to mainstream U.S. law justified by border conditions to be applied much more broadly.
- *Change* In the area of change, U.S. policy is currently somewhat confused and often self-contradictory. Despite an announced goal of remaining a global leader in the development of scientific and technical knowledge, many current policies dealing with information and information technology not only will make that unlikely, but may well reverse advances already accomplished. The same can be said regarding democratic processes of social change.

It is at the next level of detail that the contributions of specific information policies to these large-scale social trends become clear. The obscurity, unfamiliarity, and technical nature of many types of information policy, however, have kept many of these developments out of public view. In some of these areas the trends not only are devastating but may be very difficult to reverse, while in others conditions of turbulence, recency, and tentativeness of a change in direction, or outright resistance, mean that the future may not look like today.

The next three chapters build the theoretical foundations for understanding just what is going on. Chapter 2 unpacks the concepts of information, power, and the state as they provide the theoretical grounding for this work. Chapter 3 provides a brief history of information policy and explains just what is included in the domain of information policy. Chapter 4 examines the twenty information policy principles found in the U.S. Constitution and its amendments and the social spaces they create. Chapters 5–8 examine in turn the impact of U.S. information policy on identity, structure, borders, and change. Each of these four chapters opens with a theoretical introduction to the orienting social concept before going on to explore a sampling of pertinent information policy issues. Discussion of each issue is introduced by a brief look at the background and history of current law and a concise description of the current state of the law. These contextual elements make it possible to look at trends in the development of these laws and regulations and in their effects on U.S. society. The concluding chapter explores the implications of these trends when viewed together as a whole. Extensive bibliographic essays follow that provide much more depth regarding the development of the theories applied as well as the empirical sources upon which the legal analysis is based.

Several guidelines helped choose which information policy issues would be discussed as exemplars in this book. Familiar and widely discussed issues such as intellectual property rights, privacy, and trade in services are included because it is hoped that the additional frame and conceptualization offered here will enrich those conversations. In some areas, such as the use of propaganda in support of military power, changes wrought by the use of new information technologies are fairly straightforward and adequately explored in the existing literature, and so they are not included here. The same cannot be said for such things as the incorporation of information policy tools in arms control agreements, the appearance of the category of hybrid citizenship, or the collapse of physical network structures into sheer conceptual effort. In most cases, then, the principal driving the selection of one information policy issue over another has been "lookin' where the light don't shine," the desire to draw attention to areas of information policy that are extremely influential but which are receiving relatively little attention—the "dark matter" of the law. The final factor taken into consideration was the degree to which trends in a particular area illuminate the macrolevel social trends that are the central thrust of this book's argument regarding the implications of the transformation to an informational state; the expanding use of "functionally equivalent borders," for example, falls into this category.

There are things that this book is not: More detailed discussion of changes in the world for which policy is made, both technological and social, is found elsewhere. The same is true of analysis of developments in the economics of information that underlies policy-making. Internationalization (with other states) and globalization (with both states and non-state actors) of the law affect each of the areas of information policy here but are not included in this book's discussion. The use of information and information technologies as policy tools to effect other political goals is another important trend that is outside the bounds of this book. So, too, are discussions of changes in the nature of information policy-making processes, and in the overall relationships between the law and society.

Change of State is an introduction to information policy in two senses. Closest to the ground, it provides an entrée into many of the most important information policy issues with which we will be struggling during the twenty-first century. At the most abstract level, it explores interactions between social theory and policy. It is between the two, however, that it is hoped the book will have the most impact, by providing a way of seeing the role of information policy in effecting the fundamental social changes wrought by the transition to an informational state.

2

Forms and Phases of Power: The Bias of the Informational State

The informational state is distinguished from the bureaucratic welfare state and other earlier types of political organization by its emphasis on the use of informational power. We begin here by looking at just what information is, what makes informational power different from other forms of power, and what both of those mean for the evolution of the nation-state as a political form. Together, these provide the context within which it is possible to see trends in the development of information policy as manifestations of change in the very nature of governance itself.

Information

Any approach to the study of information policy must start with the question of just what information is. There is no easy answer. A 1980s survey reported more than one hundred definitions in use for regulatory purposes alone, and since then the problem has worsened. A look at the venues in which information policy is made shows that though many institutions often deal with the same or closely related types of issues, they do so in very different ways. These can be compared and contrasted along three dimensions: the *value hierarchy* (in the terms of political science) or *preference ordering* (in the terms of economics) that drives decision-making; the *modes of argument* used; and the *operational definition* of the policy subject. Lack of agreement on the last is among the most serious of the factors that impede the ability to reach agreements on contested issues. Debates over international trade law, for example, are consistently marked by differences between those who view international information flows such as movies, television programs, and film as commodities only, and those who view these media as potent cultural forces. Ways of conceptualizing information also change over time; though information today is often treated as if it is timeless, the concept has its own history.

The very multiplicity of forms in which information exists is so problematic that some attorneys have suggested that the definitional task may be useless altogether. Information is heterogeneous, appearing in apparently infinitely variable permutations. Economists distinguish between information in its functions as a primary good (a consumer product) and a secondary good (a good used as an input into the manufacture of other products); and between information as an asset, a resource, and a commodity. Many definitions are methodologically driven; economists such as Hal Varian define information as "anything that can be digitized," while psychologists define it as that which flows between cognitive agents. As a result, many definitions are pretheoretical. An alternative response to this problem can be found in theoretical pluralism.

Theoretical Pluralism

Over the last few decades, theoretical pluralism has become the preferred stance of many social scientists because it incorporates multicausality into analysis and because processes may unfold in different ways at various levels of the social structure. Political economist Immanuel Wallerstein and historian Fernand Braudel provide models of such an approach in multilevel analyses that look at perceptions of marketplace transactions from the perspective of different positions within the social structure. For a medieval peasant, for example, a single transaction may be viewed simply as an exchange of a cow for a bolt of cloth. For members of elite trading families that managed the movement and sale of goods all the way from Asia through the Middle East and across Europe, however, the same transaction is only one piece of information that feeds into a macrolevel strategy involving complex organization across time and space. Distinctions in socioeconomic class, political position, and cultural capital enable each person to understand, use, and receive the benefits of information differently, with the advantage always accruing to those who take the longer and broader view. Franklin Ford, in an early-twentieth-century formulation that influenced sociologists John Dewey and Robert Park and presaged contemporary marketing practices, demonstrated the pragmatic utility of a theoretically pluralist approach when he pointed out that this very feature makes it possible to simultaneously market the same information differently to the individual, members of a class, and society as a whole.

Historically, legal analysts have understood the value of theoretical pluralism because of the wildly variegated contexts to which terms must be applied. As lawyer and legal scholar Felix S. Cohen noted decades ago,

> Among the difficulties that stand in the way of a comprehensive view of the legal order is the naive view of definitions as propositions which are true or false.... Once we recognize that a definition is, strictly speaking, neither true nor false but rather a resolution to use language in a certain way, we are able to pass the only judgment that ever needs to be passed on a definition, a judgment of utility or inutility. (1935, 18)

More recently, Cass Sunstein suggests theoretical pluralism when he notes that legal argument is sometimes "incompletely theorized" because there are always ambiguities latent in legal theory that require ongoing theoretical attention.

Operationalizing theoretical pluralism in defining information for policy purposes produces a definitional taxonomy that has some hierarchical features when used by policy-makers. This approach has several advantages: It incorporates all of the dimensions of the concept being explicated, as well as all of the values that must be taken into account in policy-making. Placing the elements of a taxonomy into a hierarchy makes it possible for the policy-maker to determine which definition is appropriate for a given decision-making task, and to use multiple definitions in appropriately complementary ways. The disadvantages remain that any typology involves oversimplification, and that the lines between categories are not always bright and clean.

A Taxonomy of Definitions

A taxonomy of the myriad definitions of information distinguishes among them according to several features:

- *Complexity* How complex is the social structure to which the definition is intended to apply? What is the degree to which the social structure implicit in a particular definition is articulated?
- *Scope and scale* What are the scope and scale of the social processes to which the definition is intended to apply? How broad is the range of types of social processes to which the definition might apply, and at what levels of analysis?
- *Power* How much power is granted to information and its creation, processing, flows, and use by a particular definition?

Distinguished along these dimensions, definitions of information fall into several groups: information as a resource, as a commodity, as perception of pattern, as a basin of possibility, as an agent, and as a constitutive force in society. Because any single piece of information or processing event may simultaneously be definable in more than one way, an approach to using multiple definitions of information in the policy-making process is also suggested in the following text. One of the weaknesses of information policy as it has been practiced to date is that it does not yet incorporate awareness of information in all of these forms; this is particularly the case with information as an agent.

Information as a resource Information is defined as a resource when it is treated as something that an entity—a person, an organization, or a community—must have in order to function. Information is a resource when it is an input into any decision-making, production, or bureaucratic process.

Economists provide models for measuring information, its flows, and its value that emulate those developed for physical resources. When information is a secondary good, it is information as a resource for the producing organization; information as a final good is often a resource for the buyer. Information as a resource now appears in "national accounts"—statistics regarding what resources come into or are created by society at the national level, and what is spent—today referred to in the United States as the National Income and Product Accounts (NIPA, produced by the Bureau of Economic Analysis [BEA])—as an effort to determine what is being acquired, lost, and used at the level of the nation-state. Information is treated in the same way when economists measure the flows of information across borders in the form of imports and exports and when political scientists quantify international information flows in the expectation that this will reveal political relations. The effects research that has dominated the mainstream history of the field of communication, from early work on the two-step flow, through diffusion studies, to today's work on persuasion, treat information as a resource. At the level of the individual, what researchers refer to as "information seeking" is the effort to acquire information as a resource and a "knowledge gap" occurs when such resources are insufficient for decision-making purposes.

Analysis of information as a resource is generally quantitative, measuring numbers of telephone calls, pieces of mail, or numbers of books. This type of analysis does not, therefore, include attention to content, uses, and/or effects, whether behavioral or at the level of meaning formation. Descriptions of information treated as a resource include mathematician Anthony Oettinger's treatment of it as a generic concept referring to any information content represented in any way, embodied in any format, and handled by any physical processor and Hal Varian's insistence that it is anything that can be expressed in bits. The notion of information as a resource is at the heart of the "a bit is a bit is a bit" approach to analysis of information flows, characteristic of the approach of computer scientists, electrical engineers, and economists. Those in communication, cultural studies, or political science, on the other hand, insist that a bit is *not* a bit—that is, that bits of information are *not* equivalent, because they differ in their social, cultural, and political meanings and therefore in their impacts.

Among the strengths of definitions of information as a resource is that they are relatively easy to comprehend and widely applicable. The concept of information as a resource requires only the simplest of systems. Any kind of entity, from a single cell organism on up, takes in and expels information. This type of system is typically viewed as isolated and autonomous, with clearly defined and impermeable borders. The social structure to which the definition applies is also relatively simple (or simply conceived). Information has no power in its own right. It comes in pieces unrelated to bodies of knowledge or organized information flows. Methodologically, this approach emphasizes the uses people make of information rather than its effects upon them. All of these features have made the resource approach attractive to economists and in turn, therefore, to policy-makers who rely upon economic analyses in their decision-making.

Information as a commodity Information is a commodity when it is something that we buy and sell. The growth of the information economy has vastly expanded the use of such definitions; while information about supplies and prices has been considered a commodity for hundreds of years, only in the past few decades have personal information, information that is public in the sense of having been collected by the government to serve public ends, and information about information all come to be treated as commodities.

The information economy has also multiplied the range of terms in use to refer to information in this way. In international trade agreements, such as the overarching multilateral General Agreement on Trade in Services (GATS), administered by the World Trade Organization (WTO), information and its processing and flows are referred to as "services." Because of the many problems created by efforts to analyze information using neoclassical economic concepts, the WTO doesn't offer a conceptual definition of services but, rather, just a list, and it took years to achieve a consensus over even that. (The GATS came into effect only in 1995, after long debate over whether to extend international trade law to apply to services as well as goods.) Among analysts and journalists, the most popular definition of services was offered years ago by the British news magazine *The Economist*: "Things which can be bought and sold but which you cannot drop on your foot." (1985, 20) Trade negotiators look at services for as products of economic activity that are exchanged but are not material goods. In the 1970s and 1980s the terms "TBDF" and "TDF" for "transborder data flow" were used to describe information as a commodity in the international arena, and legal scholar Anne W. Branscomb was able to identify seven variations on the theme. The sectoral approach to identifying the information industries was an effort to conceptualize information as a commodity for policy purposes in the domestic environment. In the corporate world, notions of information as a commodity appear within discussions of the "value chain" associated with a variety of economic activities.

Critics of the definition of information as a commodity are concerned that such an approach not only ignores many of its social functions, but can also destroy other forms of value. Information is often exchanged as a gift in order to strengthen social relations, for example, or is created and exchanged for ritual ends that include both individual spiritual growth and community formation. Those who study the important roles of gifts in society note that when items (including information, and stories) that have been exchanged to build or cement social relations or spiritual meaning are transformed into commodities, their earlier contributions are lost. The same critique, as applied to the communication systems that are the subject of information policy, underlies James Carey's distinction between the "transmission model" of the communication process (in which messages are basically commodities) and the "ritual model" of the communication process (in which messages are exchanged in the process of building and sustaining community). The commodity definition also precludes many of the critical processes and relations involving information as well as consideration of the effects of information creation, processing, flows, and use that should be important to policymakers.

Definitions of information that treat it as a commodity do, however, have heuristic and organizational value. The scope of the notion of information as a commodity is wider than that of information as a resource, for it incorporates information exchanges and use. The social structure implied by this approach is also, more highly articulated, comprising buyers, sellers, and the organization required to produce and distribute information within a market. With this type of definition, information is granted at least economic power.

Information as perception of pattern Definitions of information that treat it as patterned data—or data about patterns—broaden the concept by adding context and structure. Information from this perspective has a past and a future, is affected by motive and other environmental and causal factors, and itself has effects. This definitional approach is suggested in scholarly and popular discourse that focuses on differences between data and information, information and knowledge, or knowledge and wisdom, for all of these are ways of struggling with the recognition that there is an important difference between a pile of information and information organized in such a way that it affects how the world is known or understood. The ontogeny of information—where it comes from—is thus useful, because all information has a developmental history.

Definitions of this type range in complexity. The simplest focuses on the capacity of information to reduce uncertainty. In the classic statement by mathematician Claude E. Shannon, written for Bell Labs in an effort to help increase the efficiency of the telephone network, information is a measure of the predictability of the signal, the "difference that makes a difference." In Shannon's theory, a bit is defined as the minimum amount of information needed to reduce the alternatives by half, and entropy is equated with ignorance. Mathematically, this theory approaches information as a *change* in data, requiring not only the "fact" itself but also an understanding of patterned context in which it appears. From this perspective, a thermometer that registers the same temperature every day tells you nothing at all; it is only when the reported temperature changes that information is given. Information flows are thus pathways upon which a value is placed according to the degree to which uncertainty is reduced.

Reduction of uncertainty is important from the economist's point of view because it lowers the cost of search and increases the "productivity" of decision-making. In a famous and highly influential article in the 1930s, economist Ronald Coase argued that organizations came into existence for just this reason—to reduce the "transaction costs" associated with economic activity. More complex definitions that are instead driven by a concern about the making of meaning appear in diverse literatures that focus on context (semiotics); sense-making on the part of message receivers (cultural studies); and the cultural, economic, political, and social impact of knowledge architectures (information science and the sociology of knowledge). What all of these approaches have in common is respect for the way in which a bit is not a bit, as well as the awareness that content matters, and that content matters most when it brings together information into a story about the world within which we can locate ourselves and, therefore, act.

This definitional approach can be used broadly across a wide range of phenomena and processes. When information is defined as perception of pattern, a complex social structure is assumed, information has significant power in its own right, and the realm within which information exerts power is significantly broadened. As Wallerstein and Braudel demonstrated, those who perceive the broadest patterns—those who think about information within the widest contexts—have the most power.

Information as perception of pattern may appear only with a shift in scale made possible by the use of a technological innovation, by movement to another level of the social structure, or with the introduction of a new theory. The approach incorporates the context and processes within which information can be treated as a resource or commodity. The chronological progression in the ways in which the information economy has been conceptualized reveals increasing sensitivity to information as perception of pattern. The value of information as perception of pattern is most clearly acknowledged within the policy world via support for basic and applied research and for education. This definition of information is pertinent to a number of other types of policy issues, but is difficult to operationalize in ways that can usefully be incorporated into decision-making processes.

Information as an agent Until this point, each definitional approach has assumed that information is used by other entities, whether those are individuals, organizations, or governments. With recent technological developments, however, we have become more aware that sometimes information itself has agency; that is, that information can, on its own, make things happen. The economic historian Alfred D. Chandler, Jr., pointed out that this began to be so in the nineteenth century, when the automation of production lines took many decisions about manufacturing out of the hands of people and placed such decision-making into the hands of machines. A simple example of information as an agent with which we are all familiar is the thermostat, which senses the temperature in a room and, when that temperature crosses a preestablished limit, turns a heating or cooling system on or off. The role of information as an agent is even more important now that there is software that serves as "intelligent agents," capable of acting autonomously on such matters as deciding when to make trades in the stock market, or how to repair a telecommunications network.

The level of the autonomy of such intelligent agents is increasing, for three reasons. First, they are becoming responsible for ever-more complex types of decisions. Second, they are continuing to evolve and, increasingly, are allowed to do so autonomously, because those who design software are finding that programs solve problems more efficiently and effectively when they are allowed to genetically mutate in response to the environment and to learn. And third, as networked sensors become ubiquitously embedded throughout the material and organic environments, the proportion of activity triggered and managed by information and information technologies is growing. Action triggered by information via such technologies has been described as "pandemonic," referring to the medieval sense of the demon as the source of agency that is neither human nor divine and adding the sense that this type of agency is everywhere.

When information is defined as an agent, its power is clearly recognized. This definitional approach applies throughout the social structure, and that structure is understood to be highly complex. Legal thought has only begun to address issues raised by information as an agent, though as discussed in more detail elsewhere, there is some history of law and regulation that addresses technologies as a policy subject and there are laws and regulations in place designed to serve the "needs" of technologies as a value informing policy-making processes. Increasingly, however, information policy must take into account the ways in which information and information technologies are now supplementing, supplanting, and superseding human decision-making.

Information as a basin of possibility Even though information presented in statistical form is often treated as fact, it is not concretely descriptive but, rather, refers to probabilities. Today another important definition of information is as a basin of possibility.

Even our understanding of probability has grown in sophistication over time, often driven by theoretical and methodological needs of policy-makers. Accepting the role of chance marked an important moment in the maturation of modernity and the transition to postmodernity, for it was an important part of the Enlightenment turn away from the sacred and toward nature as the source of causation. With the development of statistical techniques, however, the role of chance in the material world became manageable and, therefore, acceptable. By the late nineteenth century, the "law of large numbers" came to replace the sense that it was possible to achieve absolute knowledge of individual facts, and much of the early twentieth century was spent figuring out just how to apply statistical reasoning to society.

During the second half of the twentieth century, future as well as present probabilities began to draw attention as modeling and simulation came into heavy use. Architect and social theorist Marcos Novak describes simulation as reverse empiricism, because it is the "empiricism of the possible" as opposed to that of the actual. In social theory, contingency was expressed in ideas such as sociologist Pierre Bourdieu's concept of the "habitus," which he defines as a predisposition to action that is still indeterminate—a concept important to understanding the nature of policy in today's environment.

Two recent developments have taken probability theory beyond the popular understanding as it was taught within the United States during the second half of the twentieth century. We have come to acknowledge that correctly evaluating the probability of a particular event might require analysis of a sequence of intervening, also probabilistic, events. This realization has become operationalized in the development of instruments known as "real options" that incorporate contingency into their design (currently used in calculations behind telecommunications policy) and in treatment of risk as a commodity in itself. In the world of policy analysis, this insight has made us more sensitive to what is described in what follows as precession among types of policy issues and the effects of the tools used to address them.

An additional type of uncertainty is brought into the evaluation of probabilities under conditions in which the data involved refer only to what are considered to be partial truths. To deal with this, fuzzy set theory was introduced in the 1960s. In fuzzy logic, exact reasoning is treated as a subset of more generally useful approximate reasoning, and everything is considered to be a matter of degree. From this approach, knowledge is viewed as a collection of elastic and fuzzy constraints on a collection of variables. Given the complexities of the types of knowledge—including evaluations of political and logistical possibilities under shifting conditions—fuzzy set theory certainly has a role in information policy analysis.

Definitions of information as a basin of possibility apply across the range of social processes and at every level of the social structure. They share with definitions of information as perception of pattern an emphasis upon sense-making, but differ from them in the nature of the referent. The power of information as a basin of possibilities lies in its identification of potential futures that, as a result of their expression, increase in likelihood. Interestingly, however, this approach provokes a paradox—when the world was described in qualitative terms, there was a belief in precision, but as the capacity for quantitative description increased, so did the sense that it is impossible to be completely exact.

Information as a constitutive force in society The most important definition of information from a policy-making perspective acknowledges its fundamental role as a constitutive force in society. The constitutive and the constitutional roles of information are closely related but not the same—constitutional principles describe an ideal, while constitutive forces have an empirical effect that may or may not bring society closer to the constitutional goal. Constitutional law is only one among the forces that determine the actual constitutive effects of information creation, processing, flows, and use.

While definitions of information as perception of pattern acknowledge the role of context, those that see information as a constitutive force emphasize the ability of information to actively *shape* context. Defining information as an agent can be operationalized for single instances of action, while defining information as a constitutive social force applies to the cumulative effect of numerous flows and actions. Information is not just affected by its environment, but affects its environment as well. It is for this reason that, as mentioned earlier, Laurence Tribe argued that all communication and information policy is constitutional in nature. Tribe based this analysis on the insight that while other types of law deal with relations within and between entities in categories as already defined, issues involving information and communication define the categories themselves and the relations enabled or permitted within and between them. Communications scholar Klaus Krippendorff describes the same effect in economic terms:

> In the input-output table for an economy in which exchanges between and transformations within industries (categories of industries, sectors of an economy or geographical regions) are entered, information participates in the process by changing the table. It may change the transition function within one cell (e.g., when information is geared toward a more efficient organization of the process), it may change the interaction between cells otherwise considered independent

(e.g., when industries, etc., become more informed about each other and coordinate their production and consumption) or it may add new cells, rows or columns (e.g., when information introduces new technologies, communication technology for example, that cause structural changes in the economy). In such an analysis information is seen to be about or superordinate to the economy. It guides, controls and rearranges the economic activities and has, hence, the characteristic of a meta-economic quantity that cannot easily be built into a system of analysis that is essentially flat and provides no opportunity for self-reference. ([1984] 1996, 15–16)

This definition of information appears in a wide variety of quite different literatures and is used in support of a wide variety of political positions. In even the earliest versions of systems theory, information flows shape systems and form the means by which systems adapt to their environments and influence other systems. To social psychologists, information creation and flows literally construct reality. Media sociologists operationalize such ideas as they play out in specific fact-creating situations. The base/superstructure preoccupation of critical theorists demonstrates an overall focus on the idea that information is a constitutive force in society, though that literature includes multiple ways of conceptualizing the relationship between information flows and society. This type of definition of information has played a large role in the development of mass communication theory, both directly and indirectly.

Definitions that treat information as a constitutive force in society are at the top of the definitional hierarchy presented here. They apply to the entire range of phenomena and processes in which information is involved; they can be applied to a social structure of any degree of articulation and complexity; and they grant information an enormous power in constructing our social—and ultimately, therefore, material—reality.

It is a strength of this type of definition that it is relatively friendly, enlarging the context in which users of other definitions work. Thus it is particularly easy to use this type of definition in the first and last steps of a policy analysis that in subsequent stages depends upon one or more other operational definitions. It is a weakness of this type of definition that it is difficult to operationalize for purposes of policy analysis, because often constitutive effects are qualitative rather than quantitative in nature.

Using the Taxonomy

Each of these types of definition has its own use, with several factors determining which is of the most utility in a given situation. The most important definition from the perspective of policy-making highlights the role of information as a constitutive force in society. Often, though, policy-makers are involved in multistep processes that require the use of more than one definition in the course of their work. If they do so, however, they should both start and conclude with analysis of a proposed policy or evaluation of an existing policy in light of its impact as a constitutive force.

Choosing a definition Two factors should influence the selection of a particular definition of information for use at any given stage of a decision-making process. These two factors interact in determining just which areas of the law apply to a given problem or issue.

To some extent, the perspective from which an information policy issue depends upon the empirical environment to which a decision applies. Any entity—individual, organization, community, or nation-state—that views itself as isolated, autonomous, and concerned about survival is most likely to view information as a resource. Though such perceptions are likely to be inaccurate in terms of actual causal relations in an increasingly interdependent world, they still exist, and still motivate decision-making even if the results are not optimal. Policy-making in areas such as trade and interstate commerce will need at some point to treat information as a commodity. The potential gap between perception and reality and the fact that often the use of information makes possible the exercise of multiple forms of power, irrespective of how perceived, are arguments for use of a constitutive definition of information in policy-making to ensure that all possible uses and effects are taken into account.

The choice of which definition is to be used, however, is also political. Definitions of information that treat it as a commodity work to the advantage of those who win when the game is played on economic grounds or for whom economic values are the only values. Definitions that treat information as perception of pattern begin to be sensitive to cultural, aesthetic, or religious concerns. Pattern-oriented definitions can be helpful in identifying effects of information creation, processing, flows, and use; and they may be helpful in improving the efficiency of activities at specific stages of the information production chain by drawing attention to interactions between processes at different levels of the social structure. Defining information as a constitutive force in society is the approach that has the most breadth and addresses the greatest number of concerns that should be most fundamental to policy-makers. This type of definition encompasses the concerns of all parties involved and, therefore, the entire range of values that must be taken into account in the course of decision-making. It also clarifies the political effects of information and its processing, flows, and use.

Definitional practices of policy-makers Policy-makers must place primary emphasis on the definition of information as a constitutive force in society. There will be occasions when this is the only definition that need be taken into account. In U.S. Supreme Court deliberations, this is the only issue on the table, even if thinking about a matter in constitutional terms requires, as it often does, a balancing of two or more principles and goals that have come into conflict with each other.

Most types of policy-making, however, are multistaged and may for good reason take different definitions of information into account at different stages of the process. It does not strengthen the argument of those concerned about civil liberties and other humanitarian values to deny the utility and appropriateness of definitions of information as a resource or a commodity in certain settings. Nor is it impossible to acknowledge the legitimate interests of those with an economic stake in informational activities while simultaneously requiring that those activities be carried out in ways that respect cultural sensitivities and social needs.

Of course, at a fundamental level any decision-making entity will be concerned with the resource value of information, even when other definitional approaches are used. Despite the contention by those concerned about the cultural effects of information flows that services should not be treated as commodities, for example, sometimes books, films, and data processing services *are* commodities, and admitting such does not necessarily reduce appreciation for the cultural impact of their production, flows, and use. Similarly, the realization that journal article citations and the editorial vision provided in a table of contents can be separately marked as commodities does not deny the role of such information as perception of pattern. As U.S. Supreme Court decisions have acknowledged, for example, decisions about the provision of primary and secondary education to the children of foreign nationals will inevitably take resource issues into account, but should also be evaluated in constitutive terms. In another example, via directive OMB A-130 and its offshoots, the Office of Management and Budget (OMB) requires every federal agency to examine its information collection, storage, and distribution practices using cost-benefit analysis appropriate to treating information as a resource, even though altering regulatory practices on the basis of the results of such analysis can result in contravening statutory intention and in such cases would have constitutive effect.

Those with public policy-making responsibility must first explore their goals in both constitutional and constitutive terms. At the second and subsequent stages of decision-making, however, it may be necessary and appropriate to define information as a commodity, or as a resource, and so on. The final stage of decision-making must return to evaluation of a policy in terms of its constitutive effect. Doing so may bring entirely other issues to light. A policy that looks very good from the perspective of information as a commodity, for example, may reveal itself as having unfortunate dysfunctionalities from the perspective of information as a constitutive force.

Since information policy-makers have responsibility for establishing the basic shape of society, however, analyses of information as a commodity should still be framed within the context of the effects of such policies on the constitution of society. Definitions of information as a constitutive force should provide the standard against which decisions that treat information as a commodity or other entity should ultimately be judged. Constitutional principles and constitutive effects must be the context for any decision made using other definitions of information, and ultimately the analytical standard against which any decisions made using other types of definitions must be judged.

The process of policy-making, then, may be pendulum-like, swinging back and forth between viewing decisions through the lens of information as a constitutive force in society and from the perspective offered by other types of definitions. The alternative, continued disagreement over a singular definition of information for policy-making purposes, invites a continuation of decision-making characterized by conflict rather than cooperation and the possibility that national and international regimes will be put in place by those who can most successfully wield brute force. Acceptance of a pluralistic approach to the problem of defining information, one that focuses on constitutive matters first and last, not only encourages cooperation but also keeps attention focused on the questions that should be at the heart of all information policy-making: what we're doing to ourselves.

Power

Ideas about the nature of power inform all policy, whether those ideas are well or poorly formed, explicit or implicit, and conscious or not. Though the concept of power has long been important in the social sciences, many who use the notion treat it as if it referred to something simple and singular, as if power always came in the same size and flavor. This is not the case. Political scientists typically discuss power in three forms (instrumental, structural, and symbolic), but the informatization of society has brought to our attention and vastly increased the importance of a fourth form of power: informational. Similarly, political scientists have long distinguished between power in its actual and potential states, but digital technologies have made power in its virtual state important as well. Further articulating the concept of power reveals distinctions by attributes, units, and direction. Even with such insights in place, however, the study of power can be problematic.

The Problematics of Power

Notions central to the analysis of power that have often been treated as simple are now understood to be complex. Though power is often treated as a characteristic of a country or a person, it is actually a relationship—and precisely because we are immersed in power relations, they can be difficult to perceive. Theories of power tend to the abstract and deal in universals, but the practice of power is concrete and particular. The potential for power can only be estimated, and actual power only measured post hoc. Most analytical approaches focus on the exercise of one type of power—military force, say, or propaganda—but in many cases various forms of power are enacted simultaneously and are interrelated. In order to achieve comparative analysis, therefore, there must be ways of converting measurement of one form of power into another (e.g., how many slogans equal a gun?) and of understanding relationships among forms of power (e.g., what happens to a gun when there are slogans around it?). The literature focuses on the power holder and only rarely on the subject of the exercise of power—yet the autonomy, vulnerability, and perceptions of the subject play important roles in determining the outcome of an exercise of power. Analyses of power usually assume that causal relations are linear, when often they are not.

Changes in the nature of society that derive from the process of informatization as well as other factors generate additional problems in the study of power. Many expressions of power are difficult to perceive because the effects take so long before they are recognizable, as with genetic damage. There may be no means evident to the human senses to perceive the exercise of power, as with new forms of surveillance. Some effects of the exercise of power, such as environmental problems, elude nation-state-based reporting mechanisms because they are transnational. Increasing turbulence in social relations makes it harder to understand

Table 2.1
Forms of power

Form	Definition
Instrumental	Power that shapes human behaviors by manipulating the material world via physical force.
Structural	Power that shapes human behaviors by manipulating the social world via rules and institutions.
Symbolic	Power that shapes human behaviors by manipulating the material, social, and symbolic worlds via ideas, words, and images.
Informational	Power that shapes human behaviors by manipulating the informational bases of instrumental, structural, and symbolic power.

the effects of power. Power relations may be indeterminate, leading to what sociologist Craig Calhoun describes as a loss of intelligibility; and even when determinate, we have few analytical tools to cope with the exercise of power during periods of change. The number of claimants to power is multiplying as new holders of traditional forms of power emerge (e.g., the entry of women into corporate and political worlds), previously unacknowledged forms of power become visible (e.g., the socialization power of mothers), and new forms of power empower new power holders (e.g., computer hackers proficient in computer programming).

Forms of Power

Analyses of power have typically distinguish among three forms—instrumental, structural, and symbolic. (Joseph Nye appealingly refers to these as "sharp power," "sticky power," and "soft power.") In today's information-intense society, however, a fourth form, informational power, has moved to center stage (table 2.1).

Instrumental power Instrumental power shapes human behaviors by manipulating the material world via physical force. This is the most ancient and familiar form of power, exercised by military and police forces via the use of weapons. It has been of central importance to the modern state since it began to appear in the sixteenth century. Indeed, the classic description of a state is a political entity that exercises physical control over a specified geographic space. In the second half of the twentieth century, concern about this form of power underlay the effort to achieve an international "balance of power." Military historians often provide the analyses that inspire political strategies using instrumental power.

Structural power Structural power shapes human behaviors by manipulating the social world via rules and institutions. Both rules and institutions limit the range of choices available and determine how specific activities will be undertaken, and both systematize behaviors so that there is less uncertainty and more confidence regarding expectations. Laws, treaties, and political processes themselves are all ways in which states exercise structural power. As political scientist Susan Strange has influentially argued, economic relations also provide a means of exercising structural power—whether by states or by nonstate actors. The study of structural power, however, has more often been the province of sociologists than of political scientists.

Symbolic power Symbolic power shapes human behaviors by manipulating the material, social, and symbolic worlds via ideas, words, and images. Symbolic power also has ancient roots; as military historian John Keegan has noted, even in the premodern world, war was surrounded by ritual and ceremony. The exercise of symbolic power external to the state is often referred to as "propaganda" or "public diplomacy." States exercise symbolic power internally via campaigns, efforts to massage public opinion, and through the education system. The study of symbolic power is often undertaken by those in the field of political communication.

Informational power Informational power shapes human behaviors by manipulating the informational bases of instrumental, structural, and symbolic power. Informational power dominates power in other forms, changes how they are exercised, and alters the nature of their effects. Informational power can be described as "genetic," because it appears at the genesis—the informational origins—of the materials, social structures, and symbols that are the stuff of power in its other forms. Today's "smart weapons," which can identify a target and direct themselves to it without human intervention, are examples of the effect of informational power on the exercise of instrumental power. The ability to monitor compliance with intellectual property rights law through surveillance of Internet use is an example of the influence of informational power on the exercise of structural power. The ability to tailor Web-based messages to the individual who is surfing online is an example of the impact of informational power on the exercise of symbolic power. And the ability to manipulate the data on the basis of which decisions are made—and to target individuals for special treatment by profiling on the basis of statistical analysis of data gathered from multiple sources—are examples of informational power in its own right. As is the case with other aspects of the information society, the study of informational power is taking place within multiple disciplinary homes.

Relationships among these forms of power are multiple. They are usually interdependent, often occur together, and may be cumulative. During the industrial era, for example, the growth of large arms firms tightly aligned with particular governments linked instrumental power to structural power. Often forms of power are related in compensatory ways, maximizing the use of strengths to offset weaknesses. The use of each type of power affects the environment in which other forms exist or might exist. In many cases, an increase in the use of one form of power is accompanied by a decrease in the use of other forms of power, as when heavy use of the instrumental power of police force is accompanied by a retreat from the effort to wield consensual force. Information flows that influence public perception (symbolic power) may so significantly transform modes of production (instrumental power) that organizational practices are changed (structural power) in ways that make it possible to gather and process additional types of information (informational power). The exercise of power therefore most often involves a suite of strategies.

Phases of Power

Political scientists also distinguish between power in its actual phase (as it is being exercised) and in a potential phase (power that is claimed, but not currently being used). Actual power is potential power in use, as when guns are firing, laws are implemented, and persuasive campaigns affect the vote. Potential power becomes actual only through specific practices, and information processing, distribution, and use are often necessary for the transformation of power from potential to actual. The number of tanks owned by an army, laws on the books that aren't currently being enforced, and ideas for communication campaigns are all examples of power in its potential phase.

In today's information-intense environment, it is now also possible to recognize power in a "virtual" phase (table 2.2). Following economist Roberto Scazzieri in his definition of virtual materials and processes, virtual power includes techniques of power that are not currently extant but that might be brought into existence using available resources and knowledge. It includes power that can be acquired or developed through

Table 2.2
Phases of power

Phase	Definition
Actual	Power that is currently being exercised.
Potential	Claimed resources and techniques of power that are not currently in use.
Virtual	Resources and techniques of power that are not currently extant but that might be brought into existence using available resources and knowledge.

transfers of power, use of resources, or shifts in internal or external conditions. Knowledge is so central to power in its virtual phase that every expansion of the knowledge base of a nation-state concomitantly causes a growth in the realm of potential power available to it. An example of power in its virtual phase would be government control over the development of encryption techniques or of scientific research in areas believed to be of value for national security purposes; in such instances the actual techniques or inventions do not yet exist. Power in its virtual phase is so important to national competitiveness and the ability to protect national security in the twenty-first century that research and development (R&D) are now considered key resources for the informational state.

Evaluations of the validity of claims to power in its potential and virtual phases are difficult, for they involve what political scientists refer to as capacity—the financial resources, knowledge of how to use those resources, political will, sovereign integrity, stability of administrative control, loyalty and skill among officials, infrastructure, and industrial base that are required to actually put the resources and techniques of potential and virtual power to use.

The State

The emergence of the informational state has taken place within a long history of successive state forms. The bureaucratic state and the cultural nation have separate histories; some nations are spread over several states, and it is common for states to have within them more than one nation. The effort to join the two in the nation-state was a feature of modernity. Among the ways in which different political entities can be distinguished is in the form of power in which each specializes. Thus this brief review of the history of the nation-state as a type of political organization is helpful for understanding just what the evolution of the informational state means. Again, we begin by looking at the factors that problematize analysis of the state. The section continues with a theoretical discussion of the field within which political entities become transformed, and then goes on to look at the types of nations and states out of which today's informational state has evolved.

Problematics of the State

Evidence of the analytical complexity of the state can be found in the multiplicity of definitions (David Easton counted over 140 in 1981) and typologies (in the neo-Marxist camp alone, schools of thought on the nature of the state are variously counted as two, three, five, and six). Discussion of the state tends to mix levels of analysis, as in discussion of foreign affairs that must necessarily include attention to both domestic and international matters. Modes of analysis are often also mixed; normative theories of the state often blend with descriptions. Appropriate and useful data are hard to find. Fundamental questions, such as the actual and normative constitutive roles of the state and its relationship to economic forces, are still open, and it may be that answers to those questions change over time and from circumstance to circumstance.

The uniqueness of the historical experience of each state makes it difficult to generalize. Those categorized together and described in the same general terms still differ from each other in legally important dimensions, such as the ways in which information is collected and used for purposes of policy-making and the cultural meaning attached to specific legal concepts. Even where states are strong, implementation of the law occurs through the processes of other social systems, less formal and not as well understood as the law.

It is possible for states—forms of government—to undergo change because they are complex adaptive systems produced by interactions among cultural habits, formal laws, discourse, and modes of organization within an ever-changing field of possibilities. Like other complex adaptive systems, states respond to shifts in resources and in their environments with transformations that range from very minor fluctuations through significant changes in structure or behavior all the way to turbulence, chaos, and perhaps a complete change in the nature of the system itself. One of the most important distinctions among the ways states change, which will be a theme running through this book, is the difference between changes within a system that still remains stable in its form and changes to the very nature of the state as a system itself. Theories and concepts drawn from systems theory run throughout the analysis offered here.

The fact that the nation-state has involved both cultural and bureaucratic modes of organization for the last several hundred years means that each must be understood separately in order to grasp the tensions affecting today's informational state. We look here at first the history of the culturally defined nation, the bureaucratically defined state, and the nation-state in its diverse forms in order to understand the transformation in political form—and, therefore, the law—manifested by the transformation to the informational state.

The Nation

"Nations" are communities that define themselves, or are defined by others, through cultural features. Though nationality, ethnicity, and cultural groups are all related, they are not the same thing. As political scientist Liah Greenfeld makes clear, every ethnicity is made up of many different features, no one of which is constant across all cultures. In the formation of nations into political entities, only certain features of an ethnic group or culture will be emphasized as critical to national identity—and which features those will be differs from nation to nation.

Greenfeld traces the development of the concept of the nation through five sequential stages:

- *Nation = a group of foreigners* In Rome, the Latin word *natio* was used to refer to people who came from other parts of the empire and generally stayed together socially while in Rome. At the beginning, therefore, the concept of the nation referred to the population of the political periphery and had some negative connotations.
- *Nation = a community of opinion* In the medieval world, students came from many places to study at universities. Because those who came from the same location tended to share an intellectual perspective, in the university environment the concept of the nation also came to refer to a particular worldview. As a result, the concept gained more positive connotations.
- *Nation = an elite* During the medieval period, debates over theological points became extremely important and people traveled from many universities to participate in religious disputations. Because philosophical dominance translated into political power in this era, members of the nations from universities came to be representative, to varying degrees, of

the political authority of their home regions. The nation, then, came to refer to a decision-making, or political, elite.

• *Nation = a sovereign people* The nation as a political unit first appeared in the sixteenth century with the notion that power resides in the entire population. The equation of peoplehood with nationhood was then exported around the world with the British Empire. The formation of the United States was an exemplary manifestation of this trend, for at the moment of its nationhood there was nothing else but the concept of an equation between a sovereign people and nationhood that united the population of the new country.

• *Nation = a unique people* In each case, once a nation came into being, it became associated with the particular characteristics of the group of people involved; thus, over time, the concept of the nation came to be associated with the uniqueness of each sovereign people. With this last move, the concept of the nation came to have two meanings, one particular and one nonparticular, each giving rise to different types of social behavior, culture, and political institutions.

Nationhood is intimately intertwined with ethnicity, but the relationship is not an identity. Greenfeld is again helpful here. She points out that ethnicity is composed of a myriad of characteristics, but no single characteristic or group of characteristic is necessarily part of every ethnicity, and no clear line distinguishes historically and/or empirically demonstrable characteristics from those that are constructed. Whereas diet, for example, is a distinguishing characteristic for some ethnicities, it will be irrelevant in the definition of other groups. The same ethnic group may use different characteristics to distinguish themselves in various circumstances; in the United States, for example, gypsies usually dress like others but retain their language, while in Europe gypsy dress is often distinct but often the vernacular language is spoken.

Ethnicity—and, therefore, nationality—are artifacts of statistical as well as perceptual constructions, and the history of the census in different countries makes it clear that there has been political utility in the often arbitrary definition taxonomies and redefinition taxonomies. Still, categories are translated into institutions (e.g., the establishment of different types of schools for different ethnic groups), practices (e.g., restricting access to certain types of employment to specific ethnic groups), and physical separation (e.g., ghettoization of one or more ethnic groups). As successive generations live with and are socialized by the experiences that these institutions, practices, and locales produce, even identities invented by others become very real to those to whom they have been applied. Benedict Anderson thus describes nations as "imagined communities" for which cultural forms are as important as, or more important than, historical detail.

Though the nation has long been bureaucratized by the state, the political power of national cultural identity became a locus of political agitation towards the close of the twentieth century and remains so. As political economist Immanuel Wallerstein noted in 1990, culture has become the battleground of the world system. Pressure is put on bureaucratic state structures by national groups, sometimes—as in the case of the former Yugoslavia—resulting in a redrawing of geopolitical borders. Even when existing geopolitical entities survive, national identity today continues to provide a powerful and effective organizational lure that, as sociologist Alberto Melucci points out, has widely replaced class identity for political purposes.

The State

In ancient Greece, city-states functioned geopolitically, but in its modern form, the nation-state first appeared toward the end of the sixteenth century. A number of variations on this political form and its techniques of governance have appeared since that time. The informational state is thus the latest development in a several-hundred-year evolution of the nation-state.

The premodern state In theory, the idea of a secular state was introduced by Niccolò Machiavelli (1469–1527) and Jean Bodin (1520–1596). In practice, secular lords began to operate on their own in ways that diverged from the desires of the Roman Catholic Church during the same era. The Treaty of Westphalia in 1648 marked the birth of the modern state by bringing to a close the period during which the Holy Roman Empire was the most effective political force in Europe. When geographically based political entities signed the treaty, they officially recognized each other and so the "international" system and the modern state came into being simultaneously.

Birth of the modern nation-state Philosopher Thomas Hobbes (1588–1679) further distinguished the state from civil society, meaning those areas of social life, from private life to the economy, that are organized outside the control of the state. The concept and practice of civil society opened a space between the polity (the citizenry as a political unit) and the state, and justified putting bounds on the latter. Mercantilist economic theory justified international trade by suggesting that overall wealth could be increased by emphasizing the comparative advantage of each state, with the simultaneous effect of reinforcing the notion that each state was unique. Over the next couple of centuries, states experimented both domestically and beyond their borders. There was a progressive widening, and then narrowing, of the gap between civil society and the state. Since the geographic bounding of secular states linked political entities to particular cultural groups, this type of political form became known as the nation-state.

The bureaucratic state Secular nation-states adopted a number of bureaucratic practices that had been modeled by the Catholic Church, but took them much further. Beginning in the early nineteenth century, particularly in Germany and Austria, there was a great deal of deliberate experimentation with bureaucratic form and analysis of the effectiveness of those practices. Over the course of that century, as a result of imperialism, those practices spread across Europe and North America and throughout societies around the world. Innovation in policy techniques and tools continued. The word "bureaucracy" came into use to describe these new practices, and the type of nation-state that resulted is known as the bureaucratic state.

The bureaucratic welfare state In the last decades of the nineteenth century, a number of countries around the world (as diverse as Australia, Sweden, and Brazil) began to develop support systems such as social spending policies and labor laws. Such policies multiplied in number and their use spread during the twentieth century. This form of the nation-state was attractive in part because it responded to the need for safety-net policies in response to the worldwide Depression of the 1930s. Innovations in information and communication technologies, however, also played a role in the development of the bureaucratic welfare state. During the late nineteenth and early twentieth centuries, office equipment such as the typewriter and adding machine came into use. While we do not generally perceive items such as file cabinets or genres such as statistical tables as technologies today, they were very much considered so when first introduced. Indeed, early in the twentieth century printed forms were considered "systems," and their use marked the height of sophistication in organizational practice. In order to function, the bureaucratic welfare state needed to be able to collect and process vast amounts of information, and these new technologies made such practices possible.

With such policies, the state began to intervene much more intimately in the affairs of civil society, marking another change in the nation-state toward what became known as the bureaucratic welfare state. Following World War II, the bureaucratic welfare form of governance was extended into the international arena through the first-ever establishment of a global economic system that included the World Bank, the International Monetary Fund (IMF), and the General Agreement on Tariffs and Trade (GATT). Sociologist Anthony Giddens describes the impact of welfare policies as so great that civil society in effect disappeared.

The informational state The international system put in place after World War II made it easier for corporations to grow through activity outside of their home countries. By the 1970s, multinational and transnational corporations had learned how to maximize their operations while minimizing the extent to which they were subject to the constraints put in place by any specific nation-state. Political scientists began to talk about the loss of state power relative to other types of players, with some even suggesting that the state might disappear altogether.

But of course the state did not disappear; instead, it again changed its form. In processes still playing themselves out, the state has been reasserting its strength in three ways. First, national governments are learning to master the same types of informational power that corporations and other non-state actors have been successfully using in their challenges to the strength of geopolitical entities. The expression of informational power in laws and regulations is the subject of the second half of this book. Second, states are developing techniques for extending the use of private sector entities as regulatory agents, turning private centers of power to state purposes. One example of this trend is the requirement that Internet service providers (ISPs) help national governments monitor Internet use for both national security and intellectual property rights abuses. Third, the state—like the firm—is increasingly characterized as "networked," because of the multiplicity of fundamental ways in which governments are intertwined with each other and with non-state actors. Examples here often reverse the direction of support just described, with governments taking on the responsibility of ensuring the most favorable conditions possible for corporate activities; national agreements with the World Trade Organization under the General Agreement on Trade in Services provide examples of this trend. The use of information technologies and informational power is so important to all of these ways in which the nation-state is evolving that today's dominant political form is best described as the informational state.

A Typology of States by Form of Power

Although nation-states differ greatly from each other and are in many ways each unique, they can be grouped into types about which generalizations can usefully be made according to the form of power emphasized. Culturally defined nations have specialized in symbolic power, bureaucratically defined states make great use of structural power, today's informational state is developing the techniques of informational power, and all geopolitical entities use instrumental power as appropriate and when possible. Of course these types rarely appear in a pure form; the typology offered here represents relative emphases in the use of power by each form of the state. Types can be distinguished along these dimensions:

- temporality,
- mode of organization,
- the process by which individuals are identified as members of the whole,
- the means by which the individual participates in the whole,
- the nature of borders,
- the role of communication, and
- the form of power that dominates.

Because nations are defined culturally, structure is organic to the communities involved, key features are cultural, and the temporal ideal is defined in sacred terms. Nations are bounded by cultural features such as language. The individual becomes a member of society through varying combinations of genetic inheritance and cultural practice. Communication fulfills what James Carey refers to as a ritual, rather than transmission, function. Decision-making is based on the discernment of meaning. The nation finds its greatest strength in symbolic power.

States, however, are defined in terms of the features of their bureaucratic organizations rather than in cultural terms. Their greatest strength is in the exercise of structural power. States as organizations exert their control by developing institutions, rules, and regulations based on a logic claimed to be rational. Elaborate information collection and processing systems are necessary. The temporal vision of the state is of a stable system in equilibrium. Political borders and the definition of certain behaviors as criminal or treasonous provide boundaries. The individual relates to the whole by engaging with bureaucratic structures. In Carey's typology, communication within a state fulfills a transmission function.

The modern nation-state represents the effort to bring the cultural and bureaucratic modes of organizing society together. Bureaucratic methods were increasingly used to distinguish among cultural groups within colonial environments to enforce a state-, rather than community-driven, sense of difference; language use is enforced via educational standards rather than arising naturally; and so forth. There is a wide variety of types of relationships possible between the two modes. In Britain, for example, public service broadcasting served the bureaucratic state, but in Ireland it served the cultural needs of the nation. Operationalization of specific, even arbitrary, conceptualizations of the nation can be used to serve the needs of the bureaucratic nation-state. In times of significant political change, the relationships between the two are often the subject of intense renegotiation.

The informational state is characterized by multiple interdependencies with other state and non-state entities in ways that largely require use of the global information infrastructure for information creation, processing, flows, and use. Informational states use control over information to produce and reproduce loci of power and to carve out areas of autonomous influence within the network environment. The temporal vision of the informational state is transformational in ways best described through the use of complex adaptive systems theory. Complexity, self-reflexivity, and change are key organizational features. Boundaries are mobile, permeable, and more accurately defined in terms of informational reach than of geographic space. Although Carey's typology of types of communication is sufficient for the historic dichotomy between nations and states, today's conditions require adding a third type: Communication within the network state fulfills the self-organizational functions of complex adaptive systems in addition to ritual and transmission functions. Successful decision-making procedures incorporate various kinds of learning. The informational state specializes in the use of informational power.

Though the United States provides a prototypical example of the informational state, other countries placed quite differently within the global system are also developing in this direction. Indian software policy provides a clear example of state use of informational power. India does not define the bounds of the software industry it regulates geographically, for it is neither coterminous with the country's borders nor with firms identified as Indian firms. Rather, cultural networks built through international education and permanent and temporary migration by Indian-born programmers were drawn upon to enhance foreign direct investment (FDI) in India's software operations. The government's decision to make software a national priority was thus simultaneously a shift toward the support of net-based activity as a policy tool. Encouragement of exports through "deputation" (sending people abroad) and the willingness to rely upon foreign technologies for matters fundamental to the country's economic strength are also evidence of the Indian turn toward the informational state, interdependent with other entities and focused on the global information economy for survival. Information industries are encouraged through a number of nonmarket means, such as building infrastructure, in addition to the manipulations of the market typical of the modern nation-state. The middle class is seen as a repository of technical and managerial skills essential for successfully undertaking high-technology activities; as a result, the state is more involved in technical than in mass education.

There are other examples: Estonia claims it is leapfrogging stages of political as well as technological development by making ubiquitous access to the Internet not only a priority, but a right. In countries such as the United Kingdom and Germany, experimentation with new types of information policy tools is rife, concurrent with the dissolution of longstanding governmental practices. The South African government is attempting to stake out intellectual property rights in discoveries of its citizens, and Iceland has volunteered its population as a database for investigations into genetic information. Thus traces of the informational state, sometimes more developed and sometimes less so, are found across the world.

Information Policy for the Informational State

While information has many faces, it is its role as a constitutive force in society that is most important from a policy-making perspective. It is this impact of information creation, processing, flows, and use that makes information policy so fundamental to the exercise of power. The development of meta-technologies and the increasing information intensity of society have magnified the value of policy techniques for manipulating informational power. Governments that recognize this, and maximize their ability to use informational power, have made the transition from the type of political form known as the bureaucratic welfare state to that of the informational state.

Some of the practices associated with the informational state involve information policy practices and principles that are ancient, while others are quite new. Chapter 3 looks at contemporary information policy within the context of its ancient history, reviews problems associated with telling just what is information policy and what is not, and offers an approach to bounding the domain of information policy for the twenty-first century.

3

Bounding the Domain: Information Policy for the Twenty-first Century

When the U.S. Constitution was written, protections for freedom of expression stood out starkly in a landscape otherwise inhabited by policies for the economy, defense, and other matters quite distinct from speech or press. With the transformations from an agricultural to an industrial and now to an information economy, however, that landscape has become filled with laws and regulations dealing with information and communication. Like the economy, social life, work, and leisure, the law itself has become more "information-intense" as ever-greater proportions of it are taken up with new information technologies, the content they carry, and the activities they enable. The number of laws involved is vast: Over six hundred bills dealing with the Internet alone were on the table during the 107th Congress. Various strands of law dealing with information technologies and the content they carry have come together, often burying traditional concerns within a vast policy space.

While the Constitution protected communication in order to enable the political form of democracy, much current law for information technologies and content also or predominantly serves quite other purposes. There has long been a confusion over whether government decisions in support of R&D in the electronics industry, for example, is a matter of information or industrial policy. Similarly, copyright law can be understood as fundamental to our ability to communicate—or as economic policy. How a policy issue area is identified is political because it determines who participates in decision-making, the rhetorical frames and operational definitions applied, the analytical techniques and modes of argument used, and the resources—and goals—considered pertinent. When an information technology problem is defined as an economic, industrial, or trade issue, protections for speech and other important constitutional principles may not apply. An overemphasis on what is "new" about digital technologies exacerbates the danger that fundamental principles developed over centuries to protect civil liberties and promote effective democratic processes will be lost in the electronic environment.

This chapter looks at what makes the problem of defining information policy so difficult today; provides a very short look at the long history of information policy; and reviews competing approaches to bounding the domain, identifying strengths and weaknesses of each. The chapter concludes with a suggestion for how to define information policy for the twenty-first century in a way that maximizes the strengths of each approach and that recognizes different conceptual needs at each stage of the policy-making process.

The Definitional Problem

It used to be easy. The Constitution and its amendments—via principles described in full in chapter 4—ensured that citizens were able to use oral and print means of expression to communicate with each other and with their government about the constitution of society. Because content must be distributed as well as produced (and to be useful for constitutive purposes, distribution must be multidirectional), the synchronous and copresent sharing of ideas through assembly and asynchronous and distributed communication through publishing and the postal system were constitutionally protected. Because in order to meaningfully discuss the constitution of society citizens need access to information and freedom to form their own opinions on the basis of that information, both of these were also protected. And because to be effective ideas and opinions must be communicated to those who can act, the First Amendment further protected the right to seek changes in government.

From there it got more complicated. Technological innovation created truly mass media, expanding the set of regulatory subjects and adding issues raised by interactions among media. It was only about the time the first regulatory systems were being put in place for electronic media—in the 1920s—that the very word "media" came into use. Over time, interpretation of constitutional law for the mediated environment articulated a number of dimensions along which rights and responsibilities were differentiated: *context* (public v. private); *content* (political v. economic v. cultural v. personal); *genre* (fact v. fiction, fact v. opinion, and news v. history); *speakers* (public v. private, and individual v. corporate v. governmental); *receivers* (voluntary v. involuntary, adult v. minor, and competent adult v. incompetent adult); and *political condition* (war v. peace, and elections v. between elections). Meanwhile, communication scholars gradually turned away from a focus on communication as a social process and toward communication technologies as their subject matter.

By now, at the opening of the twenty-first century, the field within which information policy operates has broadened yet again. Innovation has further transformed the fundamental nature of the technologies involved and the extent to which society is reliant upon those technologies. The directly communicative functions of the media are now a relatively small proportion of the overall role of information technologies in society. The distinction between public and private communicative contexts has become one of choice and will, rather than ownership, control, and history of use. We have come to understand that both nonpolitical content such as data and the infrastructure that carries it can be means of exercising informational power with the potential for just as much constitutive effect—or more—than is found with the exercise of power in its instrumental, structural, or symbolic forms. And we now see that the horizon along which power is exercised is ever-receding, graspable only by those who can control power in its virtual form through ownership of the very processes by which information is created, processed, and used. We opened this chapter with the U.S. Constitution, but the history that brings us to this point began much earlier.

History

Though today policy is being made for a society describable as "new" and still changing, many strands of information policy are very old. The history is sometimes, but not always, cumulative: skills once gained can be lost, new technologies may be bested by those that came before, good ideas are forgotten, and policies sometimes worsen rather than improve the human condition. Practices that fall within today's information policy field exist in all human societies, from the earliest tribal formations on, whether they appear in forms that look like law, the institutional practices of governance, or the cultural habits of governmentality. The importance of information policy to political power began to rise along with the modern nation-state in the fifteenth century and its forms have become ever-more highly articulated over time. The writing of the U.S. Constitution marked a turning point in explicit recognition of the relative importance of information policy to political form. A review of premodern and modern information policy provides a background for understanding the complexities of the field of information policy today.

Premodern Information Policy

Anthropology tells us little directly about the role of information creation, processing, flows, and use in traditional societies. Information policy tools and techniques still in use today, however, appeared not only in the tribal world, but also in cultures such as those of India, the Roman Empire, and that created by the Roman Catholic Church.

Tribal information society A longstanding bias against acknowledging the presence of anything not deemed to be "traditional" to a society under study prevented ethnographers from recording evidence of the appearance and uses of print, broadcasting, and other contemporary media in the communities they studied. Indeed, use of such media has been explicitly associated with the transition from traditional to modern society, and thus it marked the passage out of the terrain typically of interest to anthropologists. Storytelling, conversation, and communicative uses of symbols were recorded, but a secondary reading of existing anthropological literature to highlight what has been learned about these types of informational and communicative practices has not yet developed. Marshall McLuhan's romantic but provocative suggestion that technological change might cause a return to earlier modes of social organization is a reminder that undertaking an examination of information policy in traditional societies would be useful, even though, as Walter Ong pointed out, whatever forms a postliterate society takes, it will inevitably be quite different from that which was found prior to domination by print.

Eric Michaels has offered the most thorough analysis to date of information policy in an oral society. Though working on a contract with the Australian government that sought to encourage television use by remote aboriginal peoples, Michaels took up the challenge of helping the Warlpiri protect their traditional cultural tools and knowledge in the contemporary environment. He came to understand the Warlpiri as an information society, because in that culture, knowledge is the most important form of property, defining individual roles and status and providing the basis for interpersonal, group, and intergroup relationships. Strict rules govern the conditions under which information can be shared within and across Warlpiri communities, though some degree of individual freedom remains in the implementation of those rules. It is considered inappropriate, for example, to show images of those who have died, but individuals may choose to share a photograph of a deceased relative under intimate conditions. Study of the Warlpiri enlarges our understanding of the range of possible ways of organizing around familiar distinctions; in this culture, for example, open space out of doors is not necessarily public space.

The Roman Empire The Romans are credited with developing a number of information policy tools still in use today, though they were not always the first to use them. We look to the Romans as the source of our ideas about the roles of information in politics and diplomacy, for example, but there were already highly developed practices in these areas by the fifth and sixth centuries BCE in India. Many Roman tools fell into disuse during the period of political dominance by the Catholic Church, but they remain influential because they were taken up again at the time of the French Revolution as fundamental to *raison d'état* ("reason of state"), the rationales by which a government operates. Other modes of influence were cultural, as in Roman modeling of a public sphere for discourse, and philosophical, as exemplified by notions of civility that influenced John Milton and other theorists of freedom of the press.

The most obvious and well-known of Roman information policy tools were those used for command and control. Providing a model for the "post roads" included in the U.S. Constitution as necessary national infrastructure, the Romans built a ninety-thousand-mile road system to enable communications with the far reaches of their empire. Roman optical signaling systems were not improved upon until the invention of the telegraph, and the communication practices central to Roman military organization remain in use in the twenty-first century. Geographical handbooks, maps, and guides were developed to help interpret texts from various locations throughout the empire and to provide information about obstacles and resources available to soldiers as they moved about. When Roman emperors traveled, they even carried along card registrars with detailed information on their citizens, developed through extensive door-to-door mapping of individual homes. Archives useful for foreign relations grew in importance once Roman emperors stopped traveling with their troops. Because physicians were in high demand both domestically and abroad they were often used as political envoys, providing an early model for the professional diplomats. The Romans understood the political value of control over knowledge, drawing students from throughout the empire to their universities. The principle that speech could be restricted during times of war was also first expressed, and acted upon, by Roman leaders.

The Catholic Church Though the Catholic Church abandoned some information policy tools used by the Romans, it further developed others. The Romans enumerated people for taxation, but the Church made the registration of all births and burials mandatory in 1597. (It was not until 1736 that the information was gathered in duplicate so that copies could be given to secular governments.) It was the Catholic Church that launched the use of information campaigns to serve the purposes of governance when, in 1622, Pope Gregory XV organized the Congregatio de Propaganda Fide as a proselytizing organization. The relative decline in literacy levels after Roman times made it possible for the Church to control access to knowledge while simultaneously using popular culture via theater, artifice, and imagery for purposes of persuasion. The Church exercised direct censorship by labeling ideas it disliked as heretical (and punishing the proponents of those ideas, sometimes with death). It also attempted indirect censorship through a prohibition on the printing press. By the mid-seventeenth century, the Church—led by the Jesuits—had achieved near-monopoly control of higher education (itself a medium), and systematic efforts to map the land and master the languages of peoples governed by the Church were additional techniques of control via knowledge still in use by contemporary nation-states.

Early Modern Information Policy

Innovations in information structures (double-entry bookkeeping and the replacement of Roman numerals with Arabic numerals) and technologies (durable moveable type and enduring ink) made it possible for the nation-state to extend its information policy into the statistical realm. Two different approaches to statistics for the purposes of governance arose in the seventeenth century, with the Germans looking at individuals through the lens of categories defined by the state and the British starting from the details of the perceived natural order. (It is worth noting that, from the beginning, many distrusted the quantitative nature of statistics because they believed the most important features of a nation-state could not be captured in this way.)

Needs of the military stimulated the development of standardized printed forms and filing systems. Imperial governments gathered extensive data about their colonies in order to exert control and maximize economic advantage in ways that have since become embedded in information policy; these practices were so key to the imperial enterprise that Thomas Richards refers to the countries involved as "archival states." The late eighteenth century also saw the beginnings of modern mail systems, as rulers ceased leading their own troops into battle but still needed to communicate with those on the front, and as individuals linked together economically in different locations needed to keep in touch. Intellectual property rights had by then been in place for a couple of hundred years and a variety of regulations shaped narrative genres in ways that often served political ends.

By the time of the revolution that created the United States, then, many elements of what today is comprised by the domain of information policy had already come into existence, though not all were recognized as such, and not all were taken up by those who wrote the Constitution. Recognition of the centrality of information to state power led to legal innovations to protect individuals from the state as well. Legal principles and tools of this in the U.S. Constitution have since been incorporated into the texts of almost all other constitutions in the world. For this reason, the revolutionary moment in the United States marks a turning point in the history of information policy.

Modern Information Policy

With the development of the bureaucratic form of the nation-state, and its further evolution into the welfare state, the use of information policy tools expanded and became more highly articulated. This process was accelerated, of course, by the informatization of society, particularly during the last decades of the twentieth century though this process began much earlier (see table 3.1). The variety of ways of thinking about what we now refer to as the Internet exemplifies the multifaceted nature of information policy today.

Nineteenth century As information technologies continued to develop over the course of the nineteenth century, the number of information policy issues that the law needed to address first multiplied, and then exploded. The bureaucratic state required analysis of the administrative facets of governance, an information-intense process. As the bureaucratic welfare state emerged, governments expanded their activities further into the private realm in order to supply social services such as medical care and the safety net supports of the welfare system. Each of these again added to the domain of information policy by demanding detailed statistical knowledge of the populations being served, campaigns to educate citizens about the services available, and increasingly elaborate institutions to process data about the provision of services. This further bureaucratization of the state in turn drew further attention to the study

Table 3.1
Stages of the information society

Stage 1: 1830s–1900 Electrification, globalization, extreme articulation of the fact, new organizational forms (international organizations, distributed information organizations, and large corporations), concern about the effects of innovations
Stage 2: 1900–1960 Widespread experience of mass communication, professionalization of the information industries, heightened legal attention to information, continued evolution of organizational form, fact and play
Stage 3: 1960–1990 Awareness of the informatization of society, the appearance of information policy qua information policy, the second round of globalization, development of multinational and transnational corporations, attacks on the fact
Stage 4: 1990–2001 Harmonization of hardware and software protocols across systems, network organizations, the hyperreal and alternative facts
Stage 5: 2001– Ubiquitous embedded computing, merger of digital and biological entities, the informational state

of administration—the "policy science"—itself. Meanwhile the telegraph and telephone demanded regulatory attention. The nineteenth century also saw a lot of activity regarding structuring cultural aspects of the nation in ways that had policy consequences. The design of information architectures such as dictionaries, grammars, and encyclopedias and expansion of the university system became important tools of nationalism.

Early twentieth century Political, cultural, and technological developments triggered further developments in information policy in the early twentieth century. In the United States, mass resistance to government policy during World War I launched sustained attention to First Amendment analysis and the articulation of detailed policies for the treatment of political speech in a democracy. New mediums and genres appeared, such as comic books and film, that stimulated questions about censorship. Even the telephone introduced a range of social and cultural issues of concern.

It was technological innovation, however, that most significantly expanded the domain of information policy. It did so for three reasons:

- *New types of communicative activities* The use of new technologies, alone and in combination, brought into being a new means of distributing ideas that needed constitutional attention: the mass media. The organizations that produce and distribute content thus began to be seen as subjects of industrial and social policy as well as the locus of intellectual property rights.

• *New types of legal problems* Innovation raised new types of legal problems, such as regulation of interactions among media (e.g., between newspapers and radio), in addition to the need to develop additional regulatory systems to deal with electronic means of distribution (broadcasting and telecommunications).

• *New sensitivities to possible issues* New technologies heightened sensitivity to the kinds of damage that mediated communications could cause individuals as well as society at large (e.g., via invasions of privacy).

The Communications Act of 1934 completed a process that had begun in 1910 of distinguishing print, broadcast, and telecommunications for regulatory purposes. Constitutional law, particularly First Amendment jurisprudence, continued to govern communications in print. The Federal Communications Commission (FCC), created by the 1934 act, was mandated to create two completely distinct regulatory systems, one for wired communication (then telegraph and the telephone), and one for wireless (then radio and, soon, over-the-air television). As has been explained so clearly by Ithiel de Sola Pool, each of these systems started from a different regulatory assumption. For print, the fundamental rule was maximization of the free flow of information. For broadcast, the original approach was to designate those relatively few speakers who could own broadcast licenses as "trustees" for all others. Trustee responsibilities to those who did not have licenses justified some constraints and demands upon their activities not applied to those who produced print content. And for telecommunications (the telegraph and telephone), the governing principle was common carriage with its two basic rules: the same type of service must be provided to all who desired service, and the service provider should have no involvement at all in the content carried.

Because regulation of these technologies still had to take place within the First Amendment context, three justifications for asserting tighter controls on the electronic media were put forward. First, there was a need for *gatekeeping*, to determine who would be allowed to offer broadcast or telecommunications services. At the time of the 1934 Communications Act, technical limitations made it impossible for everyone who wanted to become involved with broadcasting to do so. In the oral environment, of course, anyone who wants to speak can do so, and it was believed that access to the printing press was so ubiquitous and the cost of printing so low that in effect this technology was also available to all, but the same situation did not obtain when it came to radio, and then television, broadcasting. The fact that choices had to be made about who would be allowed to broadcast, and under what conditions, justified the licensing system, even though licensing of print was forbidden. With the vast capacity for electronic communication now available—about 90 percent of the world's network infrastructure is currently unused, or "dark"—this justification for regulation no longer holds. Second, there was a need for a *traffic cop*, to keep those using the electromagnetic spectrum from interfering with each other; this justification for regulation remains valid today. And third, there was the *oomph factor*, the belief that, somehow, broadcasting had so much more effect than print that it required regulation to protect society. Here, social scientists differ regarding the extent to which they interpret research results to support this position, as well as on the question of whether effects are more importantly different in kind.

The Contemporary Environment

One hesitates to use the word "postmodern" for the contemporary information policy environment, but certainly there have been such significant changes in the regulatory subject that, combined with the transformation to an informational state, it should not be surprising that many policy issues and policy-making processes are being reconsidered. This section looks at the continuation of the history reported upon previously, spends some time focusing specifically on the Internet, and concludes by reviewing briefly the contributions of international and global decision-making to law and regulation at the national level.

The late twentieth century The last decades of the twentieth century were absorbed by reactions to technological change. Norbert Wiener, father of the field of cybernetics, warned as early as 1960 that innovation in information technologies would create a number of policy problems. While Daniel Bell's 1973 book *The Coming of Post-Industrial Society* brought such issues to popular attention, others identified the policy implications of technological innovation in the area of information and communication early on, including national security advisor Zbigniew Brzezinski and First Amendment analysts Thomas I. Emerson and David Bazelon. Communication scholar George Gerbner was among the first to argue that information policy needed to be treated as a distinct domain, larger than the terrain of law and policy typically considered to be media law, and Alan Westin began to identify potential threats to privacy and democracy from the new technologies in 1966.

The struggle to adapt legacy law for the digital environment began with an effort to place new technologies into existing categories. In an example of this type of "round peg in a square hole" effort, there was extensive debate over whether cable television was more like the telephone or more like traditional TV, even though the new technology had important characteristics that made it significantly different from either for regulatory purposes. By the mid-1990s, it was recognized that the legal field needed to be reconceptualized in order to develop an adequate policy response to the contemporary context, and new laws and regulations began to appear.

Even without the convergence of these different technologies into one technological system brought about by digitization, however, the use of disparate regulatory approaches for diverse media was legally problematic. Two Supreme Court cases made this point dramatically. In *Red Lion Broadcasting v. FCC* (1969), the Court upheld the constitutionality of the Fairness Doctrine, which at the time required broadcasters to present all sides of controversial issues of public concern if they presented those issues at all. Though the Fairness Doctrine was later abandoned as part of broadcast deregulation, in *Red Lion* the Court held that this type of constraint on regulatory discretion was justified if doing so would further the goals of the First Amendment by ensuring that a diversity of viewpoints entered public discourse. In *Miami Herald v. Tornillo* (1974), the Court was asked to rule on the constitutionality of a state statute establishing a right to reply to newspaper content, a type of constraint on editorial discretion in pursuit of First Amendment values that parallel some regulatory constraints on broadcasters. In *Miami Herald*, however, the Court took the opposite position from that which it had taken in *Red Lion*, striking the statute down as unconstitutional precisely because of its impact on the First Amendment rights of editors. The only justification for taking such diametrically opposed positions—by the same Court, and within the same time period—was that the medium involved in *Red Lion* was broadcasting and the one involved in *Miami Herald* was print.

Lee Bollinger, who at the time of this writing is the president of Columbia University, put forward the argument that these two cases established a justification for a "partial regulatory system" that supported regulatory intervention into the editorial control of one medium precisely because there was another that remained unregulated. This was an outlier position, however; for the rest, the conjunction of these two cases drew attention to a contradiction in legal treatment of different media that demanded resolution in the name of equity and fairness. The additional need to develop a legal response to digital technologies only increased the stakes and urgency of resolving a situation already perceived as untenable.

Over the course of almost two decades, beginning in the late 1960s and concluding only in the mid-1980s, the FCC began to think through the regulatory implications of the convergence of technologies via three rounds of investigations (*Computer Inquiry I*, *Computer Inquiry II*, and *Computer Inquiry III*) that focused on problems raised by the mix of regulated and unregulated flows of information through the same infrastructure. The problem was never resolved conclusively. Language in the 1934 act that gave the FCC control over matters "auxiliary" to these two communication systems, originally intended to apply to things such as telephone poles, was used by the FCC to conclude that it had the right to regulate types of information flows previously unregulated and, indeed, the entire computer industry—though it would "forebear" from doing so for the time being.

Beginning around 1970, the U.S. Congress also began to hold hearings regarding issues that had arisen, or that it believed would arise, from the use of new information technologies. Questions about whether the FCC would be the most appropriate regulator for a transformed technological environment were among the concerns that led to the change from a permanent budget authorization to temporary or multiyear authorizations. For several years, beginning in 1976, Congress held hearings every year on the possibility of establishing a comprehensive national communications policy. In 1976, two hundred members of the House of Representatives cosponsored the Communications Consumer Reform Act which, had it passed, would have ended nearly all competition in telecommunications service, an event that spurred the FCC to pay much more attention to competitive issues. Concerns went beyond regulation of the technologies themselves. Fears that innovations in information and communication technologies would weaken the competitive position of the United States globally, for example, were reasons behind the hearings in Congress in the 1970s regarding reorganization of the executive branch, and appreciation of the importance of digital technologies to the military inspired export controls that affected the information industries.

The impact of the Internet The complexities of dealing with digital technologies from a policy perspective were exemplified by debate over the digital broadband network. This discussion took place in multiple venues, each of which concentrated on a different facet of the infrastructure. It must be remembered that what we experience as the Internet is only the public face of the global information infrastructure, carrying only a small portion of the content and activities conducted via the network.

The earliest policy approach took place within the rubric of improving the speed and flexibility of the telecommunications network through global agreement upon technical standards for an Integrated Services Digital Network (ISDN). The ISDN concept was developed by technical standard-setting committees of the International Telecommunications Union (ITU) in a process started in 1980, the point at which it was believed that innovation had advanced to the degree that it was possible to envision standards for a single global broadband information infrastructure for all types of information flows, from data to voice to video. The ISDN was conceived of as a network into which one could plug any type of information and communication equipment—computers, telephones, televisions, and on—as easily as telephones were being plugged into wall jacks. It took a few years to develop the suite of standards necessary to accomplish this, but by 1985 vendors were producing ISDN equipment and the first ISDN networks were being put in place in locations such as the Wall Street area of New York City, the capitol complexes of some states, and within corporations for intraorganizational communication. By the end of the 1980s, Singapore and Hong Kong were leading the world in ISDN usage, having replaced their entire analog telecommunications networks with digital equipment. Though ISDN networks were still rare in the rest of the world, this did not mean the technology was failing. The ISDN was simultaneously the name for the set of standards being developed, actual networks being built according to those standards, and an idealized vision of a network. ISDN networks were not widely used in the United States in the 1980s, but their existence did force the FCC and other regulatory bodies to deepen their attention to digital policy issues; by the time the ISDN did become generally available in the United States, its speed had been significantly superseded, and users turned to other, faster, communication lines.

A second stream of policy discussion about the evolving information infrastructure focused on the decentralized structure of the nascent Internet. Although some of the technical concepts ultimately incorporated into the Internet first appeared elsewhere and there were a number of false starts in the direction of development of an Internet-like telecommunications system, it was the U.S. government that finally stepped forward to directly support a decentralized broadband network. Known first as ARPANet, and then as NSFNet, the announced goal was to enhance national capacity, the ability to effectively use resources in pursuit of national goals. Military needs were particularly important, for it was believed that the type of network being designed should be useful for defensive purposes by making it impossible to destroy the ability to communicate by attacking just a few selected nodes. Another announced goal was to support scientific research dependent on massive data transfers among institutions.

Though in the early 1980s there was little public awareness of either the ISDN or ARPANet, a great deal of discussion revolved around the implications of the "divestiture" of AT&T. In order to comply with antitrust law, the monopoly-like telephone company was forced to separate its long distance and local operations, keeping the former and turning the latter over to a group of regional operating companies. This was the first act in what became a global trend toward liberalization and deregulation of telecommunications networks further discussed in the section on network structure in chapter 6. Beyond antitrust concerns, of course, a number of other factors contributed to this shift, including the need to decide who would pay for upgrading the network to incorporate new technologies. Too, corporate customers of telecommunications services providers were interested in offerings not available via the infrastructure as it then stood, even though they were technically possible.

Discussion of social goals that could be served by the information infrastructure, such as education, appeared under the rubric of the National Research and Education Network (NREN). By the late 1980s, use of what we now refer to as the Internet was extended to university users beyond those in the specialist communities within which it had been developed. With NREN, researchers in a wide variety of fields were able to use the Internet to support collaborative efforts, and many within the academic world began to use email for a wide variety of types of professional communications on a regular basis. During the period in which federal support for the evolution of the network was undertaken through the NREN rubric, this concept served as a focus for discussion of universal access to the Internet.

High-definition television (HDTV) provided another focus for public and policy debate over the goals to be met by further development of the information infrastructure. In an unusual alignment of interest groups, television producers and the defense industry joined forces to urge the U.S. government to support HDTV. While those in the entertainment industry believed that it would be profitable for them to deliver high-definition programming through a fast broadband network, the military was interested in other uses of the very high-speed computer chips this technology also required, and the government saw national security advantages in both the network and the chips.

Each of these different ways of thinking about the evolving information infrastructure broadened the range of stakeholders involved in policy discussions about network design and use, but it was not until U.S. Vice President Al Gore started talking about an "information superhighway" that the telecommunications network entered public discourse and became a matter of widespread interest. Gore was not the first to think in such terms: seminal video artist Nam June Paik mentioned the concept of an information highway in the 1970s, economists and telecommunications policy analysts were thinking of the network in infrastructural terms by the mid-1980s, and Senator Mark Hatfield started to use the phrase "information superhighway" in wider policy circles in 1989. Once the notion was taken up by the White House, however, debate over the network was transformed; telecommunications issues that had long been a matter of interest only to the cognoscenti became matters of popular discussion. The information highway vision was put forward in documents by the U.S. Department of Commerce's National Telecommunications and Information Administration (NTIA), the National Information Infrastructure Advisory Council (NIIAC), and a circle of advisors in the White House.

The first time the "Internet" appeared in statutory law was in a bill proposed in the 100th Congress (1987–1988) to set up an Internet-based system to help locate unemployment insurance claims of individuals who asserted that they could not provide court-mandated child support because they were indigent. The Clinton Administration's interest in promoting the Internet began to truly take form with the proposal of two bills in the 102nd Congress (1991–1992) dealing with support for the "high performance computing and networking" that would build the infrastructure. During the 103rd Congress (1993–1994) there were four Internet-related bills, two furthering infrastructure development and two putting in place the first official federal "e-government" efforts (offering online access to texts of bills, legislative histories, and information about congressional activities). From that point on, the Internet presence in statutory law started to take off: during the 104th Congress (1995–1996), twenty-eight bills involving the Internet were under discussion; by the 107th (2001–2002), there were over six hundred. By now there has been Internet legislation dealing with the entire expanse of information policy issues, from libel to taxation to intellectual property rights and on, as well as bills that propose uses of the Internet as a tool for implementing policies of other types.

International Information Policy

Information policy at the national level has always interacted with international decision-making. A full history of international information policy is beyond the scope of this book, but a sampling of developments provides some flavor of the range of issues that have been addressed at that level and of the ways in which information policy of other countries has provided models for the United States.

There were several in the nineteenth century: The first, and longest-lived, international organization was formed to enable technical coordination of the telegraph network in the 1860s through what is now known as the International Telecommunications Union. The Paris Convention for the Protection of Industrial Property (1883) and the Berne Convention for the Protection of Literary and Artistic Works (1886) provided a basis in international law for intellectual property rights via patents and copyrights, respectively. The question of whether there should be international standards for the conduct of journalists—very much the subject of information policy discussions during debate over the possibility of a New World Information Order (NWIO) in the 1970s and 1980s—was first also raised in the 1870s, when journalists from around the world came together to discuss the possibility of agreements to manage content in such a way that peace, rather than war, would be promoted.

Access to information became an international as well as national issue at the close of World War I, when U.S. President Woodrow Wilson asked that treaty negotiations produce "open covenants openly arrived at." While neither journalists nor the public in the end did achieve access to those negotiations, the principle of openness in international relations—today referred to as "transparency"—had been successfully introduced. Following World War I, the U.S. government began to promote the concept of the free flow of information at the international level. This was partially to encourage diffusion of elements of U.S. democratic practice (Margaret Blanchard refers to the process as "exporting the First Amendment"). It was also, however, a pragmatic move, for acceptance of this principle made it harder for individual countries to barricade flows of political communication in ways that had been problematic early on in World War I, and easier for U.S.-based corporations in the information and communication industries to operate internationally.

To help member nations think about what appropriate policy responses to the informatization of society might be, the Organization for Economic and Community Development (OECD) launched a series of studies beginning in the 1960s, which were succeeded by a series of European Commission (EC) research programs on the same topic in the following decades. These programs were important not only for Europe, but for other regions as well, because they provided a map of the areas that would need attention. Countries in the developing world were keenly aware of the importance of information policy issues. An effort by the nonaligned nations during the 1960s to pursue a new international economic order gave way in the 1970s and 1980s to calls for a New World Information Order because these nations had come to realize that there would be no redistribution of material resources without a reorganization of the world's informational resources. Though the debate over the NWIO ultimately focused largely on journalism, in its earliest expressions a wide range of issues dealing with access to data and the ability to process data were also included. The Intergovernmental Bureau of Informatics (IBI)—later absorbed into other informational activities of the UN—was active during the same period, as a venue to promote the informatization of the developing world. In 1979 the ITU proposed an upgrading of the information infrastructure for the developing world (to be called GLODOM, or Global Domestic Satellite System) to the same end, though the effort foundered because of lack of financial support from developed countries. Almost thirty years later, in 2002, this proposal emerged again; this time it is more likely to be successful, because it is linked to the realization by equipment vendors and service providers that populations in the developing world are an untapped market. All of the issues raised during earlier discussion about the possibility of a NWIO are on the table during the early twenty-first-century discussions leading up to the World Summit on the Information Society, with the difference that this time there is a struggle over what type of global entity should play the lead role in governance of the Internet and other aspects of the global information infrastructure.

The Japanese government was actually the first to specifically respond to changes in the information environment, via policies promoting experimentation with the social use of new information technologies in the 1960s. The first country to comprehensively address matters of information, communication, and culture through a common policy lens was Brazil, after the military coup of 1964. Several European countries commissioned reports about the policy implications of the convergence of technologies during the 1970s and 1980s. Two national reports stand out in this regard. The Tengelin report to the Swedish government in the late 1970s first introduced the idea that increased dependence of the nation-state on electronic networks made the state vulnerable, a notion that has come to dominate political consciousness by the early twenty-first century. The Nora/Minc report of France, which appeared in English in 1980, had great political impact because it emphasized the danger if the United States were allowed to continue to control European networks; one result was intense interest in support for the information industries within European countries as well as Europe-wide collaborations.

Confounding Factors

Several classes of problems unfortunately confound the effort to identify the boundaries of the information policy domain: those raised by technologies, practices, features of the policy-making process, and characteristics of information as a specific issue area.

Technology-Based Problems

The phrase "the convergence of technologies" conflates several analytical issues. Digital technologies are qualitatively different from earlier media. They blur medium, genre, function and industry. They are ubiquitously embedded in the objects of our material world. And slow-changing structuration processes have been replaced with more rapid processes best described as "flexible."

From technology to meta-technology The law has not historically distinguished among tools, technologies, and meta-technologies, even though these differ along dimensions of legal importance.

• *Tools* Tools can be made and used by individuals working alone and make it possible to process matter or energy in single steps. The use of tools characterized the premodern era. Because communication is an inherently social act, it may only be when marks are made for the purposes of reminding oneself of something that it can be said there are communication tools.

• *Technologies* Technologies are social in their making and use; that is, they require a number of people to work together. They make it possible to link several processing steps together in the course of transforming matter or energy, but there is for each technology only one sequence in which those steps can be taken, only one or a few types of materials can be processed, and only one or a few types of outcomes can be produced. The shift from tools to technologies made industrialization possible, and the use of technologies thus characterizes the modern period. The printing press and the radio are examples of communication technologies.
• *Meta-technologies* Meta-technologies vastly expand the degrees of freedom with which humans can act in the social and material worlds. Meta-technologies enable long processing chains, and there is great flexibility in the number of steps and the sequence with which they are undertaken. Meta-technologies can process an ever-expanding range of types of inputs and can produce an essentially infinite range of outputs. They are social, but enable solo activity within the socially produced network. Their use characterizes the postmodern world. Meta-technologies are always informational, and the Internet is a premiere example of a meta-technology used for communication purposes (see table 3.2).

The shift from technologies to meta-technologies affects the scope and scale of the policy subject, as when national law must cope with global media. A vastly expanded range of alternative outcomes must be considered in the course of policy analysis; the cost of failing to do so has been demonstrated by the new vulnerabilities of information warfare made possible as a result of government-funded software research and development. Meta-technologies also involve a causal chain that is potentially much longer and more variable than those with which policy analysis has historically dealt, requiring concomitant innovations in both policy tools and methods for policy analysis. Policy-makers are most comfortable making law when they feel they understand what it is that is being regulated, but we are still just learning about the effects of the use of meta-technologies.

Convergence of communication styles Media have been distinguished from each other in the past by the number of message receivers (one, a few, or many); by the nature of interactivity, if any, between sender and receiver; and by the difference between synchronicity and asynchronicity. These dimensions together may be described as a matter of style.

Specific media were characterized by a particular style of communication. Over the air (broadcast) television is mass communication, from

Table 3.2
Types of technologies

Type	Era	Social nature	Complexity	Autonomy	Scale	Info. tech. example
Tool	Premodern	Can be made and used by individual working alone	Simple Single process	None	Local	Tallies
Technology	Modern	Requires group collaboration	Complex Multiple processes linked once launched	Autonomous within process as defined	Global	Television
Meta-technology	Postmodern	Technological system is social but enables individual use	Highly complex Multiple processes multiply linked	Potential for great autonomy	Global, enabling local	Internet

one to many; it does not permit direct interactivity between viewers and programming; and it is experienced by its entire audience at the same time, synchronously. Telephony, on the other hand, is predominantly person-to-person (one-to-one), is by definition interactive, and is synchronous. Personal letter writing is one-to-one and interactive, but asynchronous. The Internet, however, blends communicative styles in all three dimensions. During a single session, a user may communicate with a single person, small groups, and the public en masse, often fluidly switching back and forth among the three. Similarly, one-way and interactive communications, both synchronous and asynchronous, can be mixed within single sessions of activity.

This blending of communication styles is problematic for information policy, because point-to-point communication with a single receiver can no longer be excluded from discussions of media law. Under current law, several different regulatory approaches, each with its own assignation of rights and responsibilities, can concurrently apply to a single communicative act or message. Interactivity, too, must be included, because it has been deemed constitutionally worthy of protection because of the way in which it changes a discourse and the nature of information exchanged.

Blurring of medium, function, and industry The convergence of technologies confounds any expectation that particular media, functions, and industries will map onto each other. Such expectations were always unrealistic, for there has been experimental and often significant use of every medium to fill every possible type of social function. (The telephone, for example, has been used as a mass news medium and for cultural gatherings in both Europe and the United States.) In the current environment, however, experimentation and shifts in the location and form of specific social functions that once unfolded across time and place now take place simultaneously. This change confounds efforts to apply law and regulation that are industry-specific as well as efforts to use law and regulation (largely but not exclusively via antitrust law) to keep industries separate from each other. It disrupts habits of policy analysis, because typically such techniques are based on assumptions about the social functions to be served by particular media industries. And it alters the economics of each of the industries involved, further disturbing habitual analytical assumptions.

Ubiquitous embedded computing We are accustomed to treating the media as an identifiable set of objects in which communicative capacity can be found and which serve only communicative functions, distinct from other objects and from ourselves. Increasingly, however, information technologies are ubiquitously embedded throughout the material world in familiar objects such as cars, refrigerators, stoplights, and paper. And while, at the moment, such technologies are embedded in humans only at the margins—by scientists experimenting with connecting computer chips to neurons, artists treating their bodies as electronic art media, and penal systems taking advantage of new ways of tracking and restricting those who have broken the law—it is likely that in the future, information technologies will also be ubiquitously embedded in plant, animal, and human organisms as well. This change presents a conceptual and operational challenge to those making, implementing, and interpreting media law.

The media and flexible structuration Constitutive processes involve "structuration," the interaction between structure and agency, with the latter defined as the ability to effectively act on the basis of one's own intention. From this perspective, constitutional protections for the media are intended to ensure that individuals have the communicative agency necessary to participate in government. (Of course, in the late eighteenth and early nineteenth centuries, the nation-state was not the only source of structural power. The U.S. Constitution explicitly acknowledges the sustained social effectiveness of religious institutions when it relegated churches to the private sphere.) Informational power, however, blurs the distinction between agency and structure, for as discussed in chapter 2, information and informational structure can themselves exercise agency. Breaking down the distinction between structure and agency makes structuration processes far more flexible, complicating information policy in some cases by dissolving the policy subject and in all cases by introducing more complex modes of causality.

Law and regulation are always based on at least implicit assumptions about causality as direct, discernible, affected by relatively few intervening variables, occurring via single or very few causal steps, and effected by identifiable agents. United States information policy of the eighteenth and nineteenth centuries constrained and used symbolic power. During the late nineteenth and twentieth centuries, the development of antitrust law manifested the addition of structural power to the subjects of information policy and the repertoire of tools used to protect individual agency in the face of the nation-state and large corporations. Today, governments must adapt to the realities of informational power: There are agents that have not been recognized as such by the law, or there may be no identifiable agents at all. Causality may be indirect, indiscernible, affected by multiple intervening variables, and involve causal chains that are beyond analytical reach. These changes in the nature of agency and causality are evident in practice-based problems faced by those seeking to bound the domain of information policy.

Practice-Based Problems

Contemporary practices make the problem of defining information policy more difficult because there is constant innovation, genres are blurred, new alternative communication practices are appearing, and legal issues historically of concern only to information and media professionals now affect all of us.

Constant innovation Products, services, and organizational forms all continue to evolve. Examples of innovation in practice include changing Web page design in response to the number of reader hits per article and the broadcasting of news stories and documentaries by independent media groups (such as IndyMedia) on the Web. Service innovations include individually designed content and the use of intelligent agents for information seeking and delivery. Institutional and industry innovations appear when newspapers act like Internet service providers (ISPs), news-oriented media turn to entertainment, and firms in professional service industries such as the law start contract out printing services. These changes problematize information policy, because that field historically treated distinct products, services, and industries differentially and the law was applied within industries at the firm level. The process of adapting statutory and regulatory law to reflect the categories of the new industry and product classification system, which came into use only at the close of the twentieth century (see chapter 6), has not yet begun.

Blurring of genres Genre distinctions in constitutional law—between fact and fiction, fact and opinion, commentary and advertising, and news and history—are fundamental to analysis dealing with such matters as libel, commercial regulation, and postal rates. The blurring of genre thus adds conceptual problems to legal analysis. We continue to struggle with the application of standards of facticity that are important from the perspective of libel and fraud to docudrama and infotainment. The longstanding distinctions among history, fiction, and news based not only on facticity, but on the currency of information claimed to be fact, that supports differential pricing of information distribution via the post office is only one of the approaches to differential pricing of Web-based information, and it is being used in a de facto rather than de jure way.

Tactical media Tactical media practitioners work with the possibilities unleashed by the interchangeability of structure and agency. While mainstream and alternative media have historically used content to engage in political battles, the tactical media movement launched in the 1990s spurns struggles over content as a losing battle. Instead, these journalists/artists/activists take seriously Marshall McLuhan's insight that the medium *is* the message and have turned, instead, to manipulation of information production, processing and delivery systems. The goal is to alter the semiotic and electronic realities within which media operate, an exercise of informational power. Tactical media practitioners combine news and political commentary with art. Consumption, aesthetics, and humor are viewed as opportunities to enact power, often most successful in stand-alone events rather than the persuasive campaigns to which we have become accustomed. Media law and policy focused on content are inadequate in the face of tactical media. Rather, tactical media practitioners see themselves as "pre-policy," acknowledging that what they do is stimulate legal innovation.

Deprofessionalization of policy issues In the pre-digital era, most areas of information policy affected media or information professionals almost exclusively; libel law and problems of copyright infringement are good examples. In the electronic environment, however, everyone who communicates runs the danger of bumping into the same legal and regulatory issues, even when individuals perceive themselves to be involved solely in interpersonal communication. Traditional approaches to information policy that orient toward professional communicators and established media organizations must be reconsidered in this context.

Policy Process-Based Problems

Some of the problems in defining information policy today derive from the nature of policy-making itself, such as the tension between incremental and radical change, the importance of latent as well as manifest policy, invisibility, policy interdependence and precession, and relationships between public policy and other types of influential decision-making.

Transition policy Policy change can be radical, when an entire body of existing law is abandoned in favor of building anew from scratch during revolutionary periods, or incremental, in a series of small evolutionary steps. Incremental policy-making is necessary for working decision-makers in both the public and private sectors who must operate within existing law under severe time and resource constraints. Too, there is always a lag between the development of new ideas about and knowledge of social circumstances and their application in arenas as detailed and complex as the law—a lag reinforced by reliance upon precedent. Nor is it possible to understand all of the effects of new technologies in their entirety immediately. Those who analyze, make, and implement information policy today face the problem of trying to achieve incremental legal change during a period of revolutionary change in the policy subject.

Latent and manifest policy Not everything that falls within the domain of information policy is labeled as such. Thus, borrowing from the late Robert K. Merton, it is useful to distinguish between information policy that is manifest—clearly directed at what has traditionally been understood as the mass media—and that which is latent. The general notion of latent policy first appeared in the 1920s, and has since gained currency in fields ranging from technology policy to political science. Latent policy includes side effects of decisions aimed at other subjects, as when Securities and Exchange Commission (SEC) regulation of financial markets mandates the distribution of particular types of information. It can develop when its subject matter is categorized under other names, as in the "confidence- and security-building measures" (CSBMs) incorporated into arms control treaties of the 1980s and 1990s that required specific types of information exchange in support of foreign policy. Latent policy can also appear synergistically when policy from a variety of decision-making arenas interacts to produce something quite different in combination, as when the use of alternative dispute resolution systems to reduce the burden on the courts results in a loss of public access to the kinds of information about conflict resolution the Constitution recognized as so essential to a democracy. The effects of latent policy can be direct. The importance of latent forms of information policy places demands on the research agenda, for it must attend to latent as well as manifest issues, bring the latent into visibility, and explore relationships between those issues that are latent and those that are manifest.

Invisible policy Many types of information policy decisions are highly influential but little discussed, or even acknowledged. The world of information policy includes such things as presidential executive orders, decisions by federal and state attorneys general, and the practice of hiding statutory law directed at one issue within a piece of legislation commonly understood to deal with another matter. The significance of invisible sources of law and regulation to communication realities makes it necessary to take such decision-making venues into account in the process of defining the field. Invisible policy is formal and is developed within government, but has largely escaped attention.

Policy interdependence Information policy made at different levels of the social structure is highly interdependent, reflecting the emergence of networked forms of organization in all aspects of life as well as the interpenetration of political structures. Indeed, for many countries around the world, international organizations are as or more important than national governments in shaping policy, and it was in the area of the information infrastructure that what is now known as the European Commission for the first time explicitly applied Commission law to member states. Such interdependence is described as both necessary and a potential "policy trap." Some efforts to extend U.S. or European law outside its borders occur "naturally," through harmonization of legal systems or the movement of decision-making into the realm of private contracts when there is a legal vacuum rather than through the excesses of extraterritoriality (unilateral efforts by a nation-state to exert its law outside its borders). The globalization of the information infrastructure and growing appreciation of the populations in developing countries as potential markets make it more likely that developed countries will come to take the needs and concerns of developing countries into account.

Interdependence also characterizes information policy within the United States. The need to promote the national information infrastructure has been used as an argument in support of federal preemption of state law, but doing so runs counter to other forces urging decentralization of decision making. Influence runs from the bottom up as well as the top down, for even decision-making at the local level can have an influence on national policy. Interdependence requires far more consultation, cooperation, and even policy coordination in order to avoid intolerable disruptions of national and international economies. It complicates the problem of bounding the field of information policy for specific nation-states by adding the requirement that both supra- and infranational laws and regulations must be taken into account.

Policy precession Treatment of policy as a design problem must also take into account interactions among policies. This is the problem of "precession"—the need to link analysis of several types of decisions in order to understand the implications of their interactions. Precession occurs when two systems interact such that a decision or event in one changes the axis along which decisions or actions in the other can take place. The notion of path dependence suggests precession but does not incorporate sensitivity to the number of precessive steps that may be linked, the degree of complexity precession adds to the analytical problem, or differences in the angles of change. When precessive links are understood by some players but not by others, it is possible to erect barriers to meaningful participation in decision-making on one issue by foreclosing options through filters or actions designed by a related piece of legislation or regulation. An example is provided by an interaction between patent and antitrust law: the ability to assert property rights in ways of doing business through patent law, combined with the trend towards asserting property rights as early as possible in a processing chain in order to claim ownership of all products of that process, means that antitrust law may no longer be able to reach some pertinent types of anticompetitive practices. Sensitivity to precession complicates the analysis of information policy.

Public policy and other decision-making Formal policy mechanisms unfold within the broader legal field. Public policy now also interacts with decisions made by private decision-makers, often collaboratively through what is referred to as "policy networks." There are also purely private sources of decision making with constitutive impact, informal aspects of decision-making processes that are highly influential but have received relatively little analytical attention, and technological and normative trends with enormous structural force. Decisions made in all of these arenas would be included in the broadest definition of information policy, though this book restricts its analysis of laws and regulations to formal decisions of the U.S. government. Some of these nontraditional types of information policy are relatively obscure and may require specialized knowledge in order to be comprehensible, such as those made by technical standards bodies. Others are easier to understand, like the role played by ISPs in determining speech conditions for the Internet. While traditionally the word "policy" has been reserved for public sector decision making and the word "strategy" for private, the impact of the latter on the former today and the intermingling of the two types of decision-making suggests the definition of information policy may also need to include both.

Issue Area-Based Problems

Political scientists group together issues related to the same subject into what they term "issue areas." Compared to traditional issue areas, such as defense, agriculture and trade, information policy is relatively new policy and, for digital technologies, very new. Because policy is developed in response to perceived characteristics and effects of specific technologies, the fact that neither those characteristics nor their effects are yet fully understood complicates the already difficult definitional problem. Other unique characteristics of information policy include the multiplicity of players and decision-making arenas and the level of impact on other issue areas.

Multiplicity of decision-making arenas An unusually large number of players, types of players, and decision-making venues are involved in the making of information policy. While in other areas, such as tuna fishing, there is a natural limit to those with a legitimate involvement and few ambiguities regarding responsibilities, information technologies—and thus decision-making about them—are pervasive. As a result, literally dozens of entities—governmental, quasi-nongovernmental, and private—have a history of some type of involvement and, often, a stake. Within any single branch of government, several different agencies can be involved, creating conflicts. In the early 1980s, one study showed that the single issue of electronic funds transfer systems was under examination by at least four different committees of the House of Representatives, none of which had enough authority to deal with all of the technological, financial, and regulatory questions raised by the prospect of such a system, and the situation has been exacerbated since. The result is often "policy gridlock," an inability to make policy at all. It also makes it more difficult for the United States to operate internationally, for others cannot be sure with whom to work and cannot rely upon consistency in the U.S. position. Because of this multiplicity, it is inappropriate and inadequate to use a venue-based approach (e.g., "policy made by the FCC") for bounding the domain of information policy.

Impact on other policy issue areas Another unique aspect of information policy is the degree to which it influences decision-making in other issue areas through constraints on both decision-making processes and the lenses through which issues are viewed. Information policy creates the communicative space within which all public and decision-making discourses takes place; determines the kinds of information that will be available to inform those discourses; provides the stuff of the institutions within which and processes through which decision-making takes place; and offers many of the policy tools used to implement policy decisions directed at other types of social processes. The relative importance of information policy confounds the problem, because it adds pressure to the politics of the definitional process discussed. To the degree that those involved with decision-making in other issue areas *understand* the implications of what they do, there will be efforts to subsume information policy within treatment of other issue areas or to define it as something other than communication altogether in order to relieve decision makers of some of the constitutional pressure described in chapter 4.

Definitional Approaches

Confusion about just what is and what is not information policy began to be openly discussed several decades ago. A variety of definitional approaches, some implicit and some explicit, have been used to try to resolve the situation, oriented in turn around lists, legacy legal categories, industries, stages of the information production chain, and nature of the impact on society. Each has strengths and weaknesses.

Lists

Early efforts to think about information policy in the new environment simply listed areas to be included. In an influential 1984 governmental report, for example, Kenneth Leeson included technical knowledge and its diffusion, physical network components and structure, services offered and terms of network use, and regulation of content. In another example, Jeremy Tunstall during the same period included aerospace defense research and development and industrial planning as well, because they affected the nature of the infrastructure available to the media. This approach has the appeal of being relatively easy, but lists are inevitably incomplete and rapidly obsolesce. Because they are not based on a coherent logic, they do not provide a foundation from which policy analysis can be conducted.

Legacy Legal Categories

The legacy approach to defining media policy orients around the categories established by statutory and regulatory law, separately for each technology. There are strengths in this approach. It is familiar. Precedent is well developed. The terms of legacy law still govern daily activity and provide the conceptual, rhetorical, and analytical frameworks for policy discourse. Many traditional issues are still adequately addressed with legacy law—false advertising is still false advertising, and libel is still libel.

The phrase legacy law came into use, however, because inherited legal categories often no longer fit empirical realities. As discussed previously, diverse legal and regulatory systems have developed over time in response to specific technologies, each defining rights and responsibilities differently. The right to editorial control provides an example. It is unlimited in print up to the boundaries determined by constitutional law, constrained in broadcasting, and forbidden in telecommunications; in the digital environment, the same message could easily travel through all three types of systems as it is produced and delivered, and thus be simultaneously the subject of all three types of regulation. The silo habits of legacy law also impede our ability to directly confront issues that span traditional legal categories, as in the problem of regulating privately owned interfaces with the public communications network. One such interface (the mailbox) is discussed in constitutional law, while another ("customer premises equipment," or CPE, from the telephone to the computer) is a matter of telecommunications regulation within administrative law. Though the two simply present different faces of the same issue, well-developed discussions in each area of the law never reference or draw upon each other, nor are the outcomes of those discussions necessarily consistent with each other.

Industries

Because policy issues often arise when they become problematic for the corporate world, there has been experimentation with industry-oriented approaches. Such approaches are appealing because they speak directly to immediate concerns and can form the basis of discussion and operationalization via best practices within industry-specific contexts such as trade associations. There is, however, no longer any fixed map of industrial sectors, and there is not likely to be one for quite a while, if ever again. An industry-based approach also skews the discourse in favor of profit and efficiency at the cost of values such as equity, human rights, and the protection of civil liberties. From an industry perspective, those who make messages become "producers" and those who "receive" content are "consumers," rather than "citizens," or active participants in a culture. Focusing on industries also raises the risk that an approach to resolving a problem within one industry may be incompatible with techniques or interpretations used in other sectors.

Social Impact

Some advocacy groups and scholars start not from the law, but from the social impact of the law. The Center for Media Education (CME) deals with any type of communication policy that affects children (from media violence to software filtering), for example, and the Electronic Privacy Information Center (EPIC) looks at any type of policy that has an impact on personal privacy (from encryption to the USA PATRIOT Act). The value of this approach is that it turns attention away from the minutiae of existing law and regulation and towards the point of the policy-making exercise—building and maintaining the kind of society we want to live in. It offers a way of incorporating the entire range of values that need to be accommodated within the policy-making process. This approach makes it possible to bring together the historically disparate medium-specific issues within a common framework, and in turn can enrich analysis of specific problems by bringing to bear upon them pertinent discourse irrespective of originary legal realm. It offers both justification and techniques for finding the best from legacy law as law, policy, and regulation are adapted and transformed to meet today's circumstances. And it encourages the enrichment of policy thinking by theories and empirical knowledge derived from the social sciences and humanities. Often, however—as in much of the discussion about the "digital divide"—concerns are expressed in such general terms that it is difficult to identify specific laws or regulation that might usefully be the subject of attention. Bounding the domain of information policy by social impact also places significant demands on communication theory. Because most who do this start with a single issue of concern, there is no overarching framework within which to relate one issue to another or to serve as a foundation for policy analysis. A theoretical response to this problem is possible, but would be a formidable intellectual task.

The Information Production Chain

The model of an information production chain is actually the most widely used heuristic for identifying just what is, and what is not, information policy. Here the key features of this approach are summarized and its advantages and disadvantages discussed before describing each stage of the chain in some detail.

Key features Models of an information production chain are rife, though not always explicit. They are implicit in constitutional law, for example, as a means of distinguishing among types of communicative spaces for the purposes of differential application of the First Amendment. The Office of Management and Budget put forth an explicit example in its model of the "information life cycle" as a conceptual frame for interventions into the statistical practices of federal agencies. Models of such a chain are myriad, but a synthesis of versions put forward by Fritz Machlup and Kenneth Boulding has proven useful in the study of information policy.

This approach includes the stages of information creation (de novo, generation, and collection), processing (cognitive and algorithmic), storage, transportation, distribution, destruction, and seeking. Relations between stages of an information production chain change when new linkages become possible between stages of the chain, as when the Web makes it possible for producers and users of information to become directly linked; when parties at a stage of the chain lose their independent functions, as when the intermediaries between producers and users are no longer necessary; or when relations among parties change in such a way that there is reason for drastic reorganization, as when multiple information providers choose to pool their resources.

Information policy can be defined as all law and regulation pertaining to any stage of the information production chain. From this perspective, information policy is an umbrella term within which subsets of laws and regulations that pertain to specific types of communicative activities, industries, or professions can be identified. Many of these activities, industries, and professions involve various combinations of two or more stages of the information production chain. There are no messages to send without information creation and processing, information is often transported in the course of gathering inputs into message creation, storage may be combined with distribution (as in books), and destruction of the historical record created by the media is an important political issue. Thus the umbrella term "information policy" refers to all law and regulation that deals with information creation, processing, flows, and use. More colloquially, this is the domain of policy for information, communication, and culture.

Advantages and disadvantages There are a number of advantages to using the information production chain as a heuristic for bounding the field of information policy. It provides a coherent theoretical stance from which to examine diverse issues. It brings together like problems irrespective of where they have appeared in the categories of legacy law so that the entire richness of analysis can be brought to bear on the issue as it presents itself under contemporary circumstances. And it makes it possible to relate issues to each other, so that the extent, means, and consequences of policy precession can be understood.

Defining information policy in this way provides a theoretical link between the abstract and the empirical and across levels of analysis. It permits exclusion of certain types of information, actors, or modes of processing from either specific or all stages of the chain, incorporating the sensitivities of those who resist the commoditization of all information. The model of an information production chain is useful in breaking down complex communicative processes into their elements for differential analysis and legal treatment of those elements. Thus while interactive and noninteractive, synchronous and asynchronous, and intercast, narrowcast, and broadcast communications may all be mixed by users of the Internet, the concept of an information production chain can be of value in determining just how to distinctly apply legal principles. The heuristic utility of the approach has been demonstrated in analyses of laws and regulations in areas of legacy law as distant from each other as Supreme Court decisions, arms control agreements, and international trade regulations. This approach also makes it possible to understand the informational roots of familiar problems. Journalists, for example, are often concerned about access to government information, but by focusing on their use rather than the information itself they often miss the important policy question of constraints on the production of certain types of information in the first place.

There are also, of course, problems. Premiere among them is the lack of a consensus on ways of distinguishing among different types of information-processing beyond the gross distinction described here between algorithmic and cognitive modes. The analytical problem it presents can be complex, for many communication processes, phenomena, and products involve more than one stage of the chain.

Stages of the information production chain A mode of the information production chain that has been useful for policy analysis purposes follows.

• *Information creation* Information can be created in three ways: It can be the product of a genuinely original creative act and thus come out of nothingness, so to speak (creation de novo). It can be the outcome of systematic procedures for producing knowledge such as those referred to by the concept of facticity (e.g., the "facts" of journalism) or the methodologies of statistics (e.g., "data"). Information is also created when it is generated as a byproduct of other life activities and processes, such as when one interacts with an institution (e.g., registering for a class, getting a driver's license) or changes one's status (e.g., gets married). Information policy questions involving creation include intellectual property rights and access to both information and infrastructure.

• *Information processing* Information processing can be algorithmic (undertaken through procedures describable in mathematical form and thus accomplishable by computers) or cognitive (undertaken through procedures to date possible only by the human brain). Some forms of information processing may be exclusive to one or the other of these categories, while other forms of information processing (e.g., alphabetization) can be undertaken either way.

There is a plethora of ways of more finely articulating differences among types of information processing, a task of importance across policy-making venues and issues, because more subtle distinctions are critical to the interpretation and implementation of the law. The work needed to develop a set of distinctions that can achieve consensual acceptance is therefore a critical item for the research agenda. Information policy issues in this area include restrictions on information that come from defining it as not speech and therefore as not covered under the First Amendment (part of the debate over encryption), or from the government's claim that access to information in the public domain does not include the right to process that information (a claim made in a 1970s case in which the U.S. government tried to prevent publication of an article explaining how to make a nuclear bomb through prior restraint, but failed). Information processing also raises antitrust issues, as was seen in the legal challenge to Microsoft's treatment of the relationship between its browser and its operating system.

• *Information transportation* Information transportation takes place when a single message is transported (to one, a few, or many). Examples include a conversation on the street, a letter, or the production of a single documentary. This stage of the chain involves single messages. Restrictions on content or communicative behaviors put in place by ISPs as well as in non-electronic environments, including surveillance, are examples of information policy issues that can arise here.

- *Information distribution* Information distribution is distinguished from transportation because it involves regular transportation of messages over time to either narrowcast or broadcast audiences, often with a commercial aspect. Rather than single messages, distribution involves channels that handle flows of content. Information policy issues at this stage of the production chain include trying to ensure a diversity of voices in all facets of the public sphere, access to the distribution network, anonymity, and censorship via the chilling effect of surveillance.
- *Information storage* Information storage occurs through fixation in a medium and through archival and cultural practices. Storage is important because it enables the communication of ideas across space and across time and because it forms the basis of our social memory. From the information policy perspective, information storage and destruction issues are two sides of the same coin. Laws and regulation that mandate the creation, storage, and destruction of public records create the public memory so important as an input into policy-making and as a matter of identity. The reliability and security of the information infrastructure are also critical.
- *Information destruction* Just as information can be produced essentially de novo, unlike matter it can be utterly lost or destroyed as well. The fragility of digital information, and the ease with which it can be altered, have raised the salience of issues created by the risk of loss of knowledge and memory as policy issues. Loss of public memory through destruction of public records is the key information policy issue at this stage of the information production chain.
- *Information seeking* Sociologists and psychologists have brought information seeking to our attention as a distinct type of cognitive and social process worthy of attention in its own right. Information seeking has also been examined from an economic perspective, as its costs are of importance when considering research and development budgets, risk analysis, and in a number of other arenas. Incorporating sensitivity to cultural, social, personal, and cognitive differences in modes of information seeking into laws and regulations is one possible policy response. Positive support for education in media literacy is another. Surveillance is an issue here, because government knowledge of information-seeking practices can have a chilling effect.

Bounding the Domain of Information Policy: An Analytical Approach

To be useful, an approach to bounding the domain of information policy for the twenty-first century must be

- *Valid* It must map onto empirical reality.
- *Comprehensive* It must include all matters of concern.
- *Theoretically based* It must rest on a theoretical foundation that can provide a basis for thinking through positions on media policy issues.
- *Methodologically operationalizable* It must use concepts that are susceptible to analysis via social science research methods, in order to facilitate the process of informing policy positions with the results of research and advances in theory.
- *Translatable* It must be cast in terms that make it possible to translate new policy principles, tools, and specific policies into the language of legacy law in order to enable incremental legal change.

None of the definitional approaches reviewed here meets all of these criteria. Indeed, it may not be possible for a single approach to serve all of the functions that must be fulfilled—developing a theoretical framework for the field, identifying specific policy issues for attention, analyzing those issues in ways that incorporate the range of pertinent types of social science knowledge, and translating the results of that analysis into the language and genres of the legal system. Just as it is useful and appropriate to use different definitions of information at various stages of the policy-making process, as discussed in chapter 2, so it is both valid and valuable to think about information policy issues from different perspectives, depending upon where you are in decision-making. In both areas—how to think about information, and how to think about information policy—the first and last and most fundamental perspective, however, must be that of constitutive impact on society. When dealing with information policy, this goal suggests several analytical steps. The first and second steps approach information policy issues through the lens of the information production chain. The third and fourth steps analyze policy options and the effects of policies in place from the perspective of their impact on society. The final step re-engages with legacy law in order to effectively participate in change processes.

Step 1. The Policy Issue and the Information Production Chain

The first task is to identify whether a particular policy issue falls into the information policy domain by thinking through which one or more stages of the information production chain is involved in the information or communication activity out of which the issue has arisen. Some of these will be obvious; it is clear that the broadcasting and telecommunications activities regulated by the FCC will all fall into this domain, as will all First Amendment problems. Others may not be so obvious; despite the fact that Fritz Machlup began his sequence of studies of key information industries with R&D, laws and regulations that affect R&D from areas of the law that range from taxation to zoning to direct funding are rarely, if ever, treated as matters of information policy. Immigration law is information policy when it involves compelled information flows; national security restrictions are information policy when they prohibit other information flows; and so forth. Identifying just which stages of the information production chain are involved makes it possible to locate lines of analysis—wherever they are found in terms of the categories of legacy law—that will be useful.

Step 2. Link Analytically to Related Information Policy Issues

Three questions should be asked to guide analysis from both the legal and social impact perspectives. Issues raised by regulation of customer premises equipment, introduced previously, provide an example of the utility of these three questions.

What makes this policy issue like and unlike those others within its traditional legal silo? The great bulk of telecommunications regulation deals with matters internal to the network itself. While CPE are *like* telephone rates, because both have to do with the network, issues raised by CPE are *unlike* much other telecommunications regulations, because they are focused on the interface between the network and the human user. The likenesses among those telecommunications matters regulated by the FCC suggest it is appropriate for them to be addressed by the same regulatory body—but the ways in which some issues are unlike others also powerfully argues for attention to types of evidence, modes of argument, and theoretical frames suggested by their differences as well.

What other laws and regulations, irrespective of where they are located according to the categories of legacy law, raise the same issues? Once the particular type of information policy issue has been identified and distinguished from others in its traditional legal silo, the problem becomes one of locating where else one might look for insights into the same type of problem in order to learn about the types of evidence, modes of argument, and theoretical frames that may be useful. In the case of CPE, an artifact of regulatory law, a parallel can be found within constitutional law when it examines issues raised by the mailbox, also an interface between an information distribution network and the human user. Going further, one could imagine also drawing from those aspects of zoning law that deal with interactions between those receiving information and the distribution system—particularly now that digital media now increasingly appear in the course of moving through public spaces such as schools, shopping centers, and street corners devoted to other purposes. Solutions found useful in one venue or area of the law may well also be fruitful in adapting or replacing regulations in another area. Bringing together the various lines of legal precedent, types of evidence, modes of argument, and conceptualizations into a single discourse will inevitably enrich the toolkit available for addressing all of the issues that fall into this category.

With what other policy issues is this problem linked in ways that would make the effects of the law or regulation at issue precessive? Precession among policies is important both when evaluating the effects of a particular law or regulation and when recommending any changes in policy. The regulation of CPE may interact with content regulations in areas as diverse as spam and pornography, or with tax laws that affect small businesses, in such a way that decisions regarding whether or not, and if so how, to use CPE may be affected.

Step 3. Examine the Social Impact of Current Policy

The crux of the analytical problem is determining what impact the current information policy is having on society. While the temptation is to assume that the causal relation to be examined is single-step and unifaceted, in fact these relationships are more likely to be multistep and multifaceted in nature, thus requiring not one but several types of research to fully understand the effects of policies in place. In some cases, this can be achieved by synthesizing the results of research already conducted on various aspects of the problem, whether or not that research was undertaken for purposes of providing input into policy-making. Indeed, in the areas of information, communication, and culture, there are deep bodies of knowledge pertinent to policy issues rarely, if ever, brought to bear in policy debate. Where the research has not already been done, the intellectual, logistical, and resource requirements are even greater. The long history of efforts to inform communication policy-making with the results of empirical research and insights from social theory is filled with examples that identify the barriers and difficulties that problematize such efforts, but there are successes as well. It remains a normative ideal for policy-making that it should be evidence-based, and that policies once chosen should be intended for the actual environment within which they will actually be implemented.

Step 4. Develop Policy Recommendations

Whether you are choosing among policy options, recommending that the language of a law or regulation remain as it is but that implementation be altered programmatically or improved, suggesting adaptations or alterations to existing law, or arguing for abandonment of a particular type of policy tool altogether, the recommendation should be based on analysis of the information policy problem in light of its impact on the nature of society.

We have started from the position that the most important definition of information from a policy perspective is its effects as a constitutive force in society. It then follows naturally that the constitutive effects of information policy are the most fundamental and should serve as the foundation of any policy recommendations.

Step 5. Translate Recommendations into the Terms of Legacy Law

In order to achieve efficacy, the results of society-oriented analyses must finally be translated into the language, and the genres, of legacy law. It is only in this way that theoretically and empirically informed analysis of media policy issues can provide the basis for incremental legal change. One of the biggest intellectual problems faced by those involved in information policy is building bridges between the definitional approaches necessary at different stages of the policy-making process. Doing so, however, is an important element of the definition of the field. Failure to translate idealistic visions, normative wishes, or creative approaches to problem-solving into the terms of the law is one of the most common reasons why those urging reform do not succeed in the efforts.

Information Policy: Constitutive and Constitutional

After reviewing briefly the very long history of information policy, and looking in some depth at just why it is difficult to figure out what information policy is and how to think about it today, this chapter has recommended a theoretically pluralist approach to bounding the field. The result is what might be called an "enriched" definition of the field of information policy. It is all law and policy affecting information creation, processing, flows, and use—or, more casually, policy for information, communication, and culture. Identifying issues within the domain of information policy through the heuristic of the information production chain significantly broadens the range of analytical equipment that can be brought to bear and highlights elements of particular importance today that may be obscured through legal lenses developed for other social and technological worlds. Evaluation of policy options and effects remains a problem of their impact on the nature of society. And the actual legal work must take place within the language and processes of legacy law.

The focus up to this point has been on the constitutive effects of information and of information policy—that is, the actual ways in which they shape the world in which we live. While that which is constitutive is "the real," it is the job of constitutional law to define the "ideal." The next chapter uses the heuristic of the information production chain to identify all of the information policy principles in the U.S. Constitution and its amendments. These are important for the analysis of U.S. law that follows because these principles provide the standards against which laws and regulations are to be judged. Looking at the Constitution in this way also provides an efficient way of seeing what can be learned by looking across legacy categories of law when we think about information policy. A great deal of work on communication law focuses on the First Amendment alone as its constitutional ground. Explorations of privacy and of intellectual property rights have a slightly more expansive view in their own directions. Through the lens of the information production chain, however, twenty information policy principles appear in the U.S. Constitution and its amendments.

4

Constitutional Principles and the Information Spaces They Create

The modern notion of secular design for human society was translated into political terms through constitutions, texts that put in place the basic structures of the policy field of a nation-state. In the terms of complex adaptive systems theory, these are the order parameters for political life. In another language, these are the architectural principles from which the elements of information policy as social design must flow. Constitutional principles are relatively abstract, but they provide the foundation for all other law and regulation. Problems have constitutional status when they are considered fundamental to the nature of society.

Principles in constitutional texts must be translated into terms applicable to specific areas of activity. In the U.S. case, the first stage of translation takes place when statutory law—consisting of the bills passed by legislatures—puts in place specific rules and programs that make the general principles operational. When very detailed decisions must be made, or decisions that are highly technical, or decisions that must be made over and over again, an administrative agency is established to develop yet more particular regulations and handle this ongoing work. When different laws and regulations come into conflict with each other, the constitutional basis of existing laws and regulations is challenged, or the law is broken, cases go to court for evaluation by a judge and, usually, a jury comprised of peer citizens (common law). The United States is unusual in that interpretation of constitutional law can take place in any court at any level of the system, for in most other countries, this type of decision-making is reserved for a special constitutional court.

Each type of law—constitutional, statutory, administrative, and common law—ideally brings a different type of input into the legal system. Constitutions are based on ideas from philosophy and long historical experience—what we now call social theory. Statutory law, put in place by legislative bodies, is democratic in the United States in the sense that it is made by elected representatives of the people, though once elected these individuals are more free to act on their own than are party-based political figures in many other countries. Regulatory law (also called administrative law) is produced by regulatory agencies, often on the basis of specialized expertise. And common law, the decisions made by judges in the courtroom, offers an opportunity to focus on the details of specific cases as contextualized by knowledge of local circumstance.

Of course none of this is absolutely determinative of what actually takes place. No matter how clearly a law is written, there is always a gap between language and the world to which it refers. We can generalize about social forces and estimate statistical probabilities, but every event is always a unique conjuncture of factors as they converge upon a particular time, place, and person. Informal power structures are at times more important than those that are formal. Will and capacity matter because, in the end, it is only through the exercise of will to utilize existing capacity that anything happens. Implementation takes place in stages, each of which offers opportunities to deflect operationalization away from intention. Before implementation can begin, programs created by statutory law must also be funded; authorization of funds without actual allocation (these are two separate decision-making processes) is a way of effectively killing a piece of legislation after it has been approved by Congress. Once a program has been legislatively mandated, funded, and staffed, implementation problems remain at the level of the programmatic detail required to integrate projects with existing institutions and social processes. Thus the texts of constitutions and laws may be quite misleading about actual political realities.

Still, the information policy principles in the U.S. Constitution provide the basic structural features of the information architectures supportable by U.S. law. While these are principles from only one country's constitution, they are of global importance because they have been incorporated into many constitutions around the world and their influence extends beyond this type of textual acknowledgment. They are also worth knowing about because of the relative importance of the United States in crafting international law, and because the United States has been quite successful in the global competition over regulatory approaches.

It is popularly believed that the First Amendment provides the constitutional foundation for information, communication, and cultural policy in the United States. The First Amendment is certainly important, but it is far from the only source of information policy principles in the U.S. Constitution. This chapter does two things: It introduces all of the information policy principles found in the U.S. Constitution, including but going beyond the bundle of rights in the First Amendment. And it describes the informational spaces these principles create—the architecture of the information policy field. The concluding chapter of this book returns to these principles to review the ways in which technological innovation has affected how we interpret and implement them.

The Principles

There are three places where information policy principles are found in the U.S. Constitution: They are explicit in the text of the Constitution itself and in the amendments to the Constitution—most famously, but not only, in the First Amendment, one of the ten amendments that comprise the Bill of Rights. And they are implicit in the "penumbra" of constitutional texts based on an interpretive principle itself constitutionally established. (All of these principles are listed, along with their textual sources, in table 4.1.)

Principles in the Constitution

Those information policy principles embedded in the Constitution itself were put in place several years before those of the First Amendment. They are discussed here in the order in which they appear within the Constitution.

Information collection by the government The census, mandated in Article 1, Section 2, requires the government to enumerate the entire population every ten years. Because the Constitution was written during a period of significant demographic shifts (still a characteristic of the U.S. population), this provision was necessary in order to accurately apportion legislative seats and fairly distribute national resources. Making the census a constitutional matter establishes the principle that the government has both a right and a responsibility to gather information about its citizens. Just what that information should be, how it should be gathered, and how it should be used are matters of ongoing political debate. The statistical apparatus of the government has grown massively since the eighteenth century so that the census and related efforts could fill a number of additional functions.

Table 4.1
Information policy principles in the U.S. Constitution

Principle	Location
Information collection by the government	Art. 1, Sec. 2
Open government	Art. 1, Sec. 5; Art. 2, Sec. 3
Free speech within government	Art. 1, Sec. 6
Federal government control over currency	Art. 1, Sec. 8
Universal access to an information distribution system	Art. 1, Sec. 8, Cl. 7
Intellectual property rights	Art. 1, Sec. 8, Cl. 8
Restriction of civil liberties during time of war	Art. 1, Sec. 9, Cl. 2
Treason	Art. 3, Sec. 3
Freedom of opinion	1st Am.
Freedom of speech	1st Am.
Freedom of the press	1st Am.
Freedom of assembly and association	1st Am.
Freedom to petition the government for change	1st Am.
Protection against unlawful search	4th Am.
Protection against self-incrimination	5th Am.
Due process	5th Am.
Rights beyond those enumerated	9th Am.
Incorporation of federal constitution into state constitutions	14th Am.
Privacy	Penumbra of 1st Am. and 4th Am.
Right to receive information	Penumbra of Art. 1, Sec. 8, Cl. 7 and 1st Am.

Open government The general principle of open government was established in two constitutional provisions: Article 1, Section 5, requires Congress to report to the public on its activities through a "journal"; and Article 2, Section 3, requires the president to provide Congress with information regarding the conditions of the country. The first of these resulted in the *Congressional Record* and justifies access to the floor of Congress (including televised coverage of congressional activities). The second was operationalized originally through the State of the Union Address; in 1934 the *Federal Register* was created as a daily record of governmental activity; and shortly thereafter all existing laws were compiled and codified by subject matter in the U.S. Code. A manual of government operations further fulfills this constitutional requirement. In addition to these positive, or proactive, means of providing access to information about the government, since 1974 the Freedom of Information Act (FOIA) has also mandated public access to information held by federal agencies and to their decision-making processes as a reactive policy.

Free speech within government The speech and debate clause of the Constitution (Article 1, Section 6) protects members of Congress from prosecution for speech on the floor of Congress. This is an important element of the political system because it establishes the principle that even those within the government may be openly critical of it, thus encouraging the kind of robust discussion deemed essential to successful democratic practice. This provision does not, however, offer legislators absolute immunity in other contexts.

Federal government control over currency The Article 1, Section 8, prohibition on counterfeiting currency was historically a matter of information policy to the extent that it forbade particular uses of printing equipment. With the transformation of the financial system into computerized data flowing through the global electronic network, this article has become more important as an information policy principle because it can be used to criminalize certain manipulations of data.

Universal access to an information distribution system The postal provision (Article 1, Section 8, Clause 7) establishes the principle of governmental responsibility for a universally accessible information transportation and distribution system—the U.S. Post Office. Because at the time of the Constitution (and for quite a while afterwards) messages could be distributed only by physical transport, this provision also empowered the federal government to build "post roads" as necessary infrastructure for the postal system, resulting in what ultimately became the interstate highway system. The postal system was given constitutional status essential to the functioning of a representative government because those elected to office need to be able to inform their constituents of political developments and citizens, in turn, must be able to let their representatives know their wishes, needs, and concerns. Even though originally universal access to the telecommunications network was commercially motivated rather than politically mandated, as access to government information and services are increasingly provided through the information infrastructure, the postal provision also becomes a constitutional mandate for universal access to the Internet.

Intellectual property rights The right to own intellectual property is found in Article 1, Section 8, Clause 8, of the Constitution. The distinction between "authors" and "inventors" in the original language of the intellectual property rights provision led to the establishment of two separate systems of intellectual property, each with different requirements for asserting property claims. Copyright makes it possible to assert property rights in the expression of ideas in symbolic or textual form, and patent does the same for the expression of ideas in materials or processes. When the Constitution was written, it was believed that the development of new ideas and inventions by individuals was good for society as a whole. Thus in the U.S. system, copyright was intended to provide a financial incentive to authors and inventors, but limits to intellectual property rights were also put in place in order to ensure that society's needs could be met even during the period of monopoly control over an individual's creations. Fair use guidelines have thus been developed to enable limited use of intellectual property for prosocial and noncommercial purposes that do not destroy the market value of the materials used. With the informatization of society, intellectual property has arguably become the most economically valuable of all forms of property.

Restriction of civil liberties during time of war Article 1, Section 9, Clause 2, of the U.S. Constitution establishes the government's right to suspend the writ of habeas corpus in times of rebellion, invasion, or to protect the public safety. The writ of habeas corpus is the right to ask for a judicial determination as to whether one has been imprisoned unjustly, as could happen if one's speech or other expressive rights were unconstitutionally restricted or their exercise punished. This provision establishes the general principle that civil liberties may be restricted during wartime.

Treason The Constitution forbids only one class of speech: Treason, defined as levying war against the United States, "adhering" to its enemies, or providing enemies with "aid and comfort," is made illegal in Article 3, Section 3. This is one of the few criminal activities for which senators and representatives to Congress do *not* have protection from arrest even if it should take place in the course of official duties (Article 1, Section 6), and for which a president or other high elected official may be impeached. Conviction requires the testimony of two witnesses to the same overt act, or a confession in open court. Congress has determined that treason is punishable by death. While the logic of such a provision seems noncontroversial on its face, post–9/11 assertions by the U.S. attorney general's office and by some members of Congress that any expression of concern about the civil liberties implications of the war on terrorism of provides support for terrorists make it clear that this provision retains a dangerous potential for abuse.

The First Amendment

The First Amendment has been the linchpin of traditional discussions about freedom of expression in the United States. Several different rights are specified in the text:

> Congress shall make no law respecting an establishment of religion, or prohibiting the free exercise thereof; or abridging the freedom of speech, or of the press; or the right of the people peaceably to assemble, and to petition the Government for a redress of grievances.

"State action"—government involvement in an alleged restriction of free expression—is required in order for the First Amendment to be applicable. However, as discussed later in this chapter in the section on public forums, when private sector restrictions on speech take place in public spaces, constitutional standards must apply. This approach, however, has so far been applied only to spaces and not to functions. Thus as activities formerly undertaken by the government are transferred to the private sector, the state action doctrine means that First Amendment protections will not necessarily be useful.

Freedom of opinion The first clause protects the right to one's own thoughts and beliefs. When the Bill of Rights was written the greatest threats to freedom of opinion often came from religious institutions, but it has since been recognized that there are other types of issues about which people may hold unpopular or provocative opinions. Political ideas, radical scientific ideas, and even unorthodox approaches to art or entertainment have been the subject of efforts to restrict expression. Therefore this clause of the First Amendment today is understood to refer not just to freedom of religion, but also more broadly to freedom of opinion on any matter.

Freedom of speech While freedom of opinion protects your thoughts, freedom of speech gives you the right to tell others what you believe or think. Those who wrote the Constitution were thinking about face-to-face, or non-mediated, communications when they mentioned speech; such speech could take place interpersonally, in small groups, or in crowds. The phrase protects one-way flows of information, from sender to receiver, though it was clear that turn-taking in the role of sender was fundamental to democratic discourse. At the time that the Constitution was written, it was assumed that such communication took place synchronously, with all parties participating at the same time, and in the same physical space. With broadcasting, it became possible to "speak" simultaneously to vast numbers of people who were geographically dispersed. On the Internet, however, we often communicate asynchronously, with participants to a conversation joining in to learn what others are thinking and offer their own ideas at different points in time and from different places. Often, multiple different types of synchronous and asynchronous communication with individuals, small groups, and an anonymous public are engaged in simultaneously. The law is still not yet clear whether this type of communication is speech, assembly, or both.

Freedom of the press Technologically mediated communications are protected by freedom of the press, which provides the right to tell others what you think across time and space. This right vastly expands the world to which you can communicate your ideas by protecting your right to put ideas into forms that can be distributed—even globally—and/or stored for use by others at a later time. This right provides protection for asynchronous communications, in which parties to the process participate at different times and in different places.

Freedom of assembly and association Freedom of assembly is the right to get together with others for discussion. With the New England town hall of colonial times as a model, a fundamental element of participatory democracy as practiced in the United States is the opportunity for people to discuss political issues together before they vote or engage in other action. Doing so may change an individual's ideas, enable the building of a group consensus on a matter of communal concern, or facilitate the development of new ideas about governance in response to critiques of existing practices. As interpreted by the Supreme Court, this principle also extends to the right of association, since often people discuss matters with each other through the activities of organizations of which they are members rather than face-to-face. In abstract terms, this provision protects the right to interactive communication, whether synchronous or asynchronous, and whether mediated or unmediated. It also includes the freedom to *not* associate with particular individuals or groups.

Freedom to petition the government for change This is the right to ask the government to change. If individuals or groups believe the government is not acting in a way that is just or fair or serves the public interest most effectively, there is a constitutional right to ask for changes in government policy or operations. This was an important innovation in the U.S. Constitution that provides explicit protection for speech that is critical of the government. There are two types of change, however: that which occurs within the rules of a political system, and that which changes the very rules by which that system operates. Freedom to petition the government for change is generally understood to refer to change of the first type, but not necessarily the second. Thus, like the treason clause, this First Amendment principle is under great duress in the Homeland Security environment because of a shift in the government's definition of what types of change may be threatening to the system itself.

Other Constitutional Amendments

A number of other information policy principles appear elsewhere in the Bill of Rights—and in additional amendments that came later.

Protection against unlawful search The Fourth Amendment provides the core of privacy rights with its protection against unlawful search and seizure. In practice, it has also been important to freedom of the press, because search of private spaces for materials considered unacceptable is one technique that can be used to intimidate the press. The Forth Amendment has become even more important to communication today, because electronic surveillance is considered a form of search to which this principle applies. The full right to privacy, discussed later in this chapter, includes but also goes beyond this principle and relies in addition on the First Amendment.

Protection against self-incrimination The Fifth Amendment gives individuals the right to refrain from testifying against themselves or against their legal spouses to the police or in the courtroom. While exercising this right to silence does not quell suspicions, it is the only circumstance under which one may refuse to answer questions from the government without being held in contempt, itself a criminal charge.

Due process The Fifth Amendment also establishes due process, which requires the government to adhere to procedures that ensure openness and fairness in order for its own actions to be constitutional. Without such protections, any legal process can be abused. Examples of due process include rules regarding the treatment of a criminal suspect; criteria for the presentation of evidence in a courtroom and for the means by which such evidence can be collected; the right to appeal; and the requirements that judges use objective standards and explain their decisions. Because of due process, laws and regulations can be declared unconstitutional if they are applied without warning or through use of illegal means of apprehending suspects or collecting evidence about them. The Fourteenth Amendment extends the requirement of due process to the states. Analysis of due process issues has been so important to the protection of First Amendment rights that many refer specifically to "First Amendment due process."

Rights beyond those enumerated The Ninth Amendment emphasizes that the enumeration of specific rights in the Constitution does not mean that other rights are not also held by the people. This amendment provides explicit constitutional support for identification of additional policy principles and rights in what is described as the penumbra, or halo, of the Constitution's text. The full right to privacy and the right to receive information are penumbral rights of this kind. The Ninth Amendment is important in contemporary debates over the constitutional status to be accorded information processing techniques such as encryption, interactivity as a distinct type of communication requiring constitutional protection, and anonymity.

Incorporation The Fourteenth Amendment incorporates the federal constitution into the constitutions of every state; that is, every state constitution includes all of the provisions of the U.S. Constitution. This ensures a uniform floor for civil liberties throughout the country, irrespective of regional cultural and political differences. During the nineteenth century there were challenges to the application of this principle to the First Amendment, but in a series of Supreme Court decisions between 1927 and 1965 all of these arguments were rejected. Today the principle unequivocally includes the full range of informational and communicative rights introduced in this chapter. A state is free to set higher standards than those of the federal government—to provide even greater protections for free speech—but it may not set its standards lower.

The Penumbra of the Constitution

Two rights have been given constitutional status even though they are not specifically named in constitutional provisions. The concept of penumbral rights was first enunciated in an influential 1890 *Harvard Law Review* article about the right to privacy by Samuel D. Warren and Louis D. Brandeis in the late nineteenth century.

Privacy The right to privacy is based on the First and Forth Amendments. Today we recognize several different types of privacy and of invasion of privacy. This, too, is and will remain a highly contested constitutional principle in the first decades of the twenty-first century not only for political reasons but also because technological innovation has so significantly altered the means by which privacy can be invaded and, thus, the conditions under which there may reasonably be any actual expectation of privacy.

The right to receive information The right to receive information is found in the postal provision of the Constitution and in the First Amendment. The Communications Act of 1934 drew further attention to the principle by including the requirement that those given broadcasting licenses must serve as trustees for the expressive rights of the entire population and must demonstrate that programming was actually directed at the interests and needs of the audiences that received it (a requirement later abandoned during deregulation). In the last few decades, the Supreme Court has expanded upon the right to receive information, emphasizing that acquiring information is necessary in order to have something to say.

Constitutional Information Spaces

We have seen that contrary to the impression given in popular—and, often, scholarly and policy—discourse, the First Amendment includes not just one policy principle, but an entire bundle. And while the information policy provisions in the body of the Constitution itself have received less public attention, they remain important foundations for the law. These principles are only the bones of the legal framework for information policy. It is through their translation into statutes and regulations, and their interpretation by the courts, that they create the legal environment for information, communication, and culture. They do so by providing the framework for the architecture of the spaces in which information, communication, and culture unfold. In complex adaptive systems terms, these are the order parameters. Statutory and regulatory law and judicial interpretation of that law have articulated a number of different constitutional information spaces in which the law differentially applies. No constitutional principle is absolute. If any principle—such as the First Amendment—were, it would always govern when it was applicable. But many different social values have constitutional status, so often any single constitutional principle must be balanced against other important social interests.

The architecture defined by constitutional principles includes distinctions between that which is public and that which is private; among communicative spaces as delineated by medium, content, speaker, and receiver; and between communications during wartime as opposed to times of peace. Some of the information spaces created through the interpretations and application of constitutional law are enduring. Others, however, undergo reconsideration. New categories can appear, old categories can collapse into each other, and boundaries can be redefined or abandoned altogether.

Public versus Private

The idea that there should be a difference between that which is private and that which is shared with others in public seems basic to what it means to be human. Various cultures, however—even within single nation-states—draw the line differently. The same society can define what is private differently over time, or for diverse purposes. Changes in the nature of the information environment, such as those brought about by meta-technologies, can alter the meaning and effect of rules in place. Thus while the distinction between the public and the private is ancient, it needs continual reconsideration.

There has been a constant push and pull between the effort to protect spaces for expression and action in which the government does not intervene and the desire for active government involvement in the private realm that was the signature of the bureaucratic welfare state. The very word "public" came into use concurrent with the development of the administrative practices of the secular nation-state in the fifteenth century, along with the concept of administration. As a political matter, the public came to mean that realm of society that shares in common the consequences of both private and state action and that tries to act effectively in its own defense. More narrowly, the "public sector" is the government. The distinction between the private and the public is important in determining the goals of regulation, the context within which communication takes place, and ownership and control of the information infrastructure and its content.

The "public good" Information policy discourse often refers to public as opposed to private goods, but political, economic, and pragmatic definitions are often conflated. Something that is a public good in one sense may not be in another.

From a political perspective, the public good refers to decision-making with the goal of serving society as a whole. The political notion of the public good refers to an attribute of society rather than of a thing, and it is singular in nature. All of the issues raised by the problem of determining whose intention should be expressed in policy apply to the problem of figuring out just what the public good is. The concept has been translated into information policy via the regulatory phrase "the public interest," a concept that has been defined in many different ways. Mark Fowler, chair of the FCC in the early 1980s, voiced a position at one pole of the definitional spectrum when he declared that the market determined the public good. Newton Minow, chair of the FCC under President John F. Kennedy in the early 1960s, marked the other pole with the position that the public good required the government to intervene in the market to ensure the quality of broadcasting content.

To economists, on the other hand, a public good is an attribute of the good rather than of society. A public good is characterized by nonexcludability, meaning that potential users can't be excluded from public goods; and by nonrivalrous consumption, meaning that one person's use of a public good does not keep others from using the same good. Everyone can enjoy the use of a pure public good, while only the owner can use a purely private good. A good that is public in the economic sense might be provided by the public sector, a single private-sector actor, a group of private sector actors, a public-private sector partnership, or, some have argued, the market.

Nor are purely public and purely private goods the only options from an economic perspective. The telecommunications network operates in many ways like a public good, even though users can be excluded and charges can be assessed; it is thus in an intermediate position along a continuum from public to private. Similarly, the physical container for information may be a private good even when the information itself is a public good. In mixed situations, determining which is which may be tricky—the easy or free duplication of information, for example, can be described either as evidence of a public good or as a problem of private goods production under extreme economies of scale. Intermediary positions along the continuum from public to private goods can be problematic for policy analysis; in the area of broadcasting, for example, television content is treated as if it were a private good even though content is always to some degree a public good.

Pragmatically, resources—including information—that are held, controlled, or created by the government are "goods that belong to the public." From the perspective of information policy, the most familiar example of this type of public good may be the public domain in copyright, which includes materials for which copyright has lapsed, over which copyright has never been asserted, or those voluntarily placed in the public domain (as well as government documents). The argument that data collected by the government on behalf of the public—such as the images collected through satellite surveillance—should be treated as this type of public good has been important in discussions about the possible privatization of some government functions. And recently a requirement has been put in place that the data generated by federal government-supported research projects—as well as interpretations of that data—need to be made publicly available.

The public and private in social systems Public and private communicative contexts are distinguished for a variety of purposes, including the freedom with which one can engage in political speech and whether there is a reasonable expectation of privacy. Four types of environments have been distinguished: public forum, quasi-public forum, quasi-private forum, and private forum. The factors that determine the nature of a particular space include ownership and control of the space, the general and specific purposes to which the space is devoted, and the history of use of the particular space.

• *Public forum* A public forum is owned and controlled by the public (the government) and is devoted to purposes that serve the people as a whole. Its specific uses are also public in nature, and there is a history of the use of such spaces for general public purposes. Examples are public parks, sidewalks, streets, and other communal areas traditionally treated as public spaces. In such environments, speech can be restricted only when constitutional standards have been met, and there is no legitimate expectation of privacy.

- *Quasi-public forum* A quasi-public forum is owned and controlled by the government and serves the population in general but is dedicated to a specific function; there is no history of public access. Examples include prisons, public schools and universities, military bases, and nuclear energy installations. In such environments, it is constitutional to restrict speech activities if doing so is necessary to ensure that the function of the institution is fulfilled. Thus it is legitimate to forbid access to nuclear installations; to strictly limit access to military bases and prisons and to control that access when permitted; and to restrict expression on public university campuses if the speech is deemed to interfere with the educational process. Because these are still public environments, however, there is no legal expectation of privacy within them.
- *Quasi-private forum* A quasi-private forum is privately owned and controlled but serves general public functions. In general, there must be access and some freedom of expression within such environments, but restrictions are constitutionally acceptable if they are necessary to enable the entity to fulfill its specific functions. Restaurants and stores open to the general public, shopping malls owned by private parties, and company-owned towns are examples of quasi-private forums that fulfill many functions of public spaces. The degree to which one might have an expectation of privacy in a quasi-private space depends upon its specific function—in a restaurant one may have a greater expectation of privacy than in a public park, but not complete protection, while in a shopping mall the very public experience of the space means one has no expectation of privacy.
- *Private forum* A private forum is privately owned and controlled and serves private functions both in general and in particular. The home is the classic private space. There one has complete freedom of expression as well as a legal expectation of privacy.

Many of the difficulties of regulating expression in the Internet environment come from the difficulty of determining whether a given space, such as a list-based discussion group, is a public or private forum. Internet service providers present an important problem of this type because their services are necessary in order to access the Internet and thus the contractual "acceptable use agreements" or "terms of service" to which users must agree have become an important source of de facto communication regulation.

The public and private in technological systems Whether the information infrastructure is in private or public hands makes a difference because it determines the goals to be served by the network, the values according to which network decision-making will take place, the role of regulation, the linkage between content production and control over the infrastructure, and even whether there is one service provider or many.

Though infrastructure regulatory issues are not always discussed in constitutional terms, they are included here for several reasons. The extent of privatization and degree of concomitant liberalization or deregulation affect the types of policy tools that can be used to ensure that constitutional goals are achieved by the information infrastructure. With the convergence of technologies, the public interest standard of broadcasting should be pertinent to the telecommunications network as well, because the latter is increasingly the means through which the diversity of voices key to healthy public discourse in a democracy can be expressed. For the same reason, constitutionally based quasi-public and quasi-private forum arguments should pertain to much Web-based communication. Finally, the infrastructure is now among the elements of the informational environment that should be, many argue, treated as a commons; some suggest the phrase "public domain technologies" should thus be used to describe those elements of the information infrastructure that cannot be patented, that result from publicly funded research, or that have outlived their patents.

Until recently, telecommunications and broadcasting outside the United States were controlled by governments, while in the United States both types of infrastructure were in private hands (except for a brief period during World War I). Beginning in the 1980s, however, governments around the world wholly or partially privatized their communication systems. Because the infrastructure is global, privatization and deregulation of infrastructure have made it much easier to harmonize laws across nation-states and for transnational vendors and service providers to operate around the world. Even in the United States, there has been an increase in competition in telecommunications since the late 1970s. Though AT&T was never technically a monopoly, it held a monopoly-like position until 1983, when it was forced by the Antitrust Division of the U.S. Department of Justice to divest itself of its regional and local operations.

Though a relaxation of regulation—or "liberalization"—often accompanies privatization of communication systems, that is not a necessity. Some see privatization as a subset of liberalization, while others see liberalization as a subset of privatization, and the two are often confused with each other. Additional terms applied to the regulatory and ownership shifts of recent decades include commercialization, deregulation, no regulation, reregulation, and forbearance. It is worth clarifying their meanings.

Privatization is the relinquishing of government control over communication, generally through a sale of governmental assets. Privatization does not require the end of monopoly provision of infrastructure, content, and services, though in many cases this also takes place. Nor need it mean that regulation must be relaxed, though again often it is. *Commercialization*, the incorporation of formerly governmental entities and their entry into the competitive market, is the first step for many governments as they undertake the processes of privatization and deregulation.

Liberalization is a relaxation of legal constraints though some regulation remains. Content rules may become more lax, there may be greater openness to advertising, requirements to serve the public may be abandoned or reduced, license terms may be improved, and the percentage of local and national markets served by single content providers may be raised. Just as commercialization is often a step in the process of privatization, so liberalization is often a step in the process of deregulation. Many countries have undertaken liberalization in a series of steps in order to gauge effects before going further.

Deregulation entails the removal of regulatory constraints on competitive activity. Deregulation of communications in the United States began in the 1970s with the decision to permit the unbundling of customer premises equipment from the provision of network services. This was followed by a systematic loosening of regulatory constraints upon both telecommunications and broadcasting over the decades leading up to the Telecommunications Act of 1996. Deregulation has continued since then, including, notably, the raising of the cap on the reach of single content providers in 2003. In some countries in which communication systems were owned and managed by the government, there had otherwise been *no regulation.*

There is also the possibility that a government can choose not to regulate in an area in which the right to regulate has been claimed. This is called *forebearance.* As mentioned earlier, the FCC did this with the computer industry at the conclusion of its three computer inquiries undertaken from the late 1960s to the 1980s in an effort to determine whether to regulate a network that had begun to include those activities that had historically been regulated as well as those that had not. To assert the right to regulate the computer industry, the FCC relied upon the responsibility assigned by the Communications Act of 1934 to regulate those things "auxiliary" to broadcasting and telecommunications, though historically this term had applied only to such things as the wooden poles that were necessary to the telegraph and telephone networks. At the opposite end of the spectrum, some governments are finding that deregulation has gone too far; they have started processes of *reregulation*.

Deregulation and privatization are both linked to the goal of reducing the size of government. Deregulation of communications has also been promoted by those who argue that regulation interferes with the First Amendment rights of content producers such as broadcast corporations. Other arguments used to support these trends, however, can also be used to justify their reversal, such as the desire to promote innovation and to enhance the capacity of the nation-state.

The public and private in informational systems Information, or content, becomes private when intellectual property rights are asserted. Public content is that which is in the public domain or, potentially, in an information "commons." Through fair use, privately owned content is publicly accessible when it is considered to be in the public good in the political sense. Currently there is a battle, in the United States and worldwide, to expand the realm of information held in a commons rather than privately.

Spaces Defined by Medium

Earlier, the different legal systems that have grown up over time in the United States were introduced: the First Amendment "system" in response to print, broadcasting regulation in response to radio and television, and telecommunications regulation in response to telegraphy and telephony. Each of these systems defines rights and responsibilities in very different ways, creating a problematic legal situation once these technologies converged with each other. Today there are many situations in which all three bodies of law and regulation can apply to a single communicative act. Here, a few of the differences between the legal spaces as defined by medium are examined to provide some insight into just why technological innovation has raised so many information policy issues.

Regulatory target The regulatory target—not always apparent from the text of a law or regulation—is the threat against which the policy tool is designed. The writers of the U.S. Constitution were concerned about intervention into speech by church or state because it was assumed in the world of oral communication and the printing press that there were neither geographic, economic, nor cultural barriers to access otherwise. For broadcasting and telecommunications, however, economic competitors were the "other" against which regulation was designed.

Regulatory subject The subject of regulation is the entity for whom the law is put into place. The First Amendment was conceived of in response to concerns about the ability of individuals to speak and publish. Though religious and political authorities were perceived as threats to this individual right of citizens, in the print environment organizational and economic barriers were believed to be relatively low or nonexistent. Corporations, not individuals, are the subject of broadcasting and telecommunications regulation, however.

Similarly, the "user" in the print environment is the individual reader-citizen, while in broadcasting, those who receive information are described via their economic functions as members of the audience. In telecommunications, the distinction between sender and receiver disappears in favor of the user, because in interactive communications both parties play both roles. Even so, while for many years the user in telecommunications regulation was the individual, in recent years that term has come to refer to large corporations such as Citibank and American Express instead, so that corporate rather than individual needs are those primarily addressed by telecommunications regulation. Today, the user of telecommunications services is increasingly likely to be another network or technological system.

Licensing In the United States, print is not licensed because it is believed that licensing has a potential to become a form of prior restraint—if a license can be given, it can be taken away. Broadcasting and telecommunications are licensed, but according to completely different criteria, and through systems managed by separate bureaucracies. Even the justifications for licensing of the two types of communications technologies are different, as discussed in chapter 3.

The regulatory techniques used to put licensing into practice derived from these justificatory arguments. Criteria were established for broadcasting licensees and requirements put in place to ensure that broadcasters fulfilled their role as trustees of the public interest. Originally, for example, broadcast licensees were required to ensure that their programming represented the interests of their listeners and, in essence, to ensure that broadcast provided a communicative medium even for those who did not hold licenses. At the height of such requirements, the FCC's Fairness Doctrine required broadcasters to present all sides of issues of public concern when they presented any coverage of such issues at all. Each of these was abandoned in the course of deregulation.

A different set of justifications was used to institute licensing for telecommunications. Telecommunications is also known as "common carriage" because its regulation was modeled after a British approach to licensing of those who run ferries across rivers, a necessary service in days when there were very few bridges. Ferries were required to fulfill two requirements. First, the service had to be open to all comers ("common" carriage); that is, everyone who asked for the service had to be offered that service under the same conditions. The second requirement was that the licensee should have no impact at all on what was carried; that is, the condition in which someone or something got on a ferry should be exactly the condition in which that person or thing got off. As applied to telecommunications in the United States, a third principle of common carriage was limited liability for the effects of messages carried as long as there was no negligence on the part of the carrier. The basics of common carriage developed in an environment in which the services involved were monopolistic; it is more difficult to apply those principles in a highly competitive environment.

Editorial control One of the most important dimensions along which regulation differs by medium is how much editorial control over content is permitted—and therefore how much legal responsibility for that content a creator or sender of a message has. Under the print system, senders had complete editorial control; protecting this is the crux of the press clause of the First Amendment. Thus a newspaper is responsible for libelous content, a book publisher for invasions of privacy, and so forth. The prohibition on licensing was considered key to protecting this complete editorial control. In broadcasting, however, the need to license and the original definition of licensees as trustees for the general public originally carried with them some constraints on editorial control in order to ensure that licensees served the public interest. As part of the deregulation process, in recent decades some of these constraints have been weakened, though others remain in place. In telecommunications, there was historically no editorial control at all. Corporations in new industries, however—in particular, Internet service providers (ISPs)—are pressing against that wall as they seek a mix of profit maximization and liability minimization. At the time of this writing, for example, ISPs *are* held responsible for copyright infringement by users of their services if an allegation of infringement is made (under the Digital Millennium Copyright Act) and are *not* responsible for libel committed by users of their services (by court decisions). Meanwhile, most ISPs require that subscribers yield a license to information posted and/or uploaded, including the right to use such content for commercial purposes without the user's consent but with the user's name if desired.

Thus on the dimension of editorial control, there are three quite different legacies from the law: from print, the model of complete editorial control; from broadcast, the model of editorial control limited by regulatory constraints designed to serve the public interest (even though that model was later essentially abandoned); and from telecommunications, an entirely hands-off policy. All three of these can be simultaneously applicable in the contemporary environment.

The Spaces of Expression

Because constitutional protections are aimed at speech, activities determined to be something other than speech are not protected by the First Amendment. The law distinguishes between speech and things, speech and action, speech and symbolic action, and speech and information processing.

Speech versus things The distinction between expressing ideas in symbols and expressing ideas in objects or processes comes from the Constitution's distinction between intellectual property rights in symbolic expressions (copyright) and in inventions (patent). Until recently, this was considered an obvious and unproblematic distinction. Digitization, however, has created a situation in which the design of information processes and structures can be accomplished either through copyrightable text (computer code) or through patentable objects (in computers and networks themselves). Because the duration of protection and other features distinguish the two types of property rights, the choice between the two approaches to asserting property rights is now a matter of strategic choice. As a result, the patent system is now information policy not just at the level of knowledge growth, but also at the concrete levels of computer and network architectures and ownership patterns.

Speech versus action There are three constitutionally important relations between expression and action. When they are completely intertwined it is known as symbolic action, discussed in a later section. Here, two interactions between speech and action are explored: speech that intentionally leads so directly to action that the expression itself should be considered behavior (the problem of "clear and present danger") and media liability for actions related to content (the problem of "personal injury liability"). The problem of distinguishing between speech and action has plagued First Amendment interpretation since the early twentieth century.

Clear and present danger Speech that leads to unacceptable action by crowds was one of the earliest areas in which the First Amendment was interpreted by the Supreme Court. The issue was first raised in 1919 by pamphleteering meant to encourage resistance to the draft during World War I. Upholding the conviction of the defendant, Justice Oliver Wendell Holmes argued that the nature of every expression depends upon its context, and introduced the criteria of proximity and the degree to which action that might result from speech would disrupt affairs legitimately of governmental interest. The concept of clear and present danger was further refined over time. The bars for both proximity and seriousness were raised in order to ensure that political speech could be protected; a distinction was drawn between protected advocacy of abstract doctrine and unprotected advocacy of specific, illegal action; and the questions of probability and intention were added. In 1969 a test for identifying the line between pure speech and speech with the effect of action was put in place and still stands today. The clear and present danger test, sometimes known as the *Brandenburg* test after the Supreme Court case in which it was first articulated, draws the line on the basis of four criteria. The **Test for Clear and Present Danger**, then, is as follows:

1. *Incitement* Does the expression advocate the use of illegal force or violence?
2. *Intention* Does the expression actually intend to incite such illegal conduct?
3. *Imminence* Would the conduct being incited occur immediately?
4. *Probability* Is the expression actually likely to produce the illegal conduct it advocates?

Personal injury lawsuits The clear and present danger test applies to situations in which speech leads to action by crowds. In recent years, the question of the accountability of producers for actions by individuals in response to media content has also begun to receive legal attention via personal injury lawsuits. Such lawsuits can be triggered in three ways: (1) Harm through imitation: something described or shown in the media is imitated by someone in the audience, as when a group of children raped another child using a household object after seeing this done in a movie. (2) Harm from advice or instructions: the media intentionally encourages specific actions, whether via an advice column, a product instruction booklet, a political editorial, or the lyrics to a song. (3) Harm through advertising: language and/or images in advertising either encourage or model dangerous behaviors, the imitation of which can lead to harm or death.

Success in a personal injury lawsuit requires a demonstration of negligence, defined as failure to exercise the degree of care that a reasonable person would have exercised under the circumstances. Several factors are used to determine negligence in such cases. The **Test for Negligence in Personal Injury Lawsuits** is as follows:

1. *Expectation* Was there a reasonably foreseeable risk of direct harm to others?
2. *Conduct* Did the defendant fail to exercise care in the face of an expectation of possible harm?
3. *Causality* Did any actual harm occur?

Personal injury lawsuits are becoming more common, but have rarely been successful because of the difficulty of proving intention, and fear that awarding damages in such suits would launch an onslaught of cases, with the ultimate effect of chilling speech. (Speech is "chilled" when it is not directly prohibited but the legal or political environment is such that certain types of expression are strongly discouraged.) Most courts dealing with personal injury lawsuits today instead prefer to rely upon the incitement standard developed for clear and present danger.

Symbolic action Symbolic action occurs when a behavior or object is meant to be expressive, as in the burning of a flag, a sit-in, or art. Speech doesn't always accompany symbolic action, but it often does. Even when there is no language used, however, symbolic action is considered to be expression. A cross burning, for example, is considered hate speech whether or not anything additional is said.

In cases involving symbolic action, legal analysis is based on the nature of the action. Both cross burning and burning a flag are constitutionally protected political speech if there is no physical harm. If the same types of speech or symbolic behaviors are combined with action that *is* socially damaging, they will be punished as action rather than protected as speech. Hate speech combined with assault, therefore, is treated as assault—and the sentencing consequences are multiplied because the action was undertaken on hate grounds. Political speech combined with the burning of a draft card is punishable action because the action impeded the government's function of conducting the draft.

Courts use five criteria to determine whether a restriction on symbolic action is constitutional under the First Amendment; these comprise the **Test for Restrictions on Symbolic Action:**

1. *Expression* Did both speaker and audience understand the symbolic action as speech?
2. *Constitutionality* Is there a constitutional foundation for the interests that the government is seeking to protect?
3. *Substantial government interest* Is the government interest at stake important enough to be considered "substantial"?
4. *Content neutrality* Is the government interest involved unrelated to suppression of particular content?
5. *Narrow tailoring* Does the regulation restrict expression no more than is essential to protect the government interest?

Speech versus information processing Today one of the greatest threats to freedom of expression is the argument that an information flow is not speech but information processing and therefore not deserving of constitutional protections. Expression has always involved information processing in order to reach the ideas and/or create the messages expressed. Before the advent of computing, however, those stages of expression were rarely referred to other than during the training in information processing known as education. If mentioned at all, many types of information processing, and iterations of processing, were lumped together under the general term "thinking." With the exteriorization of information processing from the human to the computer, however, those stages of message creation have become much more visible. As a result, legal thinkers began to separate information processing conceptually from speech for distinct legal treatment, whether or not the processing involved was done by computers or by people, and whether or not such processing was an integral part of the formation of messages to be communicated.

The first legal distinction between speech and information processing was introduced in 1879 during a dispute, motivated by antitrust concerns, over ownership of the different patents required for transmitting voice by telephone and data by telegraphy. (To resolve the conflict, AT&T agreed to keep the telephone patents and stay out of telegraphy, and Western Union agreed to retain the telegraph patents and stay out of telephony.) The distinction retained regulatory importance, providing the foundation for the FCC's 1986 *Computer Inquiry III* distinction between activities it would regulate and those it would not in an environment in which the two types of technologies had converged. In this context, the distinction between speech and information processing did not have immediate constitutional implications, but it did draw sustained legal attention to the difference between the two types of activities.

In the 1970s—while the FCC was already in the midst of its computer inquiries—the conceptual distinction made the leap from regulatory law to constitutional law. In a case mentioned earlier, the U.S. government tried to prevent the magazine *The Progressive* from printing an article that included plans for building a hydrogen bomb, even though the information upon which the article was based was in the public domain and legally available to all. In order to justify this attempt at prior restraint, the government argued that the right to *access* information in the public domain did not necessarily include the right to *process* that information. The district court accepted this novel argument with this astonishing language:

> The government argues that its national security interest also permits it to impress classification and censorship upon information originating in the public domain . . . when drawn together, synthesized and collated. (*U.S. v. Progressive*, 1979, at 991)
>
> [D]ue recognition must be given to the human skills and expertise involved in writing this article . . . certain individuals with some knowledge, ability to reason and extraordinary perseverance may acquire additional knowledge without access to classified information, even though the information thus acquired may not be obvious to others not so equipped or motivated. (Ibid., at 993)

The issue in this case was mooted before it could be visited by the Supreme Court because the material under discussion was published elsewhere. The argument itself, however, resonated with other developments in constitutional law of the period. The same distinction between unprocessed and processed information lay at the basis of the libel defense known as "neutral reportage." This is a species of reporters' privilege that protects journalists against liability for republication of defamation in news reports of statements made in official documents and proceedings, as long as the journalists meet several requirements—including passing through the report in an unprocessed form. The claim that information processing is not speech has been central to legal claims that the First Amendment does not apply to encryption practices, even when defendants argue that they would be unable to speak without use of encryption. More recently, a 2002 Immigration and Naturalization Service (INS) directive allows the agency to seal off innocuous records that might endanger the government's interest if the information they held were combined with other innocuous information. A new category of threat to speech that involves information processing derives from concern by the intelligence establishment over what it calls "inference attacks" (the ability to infer something the government would prefer that you do not know through inference based on information to which citizens legally have access) and "aggregation attacks" (the ability to figure out something by putting two and two together).

The courts, however, have already identified a number of distinct aspects of information processing they consider to be of constitutional importance. These include collection, synthesis, and collation of information as distinct types of processing, each deserving of constitutional protection. The Supreme Court has reinforced that various ways of interacting with information make it possible to process it differently, so that reading, face-to-face debate, group discussion, and questioning are each separately worthy of constitutional protection. The number of times information has been processed can be pertinent to the way constitutional law is applied. Translation, the translation of general statements into particular statements, and anonymous speech are specific types of information processing that have all been deemed deserving of constitutional protection by the Supreme Court.

Information processing is not explicitly mentioned in the Constitution, but as mentioned earlier, the Ninth Amendment principle that rights not specifically mentioned in the Constitution are still protected provides a foundation for First Amendment protection of information processing. Interpretation of the law over the last several decades has begun to make this clear, but this is a good example of the way constitutional principles become fully translated into practice only when social tensions force the courts to elaborate upon what the Constitution's abstract ideas mean. This will be one of the key areas in which constitutional law should be expected to develop in the early twenty-first century.

The Spaces of Content

Constitutional law offers a variety of ways of distinguishing among types of content for purposes of operationalization of the law. Not all content receives the same level of constitutional protection because it is believed that different types of speech promote constitutional values to different degrees. Distinctions are made on the basis of genre, the relationship of content to facticity, the subject of a message, the nature of the message receiver, the degree to which referentiality of content is direct, and whether all or part of a text is being examined.

Genre Genres are categorized into three tiers of protection.

High protection The greatest constitutional protections are provided for speech that is political, social, cultural, and religious, and for assembly and association. Freedom from compelled speech also falls into this category.

Political speech is protected because of its centrality to the functioning of democracy. Debate over political issues and political campaigns is political speech, but so are demonstrations and protests, letters to the editor, artistic and cultural productions, and many other forms of speech. Because the forms of political speech are diverse and such speech is often combined with other content, one of the longstanding problems for the courts has been determining when speech is or is not political. Politics is about the conditions under which we live, so it is recognized that social, cultural, and even economic speech can have political implications. Thus art, popular culture such as television, and religion all fall into the category of speech that receives the highest level of constitutional protection. For the same reason, freedom of association (as in clubs) and of assembly (as in group meetings) also receive the highest level of constitutional protection.

The United States is an outlier among democracies in defining hate speech—speech that attacks groups on the basis of race, gender, ethnicity, religion, nationality, or sexual orientation—as political speech. In many countries, hate speech is prohibited because it is believed to cause illegal action (including murder), and to cause emotional and psychological harm even when limited to expression. Research by sociologists since World War II provides evidence that supports this causal expectation. Prosecution for group libel is available as a legal response to hate speech, but because such cases are successful only if they involve very small groups, each member of which is identifiable, they are rare. Three social movements since the 1960s—the racially oriented civil rights movement, the broader civil rights movement that also attended to gender and other issues, and the victims' rights movement—have drawn increasing legal attention to hate crimes. The result has been federal and state laws that require collecting information about hate crimes and increase the sentences of those convicted of crimes motivated by hate.

Compelled speech occurs when one is forced to engage in a certain type of expression. Prayer in the classroom, oaths as a condition of employment, and requiring union members to support particular political candidate via union dues are all examples of compelled speech. Freedom from compelled speech for individuals also receives the highest level of constitutional protections. (Corporations, however, may be required to engage in certain types of speech in order to correct false advertising, provide stockholders information about publicly held companies, etc.)

Regulations restricting those types of speech that receive the highest levels of constitutional protection are examined with "strict scrutiny" to determine whether they are constitutionally acceptable. In order to meet this test, the government must demonstrate that the interest it is protecting is extremely important, or "compelling"—a higher standard to meet than a "substantial" government interest. To meet the standards established by strict scrutiny, the government must answer the questions raised by the **Strict Scrutiny Test:**

1. *Compelling government interest* Does the government's interest in the matter reach the high standard of being compelling?
2. *Narrow tailoring* Is the regulation crafted in such a way that it restricts speech as little as possible?
3. *No alternative* Are there any alternatives to this regulation that might be less restrictive of First Amendment rights while still protecting the government's interest?

Intermediate protection Other kinds of expression receive some constitutional protection, but it is easier to justify their restriction. Types of speech that receive an intermediate level of protection include commercial speech, the solicitation of funds, and non-obscene sexual expression.

Commercial speech is expression that takes place in conjunction with an economic transaction, whether marketing goods and services, directly soliciting sales, effecting sales, or following up on a sale with instruction booklets, guarantees, or surveys. Subscriptions, leases, and contracts are all examples of commercial speech. The constitutional stature of commercial speech began to rise in the 1970s after the Supreme Court acknowledged that such speech can have political consequences when it has an impact on quality of life. The question that prompted this shift in perception involved the advertisement of prescription drug costs by pharmacies, which at the time was forbidden. Defendants in the key case argued that for the elderly and others on fixed incomes, the ability to comparison shop for medicine could dramatically influence the amount of income available for other needs, including food, energy, and housing.

When it is not clear whether a particular message is commercial speech, courts again look at several factors. While in the other tests introduced here every factor must be taken into consideration, in this area only one of these questions needs to be answered positively for speech to be defined as commercial for legal purposes. These are the elements of the **Test for Commercial Speech:**

1. *Payment* Did a company pay for the message?
2. *Products* Are specific products mentioned in the message?
3. *Economic motive* Did the company have an economic motive for producing the message?

Because the higher constitutional status of political speech means that such messages can be distributed in places where commercial speech cannot, some companies have tried mixing the two in the hope that their messages will be interpreted as political rather than commercial. However, courts have held that neither inclusion of political content in a commercial message, nor advertisement of goods or services in the public interest, nor incorporating educational material into products is sufficient to transform commercial speech into political speech.

While commercial speech is carried out by those who are trying to make a profit, nonprofit entities often solicit funds. This type of transaction-related speech also receives an intermediate level of constitutional protection. Campaign fund-raising and the political action committees (PACs) through which corporations can donate funds to candidates generate the leading court cases in this area.

The law distinguishes between constitutionally acceptable and unacceptable sexual speech, using the word "obscene" to refer to the latter. The dividing line between the two is determined by four factors known as the *Miller* test after the Supreme Court case in which the test was developed. This is the **Test for Obscenity**:

1. *Prurient interest* Is the work as a whole intended to excite lewd, shameful, or morbid thoughts in an average person, applying contemporary community standards?

2. *Patent offensiveness* Does the work explicitly depict or describe in a patently offensive way activities that are specifically forbidden by state law?
3. *Serious value* Is any scientific, educational, artistic, literary, or political value served by the work as a whole?

Because courts understand that cultural attitudes towards sexuality vary significantly, community standards are extremely important in evaluating the first two of these factors. The third is examined in light of national standards as determined by expert opinion. Non-obscene sexual speech receives an intermediate level of constitutional protection because it is considered normal and healthy for adults. Art and performance may fall into this category. Sensitivity to those who should not be exposed to such speech (notably children) is addressed via voluntary or imposed systems of ratings and regulation of the time, place, and manner in which such speech is conveyed. Because it is impossible to determine when children might be watching television or listening to radio, use of some specific language and images in broadcasting is forbidden as "indecent" by regulatory law.

The test for the constitutionality of restrictions on these types of speech—the intermediate scrutiny test—has three prongs. The main difference between this test and the strict scrutiny test is that here the government interest being protected at the intermediate level need only be substantial rather than compelling. Here is the **Intermediate Scrutiny Test:**

1. *Compelling government interest* Is the government's interest in the matter "substantial"?
2. *Narrow tailoring* Is the regulation crafted in such a way that it restricts speech as little as possible?
3. *No alternative* Are there no alternatives to this regulation that might be less restrictive of First Amendment rights while still protecting the government's interest?

No constitutional protections There are many types of speech that do not receive any constitutional protection at all: fighting words, falsity in a number of specified circumstances, treason, and obscenity. Any speech that promotes illegal activity or takes place during the course of it is itself illegal.

Fighting words are words that "by their very utterance inflict injury or tend to incite an immediate breach of the peace" (*Chaplinsky v. New Hampshire*, 1942, at 572). They must be so offensive as to cause acts of violence by the person or persons to whom such speech is addressed. Fighting words differ from hate speech in that they are directed at a specific individual rather than at a group, and are considered to present a specialized form of clear and present danger. The fighting words doctrine has been used somewhat less in recent years, because many of the statutes upon which its use relies have been determined to be unconstitutionally overbroad, meaning that they affect activity that is not legitimately of concern in addition to the behaviors against which the laws were put in place. The doctrine can also be difficult to apply: those who opposed a Nazi Party march in a neighborhood largely populated by Holocaust survivors claimed that to such individuals the swastika qualified as fighting words rather than political speech because in their experience the symbol was directly linked to the death of people they had known, but the courts did not agree. There is also the problem of determining when it is the speaker and when it is the audience that is hostile, as was discovered in a case in which the Supreme Court struck down the conviction of a speaker whose comments roused a large crowd opposed to racism. Under such conditions, the Court argued, it is not legitimate to punish the speaker for the effects of expression unless the clear and present danger test has been met.

The issue of truth and falsity pervades communications law. In each area of the law where the truth or falsity of a statement makes a difference—libel law, privacy, financial reporting, and advertising and other commercial speech—false speech is not constitutionally protected. The criteria taken into account to determine whether restrictions on false speech, or its punishment, are appropriate differ according to the type of legal issue involved, but several principles always apply. Here is the **Test for Falsity**:

1. *Fact* Was the false statement presented as a fact?
2. *Intention* Was the falsity intentional?
3. *Materiality* Does the false information make a difference to a decision that is made or an action taken on the basis of that information?
4. *Damage* Did any actual damage result from the false statement?

Intentionality is important because courts understand that innocent error is unavoidable. The requirements of damage and materiality ensure that the legal system is not bound up with matters that are trivial. Presentation of information as a fact is an important criterion because there are legal distinctions between falsity and opinion, fiction, parody, satire, and critique. Determining just when something has been presented as a fact as opposed to opinion irrespective of genre can itself be difficult; to do so, courts ask two questions. This, then, is the **Test for Fact versus Opinion**:

1. *Specificity* Does the statement include content that is specific?
2. *Verifiability* Does the statement state or imply a provably false statement of fact; that is, can the statement's truth be verified?

While the government can restrict the types of speech that are considered unprotected by the Constitution, it still must meet two criteria in order to do. This is the **Test for Restrictions on Forbidden Speech:**

1. *Rationality* Is there a rational basis for the restriction?
2. *Nonarbitrariness* Is the restriction being applied in a nonarbitrary manner?

Message subject There are times when the law will treat content differently depending on who it is *about.* The tort of misappropriation in privacy law is available only to the subjects of media coverage who were already famous enough to have something worth appropriating. Material about sex involving children will be treated differently from material about sex involving consenting adults. And in libel law, libelous statements about public figures are treated quite differently from statements about private figures.

Direct versus indirect Constitutional law recognizes that not all messages with impact are direct and explicit. As a result, in several areas the law distinguishes between that speech which is direct and that which is not. Libel law covers both libel per se (speech that is libelous "on its face"—that is, explicitly) and libel per quod (speech that is libelous by implication, often requiring additional information in order to be understood). When the Federal Trade Commission (FTC) examines the possibility of fraud in advertising, for example, it looks for both express falsehoods (speech in which the meaning of the words can be taken directly from the message) and implied falsehoods (advertising in which the false impressions are created by visual or verbal suggestion). In considering whether sexual speech is obscene, courts distinguish between hard-core pornography (explicit depictions of sexual activity) and soft-core pornography (references to or suggestions of sexual activity). And in privacy law, consent to enter property can be either explicit or it can be implied under a theory of custom and usage (expectations built by social habits over time).

Partial versus whole texts Courts also distinguish between fragments of texts and texts in their entirety in their interpretations of many branches of the law. In libel, obscenity, and advertising law, judgments are made on the meaning of a text as a whole. Trivial statements of falsity in libel or advertising or passing references to sexuality in potentially obscene materials will not be sufficient to restrict the expression if those details run counter to the meaning and intention of the work as a whole. Similarly, in the area of intellectual property rights, there is great attention to the portion of a work taken for fair use purposes so that the value of the work as a whole is not destroyed.

The Spaces of Content Production

There are some circumstances in which the law adapts its treatment of speech depending upon the content producer (the speaker, or sender).

Corporate versus individual Corporations are, by legal fiction, individuals in the eyes of the law. But because they usually have much greater resources than do individuals, there are some additional legal constraints upon corporate speech in order to prevent the abuse of economic power. Thus there are regulations regarding the ways in which corporations can become involved in political matters, how corporations communicate with customers and clients and, in unionized situations, the conditions of speech between management and unionized labor.

Government versus nongovernment Government employees—and governments—have speech rights as well, but they are often constrained. Higher-level government employees may not accept funds for public talks or for publications produced on their own time, for example. Federal employees may be prohibited from working on political campaigns and may be fired if there is reasonable belief that political comments were potentially disruptive of government functions. National security-driven constraints on speech that is not expressly political are more likely to affect those in government than those outside of it because of the nature of their employment, especially for those with access to classified information. Soldiers, for example, do have First Amendment rights, but their circumstances are such that the national security argument severely constrains what speech is actually permitted. Finally, and importantly, in many cases there is an affirmative responsibility on the part of the government to provide many types of information—speech in which the government must by law engage.

Distinctions by profession For years, some journalists and journalism associations have claimed that because of their social functions they have, or should have, protections under the First Amendment that go beyond those of others, such as the right to gather information without constraint. This argument was successful in exempting news organizations from government regulation under the National Industrial Recovery Act (NIRA) of 1933, an effort by the federal government to respond to the Depression by establishing standards for corporate practice industry by industry. At the time, however, acceptance of this argument was linked to acceptance of the "social responsibility" theory of journalistic practice and its assumption of self-regulation on the part of the industry. While there is still some talk about the social responsibility of the media, this approach is neither widely taught nor practiced today.

There is one area of the law in which journalists *are* treated differently from others, however. The qualified journalists' privilege permits information about confidential sources to remain confidential even when sought by the criminal justice system, if certain conditions have been met. This privilege also protects journalistic autonomy from the government, for reporters could otherwise be forced to serve as agents for law enforcement. (And, often, the privilege also protects the lives of the journalists or others involved.) Otherwise, courts do acknowledge the importance of the news media, but consistently deny that these media have a constitutional status any different from those of other citizens. (Faculty in institutions of higher education have also tried to claim special rights under the First Amendment—in their cases, to be heard in certain venues when they speak—and have also failed to have those claims acknowledged by the courts.)

Other professions have been singled out for differential treatment of speech under the law. The information processing activities of certified public accountants (CPAs) and attorneys have been contrasted, on the assumption that accountants are independent and objective while attorneys are advocates trained to be persuasive. The expressive responsibilities of accountants who play different roles have been distinguished: accountants internal to an organization provide information about the organization's financial condition, external auditors certify the internal integrity of financial statements, and decision-making based on information about an organization's financial condition provided by both internal accountants and external auditors is undertaken by management. Different roles relative to the practice of buying and selling stocks have also been distinguished for differential legal treatment.

Students Education ranks very high among the commitments the U.S. government has made to its citizens. The assumption that education is a governmental responsibility actually led to the first Supreme Court case involving higher education, in 1819, when the question of whether private universities would even be permitted was raised (obviously the answer was "yes"). Cases arising from political dissent in the 1960s and since have made clear that both high school and college students' speech outside of the class context is constitutionally protected, though as in other quasi-public or quasi-private forums expression may be restricted if it is disruptive or violates of the rights of other students. Within the classroom, however, even journalistic activity is considered to be under supervision and thus can be regulated. Since 9/11 some states have passed laws requiring libraries to share information regarding the reading habits of minors to their parents, though this trend is likely to be challenged in the courts.

Intelligence Defining an "average" adult has been at least as problematic for statisticians as it has been for attorneys. Courts often refer to an adult with ordinary intelligence, using a variety of terms such as "rational" and "reasonable," when they are seeking to establish parameters for certain types of communication under "normal" conditions rather than for extreme cases or deviant interpretations of expression. Today, for example, the impact of potentially obscene material is determined by the reactions of average adults rather than on youth or on those who are psychologically or emotionally fragile.

Free versus imprisoned The right to a fair trial includes the assurance of speech via representation in the courtroom, the right to appeal, and the right to petition—even up to the level of the president—in the case of a death sentence. The courts do have the right to refuse "frivolous" appeals, and a number of fascinating cases have gone to the Supreme Court on the question of whether illiterate appeals needed to be considered. Otherwise, prisoners do not have free speech rights.

Spaces Defined by Audience

There are many instances in which constitutional law distinguishes between types of receivers of information.

Willing versus unwilling Often behavioral regulation is aimed at ensuring that messages are not forced on those who do not want to receive them. The Supreme Court has forbidden the use of a bullhorn mounted on a truck because people were subjected to the messages delivered whether or not they wanted to be. Requirements that pornographic materials for sale be covered with plain wrappers similarly protect those who do not wish to be exposed, and ratings systems that warn of violence, sexuality, or profanity in upcoming broadcasts or in rental films are intended to serve the same purpose. Congressional support for a national "do not call" list to which households can voluntarily add themselves in order to ward off telemarketers is another example of regulation aimed at protecting those who are unwilling to receive certain types of messages.

Adult versus children In the areas of pornography, some types of student speech, and treatment of children in the courtroom, the distinction between adult and children recipients of communications is acknowledged in the law. There have been repeated statutory efforts to protect children from inappropriate broadcast and Internet content, though these are regularly struck down as unconstitutional. Ratings systems and, on the Internet, identification requirements, are at the moment the most successful tools for addressing this problem.

Many versus few The question of how many people received a message makes a difference to courts when trying to determine how much impact a false or damaging message may have had. Copyright infringement involving materials seen by only a few people will clearly have far less impact on the market of the copyrighted works than materials widely distributed. A successful suit for invasion of privacy requires publication of a message to a significant proportion of the target group. Determination of the level of damages in libel or privacy suits includes a consideration of how widely distributed the abusive messages were. Differences between delivery of stock market advice to a general audience, to newsletter subscribers, and to a single individual are also legally important.

Spaces Defined by War and Peace

The right of the government to suspend the writ of habeas corpus during time of war creates a constitutional divide between the communicative spaces of peacetime and those of wartime. As originally conceived, the line between the two conditions was bright and formal, marked by declarations of war and of peace in accordance with internationally accepted diplomatic practice. Restrictions on civil liberties during time of war took place when war had been formally declared. They were expected to be in effect for relatively short periods of time (not more than a few years), and applied to speech and behaviors that seemed to clearly threaten the nation-state either directly or through support for identifiable enemies of the nation-state. The forty-five years of the Cold War, however, began to blur the bright line between war and peace. The appearance of "low-intensity" warfare, information warfare, terrorist attacks by individuals, and other new types of military practice have also had an impact on the line between war and peace. Today, "postmodern" war can be continuous, and attacks may come from nontraditional types of enemies and in unfamiliar forms.

This change in the nature of war has had several effects on constitutional information spaces. First, nonmilitary information technologies and information may be restricted for national security reasons if they are defined as "dual-use," capable of being used for military as well as peaceful purposes. During the Cold War, the export of dual-use technologies, such as sophisticated computers and encryption technologies, was forbidden, as was the export of information about such technologies (even through travel by U.S. citizens, or access to conference sessions by foreign nationals). Since 9/11, the category of dual-use information has been significantly expanded to include data about urban infrastructure, natural resources, and the fields of biology and chemistry.

Second, there is no longer the expectation that restrictions on civil liberties on the basis of national security concerns will be of short duration. Indeed, President George W. Bush announced after 9/11 that the "war on terrorism" should be expected to last at least fifty years. If this turns out to be true and all of the provisions of the PATRIOT Act and other legal changes put in place since 9/11 are fully operationalized, it means that for at least two generations U.S. citizens will not experience many of their fundamental civil liberties.

Third, historically it was primarily freedom of speech that was curtailed to a limited degree during times of war, essentially in response to a shift in the boundaries used to determine when there is clear and present danger. Conceiving of the war on terrorism as pervasive, ubiquitous, and enduring, and the vast extension of surveillance to those whose activities are merely related to an ongoing investigation, as opposed to raising probable cause of actual involvement in illegal activity, have brought additional civil liberties under attack: freedom of association, privacy, the right to a fair trial, and access to government information.

Constitutional Principles and Their Limits

The First Amendment is not the only source of information policy in the U.S. Constitution, and even the First Amendment includes a bundle of different information policy principles. There are twenty different constitutional information policy principles that have been elaborated via statutory, regulatory, and common law to create an architecture of informational spaces distinguished from each other for differential application of the law. Some constitutional principles have received more attention than others, but all remain available for use as legacy law is extended, adapted, or replaced to fit today's conditions. The constitutional principles that underlie U.S. information policy were developed for a largely agricultural society, and much of the statutory and regulatory law through which those principles have been operationalized were created for an industrial environment. Whatever the initial conditions of a particular law or regulation, interpretation, implementation, and effects change over time.

From the perspective of complex adaptive systems theory, these principles do not attend sufficiently to the role of memory, the importance of experimentation and its archiving, or to interactions with systems supra to the nation-state. But it is clear that there is a constitutional foundation for protecting every stage of the information production chain, and legal theory developed out of existing constitutional principles can offer insight into how to think about these additional architectural matters. Meanwhile, the application of these principles to specific legal problems as they have arisen within an evolving information environment has had significant impact on social identity, structure, borders, and change. It is to these details, finally closer to the ground, that we now turn. Here legal principles hit the empirical complexities that, as limits, can serve as provocations for further development of the law.

The next four chapters address in turn a few key examples of information policy issues as they affect the identity, structure, borders, and change of society. Each chapter opens with a brief introduction to the concept around which the text is organized; those interested in pursuing the pertinent theories, concepts, and empirical research more deeply will find pathways into the literature in the bibliographic essays. Discussion of each issue begins with an overview of the history behind the current state of the law and a concise summary of where the law stands today, for those without prior background. The core of the analysis of the use of information policy in the exercise of power by the informational state is developed in the exploration of important trends in the development, interpretation, and/or implementation in the law. It is from the interactions, complementarities, and additive relations among these trends that the conclusions of each chapter are drawn.

5

Information Policy and Identity

Identity has two faces: that seen by the self, and that seen by others. The first is the source of agency, for one only acts as a figure in a story. The second constrains the field within which action may take place. Because both faces of identity are socially constructed and play key roles in the negotiation between agency and structure, and between continuity and change, identity formation and maintenance respond to changes in the communication environment—and thus in turn to information policy. The same processes that have led to changes in the nature of the nation-state and of power have also affected the ways in which identity is constructed and sustained. The loosening of traditional types of bonds, whether those of social norms and culture (for the individual) or of international political norms, practices, and agreements (for the nation-state), places a greater burden on the individual to create and sustain identity rather than being able to rely upon a given. Meta-technologies exacerbate this tension because their use disrupts existing social relations and makes it easier to develop other relations that may be networked but are often ephemeral.

Identity Theory

Identity issues have played an important role from the earliest stages of democratic theory because of their centrality to the work of John Locke. Locke's widely taught idea that legitimate governments are the result of social contracts necessarily suggests that communication among individuals and groups is fundamental to the political process. In work that is much less widely discussed, however, Locke also introduced the concept of the fact, defining it as the communication of sensory experience to others. For Locke, facts were important because what individuals would learn from their own experience could be partial, inaccurate, or perhaps misunderstood. This idea triggered a vigorous and enduring debate over just how to manage the presentation of facts, conversation about them once presented, and decision-making on the basis of that conversation—a set of questions that, much later, came to be referred to collectively as an exploration of the "marketplace of ideas." At the core of Locke's original conceptualization of the fact, however, is the insight that the organism that senses the world and communicates facts about it need not necessarily be an individual human being. The perceptual organism can also be a collectivity, whether a community or a government.

From this perspective, then, identity is critical to the nature of government and governance. Locke's work raises a number of questions. Who determines which facts should serve as the basis of decision-making? How is the perception from which facts originate being undertaken? How are struggles over facts, and methods of fact production, to be resolved? To what extent, and how, do interactions between Lockean facts and perceiving organisms determine the very identity of those entities?

Of course since Locke's time identity theory has developed greatly. After the first appearance of the individual in political thought, as the citizen, it was nineteenth-century psychoanalysis that fully and forcefully developed the concept of identity. Individual identity—when healthy—was assumed to be singular, stable across situations, and both internally and externally coherent (although psychoanalysts differed among themselves regarding the extent to which change and development were natural elements of the maturation process). Just as such ideas were being put forward, however, sociologists began to be aware of the ways in which urbanization and industrialization could make it difficult for individuals to be sufficiently embedded within a community to be able to develop and sustain their individual identities. These social changes, it was believed, explained problems such as anomie (norms regarding behavior are confused, unclear, or nonexistent) and alienation (separation from one's real nature). Over the course of the twentieth century, we learned to distinguish among the different types of interpersonal relations that connect individuals with the communities that are so important to individual identity. Primary relations are thick and densely textured, connecting individuals in multiple dimensions of their lives, while secondary relations are thin and often connect people only in the course of one type of activity, whether social, educational, religious, or work-related. In tertiary relationships, one is aware of others to whom one might be connected through the hierarchical relations of a large and distributed organization, but is not likely ever to actually have contact with those others. And in quaternary relationships, exemplified by surveillance, only one side is even aware that a relationship exists. By the early twenty-first century, we have come to understand individual identity—at least potentially—as multiple, shifting, and significantly correlated with circumstance, choice, and desire. Still, in areas such as privacy law and libel, it is clear that the ability of the individual to define, protect, and release information about his or her own identity remains fundamental to our understanding of what it is to be human.

The concept of national identity has undergone a similar transformation. At the point at which secular power in the form of the state began to be effective, the state itself—in part because it was originally so bound up with the personal identity of the monarch—was also understood to have a singular, stable, and coherent identity. In political theory, this sense was evident in notions such as raison d'état, the reason of the state, and in the Realist position in international relations. In legal practice, it was manifested in the development of an international system within which states operate as individuals. And rhetorically, the suggestion that the state is an individual underlies references to the government in singular form. While the nineteenth century saw "how to" discussions of how to make and implement political decisions, the state as a black box wasn't really opened up to for analysis until the twentieth century. Once this took place, discourse about the state took on a dual character. It was still described in popular, and often in policy, discussions as if it were a unitary actor, but both analytically and, of course, pragmatically, the state was clearly understood to be the product of complex institutional, persuasive, and instrumental processes, each one of which could be the subject of manipulation through information and other types of policy. Changes in the global political structure and in the nature of political processes during the closing decades of the twentieth century—in large part, but not exclusively, due to the effects of the use of informational meta-technologies—forced theorists to acknowledge that the state, too, is socially constructed. As the discussion of information policy and borders in chapter 7 makes clear, just as individuals now participate in multiple communities, often with an identity that shifts from situation to situation, so, too, the boundaries of state identity today vary according to the type of activity under scrutiny. The identity of the state is established through multiple means: looking back, through official memory;

in the present, through statistics and mapping; and going forward, through rhetoric and the consequences, foreseen and unforeseen, intended or not, of its decisions.

The many ways in which we have understood the mediations of individual and state identity each have their own stories. The concept of the citizen (as an inhabitant of a particular geographic area) actually preceded the appearance of the nation-state. The legal status of the citizen reinforced a theoretical bias towards treating the citizen, too, as singular, stable, and coherent, even if there was disagreement about just what rights and responsibilities the citizen did and should have. Here, too, late-twentieth-century practices that demonstrated multiple citizen-like affiliations and citizen-like practices at every level of the social structure, from the most global to the most local, stimulated a reconsideration of just what might be meant by the concept of the citizen that is still ongoing. Language policy and education are additional means by which the state attempts to reproduce itself via the development and sustenance of individual identity.

The social construction of each of these forms of identity means that they are susceptible to policy interventions. It is here where the limits to analogies between the concept of identity as it refers to individuals and nation-states become clear. The state shapes the conditions under which the communications that construct the identities of individuals take place. And although in a democracy communications among individuals, and between individuals and the state purportedly in turn constitute the state, in reality the government also creates the conditions under which information flows that might affect the identity of nature of the state itself also take place. In important ways, then, decision-making in the area of information policy is highly reflexive.

Policy issues that affect identity are intimate with matters of structure. The representations that present the identity of both the state and the individual are informational structures developed through the use of the technological structure via computerized modes of data collection and analysis. Memory, too, is a type of informational structure that is critical to both individual and collective identity. The technological structure can support or destroy community identity; just as the physical infrastructure of a freeway can break up a neighborhood by making it impossible for neighbors to move freely among their homes, so a telecommunications infrastructure that inserts long distance charges into communications between two communities that have historically had very close relations can be disruptive of those ties, both logistically and perceptually.

While the following chapters are themselves internally structured by the type of system involved, this chapter is oriented around information policy issues that affect the identity of the individual, the identity of the informational state, and mutually constitutive mediations over identity that take place in negotiations between the individual and the state.

Information law and policy that affect individual identity include libel, privacy, anonymity, and control over genetic information. National governments define their identities through the information policy tools of the census and other statistics, maps, and official memory. Information policy mediates between the individual and the state when it deals with language, education, and the vote.

Individual Identity

Four areas of the law particularly affect individual identity: libel, privacy, anonymity, and control over genetic information. The question of one's right to a particular email address or domain name is an example of another type of identity issue not explored here. In El Salvador, reflecting a history of enslavement of the indigenous population, the right to have a personal name at all is actually in the national constitution.

Libel

Libel, or defamation, is publication of a false statement of fact that damages the reputation of a person. To win a defamation suit, the plaintiff must be able to provide positive proof in six areas: defamatory content, falsity, identification, publication, fault, and harm. The criteria for each of these constitute the **Test for Libel:**

1. *Defamation* Was the language used defamatory in nature?
2. *Falsity* Did the assertion include a statement that was both verifiably false and substantial in nature?
3. *Identification* Would a third party identify the plaintiff as the subject of the statement?
4. *Publication* Was the statement made available to a party or parties other than the person who made the assertion and the person about whom the assertion was made?
5. *Fault* Was the false statement published out of fault on the part of the message producer as opposed to resulting from error?
6. *Harm* Was there any demonstrable harm to the subject of the statement as a result of its publication?

Current trends in libel law that affect identity and are of importance from the perspective of the exercise of informational power include the politicization of the personal, a weakening of the sense of facticity, examination of state of mind, and an expansion of the domain of the subjects of policy.

Politicization of the personal Libel started as a political matter, arising out of a long British history in which any criticism of those in power, whether or not based on fact, was punishable seditious libel. It was a colonial policy innovation to accept truth as an absolute defense in libel suits. As is commonly noted, this move protected political critique, and thus freedom of the press. At the same time, and less frequently noted, this shift expanded the legal right to respond to challenges to reputation to all citizens rather than being restricted to those who rule. It also marked a separation of the two types of identity within the law; while in seditious libel the individuals who govern were equated with the state itself, in U.S. libel law these two became distinguished.

Those who choose to serve in public office within a democracy do face particular demands and constraints upon their identities as seen by others: They must be in the public eye, inevitably and appropriately are linked to specific political positions, and participate in a variety of forms of political discourse that in themselves are means of exercising agency. All of these were recognized when, in 1964, libel law became "constitutionalized." In *New York Times v. Sullivan*, the Supreme Court defined a higher standard of fault for plaintiffs who were public figures. Until this point, libel law within the United States had been a matter of state statute, but with this case it was recognized that the specific features of the public identity of those who serve in public office were so critical to the functioning of a democracy that issues raised by attacks upon the identity of such individuals are of constitutional status. While acceptance of truth as a libel defense made it possible to question, challenge, or critique the government, the *New York Times v. Sullivan* standard required evidence that a defamatory statement about a public figure was actually an intentionally destructive act in order for the plaintiff to win a libel suit. This case was followed by others that ultimately distinguished several categories of public individuals for differential treatment under libel law. These categories are presented in table 5.1.

These distinctions were intended to quell the possibility of using libel for directly political purposes. Over the next couple of decades, however, the far right developed a method for indirectly using libel law to political ends. Angry at a perceived left-wing bias in media coverage of the

Table 5.1
Types of public and private figures for determining fault in libel cases

Type of figure	Qualifying criteria
Public official	Employee of government (by appointment, election, or hire) *and* contact with public *and/or* decision-making responsibility
All-purpose public figure	Person in the private sector *and* the power to make decisions that affect society at large *and/or* so much fame that decisions influence society at large
Vortex public figure	Person in the private sector *and* voluntary insertion into the public's eye around a specific issue *and* tries to influence decision-making on that issue
Involuntary public figure	Person in the private sector *and* involuntarily in the public's eye because of personal or social circumstance
Private figure	All others who are not in government

Vietnam War, conservatives established a nonprofit organization that encouraged and provided support for libel suits with the intention of destroying news organizations unfriendly to their viewpoints. Even though the media win libel suits approximately 80 percent of the time this was an effective tactic, because going to court is so expensive that it can bankrupt a news organization—particularly if required to go to court repeatedly. At the time, the burden of proof in libel suits lay with the defendant, so the cost for these suits was much higher for defendant media organizations than for plaintiffs, and the legal support provided the latter included a systematic raising of the bar for damages asked in cases in which the media lost. Finally, the Supreme Court capped damage claims in libel suits and switched the burden of proof from the defendant to the plaintiff, but by then the damage to investigative journalism, additionally fueled by other changes in the news industry that included changes in inheritance laws and the purchase of independent news organizations by large corporate conglomerates, had been accomplished.

Ironically, then, the effort to prevent libel from being used as a political tool, by first insisting that truth is a defense and then by making it more difficult for public figures to win libel suits, has been undercut. In contemporary law, personal identity has been politicized in that libel law provides an information policy tool that can be effectively used to political ends. In the post–9/11 environment, the historic notion of seditious libel, albeit under different names, becomes available again because critique of government officials or decisions in areas touching upon civil liberties has been described as treasonous.

A weakening of facticity Treatment of the fact as a specific type of statement and of factual narratives as distinct in important ways from other genres evolved out of a previously undifferentiated narrative matrix beginning with the introduction of the Lockean concept of the fact in the mid-sixteenth century. A number of economic, social, cultural, and political factors contributed to the proliferation of genres and legal differentiation among them, and we refer to the social, political, cultural, and economic effects of articulating the fact and factual narratives as "facticity." Not insignificant among the factors contributing to separating out facts and factual narratives from other types of statements and genres was the desire of those critical of government for protection under conditions in which voicing their thoughts could lead to punishment or death. The use of metaphorical language to discuss highly charged political matters, as in the work of Jonathan Swift, is, of course, quite ancient; in honor of its role in Greece, this rhetorical tool is often referred to as "Aesopian." The test used by U.S. courts to distinguish fact from fiction was introduced in chapter 4.

In recent decades, the legal distinction between fact and fiction has begun to fall. In 1984 the Supreme Court broke down the longstanding barrier between the two narrative forms by convicting an author of committing libel in a novel. As noted in a dissenting opinion, the Court's position in this case was particularly disturbing, for the basic argument was that the most extreme form of fault, actual malice (knowing falsehood or reckless disregard for the truth), was involved in the case precisely because the author and publisher knew that the book, which was fiction, was false! Today, a plaintiff can win a libel suit if the criterion of identity can be met by demonstrating that he or she served as the model for a character in a work of fiction.

While this case has not yet played an important precedential role, it remains available. If further developed, this precedent could have significant political impact. By eliminating the requirement of facticity from the legal evaluation of statements alleged to be libelous, the law returns to where it was several hundred years ago in treating diverse genres as if they are all part of an undifferentiated narrative matrix. Under such conditions, it is possible that seditious libel could in effect, if not in name, be revived, making political critique impossible, irrespective of the form it takes and of the factual foundations of the claims upon which it is based.

Examination of state of mind Genuine opinions are protected from libel suits because, in the words of the Supreme Court, "there is no such thing as a false idea," and because it is believed that protecting opinion is critical for the functioning of a democracy. Distinguishing fact from opinion, however, is not simple, and often the two are mixed. The four factors considered by courts in determining whether a given statement is fact or opinion—verifiability, ordinary meaning, social context, and textual context—were also introduced in chapter 4. Courts assume a dominant rather than an alternative or deviant understanding of words used in an allegedly defamatory statement. Words or phrases that are exaggerated or used in a figurative sense will be treated as opinion; courts do not treat rhetorical hyperbole as fact. Vagueness and ambiguity in a statement will lead to treatment of it as opinion, based on court perceptions of the ways in which such statements will be understood by the average person. Courts are also aware that words take on different meanings depending on their social context.

With the 1980 Supreme Court case of *Snepp v. U.S.*, courts began to examine state of mind in the course of the investigation of libel suits. Looking at the "mental process" of those preparing allegedly libelous statements was justified as a means of determining whether there was the "actual malice" required to successfully win a libel suit involving a public figure as a plaintiff. This opened the door to the U.S. government perusal of personal thoughts that has been taken much further in trying to identify potential or suspected terrorists in the post–9/11 Homeland Security environment in which books read, Web sites visited, and even groceries bought can be deemed indicative of actionable opinion and thought. Now that scientists can read brain activity in response to specific stimuli, the legal system could potentially require examinations of this kind as a further extension of investigations into state of mind.

Loss of the distinction between human and other types of identity Libel began in the modern conviction that human identity was worth protecting from damaging false claims. Today, however, it is also possible for the fictive individuals of corporations and other types of organizations (except for those of government) to sue for libel. Businesses can sue for defamation regarding competence or deceptive practices, nonprofits can sue if false charges affect their fund-raising ability, and unincorporated associations (such as labor unions) can sue for false stories that would damage their ability to attract members and carry out their functions. Corporations and industry associations can even sue on behalf of their products under product or trade libel. This extension of a law, designed to protect individual identity, to organizations and to objects exemplifies the expansion beyond the domain of the social as the policy subject. This shift can be used in the exercise of informational power via information policy tools when this technique is used to resist policy-making attention to issues raised by consumers.

Privacy

Privacy law in the United States is a patchwork comprised of torts, statutory law, and regulations. One of the reasons for this multiplicity is that there are four different zones of privacy: spatial (home and body), communicative (mediated communication), relational (communication with professionals and spouse), and data (disclosure and/or use of personal information). The history of privacy law in the United States further contributes to its complexity and sometime self-contradictions, for it has developed in a piecemeal way in reaction to issues raised by specific types of information rather than resulting from a deliberate and comprehensive examination of the domain as a whole. It is not coincidental that privacy law has become ever-more elaborate as new information and communication technologies have appeared, beginning with responses to forms of the mass media that first became available in the late nineteenth century because of the electrification of the printing press and the wider geographic diffusion of news stories made possible by the telegraph.

Several decades ago the then-inchoate body of common law dealing with privacy issues was organized into four categories of privacy torts that provide the basis of court evaluations today. Here are the four **Privacy Torts**; each key word in the definitions for each tort defines an element of the test used by a court to determine whether there has been an invasion of privacy for that category.

1. *Appropriation* Taking the name or likeness of another for commercial purposes without consent.
2. *True but embarrassing private facts* Public disclosure of embarrassing private facts with no news value.

Table 5.2
U.S. privacy laws

General
Privacy Act (1974)
Privacy Protection Act (1980)
Financial information
Fair Credit Reporting Act (1970)
Right to Financial Privacy Act (1978)
Electronic Funds Transfer Act (1979)
Fair Credit Billing Act (1986)
Fair Debt Collection Practices Act (1996)
Financial Modernization Services Act (1999)
Student records
Family Educational Rights and Privacy Act (1974)
Employment
Employee Polygraph Protection Act (1988)
Use of communication technologies
Cable Communications Policy Act (1984)
Electronic Communications Privacy Act (1986)
Video Privacy Protection Act (1988)
Telephone Consumer Protection Act (1991)
Telecommunications Act (1996)
Children's Online Privacy Protection Act (1998)
Driver's license information
Driver's Protection Privacy Act (1994)
Medical information
Health Insurance Portability and Accountability Act (1996)

3. *False light* Representation of an individual in a false and highly offensive way before the public.
4. *Intrusion* Unwanted intrusion into physical seclusion.

Privacy is also the subject of a stunning array of statutory laws as well as regulation by a number of federal agencies. Table 5.2 provides a list of statutory laws pertaining to privacy in the United States. In addition, a number of federal agencies have regulations pertaining to privacy issues raised by the industries or activities they regulate.

Privacy is variously defended as a claim, an entitlement, or a right. The early judicial definition of privacy as "the right to be let alone" is still useful as a commonsense shorthand to refer to issues as diverse as control over one's personal information and freedom from unauthorized observation. Privacy is important for many of the ways we are human. Only with privacy can one have solitude (the opportunity to withdraw from contact with others), anonymity (the ability to remain unnamed and unnoticed), reserve (the freedom *not* to express oneself to others), and intimacy (the ability to form interpersonal relations of a kind not possible in the presence of others)—all necessary for full personal expression, creativity, and growth. Privacy is often intertwined with but distinguishable from secrecy (the ability to protect other kinds of information from disclosure), confidentiality (disclosure of information to selected parties on the understanding that it will be transmitted no further), integrity (protection of information assets from mutilation or violation by users or owners other than the creator), authenticity (assurance that particular information has a known provenance), and liability (a standard of care required by providers or users of information to assure that innocent parties are not injured by carelessness or negligence).

Though there is a long tradition of anonymous speech, the British government acted on its fear of anonymity in political speech hundreds of years ago by establishing a licensing system for publishers and insisting that every publication include such information as authorship, date, and place of publication. One U.S. response to this experience was the rejection of licensing in the press environment. Another has been protection of anonymous speech. The Supreme Court has given several reasons to justify its consistent protection for anonymity, including the needs to protect individuals who may be associated with an unpopular political group from economic and physical threat, to promote public discourse about issues of public concern without fear of reprisal, to encourage whistle-blowing (reporting on corporate misconduct), and to encourage electronic commerce (e-commerce). Anonymity in information collection as well as distribution has also been regularly defended.

However, even prior to the existence of the Internet, the licensing of television and radio broadcasting in the United States made it impossible to legally broadcast using either of those media anonymously. The issue on the Internet is not licensing, but several factors that place pressure on anonymity in that environment: the need to locate individuals in order to determine which legal jurisdiction should apply to their activities, to surveil those who may threaten Homeland Security, and to restrict access to certain types of information such as pornography. The technological capacity to do so presents sheer temptation to identify those communicating. Anti-spam legislation has been proposed that would make online anonymity illegal, though the legislation that was ultimately passed in 2003 did not take that step. In practice, given the relative ease of government surveillance and the difficulty of understanding the ways in which private parties collect information from Internet activity, many simply assume that irrespective of intention all Web-based communication can be linked to the senders and receivers unless special protections are used. For the moment, a four-part test, based on the approach used to evaluate whether a court can constitutionally compel a reporter to reveal his or her anonymous sources, has been suggested by one court for use in determining whether to force disclosure of identities of senders of anonymous messages. Here is the **Test for Identifying Anonymous Speakers on the Internet:**

1. *Speaker response* Has the anonymous speaker been informed that the court is pursuing a release of his or her identity and had an opportunity to provide reasons why this should not be done?
2. *No alternative routes* Are there no alternative means by which the information being sought might be obtained?
3. *Importance to case* Is the identity of the speaker information that is necessary to resolve the case?
4. *First Amendment balancing* Does the government's interest in the case outweigh its interest in protecting First Amendment rights?

In no other area of the law are changes in relationships among individuals and between individuals and the nation-state so evident as in the area of privacy. The trends discussed here come in pairs: loss of any meaningful expectation of privacy, and the use of mathematics rather than space to protect privacy; a presumptive right of government surveillance, and an increase in private sector invasions of privacy for commercial purposes; privacy rights for representations, and an expansion of privacy rights to groups and governments; and the appearance of a commercial sector in privacy and anonymity, and the extension of privacy concerns to genetic information itself.

Loss of an expectation of privacy In general, the more public the surroundings—based on the categorization of types of spaces introduced in chapter 4—the less one has a reasonable expectation of privacy. History of use is particularly important for privacy in environments that are quasi-public or quasi-private; thus there is some expectation of privacy in a restaurant, because, although it is public, people often expect to be able to carry on intimate conversations over a meal. Sensory perception is more important than legal boundaries in defining a space for privacy purposes; if something that takes place within a private home can be heard or seen from the public space of a sidewalk, it is fair game, and garbage put out for collection is available for search without a warrant because it is in public view.

While one still has the right to a *legal* expectation of privacy under certain conditions, there is no longer any realistic *empirical* expectation of privacy. Technological innovations that make it possible to see into fenced backyards from a satellite, or sense the movement of individuals through a home as revealed by heat, so expand the ability to perceive from public spaces behaviors and speech carried out in private spaces that the concept of an expectation of privacy has been voided of meaning. This loss of an actual expectation of privacy affects identity like other invasions of privacy do, but also provides a species-level challenge. As biological organisms, we still feel that if we pull the blinds and whisper, we will be private, though these actions are now irrelevant to the actuality; our senses and what we need to sense no longer operate at the same scale or level of granularity. Concerns about the impact of this trend include the likelihood of "anticipatory conformity" and decreased loyalty to a surveillance-driven government, as well as a chilling of association and speech. Meanwhile, many of the techniques being used, such as software intended to identify faces, are proving to be unreliable.

Mathematics as a privacy protection While defenses against invasions of privacy in the past involved legal support for the use of geographic space and material barriers for protections, today evasive algorithms are often more important. Algorithms, the mathematics that drives computer programs, are at the heart of encryption techniques; competition between those who seek to protect the privacy of their communications with encryption and those who seek to decrypt hidden messages is therefore a battle between mathematicians. Theoretically, algorithms might also come into use as a guide to personal choices if one seeks to either avoid offering a signature that belongs to a particular profile or to present behavior that avoids detection because it is statistically predictable. Such algorithms might suggest using this word instead of that, waiting a certain time period before surfing a particular site, or adding materials to one's communicative mix to alter the picture offered.

There have always been some socioeconomic class differences in the ability to protect one's personal privacy, for sheer ownership of large amounts of space offers greater privacy for those who live in large homes on large pieces of land than is experienced by those who share small and crowded living spaces. The centrality of mathematics to privacy in the electronic environment, however, creates new privacy classes. Not only is the ability to innovate mathematically on one's own limited to a very few extremely well-trained individuals, but many of the types of software that can provide this type of protection are private property under patent law.

However, there are some widely available, relatively easy-to-use, and in some cases free software programs for encoding information so that it is comprehensible only to those to whom a decoding key has been given. Encryption is the most widely used approach to protecting communications on the Internet, but its use outside of government became legal in the United States only after many years of political struggle. This conflict was finally resolved only after one individual, Kevin Mitnick, publicly released a free and easy method for encryption on the Internet. While Mitnick did go to jail for several years for this action, he effectively mooted the government's effort to prevent encryption by private parties outside of its control. Encryption, of course, protects the content of the message but not the identity of the sender.

Legal strictures can be put in place to prevent anonymous communication on the Internet by requiring the presentation of personal information in order to contractually acquire access (whether through an ISP or an ISP-like entity such as a university). Hardware and software can also now be used for this purpose. Digital rights management (DRM) systems build restrictions on use of copyrighted material into the technologies used to access that material. Critics of the DRM approach complain that it significantly and inappropriately reduces the range of uses of the Web for content distribution and use, and there are some instances in which unauthorized efforts to access content protected by DRM can actually damage a computer system or other equipment. This is important from a privacy perspective, because one of the requirements of the DRM system is identification of the person accessing the content.

Expansion of privacy rights to groups and government entities As with libel, the concept of privacy originated in concerns about damage to an individual human being's sense of self, but is now used by groups and institutions as well. Protections for the privacy of organizational operations and data include trade secrets and exclusion of working papers from the scope of various types of evidentiary investigations (and, in the case of government agencies, from being accessed via the Freedom of Information Act, or FOIA). Companies that are privately held need not release any information to the public and must only provide the kinds of information to the government required for tax purposes and for pertinent regulation (environmental, occupational safety, etc.). The Homeland Security Act, part of the bundle of policy changes put into place since 9/11, protects government agencies involved in matters such as infrastructure or the environment from any public probing via the FOIA for information voluntarily provided to the Homeland Security Agency.

Privacy of representations The oldest notions of privacy involved protecting the biological individual, either from physical invasions of the self or private space or from inappropriate public revelation of personal matters. Today, however, appropriation and misuse of personal data are ways in which privacy now applies to representations as well. In cyberspace, it is now possible for one representation to invade the privacy of another. Appropriation, the use of the image or name of another for commercial purposes without consent, is linked to a concept of property rights in one's likeness. Statutes that explicitly establish such rights in many states protect right of publicity. And cybersquatting, made illegal in the Intellectual Property and Communications Omnibus Reform Act (1999), is use of the name of another as an Internet domain name (often done in order to sell the name back to the person or organization to whom the name belongs).

It was not a coincidence that a number of laws dealing with the privacy of different types of personal data began to appear in the 1970s, just as the computer began to make it possible to invade privacy in new ways. With networking, the increase in computing capacity available to individuals, and the development of various types of data-mining software, it has become easier and easier to inappropriately acquire information about an individual from a number of sources. When multiple types of personal data are used together to falsely represent the identity of another in transactions, or for institutional purposes, it is known as "identity theft" because it becomes possible to fully impersonate another person. Identity theft is now such a widespread problem that in the 109th Congress alone it is the subject of fifty different bills under discussion.

A new type of abuse of representations is now possible in the virtual environment, exemplified in a well-known case described by journalist Julian Dibbell in his now-famous article "A Rape in Cyberspace." Interactive electronic environments in which one is represented either textually or via a visual image called an "avatar" offer opportunities to those with programming skills to hijack one's narrative or image, or to engage in activities using the identities of others. In the story told by Dibbell, one individual took over an avatar used by another in a collaborative multiuser virtual world and used it to rape the avatars of others. Though the experience was narrative, not physical, it traumatized those whose electronic representations had been involved; they responded much as individuals would to physical rape. Up to this point, such cases have been resolved within the electronic communities, but ultimately disputants may turn to the legal system for help.

Presumptive right of government surveillance Under the conditions established by interpretation of the First and Fourth Amendments to the Constitution until 9/11, law enforcement officials needed to demonstrate to a judge that there was "probable cause" that the individual for whom a search warrant was sought was actually involved in illegal activity. Individuals being searched had to be notified of the search; those conducting the search had to leave a written record of what, if anything, was taken; and warrants were limited to a specific location (for physical search) or jurisdiction (for surveillance of electronic communication). Evidence obtained in a search related to national security concerns could not be shared with law enforcement officers concerned about other types of criminality, and vice versa. If prosecution proceeded on the basis of evidence discovered during a legal search, the defendant had the right to be presented with that evidence—as with all other evidence—in court.

Under the USA PATRIOT Act, a search warrant can be approved based only on the claim that the search would be "relevant to an ongoing investigation." The specific investigation need not be identified, nor need evidence be provided that the subject of the search is actually involved in or has any relationship to illegal activity. Prior notice of a search is not required, nor documentation of any materials that might be taken. Search warrants can be national in scope; this, in combination with the opportunity to investigate even individuals not named in a warrant, can launch a kind of surveillance "contagion"—an individual named in a search warrant may use a computer in a public library, which then in turn becomes the subject of investigation, as does anyone else who subsequently uses the same computer, and so on. Evidence acquired through a search authorized under the PATRIOT Act does not have to be presented to a defendant in court. Though this legislation was intended to be of use in fighting the war on terror, information acquired through surveillance of this kind can be shared with law enforcement officials concerned about other types of criminal matters. Indeed, the George W. Bush administration has openly announced the use of the PATRIOT Act to pursue a number of problems that have no relationship to terrorism, including drug trafficking and financial fraud. There are proposals to give the government broad powers to compel individuals (such as friends and neighbors) to turn over information about others to the government, also under a gag, and to increase the severity of sentencing for crimes if the use of encryption has been involved. And while the PATRIOT Act originally threatened freedom of association by targeting individuals for surveillance merely on the basis of relationships with others already targeted, "lone wolves" are also now suspect by the very fact of their solitude. The PATRIOT Act is not the only source of changes to privacy law since 9/11. A March 2005 analysis of the effects of the PATRIOT Act on privacy by the Electronic Privacy and Information Center identified twelve statutes that have been altered to permit greater surveillance of individual communications and behavior. Interpretations of the law by U.S. attorneys general have also been important. A summary of some of the most important ways in which privacy protections have changed since 9/11 can be found in table 5.3.

There has thus been an inversion of the relationship between individuals and the government in the area of surveillance since 9/11. While before there was a presumption that the individual was protected from surveillance unless the government could demonstrate probable cause or actual involvement with criminal activity, today there is a presumption that the government can essentially surveil at will. Even the special court involved in granting search warrants when national security issues are involved (a court established by the Federal Intelligence Surveillance Act, or FISA) has taken the position that the Federal Bureau of Investigation (FBI) has been abusive in the frequency of its requests for search warrants since the PATRIOT Act was passed. While there were sunset provisions in the PATRIOT Act, they were meaningless from this perspective because they did not apply to any "ongoing investigations," did not apply to the surveillance provisions, and did not apply to the new national database being constructed out of data currently held in different databases that cannot be "matched" against each other as a form of privacy protection. The government is pursuing additional relaxations of restrictions on government surveillance.

Table 5.3
Impact of the USA PATRIOT Act on privacy

1. *Abandonment of reasonable cause* In the past, "reasonable cause" that one was involved in a specific criminal activity was required in order to obtain a search warrant. Under the PATRIOT Act, all that is required is the assertion that the search is "relevant" to an ongoing investigation; relevance need not be demonstrated by evidence of actual behaviors of any kind.

2. *Identification* In the past, search warrants had to name specific individuals to be searched. Under the PATRIOT Act, individuals not named in a search warrant but encountered during the course of a search may also be searched.

3. *Knowledge of search* In the past, individuals who were the subject of search warrants generally had to be presented with the warrants, informed of the search, and informed of anything taken during a search. Under the PATRIOT Act, individuals need not be presented with warrants, told of a search, or told of materials or information taken during a search.

4. *Easy access to communication* In the past, a search warrant was required to acquire information such as the sites you surf on the Web or who you communicate with by email. Under the PATRIOT Act, no search warrant is required—only a declaration to a judge that the information thus acquired would be "relevant" to an ongoing investigation.

5. *Mobility and duration* In the past, search warrants were site-specific, naming particular addresses and pieces of communication equipment. Under the PATRIOT Act, a search warrant can "rove," following an individual of interest wherever he or she is or however he or she communicates. In combination with item #2, this means that if a named person communicates via public equipment, anyone subsequently using that same equipment (e.g., a computer in a public library) can then also be subjected to a search. The length of time during which a search warrant is in effect has also been extended.

6. *Knowledge of evidence used against one* The requirement that one be presented with the evidence on the basis of which one is being charged has always been fundamental to the right of a fair trial in the United States. Evidence acquired via surveillance conducted under the PATRIOT Act, however, need not be presented to a defendant in court.

Private sector invasions of privacy Two types of private sector invasion of privacy are of concern: the collection of information about consumers by marketers, and the collection of information about employees by employers.

While historically much of the concern about invasions of privacy revolved around the government, today the private sector is of active concern as well. The use of "cookies" and other techniques to gather information about visitors to Web sites, the buying and selling of databases, and spam are among the commercial invasions of privacy resented by consumers. Knowledge of the buyer has been a marketing advantage since time immemorial, but today's digital technologies so significantly change the scale at which this information can be gathered and the sophistication with which it can be used that this type of invasion of privacy is qualitatively different from historical experience.

A new challenge has appeared with radio frequency identification (RFID) tag technology, which can be incorporated into products. Manufacturers and retailers like RFID technology because it significantly eases the logistics of merchandise control, but these tags can also provide a means of tracking individuals as they wear tagged clothes or use tagged objects. Policy responses, such as requiring the tags to be turned off once an object leaves a store, are currently under discussion.

Coping with commercial invasions of consumer privacy is in the United States a matter for the Federal Trade Commission, an agency that, like others, finds its level of activity rising and falling in response to budget, presidential policy preferences, and consumer response. Just prior to the arrival of George W. Bush at the White House, the FTC had announced it would aggressively pursue those who inappropriately acquire information about consumers over the Web; since, the agency has been relatively quiescent in this regard.

The nonprofit organization Privacy Watch reported that before 9/11 at least one third of the workforce in the United States that uses networked computers was under constant surveillance by employers. Telephone calls, Web surfing, email, and computer keystrokes (including messages typed and erased) are all being recorded and analyzed. These practices are not subject to law, but they are beginning to become a part of labor-management negotiations over contracts in unionized situations.

Privacy and anonymity as a commercial sector A variety of techniques is now available to the general public for protecting the anonymity of one's communications from any but the most aggressive and powerful entities. Web sites are available that can "anonymize" communications by removing identifying information from email and Web site visits. These provide "local" as opposed to general anonymity, meaning that there is a relatively stable coalition of computers operating as a single network and observers cannot distinguish messages sent from one computer from those sent from another within the network. All communications local to the coalition are confidential and untraceable, but communications that leave it for the wider Internet bear the coalition's single IP address. The "Publius" experiment, now over, combined encryption with the packetizing of messages and the storage of packets on at least three different servers in at least three different countries as a means of making anonymous publication. In recent years, however, governments have been aggressive about trying to shut down servers involved in anonymizing activities. EPIC is supporting the development of technologies that will help protect anonymity online. A number of the services that offer anonymizing do so commercially, so it will be interesting to see how the opportunity for profit through the protection of identity will affect the political dynamics of the debate.

Extension of privacy concerns into the realm of genetic information As knowledge of the human genome—the genetic information in human DNA—deepens, the value of DNA for a variety of purposes increases. There is the temptation to use genetic information to determine insurability and fitness for certain types of employment, though genetic heritage is not solely determinative of either health or fitness in the face of actual environmental conditions and personal habits, and such uses therefore raise a number of ethical issues. For the moment, the trend in the United States appears to be not to legalize such uses of DNA, though at the time of writing the question is still under debate in Congress.

Other uses of DNA with implications for identity are now legal, however. The Supreme Court has held that patents developed from research on unhealthy body tissue belongs to the doctors, not the person from whom the tissue had been taken. If individuals do not have property rights in either their body parts or their genetic information, they can be mined for DNA, tissue, and organs of value to others. Indeed, the United States is already working with the United Nations to acquire germplasm—genetic information—from the human equivalent of endangered species, tribal groups that are about to become extinct and who have a unique genetic heritage.

Following the first successful use of DNA to solve a criminal case in 1987, Virginia became the first state in the United States to pass a law establishing a DNA databank. Though at first this databank included only samples from certain classes of offenders (sex offenders, and those guilty of some particularly violent crimes), it soon expanded to include DNA from all felons and, after the constitutionality of this law was upheld, all juvenile offenders over the age of fourteen if they committed a crime that would have been treated as a felony were they adults. By 1998, all forty-nine other states had similarly passed laws that differed only in their scope from requiring submission of the DNA from certain classes of felons, at one extreme, to including the DNA of all felons as well as some who were guilty of only misdemeanors and those who were only arrested for—not convicted of—certain crimes, at the other. The beginning of a national databank of DNA has been created by these state laws, many of which permit their information to be utilized if doing so would aid *any* criminal investigation, whether in another state or under federal law. DNA data from one state can be linked to DNA data from other states as well. Inconsistencies among state laws regarding privacy protections fall away in the face of national uses of the data. The U.S. Department of Defense now collects DNA from everyone who enters military service, and some states are even discussing collecting DNA in order to get a driver's license. There are proposals to require suspected terrorists to provide DNA samples in exchange for bail and to allow all federal agencies to collect DNA information from individuals of whom no criminal activity is suspected without either the subjects' knowledge or their consent.

Identity of the Informational State

Information policy that deals with the identity of the nation-state involves the design of statistical mechanisms for describing various aspects of the state, creating narrative and symbolic representations of a real or imagined history of the state, choosing which data and representations to remember, and deciding who has access to any of these.

The Census and Other Statistics

Rulers have kept records on the ruled since ancient times. The census took its modern form and became a permanent fixture of governments at the beginning of the eighteenth century in Europe. The size of the territories and populations of modern nation-states were larger than could be perceived via the senses of those in government, so statistical representations were necessary in order for the state to "see" itself. The census achieved constitutional status for the first time in the United States, because of the needs for congressional representation proportional to the population and to provide a basis for the provision of services and the distribution of resources. In 1840, the census began to include questions about commerce and industry, but this was a disputed practice until the Supreme Court approved its constitutionality in 1871. A permanent office to manage the census was not established until the twentieth century, and the matter of what questions to include remains the subject of congressional debate in the twenty-first. The most recent census, in 2000, was such a massive effort that it has been described as the largest peacetime mobilization effort in U.S. history.

The census was just the first of a number of statistical entities created by the U.S. government, which began to establish separate statistical offices to collect data about industry, agriculture, and the economy early in the twentieth century. This apparatus necessarily expanded significantly to support the activities of the bureaucratic welfare state when they were launched in the 1930s, for a great deal of information was needed in order to provide safety-net services to citizens and develop regulatory interventions into industry in an effort to reverse the Depression and to protect consumers. Thus in addition to the creation of standalone statistical entities such as the Bureau of Labor Statistics (BLS), each regulatory agency included a statistical function. Today over one hundred federal agencies and departments have statistical responsibilities. A mapping of the statistical activity of the U.S. government shows repeated cycles of multiplication of offices with statistical responsibilities followed by efforts to centralize such activities either though combination or through coordination.

Census content and methodology remain subject to congressional decision-making based on a series of hearings held to determine census content, methodology, and budget for every round. Census design and practice have had to balance the need to routinize the methodology, significant changes in the population being measured, and the desire of lobbying groups and legislators to use the census as a source of patronage. Despite claims that statistics are objective and politically neutral, every political tension has left a trace in debates over data categories and the methods to be used in data collection and analysis. Struggles between unions and management over appropriate contract terms for labor manifested themselves, for example, in disagreements over what was to be included in the standard "market basket" to determine the cost of living as well as the poverty line. Debates over race are revealed in transformations of categories used to distinguish ethnicity and genetic heritage. Evidence of concern over immigration can be found in decisions whether to include questions regarding location of birth and native language in the census. Like other statistical entities, the census had to account for qualitative changes in the nature of the economy due to informatization; thus, because they yielded statistical discrepancies, the Standard

Industrial Classification (SIC) codes used by government statistical offices as well as the private sector had become problematic by the late twentieth century.

By now, statistics have taken on additional, policy-relevant types of value for the nation-state. Data are a commodity that provide a profit center for municipalities, states, and other governmental units. An interest in particular types of statistics has driven passage of reporting laws, such as the Labor-Management Reporting and Disclosure Act of 1959. The detailed data that can be derived from evidence presented in court in turn fuels the development of statistical profiles for further refinement of criminal concepts and the targeting of suspects. Governments also use statistics for rhetorical purposes, as a means of asserting dominance or strength in particular areas. Still, all statistical categories are conceptually rather than empirically based; even what counts as birth and what counts as death are open questions. As a result, particular statistical systems may decrease in utility or become dysfunctional altogether as social theory, political circumstance, and empirical realities change.

Trends in the use of statistics that have an impact on the identity of the nation-state include issues raised by the accuracy of representations, lacunae in knowledge about the information society, interactions between statistical need and technological development, and statistical interventions into statutory and regulatory law.

Relaxation of concern about accuracy The constitutional language mandating the census uses the word "enumeration" to describe the task of counting every single citizen. Since the Constitution was written in the late eighteenth century, however, a great deal has been learned about statistical techniques that make it possible for analysis of portions of the whole to accurately represent the whole. Under certain conditions—including those of the census—statistical representation of the whole will be *more* accurate than the practice of enumeration. Minority groups who feel alienated from the U.S. government, those whose first language is not English, children, those who live in particularly isolated rural areas or egregiously overcrowded urban areas, migrants, and the homeless are all likely to be undercounted by enumeration. This problem does not diminish over time: the 1990 census missed 8.4 million people, the highest undercount ever recorded. This inaccuracy matters because populations that are undercounted do not receive needed government services, and they are not proportionately represented in Congress. Twice, the question of whether statistical techniques could be used for the census in order to ensure equity and fairness has been brought to the Supreme Court, and twice the Court has stood by enumeration because it is bound by the constitutional language. This is a bizarre anomaly—statistical techniques are used to draw conclusions from population samples for every other governmental purpose, but to picture itself, the government insists on using an approach that everyone agrees produces a false portrait.

There are other ways in which the goal of achieving accuracy is being lost. Data about individuals held in databases is often "perturbed"—falsified slightly—so that, ostensibly, it is more difficult to extract actual individuals from aggregate portraits. Astonishingly, in 2003 the National Crime Information Center (NCIC)—the most extensive system of criminal history records in the United States, with an average of more than 52 million transactions per day—was no longer subject to accuracy requirements imposed by the Privacy Act. In practice, this means that the FBI has been released from the legal requirement that the information upon which it acts when it chooses to surveil an individual be accurate.

Lack of knowledge about informatization The census regularly collects information about the living conditions of the U.S. population, including source of water, method of sewage disposal, and whether or not there is plumbing and air conditioning. But despite essentially universal recognition that participating in the information economy is critical to survival in the twenty-first century, the census still does *not* collect information about the degree to which households are integrated into the information society. Though public interest advocates pressed for inclusion about access to telephones, computers, and the Internet in the 2000 census—critical questions for analyzing the extent of the "digital divide" and designing policies to respond to that problem—no questions of this type were included.

Interactions between statistical need and technological innovation Just as the need of the nation-state for statistics has stimulated development of that field over the course of several hundred years, so the need of the government to process those statistics has been a "pull" factor for technological innovation. It was for the Census Bureau that the first automated punchcard tabulation machine—the most complex business technology to be marketed before World War II—was developed in 1890 by the company that ultimately became IBM. In the 1950s, it was the Census Bureau that pursued development of optical sensing systems to permit machine reading of forms marked with lead, and for the 2000 census more sophisticated optical recognition systems came into use. In the early 1990s, the agency began experimenting with parallel computing as a means of classifying long-form census applications and found that use of "memory-based reasoning," in which forms were compared to information held in a large database, was much cheaper and faster than development of an expert system for processing forms using standard processing techniques. Other technologies, such as remote sensing satellites, supplement census data. The assiduousness with which the Census Bureau has taken up the use of new information technologies has its drawbacks, however: the 1960 census tapes can be read only by two existing machines, just one of which is in the United States.

Dissolution of the individual into a probability The individual human being, with specific characteristics and an always-unique history and circumstance, is disappearing in U.S. law, to be replaced by statistical probabilities. Profiling, computerized sentencing, and related practices have a significant impact on individual identity. Inclusion of those whose behaviors are statistically unpredictable in the definition of the "enemy" according to new security theory makes this shift particularly dangerous in the Homeland Security surveillance environment. While originally profiles were carefully built from analysis of the characteristics of those who had been found guilty of the crimes involved, data matching—linking information about an individual gathered for one purpose and held in one database with other information gathered for another purpose and held in a separate database—made it possible to develop new types of profiles based only on statistical calculations.

Data matching has been regularly opposed by the U.S. Congress, but after 9/11 the national security argument (at least for the moment) overcame all barriers. Today statistical profiling is at the heart of the means by which the U.S. government is identifying citizens as targets of surveillance. Nor is its use restricted to adults potentially capable of terrorist action: the United Kingdom—which has put itself forward as a test environment for security techniques being considered by other nation-states—is profiling primary and secondary school students considered to present the potential for socially threatening behavior, perhaps because children of interest exhibit a particularly lively intelligence and curiosity. In another example of the dissolution of individual identity in favor of statistical probabilities by information policy, today immigration cases—even when they involve individuals claiming the need for political asylum—no longer receive individual attention but, rather, those involved are treated as members of classes of which members will all be treated in the same way. Implementation of the PATRIOT Act has also exacerbated this trend; because one "David Nelson" apparently raised suspicion of involvement with terrorist activities, every single David Nelson in the United States—and there are 251 in Wisconsin alone—is treated as a terrorist suspect if he should attempt to take an airplane flight.

Statistics-driven policy The bureaucratic state used statistics as input into policy-making, the design of programs for implementing policy, and evaluating programs once in place. For all of these purposes, a number of steps came between the gathering of statistics and decision-making, including consideration of political and logistical realities as well as consideration of congressional intent and normative standards. In the informational state, however, statistics now often directly drive policy, often in contravention of legislative intent and without regard for normative imperatives.

The Office of Management and Budget, which regulates the flow of government information by establishing and controlling the budgets of the agencies devoted to statistics as well as the portion of the budget devoted to statistics of all federal agencies and departments, is the most important entity in this regard. Justified by the Paperwork Reduction Act of 1980, the role of the agency was operationalized in OMB Circular A-130, first put in place in 1985, and revised several times since. Amendments to OMB A-130 in 1993 expanded the entity's purview to include private sector information collected and managed on behalf of the government as well as that produced by the government itself. The OMB uses cost-benefit analysis to determine whether information collection, processing, and distribution activities of or for units of the federal government are economically justified. Because decisions regarding the treatment of information are embedded in agency rules, the OMB has approval authority for the decision-making of all federal agencies. In recent years, the OMB's self-description has changed from "counselor" to "gatekeeper" and it admits to having the greatest influence over agency rules during "informal" review processes that do not leave a public trace but that do result in significant changes in rules or their abandonment altogether.

A Harvard study of OMB review of proposed studies by the Centers for Disease Control (CDC) in the mid-1980s found that the OMB was seven times more likely to reject studies with an environmental or health focus than those focused on conventional diseases. Other studies have found that the OMB has used cost-benefit analysis to deny agencies the right to collection of racial and ethnic data for the purpose of monitoring discrimination, whether in housing or employment; to survey uses of federal lands and attitudes towards environmental reclamation; and to acquire data required for outpatient mental health treatment. During a one-year period in the 1990s examined by the GAO (at the time the General Accounting Office, and now the Government Accountability Office), the OMB asked for changes to four hundred agency rules, including about one third of those from health, safety, and environmental agencies most active during the period—most often those from the Environmental Protection Agency (EPA). Many times, requests for changes in rules followed contact with the OMB by outside parties, and the requests made were very similar to recommendations offered by those outside parties. In the George W. Bush administration, the ultimate decision-maker in cases in which there are appeals to OMB decisions is Vice President Dick Cheney.

One result has been a chilling effect on agencies, which are said to have become so demoralized by the current process and the climate it generates that in many cases they have stopped submitting requests for approval of regulations they believe should be put in place. Another is a derailing of the law. The prevention of data collection about racial and ethnic discrimination in employment provides a clear example: Congress can issue a strong mandate in favor of equal employment opportunity and pass laws intended to provide institutional mechanisms to ensure there is such equal opportunity. Without data about actual practices, however, the statutory law—and the will of the people—are toothless.

Mapping

Mapping is a particular type of data collection effort that uses images rather than numbers to provide information about the identity of the nation-state; as digital technologies become more sophisticated, there are more and more ways of correlating images with data and analyzing the two types of information together. It was the Census Bureau that began the process of systematically mapping the United States, in 1870. In the second half of the twentieth century, a number of additional governmental units became involved, including most importantly the U.S. Geological Service (USGS), the National Imagery and Mapping Agency (NIMA), Landsat, and the National Oceanic and Atmospheric Administration (NOAA).

The earliest mapping efforts involved drawings based on oral reports, documents, and visits to areas being mapped. Today, photographs have replaced this type of visualization. Many additional types of sensory inputs are used as well, including infrared, heat, and over one hundred types of chemical, biological, and physiological information. While the earliest efforts to bring different types of data together into one computerized map ran into difficulties because of qualitative differences in the kinds of data involved, mathematical and computing developments since then have resolved many of these problems. The political issues remain.

Trends of importance from an information policy perspective include the vast expansion in mapping capacity, the tension between general and local views, repetitive mapping, real-time mapping, and the convergence of mapping with surveillance.

Expansion of mapping capacity The extraordinarily vast expansion of our capacity for maps and images has had profound cultural effect. The first images of Earth from space in the 1960s have been credited with encouragement of the environmental movement, because it was possible for the first time to see what Buckminster Fuller referred to as "Spaceship Earth" as a whole, in all of its fragility and with promotion of a sense of global citizenship. Eric Jantsch even credits such images with stimulating the development of complex adaptive systems theory because, along with other scientific developments of the era, we were able for the first time to see relations among processes unfolding at different scales. Poet Christopher Dewdney notes that with ubiquitous mapping and the ability to pinpoint individual locations using global positioning system (GPS) technologies, the feeling of being lost may itself become intoxicating. At the national level, the expansion in mapping capacity and detailed knowledge of the material environment enables the other trends being discussed here.

Tension between general and local knowledge Economist Friedrich Hayek first noted the difference between general and local knowledge in 1945 when he pointed out despite the value of statistical and scientific knowledge, every individual always knew more than anyone else about his or her local circumstances. Since then appreciation for the value of local knowledge, often but not necessarily tacit as opposed to codified, has grown. The effort to bring general and local knowledge together is today an important problem in the design of databases and knowledge management systems, and the differences in perspective on the same phenomenon, event, or place has been important in the history of mapping.

In the United States, the Census Bureau's efforts to collect information about the boundaries of local government units began in the 1940s. Originally, boundaries were defined by federal officials, but this approach produced inaccuracies as a result of a reliance on estimation or paper maps of unknown accuracy. Local boundaries as established by federal officials used features that were movable, or removable. Ultimately state, local, and tribal governments took over the functions of providing local maps for the national census. Though the success of local efforts to impose their perspective on national and global maps has not always been as successful in other settings, local knowledge is all-important at the stage of interpretation of images and maps that may have been generated by other means.

Mapping as a constant process A map used to be a one-time thing. Map collectors are interested in old maps because there were so few of them, and comparisons between maps of the same territory made at different times are revelatory of major shifts in world views and dominant narratives as well as empirical—or at least experiential—knowledge. Today mapping is an ongoing exercise with repeated iterations of information collection by satellite. As a result, maps are now dynamic, rather than static. Such repetitive mapping reveals environmental, political, cultural, social, and economic processes as they unfold.

Wireless communications, nanotechnology, and innovations in intelligent sensors are combining to produce an environment of networked intelligence based not in communication- or computing-specific devices but, rather, in the material world itself. Experimentation is currently under way with what is known as "ubiquitously embedded computing," "pervasive computing," or the "sensor web." In the future, it is to be expected that the planet will be covered with intelligent sensors that communicate with each other, including on the ocean floor, deep within the earth, and in plants and animals around the world. When this happens, "mapping" will become a stream of reportage about real-time data more like a world brain than anything that has come before. Processing and filtering that data so that it will be useful are key; programmers are currently working on a browser-like interface that would make it possible to ask natural language questions of these sensors, such as "Does my garden need watering?" or "Is this coal vein exhausted?"

The psychological and social implications of this type of intelligent and communicative environment are likely to be profound. As Ulrich Beck first noted in the late 1980s, causal chains were already so long and complex that they often evaded perception by existing statistical and other mechanisms. As a result, it can be impossible to determine the actual effects of the use of complex technologies, and to assign accountability for undesirable consequences. Beck predicted that in an environment in which causality could not be determined, people were likely to return to nonrational modes of explanation. Once pervasive computing moves from the experimental stage to widespread use, this problem will be exacerbated.

Convergence of mapping, surveillance, and intelligence Historically, distinctions were made among different types of mapping and information collection exercises undertaken for national security and criminal justice purposes. "Intelligence" referred to information-gathering about a specific individual or group whose behaviors or communications were already suspect. "Surveillance" was information collection about an environment with the purpose of identifying individuals or groups deserving of more focused attention. "Verification" involved collecting information about the activities of nation-states with the specific purpose of evaluating whether there was compliance with the provisions of bilateral or multilateral treaties. "Confidence- and security-building measures" carry out ongoing surveillance at the level of the nation-state with the intention of reducing threats to peace by increasing mutual knowledge. With "transparency," there is proactive sharing of information of specific types by a nation-state, group, or individual; that is, the subject of information collection voluntarily presents the information rather than passively—or unknowingly—being the subject of information collection activities by others. Other types of information collection and mapping for nation-state purposes, such as the gathering of information about crops being planted or uses to which forests were being put, were undertaken by task-specific organizations and, generally, used for those tasks only.

Distinctions among individuals, groups, environments, and nation-states, and between tasks, were important because information-gathering for each took place at a different level of granularity, analysis of information utilized different types of filters and information-processing techniques, each type of information-gathering focused on a particular category of information, and use of data gathered for specific purposes was often limited to users with related responsibilities. Today's digital technologies, however, collect such vast amounts of data that the same information can be analyzed using different types of information processing procedures, at multiple levels of granularity. The U.S. Department of Defense was already offering military commanders a choice of whether to see broad overviews of battlefront formations or focused detail on particular areas out of the same database as long ago as the early 1980s.

As a result, information gathered for one purpose can be used for another. A major breakthrough for the environmental movement occurred when it achieved access to satellite data collected for national security purposes in order to gain a much more comprehensive and detailed picture of environmental change around the globe. Conversely, data gathered for nonmilitary purposes, such as the mapping of community infrastructure, is now being turned to national security ends as well. General mapping exercises, such as those undertaken by satellite remote sensing, can be used both for general surveillance purposes and to follow the activities of specific individuals in response to intelligence needs. Thus there is a conflation between mapping and surveillance, and between mapping and intelligence.

Official Memory

The narrative within which an identity appears and acts has a history, a past full of events that explain the present and in conversation with which future actions will take place. Whether specific details of that history are accurate is a separate question from whether the story is told at all. History, too, is a construct, albeit one that rests upon records of empirical experience. It is a particularly important construct, because in turn it shapes contemporary political realities.

It may perhaps not be surprising that the practice of writing histories that serve as communal memories received a great boost during the period from 1763 to 1788, a period critical to the history of the modern nation-state itself, since the growth of a stable, complex, and continuous social order itself suggests the need for and in turn creates a corporate memory. This was the same period during which an identity between language, state, nation, and currency came about in Europe. There is an interesting interaction between official forms of memory for the state and the law, for until there were written records of decision-making, "living memory"—what remained in the memory of the oldest living person—provided the legal function of precedent. In 1275, a statute was actually put in place in England setting the limit of 1189 for living memory and announcing that after that date only written records would be relied upon. The statute, therefore, has itself been described by some as the formal beginning of the era of artificial memory. In a recapitulation of this event, one of the first nontechnical uses of the Internet, before it was available to the public, was with Project Gutenberg, launched with the U.S. online publication of the Declaration of Independence in 1971.

The "official memory" of a nation-state includes available systematic information about the history of the decisions, activities, and events of the nation-state claimed by the government to be accurate and of value. The constitutional requirement that Congress report to U.S. citizens on its activities produced the *Debates and Proceedings in the Congress of the United States* from 1789 to 1824, the *Register of Debates in Congress* from 1824 to 1837, and the *Congressional Globe* from 1833 to 1873. In 1873, the *Congressional Record* was launched as a daily record of proceedings and debates in Congress. The *Federal Register* was launched in 1935—after a court case was won because the defendant was able to demonstrate he had had no way of knowing that the law he had allegedly broken was in place—to provide an official daily record of the rules, proposed rules, and notices of federal agencies and organizations, as well as executive orders and other presidential documents. In 1982, detailed requirements for the *Federal Register* were enunciated. It is very difficult to reconstruct many aspects of what should be the official government record prior to the 1930s. For example, while Supreme Court opinions and other court decisions have been published from the start (though not always completely), there is no comprehensive collection of presidential executive orders before those of Franklin D. Roosevelt in the 1930s.

An official national archive for all of the other kinds of material that documents the history of the U.S. government was first established in 1934. Numerous pieces of legislation since then have responded to political developments, such as the Kennedy assassination, Watergate, and the switch to digital government records, by providing specific rules for inclusion of related material such as presidential papers in the archives. Under management of the National Archives and Records Administration (NARA), the National Archives include the history of policy-making processes, details about the implementation of government programs down to the case level, adjudication of grievances and cases, financial accounts, and the scientific reports and statistical surveys used as inputs into policy-making.

Other sources and activities fuel the formation of cultural memory at the level of popular culture. There has not been an official newspaper in the United States, other than for a very brief period following the Revolutionary War. Beginning in 1851, the *New York Times* served as a quasi-official newspaper of record, publishing key government documents and Supreme Court decisions for easy public access, but in recent years has abandoned that role. The Smithsonian Institution, established in 1846, defines its mission as complementing the official material in the National Archives by collecting material important to the cultural and material identity of the various peoples in the United States and making that material available to the public through the interfaces of its museums and publications. Statutes, memorials, stamps, and historical markers all publicly document events and people the government has decided are worth noting.

Here, the focus is on the National Archives as a particularly detailed and comprehensive source of historical memory, and as an exemplar. In theory, and as intended, the archive would provide the resources needed by historians and others irrespective of political position and perspective. In practice, the archives are incomplete, there is ambiguity regarding what information should be retained, achieving access to information held in the archives is difficult, record retention is of low priority and status within the agencies that create material of archival value, and struggles over what should be retained are highly political.

Confusion regarding what is history, and what is not Despite its importance, establishing and maintaining a national memory does not have constitutional status. It has taken a long time to develop a legal framework appropriate to the task, and that framework remains fragile. Record retention is also of low status within the government agencies and departments whose history is involved. Responsibility for records management is often a low-level clerical task, organizational training rarely highlights the importance of record retention or educates staff regarding pertinent rules in this area, and those who are closest to the records because they create them may not only be ignorant of the rules regarding their retention but also have an active interest in destroying records for personal or organizational reasons.

Though the government has been working on record retention legislation since the 1930s, there is still no statute that effectively mandates retention of all important policy documentation. The government's position has gone back and forth, reflecting struggles within the executive branch regarding who should be allowed to make decisions regarding the disposal of records and what the definition of a record should be.

The original statute creating the National Archives as an independent agency put decisions regarding what to keep in NARA's hands, but a 1943 bill permitted government agencies and departments to destroy documents if employees of those organizations felt the material had no administrative, legal, research, or other value. In 1950, legislation set standards for selective retention of records of continuing value, and then in 1955 a supplemental appropriation bill gave Congress control over record creation and destruction. In the 1968 law mandating archival storage of government records, authority was given to the archivist for final decisions regarding record retention. In 1972, however, Congress removed that authority from the archivist. Today there are general rules regarding record retention that apply across the government, and agency- or subject-specific rules are included in the legislation establishing and providing the parameters for agency activity. Decisions about whether to permanently retain materials that fall within the categories so defined are then made by the archivist, a political appointee. It was President Richard Nixon's effort to claim his recordings of telephone conversations as private property that led to legislation mandating presidential papers as public property that must be turned over to the National Archives. After Secretary of State Henry Kissinger tried to protect the transcriptions of his telephone conversations from public access via the Freedom of Information Act by turning them over to the Library of Congress, the State Department was required to develop specific rules regarding record retention and the transfer of its materials, so important to understanding—and learning from—the history of foreign policy. And it was President Ronald Reagan's request to destroy all of the electronic records produced during his presidency that forced legislative attention to the need to archive material in electronic as well as paper form.

In October 2001, President George W. Bush signed an executive order allowing either sitting or former presidents to veto the transfer of presidential records to the National Archives. Both historians and political analysts are contesting this move, which took place in combination with numerous other policy changes under the PATRIOT Act and related legislation, executive orders, and opinions of the attorney general to reduce the amount of information available to U.S. citizens about the operations of their government.

Traditional definitions of records have emerged from paper-based concepts and have merely been applied to new technologies. How the concept of a record is defined can have an enormous impact on the welfare of an organization, because it determines which types of information can be introduced as evidence in the courts or be subpoenaed. Such a definition also serves pragmatic ends, ensuring that specific forms or versions of information are recorded in order to fully document the decisions and activities of the organization.

The Uniform Rules of Evidence, in use as a matter of statutory law by most states and the federal government, defines records for the purpose of in judicial proceedings. Records include information inscribed on a tangible medium or stored in an electronic or other medium and is retrievable in perceivable form. Here is the **Test for Distinguishing Records from Hearsay:**

1. *Temporal proximity* Was the record made at or near the time of the event recorded?
2. *Knowledge* Was the record made by, or from information transmitted by, someone with knowledge of the event?
3. *In the course of business* Was the record made in the course of a regularly conducted business activity?
4. *Normal activity* Was the production of the document or data among the regular business practices of the organization?

There is further nuance. In electronic surveillance, a record is "authentic" if it is made simultaneous with the conversation that it purports to have recorded, and "accurate" if that recording has not been altered, distorted, or changed and does contain what was actually said. For the purposes of information professionals, the American Records Management Association (ARMA) defines as an official record as one that is "legally recognized as establishing a fact," where a record is "recorded information, regardless of medium or characteristics" (Shupsky 1995, 40). The Federal Records Act (1950) provides the definition of a record to be kept for historical purposes used by the National Archives:

> [A]ll books, papers, maps, photographs, machine readable [electronic] materials, or other documentary materials, regardless of physical form or characteristics, made or received by an agency of the United States Government under Federal law or in connection with the transaction of public business and preserved or appropriate for preservation by that agency ... as evidence of the organization, functions, policies, decisions, procedures, operations, or other activities of the Government or because of the informational value of data in them. (Ibid.)

Nonrecord materials are defined by the same act to include materials developed for reference or exhibition purposes, published material, and working papers such as a day file.

None of these definitions completely removes the need to exercise discretion, because the number of types of documents, images, and recordings is effectively endless. And once material is in the hands of the archivist, the decision must be made as to which of it will have enduring historical value. Here there can be no simple rule of thumb, for any type of material might be important to an historian depending upon the question asked. It is also difficult to determine just when a particular piece of information is related to government business in a way that would make it an official record.

Because working papers—drafts, jotted notes, proposals, and so on—are treated as nonrecord materials (and are also treated as exempt under the Freedom of Information Act), many organizations have developed workarounds for communications and decisions that they prefer not to be exposed to the public eye. Hallway conversations can replace meetings with recorded notes, and agreement to draft proposals achieved in a series of interpersonal meetings can replace official "decisions." Some of the technological practices described in later sections of this chapter also fall into this category of problems.

Haphazard memory storage and access At each stage of the archival process, records are vulnerable to loss. In the office where records are created they may be inadvertently destroyed or destroyed because they are believed to be unimportant; individuals take particular records of personal or perceived economic value; and with the switch to electronic record-keeping, "updating" information may mean completely replacing data that had come before. Bureaucratic resistance to any concern for the historical record is compounded by uncertainty regarding whose decision it should be regarding what should be retained. There was public discussion about fear that official records would be lost because of technological change by the mid-1980s.

Records that are saved may sit in warehouses for years before they are organized and described, steps that must be completed before the records are even accepted by the National Archives. The storage center in Suitland, Maryland, where records are kept until processed, has more than twenty rooms, each the size of a football field, crammed with tattered boxes of papers. Each day truckloads of additional material arrive, adding volume at a rate at least 50 percent greater than that of the material removed daily for handling. A decade ago, the federal government was producing as large a volume of records every four months as had been created by all administrations from George Washington through

Woodrow Wilson put together. In one example of what this means pragmatically, records about U.S. disability policy and vocational rehabilitation programs go back to the 1920s, but are still in Suitland and haven't yet made it to the archives; the records exist, but are effectively inaccessible to historians. NARA is so overwhelmed that there are times when it asks departments to destroy records though the departments involved believe that the information is of historical importance and ought to be saved. This has happened even with State Department materials essential to the understanding of foreign policy.

The same problem is faced by courts, which are accountable to the requirement that evidence be kept. Warehouses are nearing capacity, with a consequence for the types of evidence being permitted into the courtroom. Actual objects are being replaced with photographs in many cases, even though the rhetorical impact may be quite different; presentation materials prepared to clarify arguments for juries are no longer accepted; and evidence in death penalty cases is kept only until the inmate is executed or cleared on appeal.

Once materials make it into the archivist's hands, they must be organized in such a way that they are accessible for use. The only comprehensive description of the holdings offers location of the records, source of the records, quantities in cubic feet and, in some but not all cases, very general descriptors of the subject matter at the record group (record category) level. As of 2003, about 20 percent of NARA's holdings at this level of description are searchable via an electronic catalog, though there is an ambition to have the entire catalog online by 2007. Meanwhile the paper records themselves remain vulnerable to decay, to destruction by insects and animals, and to damage from extremes of humidity.

Technological vulnerability The constancy of technological innovation is a problem for historical memory because records produced to be accessible via one technology may not be legible via any others. By the late 1990s this problem had reached a crisis stage (the average life of software is now five years), and many believed that unless a solution were found the concept of a national archive would become meaningless. NARA is currently working with university-based researchers to develop an approach called "persistent object preservation," which involves digital applications independent of the technology in use at any given time because they focus on the properties of the record being preserved rather than the technologies used either to create or store it. Those involved in the project claim it should solve the problem for three to four hundred years, but it has not yet actually been put into use. Other techniques undergoing experimentation include emulation of obsolete equipment and migration of records to new software and hardware formats.

Meanwhile, in 1999 the U.S. Court of Appeals decision in *Public Citizen v. Carlin* upheld NARA's rule permitting agencies to delete electronic versions of a document once the document had been printed, in a case pressed by a public interest group that insisted paper versions of electronic records do not preserve many of the important characteristics inherent in electronic formats. Demonstrating unusual prescience, eight days before President George W. Bush took office, NARA sent out exacting criteria for archiving all government Web sites created under President Bill Clinton.

Of course in some cases digital technologies do increase the quality of archives rather than creating a vulnerability via technological obsolescence. As example, in 2003 the Government Printing Office (GPO) entered into a collaboration with NARA to serve as an archive by keeping all of its publications permanently available digitally. The GPO also now archives government Web sites that go out of existence.

Mediating the Identities of the Individual and the Informational State

Information policy mediates the identities of individuals and that of the nation-state when it affects citizenship, language, education, and the vote.

Citizenship

One of the defining moments of the emergence of the modern nation-state was the transformation of monarchical subjects into citizens. The modern standard for citizenship was established in the 1648 Treaty of Westphalia, which clarified questions of property, authority, and relationships between the leaders and the residents of a territory. Most contemporary discussions of the nature of citizenship begin with the work of T. H. Marshall, who identified three dimensions in which citizenship entails rights: (1) *civil*—freedom of action within the sphere of civil society, expressed in matters such as freedom of speech, thought, association, and movement as well as property rights; (2) *political*—opportunities to participate in the exercise of political power; and (3) *social*—achievement of a basic standard of living.

Additional ways of conceptualizing citizenship are appearing in response to changing relationships between individuals and various types of loci of power. Some have legal status, some are conceptual only, and some are meant to be metaphorical, but briefly introducing them illuminates the kinds of pressures on the nature of citizenship today that are also expressed in trends in U.S. law that affect citizenship as a mediation between the identity of the individual and that of the nation-state. The notion of "thin citizenship" has developed within the European Union to refer to the fact that the European Union provides only some of the services and forms of control traditionally associated with the nation-state; in turn, citizenship involves only a few of the types of rights and obligations with which it has traditionally been associated. The concept of "pluralist citizenship" is applied to those individuals who simultaneously identify with multiple different loci of power, whether economically, culturally, or politically based. Those who promote global civil society base their ideas and work on the assumption that "global citizenship" is a real possibility and, in a de facto way, already exists. "Cultural citizenship," in which citizenship-like rights and responsibilities arise out of participation in a culture rather than a geopolitical entity, receives attention because culturally based organizations wield so much power globally today; "cultural China," for example, has the third largest economy in the world. The combination of the privatization of many formerly governmental functions with the legalization of the organization means that private sector decision-making now often has the kind of structural effect traditionally associated with the law, and employees of an organization may take on the roles of "corporate citizenship."

Trends in information policy affecting citizenship—and transformations in our understanding of the nature of citizenship that in turn affect information policy—include changing conceptualizations of the informational needs of citizens, development of the category of hybrid citizenship, and the threats to citizenship rights of suspected terrorists who are U.S. citizens as a result of legal developments involving terrorism.

Changing conceptualizations of the informational needs of citizens In Michael Schudson's analysis, there have been four quite different conceptualizations of "the good citizen" in U.S. history, each of which entails different types of informational rights and responsibilities, and all of which coexist today:

• *The trust-based citizen* Citizenship at the time of the country's founding assumed that public life was trust-based. The good citizen of the era recognized virtue as it was defined in religious terms, understood his place in the social order, and voted in solidarity with an established community leader in whom he had trust. To be a good citizen, one needed information about the social structure of the community and one's place in it and about the personalities and power of candidates.

- *The informed citizen* It was not until 1890 that the model of the good citizen significantly changed to require knowledge of issues, policy options, and party and candidate positions. To be a good citizen, one needed to be literate and current with information circulated through the public sphere on political matters. It was this vision of the citizen—and of the role that information played in the practices of participatory democracy—that dominated as First Amendment jurisprudence first took shape. (Schudson, of course, was writing before 9/11, and one wonders whether or not he might add a fifth category today.)
- *The rights-based citizen* While the first century of U.S. law focused on the powers of government, by the 1930s attention had switched to the rights of citizens. Courts joined the vote as sites of participatory democracy. The good citizen was informed about civil rights, and it became important to understand social conditions as a basis for political action.
- *The monitorial citizen* Over the course of the past thirty years, elite-challenging political action and political groups not based in parties have grown in importance; "subgovernments" closed to the public eye with autonomy in specific areas have been theoretically dismantled; attention has turned to due process; and the mechanisms by which citizens can acquire information about the processes and practices of government have multiplied. The result has been development of a sense of the good citizen as monitorial, keeping an eye on government itself.

Hybrid citizenship Prior to 9/11 the question of U.S. citizenship was binary—one either was or was not a citizen. Someone born a U.S. citizen could lose that status only through voluntarily giving it up. (A foreign-born citizen could lose that status if perjury in the course of the citizenship process were discovered.) A citizen's civil liberties were restricted if imprisoned, but in many states were restored upon release. Since 9/11, however, a spectrum of types of citizenship status has developed through the concept of the "hybrid citizen" and ambiguity in the definition of terrorism, both discussed here. (Informational aspects of immigration are discussed in chapter 7.)

For the first time, an Office of Citizenship was established after 9/11 as part of the Homeland Security Act of 2002, with the goal of "reviving" civic identity. Historically, U.S. citizens were guaranteed greater protections of their civil liberties than were non-U.S. citizens; this was the primary reason for dividing the intelligence community between those agencies responsible for and practices applied to non-citizens (e.g., the Central Intelligence Agency, or CIA) and those agencies responsible for and practices applied to U.S. citizens (e.g., the FBI). The PATRIOT Act broke down this barrier with two provisions that affect the nature of citizenship. First, the act made it legal to apply intelligence techniques formerly used only with non-U.S. citizens against U.S. citizens, and legalized the sharing of information among intelligence units with different purposes. Second, it diminished the level of constitutional protections extended to those U.S. citizens who have connections with foreign nationals involved with an organization defined by the attorney general's office as terrorist—even if the U.S. citizen had no knowledge of the relationship with that organization, or of the organization's status, and even if there were no evidence at all that the citizen involved had any connections with terrorist groups him- or herself or had engaged in any suspect activities. These legal changes created a category of "hybrid" identity used by the government to justify the use of "hybrid" legal tools in the treatment of those individuals.

The effects of these changes in the law have been extended through practice. There was protest when the U.S. government wanted to hold trials of suspected terrorists in secret, but the government defended this practice when the individuals involved were not U.S. citizens. A case which involved a U.S. citizen and in which there was significant evidence of involvement in the planning of terrorist activities by someone who was not born in the United States, is dark of skin, and is a Moslem, however, has introduced the possibility of secret trials for U.S. citizens as well. It could get more extreme: should the legislation colloquially referred to as "PATRIOT Act II" become law, those who are currently considered hybrid citizens would lose their citizenship altogether.

Terrorism and the loss of citizenship rights The historical assumption in the United States was that one was innocent until proven guilty; due process was put in place to ensure that one was treated accordingly. However, U.S. citizens who are suspected of being terrorists lose some of their fundamental civil liberties, including the right to confidential conversations with their lawyers and the right to be presented with the evidence being used against them. Since terrorism is so key to the question of whether a U.S. citizen will in fact receive full constitutional protections, the definition of terrorism becomes fundamental to the concept of citizenship and to the nature of personal identity as mediated by the nation-state.

Terrorism first became an important part of the U.S. legal vocabulary in the early 1990s when it was included among the four categories of the "enemy" in the new security theory that developed after the close of the Cold War (the others were those involved with drugs, those who economically damage the United States, and those whose behavior does not fit existing statistical profiles). It became an everyday word following 9/11, but neither then nor now has the concept received a clear definition. Terrorism is in a sense defined by the activities included in the USA PATRIOT Act as prosecutable under that legislation, which includes damaging government property and manipulating a computer system to the extent that, cumulatively, efforts to return the system to its original status cost at least $5,000. A list of foreign terrorist organizations is published by the U.S. Department of State, with organizations appearing on and disappearing from the list fairly regularly, but the criteria used to so categorize these organizations are not presented. Activities that were legal at the time they were undertaken can now be retroactively defined as terrorist, going back fifteen years.

Long experience with the undefined term "hooliganism" in the former Soviet Union made clear that ambiguous concepts that criminalize those to whom the concepts are applied is an open invitation to use of those words to serve a variety of political ends. Ambiguity regarding the definition of terrorism on the part of the nation-state presents an ontological threat to individual identity, for one can never be certain whether an activity or communication understood to be perfectly normal and legal will endanger one's legal status now or in the future.

In several areas, attacks on the constitutional rights of citizens that have occurred under the cloak of fighting the war on terrorism are being fought in the courts and in Congress. In the domain of the right to a fair trial, these include denial of the right to confidential conversations with one's attorney (for those arrested on suspicion of terrorism) and denial of the right to be presented with the evidence upon which one is being judged (for those whose court cases involve evidence collected during the course of surveillance triggered by terrorism concerns). The right to association is severely weakened by the reawakening of "guilt by association."

Language

History is littered with efforts to control the use of language as an exercise in political power, going back at least to Roman times and probably further, to Akkadian. Control over language was certainly a key feature of the imperial exercises of modern governments as they forced cultural nations and bureaucratic states into single entities. With globalization and other pressures encouraging the separation of nations from states in the late twentieth and early twenty-first centuries, language policy has again become very much an issue.

At time of the founding of the United States, twenty languages were regularly spoken in this country, and the Articles of Confederation were printed in German as well as English. Language was first an identity issue early in the nineteenth century when the United States tried to separate itself culturally from England. During the nineteenth and early twentieth centuries, linguistic diversity grew with each successive wave of immigration; beginning in the late nineteenth century each group of immigrants also stimulated an English-only movement. Questions about language first appeared in the census in 1890. Today the salience of language as an issue is rising along with the growing size and importance of the Hispanic and Asian populations.

The range of policy options includes offering several different languages official status, each in its own region; giving speakers of any language the same rights all over the country; officially permitting "plurilingualism" but using only one language for official purposes; and official monolingualism, in which only one language is recognized, even though there are linguistic minorities. Trends in the debate over this information policy issue with relevance to the mediation of individual and national identity include the effort to use linguistic purity to counter genetic diversity, and the tensions that language policy generates between bureaucratic and cultural modes of organizing the polity.

Use of language purity to counter cultural diversity Changes in the ethnic makeup of the population clearly affect language law. New York amended its constitution to disenfranchise over one million Yiddish speakers and California did the same to disenfranchise its Chinese early in the twentieth century. Native American children have long been removed from their homes forcibly for education in English-language schools where they were forbidden to speak their native languages. And it is no coincidence that California, which in the 2000 census was revealed as the first state in the United States to have *no* ethnic majority, is a particular locus of activity promoting the English-only movement.

The English-only movement has grown in recent years. Since 1981, the number of states with English-only laws has risen to twenty-four, with Hawaii as the only officially bilingual state. State and local level legislation touches upon matters such as mandating use of the Roman alphabet on signage (thus forbidding the use of signs in Asian languages, Arabic, or Russian), forbidding the purchase of non-English books by public libraries, requiring employees to use only English on the job and/or during breaks, and forcing school children to use English in school buses as well as in classrooms. Both an English-only constitutional amendment and a statutory proposal that would require all government activities to take place only in English have been before Congress since 1981.

Opponents of the English-only movement have their own legislation, known as English Plus, already passed in four states and the city of Oakland. The American Civil Liberties Union (ACLU) takes the position that English-only laws violate the Equal Protection Clause of the Fourteenth Amendment because they can jeopardize the ability of people on trial to comprehend proceedings or to receive government services. The Equal Employment Opportunity Commission (EEOC) started tracking language-based filings in the mid-1990s, and found the number of complaints growing 500 percent between 1996 and 2000.

Language as a site for tensions between the cultural nation and the bureaucratic state Language policy marks the tension between cultural features of the nation and the bureaucratic features of the state, because strengthening the former would work to the detriment of the latter. English-only legislation is very hard to enforce. When Dade County, Florida, passed an English-only ordinance in 1980 that required the canceling of all multicultural events and bilingual services such as directional signs in the public transit system, county medical services, and 911 emergency services, public outcry in the heavily Hispanic area forced its repeal. New Mexico's constitution, which established English as the state's official language, was ironically ratified by means of a bilingual ballot. None of the states or municipalities insisting on English only have increased funding for the teaching of English, though linguist Geoffrey Nunberg found that in 1997 in Los Angeles alone there were half a million adults on waiting lists to learn English.

Economically, producing materials in multiple languages raises cost, but economists believe it is not until the number of languages involved is more than ten that translation becomes counterproductive. The investment to make marketing materials multilingual, for example, is a relatively inexpensive way of vastly expanding a market; the percentage of U.S. Fortune 100 companies with multilingual Web sites rose from one-third to almost two-thirds between 1999 and 2000. A GAO study that looked at the total number of federal documents printed in languages other than English in the 1990s, on the other hand, revealed that that number came to less than one-tenth of 1 percent. Federal law currently mandates foreign language services in only a handful of special cases, such as in migrant worker health care centers and for certain Immigration and Naturalization Service procedures.

Arguments in favor of the English-only movement, often emotional or stemming from a desire to attack not the language but its speakers, do not jibe with the facts. While promoters argue that without the legal requirement, immigrants will not become assimilated, research shows that over 95 percent of first-generation Mexican Americans are proficient in English, and nearly 90 percent of Latinos five years old or older speak English in their households. The 1990 census showed that fewer than 3 percent of the thirty-two million language minority population were not at least functionally bilingual. Perhaps most importantly, a 1992 study sponsored by the National Academy of Sciences found that bilingual education reduces the time to reach full English fluency by two to three years, compared to the learning rate in schools that insist on English only.

Education

Education—the production, reproduction, and distribution of knowledge—is an information industry that has historically played a key constitutive role for the nation-state via its contribution to what political scientists refer to as "capacity," the ability of the state to act on its intentions. Education does this by improving the quality of decision-making, training the population in core skills needed for both military service and the labor force, innovation critical to economic growth, and knowledge production. Education for the masses developed with industrialization, which required literate and skilled workers. Processes of curricular reform inevitably lag behind—but continue to respond to—projected future bottlenecks in the labor market.

It has long been understood that education creates civic identity. In the late eighteenth century, many European states practiced new ideas about the political naturalization of their citizens through the education of abandoned children. (Even Rousseau abandoned his own children to the state with the expectation that he would then never recognize them as adults!) In the original Jeffersonian vision for the United States, higher education institutions were so important to the information infrastructure that they would have been put in place at the constitutional level along with the First Amendment and the postal system. Nineteenth-century German sociologist Ferdinand Tönnes defined political publics as the linkage of educated individuals via knowledge, and John Dewey emphasized the link between the university system and the cultural expansion of citizenship.

Education contributes to the formation of civic identity by transferring the memory of the nation-state from generation to generation. Schools offer a venue within which to introduce students to modes of public discourse. Members of the general public need to be informed in order to elect representatives and participate in debate on public issues, and individuals elected or appointed to government need to be additionally trained in decision-making skills. The quality of political decision-making is linked to cognitive information processing skills and cognitive complexity. For everyone, education is important in the transition from irrational to rational decision-making, and development of the ability to build and defend complex arguments through education is key to the success of originally peripheral political groups.

The mass media and education in the service of nation-state goals have been linked by institution, infrastructure, and genre since the early nineteenth century, when some of the first publications mass produced were marketed as a form of worker education. John Dewey saw the powerful socializing influence of radio, but was concerned about its ability to distort and mislead; the question, as former chair of the FCC Newton Minow noted about television, is not whether education is taking place but, rather, what is actually being taught and learned. Much influential thinking about the effects of the use of new information technologies has been driven by educational concerns: Marshall McLuhan's *Understanding Media* (1964) started as a report commissioned by the U.S. Department of Education on the problem of teaching media effects in secondary schools. Daniel Bell's *The Coming of Post-Industrial Society* (1973) was a print version of ideas first developed in a 1966 report from a series of symposia on educational reform he organized for the American Academy of Arts and Sciences (AAAS). Jean-François Lyotard's *The Postmodern Condition* (first published in French in 1979 and translated into English in 1984) was a report commissioned by the Québécois Department of Education on the state of knowledge in fields of science and technology in advanced industrial countries. And Fritz Machlup's (1962) seminal first pass at distinguishing among the information industries included higher education; in 1980 he began his industry-by-industry analysis there.

Recent trends in education, of importance in the mediation of the identities of the individual and the nation-state, include a contraction of the role of educational institutions in and as public spheres, growing tensions between educational institutions and the nation-state, use of education as a cultural policy tool, and an emphasis on information technologies over information itself.

Contraction of the public sphere Educational institutions have both played an important role in the general public sphere (particularly those of higher education) and as venues for the public sphere themselves via open discussion in the classroom. For this reason the Supreme Court has defended speech rights on campuses and in schools within the bounds of limits provided by the nature of those institutions as either private forums or quasi-public forums. For universities, however, the widespread expansion into distance education has reduced both roles by diluting and dispersing the academic community as a coherent public. The growing interest in for-profit activities by universities inevitably reduces their presence as critical voices contributing to discourse on matters of public concern within society at large. There are trade-offs: as the property rights of universities expand, any special protections they may have tried to claim as particular arenas for public discourse and knowledge production are weakened.

Tensions between the production and reproduction of knowledge and the needs of state identity Until very recently, when digital transmission capacity so vastly expanded that it was not unrealistic to talk about storing knowledge not in specific archival sites but in the network itself, there had always been linkages between particular communities, stores of knowledge, and locales. Today, combined access to databases from across the world (and concomitant conceptual standardization), a growth in transnational collaborations in both research and teaching, and the detachment of the communities of particular universities from geographic bounds via distance education and a recrafting of institutional boundaries raise important questions about relationships between knowledge production and distribution institutions and specific geographic sites. State legislatures with the mission of devoting their resources to the people of their states, for example, are less willing to provide support to their public universities when those institutions are heavily involved in distance education that serves growing numbers of students from outside the state's borders. At the national level, some have expressed concern about the percentage of higher education resources that have gone to educate foreign nationals, though others point out that the education of professionals from around the world has been important to the quality of our international relations. (Post–9/11 monitoring of foreign students has reversed this trend.)

There are other legally driven shifts in relations between higher education and the nation-state. Under the Digital Millennium Copyright Act (DMCA), universities, like other organizations that provide access to the Internet, essentially become an arm of the state by shutting down Web access for those accused by copyright owners of infringing upon intellectual property laws—again, before those accused are found guilty. There are also disagreements over the nature of the peer review and data distribution processes associated with federally funded research. At the same time, the government would like to ensure diffusion of research findings to the commercial sector. Though the Supreme Court had long resisted examination of course content in order to determine the constitutional status of an institution, the decision in a 1978 case (*Cleland v. National College of Business*) set a dangerous precedent by sustaining indirect intervention into curricula by denying financial support for student participation in innovative courses.

A focus on information technologies rather than information literacy
Efforts to use education to adapt the labor force to the needs of an information rather than an industrial economy have been largely accomplished through policy intended to aid in the diffusion of information technologies by encouraging their use in the classroom rather than in education policy itself. Today, the use of new information technologies in education is as much a matter of telecommunications policy—via the universal service provisions of the Telecommunications Act of 1996—as it is a matter of education, culture, or economics. The same has been true in Europe. Meanwhile, failures of policy efforts to ensure a technologically literate workforce sufficient for contemporary needs has led to a reliance on immigration as a source of high-technology labor and the transfer of jobs offshore.

Mutually Constituted Identities of the Individual and the Informational State

It is in the manipulations of the gap between state and individual identity that we see the most interesting trends discussed in this chapter. It is the state that operates the statistical technologies. While it is individuals who respond to questionnaires, engage in self-report, and choose to participate in the activities about which statistics are generated, in the informational state the degrees of freedom with which those activities may be undertaken are becoming more restricted. Citizenship rights are exercised by individuals, but the state is manipulating criteria for citizenship, status categories, and both allowable and mandated behaviors. When the identity of the individual and of the state are aligned, social cohesion is high; conversely, when they are disparate, social cohesion declines. Meanwhile the state continues to intervene in ways in which public communication affects individual identity in interpersonal and group relations (via libel law) and intra-individual perceptions of the self (via privacy law).

In sum, as the personal ability to construct a meaningful, coherent and effective autonomous identity declines, that of the informational state to manage and make use of the identities of its citizens to serve its own ends goes up. The result is one of the most important markers of the informational state in its democratic form: while historically citizens determined their own identities for the purposes of political representation, in the informational state, representation—even of the individual—is determined by the government. On its surface, the formal structures of representative democracy look the same, but the means by which power is effectively exercised have changed. As a consequence, the relationship between the individual and the state is being redefined in ways that may strengthen the identity of the informational state—but undermine the social cohesion upon which its effectiveness and vitality rest.

Identity, like agency, appears in a mutually interactive dance with the structures that provide the context within which action and expression take place. Law and regulation affect both identity and structure simultaneously, for policy is a structuration process that affects the subjectivity of identity as it appears within the objective routines of daily life. Thus the ways in which information policy affect identity are intertwined with the effects of information policy upon structure, the subject of chapter 6.

6

Information Policy and Structure

Because both communal and individual identity are constructed via flows of communication, introduction of any new information or communication technology influences the ways in which we relate to each other and form into groups, from the most local to the global. Informational structures provide the architectures that enable both social and technological form. Information policy applies to the conjuncture of these three types of structures because they interact. Organizations *are* technologies, technologies embed information architectures, and information architectures create social structures. However, we tend to make policy for each type of structure as if it stands alone.

Because meta-technologies so greatly multiply the degrees of freedom with which we may act, there is currently a great deal of experimentation with all three; thus the structural implications of information policy today are particularly important, and particularly problematic. The embedding of social life within the digital network has stimulated the development of new communal and organizational forms as well as altered our perceptions of the variety of social structures of analytical, political, cultural, and economic importance. The very process of making decisions for the global information infrastructure has itself heightened awareness of the ways in which each type of structure is translated into and influences the shape of the other two systems. As a consequence, over the last few years we have begun to develop theories of the intersections, the interactions, and the homologies among social, technological, and informational systems.

Theories of Structure

Several different disciplines have thought about social structure. The first generations of anthropologists sought universal generalizations based on the relationships, activities, and material artifacts they observed within relatively isolated and traditional tribal groups. These thinkers emphasized elements that create within-group coherence, involving hierarchies typically based on familial and religious relations. Formlessness, or anarchy, when it appeared within anthropologists' reports, was fleeting and served a ritual function. Sociologists, on the other hand, gave birth to their field in the study of urbanized and industrialized societies filled with a myriad cultural and bureaucratic forms that interact at both the group and individual levels in a number of ways. When formlessness was observed, as in the cases of anomie mentioned in chapter 5's discussion of individual identity, it was viewed as destructive, or as decay. Political scientists worked between the poles of the cultural nation and the bureaucratic state, as explored in chapter 2. The larger world within which these political units operated was viewed throughout much of modern thought as anarchic, justifying the exercise of political, military, and economic power as a means of providing a shape to world affairs. While the stories told by historians focused on struggles and developments within cultural and political entities, periods of great turbulence, both within war and outside of it, were an inevitable part of their reports. Economists, meanwhile, long worked with a binary opposition between organizations (often referred to as "hierarchies") and the market. While organizations were characterized by highly structured tasks, decision-making, and information flows, the market was idealized as without form altogether. Instead, markets were characterized by decision-making for the whole out of the sum of individual decision-making based on rational self-interest (much like the view of international relations held by many political scientists) and also by perfect and equivalent knowledge on the part of all participants (a notion quite unique to neoclassical economics).

Across the social sciences, then, by the mid-twentieth century, three different ways that people might relate to each other were envisioned—through culture, or organization, or without any structured relationships at all. Four developments in the last few decades, however—two empirical and two theoretical—broadened our understanding of the vocabulary of available social forms.

The first empirical trend has everything to do with the other three, for technological innovation both facilitated experimentation with social forms and provided the computing capacity and speed to conduct analyses from theoretical foundations that could not practicably be used earlier. The second empirical trend was the evolution of new types of organization. Corporations began reconsidering which tasks should be performed within the organization and which outside; hierarchies started flattening; and appreciation for the value of collaboration and coordination, as well as competition, grew. Long-term interorganizational relationships so gained in importance that both sociologists and economists started talking in terms of the "network firm." The same phenomenon was observable in the public sector, with political scientists increasingly referring to "policy networks" involving collaborations across levels of governance as well as the private sector. Indeed, networked forms have become so important that many now prefer the label "network society" to "information society." On the theoretical side, the combined efforts of social scientists and mathematicians yielded tools of network analysis that made it possible to study and discuss these new social forms in some detail. Another important theoretical development was the application of complex adaptive systems theory to social structures, an approach that made it possible to see turbulence, and even chaos, as natural and perhaps inevitable stages in the transitions from one social structure to another.

Thus today's typology of social structures includes the community, the organization, and the network. The concept of the market provides a stand-in for the various versions of stable astructural conditions, and turbulence and chaos refer to astructural conditions that are not equilibrious. The lines between these types of social structures are not bright. Today's global information infrastructure makes it possible to form multiple diverse networks easily and to quickly move from participation in one to another. Nor do new social forms completely replace those that have come before; rather, they are layered over those that have come before as the complexity of social life continues to grow.

It is also important to remember that the appearance of one or another of these types of structure may or may not validly reflect the realities to which the models refer. The same can be said for technological systems, as we now know well in the case of the Internet: While the Internet was initially designed to be decentralized and nonhierarchical, and there is still rhetoric to this effect, the realities of social desire (how do we find each other?), commerce (how do we organize the economics of getting onto the net, using its services, and using the net as a market?), and political realities (how do we know which legal jurisdiction to apply, and prevent the use of the net by terrorists?) mean that a variety of structures have been placed upon the global information infrastructure.

There have been two dimensions along which our conceptualizations of technological structures have changed. With the addition of technologies, and then meta-technologies, to the range of tools available, the number of dimensions and effects to be taken into account has multiplied. Too, as our understanding of relations between the social and material worlds has grown in sophistication, the original focus on technologies as standalone objects has given way to appreciation of that fact that all technologies are parts of systems. There are four types of technological systems:

- *Mutually dependent systems* There are systems that come into being because the use of one type of technology is dependent upon the use of another, as use of the printing press required the technologies that make ink and paper. These relationships are significant because when there is a change in one of the technologies involved it may require changes in others. When the printing press sped up as a result of electrification, for example, paper manufacturers started producing rolls of paper rather than sheets and the quantities produced went up by orders of magnitude. An example of an indirect policy intervention possible with this type of technological system is the use of restrictions on access to paper as an effective way of preventing materials from coming into print without direct censorship.
- *Linked systems* In a linked technological system, individual technologies must actually be linked with each other in order to be functional. Physical linkages, such as the couples between railroad cars, are one way of linking technologies in this way. Electronic, or virtual, networks are another. The telephone network is an example of a linked technological system in the field of communication. The Internet is made up of many interlinked telecommunications networks, so we refer to it as a "network of networks."
- *Analytical systems* A third type of technological system develops when social and technological forms are combined for the purposes of strategy and analysis. A good example from the perspective of information policy is the European use of the concept of the *filière électronique* to refer not only to the telecommunications network but also to the organizations that exist only within and because of the network. The *filière électronique*, rather than the telecommunications network by itself, has thus become the unit of analysis for economic and policy purposes.
- *Personal systems* A fourth sense of technological system is the information environment built and used by specific users as they choose par-

ticular technologies, networks, and interfaces for their own use. We refer to the entire world of communication and information technologies from which we choose as the "information environment." Those we actually bring into our lives create a personal "information ecology." Because the technological potential becomes actual only through such choices—and the effects of technologies can be understood only within this context—this type of technological system is of growing interest to researchers.

The global information infrastructure is rife with legacy technologies, systems already in place that do not take advantage of current technological potential but that provide the context within which any future decisions must be made. Path dependency is an important factor differentiating the potential of a meta-technological system from its actuality because each design decision, once made, constrains the options available for future choices. The complexity of the information infrastructure is one reason for this path dependency; so many different technologies and meta-technologies must work together that changing any single one of them creates a risk that others may no longer work. Sunk cost, the capital invested in a particular set of resources that cannot be recouped if the system should change, is another important factor. In the case of information infrastructure, this is often literally sunk cost in the form of wires, cables, and fiber optics buried in the ground. It also includes the human cost associated with asking individuals, communities, and organizations to change the ways in which they do things. The need for technical standards also creates a bias toward incumbent technologies.

The history of wired telephone networks provides a vivid demonstration of the ways in which technological systems are intertwined with social systems. As built in the late nineteenth and early twentieth centuries, the U.S. network oriented around individual communities that became fully interconnected only once AT&T achieved—after a great deal of aggression—its monopoly-like position in the 1920s. In France, all lines led to Paris. Germany built a grid that efficiently linked urban, manufacturing, and shipping centers. And in the former Soviet Union, the telephone switching system followed Communist Party structure. A single architectural feature can exist in several different manifestations at once even within one society, as was the case in the early 1980s when ISDN was simultaneously an abstract concept, a set of technical standards, and an actual network that was being built in a few places around the world.

Definitions of information as perception of pattern, as discussed in chapter 2, lie at the heart of ideas about informational structures, and definitions of information as a constitutive force in society link those informational structures to their social effects. The extraordinary flexibility in design and use of technological structures built with today's digital meta-technologies has affected our understanding of informational structures for several reasons. The ability to implement informational structures either through the design of a piece of hardware (an object) or through use of software (a text) draws attention to the ways in which information architectures are manufactured, not given. Though historically information architectures were developed either by subject specialists (such as scientists working in a particular area) or information professionals (librarians), today participation in such processes is much more widespread; information architectures for particular communities are often the result of participatory processes. Individuals are actively creating their own informational structures, as is so often done with music stored on mobile devices. The speed and ease with which vast quantities of data can be analyzed for patterns suggestive of architectural features encourages self-aware development of informational structures. With the growth in interdisciplinary research, the need to clarify meaning across interpretive boundaries, each community of which may have its own informational structures, has stimulated interest in the categorical problems now referred to as the study of ontologies. As the appetite and capacity for computerizing knowledge grow, increasingly information that was never before made explicit (tacit knowledge) is being translated into forms that can be communicated (codified knowledge) and stored (embedded knowledge). Those interested in discerning intention in communications and actions of those who may threaten national security are interested in understanding information architectures in as wide a diversity as possible, for each architecture offers a means not only of revealing information, but also of hiding it.

Interactions, intersections, and homologies among social, technological, and informational structures become visible from a policy perspective when we examine latent as well as manifest laws and regulations that affect each type of system, and attend to the precessive effects among such laws and regulations provides entrée into the mechanisms by which mutual effects develop. In order to be able to clearly examine the ways in which trends in treatment of specific issues manifests the use of informational power by the U.S. government, however, this chapter will look separately at a few issues currently of import for each type of structure.

Information Policy and Social Structure

Many of the areas in which information policy addresses questions of social structure demonstrate the difficulty of separating informational, social, and technological systems. Antitrust law tries to prevent the formation of relationships among corporations that may be destructive, but because evaluating possible antitrust evaluations requires distinguishing among products, there is a need to make conceptual decisions regarding how to define specific technologies in the digital environment in ways that may or may not coincide with other commercial and technological ways of conceptualizing those products and services. Intellectual property rights can be considered a matter of social structure because of the impact of their ownership on the distribution of capital—but this is also an area of the law that involves control over access to and the manipulation and distribution of content, matters of informational structure. Association is more purely a social structure issue. All three of these categories of information policy issues that affect social structure are discussed here, with separate treatment for copyright and patent law to highlight interesting differences in trends within each area. Examples of information policy as it affects social structure not discussed here include reporting requirements for various types of corporations, nonprofits, and community organizations and differences in postal and telecommunications rates depending upon the type of group that is the content source.

Antitrust

Antitrust is a particularly complex area of the law that has had a cyclical history influenced by political movements, philosophical agendas, corporate climate, cultural experience, and changing political institutions. The goals of antitrust law have been variously promoted as protection of the consumer, enabling competition, or making the economy more efficient. A product of the U.S. economy and, initially, the political movement of Populism, antitrust law is now found around the world (most often referred to as "competition law").

It is the point of antitrust law to keep a single company from unfairly dominating a market, or a few companies from colluding with each other to do so. Anticompetitive pricing strategies, tying goods and products together so that a consumer must acquire all in order to have one (known as "bundling" in the communications and information industries), and inappropriate sharing of information and knowledge are key targets of antitrust investigations. There are several approaches to analyzing what constitutes monopolistic or oligopolistic control of markets. The Columbia school of antitrust theory starts from the position that unregulated markets are unlikely to function competitively, so government regulation is needed in order to pursue distributive goals. The Chicago school of antitrust theory, on the other hand, argues that unregulated markets in fact can work quite well, and that most distortions to the market are caused by government interventions that disturb its efficiency. The Harvard school of thought starts from an interest in the nature of industrial organization and incorporates noneconomic values in evaluations of the utility of antitrust as a market-correcting mechanism. This multiplicity of theoretical approaches means that there are great disagreements over how to conduct antitrust analysis. Debates over whether to treat innovation processes as sequential or simultaneous and the question of whether fairness should play an important role are particularly important to the information and communication industries.

Antitrust law has been important to the communication and information industries since within a decade of its creation in the late nineteenth century. In fact, in 1879, even before the Sherman Act put antitrust law in place, a court decision in a patent case led to an antitrust-like agreement between AT&T and Western Union to split control over voice and data communications, with AT&T taking the former and Western Union taking the latter. During the first decade of the twentieth century, AT&T tried to take over a number of competing equipment manufacturers but was stopped by antitrust law, though it did acquire Western Union in 1909. By 1913, the Justice Department demanded that AT&T divest itself of Western Union in an antitrust action that became known as the Kingsbury Commitment. This agreement again only separated the voice telephony (AT&T) and data (Western Union) businesses, but it also reinforced the notion of telephony as a local monopoly and offered AT&T the promise that antitrust pressure would lessen. The 1921 Willis-Graham Act provided further antitrust immunity for AT&T by permitting it to buy competing companies under regulatory oversight. In 1956 and 1982 antitrust actions, AT&T had to choose between selling equipment to the network or to private parties; in 1956 it chose to stay with the network, but by 1982—with a range of new services possible by technological innovation and the likelihood of another divestiture in sight—it chose private parties. The 1984 divestiture of AT&T was the largest industrial reorganization in history. More recently, an antitrust suit against Microsoft forced that corporation to unbundle its browser from its operating system.

Antitrust challenges have also been directed at other information and communication industries. In 1930, the Supreme Court held that Hollywood film producers were in violation of antitrust law because, at the time, they also owned the theaters in which films were shown. In the early 1980s, the National Association of Broadcasters (NAB) had to abandon its code of conduct because those agreements to restrict certain types of content, widely held to be damaging to society, were deemed violative of antitrust law in support of advertisers' views—but then the Television Improvement Act of 1990 provided the television industry with antitrust exemption in order to develop and disseminate voluntary guidelines to alleviate negative impact of violence in TV material. Antitrust law affected the spread of cable television, and entry of telephone companies into the cable business.

Antitrust law is at the intersection of technological and social structures because it involves the management of infrastructure and/or specific technologies. It is a matter of the information structure because, particularly in the digital environment, distinctions among products and markets are essentially conceptual. Since antitrust depends upon clear definitions of specific industries, markets, and products, it is particularly susceptible to transformations in the nature of the economy that have resulted in the blurring of industry lines, the globalization of markets, and the ability to define and redefine products conceptually.

Important recent trends in antitrust law that have an impact on structure include tensions between antitrust and the First Amendment, treatment of innovation, internationalization, and the use of antitrust remedies as a regulatory tool.

Tensions between antitrust and the First Amendment In the past, assertions of First Amendment rights convinced the Supreme Court to support defendants accused of antitrust violations, though not when the activities under discussion have prevented others from also exercising their civil liberties. However, as the extent of media concentration worsens, there is growing concern over the challenge that oligopolistic media corporations present to the First Amendment rights of society as a whole by decreasing the diversity of voices in public discourse. While the current status of media concentration is the combined result of statutory law and regulatory consideration of the antitrust implications of mergers, many today argue that First Amendment considerations need to play a larger role in decision-making in this area. There have even been free speech concerns about the impact of antitrust law on activities such as the selling of real estate and communications among health professionals.

Exemptions for innovation One argument against antitrust law has been that it prevents the sharing of intellectual property rights and resources necessary to technological innovation. By the early 1980s, this argument gained weight as the United States began to lose ground to Japan in the area of high-speed integrated chips. The National Cooperative Research Act of 1984 (NCRA) stimulated the growth of R&D consortia. Companies in the chip industry argued that not only were they not being allowed to undertake the R&D activities necessary for the next round of innovation, but that the effects of this problem extended beyond its impact on the companies involved, and the industry, to damage the U.S. position internationally, as high-speed chips are so critical to defense. By then, those responsible for evaluating antitrust issues had come to recognize the importance of economies of scale and scope, and to operationalize that in acceptance of horizontal integration when it could legitimately be claimed that such mergers ultimately yielded benefits to consumers. Congress responded to these concerns with the National Cooperative Research Act of 1984, which offered an exemption from antitrust law to research consortia whenever doing so is deemed necessary in order to successfully innovate.

A few consortia were created as a result of this act, but because the legislation clearly distinguishes between R&D and commercial activity, often closely intertwined, some argue it has not gone far enough. In the 1990s, an alternative approach was developed in which research was presented as "precompetitive" and therefore not appropriately the subject of antitrust investigations. Additional arguments in support of this position also were based on a shift in the way in which R&D is perceived. Innovation processes were described as ephemeral rather than permanent; and collaborations among corporations for purposes of innovation as the activities of communities involved in developing a consensus, not competitors. One type of consensus that is achieved in such settings, of course, is in the area of standard-setting.

Replacement of rules with case-by-case determinations Commonly, a number of different types of policy techniques can be used in response to a particular problem; antitrust has become more important in the deregulatory environment. This shift has turned attention to the crafting of remedies as a form of regulation designed for a specific situation rather than rules to be applied to a class of situations. The *U.S. v. Microsoft* (2000) case was an example of a situation in which an enormous amount of energy—including public debate—went into designing an appropriate remedy once it was determined that there had been an antitrust violation.

A variety of approaches has been suggested for choosing from among available remedies. Some would use fairness as a tie-breaker; others suggest that, at the very least, consumers should be left no worse off than they were before. A framework for choosing among remedy could include three steps. First, evaluate a proposed remedy in terms of whether its static efficiency (short-term, holding technology constant) yields a net gain. If it does, evaluate whether its dynamic efficiency (long-term, with technological change) yields a net gain. If that answer is also positive, the third step is to evaluate the remedy in terms of its enforcement costs.

Copyright

Copyright is a matter of social structure because it determines property rights. It thus can make a significant difference in the economic status of producers and/or owners of content. Copyright also affects the social construction of reality by determining who has control over whether particular content enters public discourse and, if it does, the conditions under which it does so.

In an information economy, ideas and information are the most valuable forms of property, the critical drivers of all other economic activity. In addition to increased appreciation for the economic value of intellectual property rights in the digital environment, two other differences in the nature of the practices, products, and institutions involved have changed the world to which copyright applies and the ways in which we think about it. First, while copyright was conceived in an environment in which the image of an author was an individual working on his or her own, today authorship is often the product of a collectivity. Second, in the print environment it was assumed that once a text was put in tangible form it was fixed and that, therefore, modifications of the text would require production of another text—and thus be relatively rare, and traceable. Works in digital form, however, can be both copied and altered so easily—including by the original content producer—that the scale of these activities has significantly increased. For these three reasons, it should not be surprising that copyright is currently a hotly contested area of the law.

The constitutional provision establishing intellectual property rights was immediately translated into statutory law in the Copyright Act of 1790. The law has been revised half a dozen times since and been interpreted by the courts in ways that have significantly refined its operationalization. Participation in various international treaties dealing with copyright has also been important to the development of U.S. law in this area.

Intellectual property rights cannot be asserted in facts, but they can be asserted in other symbols or texts that meet three criteria. The item in question must be an *expression*, must be *original* to the person who expressed it, and must be *reproducible* (expressed in a form that can be copied). Copyright actually involves a bundle of rights that is divisible, meaning that each of the rights can be treated separately. Further, licensing or other types of permission for use of copyrighted material can be limited to certain geographic zones, time periods, or use in very specific contexts. Control over copyright does not carry with it control over the objects in which the copyrighted material is embedded. As a result, libraries can loan out books and video stores can rent out videotapes once those items have been purchased, according to the "first sale" doctrine codified in the 1976 revision of the Copyright Act. Content produced as a "work for hire," under agreed-upon terms with an employer, whether as an employee or independent contractor, is owned by the employer, not the creator. Here are the **Elements of Copyright:**

1. *Display* The right to display a work in public.
2. *Distribution* The right to distribute a work through any distribution channel.
3. *Reproduction* The right to reproduce a work through any medium.
4. *Derivative works* The right to create a derivative work; that is, to create a new work based on an existing work through translation, adaptation, abridgement, or other processing.
5. *Performance* The right to perform a work in public.

Intellectual property rights were included in the Constitution because it was believed that new ideas, whether in texts or inventions, were a positive good for society—and that individuals would be more inclined to create new works if there were a financial incentive for doing so. This was a case, then, of establishing property rights for the individual in order to provide something for society as a whole. As the duration of copyright grew longer, courts were concerned about also making sure that the needs of society were met. Based on a doctrine elucidated by Justice William Story in an 1841 case and codified in the 1976 revision of the Copyright Act, the result was fair use, the legal right to use copyrighted materials without either license or permission, if four criteria are met. Here are the **Criteria for Fair Use of Copyrighted Material,** along with the issues examined by courts to determine whether these criteria have been met:

1. *Purpose* What is the purpose of the use?
a. must be not-for-profit *and*
b. must serve the public good (e.g., education or news) *and*
c. must be productive.
2. *Nature of copyrighted work* What are the characteristics of the copyrighted work for which fair use is being asserted? Most likely to be acceptable if
a. published rather than unpublished;
b. factual rather than fiction;
c. out of print rather than in print; *and*
d. capable of being used by many people as opposed to just once (e.g., a workbook).
3. *Portion of work used* How much of the work is being used? Determinations are
a. quantitative (percentage of the work taken in relation to the whole); *and*
b. qualitative (cannot take the "heart" of a work).
4. *Economic effect* Would the use affect the market value of the work?

Though the life of copyright has been extended, it is not infinite, and some works are never copyrighted at all. Works that are not owned by anyone but, rather, are in the public domain, can be used by anyone for any purpose—including for commercial purposes. Several different types of materials are in the public domain. From the very first legislation dealing with copyright in the United States, the availability of works in the public domain has been a fundamental element of the system. Here are the **Categories of Works in the Public Domain:**

1. *Never copyrighted* Works that have never been copyrighted are in the public domain.
2. *Expired copyright* Works on which the copyright has expired are the public domain.
3. *Voluntary* Creators of content can voluntarily choose to place their materials in the public domain rather than copyrighting them.

4. *Government-funded* Works, the production of which is funded by the government (including public records), are in the public domain unless there are special restrictions on their use.

Ever since the United States signed the Berne Convention—almost one hundred years after other countries first signed the international agreement governing copyright—those asserting copyright in the United States need not take any positive actions in order to have ownership in works once published. In order to protect copyright of either published or unpublished works against alleged infringement in court, however, several steps must be taken. A copyright notice (including the copyright symbol or the word copyright, year, and the copyright holder's name) must be placed in a prominent position on the work. A form must be filed with the Copyright Office, part of the Library of Congress, along with a small fee. Finally, copies of the work must be submitted to the Copyright Office (one copy if unpublished, two if published).

The duration of copyright, the range of types of content that can be copyrighted, and expansion of the notion of work for hire have all been means through which the copyright system has been strengthened in recent years. This trend is also being resisted, through the development of theories regarding an information commons and experimentation with institutional, legal, and economic means of sustaining such a commons. The U.S. approach to intellectual property rights had long diverged from that of the rest of the world, but with the growing importance of this type of property in international trade, the United States is now an active participant in pertinent international agreements. The last trend worth noting in this area is the treatment of alleged copyright infringers in the digital domain as if they are guilty until proven innocent.

Extension of duration The original copyright law, in 1790, established a temporary monopoly for copyright holders of fourteen years and the possibility of further extending that for another fourteen years. In the 1831 revision of the Copyright Act the time limit was extended to twenty-eight years, with the possibility of a fourteen-year extension. The extension was lengthened to twenty-eight years in 1909, and to life of the author plus fifty years in 1976. Congress amended the Copyright Act again in 1992 to make copyright renewal automatic, dramatically curtailing the entry into the public domain of works protected by copyright before 1978. The Sonny Bono Copyright Term Extension Act, passed in 1998, extended protection to life of the author plus seventy years (or ninety years, if the work is owned by a corporation). A generation is considered to be thirty years; under current U.S. copyright law, works can be owned monopolistically for four generations or more. Firms in the information industries take the position that this legal stance is necessary in order for their businesses to be profitable. Many members of the public, however, feel that this contravenes the constitutional intention that the purpose of intellectual property rights is to make new ideas available to all.

Intellectual property rights in software and databases The first time the issue of copyright for an encoded sequence of instructions was raised the technology at hand was the player piano. In 1908, the Supreme Court considered whether the rolls that encoded pieces of music for the piano were not copies of a musical work (and therefore infringing on copyright if they had been produced without permission) but, rather, parts of a machine. In its opinion in *White-Smith Music Publishing v. Apollo*, the Court stated that if such things were to be covered by copyright, Congress would need to explicitly cover them by statutory law. This Congress did, first implicitly in the 1909 revision of the Copyright Act, and then explicitly in the 1976 revision of the act that defined the criterion of fixation to include "any tangible medium of expression, now known or later developed, from which they can be perceived, reproduced, or otherwise communicated, either directly or with the aid of a machine or device."

The question of copyrighting software programs didn't appear until an active market for such works began to develop in the 1960s. The incremental and collective development of programs were problematic from the start; according to copyright law as it stood at the time, registration at the time of the first appearance of a work was required in order to assert property rights. The first attempts to copyright software took place in 1964, and the response of the Copyright Office was to consider such works the equivalent of "how-to" books, copyrightable if the acts of assembling, selecting, arranging, editing, and literary expression that went into the development of a program qualified as original authorship. (The alternative was to consider the conversion of source code to object code a type of information processing not copyrightable.) If this criterion were met, the works would have to meet the other requirements, including inclusion of the copyright notice and submission to the Copyright Office of copies of the program in a language intelligible to humans (e.g., a printout of the program).

With this decision, the copyright of computer programs became generally accepted. The Copyright Act of 1976 made this option more explicit by including a reference to works in numerical symbols, regardless of the material objects in which they are embedded (including disks or punchcards). It also qualified the term "literary" by saying that the word does not connote any criterion of literary merit or qualitative value, but also refers to catalogs, reference works, and compilations of data; software programs and computer databases were specifically mentioned. There were still concerns about the possibility of misuse of computer programs, so Congress asked the National Commission on New Technological Uses of Copyrighted Works (CONTU)—first established by Congress in 1976 to consider guidelines for fair use—to come up with more detailed recommendations; these were then adopted by Congress in an amendment of the Copyright Act in 1980. The Computer Software Rental Amendments Act of 1990 specifically limited the "first sale" provisions of the Copyright Act as applied to software; the consequence is that it is not legal to commercially lend software in the way that it *is* legal to commercially lend books or videotapes.

The accumulated result of all of these decisions is that software sales are accompanied by "shrinkwrap" licenses to which one agrees by the act of putting the software on a computer, and those licenses can be as restrictive as the software producer desires regarding the number of machines on which the software can be placed, the uses to which it can be put, and the ways in which it can be modified.

The question of whether the presentation of facts could be copyrighted first arose in 1918, when the Supreme Court prohibited another news service from publishing as its own news that had been gathered by the Associated Press in *INS v. AP*. Though influential Supreme Court Justices Holmes and Brandeis both warned against the danger of recognizing private property interests in information, the Court's opinion in this case called the news "quasi-property," which the public was free to communicate after it had been published or broadcast by a news organization. News organizations, in turn, could claim copyright only if they explicitly asserted that property right in particular expressions of facts as news.

The specific inclusion of databases in the 1976 act also made clear that databases in any format, whether print or computerized, could be copyrighted, though again only if all of the criteria for copyrightability were met. The limits of this position were tested in a 1991 case involving the compilation of a telephone directory based on information included in another directory. Here, the Supreme Court made clear that a database comprised of information held in another or other databases would be copyrightable only if there had been creativity in the selection and organization of facts, including the contextualization of data with additional information.

Expansion of "work for hire" The doctrine of assigning property rights for content created under work-for-hire agreements has long been a mainstay of copyright law. With increasing appreciation of the economic value of the expression of ideas in the information economy, however, organizations of all kinds are broadening the definition of what they consider to be works for hire. Some corporations are beginning to claim they own all intellectual work products of their employees, whether or not that work is undertaken on company time, whether or not it uses company equipment, and whether or not it pertains at all to the substance of the activities of the corporation. The time when universities permitted individuals to control the patents in discoveries achieved using university research labs is long gone, and many institutions are beginning to assert property rights in the publications, syllabi, and Web sites of their faculty members.

Growing interest in an information commons In response to the aggressive assertion of intellectual property rights in the digital environment, there is a growing movement to reverse the trend. A number of different approaches for doing so are collectively referred to as the "information commons." At one extreme, there are demands that all information should by right be freely available in an information commons. At the other extreme, some nonprofit organizations have developed techniques that make it easier for individuals to use existing copyright law to shape licenses to copyrighted materials in ways they prefer in order to maximize public access. In between come approaches that encourage content producers to voluntarily place their materials in the public domain and recommend amending copyright law in ways that will effectively expand public access to copyrighted materials, such as permitting rights to be held collectively by communities rather than by individuals.

Content and software code are two very different areas in which a commons movement is growing. Because of the differences in how each of these is created and used, diverse practices are appearing. Following is a brief description of each approach to a content commons currently in play. It includes fair use and the public domain as commons-type practices already in use before the commons movement began, as well as an introduction to open source software, so that you can compare what each set of practices yields. **Legal Approaches to an Information Commons:**

1. *Fair use* The use of copyrighted material without permission or license, if the criteria of serving the public good and not damaging the market are met.
2. *Public domain* Material is in the public domain when it has never been copyrighted, the copyright has expired, the material is voluntarily contributed to the public domain, or the government has produced the information.
3. *Creative commons* The nonprofit organization Creative Commons offers a license that does two things: publicizes the availability of copyrighted works for use by members of the public, and makes it easy for content producers to specify the conditions under which such use can take place; areas in which conditions can be specified include attribution, commercial use, and modification of the work.
4. *Founders' copyright* Creative Commons will purchase copyrights for $1.00 and release the material to the public domain after fourteen years (unless the author prefers an extension of another fourteen years—the original 1790 copyright term), thus making it easier for copyright holders to control their work for only a limited period before releasing it to the public.
5. *Copyleft* A license used to voluntarily release software to the public with the requirement that any reuse or redistribution of the information similarly be distributed freely to the public; also known as a General Public License (GPL).
6. *Open source* An open source software license makes it possible for anyone to modify and reuse source code, but requires the commitment that works produced on the basis of such code also be freely available to others.
7. *Communal ownership* The principle that intellectual property rights may be communally or collectively held, currently operationalized via contract law but under discussion for inclusion in intellectual property rights law.
8. *Pure commons* The position that all information should always be freely available for anyone for any purpose.

It is worth providing a little more detail on the open source software license as it is being promoted by the Open Source Organization and widely used, because it demonstrates the range of concerns taken into account as well as the thoroughness with which the commons approach is being thought through. Those involved in writing open source software—Linux is the prototypical example of an open source operating system upon which a great many user-oriented software programs have been based—agree to make their source code freely available to others for modification and use. Any software developed using open source code can be sold or given away as part of a bundle of software containing programs from several different sources, and any distribution of software must include free or low-cost availability of source code as well as the program in compiled form.

The terms of the open source license cannot be restricted to use of a program in a particular software product, and any other software included in a bundle that includes open source programs may not be restricted in any way. Modification of any open source programs and any derivative works created that are open source–based must also be distributable under the same terms as the original source code. Authors of code may protect their own reputations by separating their programs and their source code at the time of distribution and requiring any modification of programs to use different names. Distribution and use of open source software cannot discriminate against any individuals or groups, or against uses for any particular purposes (such as running a business or conducting genetic research). Finally, license terms cannot be dependent on a specific technology or interface.

There are arguments against treating everything as part of an information commons. Pamela Samuelson, an expert on intellectual property rights and software, points out that placing materials in the public domain is not always the most effective way of maximizing their utility to society, an argument that has been applied by others to the protection of the environment and wildlife. Corporations in the business of content production point out that their firms would not be viable without intellectual property rights, to the ultimate detriment of artists and audiences alike. (In fact, the music industry did show a decline in sales during the period in which music was freely available online, although for many years it did not—and it could be argued that the industry's profits are in any event unreasonably high.)

Some of the new approaches have been quite effective. The open source software movement, for example, counts millions of programmers among its users and adherents, and the number of corporations and governments using open source software is steadily growing. The United

Nations Conference on Trade and Development (UNCTAD) has announced its support of open source software as a means of bridging the global digital divide. In this area of the law, the fact that digital technologies share features with other meta-technologies such as biotechnology is having an impact. One of the suggestions for expanding the range of types of information freely available in an information commons, collective ownership of intellectual property rights, has developed in response to the grab for genetic information driven by biotechnology. As pharmaceutical and chemical companies have come to appreciate the value of plant and animal DNA for the development of commercial products, they have turned to the aggressive collection of genetic information from the most biodiverse regions of the world, all in developing countries. Using a seemingly self-contradictory argument, these corporations claim that genetic information they acquire belongs to a global information commons—but also that it is legitimate, once that information is processed into a product of commercial value, to sell the goods made from those resources back to the source societies at prices so high that the medicines are not affordable. A number of techniques have developed since the early 1980s in response, mostly predicated on the assumption that a government unit can contract for use of genetic information within its territory on behalf of the community that lives there. The idea of incorporating communal ownership of intellectual property rights into the law rather than dealing with it on a case-by-case basis is under discussion. Though inspired by developments in the treatment of genetic information, these trends in intellectual property rights law would also apply to creative content produced collectively, whether traditional bodies of knowledge such as stories and rituals or the work produced by contemporary artists working collectively.

Guilty until proven innocent As in other areas of U.S. law, up until 1998 someone accused of infringing upon the copyright of another was assumed innocent until proven guilty by a court of law. Occasionally, court injunctions were issued to stop distribution of disputed material in egregious cases with significant impact on the value of the material involved until a court had resolved the matter. In general, however, disputes arose over one-time publication or use of material, and responses to the matter occurred through the normal procedures of adjudication of legal disputes. With the passage of the Digital Millennium Copyright Act of 1998, this assumption was overthrown. Under this act, organizations that enable Internet access—ISPs, or ISP-like institutions such as universities—are legally liable for copyright infringement if they continue to allow someone accused of infringement by a copyright holder to continue to use the Internet through their infrastructure. This means that the mere charge that someone has abused copyright, whether or not true, can be enough to bar someone from Internet access through their accustomed means rather than requiring the conclusion of the full legal process before any justifiable punishment is levied.

Patents

The patent system, which provides property rights in the expression of ideas in objects or processes, is also constitutionally based and first was operationalized in statutory law in 1790. During the late eighteenth century, the industrial revolution was flourishing and it was clear that the patent system had been important to the British economy. A pro-patent attitude prevailed in the United States until the late nineteenth and early twentieth century, when patents began to be seen as important tools of the monopolistic corporations that were the target of then-new antitrust law. Waves of skepticism reappeared until the 1980s, when the desire for technological innovation—particularly in the information and communication industries—overcame many remaining concerns, although antitrust law and patent law continue to affect each other.

The definition of what is patentable in the United States has remained almost unchanged since the late eighteenth century: "any new and useful art, machine, manufacture or composition of matter and any new and useful improvement on any art, machine, manufacture or composition of matter." The need to clarify what it means for an invention to be "new," and to be "useful," led to further regulation in the area of patents over time. With changes in the law, the level of specificity required to describe an invention in a patent also went up—so much so that that some commentators describe the history of patent law as the history of the development of the narrative capacity to describe material objects.

In order for an invention or process to be considered patentable, it must fall into one of the categories described as patentable in statutory law, and it must be new, useful, and nonobvious. While the United States has one of the most inclusive patent systems in the world, examples of inventions that would not be patentable because they are not mentioned in statutory language include data structures or programs per se (as opposed to programs used in the manufacture or use of a specific machine or process), compilations or arrangements of nonfunctional information or storage units in which such compilations are encoded, and natural phenomena such as electricity and magnetism. All of these exceptions are considered abstract ideas or laws of nature. There are two types of patents. Utility patents, which have a duration of twenty years from date of filing, apply to tools, devices, machines, computer programs, processes, formulae, and business methods. Design patents, which have a duration of fourteen years from the date they are granted, apply to the shapes of articles, dolls, characters, and related objects, and protect only the appearance of an item.

The expansion of the patent system, the interchangeability of copyright and patent in the digital environment, and the ability to patent methods of doing business are trends worth noting for their impact on social structure. Major changes to the patent system are under consideration at the time of this writing.

Expansion of the scope of patent The scope of the patent system has expanded over the course of the twentieth century to include the assertion of property rights in living organisms as well as the patenting of software and modes of doing business.

Though rose growers started protections for the breeds they perfected in the nineteenth century, the notion of extending intellectual property rights to living organisms was long considered morally reprehensible. However, by the close of World War I, biotechnology had appeared as a form of informational meta-technology that produced commercially valuable products through manipulation of genetic material. With economic value came increased pressure on the patent system, and in 1930 the Plant Patent Act extended patent protection to asexually reproduced plants. In 1954, amendments to this act extended its provisions to cultivated sports (crosses between species), mutants, hybrids, and newly found seedlings. The Supreme Court upheld the patentability of a genetically modified bacterium in 1980, and the first transgenic species was patented in the late 1980s (the "oncomouse"). The requirement of demonstrating nonobviousness in the filing of biotechnology-related patents was removed in 1995. Today corporations own the rights to entire species of basic grain crops, and physicians can take out patents on processes discovered through working with materials removed from patients' bodies.

For more than a hundred years, the United States (like other countries) had also taken the position that business methods could not be patented. Inventors had over the years applied for patents for accounting techniques and methods for operating specific types of business, but had always been turned down by either the courts or the patent office. By 1908, patent attorneys were advising their clients not to even try. The arguments used to reject such applications were that such patents could not be competently examined by patent offices; that the most relevant "prior art" might well not be available in an organized or readily accessible form; and that the scope, content, and inventor of such an "invention" could be difficult to identify. These arguments were so well known that they were referred to as the "business methods exception" from patentability.

Computer programs for business methods faced the additional problem that up until 1981, courts had also generally struck down patents on any type of software, because such material was deemed, like mathematics and the laws of nature, inherently unpatentable. In *Diamond v. Diehr* in 1981, however, the Supreme Court reversed its position, declaring that that just because an invention uses software, it is not necessarily unpatentable. In 1998, the court decision in *State Street Bank v. Signature* held that a computerized method for transferring assets between a number of mutual funds pooled together for tax purposes should be treated as a patentable invention if the other requirements for patentability—the invention must be new, and nonobvious—were met.

As with other software patents, there are many questions about the quality of the examination process and whether it is possible to accurately determine the nature of prior art, if any. From the perspective of legal interventions into social structure, however, the explosion of patents on business methods is even more disturbing. Analysts claim that this change has taken place because the Patent and Trademark Office (PTO) has been captured by the patent community, and that this change in treatment of applications for patents for business methods runs counter to other national policies in support of electronic commerce.

Patents on business methods are at the heart of many Internet-based forms of commerce, so there has been a rush to stake out patents of this type. Meanwhile the growth in the number of business methods and other software patents has pushed the patent system itself into crisis. Such familiar techniques for e-commerce as one-click shopping, in which one enters detailed personal information into a form only once with a vendor with whom there is repeat business, are now patented. Another result is inefficiency in the world of software, because firms must keep reinventing the wheel. Business patents are process patents, like chemical formulae, because they are not physical objects. (Doctrine in *Diamond v. Chakrabarty* [1980] was that "anything under the sun made by man" may be patented.) The United States leads the world in patenting business methods.

Interchangeability of patent and copyright for software The question of the patentability of software first arose in 1966, when uncertainty regarding the legality of extending property rights to computer programs was compounded by the lack of a classification technique and the professional skills to evaluate applications for software patents—and the existence of copyright as a means of asserting property rights in software—to support the position to continue to deny such patent applications.

For the next few decades, there was a great deal of conflict between decision-makers operating in different venues over the question of whether programs should be patentable. Between 1969 and 1972, the appeals court to which those denied patent claims turned began to reverse the patent examiners and compel the issuance of computer program patents. In 1972, however, the Supreme Court—at the behest of the Patent and Trademark Office—denied the patenting of a computer program that was basically algorithmic in nature in the case of *Gottschalk v. Benson*. The appeals court responded with hostility and insistently interpreted *Benson* as narrowly as possible, with the result that very few software patents were issued between 1972 and 1981. During this period, the World Intellectual Property Organization (WIPO) proposed a new category of intellectual property rights specifically for computer programs, many European countries followed the United States lead in denying patents to software, and vendors tried to circumvent the issue by hard-wiring processes into computer parts and patenting the machines themselves instead.

This outcome was extremely costly to the user, for it meant that the market was filled with computers devoted to specialized tasks rather than general-purpose machines capable of serving a wide range of needs through the addition of different types of software. Finally, in 1981, the Supreme Court decision in *Diamond v. Diehr* opened the door to patenting of software. Over the next few years, other court cases further refined concepts to be used in determining the patentability of specific software programs, and a private consulting firm with a stake in the patenting of its customers' software, EDS, developed a software classification scheme for use by the PTO.

It is still the case that not all software programs are necessarily patentable. However, a circuit court decision in 1994, *In re Appalat*, offered a conceptual transition between abstract ideas and concrete machines that resolved much of the remaining ambiguity. Algorithms as mathematical expressions are nothing more than unpatentable abstract ideas, but their use to perform functions on a general-purpose computer turns that machine into a special-purpose computer. Thus the combination of the program and its use in a general-purpose computer becomes patentable.

Less knowledge is better knowledge The subject of a patent application will not succeed on the criterion of "newness" if there is "prior art"—earlier patents for part or all of the invention or process for which a new patent is sought. In order to demonstrate newness, therefore, analyses of patent database searches are part of the argument put forward in a patent application. In the area of software, however, there is great confusion. Programs are complex and often change, while the practice of "reuse" of portions of programs is growing. Challenges to successful products are growing from competitor organizations that claim prior art, but determination of the validity of these claims is extremely complex and often contested. Patent Office classification schemes may or may not help in the course of searching for prior art for a particular program. As it is impossible to know whether a search has in fact yielded all pertinent prior art, some applicants for software patents now skip this step, with the position that doing so allows them to say accurately that they have no knowledge of prior art.

Association

The constitutional protection for the right to assemble was originally interpreted to refer to what we would now describe as physical and synchronous meetings—that is, people getting together at the same time in the same place, face-to-face. Efforts to identify members of groups that espoused unpopular political ideas for retaliation, however, brought the importance of asynchronous and mediated assembly, or association, to attention. Association via membership in an organization is considered political assembly because it often involves communication with others, and concerted action, on public issues. Now that the tools of network analysis, and the data upon which to exercise those tools, are widely available, networked social relations are also being treated as association for legal purposes.

Guilt by association The constitutional right to association has been curtailed by the PATRIOT Act and other legal changes since 9/11.

Previously, individuals were held responsible only for their own actions. Even if one were involved with a group that included others who took part in illegal activities, association with the group and promotion of its ideas were protected as constitutional rights. (The attacks upon Communists during the 1950s period of McCarthyism were social and political, not legally based—even then it was legal to be a member of the Communist Party. The use of a loyalty oath that disallowed an involvement with Communism or relationships with Communists as a condition of employment was eventually declared unconstitutional.)

Under the provisions of the PATRIOT Act, however, one can be treated as a terrorist not just on the basis of one's own actions, but also because one is associated with a group any member of which has been involved in activity defined as terrorist—whether or not it is sanctioned by the group and whether or not one is aware of this activity. This expansive definition of terrorism makes it likely that people will become afraid to associate themselves with political groups, thus quelling political speech.

Once any foreign group has been labeled terrorist—or held to be so by the government without any public announcement of the fact—it will be criminal for any U.S. citizen to support the legal, political, or charitable activities of that group. Even the provision of goods that are clearly not "dual use," such as clothing for an orphanage operated by a designated group, would not be legal. As an example of the implications of this facet of the PATRIOT Act, had it been in place a few years ago, it would have been illegal to have provided any support for Nelson Mandela's African National Congress (ANC) in South Africa (the party that ultimately brought about the end to apartheid in that country).

The term "foreign" is not defined. Thus a group based abroad that has branches in the United States with many U.S. citizens as members might qualify as foreign. Judicial review will not adequately protect against abuse because, again, the determination to label any given organization as terrorist is likely to be based on evidence that will be kept secret.

Expansion of the associative network Whether or not it is achievable, and whether or not decisions to surveil or pursue someone would be based on this kind of information, John Ashcroft, when U.S. attorney general, announced that the goal of the databases being created to support the war on terror was to include information about relationships as distant as six degrees of separation. In the terms of network analysis, degrees of separation refer to the number of links mediating an indirect relationship between two people. If actually operationalized, such databases would then mean an individual's associative network would extend to those who had, say, rented the same apartment even if there were five other people who had rented the apartment between the two of you, or sat in the same airplane seat six flights earlier.

Information Policy and Technological Structure

Many decisions regarding technological structures take place within bodies with the responsible of determining technical standards, referring not to the quality of a technology but to the technical specifications to be used. For information and communication technologies, the most important standard-setting bodies are international but largely reflect the positions of the largest manufacturers, often serving as country champions. The politics and economics of standard-setting are enormously important, but discussions of the sources of possible disagreement are often very specific to the technology for which standards being set, and thus standards are not discussed here.

The problem of whether or not, and if so, how, the networks that started with telegraphy and now comprise the global information infrastructure should interconnect is another enduring and important policy problem. The social and political (and economic) goal of universal service is also a matter of ensuring that access to the technological infrastructure is available to all, a question that can involve intervention at several stages of the design process, including standard-setting. The roles of users in the design of technological structures is worth including here because it provides a demonstration of how differently innovation looks when technological structures are also understood to be social structures.

Interconnection

Interconnection is the connection of different information and communication networks with each other so that messages and data can flow between them in a way that is transparent, or unobservable, to the user. The nationalization of the telegraph and telephone networks during World War I provided such a vivid demonstration of the many social, economic, and political benefits of interconnection that this became a fundamental regulatory principle. As telecommunications policy expert Eli Noam notes, interconnection is in essence an extension of common carriage principles to the network level. Indeed, in the Telecommunications Act of 1996, the phrase "universal service" referred to access to a network by individuals, and "universal access" referred to access to a network by other networks.

There are three classical forms of interconnection. In parallel, or cooperative, interconnection, carriers that dominate in one territory link up with carriers dominant in other territories in a partnership that maximizes the use of resources. In vertical interconnection, a carrier with a bottleneck facility at one stage of the transmission chain permits another provider to use that bottleneck in order to provide service, as when a long-distance carrier interconnects with a local exchange carrier. And in horizontal interconnection, a more recent development, competitors for the same markets and customers link up with each other. Many interconnection arrangements today involve elements of all three of these approaches. The integration of different networks by users as they shape their personal or organizational information ecologies should be considered a fourth form of interconnection, though one that has not been the direct subject of policy. Technical standards make interconnection possible.

It is tricky to determine where the boundary lies between mandating or encouraging the level of cooperation needed to serve society, and where organizations work together so closely that they run into antitrust concerns. From an economic perspective, interconnection should increase competition by lowering barriers to access. In practice, it can decrease competition, because the strength of one firm adds to the strength of those with which it interconnects—particularly in a network economy in which cooperation and coordination are as important as direct competition for long-term economic success. The result, ideally, is design solutions that are more "Pareto-efficient"; that is, that maximize the good to the greatest number rather than maximizing the good of one participant at the cost of another. However, interconnection as a policy goal repeatedly runs afoul of intellectual property rights law as well as antitrust law. And interconnection is not always considered a social good: during the early twentieth century, when there was competition in the local telephone market in the United States, for example, socioeconomic elites did not want interconnection because it made it easier for individuals to cross class lines. In the early twenty-first century, the United States is building a separate telecommunications network for communications internal to the government that does *not* interconnect with the rest of the information infrastructure, supposedly for national security reasons.

Trends in information policy dealing with interconnection include a proliferation of techniques, shifting attitudes toward the user as a network, and identity issues for the networks themselves.

From wired to wireless Early in the twentieth century a series of agreements dealing with antitrust and intellectual property rights and the establishment of separate regulatory systems for telephony and broadcasting created a distinction between the wired communications system, used for person-to-person data and voice communications, and the wireless communications system, used for mass media broadcasting. Even during the early years, however, the two types of systems were mixed in a variety of ways: There were contexts in which AT&T used radio waves to transfer signals, specialized uses for wireless communications in certain organizational settings were allowed, and radio waves were also licensed for specific institutional uses such as Muzak in offices and elevators. With the convergence of technologies and deregulation, linkages between the wired and wireless systems became easier, as did the incorporation of additional physical media, such as fiber optics, into a network that had been initially comprised of copper wire. With mobile and cellular telephony, the use of wireless communications even for interpersonal conversations and data transfer is beginning to overtake use of wired lines. Meanwhile the FCC is considering use of the electrical network as an additional carrier of communications signals. One of the most important uses of wireless communication that is quickly growing is community-based wi-fi (short for wireless fidelity), or municipal-level commitments to ensuring that wireless access to the Internet and all of its services is available to anyone at no cost within that community.

Proliferation of techniques The specific techniques used for interconnection differ according to the type of network involved—telephone, cellular mobile, or data networks. Because voice telephony and broadcasting are migrating towards delivery via the Internet, the model for Open System Interconnection (OSI) developed by the International Standards Organization (ISO) is described here. The OSI breaks the tasks involved in network communication into seven different layers, each of which has its own standards and protocols, each of which offers opportunities for or barriers to interconnection, and each of which may separately be the subject of regulation. At the transmission layer, these include the following:

- *Physical layer* The actual physical connection of the end system to the network, and bit-transmission between nodes.
- *Data link layer* The layer involved in data transfer, addressing, and error checking.
- *Network layer* The layer at which setup, maintenance, and termination of connections takes place.

Application layers include the following:

- *Transport layer* At this layer information is transferred between end systems providers, reception is acknowledged, data transmission is corrected, and multiplexing takes place.
- *Session layer* This layer controls individual communication sessions between end users.
- *Presentation layer* At this layer, data is adapted to various presentation and display formats.
- *Application layer* At the application layer, users input data so that it can be passed to the presentation layer, and vice versa.

The range of elements that must be harmonized or standardized in order to achieve interconnection is thus seemingly endless—networks may be joined at the level of wires but still not be effectively interconnected because owners refuse to share addressing information, or addressing information might be shared but filters refuse messages from certain sources. The numerous specific mandates to promote interconnection in the Telecommunications Act of 1996 included the right to resell services acquired at wholesale rates, number portability, access to directory assistance, access to poles and rights of way, access to databases and associated signaling, and even physical collocation, where practical. Interconnection today is becoming ephemeralized; while the earliest forms of interconnection required the physical linking of wires at switching nodes, today it is often accomplished via software or contract instead.

The problem of interconnection is much like that of information sharing for purposes of promoting cooperation and reducing conflict—at the end of the day, it is a matter of will, not quantity or form. For the same reason, interconnection is easier to achieve when there is a definitional consensus about the various elements involved, but can be achieved even without this if there is the will to do so (a matter of importance when dealing with international interconnection issues).

Interconnection and network identity The number of points within a system that are interconnected is proliferating to such a degree that it is becoming increasingly difficult to discern the difference between interconnection and achieving an absolute identity of one system with another. As Internet traffic became and the architecture of the network became more complex, backbone providers found they needed to multiply the number of points at which data is transferred from one backbone to another in order to avoid a backlog and loss of packets. In addition, for truly effective transfer of information from one network to another, network topology and routing tables had to be integrated so that data transit would be seamless. Together, these practices are known as network "peering," accomplished by contract that either establishes a collaborative arrangement (among top-tier backbone providers) or customer-like arrangements (between those who control the network backbone and service providers who must lease access to that backbone). Potentially, two networks could peer at every point with each other, which would make the distinction between them meaningless.

Participatory Design

While the government cannot mandate participatory design, its policies indirectly encourage it in some cases, and respond to such practices in others. The open source movement, involvement of users in large-scale system design processes, and software-driven design processes are all ways in which information infrastructure design is becoming participatory, rather than the product of technical specialists engaged in a top-down process. Both the open source movement and the Internet suggest that top-down, centralized design processes have limits.

Open source Almost all source code for computer programs is tightly held intellectual property, enabling corporations to control the market while forcing users to adapt to a limited range of design choices. In response to these limits, the "open source" movement now makes it possible for users to develop and adapt their own software and to collaboratively develop software for general use. The Linux operating system, first released in 1991, is at the heart of the open source movement. It now claims a base of at least ten million users worldwide that is growing on an exponential trajectory. A number of governments are turning to Linux, for both economic and political reasons, as the main competitor to Linux comes from the U.S.-based Microsoft Windows operating system. The German government just released a manual for making the transition from a Windows- to a Linux-based environment that should make this switch even easier for governments, organizations, and individuals.

User input into design There are two senses in which users are now actively involved in designing the technological structure: through the formation of personal information systems, as discussed in the introduction to this chapter, and as active participants at the point of the design of technologies via their engagement with manufacturers.

For a long time the word "interconnection" also referred to connections between the telecommunications network and customer premises equipment. While AT&T held monopoly-like status, it insisted that only its equipment—rented, not sold to customers—could be connected, because anything else might bring the network down. The inventor of the Carterfone, a device that connected wireless and wired communications networks, was among those told he could not use his device with AT&T lines. Because AT&T itself had a device much like the Carterfone that it did allow customers to use, a complaint was filed with the FCC, which agreed that there was no meaningful difference between the two pieces of equipment other than the fact that AT&T owned one and not the other. In the FCC's 1968 *Carterfone* ruling, it was held that customers could connect any of their own equipment to the network as long as it did not harm the network in any way. This landmark decision opened the way to the series of antitrust measures and deregulatory steps through which AT&T's grip on the market was loosened and more genuine competition was made possible. Allowing customers to attach their own CPE to the network was also an important stimulant to the development of the enhanced services that are now such a familiar part of network use. The multitude of networks internal to organizations, often referred to as "intranets," is today one of the reasons the global information infrastructure is described as a "network of networks." Since the 1960s, then, customers have gone from being completely outside of the network structure, to sources of equipment connected to the network, to networks in themselves.

For a number of years those who design and build very large-scale computer networking systems have recognized that design processes are more successful if the users of these systems are involved as early as possible. It used to be believed that use of a technology in the field for purposes other than that for which it was designed was a diffusion failure; today this is recognized as creative adaptation that itself qualifies as innovation. The same thing is true at the level of organizations, where choosing technologies, and tailoring technological systems to particular uses, is inevitably more productive if the people who will be using these systems in always-local circumstances participate in design. Communities are beginning to experiment with means of providing input into the design of public network processes, through focus groups, hearings, and other means of exploring options and expressing their preferences.

The Internet itself offered a dramatic example of participatory design, up to the point that it became commercialized and much more widely diffused, beginning about 1993. A number of factors—sometimes unintentional or the product of chance, and sometimes deliberate; sometimes put in place for the most short-term and instrumental of purposes, and sometimes the product of long-term vision—came together to make this possible. The Internet story also demonstrates the range of values that can be brought into design processes by different types of stakeholders: the military sought survivability, flexibility, and high performance; academics tried to maximize collegiality, decentralization of authority, and the open exchange of information; and the commercial world sought low cost, simplicity, and commercial appeal.

Software-driven design With the use of software-driven design, in which computer programs autonomously evolve software for specific purposes and evaluate and fix technical problems on their own, it can be said that the infrastructure itself is now participating in the design process. Many of the most promising approaches to development of technology-based intelligence, whether under the rubric of artificial intelligence, artificial life, or electronic software design, now evolve in a bottom-up manner so suggestive of evolution that the phrase "genetic algorithms" is used to describe the mathematics behind such programs, and require little human involvement once an environment is established and a few rules—or, better, capacities—are put in place. Doing so can lead to some surprising design principles; permitting randomness, for example, has turned out to be invaluable in network design, because a machine that is large enough will then contain every network that might ever be required.

Universal Service

Universal service is a design issue at the interface of the technological and social systems, for it involves ensuring that the infrastructure is effectively accessible to the entire population. It affects informational systems, for conditions of access determine who can contribute information to our knowledge stores and what types of information become available to all, and they influence how informational systems are structured. Universal service is a set of policies and practices to ensure that everyone has equal access to use of the telecommunications network. It aims to minimize barriers between socioeconomic and informational classes within the social structure and to ensure that everyone can participate in public debate about public issues. The technological architecture can facilitate or impede provision of universal service. And it is a matter of informational structure, because it affects the kinds of voices that are able to contribute to the communal knowledge base.

From the beginning of the information society, visions of connecting everyone within and across societies have driven those who build and run communications systems. Samuel Morse, inventor of the telegraph, coined the phrase "global village" during his plea in 1838 for congressional funds. The first president of AT&T, Theodore Vail, used the slogan "One system, one policy, and universal service" to promote his company, and the same dream was expressed by David Sarnoff in the early days of television.

Today, complementary social, political, economic, and national security arguments are put forward in support of universal service. Because the value of a network grows as the number of people using the network gets larger, private sector entities do have selfish reasons to make sure that as large a proportion of the population as possible is on a network. Indeed, during the long period when AT&T had a monopoly-like presence, it subsidized rural telephony even though reaching those customers was very costly. In today's environment, universal service is increasingly critical for full participation in the economy as well as in social, cultural, and political processes. The U.S. government has even said it is moving towards the provision of government services solely through the Internet.

There are also arguments against promotion of universal service through government policy. There is some question as to the actual universality of demand; the concept of "clubs" has been introduced to describe infrastructural collaborations among users with unusually large demand for capacity and speed (such as among research centers that exchange scientific data). Providers insist that fulfilling universal service obligations slows down innovation by absorbing resources. Some claim that there is no universal service issue at all, but merely bottleneck monopolies for local service that would be resolved were the environment to become truly competitive, even at the local level. Others argue against universal service on the grounds of implementation problems. There is certainly the question of who should pay for universal service—service providers, the government, users, or "the market." And there is some skepticism regarding the validity of measuring universality of service by penetration.

Trends in information policy for universal service include a raising of the definitional bar, the realization that information and technology literacy are required in order for universal service to be meaningful, a blurring of the line between access to infrastructure and access to content, and questions about whether it is appropriate to insist that everyone be connected to the Internet.

A raising of the bar Universal service joins concepts such as equal access to education and equal opportunity in the job market in being easier to agree upon in the abstract than in the particulars. Even in the single-service environment of the telephone, access involved multiple factors, such as geographic penetration and cost. In today's multiple-service environment, available services range from very fast data transfer, practicably of use only to those who must exchange large amounts of data for research purposes, to email and Web-surfing functions necessary for everyone who wants to communicate, engage in commerce, and access government functions and educational materials via the Internet. (Just how fast: "very fast" is, of course, keeps changing in response to continual technological innovation. And the population that would like access to the fastest network services available will expand as entertainment uses—such as Web-based film, television, and interactive gaming—continue to grow.) Those with any sophistication regarding the technical nature of the information infrastructure agree that defining the bundle of features to be included in universal service at the maximum of contemporary technological potential is inappropriate because in a majority of cases there is no need, the cutting edge is constantly moving, and it may not be logistically or financially possible to meet that goal as defined at any single point in time. The definitional problem thus involves determining a floor of functions that should be universally available within the context of constantly shifting functionality.

Eli Noam, noting that government intervention may be required in order to achieve universal service both when a new technology is first launched and in order to reach the last few users after it has been widely diffused, identifies two criteria that can be used to make that determination. The criterion of neutrality requires that universal service be neutral across technologies, companies, applications, content, geography, structural matters, and jurisdictions. The criterion of friendliness should be applied to how a policy is experienced, how easily it is integrated into the existing regulatory and technological infrastructures, its impact on productivity, and the ease with which funds to support universal service can be collected. Together these yield several factors to be examined in evaluating whether a given service already in existence should be universally available: Has the service reached, through its own self-sustained growth in the market, the private optimum beyond which further growth will not occur on its own? Are there still net benefits to be gained from further growth? Are there enough people excluded from the particular service to generate a political opening for extending the definition of universal service to include that feature? For services newly made available, these questions would be a bit different: Does this service enable social processes, whether economic, educational, or political, considered to be in the public good? Is it logistically and economically feasible to make this service universally available? Would including this service in the bundle of features included in universal service place other additional requirements upon the network?

These questions became the foundation for the approach to determining what is and is not to be included in requirements for universal service in the Telecommunications Act of 1996. With some adaptation, these are the current federal **Criteria for Universal Service:**

1. *Value to society* Does the service involve education, public health, or public safety?
2. *"Natural" diffusion* Has the service been voluntarily subscribed to by a substantial majority of residential customers?
3. *Achievability* Is the service available via public telecommunications networks, so that it is logistically and economically feasible to make the service universally available?
4. *Public interest* Is provision of this service consistent with the public interest, convenience, and necessity?

Policy goals in the Telecommunications Act also include the provision of services of high quality at affordable rates; geographic equity; contributions by all telecommunications providers to the support of universal service; and provision of service to all libraries, schools, and medical institutions.

Information literacy and universal service Because technological and social structures are intertwined, the effort to achieve universal service in an intelligent network environment raises the question: What must people know in order to make meaningful use of the Internet and other digital services? Physical and economic access are meaningless if one does not know how to use the technologies involved, or is not comfortable with them. Literacy in the classical sense of being able to read and write has long been a goal of U.S. information policy. Under various rubrics—information literacy, technology literacy, and media literacy—this concept is currently being expanded to include familiarity with technology and knowledge of how to search for and use information. From this perspective, support for incorporation of the use of technologies in K–12 and higher education curricula, ensuring Internet access in all schools, and development of specific courses in information and technology literacy should all be considered facets of the drive toward effective universal service.

There is disagreement, however, about precisely how to define technological or information literacy. Lists of specific competencies run the danger of obsolescing quickly and do not necessarily prepare individuals to take up new applications when they come along. They can differ significantly in their levels of relative ambition, and in the kinds of skills they emphasize. One way of thinking about information literacy is "functional," in analogy with the definition of "functional literacy" as the ability to carry out certain activities that are necessary as part of daily life. Approached from this perspective, information literacy can be defined as the ability to carry out such functions as the ability to locate and use information as needed to participate in political activity, become educated, perform one's job, and manage financial affairs. A second approach to information literacy focuses on specific skills, such as the abilities to retrieve, evaluate, organize, manipulate, and present information. A third approach is cognitive in orientation, emphasizing the understanding of connectivity (how is information transferred, who sees it while I am transferring it, and how do I establish levels of trust?), basic logical operations and data structures, the functions of generic tools such as correction tools and search engines, and the ability to master various types of interfaces. The U.S. Department of Education is currently evaluating a draft report on establishment of information literacy standards for the postsecondary level.

Merging access to infrastructure and access to content Universal service obligations regarding content have historically been discussed in a number of different contexts, including the right to receive information, access to governmental information, public service broadcasting, and the public education system. In the Internet environment, access to the infrastructure is increasingly understood to be access to information because so much information is becoming available digitally and because much of that information is available *only* online.

The federal government is among those who have put significant funds into the development of digital libraries, promoting the digitization of print materials so that they can be made electronically available as well as development of the institutional, economic, and legal structures necessary to make the sharing of materials in this way practicable. While such libraries have gone an extraordinary distance toward minimizing barriers to access to information by those who are geographically remote or institutionally peripheral, in most cases one must still be a part of a specific institutional community in order to access these libraries. At the same time, those same institutions are abandoning print resources that had also historically been available to the general public—at least for on-site reading—as resources are moved to electronic formats. The commons movement, discussed further later in this chapter, encourages voluntary submission of information to the public domain and lobbies for changes to the intellectual property rights system to maximize public access to information, and promotes universal access to information that is not as sensitive to community or institutional relationships.

Achieving universal access to information does have implications for the technological design of the information infrastructure, such as ensuring that directory or navigation systems aren't limited to those offered by a single service provider (e.g., Microsoft) and protections for privacy and from theft of services. The U.S. Telecommunications Act of 1996 mentions both information services and telecommunications, though the universal service obligations are generally understood to apply only to telecommunications services. More might be made of the constitutional underpinnings of the right to receive information for this purpose.

Universal access versus mandated connection While we are accustomed to thinking of universal service as a social and political good, it may not be experienced as such by everyone. Research has shown that at every economic level, about 2 percent of the population chooses not to have a telephone in the home, so access is not a matter only of cost relative to one's budget. There can be very good reasons for preferring not to be on the Internet, including protection of personal privacy, ensuring a filter on types of information encountered, and a preference for other types of activities. Before the government requires everyone to be on the Internet in order to operate financially, to participate in government, and to receive government services, there should be general public debate over the desirability of a forced connection to the network.

Information Policy and Informational Structure

Of the types of structure discussed in this chapter, we are least accustomed to thinking about informational structure. Access to government information is one of the most important information policy issues that both shapes and is affected by informational structures, particularly in the course of classification. The government plays a large role in determining just how accounting systems are used, including how to structure and analyze the data they report. Metadata—the effort to develop a way of labeling data itself—provides an example of the development of new information structures that is particularly interesting because we can watch this effort in action from the start, because it is inherently an international rather than national endeavor, and because of the extent to which development of metadata is participatory. Examples of information policy issues that affect informational structure for which there is no room to discuss here include constraints that may be placed upon Web browsers, the various legal mandates and constraints upon making scientific and technical information available, the extent to which government resources are committed to the development of the semantic Web, and government efforts to diffuse U.S.-based information architectures globally.

Access to Government Information

While access to formal decisions of Congress is mandated by the Constitution, it was only with passage of the Freedom of Information Act in 1974 that citizens gained statutory access to information held by federal agencies (created by congressional statute but part of the executive branch of government) before that information effectively reached archival status. Agency records that must be produced in response to a request are those that have been created by and are in the possession of the agency; records can be in any form.

Under the act as originally passed, no explanation of why the information is sought need be provided, but requests must be specific. Material exempted from access under the FOIA include national defense and foreign policy secrets, internal agency personnel rules and practices, information specifically exempted by other statutes, trade secrets and commercial or financial information obtained in confidence, internal agency memos and policy discussions, personal information, law enforcement investigative information, federally regulated financial institutions, and (demonstrating the power of lobbyists) oil and gas well data of private companies. Use of the exemptions is discretionary, but if an exemption is used, all other information requested must be released and the agency must cite the exemption used. The withholding of information can be challenged both within the agency and in court; if a case went to court, the agency had to demonstrate the harm that might take place were the information released. Historically, contesting such refusals has been quite successful in gaining access to additional information, even if not all of the information originally requested was released. The Federal Advisory Committee Act (1972) provides similar kinds of access to information about advisory committees through which government agencies obtain advice from private individuals.

Information policy trends in the area of access to government information worth noting include the classification of information, the impact of technological innovation on access to information, and the dramatic diminution of the amount of information available in the Homeland Security environment that has developed since 9/11.

Classification Information that has been classified because of its importance to national security is exempt from public access. How much information is classified, how many people have access to that information, and the various categories of classification change, often from administration to administration. President Clinton declassified large amounts of material that has enabled historians to unravel critical events such as the Cuban missile crisis of 1962 and efforts to plot a coup in Vietnam during the same decade. Under President George W. Bush, classification policy has gone the other way. Not only is more information becoming classified, but information that was declassified under Clinton is actually being reclassified under President Bush. The Bush approach also makes it possible to classify compilations of unclassified information if the act of compilation reveals relationships between data not otherwise visible. The Bush scheme uses a three-tier categorization, in which "top-secret" information is that which could cause grave damage to national security that the classifying authority could identify, "secret" information could cause serious damage, and "confidential" information could cause damage. Among the categories of information that can be so classified are scientific, technological, or economic matters. Foreign government information is presumptively classified, while under other presidents decisions were made, as about U.S. government information, on a case-by-case basis. President Bush has also slowed down the declassification for at least three years of millions of documents that should be declassified because they are twenty-five years old.

Impact of technology When government records were first kept in electronic form, there were claims that the Freedom of Information Act applied only to paper records. The Electronic Freedom of Information Act (1996) was required to specifically extend the FOIA to electronic records. This act makes it possible to request data from a database in any form—including data and formats not published or preferred by the government—as long as providing such data is possible given the software in use. Public records must be made available electronically within a year of their creation, agencies and departments must create indexes of records available by computers, and agencies have an affirmative responsibility to publish certain information online, including final opinions, policies, and any requested, nonexempt material that is likely to be requested again. The need to comply with these requirements was a major stimulus to e-government practices of establishing government Web sites for information provision as well as, increasingly, service provision. While the FOIA was experienced only as an unwelcome cost in the pre-electronic environment, Web sites that comply with requirements of the Electronic FOIA are also now being used proactively for public relations purposes.

Access to information since 9/11 A combination of executive orders and attorney general's opinions in three different areas—classified information, rules for implementation of the FOIA, and presidential records—has significantly reduced the amount of information available since 9/11.

The national security exemption under the FOIA has been widened dramatically to include such matters as information about urban infrastructure and environmental affairs, and there is no longer any requirement that an agency demonstrate what harm could ensue were information withheld under this exemption released. Any information about "critical infrastructure" (defined as including water, transportation, energy, and any other industries critical to the national economy) that is provided to the Department of Homeland Security is exempted from the requirement to respond to FOIA requests. Both environmental groups and the GAO have already experienced what these changes in access to information mean: multiple efforts by both to gain access to information about an energy task force that is advising President Bush have failed. Requests for access to presidential records held in the National Archives must be accompanied by statements of need to justify that access; President Bush had attempted to insist that the archive withhold all information from presidential records to which any of the exemptions might apply, but ultimately yielded on that point.

The government is also taking a proactive stance regarding restricting public access to information by withdrawing from the public domain information that had long been available. Information has been removed from Web sites of the U.S. Geological Survey, the Bureau of Transportation Statistics, the Environmental Protection Agency, the National Archives and Records Administration, the Internal Revenue Service, and many others. There are also allegations that reports of research findings that do not support the education plan of President Bush have been removed from Web sites of the Department of Education.

More than 6,500 scientific and technical documents previously available from the National Technical and Information Service (NTIS) have also been withdrawn. Pressure is being put on the scientific community not to publish information that may have national security implications, and prestigious journals such as *Science*, published by the American Association for the Advancement of Science (AAAS) have admitted that national security review has been inserted into the peer review process and that some articles and portions of articles have already been denied publication on these grounds.

Other types of restrictions on access to government information put in place since 9/11 have been discussed in other sections of this book. Table 6.1 puts these together for an overall summary.

Accounting Systems

The earliest bookkeeping records, in ancient Middle Eastern cultures, were already examples of codification practices that made tacit knowledge explicit and shareable; the very first accounts reveal a complex economic system that was already well developed. The first accounting textbook, in the late fifteenth century, introduced double-entry bookkeeping to support the international trade centered in Venice, and this invention made the modern corporation possible. Double-entry bookkeeping is still used today, though additional accounting techniques came into use in the twentieth century.

The history of the development of accounting systems again demonstrates the interactions among innovations in social, technological,

Table 6.1
Restrictions on access to information since 9/11

1. *Broadening of national security exemption* The national security exemption in the Freedom of Information Act has been broadened to include many additional types of information, including environmental data and information about urban infrastructure and energy.

2. *Foreseeable harm* If the refusal to supply information requested under the Freedom of Information Act is challenged, agencies no longer need to provide evidence of the "foreseeable harm" that might result from release of the disputed information.

3. *Reasons for access* Individuals requesting information under the Freedom of Information Act now may be required to provide an explanation of why they need the information, on the basis of which a request may also be denied.

4. *Homeland Security quid pro quo* Data voluntarily provided by municipalities and states to the Homeland Security Department is exempted from access via the Freedom of Information Act. (The government units involved are also protected from prosecution that might have been triggered by any of that information.)

5. *Access to scientific information* The government is now restricting access to scientific information in fields such as biology, chemistry, and environmental studies; the result is censorship of scientific publications, removal of data from Web sites, and restrictions on other means of accessing this information.

6. *Increase in classification* Information already declassified is being reclassified. Information that by law should be declassified because of its age is still being withheld from the public.

7. *Presidential records* Sitting and former presidents can unilaterally decide to close presidential records.

8. *Evidence* Individuals charged with crimes on the basis of evidence gathered via PATRIOT Act–justified surveillance will not have access to that evidence, or to information about it.

and informational systems. In the nineteenth century, changes in military command structures (later transferred to the commercial sector) created a growing dependence on detailed and constant information flows. The first technologies created to deal with these flows were organizational, resulting in elaborate hierarchies of clerical and managerial staff, each level of which was responsible for a particular type of information processing. By the close of the nineteenth century, material technologies to process and distribute information—the typewriter, carbon paper, the cash register, and the adding machine—were also coming into use.

Narrative developments also helped: through the nineteenth century, only the barest of financial records were kept in the format of books; all other business information was in documents written by hand on blank paper. This practice was time-consuming and error-prone, and it created texts in which it was difficult to locate figures of importance. The development of printed forms, later typed and duplicated with carbon paper, made it much easier to standardize and locate information. Numerical tables were another narrative invention, made much easier by the tab function on the typewriter. All of these reduced time spent recording and analyzing information. Forms and tables made such a difference to business practices that they were referred to as "systems," and in the first decades of the twentieth century, they were considered to be signs of modern management practices. The notion of treating mathematical techniques for analyzing data as technologies was already inherent in the nineteenth-century insurance industry practice of referring to such approaches as "combinations" to be undertaken by a series of steps, just as a machine combined materials in a series of steps. Ratio analysis and cost accounting techniques, both now ubiquitously used, are examples of analytical procedures that place demands upon information architectures with structural effect.

Two developments in accounting systems that are intertwined with information policy have had widespread impact through the restructuring of information architectures: reporting requirements for publicly held companies and the recent transformation in the categorization of industries for accounting purposes.

Accounting by publicly held corporations Historically, the most important stimulus for innovation in accounting techniques was the appearance of the stock market and its movement to the center of the economic stage. Once firms start selling their shares on the stock market, they need to produce data for new audiences—investors and potential investors, external auditors, and, ultimately, the Securities and Exchange Commission (SEC). As the number of firms involved in the stock market began to grow, around the turn of the twentieth century, new approaches to accounting developed that became reified by World War II. Because the proportion of economic activity governed by publicly held corporations was so large, these new approaches to accounting became the standard for all organizations. The development of these new approaches to accounting accompanied the transition from family-based management to professional management, the development of higher education curricula in accounting and business, and the separation of accounting functions from other activities of the firm.

Traditionally, data had been collected at the level of the individual worker and the unit in order to provide managers with information necessary to actively monitor cost effectiveness and efficiency. Publicly held firms, however, needed firm-level data comprehensible to outsiders. Instead of being oriented to the specifics of the firm context, information had to be generic, comparable across firms and industries, and manipulable in a number of ways. This practice created such a separation of managers from detailed knowledge of operations on the floor that economic historians have described as "management by remote control." Such a decision-making environment encourages production for its own sake and a focus on the short-term horizon. This problem was exacerbated by demands from regulatory agencies for additional types of data that had to be produced for the government but that weren't necessarily useful for managerial decision-making. Some corporations, as a result, began to develop multiple information systems—one to meet regulatory requirements, and one for decision-making purposes.

With the transition from an industrial to an information economy, the accounting system mandated for use by corporations became even more problematic because it focused on tangible assets rather than on the intangible assets so important in an information society. Banks noticed, for example, that when they committed to loans on the basis of traditional criteria, such as committing funds to those with resources like real estate (e.g., a shopping mall or manufacturing firm) but not to those with no tangible assets (e.g., a software company or data-processing service provider), they were losing money. The concept of "intellectual capital" began to take sway, and by the mid-1980s, many companies began to experiment with alternative accounting systems that were more sensitive to the value of intangible assets and shifting industrial realities of the information economy. Some corporations even started issuing two types of annual reports: one that met regulatory needs, and one that offered what they believed were more valid depictions of the state of corporate affairs.

Industry categorization systems Ultimately governments, too, began to acknowledge the problems raised by trying to apply traditional accounting categorizations of economic activity to the information economy. As mentioned in chapter 6, in the 1930s the U.S. government developed a classification system for all economic activity known as Standard

Industrial Classification (SIC) codes. (The same system was later taken up for global use as International Standard Industrial Classification [ISIC] codes.) The first, and still dominant, approach to defining the information economy used the SIC codes to identify which activities should be considered in the information sector.

This approach was problematic from the start because so many informational activities of economic importance are embedded in relations, not in goods, and because often the decision as to whether an activity should be considered informational was essentially arbitrary. Problems with use of the SIC codes as a basic for accountancy grew as new types of informational goods and services appeared that had no presence in the existing system. Industry lines began to blur in what is still a continuing negotiation regarding control by different types of organizations and professions over various informational activities and resources. The need to completely harmonize accounting systems within the three countries involved in the North American Free Trade Association (NAFTA) (the United States, Canada, and Mexico) provided an additional provocation to the existing system of industrial codes.

While SIC codes did get revised from time to time—most recently in 1987—the government finally acknowledged that a complete overhaul was needed and began this effort in the mid-1990s. In 1997, the OMB adopted the new system, the North American Industry Classification Codes (NAICS) for use by the statistical agencies of the government. Earlier approaches to the analysis of industrial activities focused on the worker, the product, or the task (the activity undertaken by a single worker); the SIC codes mixed identification of industries by demand and by product. The NAICS uses a single organizing economic concept: the processes involved in a particular industry. A production-oriented system was first theoretically proposed by Italian economist Roberto Scazzieri in 1993; as operationalized in the NAICS, it results in grouping together economic units that use the same processes or services to distinguish industrial categories.

The system was released before all of its details were worked out. Not surprisingly, distinguishing among industries in the areas of information, communication, and culture was among the last problems to be addressed. During the transition period, the SIC and NAICS codes can be simultaneously used, and translation charts are provided by the government to assist in the change from one system to the other. The U.S. Census Bureau was the first government entity to issue reports using the NAICS, and more agencies are doing so every year. Meanwhile negotiations are underway in the international arena to similarly adapt the ISIC, although proposals currently on the table would do so in ways that diverge from the North American approach. The U.S. government announced in 1998 that it would reconsider and revise the NAICS regularly.

Many industries that deal with information, communication, and culture are described as "service" industries, though that term also includes services such as the hotel and fast food industries. (For this reason, some prefer the phrase "service economy" to information economy, and it was for this reason that the new international arrangement dealing with international information flows is titled the General Agreements on Trade in Services [GATS].) The SIC codes in their last incarnation had 1,004 industries, of which 416 were service-related; of its 10 sectors, 5 were service-related. The NAICS has 1,170 industries, of which 565 are service-based; of its 20 sectors, 16 are service-related. Another difference between the NAICS and the SIC codes is the level of detail—the NAICS uses 6 digits rather than 4, allowing for more precise distinctions at the level of industry subgroups. In the NAICS, the first 5 digits are standardized across countries, while the sixth can be used for detail particular to individual countries.

In its marketing of the NAICS, the U.S. government emphasizes that with this system, it will have accurate data on the information sector for the first time. Among the new information industries included in the NAICS are semiconductor machinery manufacturing; fiber-optic cable manufacturing; reproduction of computer software; manufacture of compact discs; cable networks; satellite communications, paging, cellular and other wireless communications; telecommunication resellers; and telemarketing bureaus. For two examples of the NAICS hierarchy of industries from the information sector, see table 6.2.

Several NAICS sectors fall within the purview of this book, but the defining characteristics of industries that fall within the "Information" sector are revelatory of just how far economic thinking about the information economy has come. This sector includes three types of organizations: those that produce and distribute information and cultural products; those that provide the means of transmitting or distributing these products, as well as data and communications; and those that process data. "Cultural products" are defined as those that directly express attitudes, opinions, ideas, values, and artistic creativity; provide entertainment; or offer information and analysis concerning the past and present.

Table 6.2
Examples of NAICS hierarchy

NAICS level	NAICS code	Description
Sector	**31–33**	**Manufacturing**
Subsector	334	Computer and electronic product manufacturing
Industry Group	3346	Manufacturing and reproduction of magnetic and optical media
Industry	33461	Manufacturing and reproduction of magnetic and optical media
U.S. Industry	334611	Reproduction of software
Sector	**51**	**Information**
Subsector	513	Broadcasting and telecommunications
Industry Group	5133	Telecommunications
Industry	51332	Wireless telecommunications carriers, except satellite
U.S. Industry	513321	Paging

Source: Compiled from U.S. Census Bureau, www.census.gov/epcd/naicsoz/naicodoz.htm.

The government emphasizes that the products of both popular ("low" art forms such as television and rock music) and "high" culture ("fine arts" such as opera and oil paintings) fall into the category of cultural products, and that the category includes both those goods and services that are final products purchased by consumers (primary goods) and those that provide inputs into processes used to produce other final products (secondary goods). It also notes that the traditional sequence of manufacturing and distribution may be reversed for these industries, since material delivered online might be printed out by the user rather than the content producer.

What are described as the characteristics of industries in this sector project almost a desperation regarding retention of property rights in the goods and services involved:

- *Intangibility* These products are not necessarily tangible and are not necessarily linked to specific forms (e.g., a sound recording can be aired on the radio, embedded in multimedia products, or sold as a CD in a store).
- *Indirect transactions* The delivery of these services does not necessarily require direct contact between the supplier and the customer.

- *Symbolic value* The value of these products lies in their informational, educational, cultural, or entertainment content, not in their format.
- *Property rights as production controls* Because these products are intangible, the processes involved in their production and distribution are very different from those of traditional products. Only those possessing rights to these works are authorized to reproduce, alter, improve, and distribute them—irrespective of the technologies involved.
- *Value added by users* Distributors of information and cultural products can easily add value to the products they distribute that may be far greater than the original value of the information. Examples of this used by the Census Bureau include the addition of advertising to broadcast content, and the addition of search tools to mailing lists.

Metadata

Diverse practices in the design of information architectures receive a frame, or grammar, through the use of metadata. Metadata are data about other data—descriptive information used to catalog, describe, identify, and locate informational resources. Metadata have been in existence ever since librarians started cataloguing items included in a library, beginning with handwritten lists of scrolls on a shelf. While the first effort to use computers to index materials in the 1950s was highly controversial because it was believed to require a sensitivity to content beyond what computers could achieve, with the Internet interest in metadata has exploded. Three factors account for this: (1) the proliferation of information makes it more difficult to identify the information being sought ("information overload"); (2) collaboration in the development of digital libraries makes it necessary to develop forms of metadata that can transcend languages, subject matter, and practices; and (3) tools used to identify information need to be interoperable, meaning that they can be used irrespective of the technology involved in locating, accessing, and processing information. Metadata may be placed in records separate from the items described (as in a library catalog), or embedded in records themselves (as in the data printed on the verso of a book's title page or the header of an electronic text).

A number of metadata initiatives are under way. Information scientists from around the world with experience in structuring information for human use and the institutional need to find a way of doing so in the electronic environment, have been participating in development of a metadata grammar called the Dublin Core. Governments, including the U.S. government, have developed their own metadata initiatives. The

World Wide Web Consortium (W3C), a group of institutions that have been active in the design and building of the information infrastructure that carries the information for which architectures are being designed, are engaged in their own effort to develop a metadata grammar for use in the management of digital information. This consortium is linked to a semantically oriented effort, called the "semantic web," led by the person who was played a key role in development of the hypermedia capabilities of the Web, Tim Berners-Lee. Some individuals have their own approaches, such as Pierre Lévy and his "collective intelligence." Trends in the development of metadata for digital information, and in their use in the crafting of other types of information architectures, include international collaboration, the enabling and encouragement of participatory information architecture design, and the development of connections among metadata known as "ontologies."

International collaboration The Dublin Core Metadata Initiative is a collaborative global effort to develop metadata for electronic information resources. The Dublin Core has produced a simple but effective language for describing networked resources. The standard includes two forms: the Simple Dublin Core includes fifteen elements and the Qualified Dublin Core includes a sixteenth (audience) as well as a set of refinements called "qualifiers" that elaborate upon the semantics of the elements in a way that can enhance discovery. Put another way, the Dublin Core is a simple language that can express basic concepts but not complex relationships, using elements (nouns) and qualifiers (adjectives).

Several principles were used to design the Dublin Core. According to the "one-to-one" principle, metadata describe a particular manifestation of a resource as opposed to assuming that different manifestations stand in for one another. Thus while a digital image of the Mona Lisa is related to the original oil painting, it is not the same thing; the relationship between the two is part of the metadata description, which can help the user determine whether he or she can rely upon the digital image or needs to go to the Louvre to see the original. The "dumb down" principle identifies the ability to successfully use unqualified elements even though some specificity is lost in doing so. The principle of "appropriate values" emphasizes that while best practice for a particular element or qualifier may vary by context, someone implementing the Dublin Core should assume a wide variety of contexts that include both machines and humans as users of the metadata.

The goals of the Dublin Core include simplicity of creation and maintenance, commonly understood semantics, international scope, and extensibility (the ability to add metadata sets for particular needs, types of resources, and or communities of use). The process through which the Dublin Core has been developed has striven to be consensual; international; neutral regarding purposes, business models, and technologies; and interdisciplinary.

There are three categories of metadata in the Dublin Core: elements that refer to content (coverage, description, type, relation, source, subject, title, and audience), aspects of intellectual property rights (contributor, creator, publisher, and rights), and instantiation (date, format, identifier, and language). It is understood that some information may appear to belong in more than one metadata element, so that while normally there will be a clear choice, in some cases judgment will be required to assign elements. The **Elements of Metadata** include the following:

1. *Title* The name given to a resource, often formal.
2. *Subject* The topic of the content, usually in the form of keywords or phrases.
3. *Description* A description of resource content that may include an abstract, table of contents, narrative account of the content, or graphical representation.
4. *Type* The nature or genre of content, generally drawn from a restricted vocabulary (e.g., image, sound, or text).
5. *Source* A resource from which present resource is derived, generally in the terms of a formal identification system such as library call numbers.
6. *Relation* At least one reference to a related resource (e.g., a collection of related items, or a version of something).
7. *Coverage* The extent or scope of the content, typically including geographic location, temporal duration, and jurisdiction.
8. *Creator* The entity responsible for producing the content of the resource, whether an individual, organization, or service.
9. *Publisher* The entity responsible for making the resource available, whether an individual, organization, or service.
10. *Contributor* The entity responsible for making contributions to the content of a resource, whether an individual, organization, or service.
11. *Rights* Information about intellectual property rights held in and over the resource and entity responsible for rights management.

12. *Date* A date associated with the life cycle of a resource, typically when it was created or made available.
13. *Format* The physical or digital manifestation of the resource; if physical, this would include medium and dimensions (e.g., size and duration) and if digital, this would include software, hardware, or other equipment used to display or operate the resource.
14. *Identifier* An unambiguous reference to the resource within a given context, such as the Uniform Resource Locator (URL, for a Web site) or ISBN (International Standard Book Number, for a book).
15. *Language* The language of the intellectual content of the resource.
16. *Audience* The class of entity for whom the resource is intended or useful, as determined by the creator, the publisher, or a third party (e.g., elementary school students, or deaf adults).

The Dublin Core is the product of an international collaboration. The U.S. government participated directly in the development of this information architecture through the involvement of the Library of Congress and the National Science Foundation (NSF), and indirectly through the involvement of units funded by the U.S. government such as the National Center for Supercomputing Applications (NCSA) at the University of Illinois-Urbana, the Coalition for Networked Information (CNI, representing several organizations involved in higher education), and the Online Computer Library Center (OCLC, a non-profit organization devoted to bibliographic support of libraries worldwide).

The U.S. Government Information Locator Service (GILS) provides a means of locating publicly accessible resources held in a decentralized collection of agency-based information, using international standards. Its development was first mandated in 1994, it was made statutory law in the Paperwork Reduction Act of 1996, and it was operationalized in OMB Bulletin 95-01. This system is an early example of the use of metadata, but a 1997 analysis found its use and application spotty, coverage uneven, accuracy doubtful, and use across agencies inconsistent. The GILS system differs from the Dublin Core in its distinction between controlled and uncontrolled subject terms and inclusion of items such as database coordinates that are meaningless to users.

Agencies within the U.S. government are now turning to the Dublin Core for new records added to databases, and software has become available to make sure that databases that include information input via two different metadata schemes are usable within a common frame. "Crosswalks" provide verbal descriptions of the relationships between elements in different schema.

Participatory design By using these metadata grammars, many different types of information architectures may be constructed for particular purposes—with the advantage that they will be comprehensible to each other and translatable into common terms. In the past, professional librarians were responsible for designing information architectures—even for well-developed disciplines such as chemistry or electrical engineering; today, participants in various epistemic communities can establish their own information architectures simply through the practices of daily use.

Ontologies Metadata rely upon the taxonomies of information architectures, but taxonomies can be insufficient for work that is interdisciplinary (and thus draws upon multiple taxonomies), deals with emergent knowledge subjects, necessarily involves changes in response to flows, and/or yields data intended to be available in future for reuse by researchers working on a types of questions quite different from those which generated the information. Thus, after engaging with the development of taxonomies used by statistical systems, and metadata used by those computerizing multiple taxonomies for wide use, the U.S. government is now supporting efforts to develop what are being called ontologies that will facilitate interoperability among computing systems, databases, and software applications at the levels of semantics, concepts, and language use across disciplines and taxonomies. This effort involves researchers in many types of organizations in the public and private sectors, inside the United States and without. The government's involvement takes place via support for research on ontology development through DARPA and, because success with ontologies involves computing standards as well as decisions about information architectures, with the International Standards Organization and the World Wide Web Consortium as well. This work builds upon both the participatory design and metadata trends because many of the techniques by which ontologies are being developed involve bottom-up contributions from those engaged in particular types of research.

Information Policy and New Structural Formations

This look at ways in which information policy affects the structures of social, technological, and informational systems makes clear the extent to which the three interact in mutually constitutive ways. In the digital environment, there are many circumstances in which they are indistinguishable from each other. Yet under legacy law, regulatory interventions are generally designed to affect only one. This gap between reality and legal habits emphasizes the importance of thinking in terms of policy precession, and of incorporating social theory and the results of empirical research on social processes involving the regulatory subject, in legal analyses.

In large part, though not exclusively, as a result of the use of digital meta-technologies, all three types of systems have been characterized by fluidity, and even turbulence, in recent decades. With the change of state, however, the outlines of a new equilibrium have been identified; as will be seen in chapter 8, on change, the structures of the social and technological systems are idealized as more rigid than has historically been the case in the United States. Even so, the desire to promote innovation justifies exemptions from structural regulation—or case-by-case determinations rather than the application of rules—when doing so serves other goals of the government.

The theoretical inability to clearly and consistently distinguish among different types of information processing, first introduced in chapter 2's discussion of the information production chain, continues to present legal problems. Two examples from this chapter: Difficulties determining prior art in patent law highlight the inadequacy of our ability to theorize differences in types of information processing for legal purposes. And the problem of drawing lines between different informational goods and services for accounting purposes has been the most difficult to resolve in the development of the statistical frameworks used for accounting purposes. The same problem underlies, or contributes to, a number of the other issues discussed throughout the book, such as disagreements regarding exactly when a communication constitutes association, or to what extent constitutional protections apply to interactivity per se.

Other points can be taken away from this chapter: (1) Because the technologies that shape social and informational structures are increasingly mathematical in nature, new regulatory tools that are also mathematical in nature are being developed; and (2) the possibilities of participatory design provide new challenges to democratic theory and practice.

The structures explored in this chapter are those internal to a system. The parameters, or the boundaries, of a system are also a part of its structure, and it is to the borders of the informational state that we now turn.

7

Information Policy and Borders

The concept of a "border" first took on geopolitical meaning with the formation of the modern nation-state in the fifteenth century—a couple of hundred years after the word "citizen" appears in reference to the association of an individual with a particular community. There are over three hundred contiguous land borders between states in today's international system, yet the concept of a border has been the least theorized of the four aspects of the state—identity, structure, borders, and change—being explored here. Perhaps the nature of a border seemed self-evident once identity and structure were in place. Perhaps, like so many things, they become visible only once they start to break down, as has happened with geopolitical borders as a result of globalization. Or perhaps borders don't really become an analytical as well as a practical problem until there has been a change of scale, so that both sides are seen simultaneously as internal to a larger system.

Because any system operates at multiple scales, there are actually many different kinds of borders, involving not only relationships with other systems of the same type (here, the state), but also with those that are supra to the type of system (the international and global systems) and infra to the system type (individual identity, as well as internal political divisions). The focus of this chapter is on the borders of the state vis-à-vis other states, but it is precisely the point that, today, doing so inevitably involves cross-scale processes as well. The very possibilities of producing scales that diverge from those that are geopolitically defined, abrogating boundaries, and jumping scales all offer political opportunities in themselves.

Border Theory

Border studies encompasses a literature that focuses on borders as its central subject of analysis rather than as features of other focal analytical subjects. Border theory is very much a twentieth-century development, appearing originally in response to the "problem" of the U.S.-Mexico relationship. Several empirical trends fueled interest—the decline of the former Soviet Union and the consequent need to renegotiate borders in its territories; the growing economic and cultural importance of the regions now commonly referred to as "borderlands"; increasing concern about the inability of nation-states to control flows of both capital and information across their borders; and, most recently, the high drama of the wall being built between Israeli and Palestinian territories. Theories of globalization drew attention to borders as a premiere site for examining the collision of concept and experience. Contemporary border studies draws not only on anthropology and sociology, but also on work in the disciplines of political science, economics, communication, and cultural studies. The impact of digital technologies on flows of information across borders make locating pertinent work a bit more complex because the scope of policy issues has frequently changed over the last few decades, as has the terminology used to discuss them. The singular problem of "transborder data flow" of the 1970s and 1980s, for example, is now the multiple problems—and literatures—of trade in services in international trade law, data privacy within the network and as an aspect of globally distributed economic activity, agreements among states regarding profit-sharing for revenues generated through international data and voice flows, and the question of how the Internet should be regulated.

Though the study of the movement and formation of social groups across borders initially framed issues in terms of "sending" and "settling" communities, these processes are now understood to be constant, and interactive. Because so many critical dimensions of community life are transmitted across space via interpersonal and mass communication, today the question often is the way in which community is recreated across distance—but rules and practices for the transmission of media content across borders differ depending upon genre.

It is for cultural reasons that borders have a phenomenological dimension, for while one knows when one has encountered a different culture it is not clear just where the boundary at which that occurs is located. Because cultures are so complex, there is no single dimension of social life that inevitably marks boundaries between cultural groups. Jacques Derrida's 1992 meditation on the macrolevel cultural impacts on national identity and social memory of the regionalization of Europe laid out a research agenda that is still being worked through across the social sciences in numerous case studies, social dimension by social dimension, and border by border. Cultural differences, whether expressed in rhetoric or boundary-drawing practice, fuel debates over contested borders, and at times cultural affairs are used as justifications for abrogating border rules. Such tensions can develop their own behavioral practices: In European history, witch-hunting typically occurred in culturally contested border regions. The study of borders has itself stimulated cultural theory because it encourages particularly sophisticated and complex thinking about issues raised by the mingling of societies, has historically played a role in expanding the diversity of scholars working in the social sciences, and has provided leadership in analysis of a research problem from both sides of a border, whether geopolitical, cultural, social, or economic.

Often, of course, the results of the analysis of borders have immediate political value, as in efforts to resolve tensions between economic and political imperatives in the new Europe. Political scientists, and politicians, treat policies that regulate the flow of people and ideas across borders as a form of adaptive behavior. It is understood that altering trade relationships affects national identity. There is a paradox—making it easier for goods and services to flow across borders can increase risk in some dimensions, while reducing the likelihood of conflict in others. Thus trade regimes and other aspects of interstate relationships shift in response to changes in perception of what is needed to protect the integrity of the state, even if doing so requires translating political relations into economic relations via the replacement of theories with contracts. Even those who take the Realist position in international relations, insisting that states are autonomous and unitary actors, acknowledge that borders are open to others, though ideally under situations the state controlled (James Rosenau thus prefers the metaphor of a moat for borders). Borders can also be sites for experimentation with various types of policies, as several argue has been the case with techniques of low-intensity conflict subsequently taken up for use in the interiors of countries. And of course the reliance upon digital technologies can induce risk when one state must rely upon know-how or systems of another via the essentially border less global information infrastructure.

When economists started thinking about the spatial distribution of economic activity, the border stopped being a bright line and began to be viewed as an economic space of variable width dependent on the nature of the supporting infrastructure, the type of economic activity under consideration, and the extent to which (and ways in which) that activity is regulated. Thinking about borders has stimulated development of economic theory in areas such as the "cultural discount" and costs to network efficiency at border crossings. The distribution of production processes made possible with meta-technologies also increases risk simply by expanding the volume of cross-border flows. The second of these has long been recognized as a problem, having given rise to the first international organization in order to increase network efficiency for telegraph systems that crossed borders. From the perspective of location and growth pole theory, border regions were typically seen as problematic, but by the late 1970s such regions had clearly become sites of increased international economic integration and contributed to the decentralization of economic decision-making. Economic activity specific to border regions includes trading activity, storage of goods, collection of duties, and transfrontier investments to avoid customs duties; by the late 1960s, several legal maneuvers (discussed later in this chapter) were in use to maximize these advantages. By now there are there are multiple other ways in which individuals and organizations are permanently linked across borders, creating value jointly rather than simply transferring goods, services, and capital back and forth. Indeed, just as corporations are downsizing through outsourcing many of their activities, so some states are now doing the same. As Richard Rosecrance has pointed out, by the mid-1990s, Switzerland and the Netherlands were producing most of their goods outside of their national borders, and the United Kingdom was moving in that direction. Finally, border policies have been instrumental in shaping a labor force to meet particular needs.

There is a long history of interplay between technologies and geopolitical borders. In response to Martin Luther's aggressive use of the printing press to spread Protestantism, in 1535 François I banned the printing of any books in France on pain of death by hanging—with the result that at the time of his death, his eastern borders were ringed with Protestant states and cities producing a massive stream of smuggleable print. A range of developments in the transmission of information across borders, ranging from agreements on official diplomatic practices and the development of professional armies but including the establishment of material barriers along borders that clarified what was "front" and what was "rear," generated new stability to the interstate system by the late 1700s. In 1948, the Canadian Massey Commission described U.S. television as a foreign technological invasion. Satellites made it possible to communicate from a single point within one state to multiple points in another, significantly changing the possibilities for hard propaganda, soft diplomacy, and de facto cultural influence.

The role of innovation in national competitiveness has changed. National boundaries are rapidly losing significance as natural domains within which innovations are generated, so the ability of governments to control technological outcomes unilaterally within its borders is weakened. There have been three policy responses: First, states are joining in alliances of various types for purposes of engaging in research and development; this was quite significant among the motives for the regionalization of Europe. Second, competition has shifted the rate at which innovations are diffused. Third, intellectual property rights are taking up some of the functions of trade barriers. With allegiance to national champions during international negotiations over technical standards, the firm-specificity of some technological structures of interest to organizational sociologists and economists are now national and regional differences regarding basic decisions for some aspects of the information infrastructure, especially in mass consumption products. Because electronically based modes of organizing social activity can now be owned by patent and/or copyright, these differences in technological structure are becoming manifest in regional blocs distinguished by organizational form and informational practice rather than political ideology.

There is a larger sense in which information technologies have shaped the ways in which we understand borders. It is only because of digital technologies that it has become possible to truly envision our shared environment as a global species—globality—through computer modeling, simulation, and machinic visions of the earth from space that have the planet itself visible. While the nature of transnational political movements is largely beyond the scope of this book, it may be useful to note that sociologists have found that Internet-based transnational movements exhibit less ideological crystallization and more issue-orientation than those within states. The very existence of technologies capable of global surveillance has itself contributed to the increase in research on border areas because it is possible to gather data of new kinds. They have also made it easier to see what is going on inside of countries with closed borders, or in critical areas undergoing war or natural catastrophe. The first news media use of commercial satellite imagery, in 1986, provided a powerful example of this by showing images of the Chernobyl nuclear explosion at a time when the Soviet government was still denying that anything had taken place. A final way in which these technologies affect information flows across political borders was demonstrated by the Tiananmen Square experience in 1989. Though people outside of China were sending news of the demonstrations into the country, fueling the political activity with cascading effect, the Chinese government was unwilling to shut down those flows because doing so would have required bringing the entire telecommunication system—which also served ongoing economic and other needs—to a halt.

Despite our ability to gather more data, and more kinds of data, than ever before, the analytical organs are those of states, and thus, as Ulrich Beck has persuasively argued, are often inadequate for understanding complex transborder processes, particularly those that are also transgenerational in creating their effects. Thus informational structures may still not map completely onto the world that they are trying to grasp. We do know, though, that codification of knowledge, including the development of information architectures, helps extend the influence and diffusion of science across borders. The question of what information Europeans need in order to function as European (rather than national) citizens provides an interesting example of the development of new informational structures in response to an alteration in the location and nature of geopolitical borders.

While information policy and other types of laws and regulations affect the nature of borders, the reverse is also true. Criteria for citizenship differ widely, and when new borders are drawn, a process for establishing criteria for the new geopolitical entity must be undertaken. There are often shifts in constitutional law in postindependence states, influenced by developments in other states and global trends in the market for law. The Albanian Constitution, written in 1998, provides a dramatic example, for it protects the rights of Albanian people who live outside of its borders and specifies that borders can't be changed without first hearing the opinions of those in the area under discussion. In some circumstances, states may have to negotiate with those responsible for international law for the very right to defend their borders.

Extraterritoriality is the process by which states attempt to apply their law to entities and processes outside their geopolitical boundaries; given the history of multinational and transnational corporations, it is perhaps not surprising that decision-making about when extraterritoriality is acceptable and when it is not has largely taken place within the context of antitrust (competition) law. Notions of the national interest underlie interpretations and applications of the law; because economic and political definitions of that interest often come into conflict in border regions, some suggest that the national interest itself needs to be reconceptualized—at least for that use—in order to resolve ongoing internal inconsistencies in the law. Meanwhile, the development of computerized databases of laws, regulations, and court decisions makes legal analysis across jurisdictions easier than ever before.

The structural issues discussed in chapter 6 involved matters internal to particular systems, while the border issues discussed here focus on the parameters of those same types of systems. Thus this chapter, too, approaches pertinent trends in information policy through the lenses of technological, social, and informational systems. And here, too, developments within each affect the others. Some of the information policy issues raised by borders are long familiar and obvious, such as diplomatic and public information practices in which nation-states engage in order to communicate their preferred identities and goals externally. Others—such as international trade—were not the subject of study within the fields of information, communication, and culture for many years but have become so since the 1980s in response to shifts in the international trade environment. Yet others, such as the incorporation of information policy tools within legal instruments used in quite other issue areas—for example, the informational provisions of arms control agreements so important in the area of defense—are quite new to those who are not topical specialists and even, often, to those who are.

Borders of Social Systems

Two very large issue areas in which information policy plays a role in the definition and crossing of borders are the informational aspects of geopolitical borders themselves, and international trade. The difficulty of separating out that which is social from that which is informational and that which is technological is clearly evident here, for much of what has changed about the treatment of the geopolitical border has been the result of the use of new information technologies, and the transformation of international trade law was the direct result of an attempt to establish favorable global conditions for those in the information, communication, and culture industries. Among the many border-related information policy issues involving social systems for which there is insufficient room here are interactions between domestic and international technical standard-setting; treatment of antitrust matters when corporate sites in multiple countries are involved; the development of law for satellites, the geosynchronous satellite orbit, and satellite-generated data; and the question of the role the United States should play in combating the reproduction of socioeconomic differences internationally as a result of differential access to the information infrastructure and the content it carries.

Geopolitical Borders

The borders of the United States, like those of most states, were established by war and treaty over a long period of time that included moments of redefinition and ongoing disputes. Indeed, the very question of where the border between the United States and Mexico actually lies, already the source of war and the problem that gave rise to border studies altogether, remains alive today among those who use the phrase "Spanish Borderlands" to refer to the American Southwest and who continue to seek to pry control of that area away from the United States.

The United States has been trying to coordinate its border activities with other countries at least since 1894, and achieved joint coverage of the northern border by 1908. The 1924 Immigration Act enabled more aggressive informational activities at U.S. borders because it made the role of border agents more important in preventing illegal immigration and created a border patrol. The twentieth century saw a great deal of experimentation with techniques for monitoring borders, from issuance of various kinds of ID cards to expansion of the types of information that had to be provided to gain entry and to stay. Many of the racial and ethnic categorization issues discussed in chapter 5's treatment of individual identity were raised in the course of trying to implement immigration laws.

Illegal border crossings have been more of an issue along the southern than the northern border. Explicit U.S. and Mexican policies encouraging cross-border activity and the creation of transborder communities, however, have been heavily responsible for encouraging such movement. In 1942, the United States launched the Bracero program to entice Mexican workers across the border with the argument that their labor was needed in order to replace that of U.S. citizens who had gone to war. The result is now familiar from "guest worker" programs all over the world. The program was popular because the economic appeal to Mexicans was great; a few months' work in agriculture in the United States often generated enough capital to support not only one's family, but in some cases one's entire village in Mexico. Because Mexicans were willing to work for far less than U.S. citizens (and because they were often unable to challenge abuses regarding pay), the program was also popular with U.S. employers. Thus when the Bracero program ended in the 1960s but the work remained, illegal border crossings from Mexico started to increase, as did struggles to enforce the border. The development of free trade zones, so important to the development of maquiladoras (see following discussion) was not sufficient to absorb all of the Mexicans seeking work within the U.S. economy. There are disagreements, however, regarding the extent to which apprehensions work as a deterrent. And while each improvement in communication and transportation technologies made the work of border patrols more effective, the same technologies also served those who were trying to cross borders.

Trends in the treatment of U.S. geopolitical borders of particular importance from an information policy perspective include the extent to which they are increasingly information-intense, the growing use of the notion of functionally equivalent borders, and the creation of free trade zones. It is possible that 2005 legislation giving the Department of Homeland Security the power to waive all law in order to protect the border will also have First Amendment and other information policy implications.

Increasing information intensivity of borders Inspection and information collection are ancient border activities that have been a part of U.S. practices from the start. A mandate to automate these processes was part of the Illegal Immigration Reform and Immigrant Responsibility Act of 1996, though this provision was not implemented until after 9/11. In December 2001, the United States signed a thirty-point action plan in support of a U.S.-Canada "Smart Border Declaration"; in January 2002, President George W. Bush announced a more general smart borders initiative; and by March 2002, a twenty-two-point smart border agreement had been reached with Mexico. The combined goals of the smart borders plan are to improve the ability of the United States to repel threats while simultaneously increasing the efficiency of border crossing for individuals, information, and goods. The integrated "border management" system includes screening goods and people abroad prior to their entry into the United States, inspections at the U.S. border and within the United States to ensure compliance with entry and import permits, and trying to achieve seamless communication among border control agencies and between those agencies and the criminal justice and intelligence communities. Advanced technologies to track the movements of goods and people are fundamental to smart borders; the word "smart," of course here refers to an effort to make borders more intelligent through the use of computing. In September 2002, the U.S.-Canada plan expanded by two additional items, involving cooperative research and development in the area of biosecurity in particular and across a range of science and technology issues more broadly. Other elements of these agreements include harmonization of immigration and air flight databases and of commercial processing, establishment of joint inspection facilities, a regular exchange of customs data, the development of smart transportation systems that would include inspection-related data collection equipment, and integration of intelligence units across governments.

As an example of the technologies being used as part of this program, a technique called "pulsed fast neutron analysis" uses a pulsed beam scanned on vehicular traffic to examine cargo. The pulsed neutrons interact with the elements of scanned objects, creating distinctive gamma rays that respond to particular chemical elements (e.g., explosive chemicals). Each machine cost $10 million at the time that it reached experimentation stage. The manufacturer claims that the error rate is less than one percent, but when put into use, its actual error rate under working conditions is unknown. In ideal conditions, each truck can be processed in three minutes, but even so at a rate of sixty trucks per hour per point of entry, this process will inevitably lead to backups. This technology was first developed for drug interdiction in the 1990s, but was shelved because of its cost, the amount of physical space needed to install it, and the time required to use it.

Other informational technologies being used to make borders intelligent use biometrics for identification and verification of people. Biometrics are already in use in some permanent resident ("green") cards and in all border crossing cards (BCCs), or "micas," used by Mexican citizens who wish to cross into a twenty-five-mile border zone for up to seventy-two hours. Embedded in each card is unalterable personal information, including fingerprints and a digital photograph. In future, the United States will embed biometric information in radio frequency ID chips in passports, a development that is being protested because the particular form of RFID tag technology being used can be read from a distance by anyone with a reader. In an exercise of extraterritoriality, the United States has also demanded that those countries for which visas are not required for people entering the United States similarly embed biometric information in their passports.

To make decisions about the information technology aspects of the smart borders initiative, the Department of Homeland Security established a new agency, Customs and Border Protection, that has taken on a number of functions that were previously the responsibility of the U.S. Border Patrol and the Immigration and Naturalization Service. Decision-making for this unit is supported by an advisory committee comprised of representatives from high-technology companies. Further, the secretary of homeland security has the discretionary power to protect antiterrorism technologies against any liability claims that may result from the use of such technologies. Data created through such techniques is entered into the FBI-run National Crime Information Center (NCIC) database—the same database for which the FBI was released from the requirement that the information be accurate, as discussed in chapter 5. Meanwhile a 2002 report from the Government Accounting Office concluded that the INS was already unable to manage its information technology (IT) system, with only one person overseeing 107 separate IT systems and no knowledge regarding whether those systems actually worked. The evaluation of analysts is that further rounds of improvement are likely to be even less practicable and affordable.

Because treatment of a border is necessarily a bilateral affair, differences between the treatment of the Canadian and Mexican borders with the United States are likely to remain. On the Canadian side, longstanding differences regarding the extent to which personal data are afforded privacy protections remain problematic regarding border data. On the Mexican side, there is concern that collaborative efforts regarding treatment of the labor force launched four decades earlier were being pushed aside.

Creation of free trade zones Two types of free trade zones have been created by the U.S. government, both affecting the nature of the border. Foreign Trade Zones are located all over the country, with a border nexus justified by the presence of customs agents in each state. Maquiladoras are specific to the U.S.-Mexico border, and involve cross-border communities. Both have information policy implications because they influence the ways in which information flows into, out of, and with them, and because both have been very heavily used for manufacturing purposes by the information industries.

The Foreign Trade Zones program was created by the Foreign-Trade Zones Act of 1934 in an effort to counteract some of what were perceived to be the destructive effects of tariffs put in place in 1930. It was designed to encourage foreign commerce in the United States by making it easier and cheaper through the designation of geographic areas free of customs duties and related taxes. From 1934 to 1950, manufacturing within these regions was prohibited and the zones were virtually unused. The creation of an international trading system, the General Agreements on Tariffs and Trade, in 1946 provided a tremendous stimulus to international trade, changing the context of free trade zones. In 1950, manufacturing became permitted in the zones, at first only with approval on a case-by-case basis and with full tariffs and taxes upon the entry of goods produced in these zones into the domestic economy (the "island" model). Over the next couple of decades, tariffs continued to be lowered, while manufacturers began to distribute their manufacturing processes around the world, coordinating their activities with the use of new information technologies. These changes resulted in an odd situation that created a strong incentive to move all production overseas: in many cases, manufacturers had to pay more to import parts than buyers in another country would pay to import the finished product, biasing against domestic production as opposed to moving production overseas. In 1980, the foreign trade zone rules were changed so that goods manufactured in that environment would not be assessed on the value added in the United States, whether for materials, parts, labor, overhead, or profit. The result is that foreign-sourced parts or materials can be brought into a free trade zone without paying any duty, incorporated into finished products using U.S. parts and labor, and then enter the U.S. market with duty on the value of the foreign non-duty-paid content only. This "integrated" model of foreign trade zones has been very popular; in 1970, there were only eight free trade zones, but by March 2005, there were 248—at least one in every state and in Puerto Rico, almost all used by firms in the information industries.

At the time that the United States created the Bracero program to bring Mexican laborers into the United States, the Mexican government simultaneously put in place its own program to develop its northern frontier to be a "window on Mexico" through which the United States might gaze. Tijuana received a lot of attention for this purpose, as it was already a free trade zone. In 1965, however, the Mexican government went further, with the Border Industrialization Program, intended to create jobs lost after the United States discontinued its Bracero program. The new terms lured U.S. manufacturers to Mexico because they could use Mexican labor, paid at Mexican rates in U.S.-run factories, to manufacture goods for sale in the United States that would be taxed only on the value added in Mexico as evaluated in terms of pesos. The number and size of maquiladoras exploded in the early 1970s, with the number of plants involved almost doubling in 1973 and 1974. The creation of a maquiladora-specific government unit and repeated rounds of devaluation of the peso made the combined use of free trade zones on the U.S. side and maquiladoras on the Mexican side ever more attractive to U.S. firms, with a consequence for Mexican workers, who found they had to work four times as long to purchase a basic market basket in 2004 than was the case in 1987. In the late 1990s, governments in both countries—often at the municipal rather than national level—began discussing the possibility of completely merging the Mexican and U.S. telecommunications systems in cross-border maquiladora cities in order to even more efficiently support manufacturing processes there. Setting up a telecommunications regulatory system specific to these communities is a part of the discussion about this option that is still under way.

Functionally equivalent borders It has long been held that the Fourth Amendment's restrictions on searches don't apply to those entering the country; anyone can be subjected to a nonroutine search at the border without a warrant and without any requirement of showing probable cause. Originally this exemption from Fourth Amendment protections against inappropriate search was applied only to those coming into the United States, but by the mid-1990s, it was also being applied to people leaving the country.

The Supreme Court has determined that it is acceptable to do this anywhere that is a "functional border equivalent," but has not defined just what that is. As applied to populations such as airplane passengers who cross a border in flight and go through customs upon arrival irrespective of the location of the arrival city, the concept seems unproblematic. As used to justify search of any Mexican immigrant at any time and at any location, it becomes more difficult. The notion of functionally equivalent borders was important to antiterrorism efforts in the period between 9/11 and the passage of the PATRIOT Act and related changes in the law that have made it easier to search anyone.

Waiving law at the borders In 2005, a bill was passed by the U.S. Congress and signed into law that makes it legal for the Department of Homeland Security (DHS) to *waive* all law when securing U.S. borders; the DHS, that is, is now free to act *above the law* in matters involving protection of the border. The immediate problem used rhetorically to justify the law—which passed as a rider to a bill providing a supplemental budget for the war in Iraq because it was believed there would otherwise have been too much resistance to it—was the desire to build a fourteen-mile fence in the San Diego area without contending with environmental impact issues. The language of the statute, however, does not limit possible uses of this power to such circumstances. Rather, this law, which is unprecedented in the United States, gives the DHS the ability to waive any and all law anywhere in the vicinity of the borders in order to expedite construction of fences and barriers and remove any obstacles to the detection of illegal immigration. The availability of the concept of functionally equivalent borders, combined with the global network for surveillance of communications that might pertain to illegal immigration, means that the geographic scope of the power unleashed by this bill might be interpreted to be global. An early version of this bill would have denied the courts any right to hear cases arising from actions based on decisions to waive law, but as it stands courts will be permitted to deal with constitutional issues. The DHS is required to publish its intentions to waive the law in the *Federal Register* before acting on such decisions.

The first use of this law demonstrated the open-endedness of what is permitted given the logistical complexities of even the seemingly limited and concrete problem of building a fence. Though the bill became law in May, the DHS waited until September 19, 2005, to announce its intent to waive all law in order to expedite construction of border fencing near San Diego. OMBWatch (www.ombwatch.org), a nonprofit organization devoted to serving the public interest, notes that at that point this historic move received little media attention because all eyes were on Hurricane Katrina and its aftermath. The DHS did specify which environmental laws it would be waiving to build this fence and did not eliminate the possibility that other laws would also be waived. There is concern that laws such as Davis-Bacon Act requirements that federal contractors hire construction workers at the area's prevailing wage, Occupational Safety and Health Act requirements for job safety, and requirements for maximum hours of service for truck drivers delivering equipment or materials to the border zone might also be waived. Protections of the free speech of those critical of DHS activities might also come under attack.

Trade in Services

The global economic system set up after World War II, which included the establishment of the World Bank and the IMF, had as its centerpiece the GATT, a suite of rules and regulations regarding trade in goods based on the longstanding belief that reducing tariffs is always to every country's advantage. While some informational goods and services were included under the GATT, a large proportion were not, and because the GATT was designed to manage goods, the rules were not always completely appropriate when applied to information flows. The United States in particular by the 1980s thus became concerned that the trading system needed to be expanded to include the industries important in an information economy.

The perception that international law was inadequate for the contemporary economy was not based on abstractions. In the mid-1970s, it became evident that lacunae in national and international laws, overlapping and sometimes mutually exclusive types of international and domestic law that might apply, and differences between laws at the national level regarding treatment of international information flows made carrying out business extremely problematic, both for those in the information industries and for those in other sectors of the economy reliant upon information flows to sustain distributed operations and transactions taking place all over the world.

By 1979, seventy-five countries in Europe and around the world had passed laws that restricted the free flow of electronic information across borders. West Germany, for example, insisted that computer data could enter that country only through a single hard-wired leased line, and that data had to receive further processing in Germany before being further distributed there. The Japanese government demanded the provision of encryption keys for all commercial data entering Japan. Other techniques being used were usage-sensitive pricing even for privately owned lines, local content laws, insistence upon incompatible technical standards, foreign government monitoring of proprietary information, outlawing of encryption, and denial of access to the foreign national's communication system. Because of the military background of U.S. actions even in areas such as standards for color television, efforts to negotiate such restrictions were met with suspicion.

There were other reasons for Europeans to fear U.S. actions, even though the United States was not, even then, the most technologically advanced country with regard to its telecommunications network—Japan announced its commitment to going all-digital in 1981, and South Korea was the first to achieve universal broadband. The U.S. practice of determining for other countries just where and how international telecommunications cables would be located, the 1972 refusal of the United States to sign a U.N. proclamation regarding principles for direct broadcasting as one aspect of peaceful uses of outer space, and the sense that the United States practiced a double standard in terms of communication policy principles within and outside the United States raised resistance. The Nora/Minc report on the effects of the computerization of society to the French government in the late 1970s had warned that, with digitization, the United States was developing a position of control over all European communications and data processing, and there was concern that the divestiture of AT&T and deregulation of communications in the United States would only make U.S.-based corporations more competitive globally. There was every sign that the FCC would try to enforce its distinction between communication and non-communication processes, and between processed and unprocessed communication flows (the outcome of the Computer Inquiries discussed in chapter 3) in international transactions, even though other countries treated both types of information flows in the same way.

Discussion of international information policy issues outside of the trade context referred to the flows involved as TBDF, or trans-border data flow, at the time. An extraordinary range of types of law applied to TBDF, even if indirectly, including postal, space, intellectual property, culture and education, national security and law enforcement, and telecommunications regulation, as well as the GATT. Domestic laws also affected the international environment; the 1980 Canadian Bank Act, for example, required all data generated in Canadian banks to be processed in Canada. Disagreements over how to treat international flows of communication, information, and culture in digital form manifested themselves in debates over spectrum allocation, the question of whether corporations were legal persons for the purposes of data privacy legislation, the design of tariff frameworks for processed data, interactions between data privacy and human rights, and cultural policy.

Once the United States introduced the idea of extending the GATT system to include trade in services, debate over this change in policy was so intense that the next scheduled meeting to discuss international trade matters, called the Uruguay Round of GATT talks, was put off for a number of years. One question was how to define services, as each country did so differently. The conclusion of that decision-making process was a list of twelve sectors, ranging from communication to energy to the movement of natural persons. In some cases, the informational aspect of these services is embedded in the knowledge transferred, as with health and social services. Other sectors more obviously deal with information, communication, and culture. The business and professional services sector includes accountancy, advertising, and computer and related services, along with architectural, engineering, and legal services. The communication services sector includes the audiovisual industries (television and film), postal services, and telecommunications. The best colloquial definition of services, though, remains that offered by the British news magazine *The Economist* twenty years ago: "Anything that can be bought and sold that cannot be dropped on your foot" (1985, 20).

The more difficult problem was reassuring various governments that their societies would not be damaged by a trade regime that included services. Developing countries with economies largely based in agriculture were concerned that an international trading system oriented toward information industries would prove even less congenial to their needs than that already in place. Governments in well-developed countries, such as Canada and France, believed that the approach being promoted by the United States would yield results damaging to their cultures. Finally, after a number of years of difficult negotiations, the World Trade Organization was established in 1994 to manage agreements dealing with trade in goods (under the GATT), trade in services (under the GATS), and intellectual property rights (under the Agreement on Trade-Related Intellectual Property Rights, or TRIPS). Under the WTO, each country negotiates its own approach to regulating trade, sector by sector, with the international organization.

Particularly important trends in information policy within this extremely complex set of activities include a boost to the commoditization of information, and use of trade law to expand the boundaries of the U.S. legal system in a de facto way. Two other developments are worth mentioning: There is a long history of political use of international affairs as a means of effecting legal changes within the United States, but this has been a particular feature of U.S. negotiations with the WTO; one example was President George W. Bush's (failed) attempt to use WTO principles to dismantle the domestic postal system. Reliance upon economic approaches to decision-making and high regard for economic values also have been characteristics of the U.S. legal system since its inception, but again the WTO framework provides openings for increasing pressure on the legal value hierarchy in the economic direction. One form of such pressure was an effort a few years ago to map classification schemes and operating rules that had been agreed upon by accounting firms onto the legal profession.

Commoditization of information As was discussed in chapter 2, there are many different ways of defining information, and all of them have legal implications. The crux of political resistance to inclusion of flows of information, communication, and culture under trade law from developed states came from differences in just how these international flows should be defined. For many countries such flows are more a matter of culture than of economics, and social and cultural values thus dominated their approaches to law and regulation in these areas. Television and film, which both fall under the audiovisual sector of the GATS today, provide vivid examples of areas in which there was fierce contention for this reason. Of course the governments of countries such as Canada and France, which resisted extension of trade law to services, did not take the position that these industries did not have an economic dimension—but they did insist that other factors were additionally, and importantly, taken into account in their policy-making regarding these cultural products. Any material item or activity that is the subject of trade law is defined legally in economic terms, raising the relative importance of that definitional approach in the value hierarchy for decision-makers. Discussions about other aspects of regulation of the global information infrastructure and its content that has taken place since the GATS was put in place demonstrate that the effects of including trade in services under trade law have not been trivial, even in areas in which many believe the constitutive definition should govern.

Expansion of the U.S. legal system In discussions of the law, the term "harmonization" refers to the alignment of legal systems of different states with each other. For corporations, adapting activities to differences in legal systems is costly in many ways, so with the growth of multinational and transnational corporations, interest in harmonizing legal systems grew. Deregulation and liberalization of telecommunications systems during the 1980s and 1990s is one example of such harmonization in the area of the regulation of the technological infrastructure; indeed, this combined technological and legal harmonization is one of the key features of the fourth stage of the development of the information society.

Harmonization of legal systems takes place through a number of different processes, many of which may take place in combination. Imitation is one process, with governments that have been innovators in particular areas of the law providing models that other governments later take up. Education and persuasion sometimes come together, as in the aggressive practices by U.S.-based entities to "consult" with the transition governments of the states formerly part of the Soviet Union during the 1990s regarding the kinds of constitutions, laws, and regulations they should put in place. Direct pressure occurs when an entity such as the International Monetary Fund insists upon a particular regulatory configuration as a condition for substantial loans to governments. There is the spread of legal ideas from private contract law to government statutes, which has been particularly important in the many areas dealing with digital technologies for which there was no pre-existing law. With GATS, it became easier for U.S.-based accounting and legal firms to operate around the world, carrying with them another technique for harmonization, the influence of technical expertise.

Borders of the Technological System

The premiere characteristic of borders within the electronic network is that they are first and foremost conceptual, rather than physical. This was not always the case; before interconnection was introduced as a legal mandate and then came to be understood to be as a desirable practice (discussed in chapter 6), there were telephone systems with clear technological borders. In the analog era, it was possible to create a network or content border through sheer refusal to engage with certain customers, as happened when the British excluded so many parties from use of its telegraph system during World War I that other governments turned to radio as an alternative medium. Efforts to create a technological border by legal mandate where none naturally exists and where those who control the technologies do not themselves agree with the policy, however, was shown to be impossible, even with the printing press several hundred years ago. In today's global digital network, it is no more possible, as communication about the Tiananmen Square event in China in 1989 made clear.

Paradoxically, while developing societies have not succeeded in shaping discourse over global regulation of the Internet in such a way that their needs are adequately and persuasively represented, techniques for blocking access to Internet content created in support of Chinese and Saudi Arabian policies are now being taken up by the U.S. government to serve its own purposes. The end of this censorship story, however, is not yet evident. Just as the radio allowed those who were not allied with the British to communicate despite the lack of British cooperation during World War I, innovation has continued to trump efforts to set technological borders since then. There have been many times when the desire to enforce content restrictions was dependent upon the ability to set technological borders: Within the United States, Oklahoma's cultural preference to forbid liquor advertising on television was overridden by the Supreme Court, with the logic that insisting on such state regulation would prevent the cable television system from expanding nationally. Canada's bias against advertising on television became unenforceable as soon as Canadian territory fell within the satellite footprint of broadcasters. Germany's restriction on the production of Nazi materials is now toothless, because that content can be, and is, produced in the United States and then distributed in Germany via the Internet. Today the censorship/counter-censorship battle, just like the struggle over privacy, is often fought mathematically, via the design of computer programs.

The conceptual nature of borders in an electronic network environment has created a quite various range of legal problems. In the 1980s, the question of where to locate the transactions that take place in the course of foreign direct investment. Difficulty in answering the same question is a key reason (though not the only reason) for the reluctance to tax Internet-based transactions, known as e-commerce. "Settlements," the policy for dividing payment for communications that take place between corporations in two countries, are also purely conceptual. Jurisdictional issues regarding such matters as content and certain types of content remain rife, because they cannot be resolved by simply bounding the technological system.

Three examples of information policy issues that arise from the need, or desire, to establish borders within the boundary-less global digital technology system, will be discussed here. The first is historical, involving the definition of the U.S. border for communications purposes as it was shaped during the period in which voice and data flows were carried through physical wires. The second involves the establishment of borders between networks for the purposes of rate-setting. And the third, export controls, provides an example of a political effort to prevent certain technologies from crossing the U.S. border for national security reasons. Restrictions on foreign ownership of the U.S. communication infrastructure is one example of an issue involving the borders of the technological system not discussed here.

Network Borders

Three laws provide the basis of the FCC's activities dealing with international communication via the telecommunications network, the focus of the discussion here. The 1921 Cable Landing License Act gave the president authority to control licenses for submarine cables between the United States and other countries, an authority delegated to the FCC by executive order in 1954. The 1934 Communications Act, as amended by the 1996 Telecommunications Act, includes several provisions that give the agency international responsibilities. And the 1962 Communications Satellite Act extends its purview to that then-new technology. The governing definition for the public interest on international matters was enunciated in 1971, with four guiding principles. As summarized in contemporary language, these were:

- *Redundancy* Left on their own, telecommunications providers would decide which technologies to use according to economic criteria, although some technologies are more vulnerable to attack than others, and each type of technology is vulnerable in a different way. The FCC has the responsibility to ensure that the national communication network is as resistant to attack as possible and thus requires corporations to simultaneously invest in different types of technologies. This principle was inspired by the attraction of telecommunications providers to satellites, sensitive even to changes in weather and sunspots but capable of quickly recuperating without any intervention. Undersea cables are rugged, subject only very rarely to attack for military reasons, and occasionally disrupted by natural events, but when cut, they are very difficult and time-consuming to repair. At the time that this principle was put in place, providers were required to invest equally in cables and satellites if they were expanding capacity in any way.
- *Innovation* It is deemed to be in the public interest for telecommunications providers to use "the most modern and effective technology."
- *Simplicity* At a time when most international traffic was being generated by the United States, the principle was established that "artificial" formulae should not be used to determine rate structures for messages and data also handled by foreign carriers.
- *Price reduction* Expecting technological innovation to continue, and with the assumption that the agency would continue to regulate pricing, the FCC defined the public interest in international telecommunications to include the requirement that economies from the use of new technologies be reflected in a lowering of charges for service.

Many parties are actually involved in any negotiations involving international telecommunications: the U.S.-based corporate network provider, the foreign network provider, the FCC in its monitoring and licensing roles, the foreign government in its regulatory roles, and the International Telecommunications Union. The ITU was incorporated into the WTO at its inception, and the U.S. agreement with the WTO regarding the telecommunications sector is among the public documents on the FCC's Web site. Telecommunications matters are so complex that the ITU, the FCC, the U.S. National Telecommunications and Information Administration of the Department of Commerce, and the U.S. Department of State have actually developed a list of ten criteria to be used to determine whether any given international communication problem actually has regulatory status. As the amount of international communication traffic has risen—and its importance to the U.S. economy has grown—international activities have risen in salience for the FCC as an organization, though both internal and external evaluations regularly report that it is underfunded and understaffed in this area.

The long history of U.S. involvement in international and bilateral decision-making for communications goes far toward explaining resentments that affect current negotiations. The United States as odd man out began with a refusal to participate in the ITU when it was formed in the 1860s because telegraphy, and then telephony and broadcast, were in the hands of the private sector, while elsewhere, until the privatization rush of the 1980s, these activities were in the hands of government. (The ITU yielded on permitting individuals from the private sector to represent the United States in the 1920s, recognizing that the country had become such an international force that it would be to everyone's disadvantage were the United States not to take part.) Until the last couple of decades, the United States also demanded that communication partner states locate their end of submarine cables according to U.S. preference, a practice that reasonably generated enormous and enduring resentment. Most recently, U.S.-based and government-supported entities have dominated policy-making for the international satellite system (by INTELSAT) and for the Internet (via ICANN).

Aspects of the FCC's policy-making regarding international telecommunications matters of interest from the perspective of their impact on the nature of the border include: the linkage of corporate and geopolitical form, the role of technologies in locating the border, and an increase in the permeability of the border.

Corporate structure and the telecommunications border As long as the same companies managed both domestic and international communication, the FCC had no need to officially define the border between the two. In 1943, however, an antitrust action against Western Union forced that company to divest itself of its international activities, a process that took twenty years, new statutory law, and a regulatory decision regarding the nature of the border to complete.

Managing competition among carriers, and responses to carrier demands for less regulation and more competition altogether, have continued to play important roles in FCC definitions of the U.S. border. Five border crossing points were named ("gateway cities"), essentially codifying the existing locations of international cables—New York, Miami, New Orleans, San Francisco, and Washington, DC—and specific "international record carriers" were allowed to operate out of each. The requirement to hand off messages between international and domestic carriers in these cities helped design the competitive map of U.S. telecommunications by allowing those corporations appropriately situated to gain in market share with statutory and regulatory sanction. Setting up multiple carriers to handle international messages also raised prices for U.S. consumers, and for business customers often meant working with multiple technologies, each communicating with a separate carrier, with great logistical difficulty and cost.

Border definition by technology When forced to do so in 1943, the FCC chose to delineate the U.S. border in terms of the technological network rather than geopolitically. Communication within the forty-eight contiguous states—and Canada and Mexico—was defined as domestic, because the same network technologies were used throughout that space, even though that space included the territories of two other sovereign governments. Communication with the states of Alaska, Hawaii, and the U.S. territory of Puerto Rico, as well as with all other countries in the world, was defined as international, because communication with those places could not be reached via the same land network but, rather, required the introduction of the different technology of submarine cables.

Border permeability Once satellites were introduced, so that this technological distinction was much less important (though because of the redundancy principle, still pertinent), the FCC decided to keep the concept of gateway cities in place. Telecommunications providers, expanding their business, wanted additional cities to be designated as gateways, and both technological change and the growth in international information flows placed pressure on the FCC to do so. In 1974, the FCC finally acknowledged the role of every node in the network in international communications, but it was not until 1980 that the agency began to allow international communications from any location that had a satellite uplink. At that point, the question of whether to keep the antitrust barrier to permitting single corporations to handle both domestic and international communications revived, a story that continued to be played out in various forms until the establishment of the WTO and agreements under the GATS shaped current operating conditions.

Export Controls

Export controls are an interesting example of an area in which it is difficult to separate technological systems and informational systems, for the regulations designed to prevent the export of technologies that might be used for military purposes by others also apply to knowledge *about* those technologies, whether embedded in technologies, databases, or humans seeking to travel. There is a long history of U.S. efforts to control the transfer of scientific and technical knowledge across its borders. The most important legal arrangements for export controls after World War II were originally designed to prevent the former Soviet Union from closing the technology gap. Both multilateral (Coordinating Committee for Multilateral Export Controls [CoCom]) and unilateral (Export Arms Regulations [EAR] and International Traffic in Arms Regulations [ITAR]) agreements were used.

The Coordinating Committee for Multilateral Export Controls was created in 1948, and involved Japan and all NATO states except Iceland. It was coordinated by a small committee in Paris, but no official treaty binds its members and both its budget and staff are supposed to be secret, buried in embassy and OECD buildings and documents. CoCom annually refined its list of items to be subjected to export control, and for a long time dealt weekly with requests for exceptions. While many believed CoCom would be dissolved when the Soviet Union broke apart, it has continued to exist in the form of a more formal arrangement, the Wassenaar Arrangement on Export Controls for Conventional Arms and Dual-Use Goods and Technologies. Continued security concerns, self-interested bargaining among states, and norms of appropriate post–Cold War behavior have all been offered as justifications for this agreement, which was designed in the course of five rounds of negotiations between 1994 and 1996. Much of the shape of the Wassenaar Arrangement was derived directly from CoCom.

CoCom and the Wassenaar Arrangement obviously only orient toward security goals, but U.S. export controls also involve the Departments of Commerce and State. Some believe this involvement was necessary once information was recognized as the most valuable part of technology, in the 1970s, as control over technological information at the time was beyond the purview of the traditional constituencies of the Department of Defense. Recommendations for such controls were presented in the Defense Science Board's Bucy Report of 1976, and almost all of those recommendations were translated into the Export Administration Act of 1979. Among the most important of these recommendations was creation of the category of "dual-use" technologies; that is, technologies that can be used either for military or for nonmilitary purposes, unlike weapons. Each of the categories of technologies termed dual-use was itself very broadly defined, with the consequence that essentially any advanced information or communication technology is potentially subject to export controls. (Biotechnology was added to the dual-use list when it was amended in 1986.) The determination as to whether any specific item (or, more recently, service) should be designated as dual-use is made by government officials on the basis of their (often ad hoc) evaluations of likely or possible use; whether the purchaser is in the public or private sector is irrelevant to this decision. Operationally, creation of the legal category of dual-use technologies required harmonization of some of the classification schemes and activities of the Departments of Commerce and Defense. The same treatment of dual-use technologies appears in the State Department's International Traffic in Arms Regulations.

It was probably cryptography that first brought digital technologies and knowledge about them to the keen attention of those involved with export controls. In 1975, the National Security Agency (NSA) tried to stop all work on cryptology other than its own simply by asserting that it was the only entity with the right to do work in this area and seeking to prevent the National Science Foundation from giving any grants in this area. In 1977, in one of the first uses of export controls to try to restrict speech, the NSA stepped up its efforts by warning the Institute of Electrical and Electronics Engineers (IEEE) that its scheduled conference on cryptography would be criminally violating the ITAR if it did not get a license to hold the conference ahead of time.

Today the complete list of arms control regulations includes not only ITAR and regulations under the Arms Export Control Act (AECA), but also Defense Trade Security Initiatives (DTSI) and criteria for production and export licensing. Specific initiatives have been put in place (in order to support the exports necessary for U.S. involvements in Iraq) that sped up approval procedures and made it possible for exports to take place without all of the required paperwork in place; on a case-by-case basis, it has been possible to waive ITAR requirements altogether as part of "Operation Enduring Freedom."

External ineffectiveness There are at least four reasons why many question the effectiveness of first CoCom, and now the Wassenaar Arrangement, in achieving stated goals—nonadherence, nontrade options for acquiring listed technologies and information, the spread of expertise in research and development in areas of interest, and the existence of information flows within organizations.

The question of adherence to CoCom in its original form was always complex, given that it had no formal legal status, the agreement wasn't binding, and there were no costs—other than, potentially, political—for those who chose to abrogate its terms. Both discomfort at U.S. dominance of CoCom and concern about going too far in intruding into critical internal affairs of member countries drove the somewhat laissez-faire approach to acting on CoCom's decisions. Because each country provided its own list of technologies of concern and decided whether to pass requests for exemption on to CoCom, most discretion continued to lie with individual governments rather than the multilateral group. As member countries besides the United States gained in technological strength and the Soviet threat appeared to weaken, the desire to support their own economies through export made it more and more likely that CoCom's greatest strength was symbolic rather than operational. By the close of the Cold War period, many believed that only the United States was strictly adhering to CoCom principles.

The U.S. Panel on the Impact of National Security Controls on International Technology Transfer identified three strategies frequently employed to gain access to high-technology information and equipment, all of which might be used simultaneously by the same country or group: espionage, diversion (shipment of militarily significant dual-use products and technology to unapproved end users, either directly through export of controlled products without a license [smuggling], or indirectly through transshipment using a complex chain of increasingly untraceable reexports), and legal sales. Of course CoCom and Wassenaar can only affect the last of these. It is believed that the proportion of transfer of technologies and information of military use through the indirect means of diversion is quite large.

By the early 1990s, the U.S. government also had to admit that the argument for CoCom had been seriously weakened by the sheer fact that the United States was no longer necessarily the most technologically sophisticated country in many of the areas of interest. Finally, border issues interact with structural matters in an interesting way when information is involved: intra-organizational knowledge flows, particularly in support of cross-border innovative efforts, is one way in which information about advanced technologies crosses borders irrespective of national concerns.

Internal effectiveness Whatever the effectiveness of arms control externally, there have been clear effects internally. This concern had been there from the start, but it was not until the political situation in the Soviet Union began to change that even U.S. leaders of CoCom began to admit that care had to be taken to ensure that export controls did not cramp the competitiveness of U.S. information industries. Pressure from manufacturers concerned about the impact on their commercial viability—especially as manufacturers from other countries met and surpassed the level of technological sophistication found in the United States—did finally result in a relaxation of rules regarding the export of technologies with encryption mechanisms built in, but the issue remains.

Export controls have also had the effect of restricting the flow of scientific and technical information even within the United States. The definition of technical data subject to ITAR covers any unclassified information that can be used, or adapted for use, in the production, maintenance, or operation of instruments of war as defined by the U.S. government's Munitions List, or any technology that advances the state of the art or establishes a new art in an area of significant military applicability in the United States. As one commentator noted, the treatment of "technical data" by ITAR was so broad that it was difficult to determine what might *not* be included. Both ITAR and the EAR consider an export to have taken place when information is disclosed to a foreign national, including to students via academic instruction, in scientific symposia, or even as a result of publication. The ITAR exemption for information that is publicly available does not apply to new information, or to old ideas combined in a new way.

Militarization of the information industries Of course security needs have always been important drivers of the development of digital technologies and of scientific and technical information, but until the dual-use label came into use it was possible for companies and researchers to choose whether to participate in defense-related contracts. For the U.S.

government, it is an advantage to be able to procure technologies needed for military purposes in the open commercial market rather than having to "command" their production. For those in the commercial or academic sectors, however, the dual-use designation removes the option of nonparticipation in defense-related matters if they work in any of the broadly defined areas that have been labelled in this way.

Confusion Aside from the fact that some of the munitions lists have been or are secret, there are two additional sources of confusion regarding export controls. First, the Export Administration Act (EAA) has been allowed to lapse numerous times, meaning that the same information or information technology may or may not be allowed to leave the country, depending upon when permission is sought. Second, when restrictions on the export of scientific and technical information were originally challenged on First Amendment grounds, in the early 1980s, courts agreed that constitutional issues were a concern and established a high level of scrutiny. The bias had already been moving in the other direction prior to 9/11, but today the barriers are very low. Thus longstanding practices, especially regarding treatment of scientific and technical information, have recently become suspect or illegal.

Informational Borders

Borders of informational systems are created when certain types of speech are deemed unacceptable, as discussed in the review of the informational spaces created by constitutional law in the United States in chapter 4. Border crossings are literally used as sites and moments in which certain ideas and information may be prevented from entering the country, or from leaving it. Both political speech and scientific and technical information receive attention of these kinds. An overarching topic of importance beyond the scope of this work, but underlying it, is the growing importance of transparency as a policy principle across diverse arenas of international relations.

Political Speech

The same McCarran-Walter Act that created a category of visas for temporary workers also included provisions that made it possible to prevent those who either espouse communist or anarchist ideas or who belong to organizations that do from entering the United States at all. Under some circumstances the attorney general may choose to waive excludability;

under others even this discretion is not an option. Decisions are made on the basis of a computerized list of names reportedly derived from suggestions by informants, foreign police, and the CIA, though the government has never officially described how the list is compiled. One report on this list in 1987 mentions that at the time it included over two million names. Though the intention of these provisions is to prevent active subversion of the U.S. government, that notion has been generously interpreted to include merely giving talks on a speaking tour. Prior to 9/11, several hundred individuals a year were being stopped at the border because of their political speech and/or beliefs. Writers who have been refused entry for these reasons include Gabriel García Márquez, Carlos Fuentes, Pablo Neruda, and Jorge Luis Borges.

Border activity structures domestic political debate Because denying entry to the United States affects not only those individuals involved but also the structure and content of political debate within the country, this practice is of constitutional concern. One Supreme Court decision in a case challenging the attorney general's choice to waive excludability for an individual invited to speak on several university campuses—*Kleindienst v. Mandel* (1972)—established important precedent regarding the right to receive information under the First Amendment and importantly distinguished interactivity as a specific type of information collection and processing, different in kind from passive information reception for legal purposes. In the early 1980s, courts—concerned about the damage to free speech presented by these visa denials—increased the level of activity required, but discussion about strengthening visa restrictions again began in Congress not long after the first effort to bomb the World Trade Center. In June 2001, specific recommendations for doing so were offered by the Congressional Research Service and others, and after 9/11 these additional techniques, many discussed here, were put into place. Many are concerned about the impact of these changes on U.S. citizens' right to receive information.

Strengthening of the border against unwelcome political ideas Use of the restricted list to prevent entry has significantly increased since 9/11, another dimension of the effort to strengthen U.S. borders. One striking consequence of this trend has been that many individuals who have been welcome in the United States previously are now being turned away. In one highly publicized example, a Nicaraguan woman was in this way prevented from taking a position she had accepted on the faculty of

Harvard University. Often these individuals are attempting to come to the United States in order to take part in activities that have nothing to do with political affairs. Aware of the cost of these practices to U.S. knowledge production, the Federation of American Scientists (FAS) maintains a list of the scientists who have been refused visas for political reasons.

Arms Control Treaties

Other than the role of national security in identifying speech that receives no constitutional protection because it is defined as treasonous and in marking the boundaries of acceptable and unacceptable political speech, we have not typically thought about the defense arena as a source of information policy. The formalization of diplomatic practice, however, with consensually understood implications of specific types of communications as stages in the movement towards open conflict, can be understood as the first stage in development of information policy tools for peacemaking and peacekeeping purposes. A detailed analysis of the information policy principles incorporated into arms control treaties and related agreements reveals that over the last few decades there has been a steady expansion of the role of mandates regarding information collection, processing, and flows in arms control agreements, referred to collectively as confidence- and security-building measures.

The chronology starts in 1944, when a multilateral agreement to outlaw aerial reconnaissance was signed and then immediately ignored by all signatories. In 1946, U.S. statesman Bernard Baruch suggested setting up inspection teams to prevent the further development of nuclear weapons, but Josef Stalin rejected this possibility as a cover for espionage. The first arms-related agreement that included an information policy provision was the Hotline Agreement between the United States and the Soviet Union in 1963. From that point on, every treaty or agreement included at least one information policy provision, with a high point in reliance on informational tools in the Commission on Security and Cooperation in Europe (CSCE) documents produced by the Stockholm Conference in 1986. The relationship with formal agreements or treaties is critical to understanding the nature of CSBMs, for they are devoted to verification of compliance with other treaty provisions, not other intelligence or surveillance purposes.

The twenty-five types of provisions found in treaties, agreements, or proposals between 1928 and 1990 fall into six categories:

- *General principles* Reference to the role of information flows in security theory, inclusion of informational goals in the purpose of agreements, attention to the impact of the use of such provisions on the development of weapons, doctrinal discussions, and other general points.
- *Data reporting* Notification of activities, reporting on activities, fact-finding, data exchange, and communication regarding weapons-related calendars.
- *The role of personnel* Observers, factory and laboratory personnel exchange, and onsite inspections.
- *The role of technologies* "National technical means" (the use of technology-based intelligence and surveillance techniques), production line monitoring, and monitoring of storage sites.
- *Management* Consultation, management, and data verification.
- *Communications processes* Access to sites by the media, prohibition of propaganda, a mandate to avoid deception, establishment of crisis communication programs, the general goal of improving communications among states, and the ideal of setting up a global database center for conflict-related information that would be available to all.

Among the thirteen additional information policy tools suggested but not incorporated into any agreements by 1990 were banning all encrypted radio traffic, establishment of joint teams for data-sharing and examination of nuclear detonations of unknown origin, perimeter and portal monitoring, continuous transfer point (border) monitoring, calculation verification, creation of a global equipment pool, and universal access—by individuals as well as governments—to all information from a global surveillance system.

The last few decades of the twentieth century saw a great deal of experimentation with the use of information policy tools for security purposes. Technological innovation and shifts in the political context continue to stimulate experimentation in the twenty-first. Trends worth noting include the role of political will in determining data sufficiency, the perhaps unexpected role of civil society, and the resistance of the United States to inspections on its own soil even though it demands that other states accept the practice.

Sufficiency determined by political will, not quantity The general notion that empirical data can provide evidence of intention on the part of unfriendly states rests on the beliefs that the research methods used are both valid and reliable, that qualitative conditions can be understood through quantitative means, that analytical techniques are in themselves neutral, that empirical data can be interpreted in only one way, and that states make decisions on the basis of empirical evidence. Put together, these assumptions are translated into CSBMs in order to achieve the "better data" that comes from "more data." Many of these basic ideas are questioned today, however, and others—such as the confidence that political decisions will be evidence-based—have been dismantled by changes in U.S. political life. Certainly the same data can be interpreted in multiple ways; an example often mentioned in the literature on intelligence was the disagreement regarding how to read satellite photos of Soviet ship cargo to Cuba that launched the Cuban Missile Crisis. Recent U.S. experience demonstrates the political uses to which analyses, or avoidance of analyses, or design of analyses, of data can be put. In sum, irrespective of how many information policy principles are included in arms control treaties and other security-related agreements and laws, in the end it is political will, not quantity of data, that determines whether one state believes it can trust the messages regarding intentions that it is receiving from another.

The role of civil society The biggest surprise in the history of CSBMs is the critical role played by a nonprofit organization, the Natural Resources Defense Council (NRDC), in breaking the decades-old deadlock regarding whether to monitor nuclear production and testing. The argument with which Stalin originally resisted the 1946 suggestion for such monitoring—that it would be a cover for espionage—continued to be replayed every time recommendations of this kind came up. Other justifications for declining to experiment with such techniques were added: it costs too much, the technologies needed don't exist, the other party would never go along with it.

After yet one more round of a failed effort at including CSBMs in an arms control agreement, leaders of the NRDC sat around late at night joking that perhaps they should just set the process going. As environmentalists, nuclear production and testing were of critical concern because of their inevitable impact on the environment when things go as planned, and because of the devastation that could occur if and when things do not go as planned. While this idea was first treated as what it was, a late-night fantasy, by light of day it came to seem like a realistic possibility. They contacted Soviet scientists, and within three months there were inspectors on the ground in the Soviet Union setting up nuclear test monitoring devices—scientist to scientist, rather than government to government. (In contrast, it is worth emphasizing, it took much longer for the reciprocal process to get established in the United States because of resistance from the U.S. government based on fear of espionage, and from the organizations involved concerned about loss of intellectual property and trade secrets.) Once the door was opened in this way, many of the arguments against incorporating CSBMs into arms control treaties fell away. The technologies did exist (and innovation in this area proceeded rapidly once the political use of the results had been accepted). The other party *would* play along. It appeared to be possible to carry out inspections with integrity. The experimentation with a wide variety of techniques detailed here was the result.

This progress did not, of course, mean that problems did not remain. In fact such programs are very costly, and it is difficult to find people with both the training necessary in order to undertake the work and the willingness to undergo the constant travel involved. The use of CSBMs to increase transparency also stimulated further innovation in order to hide information in new ways. Disparities in the technological capacity of states resulted, in the sense that the playing field was not level for those governments involved in inspections that had to rely on less-sophisticated equipment. There were disagreements regarding how often, and in response to what kinds of triggers, inspections should take place. And there is protocol, always protocol; as one reads through arms control treaties across time, one of the most striking feature is that they are ever-more elaborate, largely as a result of the need to articulate protocol, often involving CSBMs, at a finer and finer level.

The history of citizen-based resistance to nuclear weapons goes back to the explosion in Hiroshima (the development of the weapons was secret up until that point). Numbers of participants rose and fell, and activity levels climbed and dropped, but this move by the NRDC was by far the most effective action undertaken by any civil society group struggling with this issue. From the perspective of the growth in globalized civil society organization, action, rhetoric, and theory over the last decade, the NRDC's role in opening up the use of CSBMs for peacemaking and peacekeeping purposes can also be seen as a turning point in the history of global civil society.

Inability to apply techniques to non-state actors However successful the experiments with CSBMs, and however well-developed the technologies and institutions required to implement these information policy tools, they are ineffective when the unfriendly parties of concern are not other states. Verification practices obviously mean little during a war on terrorism, in which there are neither treaties for which compliance might be verified nor parties with whom—in a state-based international system—it is appropriate to sign agreements. There is a complex nexus, however, between the verification activities of the search for weapons of mass destruction in Iraq as a justification for U.S. aggression in the area and the war on terrorism that provided the initial rhetorical argument. As the domain of areas of concern that can be treated with verification procedures shrinks, the use of intelligence and surveillance techniques grows.

Importing Knowledge Workers

Manipulation of immigration criteria has long been a means of trying to ensure that the necessary skills and knowlege are available in the labor force. Until 1885, the United States admitted temporary workers as contract laborers, providing much of the unskilled labor that built the railroads and supported the shipping, fish canneries, and gold mining industries. This practice stopped almost completely with the advent of legally recognized unionization. Temporary workers were not admitted into the United States again except for during extreme labor shortages until the McCarren-Walter Act of 1952 authorized the H-1 specialty visa program. That law distinguished between skilled and unskilled workers for visa purposes, but failed to define just what was meant by "skilled." Until 1990, this same skill-based visa category was used by everyone from entertainers through those in the health occupations to professors. The Immigration Act of 1990 created further divisions among types of temporary workers, resulting in nineteen temporary visa categories. The most important from the perspective of its contribution to the U.S. knowledge base is the H-1B, with certain individuals and organizations exempt from the H-1B cap. Special visa categories have been established for the NAFTA countries, with higher requirements for those coming in from Mexico than from Canada. The United States is unique among the countries who receive large numbers of immigrants in requiring a worker to be sponsored by an employer.

The H-1B visa is of keen interest to the computing industry in particular, for it can be used by programmers and those with related knowledge. The same visa category, however, is used by Department of Defense workers—and by fashion models. Initially, a cap of 65,000 visas per year was put in place. This cap was later relaxed in response to pressure from the computer industry, and in 2000, 355,605 people entered the United States under H-1B visas. The cap was returned to 65,000 for 2004 and 2005, in large part because of pressure to protect information industry jobs needed by American workers who became unemployed during the dot-com crash. The top countries of origin for temporary workers entering under H-1B visas include India (almost 50 percent), China, Canada, and the United Kingdom. Holders of these visas stay for different lengths of time, and many ultimately become permanent residents. In 2003, the GAO recommended that the Department of Homeland Security gather more detailed information regarding the activities of H-1B workers and the lengths of their stays and issue regulations limiting the duration of U.S. employment.

Temporary visas are not the only means by which non-U.S. citizens bring their knowledge into the U.S. labor force. In 2000, 13 percent of all college graduates in the civilian labor force were foreign-born. A higher percentage of college-educated foreign-born employees holds postgraduate degrees than do native-born employees, and the foreign-born who are highly educated are more likely to be found in the high-technology, science, and engineering occupations. In 2002, almost one million foreign students and exchange visitors entered the United States as on student visas, but changes in the legal situation after 9/11 made the United States less welcoming and the 2002 number was down 7 percent from a year earlier. By the close of 2004, the number of foreign students in U.S. universities had dropped 30 percent from the level prior to 9/11. A new tracking system to monitor all foreign students, the Student and Exchange Visitor Information Program (SEVIS), was launched in August 2003. The top three source countries for foreign students remain Japan, South Korea, and China, but over 220 countries are represented in U.S. universities.

Border Rhetoric versus Border Realities

Quite aside from publicly acknowledged border disputes, rhetoric about the clarity of U.S. borders of various kinds was never completely supported by historical reality. Nor is the claimed unity of the borders of the geopolitically defined nation-state across types of activities an actuality. Today we know that geopolitical borders do not necessarily map onto borders that are economic, cultural, communicative, or informational in nature. Indeed, it is precisely the differences in the borders of the nation-state as viewed from each of these and more diverse perspectives that create and manifest the interpenetration of political structures discussed in chapter 2.

Borders are of course very much the stuff of identity and structure. One of the most interesting problems for policy-makers today is whether—and if so, when and how—to insist upon creation or maintenance of borders in situations in which they have in fact resolved into an identity in its other sense, the mapping of formerly separate systems onto each other in such a complete way that they are no longer distinct. This question is premiere in consideration of technological structures, and appears in various ways in discussions about social and informational structures as well. Some of the multiplicity of types of borders derives from the fact that new social forms do not replace, but become layered over, the old. New closures mark the appearance of new types of borders; thus when states began to close their borders to the export of germplasm in the early 1980s, it marked not only the beginning of the "seed wars," but also the marking of a new type of state boundary.

Borders are rarely, if ever, bright and clearly demarcated lines; rather, the effective width and texture of a border varies according to the dimensions of interest and responds to changes in conditions. It is this susceptibility to context that makes borders amenable to policy interventions. The geopolitical border itself is an outline of an object that is just one of its instantiations. In many other instantiations, the actual border is more often a region than a line, and the breadth and undulations of that border narrow and widen depending on the type of activity, the regulatory environment, the nature of the pertinent infrastructure, and political mood. Border cities such as maquiladoras are so significant in terms of size, economic importance, and locally specific cultural forms that they are not only places in which some national laws are lifted but, in some cases, the subject of region-specific laws of their own. Some use the word "postnationalist" to describe to the cultures of these cross-border urban environments.

As the long history of the "elastic border" concept tells us, such experiences are not new. In rural areas of Afghanistan, the modern bureaucratic state governs a forty-meter swath along each of the roads, but tribal governments govern the land between. The Soviet Union maintained secret cities in its "nuclear archipelago" that never showed up on maps. In the United States, communities on tribal reservations have a dual experience when it comes to sovereignty, declaring themselves independent of the United States for some purposes (e.g., the requirement to pay sales taxes on the consumption of goods such as tobacco), but a part of the United States for other purposes (e.g., as a justification for requests for financial support from the U.S. government). Whether Puerto Rico is inside, or outside, the U.S. border has never been quite clear. In Europe, confusion regarding just what is near to and what is far from a particular state under today's conditions leads to use of the term "fuzzy borders." The distinctions in border studies between borders, frontiers, and borderlands captures some of this fuzziness.

Since 9/11, there has been a significant expansion of U.S. informational borders in this way, with the placement of U.S. customs agents in airports and seaports of other countries to surveil goods and people abroad before they even begin their transport to the United States. While this development had its conceptual and legal predecessors, the extent to which it is being practiced and the interactions of this trend with other approaches to harmonization of the laws of other states with those of the United States, are new and specific to the informational state. Because border movements, shapes, and permeability of all of these kinds are almost exclusively reliant on flows of information, communication, and culture, they are both the subjects and the effects of information policy.

Changes in the nature of the informational borders of the United States, as discussed in this chapter, particularly in the areas of restrictions on the flows of scientific, technical, and political information, can undercut governmental efforts to effect other types of change in social, technological, and informational systems. Chapter 8 examines information policy for these other types of change.

8

Information Policy and Change

The society envisioned by the authors of the U.S. Constitution welcomed new ideas and inventions and involved all citizens in the ongoing processes of refinement of the political system and selection of leaders to manage that system. President Woodrow Wilson articulated what this meant for "policy science" in 1887 when he included the education of citizens to the benefits of change among the fundamental policy principles for a government in its operational, rather than constitutional, phase. The nature of change, however, is among the most ancient of philosophical problems; in the Western tradition, the debate began with detailed and diverse approaches by the pre-Socratic thinkers and has not stopped since.

Theories of Change

Irrespective of the type of system that may be subjected to change, a series of fundamental questions can be asked. These identify dimensions along which the trends in information policy vis-à-vis change can be analyzed:

• *Change versus no change* The question of whether change has occurred is really a bundle of problems. Is change in a particular system possible? If change is possible, is it apparent? Is change actually occurring in a specific system of interest? Is what appears to be change actual change, as opposed to merely shifting representations of an unchanging referent? *Should* change take place? The last, normative, question is critical to information policy debates over matters such as the extent to which critical speech should be tolerated. The distinction between actual change and its representations offers opportunities to use policy discourse as a policy tool in its own right.

- *Episodic versus cyclical versus constant change* Does the change process being observed or designed take place only once (episodic), regularly according to a given schedule or in response to particular stimuli (cyclical), or all the time (constant)? All of these possibilities are designed into the U.S. political system, and all are available as selection that can be made in the selection of particular information policy tools.
- *Incremental versus radical change* Does the change have only a minor effect on a system or a part of a system (incremental change) or does it significantly create significantly different circumstances (radical change)? An example of this distinction in current popular discourse is identification of some technological innovations as "disruptive," while others are not. While in some cases the difference between incremental and radical change is obvious, in many circumstances it can be difficult to reach agreement on this line.
- *Nonparametric versus parametric change* Change is more commonly accepted when it takes place within the rules and structures of a particular system (nonparametric change) than when it causes fundamental change to the nature of the very system itself (parametric change). Changing the dominant political party within the United States through a normal electoral process is nonparametric change to the political system. Changing the dominant political party through violent overthrow of the government, resulting in abandonment of the normal electoral process, would be parametric change to the political system.
- *Genetic change versus epigenetic change* Over the long history of theoretical debate over the nature of change, it has largely been assumed that the processes involved took place over time and were locatable in space (genetic change). Today, however, three developments—complex adaptive systems theory, growing interest in environmental interactions approaches across the social and natural sciences, and the experiences of globalization—have created an interest as well in change that takes place across space at a single point in time (epigenetic change). Current developments in information technologies and in their uses will make epigenetic processes very important targets and tools of information policy in the future.
- *Equilibrious versus nonequilibrious change* When change to a system results in a return to conditions of stability once the processes of transformation are completed, it can be said that change has been equilibrious—the system has gone from one equilibrium to another. We now know, however, that it is not always the case that periods of turbulence and chaos will necessarily result in a new system that is able to sus-

tain itself in a stable manner for an extensive period. It is also possible for a system to dissolve altogether into its constituent parts, revert to chaos altogether, or develop conditions in which the system will oscillate repeatedly among two or more configurations. When any of these three outcomes results, change has been non-equilibrious.

Change can be difficult to perceive and to understand. It can take a long time to gain sufficient analytical distance from major transformations for the outlines of change to become visible. Lines of causality may be so long that they are hard to trace, or they may be imperceptible altogether because they operate on a scale beyond that of our perceptual systems. Change may operate upon parameters of which we are unaware or which we do not understand. We habitually look for intended consequences of our actions, but change may result from unintended consequences. The greatest innovative leaps, whether in society, ideas, or technologies, often come about via spandrels, the use of something put in place for one purpose that later serves another end.

Over time, the distinction between incremental and radical change became translated into a policy differentiation between those technologies that are considered "critical" because they will radically change state capacity in some important way, and those that are not. The distinction between nonparametric and parametric change became manifested in the use of interventions into organizational form (as in antitrust law, as discussed in chapter 6) in order to transform the fundamental nature of the telecommunications network, the goal now widely understood to have driven the divestiture of AT&T in the 1980s. The goal of developing epigenetic decision-making processes, which make it possible to respond in real time to situations about which there is total and instantaneous knowledge, drives a fair amount of the contemporary R&D that contributes so importantly to change in informational structures. Theories of change specific to the three types of systems of importance to information policy have developed independent of each other. Each of the ways of thinking about structure introduced in chapter 6 implies a theory of change.

Information policy affects change in social systems through the ways in which it creates the context within which political speech takes place. Political speech receives the highest level of protection under the U.S. Constitution because it is the means by which the social system is created, sustained, and changed. There are enduring tensions in the area of political speech—between the government and those critical of the government, between groups whose political views differ, and between the support for multiple goals of constitutional status that cannot simultaneously be achieved. Information policy in this area can be broken down into that which deals with the potential for change to the parameters of the system itself (periods of war), that which deals with the potential for change within the parameters of the system (efforts to pass new legislation, and the vote), and that designed for periods of stability in which change is not the focus (ongoing political discourse). The two conditions that have historically drawn attention for their potential for parametric change have been the conditions of revolution and war, often closely intertwined. Trends in information policy with implications for parametric change of social systems include an expansion in the use of protection of national security as a policy principle, a change in the conditions understood to present a clear and present danger in speech, use of gag orders as a form of widespread prior restraint, experimentation with restrictions on the press during war, and redefinition of the concept of the enemy capable of providing a parametric threat.

Technological innovation became an issue area for policy-makers in the twentieth century in response to three theoretical developments in the field of economics. In 1911, Joseph Schumpeter pointed out that basic innovations are fundamental to economic success. Longitudinal data about economic history reveals several "long waves," called Kondratiev waves, of economic growth, each of which was launched by the appearance of a significant new technology. In the 1930s, John Maynard Keynes reversed the longstanding assumption that encouraging the accumulation of capital by producers was the most successful way of stimulating economic activity (the "push" approach). Instead, Keynes argued, a healthy economy is driven by consumption (the "pull" approach). Consumption in turn is encouraged by attending to the income of ordinary individuals as opposed to just the wealthiest—and by repeated cycles of product innovation so that consumption will take place repeatedly. The first exercise in technological assessment, by the Roosevelt Administration in 1937, recognized the cultural gap between introduction of a new technology and manifestation of its social consequences, a gap that in itself explained some of the lack of coherent policy regarding technological change. The final piece of economic theory that provided a foundation for development of policies for technological change was offered by Walter Rostow in the 1970s. Rostow's model of successive leading industry complexes suggested that the economy is stimulated when there is a shift in dominance from one industry to another. After the launch of the first satellite, Sputnik, by the Soviet Union in 1957, economic arguments about technological innovation were complemented by the movement of technological innovation to the center of national claims to capacity and power.

Once policy-makers became committed to technological innovation as a positive goal for the government, additional theoretical, historical, and contemporary empirical work had to be done to determine which types of innovation should be encouraged and just how that encouragement might be successfully undertaken. A few among the discoveries that this work produced: Users of technologies are themselves important innovators (and can valuably be incorporated into R&D processes). Somewhat counterintuitively for some, innovation arises more successfully when networked organizations share intellectual property rights than when individual organizations hold their intellectual property rights closely. Despite the globalization of R&D and common reliance on geographically distributed collaborative work processes, dense geographic concentrations of activity on particular types of R&D problems are extremely productive. In today's meta-technological environment, innovations in processes are often more important in the long run than are innovations in products. Cultural factors, within specific organizations, particular knowledge communities, and in society at large, also affect the pace, direction, and success of efforts to innovate.

There are theories about change to informational structures at diverse levels of analysis. At the most macro level, studies in the history of the sociology of knowledge provide very broad-brushstroke views of interactions among various social processes, technological developments, and knowledge architectures. At the micro level, work by psychologists on cognitive information processing yields an understanding of how individuals acquire new information and incorporate it into their personal internal knowledge structures. Research by sociologists and anthropologists provides insight into how individuals shape their personal information ecologies to maximize meaning, access to the information considered most desirable, and pleasure. And at the meso level, work by sociologists in the relatively new area of science and technology studies looks at how informational architectures are created, sustained, and changed within particular knowledge production and interpretive communities. Relatively little theory in these areas, however, has made its way into the policy arena. Beyond appreciation of the fact that a consensus regarding information protocols is necessary in order to achieve or effectively use digital information technology systems, political motives and religious belief appear to be driving information policy-making directed at informational architectures.

Many of the areas in which information policy affects and effects change have already been explored in other chapters. Education provides the knowledge base and intellectual preparation for innovative ideas in addition to being critical to identity. Copyright and patent law are meant to stimulate change in ideas and technologies in addition to playing a significant role in the structure of the social system. The ideas, objects, and people who cross the country's borders change what happens in the United States, and so forth. This chapter will focus on additional areas of information policy important from the perspective of their role as change agents: Laws and regulations dealing with innovation affect the technological system, treatment of political speech affects the social system, and policy regulating access to and the diffusion of scientific and technical information manages change in information systems.

Information Policy and Change in Social Systems

The distinction between incremental and radical change introduced as it pertains to the legal system in chapter 3 is critical to understanding change more broadly in social systems. Under modernity, with its built-in expectation of "progress," it is assumed that some amount of social change takes place regularly. Indeed, incremental change undertaken within normative and legal parameters is simply understood to be normal social process. Change that takes place faster than is considered normal, or in an atypical direction, or using nontraditional processes to effect the change, may alternatively be viewed as radical, or revolutionary, in nature. Policies directed at change in social systems generally are efforts to channel the nature, direction, and rate at which that takes place.

Types of information policy that affect change in social systems include regulating the balance between freedom of speech and the need to protect national security and the vote. Information policies that affect change in the social system but are not discussed here include the use of media campaigns—both those directly supported in the federal budget and those that take place through information subsidies—by the government, and treatment of private sector entities such as ISPs as agents of the government to restrict forms of communication deemed unacceptable.

Freedom of Speech versus National Security

While it is often and inevitably the case that constitutional principles must be balanced against each other, as when there is the possibility that freedom of the press may impinge upon the right to a fair trial, national security is the "trump card" of policy principles for two reasons: When it is played, other policy principles are often overridden rather than balanced against it. And when national security interests are claimed, the information upon which a decision is made need not be revealed to others, such as legislators, judges, or citizens, who may have wanted to be or understood themselves to be legally required to be involved in a decision regarding the appropriate balance between constitutional goals in a specific instance.

Because national security goes to the heart of the political enterprise, many constitutions in the world include a provision permitting their provisions to be set aside, if need be, to ensure the survival of the state. In the U.S. Constitution, this is accomplished through the provision that the writ of habeas corpus may be suspended if required in cases of rebellion or invasion. This provision means that imprisonment on the basis of the exercise of other civil liberties, such as free speech or freedom of association, cannot be challenged under conditions in which there is claimed to be a threat to national security. The result is that even radical reinterpretations of other constitutional principles are possible, depending upon how national security is defined. In recent years, protection of the environment and food supplies have been defined as matters of national security; since 9/11, so have knowledge about national infrastructure and access to many types of scientific information.

The threat of parametric change has meant that each period of military engagement in the United States has stimulated legal attention to matters of free speech. This stage began just after the successful revolutionary activity that resulted in the creation of the United States, when those in the new government had to deal with the question of whether that government could tolerate the type of criticism that they themselves had levelled at the British government. For a brief period (1798–1800), hotly contested legislation was put in place that did not. The Alien Act made it possible to deport anyone who was "dangerous to the peace" or suspected of "secret machinations against the government." The Sedition Act made it a crime to conspire to oppose the government and to publish "any false, scandalous and malicious writing" against the government or government officials. When this legislation was in fact used to imprison individuals who opposed policies of the government then in power, it was felt that criticisms of the approach had been justified and, as a consequence, when the laws lapsed they were not renewed.

During the Civil War era, use of state laws as well as physical intimidation and censorship to restrain the speech of those who opposed the Confederate position inspired the Fourteenth Amendment to the Constitution, which established a uniform floor for civil liberties throughout the country via the technique of incorporation of the U.S. Constitution into every state constitution. World War I, the first time the United States became significantly involved in international affairs, brought the largest antiwar and antidraft movements in U.S. history. The successful Russian Revolution of the same period made new socialist ideas about economics and political structure quite popular during the 1920s; these ideas would grow even more popular in response to the economic Depression of the 1930s. The first few decades of the twentieth century therefore saw a great spurt of attention to First Amendment interpretation, particularly in the area the treatment of political speech. Theories about socialism and communism combined with the actual military threat posed by the Cold War to again draw Supreme Court attention to political speech matters during the 1950s. There was another burst of attention to information flows that might lead to change in the social system during the 1960s and 1970s, in response to the widespread political protests of the time. During this period, the Supreme Court further articulated ways in which political speech might or might not be constrained, and a rash of new statutory law mandated greater governmental openness.

Since 9/11, civil liberties have been significantly curtailed. Though every period of war has led to a tightening of the definition used to operationalize dangerous speech, there are a number of ways in which changes in the law and in the interpretation of the law since 9/11 differ significantly from anything that has been experienced in U.S. history before. In the first year following 9/11, twenty-one laws were passed by Congress in direct response, some of them—like the PATRIOT Act—extremely complex pieces of legislation touching upon many different types of activities and forms of expression. In addition, many of the most important changes in the legal environment have come about not through congressional action, but through executive orders and opinions of the attorney general. In order to fully comprehend the extent to which these decisions, orders, and laws have transformed the legal environment, analysis must take into account policy precession, the interaction between different laws and regulations that creates the actual constraints upon social life as they are experienced.

Implications of the state of emergency President Bush did declare a national emergency of this constitutional status on September 14, 2001. Despite the fact that diplomatic practices in place for several hundred years require a formal declaration of war, Bush had judicial support for describing this emergency as a War on Terrorism, based on an 1862 Supreme Court decision that concluded that a state of actual war may exist without any formal declaration of it by any party involved. The current situation differs from experiences of the past during wartime, however, in several ways:

- *Action versus suspicion or association* Historically, civil liberties were restricted in response to actual actions on the part of individuals. During the current war on terror, the government can act on suspicion or association.
- *Short-term versus long-term* Restrictions on speech during periods of war in the past were always of short duration, a few years at most. The war on terror, we are told, will last at least fifty years and potentially longer.
- *Few versus many civil liberties restricted* During past periods of war, only speech rights have been restricted. During the war on terror, several additional civil liberties have come under attack, including the right to a fair trial, the right to privacy, the right to association, and the right to access government information.

Transformation of the clear and present danger doctrine Though the Alien and Sedition Acts passed right after the American Revolution lapsed, concern about the possibility that speech could present a serious threat to either the government or to society at large generated both statutory and judicial responses. In 1917, after declaration of war against Germany, the Espionage Act was passed, making it illegal to encourage insubordination in the military or obstruction of the draft. About 1,900 people were prosecuted under this act, and about 100 newspapers and periodicals were barred from the mails. During the same period, many states passed laws against "criminal syndicalism," or "criminal sedition," law also designed to constrain speech directed towards overthrow of the government. Most of those prosecuted were aligned with the political left and believed in socialism and/or communism. Because prosecution was linked to the expression of particular ideas, a number of court cases resulted that involved interpretation of the First Amendment.

Though the clear and present danger test was discussed earlier in the book, its importance warrants more detailed discussion. Evolution of the test began with Justice Oliver Wendell Holmes's decision in *Schenck v. U.S.*, a Supreme Court case of 1919 that enunciated actual danger to the country as the only justification for restricting political speech. This case involved prosecution under the Espionage Act for distribution of antidraft leaflets. The phrase "clear and present danger" was included in a very famous passage from this opinion:

> [T]he character of every act depends upon the circumstances in which it is done. The most stringent protection of free speech would not protect a man in falsely shouting fire in a theatre and causing a panic. It does not even protect a man from an injunction against uttering words that may have all the effect of force. The question in every case is whether the words used are used in such circumstances and are of such a nature as to create a clear and present danger that they will bring about the substantive evils that Congress has a right to prevent. It is a question of proximity and degree. (at 52)

This decision highlighted several concepts that have been important to the treatment of political speech in the United States ever since:

- *Context* It provided an example of use of the national security argument for restricting speech that might well have been tolerated had national security concerns not been in place—a matter of context.
- *Intention* It argued that there were important differences in degree of danger of speech. Intention was identified as important to analysis of the speech under question.
- *Speech as action* The opinion introduced the recurring problem of determining when speech can be punished as if it were action.
- *Proximity* The question of the proximity of danger—how near in time it was likely to happen—was also introduced.

The clear and present danger test reached its most extreme expression in 1951, at the height of the pursuit of members of the Communist Party and communist sympathizers, known as McCarthyism after the campaigns led by Senator Joseph McCarthy. The Smith Act had been passed in 1939, making it a crime to conspire to teach and advocate the overthrow of the U.S. government by force. Under the Smith Act, the Supreme Court upheld the conviction of eleven people for conspiracy (joint decision-making) and advocacy in *Dennis v. U.S.* (1951).

In discussing the clear and present danger test, the decision commented,

> The words cannot mean that before the Government may act, it must wait until the putsch is about to be executed, the plans have been laid and the signal awaited. If Government is aware that a group aiming at its overthrow is attempt-

ing to indoctrinate its members and to commit them to a course whereby they will strike when the leaders feel the circumstances permit, action by the Government is required. Certainly an attempt to overthrow the Government by force, even though doomed from the outset because of inadequate numbers or power of the revolutionists, is a sufficient evil for Congress to prevent. The damage which such attempts create both physically and politically to a nation makes it impossible to measure the validity in terms of the probability of success, or the immediacy of a successful attempt. (at 494)

McCarthyism soon waned, however, and so did use of the clear and present danger test to repress speech. By 1957, the doctrine was overthrown in a case in which the Court introduced one more distinction important to analysis of whether there is clear and present danger:

- *Advocacy of direct action* There is a difference between advocacy of direct action and advocacy of abstract doctrine. While the former could be restricted, the latter remained protected under the First Amendment as political speech.

The clear and present danger test was put into its final form in the Supreme Court case *Brandenburg v. Ohio*, which involved a leader of the Ku Klux Klan who had been convicted under Ohio's criminal syndicalism statute. The case was based on films and testimony regarding a Klan rally at which a cross was burned and speeches were made that were filled with racial and religious slurs. Here the Supreme Court introduced two new principles:

- *Imminence* Advocacy may not be banned unless it is an attempt to incite or produce imminent lawless action.
- *Probability* Advocacy may not be banned unless it is likely to incite or produce imminent lawless action.

Three aspects of the concept of clear and present danger as used to identify subjects of surveillance have been affected by legal changes since 9/11. First, the distinction between advocacy of abstract doctrine as opposed to specific immediate action is no longer important. Second, intention is no longer a requirement. And third, association in itself is enough to trigger identification as a "suspected terrorist." While these changes do not in themselves make certain types of speech illegal, they can have a significant chilling effect on speech.

Gag orders as a form of prior restraint Prior restraint involves preventing expression before it happens; this practice is usually attempted through the use of a court injunction to forbid an individual actor from engaging in specified speech. The constitutional bias against prior restraint has already been introduced. Efforts on the part of the U.S. government to exercise prior restraint appear most often when there are national security concerns, though often these efforts fail.

In the *Pentagon Papers* case (*New York Times v. U.S.* [1971]), for example, the government tried to prevent the *New York Times* from publishing classified papers detailing how decisions regarding the Vietnam War were made. A temporary restraining order was issued against the newspaper, but when the federal government requested a permanent injunction, the district court judge refused in a stirring decision: "A cantankerous press, an obstinate press, a ubiquitous press, must be suffered by those in authority in order to preserve the even greater values of freedom of expression and the right of the people to know." This decision was reversed by the appellate court, which called for further hearings in the matter. During this period, the temporary injunction against the *New York Times* remained in effect, but the papers were also given to the *Washington Post.* Again the government sought a restraining order, but the district court judge for the District of Columbia refused to grant one, and the appellate court upheld this refusal. As a result, the *Washington Post* was able to print the papers, while the *New York Times* was not. The *Times* did pursue the legitimacy of the prior restraint exercised against it by the government all the way to the Supreme Court, where the newspaper's position was supported on the basis of the argument that the government had not sufficiently demonstrated any actual threat to national security.

Prior restraint can also be effectively put in place via contracts, even when freely signed, particularly if the contract is with the government. (Cases in this area have involved former CIA employees who wanted to publish details of events in which they had been involved.) The policy innovation since 9/11 in the area of prior restraint is the insistence that private parties asked to cooperate in placement of surveillance technologies or in turning over information about specific individuals must not only comply with such requests but are forbidden to tell anyone—including the individual whose information has been requested or who will be surveilled—about the action. On November 21, 2003, the number of those who are likely to be affected by this form of prior restraint went up dramatically, with passage of legislation that gave the FBI permission to request financial information from any type of business without a subpoena. (The FBI need only write itself a letter saying that the collection of this information is needed because it is pertinent to an ongoing investigation involving terrorism.)

Experimentation with restrictions on reportage during wartime Controls on media access to war zones have been successfully imposed without a successful court challenge as yet. It was not until after the Vietnam War, when some believed that criticism of the war had been due to unfriendly reportage, that restrictions on reportage appeared.

In 1983, this meant that reporters were excluded altogether from the Caribbean island of Grenada when the U.S. Marines went in to force a Marxist government out. Though journalists did approach the island in private boats, a military blockade kept them out. One First Amendment lawsuit was filed against the U.S. Department of Defense based on this action, but because the ban on reporting was lifted before the case went to court, the case was declared moot. By the time of the Persian Gulf War in 1991, a set of rules had been put in place. There is disagreement about the source and acceptability of these restrictions—while the government insists that they were developed consensually with and have been accepted by the press, elements of the restrictions have never been accepted by the journalism community. Experimentation with these techniques continues. Here are the **Restrictions on the Press in War Zones:**

1. *Press Pool* Reporting will take place only through pools of reporters selected by the Defense Department. Every member of a media pool must agree to share all information with reporters not in the pool.
2. *Military escort* Each media pool will be headed and always accompanied by a military escort who will determine when and where there will be access.
3. *Attended interviews* A military escort will be present during every interview with a source.
4. *Prepublication review* Everything reported by a pool member must first be reviewed by the military to determine whether it includes any "sensitive" information.

While it is to be expected that court challenges to application of these techniques in war zones will appear, as they did unsuccessfully after the Persian Gulf War of 1991, there is a larger question: How might such rules be applied during an ongoing War on Terrorism in which there is no identifiable war zone because the front is everywhere? Arguably, all media activities could be restricted and content censored by this argument. The ubiquity of danger is precisely the argument being used by the U.S. government to justify its global, satellite-based Echelon and Carnivore communications surveillance programs, and to support its position against permitting the use of encryption tools by those in the private sector.

Redefining treason For a long time, the concept of the enemy was limited to those whose behaviors threatened to physically undermine the government and/or attacked its citizens and institutions, and expression became a threat when it enabled or inspired this type of physical action. During the twentieth century, alignment with certain ideological positions became suspect, though except for moments of extremism from which the nation recuperated, deleterious action was required in addition to belief in order to trigger a legal response. In the U.S. Constitution, treason is defined as actually levying war against the United States, "adhering" to enemies of the United States, or "giving aid and comfort" to enemies of the United States.

There have been fewer than forty federal prosecutions for treason, and even fewer convictions. George Washington pardoned several men convicted of treason in association with the Whiskey Rebellion in 1794, and the most famous early treason case, involving Aaron Burr, resulted in acquittal. In the mid-nineteenth century there were several politically motivated attempts to use treason, all of which failed. In the twentieth century, treason became mostly a wartime matter, though there have been few cases of great significance. In recent years, transfer of information regarding high technology has led to most charges of treason outside of the circumstances of war. Most states also have treason provisions in their constitutions, though there have been only two successful prosecutions for treason at the state level.

This commonsense approach to defining national security became problematic in the last decade of the twentieth century, as three factors converged. The apparent close of the fifty years of the Cold War suddenly removed what had long been the focal enemy and required a conceptual and strategic effort to define the enemy during the new era. The multiple dimensions of globalization had created a situation in which international relations had become as much or more a matter of interdependency as of dealing with the "other." And the possibility of information warfare turned communications themselves into potential threats.

A first pass at defining the enemy (and therefore what constitutes a threat to national security) under the new conditions was undertaken in the early 1990s, yielding four categories. The first of these, drugs, may be consensually agreed upon as detrimental to society but had not historically been deemed to be a threat to national security, and it is interesting that this shift in legal treatment has taken place just as the international entity that pursues drug traffickers, Interpol, began to be criticized for operating not only separately from the governments of the nation-states in which drugs were made or through which they passed, but sometimes in direct opposition to the laws of those governments. Because the second of these, terrorism, is undefined, it remained available as a category to be filled with whatever content might later be desired. The third category, economic harm, has long been the subject of international trade negotiations, but again has not historically been treated as a matter of national security other than under circumstances when there was a possibility that an entire economy might be undermined. The last category, those whose behavior is statistically unpredictable, is a new concept in political and legal thought and is of significant interest from the perspective of the negotiation over individual identity between the individual and the nation-state discussed in chapter 5.

Translation of disturbing the peace into terrorism One of the most effective means of curbing political speech has been to take the content-neutral approach that the government is merely protecting society from disturbances of the peace. Laws dealing with symbolic speech, with the distinction between public and private forums, with littering, and with speech in school and university settings all take this approach. Political demonstrators often distribute leaflets and flyers explaining their point of view—and those leaflets and flyers frequently wind up scattered all over the ground. Communities do have the right to restrict such press activities if they have in place ordinances against littering. Those engaged in political speech can of course get around such restrictions by training those involved to pick up any that fall on the ground—as long as the leaflets are going from hand to hand they will still be permitted.

Threats to protection for unpopular opinions Judicial interpretation of the Constitution has consistently upheld protection for the expression of unpopular ideas. In 1938, the Supreme Court overturned municipal ordinances forbidding the door-to-door distribution of printed materials that had been put in place in response to the proselytizing activities of the Jehovah's Witnesses. In 1940, distribution of unpopular ideas orally, in the course of picketing, was also protected by the Supreme Court. And in 1977, even the right of Nazis to march in a community filled with survivors of the Nazi camps (Skokie, Illinois) was upheld by the U.S. Supreme Court.

In the homeland security environment, however, the attorney general has suggested that the expression of concern over restrictions on civil liberties since 9/11 is a form of support for terrorists. Many of the changes in the law described previously erode support for the expression of unpopular ideas by creating a chilling environment for such speech. And in the hours after the attack on the World Trade Center in 2001, individuals in U.S. prisons known to be political dissidents—largely involved with the peace movement and/or associated with the political left—were removed from their ordinary cells and placed in secure housing units; many were denied communication with their attorneys. Six weeks later, Attorney General John Ashcroft issued an interim order providing a justification for this action based on national security concerns.

The Vote

The vote is the system established by the U.S. Constitution for democratic participation in ongoing, nonparametric change whether directly (in referenda) or indirectly (through choosing representatives to Congress). Information policy affects the process of the vote in four ways: limitations on the political speech of those with the most economic power, reporting requirements on those who attempt to affect legislation on behalf of special interests, the role of information in the design of congressional districts, and the use of digital technologies for the vote (e-voting).

Protections from abuse of economic power Corporations were not much in the minds of those who wrote the Constitution, but by the late nineteenth century, it was clear that the economic power of those organizations offered the potential for inappropriate interventions into politics. In the area of political speech, therefore, media corporations, non-media corporations, and nonprofit corporations are all treated somewhat differently.

The first question to be addressed when evaluating whether any particular communications inappropriately use economic power to affect the vote is whether the speech involved is commercial or political in nature. The Supreme Court has developed a test to determine whether a particular message should be treated as political speech (and therefore deserving of the highest levels of constitutional protection) or as commercial speech (and therefore deserving of the intermediate level of constitutional protection). (The test for commercial speech can be found in chapter 4.) Reference to a political issue does not transform a commercial message into a political one; neither does advertisement of products or services that are of public interest. Inclusion of informative brochures with commercial products also does not affect the commercial nature of the expression. The First Amendment status of commercial speech has risen in recent years, with growing appreciation of the contribution of such messages to the ability to make informed decisions about the conditions in which one lives, an inherently political matter.

Corporations do have a right to participate fully in public debate over issues being voted upon in referenda because the Supreme Court has held that citizens have a right to receive all political speech, including that of corporations. Of course corporations have media available that may not be available to others. Utility bills—particularly in situations where there is no competition for energy of water—are, for example, a mass medium that reaches essentially everyone and can include newsletters with discussion of political issues. Efforts to force utilities to include alternative political views through this medium have all been struck down as unconstitutional efforts to compel speech.

The situation is very different, however, when it comes to elections. The Supreme Court has held that special privileges granted by the government to corporations—such as perpetual life and favorable tax treatment—enhance their power in such ways that they could unfairly dominate the political environment if not constrained. Thus corporations may *not* make direct contributions of money or services to a candidate or provide indirect support to a candidate by making expenditures on a candidate's behalf. Corporations *may*, however, directly and indirectly provide support to a political candidate among management (as opposed to union) employees within their own organizations. Corporations are free to provide support for the election process itself (through get-out-the-vote drives and related activities) or for election issues (through support for groups involved with issues). And corporations can form or participate in political action committees that provide channels through which funds can be legitimately made available for lobbying and election support activities via organizations that act on their behalf.

In acknowledgment of their role in providing a venue for political debate, media corporations are permitted to specifically support or critique candidates through news stories, commentary, or editorials—as long as the media corporation is not owned or controlled by political parties or the candidates themselves. Certain types of support for candidates are still forbidden to media corporations, however, including free air time, the gift of taped interviews to a broadcaster, and free advertising campaigns. An FCC regulation—the "equal time" provision—requires broadcasters to provide the same access to air time to any candidate.

Nonprofit corporations are not under the same types of constraints on their roles in elections. It is believed that they do not present a threat to the integrity of election processes because nonprofits are organized to promote ideas, not to accumulate capital, and thus do not usually have the type of economic clout that is feared from corporations.

To prevent wealthy individuals from skewing elections because of their own economic power, and to ensure that the public is aware of the sources of support for candidates, all contributions over $50 to a candidate must be identified by source, date, and amount, according to the disclosure provisions of the Federal Election Campaign Act. All sources of funding for advertising that either directly supports a candidate or solicits funds for a candidate must also be disclosed.

Constraints on lobbying Efforts to influence the government by having an impact on the decision-making of legislators—lobbying—is protected by the First Amendment right to petition the government for redress of grievances. Corporations (including nonprofits), unions, and individuals may lobby. To prevent corruption via the lobbying process, legislation since the mid-1940s has established the terms by which this type of political speech may be carried out. In 1995, the Lobbying Disclosure Act refined these rules in an effort to make oversight more effective and to increase public confidence in government. Rather than preventing speech intended to influence political decision-making, the government prefers to encourage disclosure of such activities, so that all may be aware of such potential sources of influence.

Thus any person whose total income from lobbying contacts is expected to exceed $5,000 over a six-month reporting period must register as a lobbyist. A lobbying contact is any oral or written communication, including electronic communication, with legislative or executive branch officials. By this definition, efforts to influence public opinion through the mass media, sometimes called grassroots lobbying, are not covered by the act. Organizations must also register if they maintain in-house lobbyists whose lobbying expenses will be more than $20,000 over six months. Nonprofit organizations, including labor unions and trade associations, often must register because their principal purpose is to influence legislation. Those in public relations and advertising often have to register as lobbyists, but journalists do not. Persons who testify on legislation before congressional committees do not, because Congress was concerned that requiring such registration would discourage people from testifying. Public officials acting in an official capacity are also excluded. And people for whom lobbying constitutes less than 20 percent of their work for a particular client also do not need to register.

Registered lobbyists must file semiannual statements reporting names of clients, general issues on which they have lobbied, specific issues on which they have lobbied, specific bill numbers and executive branch actions towards which lobbying efforts have been directed, and estimates of income and expenses. They do not have to report on names of the legislators or executive branch officials individually lobbied. Violation of the Lobbying Disclosure Act can result in a fine of up to $50,000.

Gerrymandering Gerrymandering is a very old way of manipulating the effectiveness of the vote. It operates at the group level of voting districts. The practice combines two types of information policy techniques discussed here: the data collection of the census and mapping. Following each census, congressional seats are reapportioned among the states and each state must then remap its legislative districts accordingly. This responsibility offers an opportunity to the dominant political party to prolong its position by setting up congressional districts likely to result in voting patterns in its favor.

Three techniques are used in gerrymandering. The "excess vote" method concentrates opposition votes in just a few districts, resulting in a dilution of effective opposition elsewhere. The "wasted vote" method spreads opposition votes thinly across many districts so that they will dominate in as few as possible. The "stacked" method draws bizarre district lines so that dominant power votes become the majority in as many districts as possible. Both congress and the Supreme Court have forbidden the practice of gerrymandering, but because the evaluation of whether a particular mapping is inappropriate is to some degree subjective and can be contested, the practice continues.

Electronic voting Electronic voting now offers another means of manipulating the vote, in this case by working with individual votes rather than the definition of electoral regions. Following the confusions of the 2000 election tally in Florida, the U.S. Congress passed the Voting Technology Standards Act of 2001, which authorized the spending of over $4 billion on electronic voting machines. However, that act did not mandate maintenance of either a physical audit trail of votes or a means by which individuals can review the information they have entered to make sure it is correct before submitting their votes. While the presidential election of 2000 made clear that even the results of physically punched votes can be open to interpretation, the relative ease with which digital information can be altered is raising great unease over the use of electronic voting machines. Those on the political right describe such concerns as ill-founded fears by those with little technical knowledge, but engineers from communities such as Los Alamos and Silicon Valley and researchers at institutions such as Stanford University are leading the way in citizen efforts to ensure that such machines will in the future let voters know what votes are actually being recorded and provide a physical means of reviewing that record after the fact. The state of California, concerned about reports of problems with electronic voting machines, did issue a requirement that beginning in 1996 all electronic voting machines already in place must be retrofitted to produce a hard-copy audit trail, and after mid-1995 all new machines put in place in the state must have this capacity. Thus despite this acknowledgment that the use of electronic voting machines may yield unreliable voting results, electronic voting machines with no audit trail were left in place for the 2004 presidential elections.

At the time of writing, there is a national movement to demand voter-verified records of votes so that there will be a trustworthy audit trail. Twenty-seven states require this by either executive order or statute, and the rest are currently debating legislation that would do the same. Bills have been introduced in both the House and the Senate that would do the same for federal elections. In response to news reports of election abuses, rigorous scientific research into the ways that non-auditable electronic voting machines could give and have yielded distorted election results, and technical work on ways to improve electronic voting machines, support for such legislation is growing.

Information Policy and Change in Technological Systems

Policies to support technological innovation have appeared under several different rubrics. The notion of science policy appeared after World War II, providing the justification for launching the National Science Foundation. Science policy, however, was often a difficult sell, because so few politicians understand either the nature of scientific research or its importance. (The phrase "behavioral science" replaced "social science" for policy purposes precisely for this reason: when the creation of the NSF was being debated, some legislators believed the agency would support "socialist science" and thus resisted its formation.) The concept of industrial policy, which included technology policy, appeared in the late 1970s in debates about how to improve national competitiveness. This conceptual frame was critiqued because it drew attention to the fact that some industries would be winners and others would be losers. By the 1990s, rhetoric had shifted to innovation policy. The federal government now focuses on supporting R&D in order to ensure that the U.S. economy—and the U.S. military—are competitive.

All presidents since Franklin D. Roosevelt have recognized the national importance of science and engineering, though this was first expressly announced as a policy goal for the country by President Harry S. Truman in 1948, at the one-hundredth anniversary meeting of the American Association for the Advancement of Science. It was not until 1976 that R&D in support of technological innovation other than to serve military ends was the subject of government policy. In that year, the National Science and Technology Policy, Organization, and Priorities Act established an Office of Science and Technology Policy (OSTP) in the White House and created a category of "critical technologies" deserving of government support. Critical technologies are scientific and technological efforts expected to provide results of importance to the nation but which the private sector may be unwilling or unable to support. While previously technological innovation supported by the government had to be mission-specific, for critical technologies' cost-benefit analysis regarding the utility of an innovation to enhance national capacity in general is used to justify support.

The question of the role of the federal government in managing the scientific and technical information it had helped produce, including translating the findings of basic research into usable applications, came to the fore in 1960s. After the Soviets successfully launched Sputnik, the first satellite, the U.S. government drew attention to question of transfer and distribution of scientific and technical information as inseparable part of the research and development process. The 1963 Weinberg report entitled "Science, Government, and Information" identified transfer of information as an integral part of the R&D process and described scientists and engineers, along with conventional information handlers, as part of a new information community in the era of "Big Science." The Baker Panel examined both the government and nongovernment information communities. The Crawford Panel called for a central authority to manage science and technology information within the federal government. Hubert Humphrey led Congress in a decade of development of science and technology programs and initiatives that promoted collaboration between the federal government, universities, and the private sector. The NSF was encouraged to support the development of private information services and to promote uniform abstracting and indexing practices. Each federal agency was charged with the responsibility of fostering information activities within its own field, and of collaborating with the private sector, and the 1965 Brooks Act required federal agencies to meet standards for both computer management planning and technology administration.

The degree to which such efforts were centralized and coordinated, and their relative importance to the executive branch, changed with each administration. Though in the 1960s it was considered crucial for the president to have a high-level science advisor and scientific and technical information management activities were coordinated out of the White House, President Richard Nixon abolished the executive branch's Office of Science and Technology Policy, got rid of the science advisor, and transferred control over information management to the NSF. In 1975, the science advisor and office were reinstated. Technological innovation was high on the Clinton administration's agenda, but is not of much interest to George W. Bush. President Bush disbanded a subcommittee of the OSTP—the Presidential Information Technology Advisory Committee (PITAC)—in June 2005 after the group issued a report warning that without a change in federal government policies regarding support for research computation, the already-eroding competitive position of the United States in science and technology would continue to decline.

By the 1980s, the problem of management of scientific and technical information began to collide with the desire to reduce the size of government and to eradicate paperwork where possible. The executive branch's Office of Management and Budget became the de facto information manager for the government. The decade was marked by disarray and disagreement regarding specifically how information should be handled. A 1989 report from the National Academy of Sciences, *Information Technology and the Conduct of Research*, pointed the way to broader use of the Internet as a solution by drawing attention to the ways in which technology could be used for communication not only within the research community, but also between the research community, society, and the government.

The use of exemptions from antitrust laws to stimulate technological innovation was discussed in chapter 6. Direct funding of research, tax credits, and procurement are other information policy tools used for this purpose that are discussed here. Information policies that are also pertinent but that are not included here include interventions into curricula, the establishment of educational standards, and efforts to influence the staffing and freedom of speech of those on faculties of higher education institutions. The extremely important area of restrictions on the free flow of scientific and technical information was discussed in chapter 7.

Direct Funding of Research

Research and development is both a deliberate means of encouraging change in technologies as a way of bringing about change in society and the economy and an economic sector in its own right. There is a long history of government support for research to serve various purposes. In the nineteenth century, the Patent Office was involved in agricultural research; in the early twentieth century, the military supported communications research; and the government's statistical agencies have long investigated social and economic trends. Until World War II, however, industry was the principal site of R&D, accounting for about two thirds of the budget devoted to this purpose. The war spurred interest in government support for basic research because of its many research-based military successes. Prior to this, U.S. scientists had relied upon the results of basic research in Europe as the foundations of their applied research, but a significant percentage of European research capacity was destroyed during the war. A 1944 report from Vannevar Bush to President Roosevelt on the role of science and engineering in peacetime, and support for government funding of research by the congressional Kilgore Committee, led to the establishment of the NSF in 1950. Topic-specific research programs were put in place in the National Institutes of Health (NIH) and within several government departments, and Korean War conditions kept attention on the contributions R&D might make to the military.

By 1951, the infrastructure for policy for R&D was in place—a proto-presidential advisory commission, and the six agencies that were to carry the bulk of the load. In following years, other research-oriented entities such as the National Aeronautics and Space Administration (NASA), were either created de novo or evolved out of existing organizations. The level of government funding for R&D went up significantly, however, when Congress realized that technological innovation was a critical battleground in the Cold War after the Soviet launch of the Sputnik satellite in 1957. In 1959, the government spent $8 billion on scientific research, nearly equaling the total spent on science from 1776 through World War II. R&D funding was only 0.025 percent of the federal budget in 1950, but rose by 1960 to 10 percent of the budget to account for more than two thirds of all R&D funds spent in the United States.

Today NASA and the Defense, Energy, and Homeland Security Departments receive the bulk of federal dollars for R&D. Other agencies that conduct R&D, however, include the Environmental Protection Agency, the Agency for International Development, and the departments of Commerce, the Interior, Education, and Transportation. Although the NSF accounts for only 20 percent of the funds the federal government commits to supporting R&D, it receives the most public attention because it is the only entity responsible for funding across the entire range of the sciences and because much of the work of the dominant agencies in R&D, such as that of the Defense and Energy departments, is classified. The government also maintains its own laboratories, called Federally Funded Research and Development Centers, that include such facilities as those at Livermore, Sandia, and Los Alamos. It isn't always clear what type of research will be conducted by a particular agency; the Department of Commerce is involved in research on natural resources and the environment, NASA supports research on transportation, the Department of Labor sponsors research on health issues, and the Department of Health provides grants for research on education.

R&D has remained a significant proportion of the discretionary federal budget, but the size of that budget has declined as the cost of entitlements and military commitments rises (Norberg and O'Neill 1996). In 1953, total U.S. R&D was just under 1.5 percent of the gross national product (GNP), with the federal government supplying just slightly over half of the funds. Today, R&D consumes almost 3 percent of GNP, with industry providing two thirds of the financial support. Though in the 1960s the greatest percentage of nondefense R&D support went to space projects, today about two-thirds of the resources that go to nondefense R&D projects are in the area of health. Announcements of areas in which the federal government will fund R&D have been becoming ever more specific. By 2006, support for R&D was not keeping up with inflation and ever-larger portions of the $129.5 billion budget are devoted to weapons development and homeland security; the same trend is continuing in the proposed budget of $136.9 billion for 2007.

Trends of importance include policy-making on scientific matters without input from scientists, dominance of the research agenda by defense concerns failure to remain competitive in research-related computation, government intrusion into the research process, and the impact of federal funding on universities.

Reduction of input of scientists into science-related decisions The importance of science advisors has risen and waned since World War II. The success of the Manhattan Project in developing the atomic bomb convinced a generation that scientific expertise was critical to national security. President Dwight Eisenhower appointed the first full-time presidential science advisor. President John F. Kennedy's advisor, Jerome B. Wiesner, was considered one of the most influential ever, but he quit over the administration's failure to take his advice regarding the environmental impact of atmospheric testing of nuclear weapons. President Richard Nixon abolished the science advisor's office after disputes over several issues. In 1985, Secretary of State George P. Shultz publicly rebuked scientists for their opposition to research on "Star Wars," the planned ballistic missile defense system; though opposition was motivated by the scientific evaluation that the plan was unworkable, Shultz insisted that such an evaluation was beyond the expertise and authority of scientists. President Bill Clinton returned attention to science, though concerns over the budget deficit placed limits on the extent to which funding was increased. Clinton's interest in technology as a means of pulling the country out of recession translated into an emphasis on applied as opposed to basic research throughout much of his administration, though funding for basic research did rise again towards the end of his second term.

During the George W. Bush administration, the overall trend of making science-related decisions without scientific input has been exacerbated. Early examples that set the tone include rejection of the Kyoto accord on climate change, implementation of controls on stem-cell research, and support for a national missile defense system in the face of evidence that the technologies involved do not work. Delay in making key appointments in federal agencies involved with science, restrictions on ways in which research can be carried out, and the insistence that raw data be released without expert analysis are all facets of this same attitude.

Some of the inability of scientists to influence science-related policy may be attributed to a lack of sophistication regarding interpretation of the results of scientific research on the part of politicians, or to a preference for ideologically or politically driven decisions even regarding matters of science. Other factors that contribute to the situation, however, include perceptions of a sense of privilege on the part of many scientists since World War II, an inability to translate the results of research into lay terms, a professional culture that does not include communicating with policy-makers among criteria that build reputations, the fear that political activity might compromise scientific objectivity, and the financial hunger of big science, with its dependence on elaborate technologies.

Defense dominance of R&D During the Cold War, and particularly during the 1980s, the proportion of funding dollars for R&D spent on defense far outstripped that spent on nondefense research problems. During the 1990s the two sectors converged, but since 9/11 support for defense relative to other needs has again risen. While it has long been claimed that defense-related R&D has "trickle-down" effects for scientists working in other areas, in the past few years almost all of the defense-related budget has gone into development of weapons systems rather than either basic or applied research. The 2006 budget further cut defense-related basic and applied research. Defense-related R&D is carried out by the Department of Energy and the Department of Homeland Security as well as the Department of Defense.

Nondefense R&D funding has remained stagnant for the last fifteen years. The proposed 2006 budget would receive real cuts for the third year in a row and fail to keep up with inflation. A commitment to double the budget of the National Institutes of Health between 1998 and 2003 was completed, but since for the last couple of years its funding has remained flat and in 2006 the R&D budget for the NIH would fail to match inflation for the first time in twenty-four years.

Existing treaties forbid offensive weapons research in biology and chemistry, but allow defensive research. It is hard to distinguish between the two, however, for while transforming an infectious substance into a biological warfare agent is offense and developing a vaccine to use against that agent is defense, the research path leading to both is virtually the same. Prior to 9/11, two criteria were used to determine whether a given program was offensive or defensive. "Small" projects were considered defensive and "large" projects offensive, because the latter create quantities of material beyond what is needed for research. The expressed intent of the nation conducting research was also taken into account.

Since 9/11, the United States has considered all of its research on biological and chemical weapons as defensive.

Failure to remain competitive in research-oriented computation All types of R&D have become more computationally intense since World War II. The ability to remain scientifically competitive, therefore, is inextricably tied to the extent to which the research community of an informational state has access to the most sophisticated computational facilities possible. The drop in U.S. support for the research computational infrastructure has been so severe in recent years that the President's Information Technology Advisory Council issued a report in 2005, entitled *Computational Science: Ensuring America's Competitiveness*, warning that without a significant increase in funding for research-oriented computation the United States would lose its competitive global position in science. This report was followed by a presidential decision to disband the advisory council that issued it, but concern about the same problem remains widespread.

Government intrusion into research process A number of new restrictions have been attached to federal grants since 9/11. In many cases, foreign students (by far the majority of graduate students in the United States in recent decades until 9/11) cannot be involved in grant-supported projects, foreign travel funded by grants must receive approval ahead of time, and in some cases foreign students must have government officials sign off on research results before they are published. Universities complain that a new category of scientific information is being created that is neither classified nor unclassified, and some universities are beginning to refuse to accept money under these new terms. The government insists that these restrictions are being attached only to "advanced" research projects, and not to funds going to basic and applied research, but many universities do not agree that this is a meaningful distinction.

The Government Performance and Results Act (GPRA) of 1993 provides a mandate to all federal agencies to account for program results through integration of strategic planning, budgeting, and performance measurement. In response, the NSF began to speak of its activities in terms of development of intellectual capital, integration of research and education, promotion of partnerships, and the social impact of the research it funds. Though the NSF uses peer review to award more of its research dollars than other agencies—94 percent, compared to 83 percent by the National Institutes of Health and only 24 percent of grants awarded by the Department of Energy—the most recent performance reports expressed concern over the quality of the peer review process, highlighting disparities across individuals both in terms of genre (narrative, anecdotal evidence, or scientific support for evaluations) and outcomes (some reviews include specific criticisms and recommendations for improvements, while others do not). The NSF has received the charge of developing alternative mechanisms for obtaining and reviewing proposals and must present indicators of the success of the projects it has funded in areas such as the extent to which ideas are published and taken up by others for use; the role of research in stimulating innovation and policy development; creation of new knowledge tools such as databases, software, instrumentation, data, samples, and germlines; and increased operating efficiency of shared-use facilities.

Once projects are approved by the NSF, the foundation must negotiate with the OMB regarding which ones will actually get funded to move forward. Raw data must now be released. In many cases government officials must sign off before publication.

Impact on universities Support for the U.S. university system—and ensuring sufficient human resources in science and engineering—have been considered essential to development and sustenance of a national research capacity, with the value of collaboration coming to be appreciated in particular in recent years. Education was a part of the NSF mission from the start, but became more important in the early 1970s when concern about computer literacy came onto the public agenda. Some NSF grant programs are specifically intended to enhance education in areas such as (currently) mathematics. And since the early 1990s, the NSF has required heavily funded science and technology centers to provide support for K–12 education among other educational tasks added to the activities designated by the research agenda.

The proportion of a university budget that comes from government grants varies enormously across the various categories of institutions of higher education, but grants have become more important as the level of state government support for public universities has declined. The Bayh-Dole Act, passed in 1980, provided a significant economic boost to institutions with research programs in science and engineering because it eased the conditions under which universities could claim patents to innovations that result from their work instead of turning the intellectual property rights over to the granting agency. Also known as the Patent and Trademark Law Amendments Act, this legislation made possible a new form of R&D limited partnership that helped bridge the investment and academic communities.

Tax Credits

Tax laws can encourage R&D efforts through tax reductions and/or enabling new types of financing arrangements. Tax laws can be critical to efforts to encourage development of new infrastructure, and can be particularly of interest to transnational corporations that might establish operations in any of a number of locations. Tax laws can also affect international competitiveness in the information industries; during the period from 1967 to 1980 when R&D expenditures in the United States as a percentage of GNP dropped 20 percent, analysts noted that many major trading partners allow immediate expensive of R&D costs for tax purposes, as well as other tax incentives for R&D. In an environment in which many of the corporations involved in R&D are transnational, however, the national strategic incentive to subsidize R&D must be balanced against a national corrective incentive to tax R&D when corporations conducting R&D in many nation-states are involved. Economists provide a theoretical justification for tax laws favorable to R&D when they point out that the externalities associated with R&D make its social rate of return greater than the return to those undertaking R&D—although in periods of rapid innovation a successful first mover often does acquire an economic advantage in the marketplace.

Trends in the use of tax laws to promote technological innovation include the use of tax credits, promotion of new forms of limited partnerships, and new tax-like opportunities that have appeared in the internet environment.

Tax credits to promote innovation The Economic Recovery Tax Act of 1981 included a 25 percent tax credit for increases in R&D expenditures through 1985, when it was extended. Qualified research expenditures include payments for qualified research services and supplies, rights to use computers, and 65 percent of payments made for contract research done on behalf of taxpayers; the credit is available to all companies, regardless of size. This was a complex piece of legislation that based analysis of the permissible tax credit on firm-specific histories of investment in R&D. One problem with the act was that new firms couldn't take advantage of the tax credit because they lacked the necessary historical baseline. Some argued the credit should have been linked to output, but this is notoriously difficult to measure in the area of R&D. In 1990, and 1996 Congress altered the base of the credit, making it significantly more complex and more difficult to understand. There have been gaps in coverage in renewals of tax credit over time, many of which were retroactively filled. There was an unprecedented extension during the period from 1999 to 2004, including a 1 percent increase in rates for the alternative incremental research credit that benefits companies that no longer qualify for the traditional credit.

There is disagreement about the actual effect of this tax credit, partially because it is so difficult to measure the return on investment for R&D. While some corporations, such as Hewlett-Packard, gave direct credit to the act for encouraging an increase in investment in R&D, others claim that there was no discernible impact on the national level of R&D in the years following passage of the act. At the end of 1980s, it did appear that the tax incentive had encouraged a longer time horizon for R&D—the mean share of R&D devoted to long-term projects (those with no expected payoffs within next five years) was 21.1 percent up about 3 percent from ten years earlier. Research produces wildly differing results regarding the effects of these tax credits. At the time of writing, another bill is before Congress that would permanently extend the tax credit, claiming it is necessary in order to be competitive with tax incentives offered by Canada, the United Kingdom, France, Japan, India, and Singapore.

New tax-like opportunities with the Internet The struggle over control over domain names in the Internet has mixed taxing functions with direct investment in R&D. When the NSF decided in 1995 to allow one of its contractors to begin charging fees for domain name registration, the agency was effectively setting itself up as a taxing authority, with $15 of the original $50 annual charge going to an "intellectual infrastructure fund" to be administered by the NSF. The fee generated tens of millions of dollars before being challenged legally in 1998.

Procurement

Procurement—the purchase of technologies and services by government—is considered a traditional policy tool for the encouragement of innovation. The GAO reports that every minute of every business day the government buys an average of $1.9 million in goods and services. In fiscal year 2000, federal agencies spent $88 billion on services, more than all other acquisition categories. About three quarters of all government procurement is undertaken by the Department of Defense; in 2004, the Department of Defense will spend $66 billion on R&D alone, with most of that going to the development of new weapons systems. About 6 percent of procurement funds that go outside of government are spent on educational institutions and other nonprofits, 20 percent on small businesses, and the rest on other private sector vendors.

Purchases of goods and services by state, county, municipal, and school district governments also accounted for approximately 11 percent of the U.S. gross domestic product (GDP) according to the 2000 census. Mega-governments, such as those of the state of California or New York City, have financial activity equivalent to the largest private businesses of the Fortune 500. The logistics of procurement are so problematic for governments that the GAO issued over 400 reports between 1997 and 2001 on issues raised by the acquisition of information technology and software.

From an international perspective, procurement is a nontariff trade barrier. (Others include customs procedures, health and safety regulations, and national technical standards.) Multinational and transnational firms will not succeed in markets in which government procurement practices are traditionally directed at nationally based vendors. In 1989, the U.S. Department of State estimated that the extent of European funds in procurement at that time was about $550 billion annually, with only 20 percent of that subject to open tendering and only 2 percent granted to nontraditional firms. These policies were therefore considered a real market barrier in telecommunications, and the first step of transparency of public procurement procedures in European telecommunications was considered important. Thus in the early 1990s, international trade agreements began to include provisions regarding liberalization of procurement, including in the areas of CPE and network equipment so important to information policy. Because procurement often results from informal processes, longstanding interpersonal relationships, and unrecorded conversations, it can be a difficult site for regulatory intervention.

From the perspective of the nation-state, however, procurement is an important means of ensuring that necessary national capacity is supported. Thus the Buy America Act, first passed in 1933, established a public sector preference for public sector procurement—even though by the mid-1980s it was estimated that buying in accordance with this principle could add 5 percent to the cost of what might be otherwise acquired from foreign competition, 12 percent to the cost if procurement were also used to bring manufacturing capacity to a depressed region, and up to 50 percent more in cost for the defense market. Analysts argued that U.S. capacity for military technologies had been damaged by the devoting of military resources to the Vietnam War during the 1960s and 1970s, and the overall decline in R&D and procurement funding in the 1970s. Thus in the 1980s, funding and procurement began to rise again, doubling yearly for a period. This was also one among the arguments used to justify the innovation exemption from antitrust law in one of its first applications, to the high-speed semiconductor chip industry, as there was fear that otherwise the United States would come to rely on suppliers from other countries for this fundamentally necessary technology. The need to justify sustaining these budgets in the 1990s, once the Cold War was ostensibly over, was one of the drivers behind the development of new security theory, with its redefinition of the enemy, as well as the claimed need to defend the planet against possible meteorite hits. The war on terrorism, of course, now provides the justification required to sustain high military procurement budgets.

The importance of procurement to the establishment and maintenance of national capacity makes inefficiencies in the system a matter of concern. Both the GAO and the Office of Technology Assessment have reported that there are limits to the usefulness of procurement because the practice generally considers only current rather than future needs, is overly reliant on a single or a few vendors in particular product areas, takes insufficient advantage of the opportunity for "cross-servicing" within government (the purchase of services from one governmental unit by another), and is inconsistenct in its decision-making processes. Since the mid-1990s there have been a number of efforts intended to centralize and increase the efficiency of procurement, in the hopes that doing so would have the additional value of ensuring that systems purchased by government were interoperable. The War on Drugs was seen, among other things, as an opportunity to develop, test, and refine new processes for allocating resources and restructuring procurement capabilities under what the intelligence community described as "revolutionary" conditions. Overall contracting dollars declined in the last decades of the twentieth century (from $266 billion in 1985 to $204 billion in 2000), but are rising again in the Homeland Security environment. (A lot of the decline had been in the areas of equipment modification, equipment maintenance, and operation of government-owned facilities.) There has been a dramatic shift from contracting for goods to contracting for services (largely for computing and for special studies not considered R&D), and the acquisition workforce overall is declining.

The procurement process is, among other things, a rhetorical practice involving persuading Congress and the public to accept devotion of large amounts of money to the acquisition of goods—particularly weapons systems. The persuasive aspects of the process have an impact on the technologies that are produced, however, for complex systems that are highly innovative are more appealing to those in Congress, and to the voter, than are systems for mundane logistical support or traditional types of military goods of enduring value.

Bargaining with vendors A new approach to procurement in recent decades has been that of bargaining with the companies that control the development of technology. This practice has been forced upon the government by the need to access the technologies that these companies control. It is also revelatory of the growth of corporate power relative to that of the nation-state, for bargaining per se is a dilution of state autonomy, and no government freely chooses to negotiate for access to that which it considers fundamental for survival. Of course, to some degree, those involved in procurement have long been captive to a vision of technological possibility offered by vendors, for innovation has been proceeding at such a pace, and so constantly, that no one not involved with the development of new products on the ground can possibly keep up with developments.

Loss of institutional knowledge Procurement procedures, including the development of very technical specifications, are complex, highly detailed, and—when well done—require deep knowledge of the technologies involved. Almost two-thirds of the personnel in the federal government involved with procurement procedures have left government for one reason or another since 2000, taking with them their long and deep institutional knowledge. There is always concern about the extent to which those responsible for procurement have been "captured," whether honestly through information subsidies or dishonestly through other types of influence, by those who receive large government contracts. It is certainly possible that an inexperienced staff may well be more susceptible than those more experienced to decision-making on ideological or religious grounds, in response to direct attempts to exert influence.

Export controls as a procurement practice Restrictions on the export of high technology have been in place since the beginning of the Cold War, as discussed in chapter 10. Industry, of course, has always been concerned about the limitations on markets established by export controls. In response, a 1976 Defense Science Board Task Force report (the Bucy Report) argued that the use of export controls actually saves the United States $20–$50 billion per year in what would otherwise have to be spent in defense procurement if other countries around the world had access to state-of-the-art technologies from the United States that are capable of dual-use. The 1987 report *Balancing the National Interest* from the National Academy of Sciences, however, offered a different picture. The NAS found that U.S. export controls cost the country $8.3 billion annually, and 188,000 lost jobs in 1985. Fear of leakage of U.S.-based technologies and technological knowledge to other countries continues to provide a justification for incorporation of high levels of funding for R&D as part of U.S. government procurement practices.

Use of procurement as a policy tool One of the most contentious elements of the PATRIOT Act has been formation of a national database that incorporates into one database data of all kinds about individuals from diverse sources. This type of database has long been proposed by the national security community, and long been resisted by Congress, which has repeatedly taken the position that the kind of "data-matching" such a database makes possible would create unacceptable invasions of privacy. With passage of the PATRIOT Act, shortly after the 9/11 experience and with little public debate, the database was approved, but many around the country are still concerned about its possible impact on privacy. The Department of Homeland Security, on the other hand, is anxious to begin computerizing its watch list by automating scanning for individuals whose personal data fit particular profiles of interest. The logistics of establishing such a database include the acquisition of massive new computer systems by the government; the GAO has said that all such purchases must still be approved by that agency, and in so doing has slowed down the process of putting the database in place. From the perspective of overall management of the federal budget, this was, of course, a completely appropriate request from the GAO. Politically, however, it is also true that the longer it takes to put the database in place, the more opportunity there is to build an effective political response to counter this move.

Information Policy and Change in Information Systems

It is hard to separate information policies that yield or direct change in information systems from other activities. Education could just as well have been categorized here as in chapter 5, as a matter of negotiation between state and individual identity, for education is the first step in the production of new knowledge and the change that inevitably brings. Direct funding for research and development, involves the development of new knowledge as well as technologies, and so forth. The two examples discussed in this section include federal government treatment of the arts and its role in proactive dissemination of information.

The Arts

The role of art as an information system was demonstrated in the eighteenth century, when different genres were placed into a taxonomy that was codified in Diderot's *Encyclopedia* and in the then newly emerging philosophy of aesthetics. Museums, of course, exemplify a variety of means of classification of artistic information—by culture, by artist, by medium, by school, and so forth. The arts also convey information in the sense that they provide indicators of taste (sociologist Emile Durkheim used the arts analytically for this purpose, along with statistics), and of the image an entity has of itself.

With the informatization of society, the arts have come to take on new roles. Historically, artists produced works in tribute to or under the direction of those in power. In late modernity, artists were often outsiders, but in filling that role also provided alternative visions of social life. Today, digital artists are involved in technological innovation itself, writing software programs, creating new types of human-computer interfaces, and even designing computer chips. All three of these roles—celebrant of existing power relations, visionary of alternative social forms, and technological innovator—have implications for information policy.

Ongoing government support for the arts is a twentieth-century phenomenon. The celebratory function of the arts has had a policy presence in the United States since 1790, when Congress established the U.S. Marine Band. (In the 1980s, this band was still receiving more support than was the entire National Endowment for the Arts.) Discussion about providing permanent support for the arts began in 1826, and continued off and on through the rest of the nineteenth and early twentieth centuries.

In 1846, Congress accepted a bequest that founded the Smithsonian Institution, which in turn served as a receptacle for further bequests of artworks to the nation. In 1934, President Franklin D. Roosevelt established the Treasury Department's Section on Painting and Sculpture to commission art for federal buildings around the country.

The role of the artist as visionary began to appear after World War II, when affiliation with the arts began to be seen as a sign of a "modern" society. This did not achieve a policy presence in the United States, however, until a 1963 speech by President Kennedy, that announced a new cultural policy linking reconstruction of the identity of the artist to that of the nation-state. Kennedy stressed the value of artistic vision to the nation, and opposed this individualism to suppression of individual rights under communism. Cultural progress was rhetorically allied with progress in other fields, and government officials were urged to consider cultural welfare to be as important as more traditional health and education areas. With this encouragement, interest in sustained public funding for the arts was reinvigorated, and in 1965, under President Lyndon Johnson, the National Foundation for the Arts and Humanities—now two entities, the National Endowment for the Arts and the National Endowment for the Humanities—was launched to provide direct funding to artists and arts organizations.

The third role, the artist as innovator, has presented three different faces, depending on whether the innovation involved is in the area of science, technology, or politics. With high-speed and high-capacity computing, it became possible to create visual images of scientific data. Visualization, it turned out, in turn helped scientists achieve new conceptualizations and insights into their material because they were literally able to see the subjects of their research in new ways. Development and refinement of techniques for visualization itself have themselves become the subjects of federal R&D funding (and the beauty of these visualizations has led to presentation of this scientific work as art itself). The private sector has taken the lead in offering opportunities for artists to experiment with emerging technologies, knowing that in turn further innovation would result. The research unit Xerox PARC, for example, had a program for many years in which artists were brought onto campus to work full time with engineers; the artists would describe what they wanted to do, the engineers would design the technologies needed by the artists, and in the end the artists would keep the intellectual property rights to the artworks they produced, while Xerox PARC kept the patents in the technologies produced.

Despite the political role for artists envisioned by President Kennedy, federal and state support for artistic activity in the public sphere has largely been confined to the creation of public art (works of art placed on public sites), arts education and performance in social support institutions, and arts education in the schools. Many artists themselves, however, have taken on political leadership as a goal. The results range from collective art production as a model of social organization to the provocations of those engaged in "tactical media" or "hacktivism" practices. These are manipulations of the information infrastructure itself as a form of political argument, understood by practitioners to be pre-policy, in the sense that they expect regulation of certain activities may be a likely response.

Not everyone considers U.S. art policy a success. It is critiqued for basing decisions on an inadequate understanding of the real problems facing those in the arts. Many argue that majoritarian decision rules are not the most appropriate for making arts-related decisions. A number of tensions appear as a result of conflicting goals of different policies, as between the desire for privacy and requirements for disclosure; between industrial policy and cultural policy; between preservation of heritage and service to newer art forms; and between an intellectual property rights system that supports creativity and one that protects the profits of large corporate content providers. Art presents a profound challenge to policy-makers because of its multiple relationships to power, both supportive and challenging at the same time. Arts institutions play dual roles as well, providing a distribution medium at the same time that they create value in particular works, both for the artists and for themselves.

In the 1990s, economists began to pay attention to the economic importance of the arts, which create jobs, generates tax revenues, and provides a lot of support to communities in which arts facilities are located via use of service industries such as hotels, restaurants, and parking. In 2001, according to the Bureau of Economic Analysis, consumers spent $10.6 billion, or $37.30 per person, at performing arts events—$1.9 billion more than outlays for tickets to movie theaters and $500 million more than admissions to spectator sports events. Adjusted for inflation, this was a 3.6 percent increase over the year before. A 2002 survey also showed that 39 percent of adults in the United States attend a fine art event or a museum annually. As spending on videos and computers has gone up as a percentage of spending on leisure, the amount spent on "commercial participant amusements" such as bowling, billiards, casino gambling, and amusement parks declined. (Television watching is also declining with growing computer use.) Of the nine categories of income spent on leisure activities tracked statistically (from reading to gardening), the categories sustaining the most spending are video and audio goods and musical instruments at 13.1 percent.

Such trends don't, of course, always translate into economic support for individual artists. Artists generally earn less than others with the same level of education and professional status, but the census reported a 127 percent increase in the number of people who identified themselves as artists from 1970 to 1990. According to the Bureau of Labor Statistics, however, *un*employment among artists is also rising, from 3.5 percent to 5.5 percent from 2000 to 2002, roughly twice the rate found across professional workers. As with all unemployment statistics, these figures do not reflect the thousands of people who left the labor market altogether; the BLS does note that where unemployment did not rise in the arts professions, it was due to abandonment of the field. Many artists work two jobs in order to sustain themselves (e.g., 37.2 percent of musicians and singers).

Information policy trends that affect the way in which the arts produce change in the information environment include analytical confusion, the funding response to particular artistic content, an expansion of the range of policy issues of importance to the arts, and a reaffirmation of the importance of the arts in K–12 education.

Analytical confusion There are two types of analytical confusion that provide difficulties for policy-making for the arts, both having to do with efforts to fully grasp the subject matter. The first stems from endemic problems applying economic concepts to informational and cultural goods and services that are exacerbated by changes in the nature of artistic practice, products, and institutions as a result of digitization. The second has a long history deriving from the linkage of certain art forms with socioeconomic class and political power.

The arts provide a premiere example of the difficulties of policy analysis in an information society. Economically, art has been viewed as a resource, a commodity, a process, a secondary good, and a source of technological innovation. With the development of efforts to quantify intellectual, social, human, and cultural capital, it has also become clear that art is an important form of capital. Among trends in the economic treatment of art today are a growing appreciation of art as a source of innovation rather than for art products as commodities in themselves, and recognition that art as a product can provide minority or marginalized communities with niches in the economy. Among artists there is a growing sense that it is they, not their works, that are the actual products, because so much of their income comes from the provision of services after a purchase (e.g., public talks and training). Meanwhile, though it is obvious to think of art as innovation, there are almost no analyses of the diffusion of artistic objects, practices, or ideas out of the many thousands of diffusion studies that have been done.

For a long time economists distinguished among three types of cultural commodities: unique products, reproducible products, and nonmaterial performances. In the digital environment, however, there are now additional categories, including constantly mutating digital works, works that simultaneously display multiple faces, and works that never reach a tangible form at all. How the economists, and the market, view art has an impact because perceptions alter the ways people think about material objects, the formation of meaning, and the creation of value.

Lewis Hyde points out that works of art exist simultaneously in two economies: the market economy and the gift economy. He argues that only one of these is essential, however, for "a work of art can survive without the market, but where there is no gift there is no art" (1983, p. xi). It is precisely the "gift" aspect of art that makes it so difficult to accurately measure the utility of the arts in terms that can make sense for economists. Understanding the world in a new way, being stimulated to greater creativity in one's own life, achieving a breakthrough in perception of someone from another culture, strengthening community, and growth in the cognitive ability to perceive patterns that then extends to other areas of learning are invaluable but not measurable quantitatively.

The categorization of the arts professions used for statistical purposes is revelatory of the relative importance of popular entertainment relative to either fine, folk, or "street" arts from an economic perspective. It also highlights the lack of fit between statistical categories and actual practices in the digital environment, for it is hard to know where in this categorization Web designers, digital artists, and those who use the information infrastructure as a medium itself would fit. The census offers these choices: architects; art directors, fine artists, and animators; designers; actors; producers and directors; dancers and choreographers; musicians and singers; announcers; writers and authors; photographers; and other artists and entertainers. A number of the arts are included in the NAICS (see chapter 5); see table 8.1 for an example of how artistic practices look from an industrial perspective.

Table 8.1
Categories and subcategories for sculpture in the NAICS

Category	Subcategory
Sculptors, independent	Independent artists, writers, and performers
Sculpture instruction	Fine arts schools (except academic) sculpture instruction (art, drama, and music schools)
Sculptures (e.g., gypsum, plaster of paris), manufacturing	Gypsum product manufacturing
Sculptures, architectural, clay, manufacturing	Vitreous china, fine earthenware, and other pottery product manufacturing
Monument (i.e., burial marker), dealers	All other miscellaneous store retailers (except tobacco stores)
Monuments and grave markers, wholesaling	Other miscellaneous durable goods wholesalers
Monuments and tombstone, cut stone (except finishing or lettering to order only) manufacturing	Cut stone and stone product manufacturing
Art goods wholesale	Establishments primarily engaged in the wholesale distribution of art goods such as artists' supplies, curios, and souvenirs
Museums, historical sites, and similar institutions	museums historical sites zoos and botanical gardens nature parks and other similar institutions

The second set of confusions arises out of an inability to fully cope with distinctions between "high" and "low" culture and their respective art forms, "fine" and "popular" art. The development of the arts as a set of institutions differs enormously from culture to culture. In Europe, high culture arose in royal courts, but in the United States the institutions of high culture emerged as part of a larger process of upper-class formation by urban elites familiar with recent European precedents. Those who take the position that only the genres of high culture deserve the designation of art find it difficult to acknowledge the enormous creativity that comes from the street up in a wide variety of genres, often themselves rapidly changing. Just a few contemporary examples include graffiti, new forms of music, fashion as art, and the multiple ways in which those with little money create aesthetic living environments. Statistical reports that claim that adult white women dominate the arts because they represent the largest percentage of people who go to the ballet completely miss the vibrant and ubiquitous practice of the arts community-wide in many, many places in this country.

This blindness to the actual artistic practices of daily life by a large proportion of the U.S. population has a policy consequence because the needs of these individuals and communities are not taken into account. In a 1995 national task force report that was one of the first explorations of the implications of the Internet for the arts and humanities and possible policy responses to it, for example, there was a clear division of opinion: On the one hand, those who defined art only in high-culture terms believed the Internet was important to the arts because it made it easier to access elite museum collections in Europe, and identified as policy options support for development of finding aids and search tools for databases involving images. On the other hand, those whose definition of art included art produced by the members of any community, irrespective of how labelled, believed the Internet was important because it enabled new types of artistic practice and opened up new distribution channels for artists and arts organizations of all kinds. The important policy tool for those in this second group was ensuring that broadband access into the home was two-way, so that artists could send their work out as well as receiving content from corporate producers.

The funding response to content Conventional economic arguments for government support for the arts include the unwillingness or inability of audiences to bear the full costs, treatment of the arts as "merit goods" with intrinsic value, and equity considerations (the desire to ensure an equality of opportunity for both producers and consumers). Arguments on the other side include the possibility that public funding for the arts is actually a transfer from the poor to the rich; that it crowds the private sector; that it promotes inefficiently centralized decision-making that has the effect of limiting public choice; and that it commercializes indigenous artforms in a manipulation of ethnicity. While economic arguments for supporting the arts do have persuasive power with policy-makers, they never stand alone in justifying funding decisions. Rather, funds are devoted to sustaining the arts when they are perceived as serving other social goals, from community development to enhancement of the national image. Around the world, some countries are increasing their per-capita spending in the arts while others are decreasing it. A comparative analysis of per-capita spending on the arts and museums in ten nation-states placed the United States at the bottom with $6 per person, compared to $91 in Finland, $85 in Germany, $46 in Canada, and about $25 in both Australia and the United Kingdom.

Most, but not all, funding for the arts in the United States comes from the National Endowment for the Arts (NEA) funding for scholarship and other infrastructural supports for the arts, such as databases, can also come from the National Endowment for the Humanities. From the agency's founding in 1965 until 2001, over 111,000 grants were provided to artists and arts organizations. The first appropriations bill was for $2.5 million in half a dozen programs. Over time, the range of programs receiving support kept expanding, as did funding. The largest budget ever given to the NEA was in 1992, at $175,954,680. At that point, the NEA's funding of some very extreme forms of art, including work that was politically critical; blasphemous; obscene, in the sense of involving what are widely viewed as distasteful bodily functions; and, depending on one's viewpoint, sexually obscene, had a funding impact. Claims that loss of funding for particular works and/or artists was unconstitutional censorship lost in the courts, Congress placed content restrictions on what the NEA could fund, and the NEA budget was cut. The sudden growth of interest in providing evidence of the economic value of the arts in the 1990s should be understood as a strategic response to these events. In 2004, the latest year for which an annual report is available, the agency received almost $129 million. Arts funding at the state level was severely cut in the early 1990s, but is beginning to achieve a modest recuperation, and there is anecdotal but not hard evidence of an increase in support from local funding sources.

Federal government funding is complemented to some extent by donations to arts organizations and artists by foundations, but these portfolios also tend to be small relative to the levels of funding provided by foundations to social welfare projects. The importance of individual donors is not often recognized, but of the $190 billion of charitable giving in 1999, individuals donors accounted for nearly $144 billion, while foundations gave only $20 billion, with the remainder coming from corporations. The importance of individual donors to arts organizations is one of the reasons that funding at the local level is growing in relative importance.

Expansion of policy tools used to support the arts With growing appreciation for the role of the arts in community life and to the economy, a number of new types of policy tools have come into use. Support today comes not only from cultural agencies of municipalities and states, but also from agencies responsible for transportation, criminal justice, housing, and small business. It is understood that involvement with the arts reduces juvenile delinquency, and that small businesses in the arts can contribute strongly to the local economy. Community arts facilities offer training in employable skills. A portion of public housing subsidies can be devoted to creating artists' communities. Tax credits for arts facilities are useful. In some municipalities, citizens have voted themselves a small annual tax through bond issues that supports cultural institutions, and in others a tax on video rentals and sales of CDs and tapes supports public arts. Tax "checkoff" (donations via a deduction on the income tax), proceeds from lotteries, sales of property seized from organized crime, and vanity license plate sales have all been used to support the arts.

The Center for Arts and Culture, a nonprofit organization put together a list in 2003 of landmark legislation important to the arts. Divided into the categories of investment, community, education and the creative workforce, access and equity, globalization, heritage, and diversity, the more than sixty pieces of legislation on the list demonstrate the breadth of the range of policies understood today to affect the arts. Bills under consideration include a range of approaches to enhancing diversity in telecommunications and broadcasting, support for libraries and museums, changes in tax law related to charitable giving, a requirement for sectoral market assessment in the design of regional training programs, a National Language Act, several bills relating to access to the Internet and to intellectual property rights in the digital environment, protection for Iraqi cultural antiquities, legislation dealing with national parks, establishment of historical archives, religious liberties, privacy, arts education, and on. Recognizing that improvement of the living conditions of artists is an important category of arts policy, other nonprofits provide information on such matters as health insurance for those who are not covered by employing organizations.

Art and education The arts were among the first disciplines to develop educational goals and standards as part of the national curricular reform that began in 2000. Research has shown that education does play a significant role in development of a market for the arts, there is a positive correlation between exposure to the arts in the K–12 years and participation in the arts in adult life, and individuals recognize the linkage between appreciation of the fine arts and socioeconomic class. Arguments for the arts in education that came out of public forums held by the NEA around the country a few years ago include the importance of the arts as a subject in themselves; as a means of enhancing the study of other areas in the basic curriculum, acquiring vocational skills and competencies needed to function in an information society, and improving student retention; and as a contribution to family unity and growth.

Government Dissemination of Information

Information systems change not only when they are restructured, but also when new information becomes available. Technological change yields not only objects and processes that can be used by government and by consumers, as discussed previously, but also scientific and technical information that alters the information environment. Processes of social change, including political debate, also generate information that should become available throughout society. The key entities involved in dissemination of scientific and technical information are the NSF itself and the National Technical Information System. The Government Printing Office is responsible for distribution of other types of reports generated by government agencies and departments, documents produced in the course of political debate, and laws and regulation. Two other entities synthesize and analyze information and make it available to Congress and to the public: the Congressional Research Service (originally launched as the Legislative Reference Service in 1946), and the Office of Technology Assessment. The latter, still authorized but no longer funded, offered analysis of emerging technological issues with policy implications to Congress from 1974 to 1995.

Since the earliest years of the United States, there has been statutory provision for the printing and distribution of laws and treaties, preservation of state papers, and maintenance of official files in new departments. Benjamin Franklin printed official documents of the colonies, and during the first year of Congress the House invited proposals for the printing of its proceedings and laws. By 1794, congressional appropriations included funds for printing not only for Congress, but also specific allocations for printing for the State Department, the Treasury Department, and the War Department. Local printers were used until 1819, and after 1819, the House and Senate each elected printers to serve national functions. By 1846, a superintendent of public printing was designated; in 1861, the Government Printing Office was established; in 1873, the GPO took over the *Congressional Record*; and in 1895, the role of the GPO was codified in the Printing Act, which has remained the core of law pertaining to public printing since that time. Publication of government documents was linked to their distribution early on. A system of federal depository libraries was established 1813, and the Printing Act of 1895 mandated distribution of federal documents to these libraries, launched publication of a monthly catalog of government documents, and led to the development of a classification system for government documents.

With the expansion of the bureaucratic state early in the twentieth century, the GPO took on the responsibilities of ensuring that all rules, regulations, and legal instruments were published in a codified manner. Each world war, too, added to the volume of materials that had to be handled by the GPO because they added to government paperwork. By the 1970s, it was estimated that the GPO was publishing 2.5 million forms per year to support government procedures. In the mid-1990s, under congressional mandate, the GPO began to transform itself in order to take advantage of the electronic environment, though many in the librarianship community were concerned that the enabling legislation did not pay enough attention to operationalizing principles such as permanent and universal access to government information.

The NTIS was launched in 1950 in response to three motivations. First, President Truman wanted the scientific and technical documents produced during the war—both by the United States, and those captured from the Axis countries—reviewed for their utility to industry and the general public. Second, inspired by Senator William Fulbright, there was interest in reducing the gap between large and small businesses in access to knowledge. And third, it was believed that Soviet successes were due to the Soviet Union's renowned clearinghouse, the All-Union Institute of Scientific and Technical Information, which systematically abstracted and indexed 8,000 scientific journals (including 1,800 from the United States) and provided full texts upon demand. In 1950, therefore, Congress mandated the establishment of a national clearinghouse to collect and distribute scientific and technical information. In doing so, it ignored the GPO and turned to the Department of Commerce, though this was not an entirely friendly fit because the secretary of commerce at the time was quite uncomfortable with the notion of the government as printer and publisher.

The need for a centralized information collection and distribution function only grew during the post-war years. In 1956, thirty-eight agencies had science functions and all had mechanisms for distributing documents. By 1960, government agencies involved with science and technology were issuing between 100,000 and 500,000 reports annually. While some of the research funded by the government did find its way into the open literature through journal publication, not all detail was appropriate for this venue, and sometimes it was felt that the delays between concluding research and publication—which could be several years—were simply too long. "Progress" or "interim" reports are considered of particular value, in part because often they may be the only source of negative information about failed methods and unproductive techniques. During the 1950s and 1960s, the Department of Defense, NASA, and the Atomic Energy Commission accounted for 90 percent of total R&D budget, but it was estimated that only about 7 percent of the 500,000 unclassified technical reports they published annually were announced publicly. In a 1960 study, only 22 percent of 2,295 federally generated reports had been published in whole or in part, and only 61 percent of those were indexed.

The process of collecting information became more systematic in 1992, when the American Technology Preeminence Act issued the mandate that all federally produced or financed information must be provided to NTIS in a timely manner. Unclassified documents from the Departments of Defense and Energy and from NASA comprise the largest bulk of contributions. About 25 percent of all new titles come from foreign sources through various international exchange agreements, with the highest percentage coming from Canada and Germany, followed by the Netherlands, Japan, France, and the United Kingdom, and then international organizations. The collection consists almost exclusively of unclassified reports and computer products, as opposed to journal articles available in the open literature. An online database provides access to materials from 1964 on, with print and microform indexes for materials produced before then. NTIS now has the responsibility of transferring materials to depository libraries.

NTIS was threatened with closure or privatization during the 1990s, but today it remains an agency of the Department of Commerce that supports itself through fees generated by the sale of individual reports or ongoing subscriptions to its service. By now, about 2.5 million titles are available from NTIS, with about 70,000–80,000 titles added each year. Bibliographic detail about items produced since 1990—numbering approximately 750,000—is searchable online. There are fees for searching and for purchase of documents, but they are affordable to individual scholars and small businesses as well as large corporations—it costs $15 for a day pass for searching, and documents are usually priced in the tens of dollars.

The National Science Foundation was also created in 1950, and among its roles, too, was strengthening the role of government as a clearinghouse for scientific information. In part, this was done through subsidization of existing vehicles such as the Library of Congress and private publishing houses. In addition, the NSF began to collect data on science, engineering, research, and education. This function was expanded in 1972, when it took on the additional function of providing statistical support for policy decisions in the areas of R&D and education.

Information policy trends of importance in terms of their impact on changes in the information environment include the impact of centralization on interagency rivalries, a struggle between the executive and legislative branches over control of distribution of government information, public release of scientific data as opposed to expert analysis of that data, executive branch intervention into the use of scientific data by federal agencies, a blurring of genre, and the disappearance of materials post–9/11.

Centralization and interagency rivalries Today it is a commonplace that turf battles within organizations are one of the biggest barriers to successfully instituting computerized information systems. The same problem was faced by the U.S. government, which found for years that efforts to get agencies to release their materials publicly would founder on interagency rivalries. This problem was exacerbated from the 1940s on, after the government began to turn to private industry for help, because individuals working on government contracts still had private careers and corporate interests to take into consideration. At one time it was estimated that Department of Defense contractors annually withheld about four fifths of their annual reports, and agencies were fearful of demanding compliance regarding publication because they were afraid to provoke contractors. Efforts by the Department of Defense to establish its own integrated program of scientific and technical report services therefore failed. The 1992 statutory requirement that all reports be submitted to NTIS has made a significant difference in terms of the availability of information.

Tensions between the executive and legislative branches Conflict between the executive and legislative branches over control of the GPO began during the agency's first decade of existence. The crux of the issue is control: Is it constitutional for Congress to dictate to the executive branch how it should manage itself? (The two most successful public printers, who managed the GPO in the 1930s and 1940s, declared themselves independent of both branches of government, and got away with it, because neither branch could muster sufficient political weight to provide a challenge to that independence.)

By the 1950s, jealous of the superior ability of the executive branch to generate information, Congress was habitually denying federal agencies and departments funds for printing. This tactic of course did not stop printing activities, for agencies simply abandoned the GPO as the authorized channel for printing and established printing plants of their own with funds from other lines in their budgets. Limitations on the GPO's budget, too, meant that it couldn't keep up with the manuscripts it was given, and had to either stockpile manuscripts or use commercial printers. The debate was not merely "academic," for in the applied sciences backlogging information renders research useless. Though budget arguments were used to justify these restrictions, in fact they raised the cost of government enormously, because millions of dollars were spent reproducing research that had been conducted already, but was inaccessible and therefore unknown. In 1959, for example, both NASA and the Air Force spent a year and $8 million apiece developing very similar space vehicles. According to one 1958 estimate, 30–85 percent of Department of Defense contractor research was duplicative. The effort spent on literature reviews in hopes of avoiding such duplication was extraordinary; at one point, the Army said that if a research project cost less than $100,000, it cost less to do it than to run a literature search to see if the work had been done before.

The struggle between the executive and legislative branches of government over the production and distribution of government documents took a new form with passage of the Paperwork Reduction Act of 1980. With this new statutory support for the executive branch position, the OMB took on the role of point man for the White House, aggressively challenging the GPO by issuing rules encouraging agencies to go elsewhere for their printing. Congress responded with inclusion of specific language in several appropriation laws mandating use of the GPO, and there is now a debate over whether the "monopoly" of the public printing office should be broken. The public interest argument, voiced most clearly by the librarianship community, is that with the GPO the production and distribution of information are linked, ensuring both permanency and universality of access. The OMB position is based on cost efficiencies alone, without regard to political and social consequences. Testimony by the GPO before Congress regarding usage of its materials, however, so grossly understated actual use that critics of the analysis concluded that either the GPO did not want to assume the necessary financial commitment to continue its activities, or that its staff actually had such little training in research methods that it did not understand that invalid procedures were used to generate the figures reported.

The movement to electronic government changed the rules of the old game. This shift was launched with the Electronic Freedom of Information Act of 1996, furthered by a number of rules issued by the OMB, and took another important step forward when President George W. Bush signed the E-Government Act of 2002. The approach to electronic government that has developed decentralizes publication and distribution of information in the sense that agencies and departments are responsible for providing information on their own Web sites, but centralizes it in the sense that the OMB serves as overall manager. Functions of the OMB under the new e-government legislation include developing an indexing system that can be used across Web sites. The biggest concern, of course, is that permitting the OMB to determine which information should be made available to the public will result in a significant constriction of access. Analysts who are watching these moves do so within the context of an executive branch that is asserting itself via the other branches of government in multiple ways, and considers the information available to others to be a powerful means of enhancing its own position.

The government and scholarly publication The history of the scholarly publication system in the United States has been influenced in part by the financing and political struggles of the GPO. In 1924, the comptroller general interpreted the pertinent title of the U.S. Code to mean that agencies need to publish documents they produced with the government when the government bore all costs of printing and distributing. Agencies were free to turn to the private sector if it bore all of the printing and distributing costs; in turn, private publishers could take both copyrights and profits. This soon became common practice. Even though a 1932 report on federal research concluded that authors took great pride in publishing with the government and were demoralized by going to private sources, the report still urged decentralization of publication through this means. By 1954, government grants subsidized journal production through coverage of page charges for publication, and in the 1960s the NSF established a policy that authorized agencies to pay journal costs and abstracting charges. A presidential task force encouraged all R&D agencies to urge authors to publish in conventional scholarly journals, and for a period this was the only venue through which research supported by the federal government could be published. Agencies liked to work with professional societies because they had better marketing approaches and improved the quality of published work through the peer review process, though this added to the cost of research.

National security One issue raised by public access to government information—both scientific and technical information and information about the government itself—is the possibility that that information might get into the hands of parties dangerous to the United States to use to further their own R&D. This concern was first expressed in the 1920s, based on suspicions that Presidents Wilson and Roosevelt had been using government programs to further the careers of particular individuals and their own through the growth of the bureaucratic state. In the 1920s there was a concerted congressional effort to stop government publishing, further fueled during the 1930s and 1940s by specific policies. Each time, however, attacks were aimed at Democratic presidential administrations. The response was that without publication of this information, Congress was deprived of expert opinion independent of the regulatory agencies, themselves potentially captured by the industries they were regulating. Oddly, there was also political resistance to centralized distribution center precisely because it was the Soviet way, and the "American" way was considered then to be decentralized, private, and often voluntary.

Executive branch intervention into use of scientific data by agencies The George W. Bush administration issued new standards in September 2001 that govern the "quality" and "objectivity" of scientific information released by federal agencies. Supporters argue that this is a way of controlling agencies that use inaccurate scientific information to justify regulatory actions, as agencies would have to ensure that any scientific results released could be substantially reproduced and thus verified independently. Agencies were given one year to develop standards for compliance. There is a lot of concern, however, that these rules could result in costly and time-consuming double-checking of studies that have already undergone peer review. In response to any complaint, agencies are required to respond, review the study, correct it if it is found to be in error, and repeat if necessary. That extra time and expense could discourage agencies from publishing results of studies—much as the cost of presenting "all" sides of public issues discouraged many broadcasters from presenting information on public issues during the period in which the Fairness Doctrine was in effect (1949–1985). This move is linked to calls for the release of raw data from federally funded research—as opposed to access to the results of research as analyzed by experts—because in both cases there is suspicion of what critics describe as the "back room" nature of the peer review process.

This was just one in a series of moves by the Office of Management and Budget that has influenced the ways in which the U.S. government and American citizens can access and make use of the results of scientific research. The White House office was created in 1921 to be the government's "office manager," organizing its statistical activities, but beginning under President Richard Nixon has been used for what appear to be explicitly political purposes. The Paperwork Reduction Act of 1980 provided explicit authority for OMB activities in this area. Two executive orders (EO 12472, in 1984, and EO 13011, in 1996) and nine subsequent pieces of legislation—the Paperwork Reduction Act of 1995, the Information Technology Management Reform Act of 1996, the Privacy Act, the Chief Financial Officers Act, the Federal Property and Administrative Services Act, the Budget and Accounting Act, the Government Performance and Results Act, the Office of Federal Procurement Policy Act, and the Government Paperwork Elimination Act of 1998—have provided additional authority to the OMB and justified amending OMB rules already in place.

The OMB issues its mandates—which have the force of law—via "circulars" that are instructions or information issued to federal agencies and via memoranda that provide "guidelines." OMB A-130, originally issued to implement the Paperwork Reduction Act of 1980 and amended multiple times since (most recently in 2000), requires agencies to appoint chief information officers (CIOs), develop information management systems in line with OMB rules and other regulations, and follow basic principles for treatment of information and information technologies. Through this circular, the OMB establishes the framework of an information life cycle. The basic principle that will guide the OMB's evaluations of the treatment of information by federal agencies is linkage of mission needs, information, and use of information technology in an effective and efficient manner. This circular's general prescription to use cost-benefit analysis principles when deciding which information an agency should collect, how to process, and whether to disseminate it publicly in a proactive manner was made much more specific in OMB A-131 (1993), which requires agencies to use a particular analytical tool called value engineering—borrowed from industry—to conduct those cost-benefit analyses. A technique used to implement constitutional, statutory, or regulatory requirements is considered to have "best value" when it performs the basic required function at the lowest total cost.

There are other OMB circulars that operationalize the use of informational power by the U.S. government. OMB A-76, issued in the mid-1980s, defines government information collection, processing, and distribution activities as matters of the efficient use of information technologies (rather than implementation of congressional will, the necessity to ground regulatory action on knowledge of the empirical environment affected, or constitutionally based rights of access to information). In the late 1990s, the OMB began requiring cost-benefit analyses of specific regulations. In OMB A-4 (2003), that became a condition of White House pre-approval of regulations that agencies were considering putting into effect; this pre-approval also announced that approval would be dependent on adherence to such principles as a presumption against economic regulation, the requirement that market failure be demonstrated, and a positive demonstration that regulation at the federal level is the best solution.

The most recent step down the path of White House control over which research results federal agencies can use as a foundation for regulation came in December 2004, when the OMB issued its Final Information Quality Bulletin for Peer Review. This document presents guidelines for agency use of peer review to evaluate research results. An earlier draft of this bulletin would have banned the use of all academically based scientists who had ever received funding from the federal government on agency research peer review panels—even though scientists based in corporations (even those in industries to which proposed regulation would be directed) would have been permitted to serve. (In some areas of the physical and biological sciences, of course, anyone who is doing research from a university base is funded at least in part by the federal government.) In this case, vociferous critique from the community of scientists forced the White House to back down from this extreme position though the bulletin that was ultimately issued did strongly encourage adherence to executive branch preferences in this regard.

Ambivalence and Inconsistency

U.S. information policy regarding change seems deeply ambivalent. It is based in an understanding that incremental political and social change are normal in a bottom-up participatory democracy, but many current laws, regulations, and implementation practices will have the effect of channeling those processes in a specified direction under strict top-down controls. It is understood that technological change is not only a good thing, but necessary for global competitiveness, but the translation of national security concerns into restrictions on research practices and the dissemination of information make this more difficult to accomplish. Positions on the arts, and on the dissemination of information, are marked by inconsistency, though the stance in the early twenty-first century on both could be best characterized as reluctant—except in those cases in which art feeds desired technological innovation.

To some extent, these trends are manifestations of deep paradoxes within modern culture and the complexities of participatory democracy as a type of political process. But they are also signs of ways in which those making decisions for the informational state are groping to understand the ways in which policy can most effectively and efficiently be used to manage informational power at a time concurrently shaped by a shift in political mood.

9

Information, Policy, and Power in the Informational State

The question asked at the beginning of this book was, What are we doing to ourselves? That question has unfolded into several others:

- *What are the trends in information policy, and what are their effects on society?*
- *How do the interactions between and combined effects of these legal trends—policy precession—affect the identity, structure, borders, and change of U.S. society from the state down to the individual level?*
- *Given that the effects of information policy are constitutive in nature, how do these legal trends influence how we interpret and act upon constitutional information policy principles?*
- *What do the exemplars of policy trends discussed here tell us about information policy itself?*
- *What are the relationships between social theory and information policy?*

The first of these is discussed in the detail of leaving the detail of developments within specific areas of the law to chapters 5 through 8. This concluding chapter reviews what we have learned in each of the other four areas. It begins by identifying the overarching conclusions that can be drawn regarding the combined effects of information policy trends on the nature of society and on the informational state. It goes on to summarize how these developments reflect and influence our interpretation and application of the twenty information policy principles in the U.S. Constitution. The third section reviews what we have learned about information policy itself. And the fourth looks at the different strategies of policy-makers as they make use of, or ignore, dominant themes in contemporary social theory. Together, these analyses provide a picture of what makes the informational state distinct as a political form that specializes in the use of informational power.

The Social Impact of Information Policy Trends

Throughout much of this book, developments dealing with social, technological, and informational systems have been treated separately, reflecting their isolation from each other in legacy law and in order to heighten sensitivity to the multiple causal relations among the three. A warning bell that these cannot be empirically separated, however, has also been rung loudly and often. To gain the broadest view in these concluding remarks, therefore, the combined effects of developments in information policy across these different systems as well as across bodies of legacy law will be discussed as a whole, just as we experience them.

The informational state knows more and more about individuals, while individuals know less and less about the state. The model of representative democracy requires individual knowledge of the processes and activities of government, and at least enough government knowledge about citizens to apportion representation and resources. With the bureaucratic welfare state, the informational requirements of the nation-state increased in order to have in hand the knowledge of particular individuals, groups, and communities needed to implement policy. In the decades following the establishment of regulatory agencies and safety net programs, laws and regulations were also put in place that increased the symmetry between citizen knowledge of the state and state knowledge of the citizen. Of course there was never either absolute symmetry or complete transparency in either direction, for the need to protect national security has always kept some critical information about government out of citizens' hands and privacy laws protected some personal information from the eyes of government. With the informational state, however, the capacity of the state to gather and process information about its citizens and about the resources and activities within its space is growing by orders of magnitude. At the same time, the ability of citizens to learn about what the government is doing is declining.

In the informational state, the panspectron has replaced the panopticon. The concept of the panopticon refers to surveillance practices in which the individual subject of surveillance is first identified and then multiple techniques and technologies of observation are directed upon the subject. The use of surveillance techniques as a means of control under modernity is often described as panoptic, and this accurately summarizes the cumulative effect of many of the practices of the bureaucratic state. In the informational state the panopticon has been replaced with the panspectron, in which information is gathered about everything, all the time, and particular subjects become visible only in response to the asking of a question. The panspectron is also a control mechanism, with the additional features that it can manage many more subjects at once, and that the subjects of surveillance never know when, how, or why they might become visible on the panspectral screen.

There is a gap between the identity of the informational state as perceived by those in government and as perceived by citizens. Constitutional provisions regarding relationships and communications between citizens and the government suggest that a shared vision of the identity of the state was an ideal. Today, however, the informational state described earlier means the self-perception of the state through its proprioceptive mechanisms is growing distant from the identity of the United States as understood by its citizens. This trend may well generate what is described within complex adaptive systems theory as a deviation-amplifying process in which government and polity grow increasingly distant from each other, decreasing the stability of the system as a whole.

The use of digital technologies may actually decrease, rather than increase, the possibilities of meaningful participatory democracy. When the most important information technologies for political practice were oral conversation and written text, achieving classical literacy was sufficient for access to the knowledge and discourses upon which political decision making was based. Now that highly complex digital technologies provide most of the knowledge input into political decision-making, access has become restricted to very few for a complex of reasons. So, too, has much of the critical discourse that is pertinent, for that conversation now revolves around the technological issues involved in the collection and processing of information to be used for political purposes and is also not now generally accessible. The result is a citizenry that is less and less capable of participating in decision-making that can be meaningfully described as democratic. Schudson's concept of the monitorial citizen, therefore, does accurately describe the kinds of knowledge necessary to be an informed citizen in the twenty-first century, but it is overly optimistic about—indeed, does not actually deal with—the logistical barriers to actually achieving that situation under contemporary conditions. We have not yet developed either the educational systems, or the modes and venues of appropriate public discourse, for political participation that must start with design of the structures of technological systems rather than engaging with the constitutionally designed political processes of the social system. The participatory design practices mentioned in this book are the first steps in this direction.

While digital technologies could have expanded possibilities for public participation in voting via referenda, the technologies of today's electronic voting machines reduce the confidence of individual voters that their votes will be accurately recorded and remain unmanipulated. Today's electronic voting machines introduce uncertainty at several stages of the voting process, from the actual recording of the vote by individuals to statistical treatment of the vote at various levels of government once an election is over. Habitual conceptions of mobilization of political power rest on assumptions about the validity of the voting record. With that assumption gone, the vote itself can become a meaningless exercise or worse—the very fact of a vote can be used to justify political decisions, even though the statistical outcomes have been manipulated.

The individual disappears in the informational state into a probability. While statistical portraits can provide some useful information about individuals—*if* valid and reliable—the picture they provide is partial at best, and distorting or false at worst. Yet the use of statistical approaches to legal treatment of the individual, from sentencing in the courtroom to identification as a surveillance target, to consideration of immigration requests to, again, the possibility that electronic vote results may be manipulated, all reflect the disappearance of the individual human into probabilities. The human cost of this change can go well beyond the results of inaccuracies: Statistics do not have either human rights or civil liberties.

Access to information is used by the informational state for proactive persuasive purposes. In a series of steps over the last few decades, the U.S. government has mandated a shift to the Web in access to government information and has simultaneously increased its control over what information is presented, and how, and even what data is collected by "independent" agencies. Historical revisionism is of course easier in the digital environment, because changes can be made globally much more easily than could be accomplished in a print context in which individual copies of items must be removed from shelves, institution by institution.

The clarity with which those within the United States have understood whether they are, or are not, citizens has given way to uncertainty regarding both that identity and what it means in terms of rights and responsibilities. The creation of the category of hybrid citizenship; the threat that it may soon become possible to lose one's citizenship due to actual or imagined speech and behavior that fell within the pale in the past; the extension of the border exceptions to U.S. law throughout the country's geographic space; the need to struggle for sustenance of due process; and the growing realm of secrecy in government operations all combine to undermine the confidence in one's identity as a U.S. citizen.

Information policy responses to the fact that all three types of systems have been characterized by fluidity, experimentation, and sometimes turbulence as a result of the use of meta-technologies have varied from efforts to enforce rigid structures to exempting activity from rules altogether, depending upon the goals of the government. The overarching tendency within the last few years has been toward increasing use of structural regulation. However, in simultaneous pursuit of particular goals, such as promoting technological innovation, exemptions from structural regulation are granted. In domains in which there is a great deal of variance and continued experimentation, decisions are often made on a case-by-case basis rather than via generally applicable rules.

Theoretical difficulties distinguishing types of information processing present legal problems. At least two examples of this type of legal problem have been discussed here. Difficulties determining prior art in patent law highlight the inadequacy of our ability to theorize differences in types of information processing for legal purposes. And the problem of drawing lines between different informational goods and services for accounting purposes has been the most difficult to resolve in the development of the new NAICS. The same problem underlies, or contributes to, a number of the other issues discussed here, such as disagreements regarding exactly when a communication constitutes association, or to what extent constitutional protections apply to interactivity per se.

Because the technologies that shape social and informational structures are increasingly mathematical in nature, new regulatory tools that are also mathematical in nature are being developed. And because those tools come in a form over which property rights may be asserted, the privatization of formerly public power is exacerbated in the informational state. In our image of democratic decision-making, the same techniques for developing positions and acting on them were available to all groups of stakeholders involved in any given issue. And while there may have been differences in resources from one group to another, every political party could get together, debate, exchange information, and organize to try to pass or change laws in the same ways. Now that modes of organizing, organizational structures, and transactional processes can all be patented, the situation has changed. In some cases government use of computer programs to accomplish regulatory ends may generate a dependency upon private sector entities that shares some similarities with but is also different in kind from the long-standing informational dependency of regulatory agencies upon corporations in the industries they are regulating. In other cases reliance upon such programs creates a de facto privatization of some forms of previously public power. For citizens, the political playing field has become more uneven since there are now ways of engaging in political discussion and acting on decisions made through such discourse that are available to some groups of stakeholders, but not to others.

Though the borders of the state were never purely material or cleanly drawn, today more than ever before they are conceptual in nature and their extent and shape varies with the type of informational or other activity involved. In the past, geopolitical borders were often contested, but demarcations of their locations as claimed could be mapped geographically and as defined they were clean and bright lines. Current research shows that, particularly in a globalized world, the concept of the border can be replaced with the notion of border zones of varying width if one is talking about the cultural, social, and economic experience of boundaries between states. More important, however, is the appearance of a number of additional borders that are not geographic in nature but, rather, map onto technological systems and informational systems. When personal information of those who would like to enter the United States is examined in foreign countries at the point of embarkation, on the one hand, and exemptions from U.S. law at the border can be practiced within the country anywhere there are functional border equivalents, on the other, it becomes clear that the borders of technological and informational systems that do not map onto geopolitical borders are being put to use in support of the latter. The expansion of the boundaries of the informational state beyond its geopolitical borders has been used by the United States to justify interventions anywhere in the world even without referring to extraterritoriality based on the right to define injuries and articulate chains of causation that can be the basis of action where none existed before.

The informational state has much more knowledge about forces simultaneously interacting across the globe in the present than it does about history. The memory of the informational state—knowledge of genetic change, in systems theory terms—is fragmented, incoherent, and often nonexistent. Awareness of current conditions—epigenetic change—is much greater. The political consequences of this are significant, for knowledge of the past provides insight into the causal forces that have created present circumstances, providing valuable input into future planning. Knowledge of the present serves control purposes but unless archived and made accessible, does not support the planning function. While the combination of knowledge of the past and of the present would be ideal, and knowledge of the past as analyzed through a variety of theoretical lenses is invaluable to decision-makers, knowledge of the present alone creates a planning environment subject to the whims of those in a position to manipulate stories told about the past.

The informational state has a better data, visual, and, increasingly, sensory memory than it does a narrative memory. The sensory range of digital intelligence, in terms of scale and scope, and in terms of the types of data collected, keeps increasing. Current experimentation with microscopic intelligent sensors capable of self-organizing into networks for the exchange of information has brought the possibility of ubiquitously blanketing the globe with data-gathering equipment. We create our world, however, not through data but through the collaborative development of the narratives by which we live our lives. In the terms of complex adaptive systems theory, healthy social change requires narratives that are themselves complex and open to adaptation through mutual interaction. The informational state in its current incarnation, however, is driving toward narrative simplicity, even as the data upon which state narratives are placed become more diverse and complex.

U.S. information policy regarding treatment of change is confused, self-contradictory, and in many ways self-defeating. The rhetoric of participatory democracy continues to be used but, at least for the moment, change in only one direction is being tolerated. The goal of retaining technological leadership is still espoused, but a number of policies are in place that are making it difficult, if not impossible, to hold that spot. Similarly, while knowledge production remains a part of the informational state's mission, many laws and regulations discourage the processes involved by inhibiting the efforts of researchers, preventing the diffusion of knowledge throughout society so that it can be used, and declining to use the results of research as inputs into public decision making.

Information policy tools have been particularly effective as enablements of the trend away from evidence-based policy-making. A key characteristic of the modern nation-state since its inception has been its reliance upon evidence about actual social conditions as inputs into decision-making. This feature first appeared in the late eighteenth century as a pragmatic consequence of the French government's post-revolution interest in serving the people, and it only became stronger as research methods became more sophisticated, computing capacity and speed increased, and the services of the nation-state in its bureaucratic form became even more dependent upon data for their provision. The move to downsize government and reduce its paperwork that began in the late 1970s has combined with other trends—such as the progressive, conservative, and religious versions of belief in post-normal science—in a turn away from evidence-based decision-making. Information policy tools, such as those used by the OMB to intervene in agency information collection, processing, and distribution practices, are a key means by which this change in political stance has become embedded in the law.

The range of types of threats to freedom of speech is expanding. Traditional threats to freedom of speech remain in the twenty-first century environment through both direct censorship and indirect chilling effects. New issues have also arisen, including importantly the removal of constitutional protections from speech that is defined as information processing rather than communicative activity, and efforts to assert property rights in storylines and plots. Replacement of action with purported intention and association as justifications for alleging criminality also restricts speech rights.

Informational rights are becoming commoditized. One of the reasons today's economy is described as an information economy is that many types of information never before commoditized have become so. Trends reported upon here expand upon that insight with details about how informational rights are also becoming commoditized. The right to privacy provides a premiere example: While in the past one could assert a right of privacy to repel unwarranted invasions of privacy in the courts, today one must either purchase the education needed in order to protect the privacy of one's space and communications technologically, or purchase the software and technologies needed to do so from others.

The Current Status of Constitutional Information Policy Principles

Another way of thinking about the ways in which the transition to an informational state has affected how we live is to look at the impact of recent trends on interpretation and implementation of each of the information policy principles in the U.S. Constitution. Most of the effects briefly summarized here have been explored in earlier chapters, with some of the themes cross-cutting material oriented around more than one of the specific issues addressed. The status of each constitutional principle for information policy, in the order in which they were introduced in chapter 2, is reviewed here for completeness and as a stimulus to further research.

Information collection by the government Operationalization of the constitutional mandate for a census appears to be self-contradictory today, for the government has chosen to *not* maximize its ability to achieve the kinds of statistical accuracy that would ensure fairness in use of census statistics while it *is* maximizing its ability to collect information about individuals.

Open government The decades-long trend toward increased access to government information, theoretically made much easier with the use of digital technologies, has been reversed via expansion of the definition of the types of information use of which may threaten national security.

Free speech within government Though the free speech of government officials is constitutionally protected, current administration officials have accused members of Congress who express concern about the impact of the PATRIOT Act and related changes in the law since 9/11 of treasonous behavior, chilling political discourse.

Federal government control over currency As the virtual economies of game environments increasingly intersect with the "real" economy, the constitutional right of the government to control currency may provide a new justification for intervention into the content of popular culture.

Universal access to an information distribution system This constitutional principle could be used to support efforts to achieve universal access to the Internet, but so far has not. Instead, the current Bush administration has attempted to use the U.S. agreement with the WTO regarding trade in services to dismantle the U.S. Postal Service, and the universal access provisions of the Telecommunications Act of 1996 are being undercut by both private and public sector reluctance to enforce the rules.

Intellectual property rights Both the ability to access and manipulate intellectual property owned by others and the ability to monitor the use of content have increased in the electronic environment. The constitutional rubric for intellectual property rights remains in place, but extension of the duration of copyright, and expansion of the domain of patentable material and uses interpreted as infringing, have significantly reduced the social goals of this constitutional principle, while strengthening the ability of dominant players to extract profit from control over these informational resources.

Restriction of civil liberties during time of war This principle is being heavily relied upon.

Treason The definition of treasonous speech and activity has broadened, and government capacity to discern when potentially treasonous communications and behaviors take place has increased.

Freedom of opinion In the past, we needed protections for freedom of opinion as expressed publicly. Today, we need protections for opinions expressed privately, or never communicated at all.

Freedom of speech Several trends are combining to chill free speech in today's environment, including the fact that very little speech, if any, can be conducted in private, the compactness of the range of ideas in mass discourse relative to the possible terrain of points of view, the heavy weighting of the national security side of the scale when balanced against civil liberties, and expanded notions of just what might threaten that security.

Freedom of the press While the good news is that new forms of journalism are developing involving many more people than ever before, the bad news is that the current trend is away from providing many of today's most widely used news providers, including bloggers and groups described as "independent media," with First Amendment protections because those involved are not members of a formally recognized "press."

Freedom of assembly The extension of freedom of assembly to include association has become even more important, and even more threatened, in the electronic environment.

Freedom to petition the government for change This right is under threat in the Homeland Security environment, because concern about the impact of antiterrorism measures on civil liberties has itself been defined as unacceptable.

Protection against unlawful search/privacy While the right to privacy remains intact in theoretical terms, pragmatically it is next to impossible to achieve in today's technological environment. Under Homeland Security policies, the balance between the right to privacy and the claimed need of the government to surveil has tipped heavily in the latter direction.

Protection against self-incrimination Post–9/11 changes in the law, the use of statistical profiling based on data gathered from many different public and private databases, and ambiguous, even often secret, definitions of what constitutes "terrorist" activity make it possible to identify oneself as a subject of surveillance completely unwittingly. Because evidence of state of mind and purported intentions to engage in certain activity, rather than actual behaviors, are now used for criminal justice purposes, it is even possible to incriminate oneself unknowingly and irrespective of actual intentions and behaviors. And because evidence acquired in the course of a search authorized by the PATRIOT Act need not be presented to a defendant in court, it is possible to be convicted of a crime without even knowing what the evidence considered incriminating was.

Due process The War on Terrorism is being used to justify changes in legal procedure that some believe abrogate the protections of due process. The question of the constitutionality of these practices is still being contested in the courts. First Amendment due process was explicitly retained as a feature of the PATRIOT Act.

Rights beyond those enumerated Articulation and protection of rights in addition to those implied by, but not specifically identified in, the Constitution or its amendments depend upon interpretations by the courts. Such rights are likely to receive less protection, or to be rejected altogether, should the current replacement of traditional criteria for judicial appointments with ideological and religious standards be successful in the long term.

Incorporation This principle has not been affected.

The right to receive information The combination of a vastly increased ability to track the information that individuals choose to receive with the use of profiling methods to determine intention and state of mind seriously threatens the right to receive information.

The Nature of Information Policy

At another level, the material presented here can be read for what it tells us about the nature of information policy itself and about its relationship to the informational state.

Information policy tools are interchangeable for the informational state, even though the impact of different tools on individuals, and the social and cultural effects of the use of different tools, vary significantly. To the state, supplying programming capacity via the domestic educational system or by importing skilled labor from elsewhere on special visas yields the same result, though the impact on U.S. citizens and on the intellectual capital of society as a whole are quite different. Achieving transparency in the exchange of commercial information with other countries via arms control agreements, as opposed to via international trade law, achieves the same end for the state, but doing so in the military arena simplifies the conversation by excluding many parties from the table and reducing the range of values that will be brought into the negotiations.

Information policy is the self-reflexive organ of the informational state. Information policy is self-reflexive in three ways. First, it appears at the boundary between incremental and radical change. Reliance upon legacy law in information policy involves using the parameters of existing legal structures and processes to design parameters for new structures and processes. Second, as described in the language of complex adaptive systems theory, the transformation from a bureaucratic state to an informational state is a point of bifurcation at which political choice has particular impact, because policy, like technological development, is path-dependent—decisions made at one point determine the range of possible further options available. And third, information policy affects the nature of facticity, meaning the ways in which data treated as "facts" are created, perceived, and incorporated into decision-making.

Policy-making is no longer a matter of intentional and procedural design that is social in its goals and human in its processes. Today, policy-making is a matter of emergent parametric change to the nature and conditions of agency, conducted for a social, technological, and natural environment via a human-technology collaboration. A combination of empirical and perceptual factors has changed the nature of even the formal policy-making processes of government. The norm of intentionality in policy-making remains in place, but the reality is that the appearance of policies is just as likely to be emergent. We continue to think that we are designing specific rules, institutions, and programs when we create laws and regulations, but the biggest impact from interventions in the information environment is to alter the very conditions and possibilities of agency. The procedures of policy-making are being used to effect parametric change to the very political system itself. The environment for which policy is made now includes the natural and machinic worlds as well as the social, and policy for the human world is increasingly likely to be made by various forms of electronic intelligence. And while we continue to use the language of facts, their role in policy-making is more likely to belong to the rhetoric of decision-making processes rather than their content.

The process of regime formation is still under way for the informational state. Although the events of 9/11 and their aftermath provided a shock to the state that brought a period of experimentation to a close, negotiation over the information policy regime continues. Another insight from complex adaptive systems theory is that an equilibrium is not necessarily stable—complex systems can oscillate between two (or more) conditions, an equilibrium can dissolve into turbulence again, or a complex adaptive system like the state can destroy itself. The possibility of successful self-organization and morphogenetic change does not mean that either is necessary or inevitable.

It is important to recall what has been learned about the processes by which the information policy regime is being formed. Several elements of the regime being put in place have not yet been fully actualized. Key regime features are not always visible, particularly when cast within the terms of legacy law. Policy *for* the infrastructure helps *create* that infrastructure. The emergent regime presents challenges to the very nature of governance, by use of contract law and national security to "deputize" private sector institutions, moving critical decision-making into venues not touched by democratic principles, and suggesting financial stakeholding as a criterion of standing in political decision-making bodies. Meanwhile, the legal infrastructure itself is expanding as a result of the emergence of the information policy regime, through a deepening of private regulation and the contracting out of regulatory responsibilities, a broadening of governmental activities on an ad hoc basis, and an expansion of the governmental features of private sector entities. However, the role of procedural constraints upon decision-makers is diminishing in the processes of information policy regime formation. While all of these processes interact, they do not proceed at the same pace. And even though the emphasis in this book has been on policy innovations, there are both continuities and discontinuities with the past.

Policy and Social Theory

This book's exemplars reveal diverse strategies for the use (or rejection) of social theory in information policy:

• ***Though identity is now understood to be conceptual, fluid, socially constructed, and often multiple, contemporary information policy treats identity as fixed, empirically based, and quantifiable. This approach is*** *a denial of theory and a rejection of the results of social science research.*

- *Efforts to treat structures as fixed, enduring, and inevitable are falling away in the face of experience with changing forms and the inability of policy to keep up with those realities despite efforts to reassert rigid structural lines. This is rearguard and self-contradictory action undertaken as one among many techniques used by players who understand very well the degrees of freedom made possible by the use of metatechnologies as described by theorists, and who simultaneously take advantage of the opportunity to manipulate structures when doing so more successfully achieves particular goals.*
- *The flexibility and conceptual foundations of contemporary treatment of the many different kinds of U.S. borders is in line with contemporary social theory regarding the nature of border regions.*
- *Contemporary information policy practices dealing with change are so diverse and often self-canceling that it cannot be said that in this area there is any strategy at all.*

The Future of the Informational State

In his seminal work of more than twenty years ago, Ithiel de Sola Pool correctly predicted that as the regulatory systems for print, broadcasting, and telecommunications converged, the resulting legal framework would be shaped by the most restrictive—rather than the least restrictive—elements out of all of those available. What Pool was not able to predict was the way in which this change in the legal system would ultimately produce a new political form: the informational state.

While the trends reported upon here have been long developing, we can say that there has been a change of state in complex adaptive systems terms over the last few years, because the U.S. government has become much more aware of the utility, range, and power of informational policy tools at its disposal and is using those tools much more systematically and broadly. From a systems theory perspective, periods of turbulence such as we have experienced in recent decades can lead to a range of possible outcomes. They may resolve into a new and stable equilibrium that can be expected to have a long life. They may lead to oscillating equilibria, a condition in which the social system snaps back and forth between two extremes. Or what appears to be an end to turbulence may be only another period of experimentation in an adaptational process that is still under way.

Whether or not the informational state as it is currently shaped is the only political form available with the current policy tools of informational power, we do not yet know. Certainly the conclusion of the current U.S. political story has yet to be reached. Within the broad legal field, drawing upon all the tools of governance and governmentality as well as government, there are sites where political activity may still effectively take place: where there are lags among the rates at which diverse processes unfold, where a simple narrative can be made complex, where lost memory can be regained, where knowledge can be collocated with power, where awareness of indeterminacy and nonlinearity expands our sense of what might be determinate, and where small actions can have large effects.

Bibliographic Essays

Notes

These essays do not attempt to comprehensively discuss each of the multiple literatures upon which this work has been built over a twenty-year period but, rather, seek to provide conceptual and historical overviews of each that highlight seminal and/or exemplary items, with special attention to the inclusion of publications that will themselves take readers more deeply bibliographically into areas of particular interest. Certain topics of course appear in more than one chapter, but the work of particular authors is usually discussed only in the essay for the first chapter to which the material applies. Sources of value across the range of the law are included in the bibliographic essay for chapter 5.

In some cases an inverse relationship exists between the number of citations and the richness of the literature, for there are often well-developed syntheses that summarize and theoretically envelop mature streams of work, while areas that are thinner, or more recent, may not have yet benefited from such treatment. In this sense the book, and these essays, present a research agenda. The essays unfold outward, for where there are useful review essays, bibliographies, and related items, they are cited here in lieu of repeating their content. The same can be said for many elements of the argument of this book developed by this author more fully elsewhere but cited here.

Because one of the most serious weaknesses in much contemporary information policy analysis is a lack of historical knowledge regarding the development of particular issues, diverse approaches that have been tried in the past, and the variety of ways of thinking about a problem that have appeared over time, these essays provide as long a view of the literature in each area as this author was able to muster.

1 An Introduction to Information Policy

The mise-en-scène of this chapter, and of the book—the articulation of the space within which it resides—emerges at the intersection of three histories: of the information society, of the U.S. legal system, and of the nature of power as exercised by the U.S. government through its legal system. The bibliographic essay for this chapter discusses the first two of these; the third is included in the bibliographic essay for the next chapter. A full discussion of the ways in which the law, as a complex adaptive system, develops and changes in relation to a broad legal field can be found in Braman (2004a).

The Information Society

The literature on the information society qua information society is an example of attention to a topic that forces itself onto the agenda because of dramatic change in the subject matter of many disciplines, receives great discussion for a couple of decades, and then wanes because the issues with which it is concerned suffuse scholarship altogether. Issues discussed in this literature have of course appeared over a much longer span of time under other names. Both David Sarnoff (1915–1916), credited with many for creating the television industry, and John J. Carty, first chief engineer of AT&T ([1922] 1924), shared utopian visions of the social possibilities of networked communication found in much of the optimistic literature on the information society at the close of the twentieth century. Dystopian views about what we currently refer to as the information society also showed up quite early. Frederick Tönnies and other nineteenth-century sociologists explored the effects of receiving more information and faster information on individuals and groups (Hardt 1979), and by the time of the Civil War there were already complaints about the negative effects on the quality of decision-making generated by the same processes (Headrick 1990). Historical work is retrieving, in some cases through reinterpretation and in others through attention to detail never before the subject of study, even earlier developments in U.S. history as establishing the conditions under which the information society could flourish (Chandler and Cortada 2000) as well as the dimensions along which that society might be problematic (Marvin 1988). The most comprehensive work on the social, political, and economic processes that created the conditions we refer to as the information society is the three-volume set by Castells (1996, 1997a, 1997b). As understanding of the historical precedents of contemporary developments deepens, periodizations of the history of the information society appear (Braman 1995).

The "classical" era of literature on the information society began in Japan in the early 1960s with the first suggestion that an information society was replacing industrial society in a sequence that began with agricultural society (Ito 1991), though this perspective did not become available to the English-speaking world until publication of Masuda's work in 1981. Daniel Bell (1966, 1973) influentially introduced the idea of a "post-industrial" society to the English-speaking world, and from that point on the literature quickly multiplied—by 1985, Jorge Schement and his colleagues were able to compile a bibliography of several hundred items dealing with the topic, and there was an audience for the Machlup and Mansfield (1983) collection of work on the concept of information itself from a wide variety of disciplines. The Cawkell (1987) collection includes a number of fascinating pieces representing different phases of the history of thinking about information society-type issues from the early twentieth century through the 1980s.

In addition to the desire to think through the implications of social change for education further discussed in chapter 5, there were other stimuli to this literature from the political and economic goals to be served by talking about an "information revolution" (Brants 1989), to the ancient human need for myth (Carey and Quirk 1970), to the pragmatic desire to solve organizational problems under conditions different from those under which leadership had trained (Cleveland 1985), to the government need to figure out just what was going on for policy purposes (Porat 1977). Much of the work on the information society is critical (for classic examples, see Webster and Robins 1986; Traber 1986).

The concept of the information society is still used by those interested in speaking to non-academic audiences about operational issues (e.g., Lan 2005)—particularly policy-makers (van Dijk 2005)—or in turning academic attention to matters that have not yet received much attention in the information society literature (e.g., Mansell and Collins 2005). However, much of the richer theoretical and empirical work is just as likely to be found under other rubrics in tacit admission of the fact that the process of informatization is now a part of every subject of study. Thus the cultural questions raised by McLuhan in the 1960s are now being addressed by works that deal with the question up close, as in items directed at content producers (Klinenberg 2005), as well as in literature that deals with the question from afar, as in the vast globalization literature that expands upon McLuhan's prediction that a global village would appear. Sociological questions are now treated in works with titles like *The Social Life of Information* (Brown and Duguid 2002) and *Information Ecologies* (Nardi and O'Day 2000). Discussion of the information economy has bifurcated into literatures on the infrastructure and on content (Dunning 2000; Mokyr 2002). Individual subjects within the overall rubric of the information society of course have their own intellectual histories. In just two examples, there has been a series of conceptualization of the information economy at the macro-level (Braman 1993), Donald Lamberton (1971, 1984, 1992) has documented the coalescence of a subdiscipline of the micro-economics of information over the years, and it is now possible to see the intellectual history of both the macro- and the microeconomics of information within a single frame (Braman 2005).

There have been two very different streams of work on the impact of the informatization of society at the global level. A discussion that began with concern about the inability of dependent societies to tell their own stories as a result of the organization of international news flows (Nordenstreng and Varis 1973) grew into the wider concern about informational imbalances (Cruise O'Brien 1977). In the 1970s, the nonaligned nations (a coalition of about 70 developing countries) issued a call for a New World Information Order (NWIO) in hopes of achieving a redistribution of informational resources in support of the effort to reduce socioeconomic gaps between groups of countries. Twenty years after this conversation died when the United States pulled out of UNESCO, the primary venue for debate over the NWIO, it is under way again under the rubric of the World Summit on the Information Society (WSIS). Meanwhile, development efforts to both build and make use of the information infrastructure continued throughout the period in work synthesized by Mansell and Wehn (1998).

The second stream of work dealing with the information society at the global level derived from the initial insight of the 1970s that the use of digital technologies could introduce new vulnerabilities for particular nation-states (Tengelin 1981) and regions (Nora and Minc 1980). This concern has been transformed into discussion of information warfare (Arquilla and Ronfeldt 2001; Khalilzad and White 1999; Thomas 1998). Interestingly, from the perspective of the history of the sociology of knowledge, once the importance of information technologies for national security became salient, a significant literature developed revisiting the history of military organization, tactics and strategy, and weaponry from the perspective of information and information technologies (de Landa 1991; Demchak 1991; Dudley 1991; Lee 1993; Pearton 1984; van Creveld 1991).

The height of attention to the informatization of society has passed with its normalization, and the more detailed work of figuring out just what is going on is now under way. The information society literature, and the empirical changes inspiring that work, have, however, had enduring impact. The intellectual terrain of library schools has become the much richer world of "information science," engaged in theoretical debates at the heart of many of the social sciences at a much more abstract level than was historically the case (Hahn and Buckland 1998; Buckland and Liu 1998). Cognate fields continuously struggle with their relationship to information and informational processes; conference sessions of the International Communication Association (ICA), for example, have repeatedly addressed the question of how to define information. While there is no "theory of the information society" per se, many important theoretical developments in recent years, in the social sciences in particular, have derived from struggles to cope with qualitative changes in the nature of society that have been influenced by technological change. Since it took almost five hundred years to see clearly the impact of the reinvention of the printing press on knowledge production and practice in Western Europe (Eisenstein 1979), it should not be suprising if it is several decades before the impact of the informatization of society and the information society literature on theory and research can clearly and comprehensively be seen.

The History of U.S. Law

The more general historical context for the changes in U.S. law discussed here can be found in the premiere works on the history of U.S. law by Lawrence M. Friedman (1985) and Milton J. Horwitz (1992). Other historical work on U.S. law of use in understanding the policy impact of the informatization of society includes the writing of Ackerman (1984), Lawson and Seidman (2004), and Skocpol (1992). Robert Horwitz (1989) offers an intellectually sophisticated and detailed history of fifty years of U.S. broadcasting and telecommunications regulation. Rich social, institutional, and cultural histories of the period leading up to the formation of the regulatory system for broadcasting and telecommunications in the United States (Douglas 1989; Horwitz 1989; McChesney 1993; Streeter 1996) exists, but the same work has not been undertaken as comprehensively for subsequent periods. Topic-specific histories, casebooks, treatises, and focused analyses are discussed in bibliographic essays for later chapters of this book.

Changes in the practices as opposed to the content of the law are beyond the scope of this book, but this important literature includes attention to the growing importance of private law and the consequences of internationalization of the law in areas dealing with information (Dezalay and Garth 1996); analysis of the impact of information technologies on the knowledge structures of the law historically (Grossman 1994) and in the contemporary environment (Katsh 1989); and studies of the impact of new information technologies on daily practice (Susskind 1996; Sedona Conference 2005). Ease of computerization has become an important element in determining the outcome when there is a choice of alternative policy tools (Karpf 1989).

While the concepts of "government" and "governance" have been so widely used for such a long time that they are commonplace, the concept of "governmentality" was first articulated by Michel Foucault (Burchell, Gordon, and Miller 1991; Flew 1999; Foucault 1980; Hunt and Wickham 1994; Pal 1990). Proprioception—the ability of the body to sense itself—was first applied to society as a whole by the poet Charles Olson (1965). Foucault referred to one aspect of proprioception on the part of the state when he described statistical practices (discussed in chapter 5) as development of the sensorium of Leviathan, the term Thomas Hobbes ([1651] 1991) used to refer to the state.

The phrases "legacy systems" and "legacy technologies" have come into popular use to refer to the problem faced by organizations that find their technological systems are outdated but must continue to be used, with or without the addition of new technologies. The phrases "legacy law" and "legacy regulation" have similarly come into use in recent years to refer to the problem faced by legal and regulatory systems that must work with existing, perhaps obsolete, policy in the course of incrementally developing new approaches. For examples of a reliance upon the concept of legacy law by commissioners of the FCC, see Abernathy (2001) and Ness (1998).

An extended bibliographic essay on the stages through which the legal reaction to innovation in information and communication technologies occurred can be found in Braman (1995). Other discussions of this developmental effort include both those that start with the subject matter (e.g., Dunn 1982; Trauth 1986) and those that start with the terminology (Browne 1997a, 1997b). Relatively early suggestions that policy change would be needed include Owen (1970), Gerbner, Gross, and Melody (1973), Bazelon (1979), and Robinson (1978). Branscomb (1986) provided the first comprehensive overview of pertinent international legal agreements.

Ithiel de Sola Pool (1983) gets credit for first providing a comprehensive (and highly influential) overview of the history of and relationships between the three bodies of U.S. law that are oriented specifically around information and communication technologies—constitutional law as it has developed around the print-oriented First Amendment, and telecommunications and broadcasting regulation as two separate systems managed by the FCC. Many of Pool's students went on to play leading roles in the development of regulatory responses to the convergence of computing and communication technologies, and because his histories of legal responses to diverse technologies placed bodies of law previously perceived as distinct within a common frame, this book also inspired a number of scholars' research agendas. Laurence Tribe's insights (1985a) into the constitutional importance of the subject matter of this book emerged out of a larger investigation into the nature of constitutional decision-making (Tribe 1985b) undertaken simultaneously with attention to the implications of the effects of new technologies on the law (Tribe 1973) that continued to be a theme in his work (Tribe 1991).

While some had recognized the need to reconceptualize the information policy from the ground up since the early 1980s, by the mid-1990s this perspective had become widely accepted. (For an example of this kind of gesture motivated by concern about one specific policy issue, treatment of cable television, see Stern, Krasnow, and Senkowski 1983). Presidential rhetoric about an "information superhighway" was likely to have contributed to this change in public discourse, and experience struggling with specific legal issues surely encouraged this point of view among scholars and legal practitioners. Pamela Samuelson (1995), an expert on software-related law, was a highly visible representative of the latter category in her call for an entirely new legal regime. Recent efforts to locate a theoretical ground upon which to ground a coherent approach to information policy in the twenty-first century include those by Lessig (1999) and Biegel (2001). Benkler (2000) provided a gross categorization of Internet-related legislative proposals as a way of identifying general areas in which such an effort might start, using the ideas of economist Ronald Coase as a foundation upon which to offer a coherent regulatory framework for information policy. Balkin (2004) argues that we need to rethink our theories of freedom of expression for today's environment, starting with the problem of how to achieve a democratic society, for Meiklejohn (1961) and other important theoriests were responding to that problem as it manifested itself under very different conditions. And Boyle (1996) uses a few particularly interesting developments in areas such as biotechnology and the treatment of traditional bodies of knowledge via intellectual property rights to encourage broader thinking about the role the law plays not just in responding to, but in creating, the information society. In the popular literature, too often all electronic information and communication are treated as the same, but articulating distinctions among the various types of communication processes that take place in the electronic environment—just as they do in physical space—is necessary (Schlachter 1993).

Other efforts have focused on the processes by which adaptation of the legal structure might take place (Blackman 1998; Cate 1994; Dervin and Clark 1993). Mueller and Thompson (2003) importantly point out that there are continuities as well as discontinuities between the formation of ICANN and that of INTELSAT. This is not always a steady movement forward. Bollinger (1977) suggested that no coherent approach need be developed. John Peter Barlow (1996) presented a much-cited manifesto used by those who claim that there should be no regulation of cyberspace. For a description of the latest actual attempt to deal comprehensively with changes in the technologies being regulated via statutory law, see Aufderheide (1999), and for a review of the development of key regulatory concepts in the implementation of earlier pertinent statutory law at the FCC up to that point, see Napoli (2001). Abbate (1999) provides insight into the complexity of the multinational legal and regulatory context within which the global information infrastructure was actually developed. Other works discussing the tensions by which a regulatory regime for this environment is being developed include Braman (2004a) and Mueller (2002).

The argument that information policymaking must be informed by empirical evidence and contemporary social theory is made by Braman (2003), Brennan (1992b), Entman and Wildman (1990), Mueller (1995), and Noam (1993).

2 Forms and Phases of Power: The Bias of the Informational State

The bibliographic essay for chapter 2 maps onto the major sections of the text, dealing in turn with the literature on definitions of information, on power, and on the nation-state.

Information

The approach to defining information used in this book is based upon a typology developed from analysis of a couple of hundred conceptualizations of information first published in 1989; this typology included information as a resource, a commodity, perception of pattern, and a constitutive force in society (Braman 1989). That typology is further elaborated here to include the two additional definitional categories: information as an agent and information as a basin of possibility. The effort to develop this theoretically pluralist approach was motivated by recognition that, in general, it was essentially hopeless to try to identify a single conceptualization that would be both universally valid and useful (Bruce 1983) and, specifically, that legal operationalizations of definitions of information are multiple both within and across societies (Bruce, Cunard, and Director 1986). While methodologically driven approaches are used in disciplines as disparate as economics (Shapiro and Varian 1999) and psychology (MacKay 1983)—Machlup and Mansfield (1983) identified forty such disciplines—these offer little to the building of a theoretical framework. (Peters [1988] provides an overview of treatment of the word "information" within the field of communication.)

The theoretically pluralist position taken here was first enunciated by Robert K. Merton (1981), one of the most influential of twentieth-century sociologists, and by other authors in an edited collection of the same period (Blau and Merton 1981). While this specific phrase is not used in their work, examples of the utility of this approach in work that deals with multiple levels of analysis can be found in Wallerstein (1984) and Braudel (1977). Examples in legal analysis include arguments put forward by Cohen (1950) and Sunstein (1995). Skocpol (1985) uses a theoretically pluralist approach to analysis of the nation-state, and Ackerman (1984) does so in his work on the history of American law. Bohman (1999) described theoretical pluralism as a hallmark of the social sciences by the close of the twentieth century, and Wittrock and Wagner (1990) approach theoretical pluralism in terms of conceptual constellations.

In addition to the examples of treatment of information as a resource cited in the text (Oettinger 1980; Shapiro and Varian 1999), such approaches are common in economics, where they underlie models for measuring the growth of stocks of information (Jonscher 1982); in mass communication, where they are implicit in such areas as analyses of processes such as the two-step flow (Lazarsfeld, Berelson, and Gaudet 1984), and of the political consequences of development communication (for a classic example see Pye [1956]).

Definitions of information as a commodity are explicit in micro- and macroeconomic analyses of information as a primary good, as in Feketekuty's (1986) definition for the purposes of trade negotiations. Classic works in this vein include the analyses by Machlup (1980) and Porat (1977) of the information industries. For an extensive discussion of the development of this literature, see Braman (2005), though it is important to note that not all ways of conceptualizing the information economy revolve around treating information as a commodity (Braman 1997).

Definitions of information as perception of pattern appear in very different literatures. One dominant strain derives from the work on electrical signals by Claude Shannon (1948) that made thinking in terms of information so popular once it was translated into terms appropriate to the study of human communication (Shannon and Weaver 1949). At the opposite extreme are approaches drawn from semiotics (for an unusually accessible introduction to semiotics, see Fiske 1982). The importance of this approach from the policy perspective is demonstrated by its centrality in some key works (e.g., Nora and Minc 1980) and the criticism that erupts when it has been excluded from others (e.g., the Ravault [1981]'s complaint about the exclusion of informational context from the MacBride Commission Report [1980], a key document in the NWIO debate.) Discussions about the difference between information, knowledge, and wisdom highlight the differences between bits of data in isolation and their contributions to perception of pattern; in these discourses, the term "information" is therefore replaced with "knowledge" to emphasize the architectural elements.

Two types of computing developments have made us aware of information as an agent in its own right. Intelligent agent software in use today makes decisions, engages in transactions, and otherwise acts independently of human intervention in response to information encountered. When this happens, it can be said that the information itself has made something happen, or exercised agency. Similarly, the embedding of sensors throughout the material environment that can translate information into action also makes it possible for information itself to exercise agency. Hookway (1999) provides an analysis of what this type of informational agency means from a cultural and social perspective; he describes it as "pandemonic" agency after the medieval use of the word "demonic" to refer to agency that is neither human nor divine in its source. Bradshaw (1997), Russell and Norvig (1995), and Gibbons et al. (2003) discuss software agents and distributed artificial intelligence in ways that are comprehensible to those without a technical background. A first exploration of the implications of information as an agent from a legal perspective can be found in Braman (2002b).

The notion of information as a basin of possibility is inherent in statistical thought. While textbooks on statistics explain what that means in mathematical terms, the history of the development of statistical methods provides more insight into the social, cultural, political, economic, and technological factors that influence the shape and size of that basin (Desrosieres 1998; Hacking 1999) and

Martine (1992) explores the preference for determinacy from a philosophical perspective. With the development of fuzzy set theory over the past couple of decades, the fact that probabilities are just is emphasized. The authors collected in Wang and Chang (1980) opened the question of the implications of fuzzy set theory and practice for policy analysis in particular.

The idea that information actively shapes society is inherent in definitions grounded in constructivism (Berger and Luckmann 1966), itself rooted in social psychology (Cooley 1902; Mead 1934). Hacking (1999) links the social construction of reality with the category-making work further discussed in the essay for chapter 5. This definition enters the study of communication via analyses of content production; works by Tuchman (1978) and by Ericson, Baranek, and Chan (1991) offer excellent examples of this type of analysis. Theoretical arguments for the political importance of defining information as a constitutive force in society can be found in Marxist thought, as discussed in the Aron 1965 and Held 1980 introductions to a number of critical thinkers who work from this perspective. (Of course there are great differences within this school of thought; at least four different ways of conceptualizing the relationship between information flows and society can be found in debates over the nature of, in Marxian terms, the base and the infrastructure.)

It is the use of this definition of information in liberal political thought, however, that has had the most impact on U.S. information policy. This stream of work begins with John Locke ([1690] 1979) and John Stuart Mill (1963). Works on First Amendment theory regularly rely on this definition, though many other theoretical approaches are generally taken into account as well (Baker 1981; Emerson 1977; Meiklejohn 1961; Rehnquist 1976; Schauer 1982). There are significant differences among theorists regarding both what that means for the nature of communication for legal purposes (Bunker 2001; Peters 2004; Post 2000). Interpretations of the First Amendment, discussed by courts as it affects a number of issues in chapters 5–8, vividly demonstrate differences of opinion regarding what that definition suggests for practice.

Power

Interest in the nature of power is ancient and classics endure. Sun Tzu's *The Art of War*, written in the sixth century BCE, is still studied by those who wield power in the private sector as well as those in the public sector (Sun Tzu 6th c. BCE/1963). Niccolò Machiavelli (1469–1527) wrote *The Prince* in 1515 as an analysis of how the Medici ought to exercise their power both domestically and in relations with other political powers (Machiavelli [1515] 1985). And the Prussian Carl von Clausewitz (1780–1831) produced what many still consider to be the most important book ever written on the use of power in war; the standard modern version of *On War*, first published in 1832, is the Howard/Paret translation (Clausewitz [1832] 1976). All of these focus on the use of instrumental power, though symbolic power also receives some attention.

The contemporary study of power, however, can be said to have begun with the work of Max Weber (1864–1920) in the early twentieth century. Though Weber used other terminology, his work provided the foundation from which twentieth-century political scientists elaborated their discussions of the multiple faces of power. Weber offered a theoretically rich and detailed exploration of the nature of structural power, highlighted the importance of symbolic power even in the face of institutions and weapons, and defined the nation-state most fundamentally in instrumental terms in analyses woven throughout his work. Because Weber's preferred genre was essays and there were many of them, collections of his work are widely used to access the most important of his writings. C. Wright Mills, a highly influential sociologist in his own right, edited and translated the important and useful *From Max Weber: Essays in Sociology* (Weber 1946). S. N. Eisenstadt, a political scientist who went on to write extensively about the nature of the nation-state, edited *Max Weber on Charisma and Institution Building: Selected Papers* (Weber 1968). And sociologist Talcott Parsons, so important to the functionalist school of sociology from which the analyses of organizational structure that underlie conceptualizations of organizations as technologies ultimately derive, translated *The Theory of Social and Economic Organization* ([1947] 1964). Karl Marx (1904) and Bertrand Russell (1938) were other pre–World War II thinkers whose ideas about the nature of power continue to be of importance today.

Following World War II, those interested in the nature of power turned their attention to its exercise by civil society (Almond and Verba 1963; Etzioni 1968) and special interest groups and elites (Dahl 1956, 1967; Mills 1956). As the organizational forms of political power became elaborated in the bureaucratic nation-state, March (1955, 1966), Parsons (1963), and Simon (1953) looked at the interactions between institutional structure and political power that are the stuff of power in its structural form, and Easton (1953) added systems theory as a lens on these relationships. There was attention to the problem of how to mobilize power both within societies (Deutsch 1961) and across them (Morgenthau 1954).

By the mid-1970s, the growing interdependence of states as well as theoretical developments introduced new questions into discussions of power. Baldwin (1978, 1979a, 1979b) and Keohane and Nye (1977) led the way in thinking about power under conditions of mutual influence that were increasingly perceived to be turbulent; Rosenau (1984) used the wonderfully descriptive phrase "cascading interdependence" as early as 1984, leading to his own theory about both change and continuity in world politics by 1990. Power began to be seen as an expression of preferences (Abell 1977), of social exchange (Baldwin 1978), and of relativity in social relations (Lukes 1979). Dependence (Emerson 1962), "non-decisions" (Bachrach and Baratz 1963) and "latent classes" (Bonacich and Domhoff 1981) were all understood to be sources or manifestations of power. The sense that the nature of power was changing led to a historicization of analysis of power relations (Baldwin 1979b; Ball 1975; Giddens and Held 1982; Wartenburg 1990) and, concomitantly, appreciation of the role of power in stimulating transformation (Burns and Buckley 1976; Easton 1981).

Syntheses of the massive political science literature on the nature of instrumental, structural, and symbolic power until that point can be found in Lukes 1986 and Wrong 1995. In the first edition of his book (1974), Lukes originally described his approach as "radical," because he includes in his analysis such matters as the power of the weak and of resistance. This was a radical view vis-à-vis the then-dominant "realist" view of the nature of national power as exemplified classically by Morgenthau (1954). By the 1980s, power was acknowledged as central throughout the social sciences (Mann 1986; Olsen and Marger 1993), though the concept was treated with varying degrees of sophistication, sublety, and complexity and Ball (1992), at least, described the inadequacy of all that had been offered as scandalous.

Contemporary issues in the study of power include the fact that it may be imperceptible when long and complex causal chains are involved, making accountability difficult (Beck 1992). The number of claimants to power is multiplying, along with levels of the social structure at which its exercise is possible (Leca 1992). Growing awareness of cultural aspects of power leads to appreciation of ways in which the past (Schudson 1992), speed (Virilio 1986) and biological conditions (Foucault 1983) can all influence the exercise of power or offer means of resistance. Mann (1986) and Cook and Whitmeyer (1992) were forerunners of contemporary interest in the role of networks in power relations. The concept of a virtual phase of power, original with this author, was inspired by economist Roberto Scazzieri's (1993) discussion of virtual production processes as a potential that utilizes technologies or techniques that do not currently exist but for which the resources and knowledge necessary are extant.

Harold Lasswell was a political scientist interested in the nature of power who also did a great deal of work on the nature of communication from a political perspective (Lasswell and Kaplan 1950), and the role of communication in power relations continued to receive attention (Ball 1978; Domhoff 1975). The entire subfield of political communication is focused on this problem. The same Ithiel de Sola Pool who is credited previously in this book (Pool 1983) for his seminal work on the ways in which technological convergence would necessarily force us to reconsider our approach to information policy has also been described as the founder of the field of political communication (Bennett 1998). There are reviews of the political communication literature from diverse perspectives and eras (Blumler and Kavanagh 1999; Bobrow 1973–1974; Bucy and D'Angelo 1999; Chesebro 1976; Dahlgren 2004; Garramone and Atkin 1986; Gastil 1992; Kraus 1973; McLeod, Kosicki, and Ricinski 1988; Meadow 1985; Swanson 1978). Those looking at just how communication effectively exercises power often link mass communication and interpersonal communication (McGraw and Lodge 1996; Moore 1987). Even popular culture—entertainment—can serve political ends (Jensen 1990; Merelman 1998).

Habermas (1968) drew attention to the role of knowledge in power relations, but it was Foucault (1973, 1980, 1983, 1984) who truly ignited interest in political analyses of knowledge. Unger (1975), a leading figure in the critical legal studies (CLS) movement, brought debate over knowledge as power into the heart of the legal community via the law school. Reflecting tensions in the world of social theory and the institutional home of its citizens within academia, the role of theory itself in creating and sustaining power relations became the subject of study (Alford and Friedland 1985; Goldstein 1988; Gray 1983) as did the role of myth (Neely 1981).

The notion of informational power was first suggested by philosopher of technology Jacques Ellul ([1954] 1964), whose work on technique focused attention on transformation itself as a means of exercising power. Various aspects of the importance of information to national power have been explored in recent decades. Starting from this claim, Oettinger (1977) brought the study of information policy into Harvard University's John F. Kennedy School of Government. Appreciation of the political implications of representations of information—or culture—underlie analyses of symbolic power (Anderson 1983; Bourdieu 1991); examples of case studies undertaken from this approach include examinations of the role of Indian popular cinema in formation of national identity (Chakravarty 1994); Elizabethan writing in shaping the nature of the British state (Helgerson 1992); the contribution of the theater to legitimation of the nation-state in England, France, and the United States (Kruger 1992); and studies of the political effect of literature in various countries (Paulin 1992; Shell 1993). Canclini (1988) synthesized the literature on culture and power up until that point.

Analyses of the importance of information to the exercise of structural power include works by Olsen and Marger (1993), Richards (1993), and Wildavsky (1987). Dandeker (1990) provides a look at the informational bases of the historical development of bureaucratic forms of control by the nation-state. Details about the ways in which differences in information collection and processing practices distinguish states that are generally grouped together in ways that are important to the exercise of political power can be found in Silberman 1993. Huang (1994) provides a fascinating comparison of information collection practices and their political consequences in his study of two countries similarly grouped together, the People's Republic of China and the former Soviet Union. Appreciation of the political implications of information architectures has inspired a growing literature on the political and economic effects of the design of informational practices and architectures not only by nation-states but also by corporations (Bowker 1994), and often by the two types of entities in collaboration (Temin 1991). Those whose starting point is the information society itself also often find themselves focusing on the nature of power (Luke 1989).

Davis (1983) presents the development of modern legal approaches to information and communication several hundred years ago as manipulations of cultural, social, and economic structures to serve the ends of those with political power. A special issue of the *Journal of Communication* devoted to the use of information policy by national governments in the late twentieth century as a tool of power in the international arena included a theoretical overview (Braman 1995a) and case studies of such practices by the governments of India (McDowell 1995; Mody 1995), Mexico (Barrera 1995), Ireland (Bell 1995), the Philippines (Sussman 1995), Poland (Jakubowicz 1995) and Great Britain (Sparks 1995). Magat and Viscusi (1992) provided what appears to be the first analysis of informational, as opposed to behavioral or structural, regulatory tools. The use of informational tactics in resistance to national governments (Arquilla and Ronfeldt 1999; Critical Art Ensemble 1996, 2001) is further evidence of growing awareness of the effectiveness of informational power.

This is of course a very different set of questions from those addressed in the literature that examines the continuation of traditional political practices via new media such as the Internet (e.g., Bimber 2002; R. Davis 1999; Hill and Hughes 1998; Weare 2002). Because of utopian visions of the possibility that the Internet would enable a revitalization of genuine participatory democracy, this question has received a lot of attention. A special issue of the *Journal of the American Society of Information Science* edited by Leah Lievrouw in 1994 usefully explored a wide range of positions on this issue. A spate of recent books has addressed this possibility (e.g., Norris, Bennett, and Entman 2001; Shane 2004). Actual data on the electronic practices of governments not only in the United States but also worldwide is being tracked by Democracies Online, a nonprofit organization run by Steven Clift that provides access to primary documents as well as analysis via its Web site (http://dowire.org). Laws mandating and constraining such activities are of course found at the state as well as national levels (Martin, Chamberlin, and Dmitrieva 2001; Pressman 2002).

Some authors use other terms to discuss the types of power distinguished here. Mann (1984) describes instrumental power as "despotic," and structural power as "infrastructural," and "sticky," Nye (1990) refers to structural power as "soft." One facet of informational power is the subject of discussions about biopower, first theorized by Foucault (1976) and Deleuze and Guattari (1987) as treatment of the body as a site for the expression of power and use of the body as tool of power. Examples of the use of this concept include Foster's (1993) analysis of surrealist artist fixations on the uncanny as bodily manifestations of the traumas of societal transformations and Elichirigoity's (1999) look at the shift from the national to a global orientation as the transition from geopolitical to biopolitical power. Virilio (1986) extends his argument that power has accelerated to the point that it now harvests the very dimensions of time to the body (Kroker 1992). There was legal acknowledgement of biopower in the Biodiversity Convention of 1992, in which the sovereignty of nation-states was defined to include control over indigenous genetic materials. Gottweis (1995) literally describes genetic engineering as a new means of exercising power, a notion taken further in Braman (2004b). There is also work that explores power dynamics among entities that are part machine and part organic, what Haraway (1991) calls the cyborg, Hayles (1999) the posthuman, and Dewdney (1998) the transhuman. The same idea is implicit in Branscomb's (1993) discussion of strategic concerns of what are described here as meta-technologies, Krasner's (1990), and C. Weber's (1995) statement that sovereignty itself needs an alibi.

The State

The literature on the state ebbs and flows with developments in its subject matter, additionally provoked, from time to time, by intra- and interdisciplinary tensions. In David Held's (1989) particularly rich, accessible, and comprehensive single-volume introduction to theories of the state, he points out that it is the very pervasiveness of the subject matter that makes it so difficult to understand. It is precisely because nothing is more central to political and social theory, and nothing is more contested, that we have such a boisterous and massive literature. The fact that the state is our atmosphere also makes its analysis difficult, while ideas about the state are often embedded in work primarily directed elsewhere.

Normative theories of the state and description are often mixed, and states look very different when viewed from the outside as opposed to the inside (Bueno de Mesquita 1988). The uniqueness of each state's historical experience suggests that no one theory of the state could be sufficient for all states, at all times (Tilly 1985). The very concept of the state is highly loaded and ideological (Frankel 1983).

Early works on the state appeared simultaneously with the development of the modern secular state, contributing significantly to its appearance by offering ways of thinking about the organization of power and community structures in non-religious terms. A key trio of books introduced facets of the state still of focal concern today: Machiavelli ([1515] 1985) focused on the exercise of power by those who govern; Jean Bodin ([1576] 1962) responded to Machiavelli with attention to the necessity of state responsiveness to social realities and the responsibility to achieve progress; and Thomas Hobbes ([1651] 1991) articulated a place for civil society as areas of life that are organized outside the control of the state.

A modern conversation focused on the nature of the state began in the 1920s (Dowdall 1923; MacIver 1926; MacLeod 1924) during an extremely interesting moment in the history of the state as a political form: This was after Marx and Engels had put ideas about the relationship between capitalism and the state forward (encapsulated in Feurer's [1959] collection of the political writings of these two thinkers), and after Max Weber had articulated his ideas about the ways in which a variety of forms of power shaped political and social institutions (most easily accessed as republished in 1948 and 1964)—but before the significant expansion of the bureaucratic welfare state form in the 1930s that took place as a response to the Depression—and to the increased state capacity that resulted from the development of information and communication technologies that made it possible to administer complex data-reliant programs (Neely 1981). As Ackerman (1984) points out, only during this period did it come to be believed that the common law could be analyzed for general principles to make particularities seem less arbitrary and obsolete. The situation was soon complicated, for with the development of the activist state, the emphasis was placed upon taking apart those common law principles into a host of incompatibilities whose decisional weight could be appreciated only within the narrow limits of particular cases. By late 1937, there was an entirely new legal structure that mixed abstraction with partiuclarity in an essentially random fashion.

From 1940 to 1960, ideas about the nation-state were heavily colored by the need to articulate appropriate foreign policy. As exemplified influentially in the work of Hans Morgenthau (1954) and synthetically in Brecher, Steinberg, and Stein (1969), this work emphasized what has become known in international relations theory as the Realist view of power. From this perspective, the state is a unitary and rational decision maker with one specified set of goals (Allison 1971). With the passage of colonialism in its traditional form, new types of states appeared, triggering historical and comparative work (Alavi 1974; O'Donnell 1980; Eisenstadt 1980; Wallerstein 1984; Zolberg 1980). So much literature was generated in this period among Marxists debating the precise nature of the nation-state (see, for example, reviews by Gold, Lo, and Wright [1975] and Skocpol [1980] of just some of this work) that Panitch (1980) described its production as a growth industry. Among the diverse relationships between capitalism and the state suggested were direct control of political power via capital (Ollman 1976), via the structuring of production processes (Hechter and Brustein 1980), or via the influence of profit-motivated interest groups (Smith 1993). The work of Poulantzas (1974), which emphasized two-way interactions between the state and society, has been particularly influential. Meanwhile economic historians, lead by Douglass North (1979), began to understand that certain types of economic growth in Europe were made possible only as a result of institutional changes that were the result of the nation-state (Bean 1973; Gellner 1983). Diverse explanations for the formation and survival of states were suggested, including war (Barrow 1993; Porter 1994), international trade (Krasner 1976; Rosecrance 1986), and the desire to achieve social goals (Wilensky 1975; Skocpol 1979). Beginning with the notion of economic as opposed to political sovereignty, diverse aspects of the nation-state began to be seen as operating separately from each other (Simon and Waller 1986; Vernon 1968).

By the early 1980s, the number of different ways of thinking about the nation-state was vast (Easton 1981). Not everyone found this disconcerting; Judith Goldstein (1988) suggested this multiplicity was inevitable, given the importance of both endogenous and exogenous sources of explanation of state behaviors and the multiplicity of important causal forces. Despite the wealth of writing in this area, many felt the state was still inadequately theorized. In response to a period of intense interest in non-state social forces that had dominated political science, Evans, Rueschemeyer, and Skocpol published *Bringing the State Back In* (1985). Anthony Giddens (1987) and Hechter and Brustein (1980), for example, argued that political forms were not yet well understood in sociological terms, and Jessop (1977) felt the state had been ignored among those who study market forces. Giddens predicted, however, that the need to understand globalization would broaden interest in the topic among sociologists. This in fact began to happen, not only among sociologists (Badie and Birnbaum 1983; Thomas and Meyer 1984; Veyne 1992), but also by those with a working knowledge of the changing global system such as the chief executive officer (CEO) of Citibank, Walter Wriston (1992).

Murray (1971) and Herz (1957) argue that what the former called the "territorial noncoincidence" of political power with geographic boundaries began at the close of World War II. It was not until the 1970s, however, that discussion about the deterioration of the nation-state as a political form became common. Arguments about the weakening of the state at their most extreme resulted in claims that it was being made obsolete (Brucan 1980); Wallerstein (1980) actually used the classical Marxist phrase "withering away." Fundamental questions, such as the nature of the state as a collective actor, were raised (Thomas and Meyer 1984). Others, however, argued that states were simply undergoing another in repeated cycles of reorganization of capital, technology, and organizational structure (Duvall and Freeman 1983). Schmitter (1985) attributed differences in perspective on this question to ideological orientation.

Not everyone agreed that the state was the key political entity even historically, however. For alternatives, political scientists pointed to levels of analysis both infra and supra to the state. The devolution of power to the local level was so extreme in the nineteenth century that the American state during that period was described as "distributed" (Skowronek 1982) and policy-making as "stateless" (Skocpol and Finegold 1982). Socialist theorists, on the other hand, argued that the state would disappear into the international system of capitalism (Bowles and Gintis 1982; Brucan 1980; Frankel 1983).

A theoretical argument for the centrality of communication to political form was first put forward by Locke ([1690] 1979). The familiar work on the social contract of course suggests an important role for communication in the formation and sustenance of political agreements. In addition, however, Locke's culture-changing concept of the fact, defined as the communication of experience of the world, is directly pertinent. For Locke, the perceptual organism that creates and communicates facts need not be an individual human being, but rather could be an organization, a community, or a political structure. An extended examination of the consequences of this approach for the development of narrative genres, politics, and power can be found in Braman (1984b). This core insight, however, did not receive explicit attention again until the late twentieth and early twenty-first centuries, in work on information architectures and the codification of knowledge discussed at more length in chapter 6.

Attention to the role of communication in the formation and sustenance of the state—and, therefore, by extension, communication law and policy, if only implicitly—began to appear in the 1950s in diverse literatures. Deutsch (1966) called the communication system the "nerves of government," and believed that the contribution of message and information flows to governance could be quantitatively measured. A very different approach was launched by Lerner's (1954) equation of media use and literacy with political participation in developing societies. This conceptual linkage fueled one of the most extensive torrents of research and writing on the role of communication in development—much of it well funded by national governments—that, in turn, served the purposes of the United States and other nations particularly interested in political processes in developing societies as a site of Cold War conflict. This work, of course, received critique as well (Golding 1974; Mowlana and Wilson 1990). Lasswell (1953) and Boulding (1971) emphasized the role of symbols and identification in the lives of states. Communication also played a role in systems-based approaches to the nation-state, such as those offered by Easton (1979) and, in the most elaborate formulation to date, by Luhmann (1985). Students of international communication were well aware of the role that efforts to sustain national sovereignty played (Nordenstreng and Varis 1973; Nordenstreng and Schiller 1979). Brazil was actually the first country to be deliberate and explicit in its use of communication policy as a means of reinforcing a particular form of the state (del Fiol and Farraz 1985; Mattelart and Mattelart 1990). There are multiple roles that information and communication can play vis-à-vis the state; Carey (1989) influentially distinguished between the ritual and transmission roles of communication, but from the perspective of systems theory these can also serve autopoietic functions (Luhmann 1992; Krippendorff 1984).

While Benedict Anderson (1983) is generally given credit for launching the well-developed stream of literature on the cultural aspects of the nation with his work on the state as an "imagined community," Eric Hobsbawm and Terence Ranger published an important collection on this topic in 1983 that included a number of authors already working in this area, and Hobsbawm (1990) went on to further develop his ideas about nations as myths, a topic further discussed in the bibliographic essay for chapter 5. Examples of policy analyses directed at the nation as a cultural entity include Bell's (1987) work on information policy as a means of separating out a specific group from an existing nation-state, Leong's (1989) analysis of tourism as a contribution to the manufacture of a state, and Hoppe's (1993) study of the deliberate use of "ethnicity policy." Much of the work in this area in the 1980s is reviewed by Canclini (1988). Technological change itself was one stimulus for this line of work because each new technology creates new cultural borders. Martin-Barbero (1988) went so far as to claim that popular culture itself was providing a challenge to the nation-state as the focal orientation and identity of citizens. As Smith (1991) makes clear in his analysis of the political uses of culture in Germany from 1840–1920, these relationships are not always benign. George Marcus launched a line of books on cultural aspects of states in a globalized world with his own sophisticated analysis in 1994. Other literatures, such as Mircea Eliade's (1954) work in the sociology of religion on the shared features of sacred experience as they appear in quite diverse forms across religions, cultures, and societies, can contribute to our understanding of the nation from this perspective.

Two comparative analyses of nation-states are particularly valuable to students of information policy: Greenfeld (1992) offers a detailed and complex history for those who wish to go more deeply into what makes specific contemporary nation-states profoundly different from each other. And Silberman (1993) presents a comparison of leading contemporary states that emphasizes ways in which their treatment of information provides the dimensions along which these states importantly differ from each other.

Recent trends in theories of the state include discussion of "quasi-states" (Jackson 1990), the possibility that the locus of constitutional authority should move from the nation-state to the international arena (Petersmann 1991), and incorporation of environmental concerns into the notion of national security (McNelis and Schweitzer 2001). Although discussion about the role of civil society as a source of power separate from that of the state began much earlier among those involved with nongovernmental organizations (NGOs), the fact that by the late 1990s the reality of this capacity on the part of civil society had been recognized even by those at the center of the international relations community was made clear in a journal article by the head of the Carnegie Endowment for International Peace (Matthews 1997).

There have been a variety of efforts to characterize the contemporary state in informational terms, generally referring to a much more restricted scope of activity or a much less developed theoretical framework than used here. Just a few examples: Higgs (2001) used the phrase "information state" to refer to state surveillance of the citizen beginning as early as 1500 in England. For Rosecrance (1986), the "virtual state" results from the downsizing of national economies through the outsourcing of activities—a development made possible because of digital technologies. Connors (1993) describes the state as "intelligent" because of its reliance on statistics, and Litfin (1997) refers to the United States as a "statistical state" for the same reason.

3 Bounding the Domain: Information Policy for the Twenty-first Century

An earlier version of some of this material can be found in Braman (2004c). This chapter brings together insights drawn from a wide range of sources rather than building upon one or a few sets of literatures, each of which has a coherent history of its own, reflecting the fact that—as with information economics—contemporary information policy brings together many diverse strands of the law historically treated as distinct (Braman 1995b). Peters (1986) was useful in placing this development within the context of the history of communication research in general. The distinction between tools, technologies, and meta-technologies is original with this author (Braman 2002a, 2004a, 2004b). The following discussion offers a paragraph apiece on topics raised by this chapter, roughly in the order in which the subject matter appears in the text.

History

Discussion of ancient antecedents of contemporary information policy can be found in Mowlana and Wilson (1990), Tehranian (1977), and Dinh (1987). The work of military historian Lee (1993) provides an example of the kind of detail about information policy practices of early societies that is buried in works focused on other topics. Michaels (1994) offers the only example of analysis of a traditional tribal culture from the perspective of its indigenous forms of information policy. The history of the word "media" can be found in the *Oxford English Dictionary*. Hugh Beville (1948), to my knowledge, published the first scholarly piece using the phrase "new media"—about FM radio. Ithiel de Sola Pool (1983) tells the story about the FCC's *Bunker-Ramo* case in fascinating detail. Kittross (1980) collected a number of key policy documents recording the history briefly summarized here.

By 1980, pertinent committees of the International Telecommunications Union felt that technology had developed sufficiently to make the effort of establishing global technical standards for a broadband network worthwhile. By the time most telecommunications providers were capable of providing ISDN service in the mid-1990s, however, these standards had already been superseded by systems with greater speed and capacity. For discussion of the ISDN as its development was experienced from the inside while it was still considered the most desirable option, see Cerni (1982), Cerni and Gray (1983), and Dorros (1982). Siff (1984) looked at what the ISDN would mean for the FCC policies, and Sussman (1989) explored its First Amendment implications in a utopian way. The National Research and Education Network was the first expansion of what ultimately became the Internet that was available to those beyond the few specialized research environments in which it was first developed (McClure et al. 1991; Walter and Sussman 1993; Roberts 1992). For policy discussion from diverse of the information infrastructure during the period in the mid-1990s in which Vice President Al Gore's phrase "national information infrastructure" was popular, see Cate (1994), Civille (1993), Huffman and Talcove (1995), Kahin (1991), Kettinger (1994), Maule (1994), Pelton (1994), and Weingarten (1994).

Regulatory and technological shifts in the 1980s increased the salience of the interdependence of legal systems across nation-state borders. In part, this increase was a reflection of the concern over the changing nature of the nation-state discussed in chapter 2 (Spero 1981, 1982). In part, however, it was also a concern specific to the area of communication and information policy. Every type of position appeared; Soma et al. (1983) provide an example of those who felt that such interdependence was inevitable, Pepper and Brotman (1987) described the situation as creating a policy gap, and Bruce, Cunard, and Director (1986) took the pragmatic step of comparative legal analysis, understanding that this was a necessary precursor to achieving international consensus on matters involving the global information infrastructure. Of course, policy-making in dependent, developing, and other types of politically and economically peripheral societies has always been deeply affected by decision making in the dominant countries (Mansell and Wehn 1998; Renaud 1987). Now that this interdependence is widely recognized, policy analysts are turning their attention specifically to the ways in which developments in one country or region affect those in another country or region (Heisenberg and Fandel 2004). In a federalist system such as that of the United States, there are interdependence issues domestically as well (Cherry, Wildman, and Hammond 1999; McDowell 2000; Noam 1982, 1983; Teske 1995). Interdependence between public and private sector decision makers in policy networks (Marsh 1998) is also a factor.

Confounding Factors

A variety of terms is used in the literature to discuss what is described here as "ubiquitous embedded computing." Discussion of ubiquitous computing began to appear in the early 1990s (Weiser 1993). A journal devoted to the topic, *Pervasive Computing*, was launched in 2001, and in 2002 the first international conference on the subject was held under the auspices of IEEE (2003). Familiar policy problems take on new facets in this type of environment in areas such as security (Stajano 2002) and privacy (Hunter 2002). Another phrase used to describe some aspects of ubiquitous embedded computing is the "sensor web." Pew (2003) places ubiquitous embedded computing within the history of human-computer interactions in a book for nontechnical readers.

The concept of structuration was first applied to social forms by social psychologists in the 1950s, but became important to the study of the law as a result of the influential work of Anthony Giddens (1986). Giddens found the concept useful as a way of thinking through the agent-structure problem that had absorbed so much energy in the social sciences since the appearance of functionalism, a school of thought discussed in more detail in the bibliographic essay for chapter 6. For discussions of the agent-structure problem from the perspective of political theory, see Dessler (1989) and Wendt (1987). Wittrock and Wagner (1990) and Wagner et al. (1991) explore the mutually constitutive effects of social science and formal state policy. Other work on structuration that has been important for this author's understanding of the relation between law and society includes Margaret Archer's (1982, 1988) complex adaptive systems-based analysis and Leigh Star's (1987) work on technical problem-solving.

Lawrence Lessig (1999) has been the most successful at bringing appreciation of the structural effects of computer code to popular awareness, but he was neither the first (see, for example, Braman 1993) nor has he in recent years been the only scholar to elaborate upon this important point. Biegel (2001) explores some of the policy problems and options this development brings to our attention. Klein (2004) offers an extremely clear discussion of why the architecture of the Internet offers the Internet Corporation for Assigned Names and Numbers (ICANN) such a broad range of governance opportunities.

The notion that genres have become "blurred" has become a commonplace in discussions of postmodern texts, but this language was first used in a superb and still useful piece by Clifford Geertz in 1980. Davis (1983), in work previously cited, described the process by which genre distinctions became articulated out of a previously undifferentiated matrix of narrative forms several hundred years ago in response to a complex of political, economic, and social factors. Geertz's contribution appeared a couple of decades into discussion of the loss of the historical genre lines discussed by Davis, driven in large part—though not exclusively—by concern about the appearance of new genres in journalism (Hellmann 1981; Hollowell 1977).

Technology-oriented alternative media practices were given the name "tactical media" by the community of media activists and artists in Amsterdam, whose use of the term to title a series of international conferences—the Next 5 Minute conferences on Tactical Media—brought it into global use very quickly. David Garcia and Geert Lovink (1997) developed a tactical media theory in essays distributed first through the listserv *nettime* and then prodigiously republished on other lists. The Critical Art Ensemble (2001) discussed the "pre-policy" policy implications of tactical media work.

Robert Merton introduced his distinction between latent and manifest social forms, processes, and effects in "A Paradigm for the Study of the Sociology of Knowledge" (1955). Though this language was not used at the time, the concept of latent policy is impicit in Benjamin Cardozo's (1921) discussion of the interaction between general principles as rules and the facts of specific cases. For an early example of attention to latent as well as manifest policy in the area of technology see Lambright (1976); Skocpol (1985) provides an example of the utility of this notion to political scientists.

The concept of policy issue areas emerged in the international relations literature when it became clear that policy-making processes differed according to the subjects of decision-making. A review of the literature about the concept can be found in Potter (1980). The phrase continues to be widely used and its meaning has been stable since Potter's review. Other detail: Complaints about the multiplicity of players and venues for information policy-making are rife, but it was Dallas Smythe (1981) who looked at the number of congressional committees dealing with the single problem of electronic funds transfer.

Definitional Approaches

The Leeson Report, which offered a listing of subject areas included under the rubric of information and communication policy, was written for the National

Telecommunications and Information Administration (NTIA) and later published in book form under the title *International Communications* (Leeson 1984). Another example of defining the policy domain by listing topics is found in Mosco (1989).

The model of the information production chain used here was first developed and used in Braman (1988). While influenced by the myriad available implicit and explicit examples of ways of describing an information production chain, this model draws most importantly from Machlup (1980) and Boulding (1966). The utility of this model as a heuristic has been demonstrated via its use in the analysis of constitutional law (Braman 1989), international trade agreements (Braman 1990b) and arms control agreements (Braman 1990a, 1991). The U.S. government's version of the information production chain was published in a publication of the Office of Management and Budget, OMB Circular A-130. Owen and Wildman (1992) discuss some of the ways in which relationships between stages of the information production chain can change. Two examples of the use of a model of the information production to frame media discussion of information policy issues can be found in *The Economist* (1992, 1993).

A position in favor of incremental, rather than radical, legal change is taken here for a number of theoretical and pragmatic reasons. Charles Lindblom (1995) has most fully articulated the distinction between incremental and other types of change (Gregory 1989; Premfors 1992). It is likely, however, that over the next couple of decades, the cumulative effect of incremental change in many different areas of the law will actually result in a change of regime (Braman 2004a).

4 Constitutional Principles and the Information Spaces They Create

The identification of all of the information policy principles in the U.S. Constitution and its amendments is original with this author. It is not the intention of either this bibliographic essay or of the book to repeat the history of the development of the legal positions discussed, stories well told by those cited here and others. The bibliographic essay by Braman (1995b) cited previously includes significant detail regarding treatment of constitutional issues in the area of information policy raised by the impact of technology. Here, materials dealing with the role of the Supreme Court in constitutional law and traditional communication law issues are discussed.

Analyses of constitutional law tend to reflect not only developments in Supreme Court decision-making, but also trends in political thought. The "Court" is of course neither a singular nor a stable entity, changing with appointments and with the intellectual maturation of justices while they are on the Court. (When William O. Douglas was appointed, he was expected to be a conservative.) At least three swings back and forth can be identified, from a largely conservative to a largely progressive Court, and from one that does not see a proactive role for the Supreme Court to one that believes that Supreme Court decisions are inevitably political, a position summarized in descriptions of the justices as "activist." These two dimensions, however—progressive/conservative and passive/active—represent independent axes. It is possible for a progressive Court to be either active or passive, and the same can be said for a conservative Court. Thus over the long view, constitutional law is best described as dynamic rather than static (Fallon 2004) and is characterized by discontinuities (Kersch 2004). Farber and Sherry (2002) describe the effort to reach a consensus on the interpretation of the Constitution, as if there were discernible original "intentions," as misguided. Indeed, one of the most interesting aspects of constitutional law is the way in which ideas first put forward in dissenting opinions can later come to provide the basis for decisions by the Court; Lively (1992) documents those areas of the law that have developed in this way. The tension between what government is capable of doing and what the Supreme Court will permit it to do is enduring (Neely 1981).

The history of U.S. constitutional law has been examined through such diverse perspectives as its impact on the moral order (Bailey 2004), as a product or reflection of economic processes (Beard 1930; McGuire 2003), as a narrative (Fish 1989; LaRue 1995), as a particular institutional form (Grossman and Wells 1972; Murphy 1964), and as a political (Wolfe 1981)—possibly democratic (Dahl 2003; Fiss 2003)—process. The critical legal studies movement approached constitutional law from the perspective of critical theory (Dworkin 1986; Kairys 1982; Unger 1975). The effects of constitutional law are of course responsive to the dominant form of the state; for an analysis of the nature of constitutional law in an administrative state, see Rabkin (1983). For examination of what are commonly considered to be the intellectual sources upon which the Constitution draws, see Stevens (1997) and Stoner (1992), though Wills (1978) and Boyd (1992) provide alternative views. Kyvig (1996) and Levinson (1995) provide histories of the processes by which the Constitution has been amended. Justice Frankfurter (1939) described constitutional law as "applied politics," and others have explored the politics of the Supreme Court as they play out through appointments, processes internal to its decision making, and the extent to which the Court does or does not reflect swings in public opinion (Carter 1985; Corsi 1984; Ely 1980; Frankfurter 1939; Miller 1968; Miller and Howell 1960; Wolfe 1981). Witt (1984) looked at how constitutional law can be affected by shifts in administrations, using as his case the Reagan administration, and Nagel (1989) and Neely (1981) tried to evaluate the effects of constitutional law.

Overviews of constitutional law include attention to the information policy principles that are our focus here (Barron and Dienes 2003; Choper 2001; Rotunda and Nowak 1999; Stone, Sunstein, and Seidman 2005; Feeley and Krislov 1985). The literature on constitutional law is massive, but particularly influential discussions of constitutional theory and the nature of reasoning in constitutional law are available in Carter (1984), Cass (1987), Cohen (1935), Ely (1978), Fiss (1979), and Holmes (1897). That there are strong disagreements regarding how to interpret the Constitution is inevitable (Berger 1984; Horowitz 1983); a collection by Garvey and Aleinikoff (1991) includes a diverse range of contemporary theories of constitutional law. In the last few years, the argument has appeared that constitutional law is intended to be negative rather than positive; that is, rather than trying to offer a positive view of the kind of society sought, constitutional law serves only the negative function of trying to protect society from harm. This work has been of particular interest to those who promote strengthening international trade law, which some argue could itself play a global constitutional function (Jackson 1988; Petersmann 1988; Sunstein 1995). For a look at other contemporary constitutional issues that include but go beyond transformations in the technological environment, see Tushnet (2003).

The First Amendment has received a significant amount of attention in its own right, also from a variety of perspectives. Overviews of First Amendment and related law include those by Gillmor, Barron, and Simon (1998), Hemmer (2000), and Hensley (2001). Murphy (1992) provides a history of First Amendment interpretation. Theories of the First Amendment that have received significant attention have been put forward by Blasi (1986, 2002), Meiklejohn (1961), Emerson (1977), and Schauer (1982). Owen (1975), Posner (1984, 2003), and Brennan (1983, 1990, 1992a) have looked at First Amendment issues through an economic lens, and Entman (1993) looked at its political functions. Streeter (1990) discussed the application of critical legal studies to communication policy theoretically, and this theoretical approach was applied in the items collected in Allen and Jensen (1995). Bunker (2001) looked at the impact of multidisciplinary intellectual trends on analysis of constitutional law. For studies of treatment of the First Amendment under war or warlike conditions, see Rehnquist (1998) and Smith (1999). Schwartz (1990) analyzed the extent to which any of this work was cited in U.S. Supreme Court opinions from 1964 to 1986.

For details of the historical development of the legal positions summarized in chapters 5–8, including discussion of the specific court cases, regulatory debates, and statutory developments through which the current state of the law were negotiated, textbooks and casebooks will be of particular value. While one needs recently published books for current law, older items include additional detail of value when one is seeking historical trends. Works on the First Amendment include Carter, Franklin, and Wright (2003), Trager and Dickerson (1999), van Alstyne (1995, 1996 supplement), and Volokh (2003). Works that cover statutory and regulatory law that affect communication including but also going beyond the First Amendment include Franklin (2000), Holsinger and Dilts (1997), Hopkins (2004), Francois (1994), Gillmor, Barron, and Simon (1998), Middleton, Trager, and Chamberlin (2004), Moore (1999), Overbeck (2004), Pember (2003), Teeter and Loving (2004), and Zelezny (2004). Some works start from broadcast and telecommunications regulation rather than from the First Amendment in their exploration of communication law and policy, such as Black (2002), Creech (2003), and Ginsburg, Botein, and Director (1998).

Nadel (1983) offered an early effort to think through First Amendment implications of digital technology by separating the medium and message, an idea that keeps reappearing. The term "cyberlaw" came into vogue in the second half of the 1990s. It is used in book-length treatments of Internet-specific legal problems (Baumer and Poindexter 2002; Bellia et al. 2004; Ferrera et al. 2004; Girasa 2002; Helewitz 2003; Radin 2002; Rosenour 1997), and has generated enough attention to already be the subject of discussions of the identity of the "field" (Mariotti 2005). Others use the phrase "Internet law" to refer to the same set of problems and cases (Delta and Matsuura 2001; Lemley et al. 2003; Maggs, Soma, and Sprowl 2000; Reed 2004; Samorki 2001). For examples of analyses of civil liberties issues arising out of online communications or activities, see Uncapher (1991), Naughton (1992), and Schlachter (1993). There has been specific attention to First Amendment issues raised by digital technologies (Godwin 1998; Lipschultz 2000; the U.S. Office of Technology Assessment 1988; Stone, Sunstein, and Seidman 2005). We are just beginning to see the suggestion that constitutional and statutory requirements should be applied to technical standards (Benoliel 2004).

Jurisdictional issues are particularly complex and interesting. Jurisdictional problems first received extended legal analysis in the early 1980s, when the problem was where to locate foreign direct investment when it took place via transborder data flow (Sauvant 1986). Recent examples of jurisdictional issues include a replay of the twenty-year-old problem of locating the consumer and the transaction (Rustad 2004) as well as explorations of opportunities for legal innovation also offered by the Internet, such as "distributed" criminal justice (Brenner 2004) and the establishment of the offshore legal entity Sealand (Arenas 2003). Kahin and Nesson (1997) and Banisar (2002) provide overviews of jurisdictional issues.

Given the Supreme Court appointments currently being made during the George W. Bush administration, it can be expected that the swing from progressive to conservative will be intensified. In coming years, a Supreme Court with new appointees and a post-Rehnquist chief justice can also be expected to be relatively activist in its pursuit of the political program represented by the current Bush administration. Tushnet (2005) has begun to explore what these changes might mean for constitutional law, with particular attention to Justice Antonin Scalia's position on the First Amendment and to the religious right's agenda regarding religious symbolism as well as money. Whether or not the court should go in this direction is, of course, disputed (Ivers and McGuire 2004).

5 Information Policy and Identity

The essay for this chapter and each of the next three opens with a look at the theoretical literature on the orienting concept—in this case, identity—and then follows the structure for the text for which citations are being provided.

Theory

Theories regarding individual and state identity have very different histories. Theoretical work on the mediations between the two is so topic-specific that it is included in the discussion of each of those types of mediations in the following sections.

Individual identity Thought about the individual, and the self, did not appear until the modern period, with its characteristic interest in individualism. Until the beginnings of psychoanalytic ideas in the nineteenth century, the individual was most likely to show up in philosophy in the capacity of the self to experience or "know" the empirical world, as in the work of David Hume and John Locke. Histories of psychoanalytic theory (Schwartz 2001; Wallerstein 1988; Zaretsky 2004) provide insight into the various perspectives on individual identity offered by diverse psychoanalytic schools after Freud's initial seminal insights. Even psychoanalytic understandings of identity, however, continue to develop; the concept of "termination," for example, is described as "post-psychoanalytic" (Blum 1989) but is clearly important for understanding identity in the twenty-first century.

Beginning with the early twentieth-century work of social psychologists such as Cooley (1902) and Mead (1934), there was a great deal of attention to the way in which interpersonal and group interactions shape individual identity. By the 1970s, there were efforts to quantify the various dimensions of such identity-building interactions (Hooper 1976). Other approaches that linked the individual and social levels of analysis in the study of identity include studies of psychoanalysis and social evolution (Kriegman and Knight 1988), Bailey's (2000) look at the individual through the lens of the "private" in sociological thought, studies of individual identity formation and sustenance within organizations (Whetten and Godfrey 1998), and Maxwell's (1996) work on the role of marketing in ensuring that consumption is an identity-forming activity. Erikson (1968) launched an important new stream of work with his analyses of individual identities within the context of particular social and intellectual movements. Webb (1993) presents a synthesis of decades of this literature, the collections edited by Mokros (2003) and by Gergen and Davis (1985) include representative pieces on the topic, and Gergen (1992) and Leary and Tangney (2003) offer contemporary theories of individual identity against this long history. The centrality of communication in social psychology and related theories made it inevitable that a purely communication-based theory of identity should appear (Hecht 1993).

In a somewhat prescient work that linked social psychological approaches to identity with the kinds of concerns about the impact of technology on individuals, Klapp (1976) explored identity as a "playback" function. The first really thorough study of the impact of computing on the nature of individual identity, however—one that remains worth revisiting regularly for its depth of insight—was Sherry Turkle's *Life on the Screen* (1995); Allucquère Rosanne Stone (1995) also provides particularly thoughtful and provocative thoughts about digital technologies and identity in her reports about experimentation from what was then the edge. An overview of what has been learned to date about the impact of digital technologies on identity can be found in Wood and Smith (2005). Fortunati, Katz, and Riccini (2003) look at the use of the cell phone and other technologies as expressions of identity, and Feinberg, Westgate, and Burroughs (1992) point out that even technologies such as the credit card both influence and are used to express identity. Baym (1997) follows up on Stone's linkage of the digital impact on relationships with our bodies, communities, and identities in her study of a particular online community. In an interesting study of treatment of identity and community in the popular magazine *Wired*, Frau-Meiggs (2000) is able to demonstrate the acceptance of multiple identities in discourse and images.

Quite aside from direct discussions of the privacy and anonymity issues faced by policy-makers, Bunker (1996) has opened the door to a discussion of assumptions about the nature of individual identity embedded in the First Amendment and interactions between interpretations of that constitutional principle and identity, and Agre (1999) explores the ways in which market institutions shape the "architecture of identity." Given the extent to which regionalization is affecting European countries, it should not be surprising that it has largely been Europeans such as Gifreu (1986), Van den Bulck and Van Poecke (1996), Hamelink (1989), and Servaes (1989) who have looked specifically at individual identity issues from a mass communication policy perspective. The work on identity and social evolution also has policy implications, though Waisbrod (1998) argues that technology-centered discussions of the impact of globalization, even within policy circles, underplay the importance of identity issues.

State identity National identity is a specific form of collective identity (Schlesinger 1991). For explorations of why the subject is of political as well as general interest, see Ferguson and Mansbach (1996), Lapid (1995), and Rosenfeld (1994) and Castells (1997b) specifically explores the ways in which the transformation to an information society has affected the relationship between political identity and power. The work collected in Meyer, Whittier, and Robnett (2002) looks at the role of identity in efforts to change the nature of the state.

Although several diverse bodies of literature contribute to our understanding of the relationship between information and identity, few of them do so self-consciously, and the research is distinctly siloed so that there are rarely, if ever, mutual references. There are two exceptions: the sets of works on national propaganda and on the communicative aspects of "soft," or "public" diplomacy. Edward Bernays, the "father" of the profession of public relations, published his landmark book *Propaganda* in 1928 (republished in 2004) based both on his experience with the propaganda arm of the U.S. government (the Committee on Public Information) during World War I and his foresight regarding the possibilities for future use of the media to shape public thought and action. (Signitzer [1992] provides a more contemporary look at the relationship between public relations and propaganda/public diplomacy practices.) The collection by Kamalipour and Snow (2004) is unusually international in the examples of propaganda discussed. Examples of in-depth studies of specific propaganda campaigns can be found in MacArthur (2004) (on the 1991 Gulf War) and Bernhard (2003) (on the Cold War). Johnson-Cartee and Copeland (2003) analyze propaganda practices from the perspective of theories of persuasion and social influence. Taylor (2003) provides an authoritative overview of the history and practice of propaganda, and Manheim (1994) does the same for public diplomacy. For reviews of the literature on propaganda as communication from two different theoretical perspectives, see Jowett (1987) and Sproule (1987). The premiere organ of U.S. public diplomatic practices has been the U.S. Information Agency (USIA), the history of which is described in Dizard (2004). The excellent collection edited by Jonsson and Langhorne (2004) explores the role of communication in both diplomacy and public diplomacy from theory to practice. Propaganda and diplomacy are so important politically that they have been incorporated into theoretical frameworks for understanding the relationship between media and democracy (Biesecker, Mandziuk, and Nakayama 1998; Gilboa 2000; Parry-Giles 1993). Nickles (2003) offers an interesting look at how one technological innovation—the telegraph—affected diplomatic practice, and Hansen (1989), Hoffman (2002), Dinh (1987), and Peterson (2002) look at the implications of the technologies new to the late twentieth century and associated social change for diplomacy and propaganda.

A variety of cultural practices has been used to examine and assert U.S. identity (Thelen and Hoxie 1994), some simply the inevitable effects of the culture industries (Chaffee 1992; Cohen and Roeh 1992). In countries in which news agencies have been or are closely linked with governments, the news media in general play serve to articulate and reinforce national identity domestically as well (Boyd-Barrett 1980; Rantanen and Boyd-Barrett 1999). Although this was not officially the case in the United States historically, informal arrangements and overt political pressure on news agencies have meant that even news agencies and journalistic organizations have participated in identity-building in that country as well (Blanchard 1986). Asa Briggs (2004) explored the impact of both television and computers on our ability to predict the future based upon the ways in which those two information and communication technologies affect our sense of the past. The role of knowledge acquisition in shaping national identity is discussed in the bibliographic essay on borders, and the role of memory is explored in the following sections.

Information Policy and Individual Identity

Each of the specific policy issues discussed in the text receives separate bibliographic treatment here.

Libel The development of libel law is discussed in the mass communication law, media law, and First Amendment textbooks and casebooks cited previously. There are also textbooks specific to libel law (Jasper 1996; W. K. Jones 2003); it is one sign of the expansion of law dealing with information and communication that such works were more commonly published a few decades ago than they are today. Given the global nature of content distribution, comparative law is increasingly important (Amponsah 2004; Braithwaite 1995; Goldberg 1990). The Web raises problems for libel law in the basic dimensions of both time (Kumar 2003) and space (Borchers 2004), a matter recognized even before the Internet was available for use by the general public (Cutrera 1992). Shiffrin provided a preview of contemporary libel issues raised for those who are not in the media as early as 1978.

Libel law is extremely sensitive to cultural and political developments. Thus interpretive histories, such as those by Rosenberg (1986) and Smolla (1986), are useful for those trying to understand the social context within which changes in the law have taken place—and will take place. The enormous cost of defending a libel suit led to its use as a political tool by those seeking to silence investigative media voices, until the Supreme Court capped damages and switched the burden of proof (with its high costs) to the plaintiff (Dennis and Noam 1989; Gillmor 1992; Greenwald and Bernt 2000). Specific libel cases of course involve engagements of particular individuals with media organizations; Bezanson, Cranberg, and Soloski (1987) conducted empirical research on hundreds of plaintiffs in libel cases to determine why suits were filed. Of the many publications that tell the story of a case from the perspective of the person libeled, one example that is of particular interest, because it also involves Cold War political tensions, can be found in Faulk (1964).

Certain libel cases have received particular attention by scholars and historians. A colonial trial completely changed the nature of libel law by introducing truth as a defense, beginning with the words of the defendant, Peter Zenger (Zenger and Buranelli 1957). The 1964 case *New York Times v. Sullivan*, which constitutionalized libel law and, importantly, distinguished between public and private figures as a means of protecting political speech, continues to receive analysis (Hopkins 1989; Lewis 1991; Ross and Bird 2004).

Privacy R. E. Smith (2004) provides a very long history of legal approaches to privacy in the United States from colonial times. It was only in the late nineteenth century, however, that an explicit right to privacy—based in constitutional law—was first articulated (Warren and Brandeis 1890). Although there are many areas in which privacy law in the United States is now a matter of statute, for a long time it was a matter of tort law, and in many instances continues to be so. William Prosser (1971, 1984), in his works on the law of torts, is responsible for conceptualizing the categories of invasions of privacy used in legal analysis today. Privacy is also a topic included in the textbooks on media and communication law cited previously, as well as being the subject of specialized textbooks and casebooks (Connolly 2003; Rozenberg 2004; Solove and Rotenberg 2003; Tugendhat and Christie 2004). Cate (1997) provides a deeply knowledgeable and broad overview for the nonspecialist. In many areas of privacy law, comparative analysis is critical, because access and distribution of data and content are global (Bennett 2003; Goldberg, Prosser, and Verhulst 1998; Marcella 2003; Rotenberg 2003). Human rights concerns are among those that draw our attention to comparative and international matters in this area (Electronic Privacy Information Center and Privacy International 2003). The Electronic Privacy Information Center (2005) provides detailed analysis and documentation of ongoing policy debates in areas such as encryption at www.epic.org.

Given the multiple types of privacy, it should be no surprise that a wide variety of theoretical approaches have been offered as underpinnings for legal decision making in this area. A wide diversity of approaches to conceptualizing privacy by deeply knowledgeable thinkers is available in Schoeman (1984). DeVries (2003) argued that new theories regarding protection of privacy are needed in today's environment; Solove (2004) provides it by responding to the richness of the theoretical traditions introduced in Schoeman as they have affected the law and are in themselves recontextualized by contemporary conditions to offer an approach to conceptualizing privacy for the twenty-first century; and Marlin-Bennett (2004) specifically discusses privacy from the perspective of the impact of both its protection and invasion on power relations. Changes in the conditions of privacy have profound cultural effects; Dean (2002) explores these with particular subtlety and insight, and McGrath (2004) examines some of the very interesting cultural responses to today's threats to privacy by activists, artists, and young people simply trying to create and protect their identities under surveillance conditions. Posner (1984) offers an economic analysis of privacy but, as Hahn and Layne-Farrar (2002) point out, this type of approach rarely—if ever—deals with the costs to those about whom data is collected.

A broad overview of the specific features of today's environment that draw such attention to privacy issues appears in Agre and Rotenberg (1998). As just one example of ways in which shifts in the information industries raise new factors that must be balanced in determining policy responses to privacy issues, Akdeniz (2000) discusses the ways in which governments require that ISPs play a role in crime prevention; this particular issue is of even greater importance since 9/11 than it was when this article was written because of the additional responsibilities of ISPs regarding homeland security. There has been appreciation of the ways in which technological innovation can create new threats to privacy for decades, however. Alan F. Westin (1966, 1971, 1977; Westin and Baker 1972) led the way in the early 1970s with his discussion of the privacy implications of computerized databases and other new information technologies. Marchand (1979) and Gordon (1981) offer other examples of relatively early awareness of the privacy issues that are so pressing today. By now, however, we also know that technologies can protect privacy as well as offer the means of destroying it. Dingledine (2004) provides an overview of what are now called "privacy enhancing technologies," Levy (2004) describes the cryptography wars, and EPIC (1993) offered a snapshot of the state of the law in the midst of the battle over cryptography. The American Library Association (ALA) views technologically enhanced surveillance as a threat to First Amendment rights ([1973] 1981 policy). Because technological designs aren't inevitable but, rather, can be tailored to minimize or maximize privacy protections, differences in types of machines for processes like airport surveillance (Rosen 2004) can have important policy implications.

Technological innovation has had such a tremendous impact on privacy that there has been an explosion in the literature; a query of the bibliographic database of law reviews in LexisNexis in March 2005 yielded 286 citations for articles with the word "privacy" in their titles in just the preceding two years. Traditional difficulties remain, but new types of privacy concerns are also being raised. National security has always been a logic used to justify threats to privacy, but today that includes such new topics as the tensions between protections against bioterrorism and the privacy of health data (Bruce 2003), and between military requirements and personal privacy (Lear 2003). The commodification of information that so characterizes this era has led to an appreciation of the way in which privacy can function as a form of property rights; debates over DNA (Harlan 2004; Hibbert 2001; Nelkin and Andrews 1999; Suter 2004) are one among several areas in which this approach is explicit. This conceptual move also yields new types of policy interventions and problems, as in complaints about invasions of privacy from the use of the Digital Millennium Copyright Act to identify illegal uses of digital recordings (Boag 2004; Rowland 2003).

Another example of a new type of privacy issue in today's environment is fear of invasions of privacy through mapping processes (Flannery 2003), distributed databases (Froomkin 1996), and the temptations of "database marketing" (Hoffman, Novak, and Peralta 1999; Zwick and Dholakia 2004). The Federal Trade Commission maintains a Web site with information about federal and state laws relating to identity theft, scams in which those who have succeeded at identity theft have engaged, and ways to protect yourself. For studies of the impact on privacy of changes in the law, interpretation of the law, and implementation of the law since 9/11, see Chishti et al. (2003) and O'Harrow (2005). EPIC provides analyses of current issues and developments in the law at the international, national, and state levels.

The literature on anonymity is related to that on privacy, but has also its own history as well. G. T. Marx (1999) looks at sociology of anonymity and the authors in Griffin (2003) examine the cultural roles of anonymity as a dominant form of print culture going back to the sixteenth century. The technological ease with which anonymity is unmasked in the electronic environment has stimulated interest in the legal aspects of this problem (Ekstrand 2003; Froomkin 1999; Teich et al. 1999). Slobogin (2002) enunciates a specific right to anonymity in an environment in which constant public surveillance is not only possible but increasingly practiced, and Nicoll, Prins, and van Dellen (2003) provide a wide-ranging view of the diverse perspectives on and issues raised by the question of anonymity in the digital environment. Johnson and Miller (1998) examine the impact of such practices on trust in particular. There are technological means of protecting privacy in the digital environment (Claessens et al. 2003; Waldman, Rubin, and Cranor 2000). Nonprofit organizations such as the Electronic Frontier Foundation and the Electronic Privacy and Information Center are contributing to the development and distribution of such techniques, though Swire (1997) also warns of their limits. Ekstrand (2003) discusses criteria used by courts to decide when to protect anonymous communication on the Internet.

Information Policy and the Identity of the Informational State

Discussions of available bibliographic sources on the census and other government statistics, mapping, official memory, and access to government information are presented separately here.

The census and other statistics For the long history of the development of statistical thinking, see Desrosieres (1998) and Hacking (1984, 1990). There was concern about what was lost as well as what was gained by quantitative measurement from the start. (Desrosieres [1991] details some of the early records of such complaints several hundred years ago in the domain of the political consequences.) Oliver Sacks has similarly noted that many diseases—such as Tourette's syndrome—simply disappeared from awareness or knowledge in the nineteenth century when detailed narrative records of physicians began to be replaced by the quantitative records of clinical medicine (S. Silberman 2002). There is a rich body of work on interactions between the development of statistical methods and modes of government by the state (Brooks and Gagnon 1990;

Nowotny 1983; Wagner et al. 1991). This intertwining of activities makes it inevitable that seemingly objective and neutral technical debates over the details of statistical categories are influenced by professional and political commitments, with the consequence that how those choices are made will differ by time period, national culture, and profession. A breakthrough article by MacKenzie (1978) launched analysis of statistical methods from this perspective, and Nobles (2000) and Schweber (2001) present current examples of this type of work.

Rich and authoritative social histories of the development of specific statistical systems are available in Anderson (1988) on the census and Goldberg and Moye (1985) on the Bureau of Labor. An extensive history of the use of the census in reapportionment can be found in Schmeckebier (1941), and an historical study that contextualizes the 1997 economic census is offered by Micarelli (1998). The long history of census sampling issues is discussed in Desrosieres (1991), and Anderson and Fienberg (1999) and the National Research Council (1995) discuss recent debates in the United States in this area. Anderson (1993) looks specifically at the history of racial categories, Ryan (1992) at the history of statistical profiling, and Godin (2002) at fifty years of official science and technology statistics.

There are myriad examples of how the very conceptualization of statistical categories can affect individual identity in ways that have consequences for individual lives; for some examples of how this plays out in the United States, see Fitzgerald, Shelley, and Dail (2001) on the measurement of homelessness, and Bean et al. (2001) and Durand, Massey, and Zenteno (2001) on statistics about authorized and unauthorized Mexican migrants. Population data systems have themselves been implicated in human rights abuses (Seltzer and Anderson 2001), and the census has been critiqued for contributing to the development of consumption habits (Kysar 2002). Analysis of the political effects of census has raised interest in the possibility of actual manipulations of the methodology for political purposes (Carter and Sutch 1995). Potok (2000) describes the details of the most recent comprehensive census, in 2000.

The political aspects of government information policy began to receive the attention of nonprofit agencies over the last couple of decades, yielding a number of analytical publications. The journal *Government Information Insider* provided a critical look at these policies, and McDermott and Bass (1996) provide an overview of concerns. The statistical agencies of the government all provide detail about the methodologies they currently use on their Web sites. Chandler (2000) describes interactions between the development of new information technologies and the statistical mechanisms of the government in the early twentieth century, and Litfin (1997) pursues the same question as raised by satellites at the close of that century.

Cross-level analysis of the macroscale of places with the microscale of people allows places to be examined on different levels simultaneously (Jaeger et al. 1998; Subramanian, Duncan, and Jones 2001). The role of statistical agencies in stimulating technological development is documented well by Anderson and by Goldberg and Moye, cited previously; Thiemie (2000) provides a look at some of the contemporary stimuli to technological innovation coming from governmental statistical needs.

In March 2003, the FBI announced launched the NCIC (National Crime Information Center), the most extensive system of criminal history records in the United States (averages more than 52 million transactions per day). In December 2003, the attorney general released the FBI from the provisions of the Privacy Act that required accuracy in the data upon which it acted and modes of redress for those individuals who believed that data held about them in databases used by the criminal justice system was inaccurate. Ongoing updates of the effort to reestablish accuracy as a requirement can be found on the EPIC Web site at (www.epic.org/privacy/ncic/).

Mapping The diversity, beauty and even frequent idiosyncrasy of maps have long made them the objects of collectors as well as scholars; for a history of the study of maps, see Skelton (1972). There are several good histories of cartography (Bagrow 1964; Harley and Woodward 1987; Thrower 1972; Wilford 2000). Pickles (2004) looks at the history of maps through the lens of what they reveal about cartographic and visual reasoning, and the items collected in Goodchild and Janelle (2004) examine the impact of spatial logics on the social sciences. Mapping practices are of course deeply responsive to developments in information technologies (Bachi 1999; Silver and Balmori 2003).

Political uses of maps include their support for stewardship of national parks (Henry and Armstrong 2004), their use in law enforcement (Leipnik and Albert 2003), their contribution to the national debate over cultural diversity (U.S. Census Bureau 2002), their role in establishing property rights (Kain and Baigent 1992), and their utility as both argument and evidence in land use debates (Hoffman 1986). Maps are also useful for journalists (Herzog 2003), and for historians, whether they are looking at items singly, at comparative analyses of mapping efforts across time, or at new mapping information made possible only through the combined use of satellite surveillance and sophisticated sensory data analysis (Bender 2002; Cohen 2002; Knowles 2002).

Some of the political impact of maps is perceptual. Edward Tufte (1983, 1990), whose career started with the study of the use of data in policy analysis, has produced particularly influential work on how to present data visually in effective ways. Elichirigoity (1999) discusses the shift to conceptualizing locales within a global rather than local or national framework from a political and cultural perspective; and another shift is currently taking place as we gain the ability to map the larger astronomical universe within which our planet resides (DeVorkin 2002).

Current issues raised by the legal use of maps include concern over whether they may be misleading for judges accustomed to verbal arguments (Dellinger 1997), and disagreements over the extent to which it is legitimate to use geographic information systems (GIS) in ways that some people argue run contrary to Fourth Amendment privacy protections (Flannery 2003). There are tensions over the establishment of standards regarding the use of maps in international law (Lee 2005), perhaps in part because this process began under the aegis of the U.S. Agency for International Development (USAID), an entity accused by some of inappropriately serving the interests of the U.S. government in other countries (International Statistical Programs Center 1977). OMB Circular A-16 governs current U.S. mapping procedures.

Critiques of government use of maps appeared early (Wright et al. 1938). The Federal Geographic Data Committee published a report in 2004 announcing detailed plans for the National Spatial Data Infrastructure that has already been critiqued from a cost-benefit analysis perspective (Halsing 2004) as well as for its likely impact on social, political, economic, and cultural developments (National Research Council 2003).

Official memory Myths of origin have always supported assertions of power, but in their modern form—history—Stephen (1907) suggests theories of official memory first developed in the work of authors such as Montesquieu ([1748] 1949), Hume ([1741] 1975), and Gibbon ([1776] 1960) on historiographical methods as a support for the political form of the modern nation-state. Memories themselves have their own architectures, a characteristic taken quite literally in memory techniques used since the Greeks up through the medieval period (Yates 1966), and metaphorically today.

While individual memory and collective memory are certainly related, a superb review of the literature on the latter, our focus here—social memory studies—can be found in Olick and Robbins (1998). Other distinctions can be made: Walter Benjamin distinguished between the historicist approach to history (in which history is treated as preconstituted in a continuous chain of cause and effect) and the constructivist approach (in which the historian is an activist in construction of the historical narrative) (Peters 1999). Bruner (1990) identified three characteristics of narratives that serve as history: narrative diachronic ability (accounting for events occurring over time); a combination of canonicity and breadth; and "narrative accrual," the ability of narratives to be cobbled together into coherent histories, cultures, and traditions. Appadaurai (1993) adds another dimension with his distinction between history (that which leads outward, linking patterns of local changes to increasingly larger universes of interaction), and genealogy (that which leads inward, toward cultural dispositions embedded in local institutions and in the history of the local habitus). With the habitus we are, of course, brought to the embedding of memory in practice, drawing attention to the fact that when lifestyles change, often memory is lost (McKibben 1996). Paralleling the distinction between the cultural nation and the bureaucratic state, a final distinction can be drawn between cultural and bureaucratic forms of memory, making it quite interesting to note that Levi-Strauss's (1963) founding text of structural anthropology—which included the idea that mythic memory is a way of resolving contradictions between one's own experience and history as told—was written in Greenwich Village just a few yards (through the walls) from Claude Shannon, then working on the launch of information theory (Clifford 1988).

A theoretical linkage between state power and memory was offered by mainstream political scientist Almond (1983) before the notion became trendy, and Grossman (1994) has documented the actual history of the relationship between history, legal records, codification of the law, and publication of the law. In his analysis of decision-making processes, Herbert Simon (1979) highlighted the role of memory repositories, which can differ significantly by their nature and function (Lewis 1987), and play different roles at various points in the life cycle of an institution or process (Delaney 1993). Of course memory need not refer to real events in order to be effective for policy purposes (de Swaan 1997). Many of the rules of evidence for the law deal with how to elicit memories that are both trustable and useful (Baird, Gertner, and Picker 1994).

Studies of the British Empire have provided particularly vivid and influential examples of the use of official memory in constructing knowledge for the purposes of exercising power (Cohen 1996; Richards 1993). British efforts of the eighteenth through twentieth centuries to build archives of knowledge in support of their exercise of political power built upon a longer history, in which the development of legal and other social records was prelude to and intertwined with the development of the state as a successful political form (Clanchy 1979; Grossman 1994). World War II stimulated a set of studies of the role of memory of the past in shaping power relations in a transformed political environment (Müller 2002). Powerful examples of the political struggle over official memory in the United States include the books by Schudson (1992) on Vietnam and by Zelizer (1992) on the Kennedy assassination.

There are of course dangers from false memories (Kitzinger and Reilly 1997), "imagined" or "armchair" nostalgia as memory of things never known either individually or collectively, and even nostalgia for a present that is not available (Appadurai 1993). Concerns about the loss of memory as a result of dependence upon technologies goes back to Plato's report of Socrates' complaints (Peters 1999). As Stille (2002) points out, the use of new information technologies is rapidly destroying ancient bodies of knowledge around the world. And memory in digital form is dangerously ephemeral. Dewdney (1998), however, argues that one social consequence of constant and rapid innovation is that the advantage now, for the first time, increasingly goes to those *without* memory, for they will not have to unlearn old procedures in order to learn new ones. Memory is an important part of cultural capital (Palumbio-Liu 1993). MacKenzie and Spinardi (1995) make the point that government policy can itself destroy memory, even of large technological systems, in a piece exploring the "uninvention" of nuclear weapons.

All of the problems raised by statistical efforts on the part of governments, discussed previously, are raised in other forms of record-keeping as well, with the particularly important challenges presented by national security in regard to government archives (Wark 1992). Nowotny (1990) discusses political uses of memory for, as she points out, if conditions are not conducive to a group having power in the present, strategies may include rearranging the past, limiting access to the past, or shifting to the future for legitimation (all strategies we're currently seeing today). The value of historical records in the marketplace may prevent documents from being submitted to archives (as discussed in an interesting piece by an author willing to identify him- or herself only by initials in a discussion of the Russian archives—E. D. M. 1993)—or may contribute to the protection of cultural artifacts, because they are deemed to be financial assets for a community (Stanton 2002). Hoff (1996) and Krusten (1996) report on the difficulty of trying to do historical research when records have been withheld from the National Archive, as happened with the Nixon presidency, and Schrag (1994) tells the story of historian Edward Berkowitz, who found he couldn't study the history of U.S. disability policy in the 1990s because the records—which went back to the 1920s—were still in the warehouse, unsorted.

Technological innovation has broadened the scope of both legal and operational definitions of a record; The Uniform Rules of Evidence equate records with "writings and recordings" (interpreted to include essentially any recorded information) and the Federal Records Act defines government records as all materials that deal with government policies and activities (Skupsky 1995). The Office of the Federal Register published a guide to federal record retention requirements as they stood in 1994.

For an excellent collection of both primary and secondary material dealing with the history of the development of U.S. federal government records, see Nelson (1978). The Web site for official U.S. memory is offered by NARA (www.nara.gov). Burkert (1995) has been studying access to government information for decades, not only in the United States, but in other countries as well, and so provides superbly contextualized analyses periodically. The drive to reduce the size of government made it more difficult than it had been historically to maintain full government archives. Dugan, Hernon, and Relyea (1998) discuss recent efforts to dismantle the GPO and move control over dissemination of government documents from the legislative to the executive branch, and Fisher (2002) looks at the related story of attempts to withhold presidential documents despite mandated access. Springer (1989) explores the administrative law publication requirement that is operationalized in the *Federal Register*. Relyea (1996) has long played a leadership role in the study of treatment of and access to government information. Hernon and McClure (1988) examine the various issues faced by those who make, interpret, and implement information policies; Hernon, McClure, and Relyea (1996) describe how the U.S. federal government dealt with those issues in the 1990s; and Splichal (1996) explores in depth the particular tension between access and privacy.

The general topic of access to information can be broken into several more specialized categories. Because much of the information that the government holds is actually about corporations, there are economic as well as political reasons to seek access (Thomas 1996); corporations are actually the largest users of the Freedom of Information Act, seeking data about their competitors. For a discussion of the relative effectiveness of *un*published rules, see Newman (1995). Halstuk (2002) reviews the early history of the argument over whether members of the press have rights that go beyond those of other citizens—a question of particular importance during a period in which bloggers (authors of online personal journals, or weblogs) are being denied protections offered to journalists regarding confidential sources on the argument that bloggers are not journalists. The history of access to federally funded scientific information via the National Technical Information Service is told in Stewart (1990). *Government Computer News* is an excellent and very detailed source of unfolding stories about federal records.

Information Policy and the Mediation of Individual and State Identities

Bibliographic sources for the study of citizenship, language policy, and education as a type of information policy are presented in this section.

Citizenship Good overviews of the literature on the nature of citizenship can be found in the collections by Isin and Turner (2003) and by Aleinikoff and Klusmeyer (2002). It should not be surprising that the level of scholarly and theoretical interest in the nature of citizenship responds to struggles with the definition and bounding of political entities at the global level. Thus in practice, citizenship of course has a very long history, yet the classical work on citizenship—toward which today's conversation still orients—is T. H. Marshall's (1950/2003) post–World War II identification of three dimensions of citizenship (civil, political, and social). Marshall's work is criticized today for not adequately theorizing the state (Turner 1992) and for dealing insufficiently with culture (Mouffe 1992, 1993) and economics (Yeatman 1994).

In response to globalization and changes in the nature of the nation-state, the close of the twentieth century saw another round of scholarly activity dealing with the nature of citizenship. Some of this work involves looking back, as in explorations of the long histories of citizenship by Heater (2004) and Snethen (2000) and the more specialized historical analyses of Meyler (2001) and Kim (2001). Venator Santiago (2001), Gutierrez (2003), and Volpp (2001) point out that U.S. history includes a number of anomalies regarding its treatment of citizenship in their respective analyses of Puerto Rico, Guam, and Asian-Americans. Other newer work looks across nation-states; Korpi and Palme (2003), for example, compare the rights of citizens in eighteen countries in the final decades of the twentieth century, and the U.S. government has for the first time collected citizenship laws from around the world (U.S. Office of Personnel Management 2004). There are investigations of what might be described as "cosmopolitan" citizenship by those who live transnational lives (Erskine 2002; Linklater 2002), and the inevitable consequences of this type of citizenship upon participation in particular local communities, whether negative (Cox 2004; Gilbertson and Singer 2003) or positive (Del Castillo 2002). Tambini (2001) goes so far as to talk about "post-national" citizenship, what Bosniak (2000) describes as citizenship "denationalized."

Much contemporary work emphasizes the relational foundations of citizenship (Gergen 1991; McClure 1992) and its moderation, therefore, via association (Healey 1993; Scheufele et al. 2004). Conceptualizing the citizen as a construct contingent on its social context provides a theoretical foundation for thinking through emergent forms of citizenship beyond those linked to the modern nation-state (Elkins 1997). It was a U.S. innovation to have dual citizenship (federal and state) from the start. This approach to thinking about citizenship also facilitates the transfer of the notion to the corporate environment (Scott 1994; Selznick 1957), a matter of interest not only to organizational sociologists, but also to policy analysts, because of the importance of public-private sector linkages in the making and implementing of policy today. Estlund (2000) argues that organizational citizenship has positive benefits for society at large because of its enculturation effects (Vigoda-Gadot 2004), but the shift also entails dangers; as Leca (1992) puts it, the interpenetration of the public and private may result in a form of "negative citizenship," if private individual demands overwhelm public needs. In an interesting example of how the experience of corporate citizenship is in turn affecting political theory, Fox (2003) updates the Lockean notion of the social contract as the basis of the modern state with relational contract theory as a way of thinking about today's "multilayered" citizenship.

Utopian views regarding the political possibilities of new technologies have been around as long as there has been talk of an information society. Skepticism, however, also has a long history in this literature. Carey (1980), for example, made the important point several decades ago that simply being able to vote electronically is not sufficient evidence to claim there is democratic practice using new technologies, because an important element of that practice is public discussion about issues, though it is not always clear that citizens want the types of political participation the net theoretically could enable. Haight (1979) identified the impact of information technologies on citizens as key among policy concerns, a notion reinforced by the NTIA (Leeson 1984) in its argument supporting its intervention into the use of networks by local communities for purposes of development. Guthrie and Dutton (1992) offer the concept of a "public information utility" as a way of embedding policy in the technological infrastructure. One of the most influential figures in U.S. technology policy, Langdon Winner, thought of (1995) citizenship as taking on new characteristics in a "technological order" after several decades of working with government on related matters. Steven Clift provides a comprehensive portal to information about citizenship in the electronic environment and other "e-government" practices on his Web site at www.dowire.org. The general subject of legal treatment for information technologies themselves—which might include citizenship—is beyond the scope of this book, but Gray's (2002) speculations about the impact of the merger of humans with machines on the nature of citizenship are worth mentioning here.

What Stone (1992) calls "warranting" is the link between discursive space and physical space, which is so important to jurisdictional issues in the network environment, and so likely to get the policy response of an insistence on identification and authentication in all network communications (Biegel 2001). The alternative approach suggests that because there is no one site of state power today, the nature of citizenship itself also now dispersed (Keane 1991). Murdock and Golding (1990) warn about the impact on citizenship of the privatization of communication and information. Howard, drawing on analyses of the fragmentation of various aspects of citizenship for distribution variously to nation-states, clusters of states, and the European region as a whole (Caporaso 2000), uses the concept of "thin" citizenship to describe the impact of digital media on political campaign strategy (2005). Meanwhile governments are renewing their attention to the question of when scientific and technological knowledge should not be allowed to cross geopolitical borders in order to ensure that the knowledge-producing nation-state is globally competitive informationally (Branscomb 1993). The critique that governments are taking advantage of the information revolution to disempower citizens by providing more disinformation (Traber 1986) has also drawn renewed attention in response to practices of the George W. Bush administration. Citizenship is now also understood to be a narrative form on the part of both the citizen (Somers 1995) and the state (Weber 1995). Taylor (2004) provides an example of a faith-based citizenship theory in support of current administration practices.

While the argument that the need to have access to information and the right to participate in public discourse are essential to the practice of citizenship lies at the heart of constitutional discussions about information policy matters, Schudson (1998) points out that there have been at least four different definitions of the "good citizen" in U.S. history, each with its own informational and communicative requirements.

Language The previous decade has seen a tremendous amount of work on language policies of countries around the world, language loss as a cost of globalization, and the history of language policy in pursuit of political goals historically. (Much of this work explicitly refers to decision making in this area as "identity policy.") This discussion focuses on the question of language policy in the United States. Though the center of our attention today is the struggle over an English-only policy in which we are currently engaged, the United States has faced language policy issues since its founding. In a delightful, multifaceted, and easy-to-read work, Mencken (1921) describes what it took to distinguish American English from the English of Great Britain during the eighteenth and nineteenth centuries.

Language policy per se—as distinct from histories or analyses of specific policies—has only recently become the subject of study in work such as Ricento (2005) and Spolsky (2003). The history of the English-only movement, including its cultural, political, and economic aspects, is being documented by J. Crawford (1992, 2000) and Nunberg (1997). Schildkraut (2005) emphasizes identity issues in her analysis of the formation and expression of public opinion about language policy in the United States. Where implemented, English-only situations can have a wide range of social consequences, including environmental damage (Oakes 2001), an inability to carry out one's citizenship responsibilities by voting (Loo 1985), and a gap in educational accomplishment (Crawford 1997). Fighting the English-only movement, however, can have its value as a focus for community organizing (Hart 2003). DiChiara (1997) reviews the history of language laws in general.

The success of Spanish-language broadcasting provides an interesting counterargument to the claim that bilingualism prevents immigrants from becoming acculturated, for there is evidence that the growing audience for the multiplying Spanish-language stations (Stilling 1995) are significantly contributing to the socialization into U.S. society of Spanish-language speakers (Stilling 1997). Even though such stations receive their own commercial support from advertising, English-only supporters have tried to prevent them from being licensed (Crawford 1992).

Part of the support for an English-only policy within the United States comes from the acknowledged hegemony of English globally (Wright 2004), although of course there are variations in both the ways in which English is used elsewhere and in forms of resistance to this role (Sonntag 2003). There are also economic arguments for restricting the number of languages used in public forms of communication (Coulmas 1993).

Most of the related legal analysis focuses on the impact on business because of the availability of the remedy offered by Title VI of the Civil Rights Act, with articles looking at the effects on both the public sector (Robertson 2001) and the private sector (Jacobson 2001). McCalips (2002) suggests that a Supreme Court ruling will be necessary to untangle this area of the law. Updates on legislation at the federal and state levels, and other facets of the English-only battle, can be found on the Web sites of the ACLU, the U.S. Equal Employment Opportunities Commision, and the language policy Web site maintained by James Crawford at (http://ourworld.compuserve.com/homepages/JWCRAWFORD/).

Education The literature on education is striking for its gap between the idealism conveyed by those focused on content—even those who are critical of current educational practices—and the view of education provided by those on the administrative side. The political importance of education that is the focus of this book's text is certainly reflected in the mood of the research stream, though the very weakness of most research on and theorization about education is precisely one of its problems (Lagemann 1997, 2002). This is one field in which the cultural studies movement has had a significant impact in terms of deepening its theorization (Cohen 1999; Giroux 1992). Both higher education and K–12 (primary and secondary) education are critical to the story being told here, but this brief bibliographic essay focuses on higher education issues.

The field's literature begins to develop a presence in the first decades of the twentieth century, reflecting several decades of experience with public higher education, and reconsideration of the classical curriculum of higher education as received from Europe, in light of then-contemporary economic and political needs. Cubberly (1919) and Monroe (1918) are just two examples of the many histories of higher education in the United States to appear during that period. That history gets revisited again and again, with ever-richer types of analysis, as well as a longer period of time upon which to report. Thus the 1970s saw an interpretive history (Church and Sedlak 1976), analysis of the impact of higher education on the labor force (Lazerson and Grubb 1974), and a look at the range of economic, social, and political factors that affect what American colleges and universities do and how they do it (Brubacher and Rudy 1976). The political unrest among college students of the 1960s and the profound insights regarding both theory and praxis of Paolo Freire ([1970] 2000) were reflected in a spate of work exploring the relationship between higher education and social change from an often idealistic perspective (Dearing 1972; Dede 1975; Hazard and Rosenblum 1976).

Histories continue to appear (Lucas 1994; Pulliam and Patten 1987), but increasingly they focus on specific aspects of education-society relations. Green (1990) examines the relationship between education systems and the nation-state, Goldin and Page (1999) present detailed statistical data on the history of education in the United States, and Spring (1998) relates education to the globalization of the economy. A particularly interesting stream of work over the last dozen years looks critically at the history of histories of education in the United States, with Escolano (1996) contrasting postmodern and modern approaches to that analysis, Seller (1991) and Dekker (1990) examining the role such histories play in reproducing institutional structures, and Kliebard (1995) probing why the enterprise is worth undertaking altogether. Works by former university presidents are notable for their persuasiveness and absorption in the impact of higher education on society, as well as for their poignance. Derek Bok, for example, has written both on the long-term consequences of treatment of race in admissions processes (Bowen and Bok 2000) and of the commercialization of higher education (Bok 2004). Clark Kerr examines relations between higher education and several key contemporary issues (Kerr, Gade, and Kawaoka 1994).

The histories—especially the early ones—are often descriptive, but they also tell the stories of proactive efforts to think through what the nature of education in the United States should be. Early twentieth-century histories paid a great deal of attention to the decision by the federal government to support public institutions of higher education and to the mass literacy that was the goal of universal primary and secondary education. John Dewey ([1916] 2004) was probably the first U.S. theorist of education, with his influential argument for the central role of education in democracy. The book in which university president Robert Hutchins's (1936) ideas about a great books-oriented general education curriculum in higher education were presented has been described as the key work in higher education reform in the United States, and the movement he launched has continued to be the pivot around which curricular reform revolves (Bell 1966; Stevens 2001).

Over the course of the twentieth century, the extent to which education was seen as a means of exercising power grew. In a work that links education with statistical practices, Green and Grosvenor (1997) explore the ways in which the teaching and writing of history shape individual identity. Chun (1986) looks at the change function of education in Marxian terms. Green and Preston (2001) revisit the types of questions addressed almost a century earlier by John Dewey in their work on education and social cohesion. And Popkewitz (1991) discusses educational reform as a matter of "political sociology."

The study of higher education has played a key role in the history of the sociology of knowledge (Wallerstein 2004; Wuthnow 1980). Contemporary issues raised by the Department of Homeland Security can be contextualized by what is known about the impact of national security on higher education during and after the first and second World Wars (Rudy 1991) and, in a particularly ideology-infused effort, during the Cold War (Chomsky et al. 1998). Several outstanding analyses of the impact of new technologies on society motivated by the need to adapt curricula in response have had widespread theoretical influence (Bell 1966; Lyotard 1984; McLuhan 1964), and the first information industry to receive full scale analysis as an information industry was higher education (Machlup 1980).

Today there is another widespread round of reconsideration of curriculum in response to several factors. There is concern over a projected undersupply of scientists (Bartlett 2005). Driven in part by the government and in part by economic concerns, there is also growing pressure for curricular design that will yield quantitatively measurable results for the purposes of increased accountability. The best source of information regarding the last of these may well be the U.S. Department of Education Web site, including its revelatory statement that the research on education that had been available through that site until 2002 is now obsolete. There is the need to respond to changes in the professions for which higher education prepares people; profession-specific discussions of curricular reform include Ross and Fineberg (1998) on medical schools, Goldberg (1990) on law schools, and Shelton, Lane, and Waldhart (1999) on the field of communication. The impact of digital technologies on the practices of higher education continues to receive attention; the collection by Loader and Dutton (2002) provides an efficient introduction to the range of types of questions of interest. Changes in theory and method also have curricular implications (Wallerstein 2004). The educational impact of popular culture is also finally receiving attention (Papa et al. 2000).

For analysis of higher education law in general, see Olivas (1997, 2003). Kaplin and Lee (1995) present the law as it would be of interest to administrators, and Poskanzer (2001) does the same for faculty. Because of recent Supreme Court decisions rejecting affirmative action programs in higher education, law review articles dealing with higher education over the last couple of years have been dominated by the problem of diversity (for just one example, see Krislov 2004), and that issue has even been of interest for the general population (Stohr 2004). Another important current issue is the extent to which state legislatures can intervene in curriculum design; though, as Jeltema (2004) notes, at one extreme curricula can be deemed a form of state speech, in general, academic freedom of higher education institutions (not of the faculty) protects the design of courses and programs from political tinkering. As economic pressures on institutions of higher education go up (Bok 2004), the legislative presence declines even for public universities with a history of state support. There was deep concern about free speech on campus, even prior to 9/11 (Baez 2001; Kors and Silverglate 1999), and this concern has deepened since (Harrison 2004). Background, analyses, and news of speech-related legal developments pertinent to K–12 education, often with implications as well for higher education, can be found on the Web site of the nonprofit Student Press Law Center (SPLC). The nonprofit organization EDUCAUSE provides a more expansive version of the same as the law affects higher education on its Web site (www.educause.edu). The National Education Association (NEA) Web site (www.nea.org) is particularly useful on responses to changes in the law as it affects primary and secondary school teachers.

6 Information Policy and Structure

Theory

Irrespective of the type of system being examined—a social, technological, or informational structure—over time, theories of structure have changed from seeing structures as stand-alone, static, and rigid in form to understanding structures as transformational, flexible, and interdependent in form. In this area, also, relationships between social, technological, and informational systems are regularly reinforced, and some structures are simply impossible to characterize as one or the other at all. The postal service, for example, is simultaneously a technological structure (beginning with the mandate for a national "post roads" system in the Constitution), a social structure (requiring the formation of an organization to manage mail flows), and an informational structure (because postage rates are based on distinctions in the types of information being transmitted) (John 1995; Kielbowicz 1986, 1989). James Carey and Norman Sims (1976), in an unpublished but widely circulated paper, described the creation of the "modern" news story in the form of an inverted pyramid (informational structure) as a direct consequence of the use of the telegraph (technological structure) for news production (social structure). Rice (1987) and Weick (1977) were early examples of an ongoing conversation about the ways in which computer-mediated communication can itself lead to organizational innovation. The protocols for a broadband global digital network capable of carrying all kinds of information, from voice to data to images, were first developed as the ISDN (Integrated Services Digital Network), which were simultaneously standards established by an international body, an operational network in a few locations, and an ideal towards which telecommunications networks were striving (Rutkowski 1983). Organizations are now understood to be technologies themselves (Beniger 1990; Morgan 1986). While these structures are all intertwined, however, their theoretical histories were distinct and thus will be discussed separately.

Social structure Theories of social structure are complex, there are significant differences within general schools of thought, and key concepts require attention to subtlety and nuance in order to be fully grasped. The very brief introduction to ways in which ideas about social structure differ from each other presented here, then, presents only very broad generalizations about ideas that underlie the development of information policy at different points in U.S. history.

One of the interesting features of the history of thought about social structure is the great multiplicity of inspirational contexts. Some literatures develop through an internal conversation that moves from thesis to antithesis to synthesis. Others respond to the accrual of empirical data that force recognition of the inadequacies of existing theories. Cross-fertilization of ideas—the transfer of concepts across geopolitical, cultural, linguistic, or disciplinary borders—can also stimulate theoretical development. In the case of ideas about social structure, an additional motor for innovation in ideas has been shifts in attention from one level of analysis to another. Thus early functionalist ideas were inspired by looking at relatively small and homogenous tribal communities in nonindustrialized societies, but the structuralist perspective that succeeded functionalism in dominance appeared in response to urban environments, industrialized society, and quickly growing and changing organizational forms. Early twentieth-century ideas from social psychology about interactions between the individual and the group show up again, under other names, almost a century later as applied to society at large. Study of interdependence among businesses, a perceptual emphasis on networks driven by the Internet and related technological systems, and the development of new analytical tools turned attention to networked forms of social organization. Ideas about complex adaptive systems theory appeared first in the biological and physical sciences, and were only later taken up by social scientists.

The application of any of these ways of thinking about social structure to the state, and state-society relations via the law, then, is necessarily metaphorical. The U.S. Constitution is an expression of a theory about social structure specific to the state; interpretations of the Constitution over time have reflected the changes in the ideas influencing those making decisions. Still, using the phrase "social engineering," Wittrock (1991) takes a structure-based approach to policy-making in general when he describes it as design, and Mansell and Silverstone (1997) approach communication policy-making in particular from this perspective. Shields, too, has presented a theoretical approach (1995) to communication policy from the perspective of the structures it does and does not create.

Modern systematic thinking about social structure began with functionalism, an approach that treats each society as a bounded and self-maintaining system that maintains its equilibrium in the face of a hostile environment. Anthropologists who worked from a functionalist perspective included Malinowski (1944), who emphasized normative functions, and Radcliffe-Brown (1952), who believed that functions were determined by need. In sociology, the functionalist approach underlay the work of Durkheim (Giddens 1987) and Parsons (1951, 1963), who emphasized such functions as adaptation, goal attainment, integration, and pattern maintenance as activities in which any society must engage in order to survive. The functionalist view entered the study of communication via uses and gratifications research; for a collection of classical items in this literature, see Blumler and Katz (1974). In its ideal form, functionalism suggests that exactly the same functions will be found in every society, irrespective of differences in culture, environment, and history. Marxism is a functionalist perspective oriented around capital, rather than (as for the anthroplogists) ritual, as a means of defining critical social functions. Critics of functionalism argued that it overestimated the extent to which society was static, harmonious, stable, and coherent, and for ignoring the role of power in shaping social relations.

Merton (1949) made functionalism more flexible by relaxing its basic assumptions. He argued that social practices may be functional or dysfunctional (failing to support social structure), and that there may be several alternatives for any given function. There are latent functions as well as those that are manifest, and those that are latent are best identifed not by their ends, but by their meaning, the ways in which sense is constituted and persists. Parsons (1963) went further, developing a theory of structural-functionalism, in which there are links between a normative system and the "situation." The environment, then, is an ensemble of stable and consistent constraints in which the system of action is placed. Though this approach was more open to differences in the types of functions that might be found in a society and took the position that identifying actual functions depended on analysis of specific societies, there was still a tendency to exaggerate the congruence between structure (situation) and function (solution)—that is, to reduce structure to function.

Structuralism first appeared in linguistics before being taken up by sociology, turning attention away from functions altogether and towards relationships. In one version or another, structuralism dominated much twentieth-century social theory. A social structure could be distinguished from a mere conglomeration of elements by three features: a set of elements connected by relations to form a whole with properties not possessed by any of the elements alone, the ability to substitute new elements for old without necessarily altering the nature of the structure, and rules by which a structure is transformed. Functions may well differ across societies, but each society will have a coherent structure of its own. Because surface characteristics may be misleading regarding the most important features of the social structure, symbolic analysis—first influentially modeled by Saussure ([1913] 1959)—is particularly valuable for understanding society from this perspective. Rather than analyzing any specific social elements on their own, each must be examined in light of its relation to the whole. Important figures in the development and application of structuralist thought to different social processes include Levi-Strauss (1963), Barthes (1968), and Althusser (1984).

Long before structuralism appeared in sociology and anthropology, however, it underlay political thought. Montesquieu ([1748] 1949), for example, argued that the relations of diverse parts of a political system to a coherent whole makes certain options impossible and others particularly likely, and the same idea appears in Tocqueville ([1835] 2000). Distinctions between premodern, modern, and postmodern society are examples of structural analysis, and the very concept of structure from this perspective suggests a tension between agent and structure that has been particularly important for those who try to understand the nature of power and agency.

Though ideas about functionalism were born in efforts to identify commonalities across societies, and many of the concepts important to structuralism developed in industrialized societies by sociologists struggling to understand the rapid bureaucratization of society and the elaboration of organizational form, during the social turbulence of the last couple of decades of the twentieth century, theories of poststructuralism appeared. To poststructuralists, the rule-governed systems that shape language and society arise out of interactions between the two; poststructuralism differs from structuralism in denying that there are any enduring underlying structures in society and that it is possible to understand society objectively. Whereas structuralists looked past surface characteristics to relationships in order to determine the most important aspects of a society, poststructuralists are more likely to study texts—and to treat any type of social setting as a text. Michel Foucault, often cited here, is the premiere exemplar of poststructuralist thought, but others whose work has been important include Derrida (1976, 1992), Lyotard (1984, 1991), Baudrillard (1983), and Deleuze and Guattari (1987). In many ways, poststructuralism can be understood as an extension of ideas about the social construction of reality, introduced previously, that shares with the social psychologists the sense that meaning is socially constructed, but differs from them in emphasizing the multiple interpretations and meanings of any text.

Economists approached the question of social structure from another direction, curious about the nature of the market and the difference between activities that take place within organizations and within markets, with the seminal work by Coase (1937) emphasizing the role of structured information flows within the firm that offered the advantage over transactions in the open marketplace. This literature is pertinent to understanding the state because the state is often perceived as an organizational form and because much of what the state does is described in terms of its effects, or lack of effects, on the market. Those who managed large organizations, too, were interested in understanding them in order to make them more effective, and so the specialization of organizational sociology was born. Following Weber, important early works on a sociological approach to the study of organizations was offered by Parsons (1963). This work was synthesized along with the work of many others in the classic on organizations by March and Simon (1958). It became fashionable in the 1990s to think of organizations as communities, but this perspective was introduced at least two decades earlier (Swanson 1971).

The authors in Shultz and Whisler (1960) offer some of the earliest investigations of the impact of the use of computers on organizations, and Mohr (1971) also looked at this question relatively early on. Of course the use of these technologies immediately started changing organizations, so the literature in organizational sociology by those interested in structure began to focus on change processes, often involving technologies (Hill 1988), as well as the related questions of the role of information (March 1987) and communication (Yuan et al. 2005) in decision making about change. Thinking about the effects of the use of information technologies led to comparisons between the two types of social form (Rubinyi 1990). An interest in change processes also led in another direction, to complex adaptive systems theory, encouraging analyses of the state as a complex system (De Greene 1982; Gemmill and Smith 1985; Leifer 1989; Morgan 1986). Stinchcombe (1990) provides an excellent one-volume introduction to the diverse ways of thinking about the ways in which information, and therefore information technologies, are fundamental to organization structure and processes.

By the 1980s, however, it was clear that a third type of social structure—the networked organization—was also important from the economic perspective, and thinking in terms of networked structures is now extremely popular at all levels of analysis; for a general introduction to network theory and analysis, see Barabasi (2003) and Watts (2004); for a discussion of networks from a communication perspective, see Monge and Contractor (2003). This mode of thinking appears in policy analysis in discussions of policy networks that link private and public sector actors as well as those involved in both formal and informal modes of decision-making and action (Marsh 1998). Most recently, there has been interest in what some claim are entirely new forms of social structure known as "swarming mobs" (Rheingold 2002) that form and dissolve quickly.

Technological structure It is precisely the problem for those seeking to ensure that the technological structures of our information and communication networks support our social, political, economic, and cultural goals that most of the literature on technological structure is cast in language so technical that it is impenetrable to those in the social sciences and to policy-makers. There have been exceptions: Irwin and Ela (1981) expressed concern more than two decades ago that technologies themselves would dominate decision making, irrespective of the social consequences, and Kling and Sacchi (1982) were remarkably early with the suggestion that computing structures *are* social structures. Huber's (1987) report to the U.S. Department of Justice on antitrust implications of the divestiture of AT&T provides an unusually clear, detailed, and imaginative analysis of the legal implications of digital network architecture, and the Bruce, Cunard, and Director (1986) textbook on telecommunications law and regulation draws attention to the interaction between legal developments and network architecture throughout in a way that is particularly accessible to the nonspecialist. Noam (1987, 1989, 1990, 1994, 2001) and McGarty (1991) inaugurated the examination of alternative approaches to policy for the network from this perspective. Antonelli (1992) and others who write about the network firm are approaching the understanding of technological structure from an economic and organizational perspective.

Only recently, however, has the effort to understand the impact of the evolution of the global information infrastructure combined with developments in science and technology studies to yield theories about why change in technological structures yields social change (Woolgar 1991). For examples of the application of this approach to the analysis of specific technologies and technological systems, see Bijker et al. (1987) and Bijker and Law (1992). Examples of this type of analysis of information and communication technologies in particular include Star and Ruhleder (1996), Friedman and Nissenbaum (1996), Feng (2000), and Introna and Nissenbaum (2000).

The linkage between technological structure and social structure has become so vivid in studies of the Internet that even architects are now producing writing that provides insight into information policy issues (Hookway 1999; Novak 1997) and there is increasing interest not only in incorporating users into design processes (Norman and Draper 1986; Rohracher 2005) but also in using nontechnical modes of thinking about design issues (Coyne 1995).

Abbate (1999) provides an extremely useful history of the Internet that combines discussion of the infrastructure itself with analysis of the processes of decision-making by which that design came about. A number of works have tried, over the past several decades, simply to describe the technologies that are the subject of information and communication law and regulation in laymen's terms. These guides of course have had to be revised or replaced every few years. A few current examples include Cartwright (2005), Grant and Meadows (2004), Turner, Magill, and Marples (2004) and Mirabito and Morganstern (2004).

At the cutting edge of current thinking is the realization that it is no longer possible to think of a nonhierarchical global network (Blumenthal and Clark 2001). The technological structure of today's global information infrastructure is being determined by private and public sector intermediaries, who design a variety of different types of service and content packages to enable users to use what is now commonly being described as the "network of networks" (Noam 2001). In a ubiquitous embedded computing environment (Rheingold 1991; Weisser 1991), the discussion of technological structure conflates completely with social and informational structure.

Informational structure Scientific taxonomies are probably the oldest informational structures; dictionaries, encyclopedias, museums, and maps are others familiar to us. Headrick (2000) provides a detailed introduction to the development of each of these during the period 1700–1850. Histories of the introduction of the printing press into Western Europe (e.g., Eisenstein 1979) highlight ways in which the printing press significantly changed the ways in which information architectures were built, used, revised, and ramified. For broader and longer views of the impact of technologies on how and what we think, see Hobart and Schiffman (1998) and Bolter (1984).

Grossman (1994) documents the history of the impact of technological innovation on structuring our knowledge of the law, and Katsh's work on changes in the nature of legal practice as a result of computerization (1989) includes some attention to the question of informational and knowledge structures. Leaving aside technological issues, Amsterdam and Bruner (2000) and Greenawalt (1992) discuss the general question of the role of classification systems in legal analysis, and Sugarman (1995) explores the negotiations between two classification-dependent professions—accountancy and the law—over boundary definitions.

The bulk of the literature on information structures qua information structures is in the field of information science (see Buckland and Liu 1995, 1998). Information technologies have also long been of interest because of their impact on indexing practices (Hahn and Buckland 1998). Maynard (1977) includes attention to the impact of technological innovation in his study of interactions between scientific nomenclature, indexing practices, and the nature of medical research—this last a policy issue—in the United States. More broadly, Trolley and O'Neill (2001) provide a capsule of that history in their look at the history of the particular practice of citation indexing. Histories are also written by genre; see Bell (2001), for example, on the indexing of journals and Knight (1968) on books. Cornug (1983) documents the history of indexing technology itself, pushing the antecedents of today's technologies and practices into the early medieval period. These histories are richest within specific subject areas, as in Garfield's widely-emulated study of citation indexing for chemical patents (1957) or the Zaye, Metanomski, and Beach work on the Chemical Abstracts Service (1985).

Both technological and theoretical developments have broadened and deepened the literature on information structures in recent years. The technological front is most familiar, and in many areas has been responsible for stimulating theoretical development. It is not only a question of capacity and speed. Though historically the development of information architectures was a very slow process—for the most part controlled by disciplinary specialists with (in the twentieth century) the collaboration of information architecture specialists from the information science community—today, individuals are developing their own information architectures and indexing procedures for personal use (Abrams, Baecker, and Chignell 1998; Lin 2002). Where there used to be taxonomies based on bright lines between categories, today boundaries are more permeable and flexible, so that "relevance" has become an important indexing criterion (Mizzaro 1997). There are new types of material that can now be indexed—in some cases for the first time—such as visual images (Layne 1994;

Roberts 2001) and moving objects (Wolfson et al. 1998). The Web itself renewed interest in questions of information architecture (Rosenfeld and Morville 1998) in a literature and set of practices that have developed so quickly it now refers to itself as in a "third generation" (Evernden and Evernden 2003). The goal of those trying to develop a "semantic web" would be that indexing structures for Web content would be developed automatically in response to use and need not be enduring in nature.

Foucault (1973) theorized the political dimensions of information architectures created through indexes, taxonomies, disciplinary boundaries, and other knowledge structures. Examples of what Foucault's fundamental insight yields when combined with the work of other social theorists can be found in analyses of accounting as a social practice, see Hopwood and Miller (1994), Temin (1991), Merino (1998), and Previts and Merino (1998). Influenced in addition by the work of Latour, Woolfgar, and Salk (1986) on the sociology of knowledge production in the sciences, Bowker and Star (1999) provide a theoretical look at indexing practices themselves. For a few examples of the impact that statistical definitions of racial and ethnic identity have had on the political and social lives of individuals of specific groups, see Escobar (1999), Hart (2000), and Lott (1998). Manning (1996) specifically addresses the utility of defining ethnicities as a means of state power, and medical indexing provides important evidence for the gendered nature of the American medical profession (Long 1997).

Developing informational structures can serve the production of knowledge, illuminate cultural issues, or socialize the public to a particular perspective. Museum histories dramatize the political impact of indexing (Bennett 1995, 1997; Clavir 2002; Hooper-Greenhill 1992), as in recent struggles over museum-held skeletons of enormous scientific interest to anthropologists trying to discern the early history of human life in North America. There is relatively little work, however, that compares the utility and validity of different classification systems; thus the comparison by Bhojraj, Lee, and Oler (2003) of four different industry classification systems in terms of their utility for financial analysis and prediction provides a valuable model.

The development of very large interdisciplinary databases used to support research of many different kinds stimulated an interest in the theoretical underpinnings of taxonomic practices and the specific concepts placed into such taxonomies, a field of study currently referred to as "ontologies" (Zúñiga 2001). Ontologies are also useful in eliciting knowledge that may be available in relationships between records, and between records and legacy record-keeping systems (Wimmer 2004). Another strand of current work of particular importance is the study of codification, the process by which tacit knowledge—held by individuals, developed out of their own experience, "local" in nature, and often unexpressed (Collins 2001; Reber 1997)—can be translated into codified knowledge that can be communicated with others and embedded in technologies and/or stored in technological systems (Cohendet and Meyer-Krahmer 2001; Cohendet and Steinmueller; Foray 2004; Kahin 2004).

Development of an interest in ontologies has grown out of awareness of the limits of taxonomies for work in disciplines (e.g., ecology) in which flows, events, and transformations must also be represented (Keet 2005). It is believed that successful development of ontologies will promote global access to data (Arzberger et al. 2004), but there is concern about the usability of ontologies (Garcia-Barriocanal, Sicilia, and Sanchez-Alonso 2005), the extent to which ontologies facilitate knowledge reuse (Musen 1992), and the need to develop techniques for evaluating their quality (Burton-Jones et al. 2005). Much of the work in this area comes together under the auspices of the Web Ontology (WebONT) Working Group of the World Wide Web Consortium (www.w3.org).

Current efforts to develop ontologies—or processes by which to develop and refine ontologies—include the use of uncertain or ambiguous concepts as translation devices (Ahlqvist 2005), development of techniques for integrating the formal aspects of as they have been developed in different disciplines for different purposes and using different technical apparatus (Goguen 2005), and attention to the provenance of knowledge (Fox and Huang 2005). While there is a great deal of experimentation with use of automated data mining to discern patterns of language use across domain-specific collections of texts (Gillam and Ahmad 2005)—including development of special ontologies at the level of the federation of multiple, multiple-agent systems (Erdur et al. 2005)—some argue that this approach will remain limited because humans ("knowledge engineers") must make the ultimate ontological choices in many cases because of the multiplicity and ambiguity of meanings associated with words (Angelova 2005). An alternative approach to development of ontologies starts with collaborative efforts by those from different disciplines who work with data about the same research subjects and are interested in developing databases of use in common (Baker, Bowker, and Karasti 2002).

The field of the sociology of knowledge is itself becoming reflexive (Lynch and Fuhrman 1991; Shapin 1995). The "new" sociology of knowledge focuses on the effects of institutional structures on the sociology of knowledge rather than the positions and interests of individuals and groups (Swidler and Arditi 1994). Of course, even the sociology of knowledge is itself situated within the intellectual field and thus will reveal different histories depending upon the culture or society from which the work is written (Ringer 1990). Emotions, too, can play a role (Laslett 1990).

Informational structures show up in administrative law in the form of positive mandates to index information in order to make it accessible (Dore 1991). Digital technologies are expanding the ways in which this might be useful, as in the use of software to analyze similarities in the conditions of court cases as a means of identifying novel lines of precedent (Conrad and Dabney 2001). One of the most provocative policy issues to be raised in recent years regarding informational structures, however—inspired by the regular Web-indexing sweeps of firms such as Google—is the suggestion that there should be a right to be excluded from indexing (Elkin-Koren 2001).

Information Policy and Social Structure

Antitrust The literature on antitrust law and the technological aspects of the information infrastructure can be approached from several angles, from shifts in the political and social goals believed to underlie this body of law, to the diversity of economic theories used in its analysis, to difficulties defining and bounding such fundamental regulatory concepts as the market and the product.

Hovenkamp (1994) reviews the history of theories of antitrust, and Sullivan (1991) the history of the law itself, dividing it into three periods distinguished by their responses to changes in political institutions, the corporate climate, changes in the regulatory subject, and experience with various types of antitrust efforts. Perspectives on antitrust include Hofstadter's (1991) emphasis on its populist aspects, Millon's (1991) focus on its role in supporting individual liberty, and Fox and Halverson's (1991) insistence on a juridical approach. Pragmatic problems needing economic and organizational analysis include development of methods to determine whether there is monopolistic behavior (Elzinga 1989 argues that no one measure will do) and the nature of strategic behavior (Carlton and Gertner 2003; Holt and Scheffman 1989; Lipsky 1976).

The very nature of the information economy, characterized as it is by rapid and constant innovation, has introduced new types of antitrust problems for all industries (Ellig and Lin 2001). For analyses of how the same problem looks from the perspective of the firm, see Antonelli (1992), Grabher (1993), and Swann and Yates (1993). Pitofsky (1991) describes the "radical" relaxation of government enforcement in the merger area in the 1980s, in part because of a redefinition of the market and in part because of the recognition of the importance of shared intellectual property rights. (The Microelectronics and Computer Consortium [MECC] in the early 1980s launched a string of exemptions to antitrust law in the United States intended to stimulate the computer industry [Kanter 1991].) In addition to the need to share intellectual property rights, Hawkins (1999) identifies additional reasons why this is so: today's market structure is focused on creating technologically integrated business communities, "efficiency" rationales are not the only or necessarily the most important reasons for participating in consortia, and consortia are increasingly global rather than national in scope. There is the question of whether innovative corporations need special treatment under antitrust law (Greenstein 1998a; Ordover and Willig 1998). There are difficulties in defining the market, a problem with a long history (Pitofsky 1991) that has taken new forms in the electronic environment (Stigler and Sherman 1985).

Some of the problems that have chronically affected the communication industries from an antitrust perspective are now more widespread with the diffusion of the network structure across a wider range of productive and economic activities (Shelanski and Sidak 2001). An overview of the role that antitrust concerns have played in shaping the contemporary information infrastructure can be found on pages 199–202 of the Kellogg, Thorne, and Huber (1992) text on telecommunications regulation and in Horwitz (1989). Pool (1983) looks at antitrust as it influences the convergence of different types of communication law and regulation. Rowland (1982) highlights increased attention to antitrust law as a key feature of the shift from the Federal Regulatory Commission of the 1920s to the Federal Communications Commission of the 1930s. The use of antitrust law to dismantle AT&T's monopoly-like control over that infrastructure in the early 1980s—an important turning point in U.S. information policy—is reported upon from the inside by Brown (1983), from the outside by Horwitz (1986), and from a spot somewhere in-between by consultant Shooshan (1984). Johnson (1986) reviews the AT&T divestiture within the context of the history of such developments within telecommunications. Huber (1987) wrote a particularly clear analysis of the relationship between the telecommunication network's technological structure and its legal structure for the Antitrust Division of the U.S. Department of Justice. The communications industry is unusual in that two entities—the Department of Justice and the Federal Communications Commission—independently review proposed mergers (Russell and Wolson 2002).

For an overview of antitrust problems raised by digital media, see de Avillez Pereira (2000). These include new problems such as those raised by satellites (Brennan and Macauley 1997) and Internet domain names (Blue 2004). There are pressures to relax antitrust law in order to take advantage of new commercial opportunities on the Internet, both in general (Gottardo 1997) and in specific areas such as business-to-business marketing (Gotfredson 2001) and film distribution (Race 2003). The Microsoft case clarified the particular problems distinguishing digital products from each other, especially given the need for conformity in technical standards and protocols (Lopatka and Page 1999). Economic literature on standards developed in the 1970s in response to AT&T and IBM antitrust cases (Drahos and Maher 2004), and antitrust continues to be important in standard-setting for the Internet (Lemley 1996).

Political arguments regarding antitrust issues sometimes take on a different flavor when they are applied to firms in the communication and information industries. Owen and Braeutigam (1978) argue that the central concern of antitrust law as applied to communication firms should be fairness, and they review a number of cases in which antitrust and First Amendment concerns have come head-to-head. LeDuc (1987) feared that courts would not be sophisticated enough to protect First Amendment values in antitrust cases. First Amendment issues have been raised by corporations seeking to petition the outcomes of antitrust cases (Ku 2000), and in studies of possible antitrust issues raised by telephone company entry into the cable business (Pribis 1994). Gilmore (1988) talks about the impact of antitrust law on the free speech of health care professionals, and Myers (1994) treats the same problem as it affects those in real estate. Mitchell (2001) offers a novel analysis of federal election reform law from an antitrust perspective that treats candidates as products. There are ongoing clashes between antitrust law and intellectual property rights (Shapiro 2003; Soma and Davis 2000). Antitrust concerns come up even in efforts to get access to information, as when Dialog sued the American Chemical Society over restricted access to the information held in Chemical Abstracts (Kahin 1992).

The United States has attempted to exercise its antitrust law extraterritorially (Hay, Hilki, and Nelson 1991; Simon and Waller 1986). Petersmann (1991) argues that antitrust law was used for years by the United States domestically as a means of addressing foreign trade issues, and Tunstall (1986) unpacks the international implications of the domestic use of antitrust law in communications. Conversely, antitrust law is a stimulus for U.S.-based communication and information firms to expand into international markets when limits to U.S. markets have been reached (Mamiya 1991) and to take advantage of opportunities to vertically integrate in ways not permitted in the United States (Gerlach 1992). Soma and Weingarten (2000) suggest that antitrust law itself should be internationalized under the aegis of the WTO.

Jorde and Teece (1991) go so far as to argue that there is a need to reconceptualize antitrust law in an environment in which cooperation is understood to be key to economic success. Sullivan (1991) wonders if we're on the edge of an antitrust counterrevolution. Brennan (1995) not only suggests that antitrust concerns need to be revisited for the contemporary environment, but questions whether the theory behind the divestiture of AT&T is still appropriate.

Copyright Because of the extent to which technological innovation affects the means by which copyright can be both violated and protected, the economic importance of intellectual property rights in an information economy, the fact that copyright both affects everyone, and the relative accessibility and comprehensibility of copyright as a policy issue that can be widely grasped, the literature in this area is enormous. The goal here is to provide an overview of the historical development of various themes within that literature.

The earliest publications on copyright were simply how-to items, which began to proliferate as part of the professionalization movement early in the twentieth century. Copyright (along with patent), for example, was among the topics of publications from the Practising Law Institute sessions beginning in 1900. Early works on the history, purposes, and use of copyright often treated British and U.S. law together (Birrell 1899; Drone 1879), though the impact of the nineteenth-century round of globalization of economic activity was reflected in Putnam's collection of copyright laws from around the world in its 1891 and subsequent editions. The first compilation of all legal developments relating to copyright in the United States—which included copyright laws of the Colonial Congress, the original states, the U.S. Constitution, statutory law, presidential proclamations, and international law, was published in 1900 (Solberg 1900). A thirty-one-volume digest of pertinent court cases (Torbert 1908) appeared in 1908, about the time that Congress began to hold hearings on potential changes to the law.

The Bowker who has subsequently became so important to the publishing and library science industries published an analysis of the history and practice of copyright law in 1912, when the subject was topic was considered a part of the scholarly subject of "library economy." During this period the number of publications explaining how to protect a work globally (e.g., Colles and Hardy 1906) as well as in regions in which activity was being particularly encouraged by the U.S. government as a consequence of, for example, the Monroe Doctrine (e.g., National Committee of the United States of America on International Intellectual Cooperation 1938). Conflicts among national laws began to receive scholarly attention in 1917 in work by G. L. Clapp.

During the 1930s annual symposia specifically devoted to copyright began to take place, such as the Nathan Burkan memorial competition. In 1950 the Copyright Office acknowledged the growing literature on the topic by publishing a bibliography of works to date (Mertz 1950), and Nimmer's influential treatise on copyright law began publication in 1963 in a looseleaf format that was then updated frequently, first by himself and then in collaboration with his son, for decades. Practical interest in protecting copyright within the United States and around the world continued, but the historical purview began to lengthen its scope, as in Kirschbaum's (1946) study of copyright in England before 1640 and Ransom's (1956) study of the first, 1710, copyright statute within North America. (Ransom's work was one of the earliest signs of interest in scholarship about copyright from a university press.) Because of the Cold War, there was also work during this period emphasizing differences between U.S. copyright law and treatment of intellectual property rights in the USSR and other countries under communist governments (e.g., Bohmer 1960). Rothschild (1957) produced one of the first treatments of the economic impact of copyright law on artists and authors. Kase (1967) turned the discussion about international aspects of copyright law from description of differences among national laws to analysis of fundamental differences in philosophy. Fair use began to be the focus of works on copyright following passage of the 1976 Copyright Act with its heightened attention to exemptions to serve the public interest (e.g., Seltzer 1978). The *Copyright Report*, which documents every legal decision of importance in a regularly updated manner, began publication in 1978. Skepticism regarding the operations of the Copyright Office when complaints are issued that has become increasingly common in recent years as the level of aggression has risen appeared in a discussion of informal adjudication within that office as a means of sidestepping public access to decision-making data offered by the Freedom of Information Act in the early 1980s (Selkowitz 1983).

Just as had been the case with each new genre and medium that appeared, the success of the broadcasting industry stimulated production of works on intellectual property rights specific to that industry's needs (e.g., Warner 1953). Librarians also began to explicitly put forth their perspective on intellectual property rights following World War II (Clapp 1968). The impact of technological innovation on copyright did not first receive explicit attention, however, until the 1960s (Gipe 1967). From that point on, this literature burgeoned, with relatively early works in this genre including books focusing solely on the analysis of copyright and new media (Lawrence and Timberg 1980), offering primary materials on the subject (Bush and Dreyfuss 1979), and trying to discern congressional intentions and logics in response to innovation (Henry 1978). The word "crisis" first showed up in a title dealing with copyright in a 1976 book by Nasri. Meanwhile collections of "copyright-free" materials began to appear (e.g., Rice 1979), presaging interest in an information commons. The relationship between intellectual property rights and economic growth based on technological change quickly became evident (Mansfield 1988).

Postmodern theory that questioned the very notion of authorship triggered interesting studies of the very concept of individual ownership of intellectual property (Gaines 1991; Rose 1993; Saunders 1992). The spread of constructivist views of the nature of knowledge reached expression in analyses of copyright law in a proposal that the line between fact and expression needs to be reconsidered (Ayers 1999). Analysis of copyright as a form of cultural policy (Pang 2005) has introduced the concept of a "cultural free rider" into the conversation (Geller 2000). Though the question of whether or not facts themselves could be copyrighted has been raised at earlier points in U.S. history, the economic value of databases today makes this another area of focal interest in copyright law (Ginsburg 1990; Gorman 1963; Huse 2005; Samuelson 1989).

Other new issues to appear in the copyright literature toward the close of the twentieth century include the impact of copyright on preservation (Oakley 1990) and on higher education (Association of College and Research Libraries 2005), and historical work on predecessors to copyright (Armstrong 1990) have broadened our understanding of the dimensions of importance raised by copyright issues. Explorations of shifts in the nature of both copyright mechanisms and the context within which copyright operates in the digital environment are of course rife (for one example among many, see Stokes 2005). Comparative international issues remain important (Griffiths and Suthersanen 2005).

The concurrent rise of the information commons movement, on the one hand, and new legal and technological means of trying to protect copyright, on the other, stimulated a burst of scholarship in recent years. Discussions of the information commons range from reassertions of the importance of fair use (Burrell and Coleman 2005), to explorations of how widened notions of an information commons might be designed (Bollier and Watts 2002; Kranich 2004; Lessig 2001), to what a commons might mean for existing institutions—such as libraries—that facilitate public access to information (Haas and Robertson 2004). Samuelson's (2003) work stands out for the way in which she clarifies the need to differentially treat legal conditions for access to various categories of information. Work on the economics of copyright in the contemporary environment (Einhorn 2005; Takeyama and Gordon 2005), including its relationship to antitrust law (Brown and Denicola 2005) and the use of private international law as a means of asserting intellectual property rights (Drexl and Kur 2005), also contribute to the debate over the extent to which access to digital content should be open or closed. Interest in alternatives to contemporary copyright arrangements led some scholars back into history for models drawn from the pre-copyright era (Armstrong 1990). The use of organizational, technological, and rhetorical strategies to build fences around intellectual property has a long history (Bowker 1994), but with digital rights management techniques these have come to the foreground. Zittrain (2005) does a superb of explaining efforts to use technological means to enforce compliance with copyright law both technically and legally, and Einhorn and Rosenblatt (2005) do the same for arguments to use market tools to resolve copyright conflicts.

Patents The literature on patents has a long history; it is rich, and by now massive. Econlit, the bibliographic database for economic literature, holds citations to almost 2,000 items pertaining to patents since 2000 alone. This brief bibliographic essay notes highlights of new themes in the analysis of patents and their effects as they have shown up in print over time and current areas of focal interest. Items pertaining to theories of why patents should work to stimulate innovation are discussed in the section on change in technological systems.

How-to works on patent law showed up very early (e.g., Fessenden 1810); by the close of the nineteenth century, already work on how the public might cope with patent-based monopolies deemed not to be in the public interest emerged (Gordon 1897), and shortly thereafter the first casebooks appeared (e.g., Rogers 1914). The first decades of the twentieth century also saw works examining the economic impact of patents on industry (Prindle 1908) and the tax consequences of patents and other forms of intellectual property (Frye 1921). By the middle of the twentieth century works began to appear that began to prepare for changes to patent law by looking at the past (Fox 1947), the impact of patents on the U.S. economy as a whole (Folk 1942), interactions between patents and antitrust law (Wood 1942), public-interest aspects of patents (Toulmin 1939), and problems in the classification of patents as the speed of technological innovation began to increase (U.S. Patent and Trademark Office 1946). By the 1960s there was interest in the role of patents in other social processes, such as the conduct of research (National Research Council 1962), what we refer to today as "knowledge reuse" (Welsh 1965), the transfer of technologies to developing countries (Thant 1964), and the impact of the international patent system on foreign policy (Vernon 1962). Forman (1957) was one of the first to discuss the appropriateness and extent of government ownership and administration of patents. Machlup's (1958) economic analysis of the patent system is widely believed to have triggered his seminal interest in the information industries as a distinct economic sector. In the same year a first bibliography on the U.S. patent system appeared (Library of Congress, Legislative Reference Service 1958). Another bibliography was offered by Besterman (1971). Studies of developments in other countries provided some input into the question of the extent to which patents were actually necessary for industrialization (Schiff 1971). Interest in the role of patents in promoting technological innovation grew, with work that looked back historically (e.g., Dick 1970) and analyses of the relationship between patents and research productivity (e.g., Griliches 1984).

Issues of recent interest include the ability to use patented technologies for research purposes through an exemption (Gilat 1994), the study of patents as a means of understanding the processes of the knowledge economy (Cohen and Merrill 2003; Jaffee and Trajtenberg 2002), the question of how to maximize value from patents (Keller and Snowman 1995; Rivette and Kline 2000), and the impact of the ability to claim patents on the nature of higher education in the United States (Altbach and Berdahl 2005; Mazzoleni 2005) and elsewhere (Leydesdorff 2004). Mossoff (2003) provides an intellectual history of patents, and Khan (2005) argues that patent law has helped democratize invention processes. The question of the extent to which it should be possible to patent lifeforms—long resisted on moral grounds—has drawn attention to the ethics of staking out intellectual property rights in the human genome (Amani and Coombe 2005), the impact of patents on the ability of those in the global South to cope with disease (Adelman 2005; Shadlen 2004), issues raised by the patenting of indigenous and traditional forms of knowledge (Zerbe 2005), and the problematics of patenting information processes (Kahin 2003). The variety of theoretical lenses used to think about the economics of patents is expanding (e.g., Heald [2005] uses transaction costs theory). Searches for prior art and patent citation are highly political matters as firms jockey for position (Maurseth 2005). Even the Patent Office doesn't know how to think about items for which patents are sought; Self and Love (1991) tell a fascinating story of how the corporation EDS provided the Patent Office with a framework for categorizing the thousands of existing software patents at a time when the government agency itself was claiming it hadn't patented software at all, and Dahlin and Behrens (2005) address the interesting question of how to tell whether an invention is actually radical in nature. Because it isn't always clear when nanotechnology offers a change in communication process or product as well as in scale, this field presents its own complex set of patent issues (Sabety 2005).

Association As histories of the right of association in the United States (Fellman 1963; Guttmann 1998) make clear, it was not until the 1930s that this right became fully established in judicial language as distinct from the right of assembly, and it still remains less developed. Just as there is a tension between the desire to express one's opinions publicly and the desire to remain anonymous while doing so, there is an interesting dynamic in the history of the right of association. The attainment of legal personhood for organizations—meaning the ability to act collectively as a single agent on the basis of publicly and legally acknowledged relationships—is a defining characteristic of contemporary economic life (Clemens 2000). From the political perspective, however, it is the reverse of these two definitional characteristics that is of importance. The right of association in this context involves the ability to act independently from those with whom one is associated, or at least to be considered by the law to have done so. And the right to keep one's associational relationships secret has been an important stimulus to development of legal thought about association from a constitutional perspective.

During the first decades of the twentieth century, the right of association was driven by the effort to unionize labor and to develop new political parties. Today, this right is still raised by labor issues, though most often when immigrants are involved (Kolly 2004). Another enduring issue is the extent to which an association has the right to exclude from membership individuals who may wish to join (White 1997). The most pressing area of concern about the right of association today—the question of how to treat the right of association when terrorism is involved—actually received scholarly treatment before 9/11 (Cole 1999). Relationships between association and other constitutional rights, such as the right to hear (Eberhardt 1986), are receiving attention.

In addition to concern about terrorism, three other recent developments can be expected to stimulated further legal thinking and scholarship in this area. First, the techniques of network analysis, now being widely used across the social sciences, has brought to light informal (i.e., non-organizational) associational relationships not previously visible. Second, the ability to trace electronic communications among individuals means that an exponentially greater amount of data about associations can now be subjected to analysis. Third, the notion of "expressive association" (Fisher 2004) broadens the concept in ways that may also affect interpretation and implementation of the law.

Hate speech For overviews of the history of legal treatment of hate speech in the United States, see Jenness and Grattet (2001) and Walker (1994). Hate speech and libel remain intertwined in a complex way (Romero 2001), but there are important social as well as constitutional distinctions (Bollinger 1986).

A variety of types of social theory have been used to analyze arguments for and against regulation of hate speech, including speech acts theory (Haiman 1993), social identity theory (Leets and Giles 1997), economic theory (Dharmapala and McAdams 2005), critical theory combined with hermeneutics (Wright 2000), and social movement theory (Tsesis 2002). The last of these is particularly useful from a policy perspective, because it links hate speech to genocidal practices in places such as Rwanda (Schabas 2000) and Kosovo (Palmer 2001).

Research into the social consequences of hate speech began with Elisabeth Noelle-Neumann's (1984) study of how the Nazis came to power, which resulted in her theory of the "spiral of silence." This theory suggests that people will overestimate the amount of support for extreme positions voiced in public, with the result that counterviews are less likely to be expressed and those who are ambivalent are likely to move towards the extreme position, leading to a shift in overall public opinion. Shamir and Shamir (2000) have significantly refined and further articulated this theory on the basis of multiple studies that demonstrated that the extent to which individuals will actually respond to extreme positions depends in large part on the amount of information about the subject matter they have prior to exposure.

Demaske (2004), however, argues that contemporary sociological circumstances require a rethinking of the theoretical ground for legal treatment of hate speech. Certainly the Web environment has raised the salience of problems generated by differences in treatment of hate speech across jurisdictions (Dauterman 2002; Timofeeva 2003). At its worst, the United States could become known as a "haven for hate" (Breckheimer 2002), because types of content impermissible elsewhere—such as Nazi propaganda—are created here and then distributed globally via the Internet. The Internet is also now being used to study those who engage in hate speech (Glaser, Dixit, and Green 2002).

Interconnection Textbooks and casebooks on telecommunications regulation and on antitrust law cited earlier all deal with interconnection issues. Histories of the telephone provide insight into the social as well as the economic dynamics that first led to the development of telephone systems that operated in isolation from each other, and then to an appreciation of the value of interconnection after this practice was mandated for defense purposes during World War I (Boettinger 1976; Brooks 1976), though Mueller (1989) argues that many of these stories about AT&T romanticize the role of universal service as a policy goal in the development of interconnection in a way that is contradicted by the actual history.

Economic, social, military, and technological arguments for interconnection have all remained in play since that time, though lags between trends in each area introduce various pressures for and against the promotion of interconnection of particular types during specific periods. Economic demands for interdependence can work for technological interconnection (Hayashi 1992), but the desire to promote innovation may work against interconnection long enough to permit patent holders to accrue the benefits of new developments and private line carriers may have no interest in interconnection because their clientele prefers end-to-end service (Noam 1992).

Technological interconnection connects subnetworks into larger units, but can also facilitate the emergence of new networks that in themselves may develop competitively as market forces replace technical stimuli for network architectures (Pogorel 1992). Innovations that affect network architecture mean that the impact of open interconnection can be different at different points in history, so that there has been a swing back and forth between competition at the level of services, lines, and networks themselves (Chiron and Rehberg 1986). With Open Network Architecture, the levels at which interconnection could even take place multiplied (Huber 1987; Kellogg, Thorne, and Huber 1992). As new opportunities for interconnection appear, first agreements are crafted by contracts among players before either standardization or regulatory interventions become involved (Noam 2001).

Interconnection has been a significant stimulus to the continued growth of urban units (Abler 1977). Social pressure appears when information users at geographically distributed sites demand interconnection for their own purposes (Steinmueller 1992). Social and political arguments for interconnection appear at every level of the social structure. The international desire to promote linkages between national communication systems was evident by the 1860s. By the mid-1980s, the interconnection of networks and standardization of services had become linked together as global policy problems (Bruce 1983). The value of such interconnection remains evident today (Galbi 1998; Kikuchi 2003). At the most local level, too, there is a commitment to interconnection in order to provide necessary service to local communities (Wiley 1984).

Horwitz (1991) provides a regulatory history that links interconnection with other policy interests through the 1980s, though Irwin (1984) claims that some of the FCC's involvement with interconnection exemplifies jurisdictional drift. Today there are new forms of interconnection via peering (Gorman and Malecki 2000; Little and Wright 2000), and suggestions that nano-transactions (and the nano-regulation that such activity would lead to) may be an economic alternative to technological interconnection (Noam 2000).

Universal service As has been the case with interconnection, a complex of social, economic, and political goals have been intertwined in the history of universal service. Network externalities provide a powerful economic motivation for universal service, but the social impact of the same policy principle has political uses as well. The divestiture of AT&T—itself in large part driven by the consequences of technological change—served as a watershed in terms of approaches to universal service because the regulatory, market, and technical context so changed. For the long view, a succinct history of the classical view of universal service can be found in Aufderheide (1987, 1999), but Mueller (1996) offers a more extended and detailed analysis of the actual history behind rhetorical claims (as offered, e.g., by Berman and Oettinger [1976]) about both goals of and methods for achieving universal service by AT&T during the long century in which it held a monopoly-like position in the U.S. telecommunications system.

The question of universal service as a matter of broad political attention didn't really surface until the 1970s, when considerations of equity cast provided a social justification that was consonant with the economic desire to increase the economies of scale and scope in the provision of services newly available because of technological change (Cowhey 1990). In the years immediately following the 1983 divestiture, some believed that techniques such as subsidies or unbundling local from long distance service might be necessary for universal service because otherwise the release of regulatory limits on pricing would drive many users off the telephone network (Geller 1984). Others, however, believed that the effort to achieve genuinely universal service was actually a result of bottlenecks generated by a lack of sufficient competition (Crandall 1989). The General Accounting Office (1986) pointed out that the FCC actually had no way to monitor the extent to which universal service was actually being achieved. As competition opened up, questions as to which types of providers and networks had responsibility for universal service appeared quickly (Noam 1987). In 1991 the National Telecommunications and Information Administration examined various ways of defining universal service in response to an FCC investigation into whether it was appropriately operationalizing the principle for contemporary conditions, and the same task was updated in a special journal issue of *The Information Society* (Sawhney 2000) and by Xavier (2003).

Kaserman, Mayo, and Flynn (1990) called universal service a fairy tale. It became clear that to be politically acceptable, techniques for ensuring universal service had to be compatible with competitive markets (Entman 1999). Moore (1997) suggested that universal service might be related to the expansion of capacity and improvement of the efficiency of the network as one in a series of steps to be taken on the way to building as a coherent national information policy, and Milne (1998) points out that universal service policy goes through its own stages of development. Though the Telecommunications Act of 1996 put in place some mechanisms for funding universal service, its provision to those in rural areas remained a concern (Beachboard, McClure, and Bertot 1997; Hollifield et al. 2000), and there have been deep conflicts regarding which types of network providers are actually financially responsible under the FCC's requirements (Crandall and Waverman 2000). By this point, of course, the questions of universal service to telephony and to the Internet had become intertwined (Foros, Kind, and Sand 2005; Greenstein 1998b; Kim 1998).

Two decades after discussions about how to successfully implement the policy principle of universal service in a competitive telecommunications environment began, the issue remains (Hammond 2005; Rosston and Wimmer 2000). Recent work has looked at linkages between policies put in place to pursue the different goals of interconnection, universal service, and the lowering of entry barriers for telecommunications providers and universal service (Valetti, Steffen, and Barros 2002). Policy innovations (Jayakar and Sawhney 2004), such as tradable universal service obligations (Peha 1999) or the use of spectrum auctions to support universal service (Sorana 2000), have appeared.

Schement (1995) and Mueller and Schement (1996) have spawned a new stream of work on actual uses and conditions of those marginal populations to whom universal service policies are directed. Sociologists address the universal service problem under the guise of the digital divide. Particularly thoughtful and empirically rich work in this area can be found in Warschauer (2003), van Dijk (2005), and Norris, Bennett, and Entman (2001).

Access to government information Restrictions on access to government information come in a variety of firms: the Office of Management and Budget intervenes in data collection and dissemination processes, classification of information removes it from availability, and changing interpretations of the Freedom of Information Act reduce its effectiveness.

Ongoing analysis of the impact of OMB interventions into government data collection and dissemination activities can be found on the Web site of the nonprofit organization OMBWatch (www.ombwatch.org). Morin (1994) provides an overview of the techniques being used by the OMB in the mid-1990s, and Morrison (1986) documents the impact on both implementation of statutory law and decision-making processes of the OMB during the same period. Specific examples of how OMB interventions have had significant impact are its alteration of the criteria by which drugs are evaluated for approval by the FDA through replacement of scientific judgment for OMB administrative oversight (O'Connor 1988); its intervention into racial classifications, with consequences for immigration policy as well as the census (Toro 1995); and its key role in unraveling environmental legislation and its use of OMB techniques to censor speech by executive branch government employees (Perks 2002).

Because the effects of OMB involvement with government data collection procedures often meant curtailing, or even reversing, decisions made by Congress, these activities generated significant tension between the executive and legislative branches of government (Bowers 1993; Cooper and West 1988), exacerbating other conflicts over management of information flows between the two (Fisher 1990). During Reagan's administration, for example, OMB actions created a large gap between presidential rhetoric and reality regarding access to government information (Crawford and Stimatz 2000). Similarly, more recent use of the OMB to change the length of years over which implications of federal budget are forecast has had rhetorical value for the president (Puckett 2004).

OMBWatch is documenting post–9/11 limits on access to government information. The Association of Research Libraries (www.arl.org) tracks this information as it affects scholars and the higher education community across fields. The Society of American Archivists (www.archivists.org) is documenting and trying to intervene with what is happening at NARA. For ongoing discussion of impact on public discourse as a result of limitations on access to information since 9/11, see Reporters Committee for Freedom of the Press (www.rcfp.org; 2004).

The history of the development of OMB techniques has clearly responded to political developments (Mathiasen 1988). Some feel OMB policies since the Paperwork Reduction Act of 1980 and the NARA Act of 1984 have been so confused and ineffective that they should be scrapped altogether (Penn 1997). Little is actually known about the OMB's own decision-making processes (Kargman 1986). Analysis of OMB activities, however, should take into account that while not every decision put in place is implemented completely or consistently or immediately, once OMB mandates are in place they remain available to the government for use. Political scientists describe the effects of the OMB as so fundamental and unprecedented that they are literally changing our form of government (Jones 1998; McGarity 1991).

The current uniform system used for classifying and declassifying national security information was developed by President Clinton and presented in Executive Order 12958 in 1995. It has since been amended, most significantly by President George W. Bush in Executive Order 13292 in 2003. Full text of these executive orders and some other documents providing the authority for and details of the current information classification system can be found on the Web site of the Information Security Oversight Office (ISOO) (www.archives.gov/isoo/), a department within the National Archives with responsibility for declassification. A more complete group of documents on this topic is available through one Web page offered by the nonprofit organization the Federation of American Scientists (www.fas.org/sgp/isoo/index.html).

Demac (1984) and Theoharis (1998) provide histories of the classic political tensions that have surrounded the classification of government information in order to restrict access to what is considered sensitive. For a look at the impact on scholarship of this type of restriction on access to information as it stood several decades ago, see Barker and Fox (1972); nonprofit groups such as the Association of Research Libraries, the American Association for the Advancement of Science, and disciplinary groups are documenting contemporary issues of this kind with results usually available on their Web sites. The National Research Council (1995) reviewed Department of Energy classification policy and practice, and there are other specialized reports of this kind. The most comprehensive overview of the history of classification and other forms of government secrecy historically and as they stood in the years just prior to 9/11 can be found in a 1997 report by the late Senator Daniel Patrick Moynihan, which was also rewritten and issued as a trade book for the lay public (Moynihan 1998).

Lee (2003) explores the interrelationships among classification practices, intellectual property rights, and other techniques the government can use to reduce the amount of information that is effectively available to the public. In an interesting extension of the logic that underlies OMB mandates to federal agencies to reduce their informational activities because of cost, a 1993 GAO report suggests it would be valuable to conduct a similar exercise to evaluate the actual costs of protecting classified information in order to make the system more efficient.

The Classified Information Protection Act managed to complicate legal procedures in the process of trying to clarify how and under what conditions classified information could be acquired by those needing it to prosecute or defend clients in the course of a criminal trial (Holzer 2005; Jordan 1991; Michalec 2002/2003; Salgado 1988; Shea 1990). This problem has of course worsened with the introduction of "born classified" evidence when it is acquired under the surveillance mechanisms put in place by the PATRIOT Act (Note 2005). The same is true of other legal processes, such as immigration proceedings (Snyder 2002).

Current concerns about the extent of government secrecy go back at least to the changes in Eastern Europe and the USSR (Kaiser 1989), leading the GAO to ask in a 1993 report whether or not there was any longer any need to classify so much information. Our mood regarding the extent of possible threats to the United States has now changed again, but dismay over the expansion of the domain of classified information beyond historical levels remains (Swartz 2003).

Techniques other than explicit and direct classification contribute to the amount of government secrecy. Ellsberg (2004) explores the role of secrecy oaths as a means of protecting information in a classification-like way. The category of sensitive but unclassified information, to which access is also limited, appeared in the 1980s (Courtney 1988). The definition of "sensitive" has gotten more expansive in recent years, leading one anonymous author (Parker and Jacobs 2003) to describe an emergent category of "sort of classified" information. Technological means of confounding access to government information have ranged from the very simple production of microfiche versions of publicly available reports from the National Technical Information Service that placed pages in spiral relationships to each other (making them quite difficult to read) in the 1980s through the much more sophisticated techniques now in use. Examples of techniques being used to protect databases from inference attacks that would allow users to deduce classified information from data to which they legitimately have access include such things as modeling alternative logics that might link one piece of information with another (Binns 1993) and manipulation of indexing so that certain types of queries become more difficult (Ceselli et al. 2005; Hinke, Delugach, and Wolf 1997). Contemporary restrictions to access to scientific information were presaged by Sprehe (1995).

Documents recently declassified as a result of President Clinton's insistence upon operating in accordance with existing law regarding declassification and expansion of declassification requirements has made it possible for historians to begin to determine how political processes might have unfolded differently had pertinent information not been classified when decision-making was taking place. Boughton (2004), for example, has demonstrated that the definitive claim by the FBI that Harry Dexter White, a former Treasury Department official who was an important participant in the development of post–World War II global financial arrangements, was a spy was simply not based on credible evidence. Westerfield (1995) uses declassified articles from an internal CIA magazine as support for the argument that the psychological climate of the agency led to interpretations of data sometimes quite distant from empirical realities. Leitner and Stupak (1997) explore the sociological and psychological consequences of routine access to classified information for those within government—such as Oliver North—who are required to delivery the current administration's line. And Miller (1998) used the German case to look at society-wide adjustments to the existence of a large body of formerly secret government information once there is a radical change in the nature of its government.

Current issues include the question of the extent to which information from satellites put up for national security purposes is used for other purposes, such as environmental information gathering (Beardsley 1995; Haines and Joyce 1987); the necessary expansion of the proportion of the population that must have access to classified information if Homeland Security objectives are to be met (Kaiser 2003); and the diffusion of governmental practices regarding classification to the private sector (Eloff, Holbein, and Teufel 1996).

Accounting systems Contemporary developments in industrial classification systems are taking place within a long history of accounting taxonomies that goes back to ancient times (Nissen, Damerow, and Englund 1994). After double-entry bookkeeping was introduced in Venice, widely diffused once the first accounting textbook appeared, accounting techniques remained fairly stable for several hundred years. A number of authors have looked at the factors that first increased the volume and complexity of the information being handled, and then stimulated the development of new accounting techniques and taxonomies, including the increasingly elaborate logistical support needs of the military (de Landa 1991), articulation and growth in organizational form (Yates 1991), the appearance of new uses for data such as insurance (Temin 1992), and the role of standardization of accounting systems in industrialization (Chandler 1979).

The most comprehensive history of accounting in the United States, by Previts and Merino (1998), emphasizes the cultural significance of the legal, economic, and organizational forms that have evolved. (Chandler [2000] provides further detail regarding accounting practices during colonial times.) Since the mid-1980s, other work has also explored the social, cultural, and political impact of various accounting practices (Miller and Power 1995; Temin 1991). To emphasize that all accounting taxonomies are only one among the many statistical frameworks that have social impact, March (1987) uses the phrase "social accounting" to refer to techniques for evaluating matters that combine economic and social factors such as quality of life and cost of living.

Histories of theories of accounting can be found in Hopwood and Miller (1994). The notion of national efficiency arose around the turn of the twentieth century, when the attention of governments already involved with statistical efforts turned to the problem of establishing economic categories for accounting purposes. Accounting schemes developed by national governments, such as those discussed here, provide a means of intervening in the internal practices of organizations. Thus Johnson (1991) describes accounting as a means of enabling management by remote control, directing the work of individuals, subordinate production units, and the enterprise as a whole. At the national level, these systems are critical to regulation of a country's economy and make it possible to evaluate different economic policies (Thorbecke 1991). Florini (2000) provides detail on the emergence of the concept of transparency—today of such importance across all types of political and economic activity—as it first applied to accounting systems.

Early efforts to think about informational commodities and economic activity from an accounting perspective began with Machlup's (1962) work on the information sector, and include Uri Porat's SIC code-based analysis of the information sector in 1977, an OECD study of the information sector published (Gassmann

1981), and French efforts reported upon by Preston (2001). All of these, however, worked with existing taxonomic frameworks, but it was increasingly clear that the categories in use no longer sufficed.

Corporations involved in the intellectual capital movement preceded governments in trying to develop alternative accounting. Skandia was one of the first corporations to experiment with ways of accounting for intangible assets as well as those that are tangible in order to more accurately grasp their actual sources of value; Edvinsson and Ake (1999) report on what were already three generations of this type of experimentation by the close of the 1990s. Stewart (1994) popularized the notion of intellectual capital, which has by now received useful analyses of techniques for measurement (Sveiby 2000) and other pragmatic aspects of the treatment of intellectual capital for practicing accountants (Lilly and Reed 1999), as well as having been the subject of theory development (Mortensen 2000). This activity by the private sector provided avenues through which governments could begin thinking about how to replace the SIC codes in order to reflect an economic reality that had changed as a result of shifts in boundaries between economic sectors, expansion of the domain of economic activity, and transformations in the nature of economic processes brought about by the informatization of society.

For an analysis of the concepts used in the SIC codes as a starting point for development of the NAICS, see Economic Classification Policy Committee (1994). Kahle and Walkling (1996) discuss the implications of the NAICS framework for financial research in general; the same type of analyses have been undertaken industry by industry, with Harchaoui (2004) providing an exemplar with his study of the banking industry. Kort (2001) has looked at the impact of NAICS on the statistics used as inputs into federal decision-making. Whichard and Borga (2002) highlight the extensiveness of this impact in their study of how NAICS has affected our understanding of U.S. borders because of the system's implications for methods used in measuring trade in services.

Globalization has also played a role in the development and influence of accounting taxonomies (Dezalay 1989). With liberalization, the ability to use offshore accounting firms increased (United Nations Centre on Transnational Corporations 1991), an activity made significantly easier once accounting, as a service, became subject to the GATS agreement managed by the ATO. Howells (1987) provides some detail on the extent of British influence as late as the 1980s, and Zurkowski (1989) uses the USSR as a case to look at the export of accounting practices to countries with transition economies. Helleiner (2001) argues that fluctuations in currency markets can disrupt domestic accounting practices and force people to use abstract imaginary units of accounts.

There are explicit interactions between accounting frameworks and the industries of information, communication, and culture. Theoretical problems have long plagued accounting for telecommunications (Snow 1986). Changes in broadcasting station ownership patterns that began in the 1980s brought new management principles to the industry that had larger effects on accounting methods than on program schedules (Baker 1987). The news industry has a history of sensitivity to accounting issues because in most cases the same attorneys who handle issues related to freedom of speech and libel are the same ones who handle accounting matters and other corporate legal work that has maximizing profit as its goal (Anderson 1975).

Metadata Experimentation with metadata began only in the mid-1990s, so most of the existing literature deals with drafts of metadata frameworks, experiments with the use of metadata, and discussion of processes by which metadata systems might be developed. Weibel (1999) provides a bibliography of the literature on metadata as it developed through 1997. Lazinger and Tibbo (2001) provide a history of efforts to develop metadata systems, and Weibel and Koch (2000) introduce and provide a brief history of the Dublin Core Metadata Initiative in particular. Taylor (2004) contextualizes metadata historically. Caplan (2003) provides one example of the proliferating genre of how-to books on metadata for information professionals that should be considered relatively authoritative because it is published by the American Library Association.

Discussions of the development and use of metadata are now taking place in seemingly every discipline and for every type of application. Some items focus on possible sources of information that can be used for metadata (e.g., Michener et al. 1997, on ecology), some on the applicability of interdisciplinary metadata systems for use by specific disciplines (e.g., Wallace 2005, on information management and retrieval), and some on the uses to which metadata can be put (e.g., Woollard and Herrero 2005, on the use of metadata in television and film postproduction).

A number of technical issues remain. Basic metadata concepts are not always consensually understood by all who use them (Stumpf and McDonnell 2004). There are circumstances in which the amount of metadata actually exceeds the amount of actual data (Klensin 1995). Difficulties in achieving interdisciplinary metadata systems of actual utility to those in diverse disciplines remain frustrating, and professional career paths are not yet in place for those who would undertake the ongoing work of applying metadata to new research results as well as existing databases (Hill 2005). Other types of problems exist as well: metadata present a challenge to the legal profession, for example, because they produce an entirely new kind of evidence (Friedman 2004).

Still, metadata has already proven their value for such activities as raising the visibility of Web pages for browsers (Zhang and Dimitroff 2004) and making databases interoperable (Lee et al. 2004). In some fields, the use of metadata is making it possible to address old problems in very new ways. The use of "cultural metadata" with details about music content when tracking purchases of music online, for example, makes it possible to make positive recommendations to buyers about other potentially interesting purchases (Baumann and Hummel 2005). The addition of metadata to several hundred years of historical records about diplomatic practice enables new types of historical analysis by scholars (Williams 2005). Metadata-based modeling makes it possible to analyze interorganizational networks in ways not previously possible (Gans et al. 2005). Metadata are being put to use in the development of new types of information products and services, such as interactive TV (Lugmayr, Niiranen, and Kalli 2004). The use of metadata to support local e-government initiatives (Twynholm 2003) is particularly interesting from the perspective of information policy.

The National Information Standards Organization (2004) has put its imprimatur on the Dublin Core system. Ongoing documentation of development and uses of the Dublin Core can be found on the initiative's Web site (www.dublincore.org), and the same type of material for the Semantic Web project on its Web site (www.w3.org/2001/sw/). The Web site metadata.net serves as a portal to a number of metadata initiatives that range from very general development efforts to use- or discipline-specific endeavors.

7 Information Policy and Borders

Nowhere is the difficulty of distinguishing among social, technological, and informational borders more clear than in the study of geopolitical borders. Export controls were designed to deal with weapons in very material form but also include information about advanced technologies. International trade in services agreements that deal with information flows also apply to industries such as tourism, and make it possible for organizations that specialize in services such as the law and accounting to globalize. Guarding the geopolitical border is intended to prevent illegal migration of people and transport of goods, but in today's "smart borders" environment is very much dependent upon information technologies and the data they gather. Thus following the brief review of the development of theoretical perspectives on borders, the bibliographic essay for this chapter is organized around areas of the law as defined in legacy terms.

This has been a conversation with bifurcating paths. A number of specialized topics have developed out of the generalized discussion about "transborder data" flow of the late 1970s and early 1980s under the rubrics of trade in services, privacy, and international rate regulation. In this area, the scholarly literature has followed categories generated by the multiplication and refinement of political negotiations over information flows.

Border Theory

The study of borders is particularly intriguing, both because there is often an immediate political value for the results of research and because so many of the issues involved are conceptually rather than materially driven. It is a new field of study: The first topical journal, the *Journal of Borderland Studies*, was launched only in 1986, highlighting the recency of the development of the field. The earliest work on borders was in anthropology (Alvarez 1995), dealing with the U.S.-Mexico border. For an overview of economic, social, cultural, and political relations along the contemporary U.S.-Mexico border that drove the development of this area of research, see Wise (1998). Stoddard (1975, 1986) has documented the development of the study of borders and provided a widely used distinction among frontiers, borders, and borderlands. Falk (1988) produced a bibliography of work on the U.S.-Mexico border through the late 1980s, and Arnold (1995) provides a history of the "elastic border" concept.

A second stream of work on borders has been generated by those who are interested in the problem of the spatial distribution of economic activity (Hansen 1977). The difference between the border as a geographic line and as an economic space is dramatized in work that examines the variable width of border zones from an economic perspective (Engel and Rogers 1996). An extremely interesting stream of work looks at the translation of political relations into economic relations via the replacement of treaties with contracts (Davis, Kahn, and Zald 1990). Other economic questions of interest are whether to treat information flows across borders as if they involved primary goods, even if they serve the functions of secondary goods as inputs into production processes (Jussawalla and Cheah 1983), the problem of how to treat the creation of value when it arises from collaboration across borders (Aharoni 1993), the impact on network efficiency of border crossings (Hakansson and Johanson 1993), and the question of where to locate transactions that take place in the network (Sauvant 1986).

Both political scientists (Dallmeyer 1997; Goff 2000) and cultural theorists (Derrida 1992) have looked at relationships between international trade and national identity. Evans (1992) explores the ways in which a renewed desire to assert cultural identity can affect the treatment of borders. Rosenau (1970) discusses border policies as one of eight forms of adaptive behavior undertaken by those involved with foreign policy; for a summary of the Realist position on borders, see Rosenau and Durfee (1995). For a discussion of the relationship between trade and risk, see Petersmann (1991). James Lull (1997) argues that particularly sophisticated cultural analysis takes place along borders. Vaara, Tienari, and Saentti (2003) look at the role of metaphors in shifting perceptions of relationships across borders. Mains (2004) examines the very act of drawing political boundaries by geographers itself as a set of cultural practices. Kraidy (2005) theoretically develops the concept of hybridity as a "bordered" identity; Wuthnow's (1987) work documenting the frequency of witch hunts in European border regions provides a vivid example of how hybrid identities may be dealt with socially. While some argue that this is an entirely new form of identity breaking down pre-existing hierarchies, others insist that the two ways to thinking about identity can comfortably co-exist (Beltran 2004).

A particularly interesting stream of work from the perspective of the relationship between borders and identity is the study by Içduygu and Kaygusuz (2004) of the processes by which the first criteria for citizenship emerge in places where borders are newly drawn. Other research that looks specifically at changes in the nature of the law as a result of shifting borders in the contemporary environment include Jacobsohn's (2004) work on the ways in which constitutional law adapts in postindependence environments via the use of comparative materials and Brown's (2004) review of negotiation of state (infranational) governments with international players.

Katsh (1989) includes the impact of computers on the ability to conduct cross-jurisdictional legal analyses in his overview of the variety of ways in which digital technologies have affected legal theory practice. Simon and Waller (1986) look at the importance of antitrust law in efforts to exercise domestic laws extraterritorially, and Delaney (1993) discusses the boundary of firms as, using Williamson's (1981) term, a "technologically separable interface." Steele (1998) explores what citizenship information is for Europeans under today's conditions in which everyone is a citizen both of Europe and of his or her home country. Sidney Tarrow is the acknowledged expert on transnational political networks, and his 2002 work is the source of the points made here regarding such networks.

Smith (1993) provides a discussion of the diverse scales at which systems operate that is useful for understanding today's state borders, and Berg (1998) discusses the difference between an outline of an object and its actual borders. Stevenson (1994) discusses the difference between the experience of borders and their actual geopolitical location; this work repeats in a different form the point made by Liah Greenfeld (1992) that there is no consistency in which social dimension will determine the border of one ethnic group from another culturally. Cohen and Roeh (1992) and Roeh and Cohen (1992) look at genre differences at the point of border crossing. The political and economic implications of the several-hundred-year-long history of the movement of genetic information across borders can be found in Kloppenburg (1988) and Crosby (1994), and Kloppenburg and Kleiman (1987) discuss those issues in their contemporary form.

The most recent "case" to have drawn a lot of attention to border studies across disciplines has been the erection of the wall between Israeli and Palestinian territory. Many of the diverse perspectives introduced here can be found in the growing literature on this problem (Billig and Churchman 2003; Lagerquist 2004; Malki 2002). The growing theoretical interest in borders has stimulated a range of new types of research to test the concepts and hypotheses being put forward—and new information technologies, such as geographic information systems and various forms of satellite surveillance, make this more possible than ever before. Political scientists are investigating the relationship between the ease of interaction and the "vitalness" of borders and levels of conflict (Starr and Thomas 2005). Those interested in national identity are beginning to turn to its transformation in border regions such as those between Croatia and Slovenia (Ballinger 2002). Much of this work is historical, as in the analysis of the role of border medical inspections in supplying a labor force needed by the United States as it became industrialized (Fairchild 2003). Some analysts see borders as a site of experimentation with techniques of low-intensity conflict (Frederick 1989; Jimenez 2000). Tyndall (1999) notes, however, that the media can lose interest when borders become less problematic, as they did when the barriers between eastern and western Europe came down.

As with other legal questions of importance in the early twenty-first century, some suggest that the national interest itself needs to be reconceptualized as applied to border regions in order to resolve ongoing internal inconsistences in the law and practice that result from sometimes mutually exclusive goals (Gallegos 2004). The word "postnationalist" has been used to apply to the cultures of cross-border urban environments (Hackenberg and Alvarez 2001), and the notion of "fuzzy borders" to refer to the complexities of determining just what is near and what is far in the new Europe (Christiansen 2000).

Borders of Social Systems

Geopolitical borders The history of U.S. immigration policy since 1882 is told in Daniels (2004), of flows of persons across the U.S.-Mexico border in Heyman (1999), and of flows across the U.S.-Canada border in Smith (2000). Ackleson (2003a) reviews the literature dealing with security issues in particular. The Migration Policy Institute, a nonprofit organization, is an excellent source of data and analyses about all aspects of the movement of people across U.S. and other borders. Neuborne and Shapiro (1985) provide a history of denial of visas to individuals on the basis of their political speech up to that point.

Despite the fact that immigration policy is established at the national level in the United States, there are significant differences in operationalization at the local level, often countering, compensating for, and changing policies coming from the national core. Three facets of state complexity make this possible: multiple levels, diverse administrative branches, and decentralized agencies (Wells 2004). A first theoretical perspective on comparative immigration policies across nation-states that can be used to analyze empirical data was offered by Meyers (2004). Post-9/11 immigration policy has become subsumed to terrorism policy (use of an "immigration plus" profiling scheme targeting those from Muslim countries, and court complicity in changes in immigration law by viewing in terrorism policy context) (Turnlin 2004).

Economic (Hanson, Robertson, and Spilimbergo 2002) and social (Heyman 1999) analyses of the effects of border enforcement do not always support the arguments used to justify fierce border security. Actual effects are sometimes unexpected, as in the impact of distributing manufacturing processes across borders on innovation within U.S. corporations (Zander and Solvell 2000). A political economic analysis of maquiladoras shows the dark side of these practices (Sklair 1989).

Since 9/11, there have been changes in the legal treatment of U.S. borders (Adelman 2002; Harty 2005), including increases in both personnel and the use of information technologies for monitoring and protection purposes (Ackleson 2003b; Congressional Research Service 2001; Meyers 2003). The Invasion Clause of the U.S. Constitution has been used to further militarize the border (Blair 2003). Organizational changes, however, have not kept up with technological developments, and the General Accounting Office (2002) reports that the INS finds it difficult to manage its information technology systems, though recommendations from a 2001 report by the Congressional Research Service on the use of the automated visa lookout system were put in place following 9/11.

A legal analysis of the concept of functional equivalents of borders for purposes of privacy law is provided by Arnold (1995). In his history of the border search exception and the concept of functional border equivalence, Rosenzweig (1985) points out that while history is thought to justify border searches, it does not aid in establishing their limits. This loophole in U.S. privacy law as applied to immigrants is particularly ironic given that so many individuals cross borders in pursuit of protections for human rights (Jacobson and Ruffer 2003).

Other examples of recent work on the social dimensions of geopolitical borders include studies of the "Reconquista" movement, an effort to reconquer the Southwest for Mexico by eradicating the U.S.-Mexico border there (Ling 2004); of the role of technological systems in facilitating transborder political activity (Sieber 2003); and of the impact of migration on literacy practices in the sending country (Flores and Lankshear 2000). It is not surprising that some continue to maintain that borders are uncontrollable and that we should think differently about how to take advantage of benefits of migration, but it is news that someone like Bhagwati (2003)—long a stalwart of free trade—would take this position.

Trade in services The literatures on transborder data flow and on trade in services, just like the legal processes under study, began with separate lives before converging. The contemporary literature on regulation of international information flows got its start in the identification of the legal treatment of transborder data flows as a problem (Antonelli 1981; Ganley and Ganley 1982; Pipe 1979), the changes in the global economy that have given rise to these problems (Caporaso 1986; Gershuny and Miles 1983), and the international implications of domestic law as a result of the increased amount of data that flows across borders (Marchand 1979). Ploman (1982b) and A. W. Branscomb (1986) reviewed the various instruments in international law that could or already has been be applied to transborder data flows.

When the issue of transborder data flows was taken up in the trade arena, it was discussed under the rubric of trade in services. There was concern that trade and nontrade barriers to trade in services (Feketekuty and Aronson 1984; Gotlieb, Dalfen, and Katz 1974; Marchand 1981; Spero 1982) would only increase as reliance upon information technologies grew (Feketekuty and Hausar 1985; Krommenacker 1986). A positive argument for changing the legal context for trade in services was based on the idea that doing so would be good for the world economy (Atinc et al. 1984; Ewing 1985; Nusbaumer 1987; Ochel and Wegner 1987), though there is a long history of the use of international trade law for national political purposes as well (Dixon 1985; Haggard 1988; Krasner 1976). Shelp (1986/1987) describes the U.S. goals regarding trade in services, and Jackson (1988) and Petersmann and Hilf (1988) worked through the range of legal issues involved at the international level. Drake and Nicolaides (1992) tell the story of the negotiations as it unfolded step by step on the ground. Urry (1987) launched the stream of work on the geography of the information economy that later gained some renown with a look at the spatial aspects of services.

Expressions of concern about the cultural implications of the commoditization of information, communication, and culture that would be an inevitable concomitant of incorporating trade in services under international trade law appeared almost immediately (Acheson and Maule 1994; Becker 1986; Bernier 1988), and it was assumed that the Canada-U.S. Free Trade Agreement was a forerunner of what might be expected from a multilateral agreement involving many more countries (Mosco 1990). Attention to the specific needs of developing countries had actually begun a bit earlier, in the course of debates over the possibility of a New World Information Order (Hamelink 1979; Roach 1987). Developing countries had not done particularly well under the original GATT system, despite the claims of those who shaped those agreements that the trade practices they induced would reduce the gaps among nations (Hudec 1987). In the trade in services debate, some authors projected a positive impact on developing countries (Bergen 1987; Bhagwati and Ruggie 1984), while others believed the outcome was more likely to be negative (Cruise O'Brien 1983; Hveem 1987). Ultimately New World Information Order and trade in services concerns converged (Braman 1989). Even within the United States, there was some concern about the First Amendment implications of international law affecting flows of information (Damon 1986), contributing to what many saw as the positive value of getting out from under U.S. legal restrictions (Jackson 1984). Cogburn (2004) has been documenting the battle over how to define information—as a commodity or as a political force—in discourse related to the World Summit on the Information Society (WSIS) of 2005, a discussion focused on the question of who should regulate the Internet and how. Meanwhile, empirical support exists for the argument that cultural factors matter in data regarding the continued preference for intrastate trade even when regional agreements reduce the costs of international trade (Wei 1996).

International trade brings a lot of new players into the law, contributing to its detachment from the nation-state (Dezalay 1989). Several years into experience with GATS, there is concern that the treatment of services as a matter of trade will interfere with the ability of states to shape their domestic health-care systems (Beisky et al. 2004), restructure the global market for education (Grieshaber-Otto and Sanger 2002; Hanley and Fredriksson 2003), and contribute to environmental damage by making it more difficult for states to encourage "green" tourism (Bendell and Font 2004) and to prevent bodies of water along borders from becoming polluted (Elwell 2001). The role of technology in harmonizing economic and political systems is discussed in Braman (1995a).

Borders of Technological Systems

There is a variety of ways in which the borders of technological systems affect other dimensions of geopolitical borders. Two very different examples: Van Creveld (1991) and other military historians cited earlier touch upon the relationship between the development of weaponry and the nature of borders. Colas ([1991] 1997) focuses on the role of information technologies in shaping cultural borders in Europe, now often more important than political borders in that region.

Network borders Very little has been published about FCC treatment of international matters other than, particularly in recent years, in the area of pricing agreements. Frieden (1983b) published the most useful history of FCC international activity until the divestiture of AT&T, and Goldey (1983) produced a similar review focused solely on voice communication. During the same period, Meyers (1984) projected future legal issues that would arise in the more competitive global environment to be expected after the divestiture, and Rutkowski (1981) reviewed the history of FCC involvement in international decision-making arenas up to that point, with an eye to the consequences of that history for future negotiations. The discussion of the FCC's history of treatment of the U.S. border offered here is based almost entirely on primary materials, a reading of every FCC document pertaining to international communication through 1983, covered in much greater detail in an unpublished paper by Braman (1984a).

Overviews of the range of jurisdictional issues raised by today's global information infrastructure are found in Kahin and Nesson (1997) and in Banisar (2002).

Discussion about the problem of how to share profits from communications between parties in different countries is renewed every time a change occurs in regulatory, economic, or technological conditions; for examples of recent work in this area, see Cave and Waverman (1998) and Melody (2000). Frieden (1991, 1993, 1997, 1998) has continued to track developments in international accounting rates throughout his career. Frieden (1984) is also the source of the most complete discussion available on why it was widely believed that the FCC would try to exert its distinction between basic and enhanced communication services internationally. Grubesic and Murray (2005) point out that the settlements feature of telecommunications policy makes inaccuracies in spatial data even more confounding.

Export controls The borders of both technological and informational systems are affected by export controls. This policy tool came into use only after World War II, but has its roots in longstanding competition among governments over control of knowledge as an important form of political capacity.

The equation of national identity (and capacity) with control over knowledge received some discussion in chapter 5 and its corresponding essays. The "national encyclopedia" movement was an effort to equate national identity with the knowledge controlled by the nation-state (Cortada 2000; Headrick 2000) by linking political structures with informational structures. A method for quantifying the relative contributions of different states to the production of knowledge was developed in the 1830s by Alphonse de Candolle, a Swiss naturalist (Crawford 1992). After World War II, however, national claims to existing knowledge were overshadowed by international competition in R&D (Florida and Kenney 1994; Pearce and Singh 1992). For examples of the tension between national and international communities in specific knowledge domains, see Hadwiger (1982) on agricultural research, Blumler (1978) on communication research, and Ferguson (1986) on research about new information technologies. For its impact on a particular region (Latin America), see Sagasti (1992). The question of "trade barriers to knowledge" as a policy issue was first raised by UNESCO in 1955, providing a link between trade in services and problems of access to scientific information raised by the use of export controls.

In 2001 Kremic noted that despite the fact that a structure for export controls has been in place since 1949 (becoming formal only in the 1970s [Bingham and Johnson 1979]), there is a striking paucity of scholarly literature on the topic. Five factors, he suggested, might be at play: the dynamic nature of the topic, difficulty in ensuring accurate data, the complexity of the problem, the relatively small economic impact, and the sensitivity of the information involved. Though the empirical description of the size of the scholarly literature is correct, not everyone would agree with Kremic's suggestion that the economic costs are minimal. Macdonald's (1990) history of export controls identifies a number of ways in which they have caused economic damage, Johnson-Freese's (2000) work on their impact on satellites provides one example of what this type of regulation has meant for one industry in particular, and Burnham (1999) goes so far as to suggest that export controls were causing a national economic emergency.

Export controls were born in concern about diffusion of weapons, but ever since the 1982 Corson Report there has been keen awareness of the potential danger that the spread of scientific and technical information might pose as well. Here the economic and the political are tightly intertwined, for many believed that export controls actually served to strengthen domestic industry (Cupitt 2000; Levine, Mouzakis, and Smith 2003) even though such policies run directly counter to the value of scientific internationalism in an increasingly interdependent environment (Manzione 2000; Mendelsohn 1992) and may constitute inappropriate extraterritorial application of U.S. law (Feldman 1985).

The shape of the literature on export controls has followed shifting concerns during and after the Cold War. For an analysis of the impact of CoCom on information flows between the Soviet and NATO blocs during the Cold War, see Bischof (1989). Macdonald (1989) examined the impact of CoCom on flows of technology-related information in particular. As tensions began to wind down, discussion of the costs of restrictions on the diffusion of scientific and technical information emerged (National Academy of Sciences 1987; Wallerstein et al. 1987). During the 1990s these controls were seen as in transition (Bertsch and Elliott-Gower 1992), opening up discussions of possible alternative ways to balance the diverse values at stake (National Academy of Sciences 1991; Panofsky 2000). In 1994 Relyea produced the first history of the cost of national security controls to science itself. With establishment of the World Trade Organization in the mid-1990s, export controls were increasingly seen as one among many policy tools in a kit designed to protect the position of parties to the Wassenaar and other agreements in the global economic order (Garcia-Alonso, del Carmen, and Hartley 2003; Hoelscher and Wolffgang 1998). Lipson (1999) demonstrated the multiplicity of ways of viewing export controls in his analysis of the Wassenaar Arrangement through the lenses of three different types of international relations theory. Turning from the macro- to the microlevel, Zander and Solvell (2000) examine interactions between export controls and organizational structure. Resurrection of interest in export controls, and expansion of the types of limits placed on access to scientific information, have meanwhile revived concerns about the impact on academia and the ability of the United States to remain competitive in knowledge production (Keel 2004).

Much of the attention in the 1980s and 1990s revolved around the export of technologies that included a cryptographic capability. Still relied upon are arguments made at the opening of this debate by those who defended the position that information about cryptography, including discussion of cryptographic algorithms and implementation of cryptographic techniques in source code form, are protected by the First Amendment and therefore should not be subjected to ITAR. Kamenshine (1985) was one of the first to present the argument—later so important to those involved in protecting the right to encryption—that even mathematical formulae are protected by free speech. Rindskopf and Brown (1985) launched the counterargument that once scientific and technical information has been "reduced" to commercial application, the level of First Amendment protections for such speech is lowered. Cheh (1982) was one of the first to warn about the expansion of U.S. government controls on the export of ideas and noted that export controls also prevent ideas from circulating within the United States. Greenstein (1982) provides useful and early explorations of the impact of such measures on knowledge production, and Bass (1999) and Schwab (1990) looked at constitutional issues raised by export controls.

Branscomb (1993) provides a thorough explanation of why the U.S. government switched its export control focus to dual-use technologies, and what that shift was likely to mean for the U.S. economy. The economic argument against arms control has endured (Diebold 1987; Rudney and Anthony 1996). The *Arms Control Reporter* provides detailed reports on the activities of CoCom and the Wassenaar Arrangement, including estimations of the extent of compliance by participant states. Pierce (1984) explains just how ITAR works. Wiegele (1991) discusses treatment of biotechnology—another informational meta-technology—as dual-use for the purposes of export controls. Critiques by U.S. allies also endure, for arms control agreements create a high-technology "vulnerability trap" for countries such as Sweden (Mörth and Sundelius 1993), leading to the development of alternative approaches (Wallerstein 1991).

Quite aside from issues raised by the question of the extent to which other countries with which the United States had agreements regarding export controls were in fact compliant, a matter beyond the scope of this work, other evidence exists of the effectiveness of export controls. There are always exemptions in pursuit of other policy goals, as in the use of the "China differential" in the 1980s that permitted more favorable terms (Yuan 1995). Under current technological conditions, some aspects of export controls may simply be moot because workarounds are available (Hitchings 2003). New work in the history of science is demonstrating that even types of information not historically seen as potentially of military value, such as the study of environmental science (Doel 2003) and research on sea-floor hydrothermal vents (Oreskes 2003), was in fact driven by defense concerns, clouding our understanding of which types of knowledge are and are not of potential damage if diffused. And there have been times when citizens and U.S. corporations have voluntarily complied with government requests to limit flows of information on scientific and technological subjects, as happened with the atomic bomb (Laurence 1951).

Details of all current regulations restricting the export of information technology and of information can be found on the Web site of the Directorate of Defense Trade Controls of the U.S. Department of State (www.pmdstc.org).

Borders of Informational Systems

Political speech The analytical literature on denial of entry to the United States to foreign nationals because of their political beliefs is relatively sparse. Shapiro (1987) does provide a history of the closing of the U.S. border to individuals with whom there are political differences, and Shattuck (1986) provides a more general history of federal restrictions on the free flow of academic information and ideas.

Merelman (1988) offers a sociological analysis of efforts—often failed—to socialize aliens politically in the course of the immigration process. In his rereading of early First Amendment history, Rabban (1997) explores the impact of immigration on interpretations of free speech, and Passavant (2002) provides a history of the complexities of freedom of speech as applied to immigrants. Moschella (1995) looks at these complexities as they were generating fear among immigrants of prosecution for political speech within the courts. A flurry of publications appeared after U.S.-born Margaret Randall was threatened with deportation upon her return from Central America under the McCarran-Walter Act (Clasby 1989; Parry-Giles 1988; Scanlan 1988). The best information available on individuals currently being barred from entry into the U.S. on the basis of political speech is being collected by the nonprofit Federation of American Scientists.

Arms control treaties Though monitoring of weapons development and testing was suggested immediately after World War II as a means of preventing proliferation of nuclear arms, it was not until the mid-1980s that multilateral treaties were signed that incorporated such provisions. Techniques for verifying compliance with these agreements, often referred to as confidence- and security-building measures, therefore received their first intensive analysis during that decade. Discussions of the history and use of CSBMs are found in several sources best read in combination because of the diversity of perspectives and experiences found in different regions and using various techniques (Borawski 1986; Cohen 1990; Krehbiel 1989; Krepon and Umberger 1988; Tsipis, Hafemeister, and Janeway 1986). Various explanations were put forward for why the use of CSBMs should reduce conflict, including game theory (Brams and Davis 1987), cognitive theory (Levy 1983; Nicholson 1987), and extensions of international relations theory (Vasquez 1987). Critiques focused on the cost, the difficulty of logistical arrangements, and—from the U.S. side—questions about the constitutionality of these practices (Connolly 1988). Nongovernmental entities were also party to verification; Bruck (1988) describes the role of media, and Schrag (1989) documents the key role played by the Natural Resources Defense Council in breaking the gridlock over verification proposals. The analysis of information policy tools incorporated into arms control treaties as they stood in 1990 presented in the text summarizes research discussed in more detail in Braman (1990, 1991a, 1991b).

In the early 1990s, changed relations between the East and West drew attention away from arms control agreements, and the literature on verification accordingly dropped off. Instead, attention turned to the spread of nuclear materials to parties that are not official governments and, therefore, not signatory to treaties (Allison et al. 1996). Political scientists began to look at interactions between verification practices and domestic politics (Newmann 2001), and to experiment with theoretical lenses for understanding the diversity of approaches taken by governments to participation (Landau and Malz 2003). Sociologists of knowledge were interested in the ways certain scientific disciplines, such as seismology, were transformed by the infusion of funding (Barth 2003).

Early in the twenty-first century some historians and policy-makers remain optimistic about the potential of arms control verification (Graham 2002;

Kalinowski 2004; Krepon 2004), but others argue that Cold War-era approaches to arms control are seriously dated (Levi and O'Hanlon 2005) and point to limits. In some cases treaties have been abandoned (von Kries 2002). "Rogue states" and "outlaw regimes" will not be accountable to arms control treaties, making verification efforts useless (Newman 2004). As the experience in Iraq made painfully clear, the inapplicability of verification techniques for the chemical and biological weapons are increasingly of concern (Andemicael and Mathiason 2005; Deller and Burroughs 2003; Prelas and Peck 2005; Stern 2002). Logistical problems remain (Avenhaus and Kilgour 2004), and the organizational infrastructure for continuing verification activities must be redesigned given the overall restructuring of national security activities (Holum 2005). The use of remote sensing satellites has changed the technological context for verification protocols that had been developed in great detail for other technologies (Hettling 2003). Meanwhile, new techniques are being developed (Bellamy 2005; Committee on International Security and Arms Control 2005); financial auditing tools, for example, provide an alternative means of tracking down and investigating suspicious international arms transactions (Forden 2005).

The Stockholm International Peace Research Institute (2005) continues to publish an annual summarizing developments in this area, and the *Arms Control Reporter* provides much more daily detail on all pertinent activities.

Importing knowledge workers A number of histories of U.S. immigration policy and practices have focused on these policy tools as a means of shaping and controlling the U.S. labor force. Borjas (1999) and McClellan (1981) provide overarching histories, Daniels (2004) looks at immigration filters used since 1882, Calavita (1984) focuses on the period from 1820 to 1924, and Loescher and Scanlan (1986) describe the use of immigration filters in service to the economy from 1945–1985 as "calculated kindness." A documentary history of U.S. immigration and naturalization law can be found in LeMay and Barkan (1999). The claimed need for more high-skilled workers in recent years has drawn the attention of the U.S. government (Smith and Edmonston 1997) as well as of European governments (Tremblay 2005).

Debate over the extent to which the need for highly skilled workers for the information technology industries is real, rather than contrived to maximize corporate profits, has spawned a flurry of studies of the economic impact of temporary workers. A series of works by Lowell provides a panoramic overview of the range of interests at stake: in 1999, he edited a volume on various aspects of the issues raised by highly skilled temporary workers, in 2000 Lowell provided a succinct history of the practice of providing visas for temporary workers and of the debate over this practice, and in 2001 he reviewed the literature on the subject. Noting that the sizable increase in skilled workers since the Immigration Act of 1990 went into effect has raised the overall skill level of immigrants in the United States, Lowell makes clear that the nature of the effect of such workers on the labor force today is quite different from that of the past, when the impact of highly educated immigrants was largely felt within academia.

Zavodny (2003) provides a statistical analysis of the effects of the H-1B program on the information technology labor force. Hyde (2003) explores the human side of temporary workers in the same industries, concluding that in Silicon Valley, at least, H-1B workers are currently being abused and that making it easier for them to unionize should be among the policy responses. Vemeri (1999) points out that because it is impossible to really evaluate whether or not there is a labor shortage in any given industry using available data, the phrase "labor shortage" is used to refer to a number of different things and anecdotal evidence is often used to manipulate the category; the General Accounting Office (2003) similarly argues that we don't have the kinds of data needed to really evaluate the effects of the H-1B visa program. Watts (2001) agrees that the evidence of a domestic shortage of highly skilled labor for the information technology industries is inconclusive, and emphasizes the ways in which the H-1B visa in particular benefits the employer by binding individuals to a specific corporation. Espenshade (2001) demonstrates that the number of U.S. citizens in the highly skilled labor category is actually going up, though their salaries are going down.

8 Information Policy and Change

Theory

Any theory about the nature of society must implicitly or explicitly deal with the question of possible social change. Theories of technological change began to appear early in the twentieth century as economists and others struggled to understand the nature and effects of industrialization. Historians of the sociology of knowledge have offered theories of information change at least since World War II, and more recently the experiences of developing new information architectures and redesigning those that have previously existed have stimulated new thinking in this area.

Social change The concept of change runs throughout every branch of social theory, and almost everyone, at some time or another, weighs in. All of the ideas about social structure introduced in chapter 6 suggest, entail, or rely upon notions of social change. For functionalists, change is an adaptive response to a system's environment, often taking the form of functional differentiation in which one component will split into two new components, presumably to perform specialized functions more efficiently or well than the original single component. Change from structuralist perspective results from the transformation of relationships.

The wave of revolutions in the late eighteenth and mid-nineteenth centuries stimulated interest in political change, and political theory of the era, from liberalism to Marxism, dealt with processes of either incremental (normal) change or the necessity and justifications for revolutionary change. The notion of "adaptive politics" emerged in the late 1960s beginning with Rosenau's (1970) suggestion that political science could learn from the unit/environment relationship so important to social psychology. As with structural functionalism or first-order systems theorists, the goal of adaptation from this perspective is survival while keeping the essential structures within acceptable limits (Mouritzen 1988). Rosenau (1970) distinguished among four modes of adaptation based on the relative importance of responsiveness to their external and internal environments: responsiveness to both he referred to as "preservative," to the external environment only as "acquiescent," to the internal only as "intransigent," and to one's own value system only as "promotive." Most of Rosenau's later work on political adaptation (1990) dealt with consequences of adaptation once a mode has been chosen. There are different ways in which adaptation can be seen—as a decision (e.g., a specific foreign policy activity), a strategy (an enduring pattern of behavior, activity over a time span), a belief system (underlying particular activities, an orientation), or an outcome (of an activity). Agency could come from the state, the regime, or society at large. Gurr (1973) provides a review of relationships between theories of social change and of revolution as they had been presented up until the time of his writing. A systems-based approach to thinking about change in the nature of states was introduced by Almond (1963). Skocpol (1979) argued that the means by which states will change depends upon the outcomes sought and the structural conditions under which change takes place. Wittrock and Wagner (1990) categorize modes of change in states into modes of resource generation and resource appropriation, forms of institutional arrangements of the state apparatus proper, and genres of societal discourse. Changes in states can also be viewed from the international level, as Ikenberry does when he looks at interactions between state transformations and of the international economic system (1988), Cerny does in his analysis of the impact of globalization on change within nation-states (1995), and Chase-Dunn does in his examination of the role of the concept of hegemony in understanding social change (1994).

Mattei (1998) talks about different ways in which the law changes through his theory of legal formants, which are any legal proposition that affects the solution of a legal problem. These are not necessarily homogeneous, and it is useful to distinguish between operative rules (actually applied to solution of a given case) and definitions of principles (used by lawyers to explain their results). Competition among legal solutions spreads knowledge of legal rules, and legal transplants migrate legal propositions from one system to another, though these are often received without the texts upon which had been originally based. Competition to frame legal rules takes place not only in courts but also in the wide arena of legal culture. Legal pluralism is becoming more frequent today, with different sets of legal rules applying not only to different subjects, but also to the same subject as a result of differences in the context within which processes are unfolding. Since from an economic perspective transaction costs rise in direct proportion to the complexity of the legal situation, it may therefore be more useful to look at sectoral governance structures across states than at national frameworks for innovation when dealing with the most sophisticated information and communication technologies (Kim and Hart 1998).

Anthropologists have contributed to our understanding of social change with such ideas as the importance of role models in encouraging social change (Mead 1940) and the notion of cultural drift as a way of thinking about the fact that society is so complex that change may take place for reasons that may never be ascertained (Eggan 1963). Geertz (1957) turned to analysis of ritual as way of understanding social change even from within a functionalist or structuralist perspective with an essentially Platonic view of the relationship between that which changes and that which does not.

Ginsberg (1958) provides a snapshot of the thinking about social change mid-twentieth century with his emphasis on change as related to social structure and the need to be specific about the causal relations through which that change would come about. Despite Ryan's (1965) claim that the interest in structuralism and functionalism had slowed attention to social change for a period, there was a great deal of work developing theories of social change after World War II for purposes as diverse as understanding economic development, cultural change, and political mobilization. Another round of interest was triggered by the cultural and political social movements of the 1960s (Turner 1969).

It would seem obvious that social change should be analyzed as it unfolds over time (that is, diachronically), but under Saussure's ([1913] 1959) influence synchronic change, alterations in structures of relationships that exist at a single point in time, has also attracted interest. Eisenstadt's (1964) argument that institutional and societal differentiation and the evolution of social change are distinct axes along which movement may not occur in parallel provided further support for this position, as does Minkoff's (1997) argument that interdependence among organizations as well as population cycles are important for understanding successive stages of social movements. And while Foucault (in work cited previously) stimulated the important recent work on the discontinuities as well as the continuities of social change, Moore (1964) introduced this notion even earlier based on his realization that we are unable to predict rates of change, changes in direction, and the large-scale alterations and discontinuities typified by revolutions because of multiplier effects of innovations.

The distinction between epigenetic and genetic change (change across space as opposed to change across time) important to complex adaptive systems theory develops synchronic approaches more fully; this understanding of social change is particularly important in the analysis of informational power, because globalization, networked forms of organization, international harmonization of legal systems, and the use of data collected by global surveillance mechanisms have had such an impact on the exercise of power that the term "geopolitics" (the politics of geographically based power) is now often accompanied—or replaced—by the term "chronopolitics" (the politics of time-based power). Other contributions from complex adaptive systems theory to understanding social change include the importance of nonlinear as well as linear modes of causality and recognition of the fact that under nonlinear conditions, effects are not necessarily proportional to cause. Nor is it necessarily the case that the same cause will lead to the same effect across circumstances.

Additional dimensions of theories of change introduced since that time include the tension between understanding transformation processes metaphorically as opposed to empirically (Lenski 1976), at one extreme, and efforts to model social change mathematically (Land 1980), at the other. The range of approaches used today to study social movements include resource mobilization theory (Jenkins 1983), political generation and cohort replacement theory (Whittier 1997), pursuit of individual rights (Foweraker and Landman 1999), the effects of access to narrative space (Couto 1993), emotions (Jasper 1998), and commitment

(Gamson 1991). While network theory has only recently become fashionable, it was being introduced as a way of theorizing social movements at least as early as 1980 (Snow, Zurcher, and Ekland-Olson 1980), with Klanderman and Oegema (1987) distinguishing between the functions and effects of networks at different stages of the development of a movement and Rosenthal et al. (1985) providing a case study example of this type of analysis.

Tilly (1983) identified a number of ways in which ordinary people were able to express themselves politically without elections, surveys, or social movements, including repeated adoption of irreverent symbolism, use of public celebrations and assemblies to present grievances and demands, appeals to power patrons, representation of entire communities rather than special interests, appearance at sites of power, and use of authorities' normal means of action either by assuming the prerogative on behalf of the local community or through caricature. Zhao (1998) looks at the role of spatial restrictions in stimulating growth of networks, and Davis (1999)—starting from the position that theories of social change must be culturally specific—develops a theory of social movements based on various dimensions along which those who seek change are distanced from the state. Melucci (1996) offers the most fully developed argument of the popular view that identity rather than class is most likely to instigate social change today, and even those who sustain an interest in class, such as Kolankiewicz (1996), incorporate contemporary notions of social capital and networks into their analyses.

In a piece with a surprisingly contemporary feel, House looked at interactions between social trends and developments in social theory in 1928. Scientific research itself can be a trigger to change. For a recent review of thinking about interactions between research on social movements and changes in the field of sociology, see Fuchs and Plass (1999). Nissel (1995) reviews twenty-five years of analysis of social change from a statistical perspective, discussing the effect that available statistics have on our perceptions of the nature and direction of social change.

Charles H. Cooley linked biological and social change with the influence of communication upon the process in 1897, predecessor to development of the ideas that led to appreciation of the social construction of reality. It was of course the possibility that deliberate uses of communication might stimulate social change that initially led to government funding for research on communication early in the twentieth century, and that belief has continued to provide much of the motor for that field; theories of persuasion and communication campaigns can all be considered theories of social change. Contemporary work from a political science perspective that emphasizes the role of information and communication in social change includes work on information gaps (Deng 1997) and cascades (Lohmann 1994).

The assumption that deliberate action on the part of the state could effect social change via legal decision-making underlies many of the activities of the bureaucratic state. Woodrow Wilson ([1887] 1955), in a work that also identified several areas in which policy-makers needed to know more about information creation, processing, flows, and use in order to govern well, articulated this position when he commented that whoever wants to effect a change in modern constitutional government must first educate fellow citizens to want change at all, and then identify the specific changes sought. The opposite view was put forward by William Graham Sumner (1840–1910), who argued in 1907 that it was useless to believe that law could change behavior, because it cannot affect societal norms based on beliefs, perceptions, and emotions (Ball, Simpson, and Ikeda 1962). Still, many twentieth-century legal programs were designed to do just that, as in efforts to end racial segregation (Tumin and Rotberg 1957). Dror (1976) contrasts the use of cost-benefit analysis to choose from existing policy alternatives and enlargement of the set of policy alternatives by innovation, which is by definition extrarational and creative. Empirical research that focuses on the variables that shape the actual degrees of innovation in policy alternatives provide an interface among descriptive, explanatory, and prescriptive policy studies. Possible innovative methods might include systematic utilization of the experiences of working policy-makers, consultative participation, reprocessing of historic data with modern policy-making models, and shared experimentation.

Gouldner (1976) suggests that those who are outside normal politics use ideological innovation and adaptation to mobilize change forces since successful ideological projections may circumvent existing political institutions even without mainstream skills, connections, or resources. Specific individuals may be responsible for effecting change in political institutions, as Haas (1990) notes in his analysis of international organizations.

"New" social movement theory, reviewed by Pichardo (1997), argues that social change today operates differently from how it has in earlier eras, but critiques of this argument (D'Anieri, Ernst, and Kier 1990) make the point that that perception most probably stems from inadequately rich or sensitive analyses of change under other conditions. The four reasons Boudon (1983) put forward two decades ago for the failure of theories about social change to be predictively useful still hold: a belief that the social structure is more coherent than it actually is, the assumption that it is possible to find nomological generalizations across always-unique social circumstances, the belief that only structural features are pertinent to understanding social change, and the assumption that it is not only possible to identify which features of social life are responsible for change but also that the same features are always so responsible.

Technological change The extent and speed of technological change present particular challenges to social theories, however; it is the inability of regime theory to cope with this type of change, for example, that leads Strange (1982) to reject regime analysis. While they often reference each other and sometimes conflate processes, the literatures on invention, innovation, and diffusion are distinct, and only that on innovation is discussed here. Invention, which deals with the development of new ideas and thus might be considered a subset of theories of informational change, is the stage of the process that involves informational change, and diffusion, which is the process by which individuals, groups, and societies take up and use new technologies, is a matter of social change.

Mokyr (1990) has produced the best single-volume introduction to the range of theories about technological change that is accessible to those without a specialized background in either technologies or economics. He defines innovation as the process by which new technological information is developed, and technological change takes place whenever technological information resources are either created or destroyed, or when the availability of those resources changes in the economy. Societal factors that affect innovation include labor scarcity, demand, intellectual property rights, war, path dependency, technological drift, institutions, demography, geography, evolution, attitudes towards change, religious factors, values, politics, and state priorities. Individual-level factors of importance include life expectancy, nutrition, and willingness to bear risk. Economists think about the stimulation of growth and factor substitution, institutional theorists focus on the role of organizations and market design in stimulating innovation, cultural analysts and sociologists focus on the social factors that are likely to lead to innovation and on the processes by which new technologies are taken up, and policy analysts think about incentives. For a review of the history of economic thinking about technological change in more depth, see Dosi (1997). Roland (1992) identifies conceptual similarities underlying semantic differences across the disciplines and schools of thought that deal with technological change.

Theories about technological change began to appear in the nineteenth century, the period which saw, as van Creveld (1991) puts it, the invention of invention. Technological change was a tempting answer to the problem of the "residual," the part of economic growth that can't be explained by more capital or more labor. An overview of theories of economic change can be found in the collection edited by North and Mokyr (2005). Marx, of course, dealt with technology indirectly as a means of production, but had little to say about innovation itself. Kondratiev (1998), however, took advantage of the fact that for the first time in history longitudinal economic data were available, and identified long "waves" of economic cycles (now known as Kondratiev waves) each launched by the appearance of a key new technology. Blaug (1997) and Landreth and Colander (2001) introduce Kondratiev and the influence his work has had on economic thought.

Schumpeter (1911), probably the single most important writer on technological change, took up this insight and elaborated on what it meant for innovation to be the driving force of the economy. For Schumpeter, an innovation was defined as something that causes a disturbance to the economic equilibrium that would have been impossible to achieve by incremental change; famously, innovations that have this effect cause "creative destruction" of former ways of doing things. In a manner presaging contemporary thinking, for Schumpeter an innovation did not have to be a technology but could be a new way of doing any number of things, from serving as a supply source to organizing an industry.

This insight was followed by a number of efforts to figure out what led to the innovations that triggered such economic growth. The 1950s saw a series of studies on relationships between technological change and economic growth (Mansfield 1988); Solow won a Nobel Prize during this period for his work suggesting a means of quantifying technological change; for his current thinking on this topic, see Solow (2004). Burns (1960) began to look at what it would take for an organization to sustain an innovation stream. Vernon (1966) suggested a product life cycle theory that provided an explanation for the growth of multinational corporations as a means of diffusing innovations while simultaneously minimizing the costs of production and distribution at various stages in the diffusion and adoption of a new technology. There were other economic arguments for the position that innovation takes place only in response to economic need, but there were also critiques, notably that needs are ubiquitous and often there is no innovation (Kline and Rosenberg 1986; Scazzieri 1993).

The work by Dosi et al. in 1988—sometimes described as "neo-Schumpeterian"—was thus seen as a breakthrough. In his contribution to this volume, Dosi put forth the idea of "technological paradigms," which include the social context, the knowledge base, and the specific materials and technologies that will be used to generate an innovation. The Freeman and Perez (1988) contribution to the concept of a techno-economic paradigm emphasized the interrelation between product and process innovations and the argument that a combination of technical, organizational, and managerial innovation can lead to quantum leaps in economic productivity. For this group, the characteristics of innovation include a fundamental element of uncertainty, increasing reliance on the growth of scientific knowleddge; on the trend away from individual innovators and towards organizations, because of the increasing complexity of research and innovative activities; on the importance of tacit knowledge and of practice to innovation; and on the fact that technical change is a cumulative activity. Sternberg (1992) discusses photonics as an example of this type of technological paradigm. Others from backgrounds as diverse as military history (van Creveld 1991) and philosophy (Ellul [1954] 1964) add that technology is also a philosophical system or, as Nelson (1987) put it, epistemological in nature.

Innovation has been recognized as its own subfield within information economics since at least 1980 (Machlup 1980). Technology defines the limits of the set of products and processes potentially available in an economy at any given time. Innovation is recognized as so important to the economy today that, as Monk (1992) put it, the distribution of wealth now includes access to knowledge and information, with technology itself defined as information. Research over the last couple of decades shows that those industry groups that are most R&D-intensive account for a disproportionate share of U.S. exports, and that the level of national innovative efforts as measured by patents in the United States also was correlated with economic success at the state level (Scherer 1992). How to best encourage it, however, is still unclear. This matters, because as Arrow (1962) pointed out, without incentives a society will underinvest in innovation, because the results can't be predicted and because the private rates of return don't equal public rates of return. Still, as North put it, "if you want to realize the potential of modern technology you cannot do with the state, but you cannot do without it either" (1984, p. 260).

There appears to be a zone within which some competition is a stimulus, but too much is discouraging. There is a role for government in providing incentives, but if the government plays too much of a role, it can prevent innovation as work becomes limited to established formats (Simpson 2004). Increasingly, it appears, innovation is most likely to emerge when intellectual property rights are shared and efforts are collaborative across organizational and even national boundaries (Dodgson 1993; Grabher 1993; Hilpert 1992; Kanter 1991), but the network benefits of existing technological systems are part of their sunk cost that prevents the market from taking up small innovations if they are not compatible with those already in use. There has been an explosion in the number of experiments with the design of institutions specifically to promote innovation over the last few decades, but few of these efforts have worked; Massey, Quintas, and Wield (1992), for example, review the efforts to achieve this goal with science parks. Research and development are now globalized, but innovation often emerges at a higher rate in areas with dense industry-specific concentrations of personnel (Pioreand Sabel 1986). Collaboration and coordination among firms are valuable, but the vitality of industrial districts depends in part on the quality of conflict resolution processes (Sabel 1991). Even in capital-intensive industries subject to economies of scale, radical innovations can still be developed that offer a temporary advantage to the smaller firm; without these advantages, such radical innovations may take place more slowly at the smaller firm, if at all (Swann and Gill 1993). Increasingly, innovation takes place within corporations, but practices that successfullly lead to innovation often run counter to traditional corporate practice, because of the extent to which individuals must be allowed to have independence (McCurdy 1993). Organizations want to plan innovation processes, but Bastien and Hostager (1988) use the metaphor of jazz to describe the turbulent and only marginally predictable behaviors that actually lead to innovation.

There are a number of very interesting current trends. By changing the ways in which we conduct research, with mathematical screening now taking the place of laboratory experiments in many fields, the very nature of the innovation process is changing. The role of the user in innovation is receiving attention (Lundvall 1993; von Hippel 1988), as is the possibility that innovation can emerge from community experimentation as well as from professional efforts (Qvortrup 1988). Evolutionary views that first appeared during the nineteenth century have been revived with parallels between the development of new ideas and mutations on genetic information, with some suggesting that R&D could be treated as an economic proxy for species (Sedjo and Simpson 1995). In the economically, politically, and intellectually significant area of biotechnology, it can be difficult to distinguish between inventions and discoveries. Increasingly, it is recognized that not all technological innovation brings progress; as Freudenberg and Gramling (1992) put it, even new technologies that appear to be functional for a particular community in the short term may be dysfunctional in the long term. Nelson and Winter (2000) stress the value of routines in the innovation process, and Kay and Willman (1993) stress that it is more important to have a permanent strategy of change than a particular structural context.

Pointing out that it is often difficult to maintain a clear distinction between actual technological innovations and diffusion and use practices, Wright (1997) argues that more historical work needs to be done to fully understand innovation and diffusion processes. And in another link between technological structures and informational structures, it is now recognized that many innovations stem from increasingly precise measurements (Beaumont 1994). The depth of impact of a technology is determined by how great a transformation is that occurs within a single sector; and its breadth by how many sectors are affected (Krimsky 1991).

Change in information systems There are a variety of ways in which the arts are understood to be related to change in information systems, either directly or indirectly. This is again an area in which informational, technological, and social systems are intertwined, for art that has social impact often includes all three dimensions and it may be due to informational and technological developments that art at times does influence society.

The arts are perceived to be innovative in a number of dimensions that are important for political change, including memetic (Brook 2004), conceptual (Galenson 2005), and intellectual (Peach 2004). For some, art is political action in itself (Askew 2003; Rosler 2004); Martin-Barbero (1988, 1993), for example, documents artistic practices intended to have political effect in Latin America in the last decades of the twentieth century. Peach (2004) describes the arts as a public sphere in which it is possible to engage in abstract and cultural discourse about political matters, observing and experiencing political life in ways not otherwise available. There are theories of "aestheticized politics," but Wheeler (2002) suggests that it is the autonomy (or semblance of autonomy) of the practice of art that is most effective in providing a hopeful model of politics. Interestingly, a study of the relationship between participation in group activities and democratic engagement in eleven European countries shows differences by type of social group, with those participating in arts-related groups ranking the highest in political participation (Bowler, Donovan, and Hanneman 2003).

Art can also serve as an inspiration to political action, though there is some disagreement over whether successful stimulation derives largely from the content or artworks or from the aesthetic or technical innovations involved (Carroll 2002). Art can be a de facto cause of social change, as when arts-rich neighborhoods contribute to urban development (Lloyd 2002) or artisans either use crafts to construct an economic niche for themselves (Colloredo-Mansfeld 2002) or, more negatively, are forced into this position by others in an exploitative manner (Carruthers 2001). In some cases, the details of the personal circumstances of the artist throw light on general political problems (Shane 2004). In recent years, it has been more common to encounter artists who are also literal politicians (Street 2002) and artists who use the legal system as found material for art (Klein and Russ 2001). The complexities of political stances by certain artistic movements, however, can lead those involved to critique or reject work with which they are aesthetically in line (Rasmussen 2004).

Artistic innovations now being analyzed and borrowed as models for innovation in other areas, including organizations (Bastien and Hostager 1988) and products (Kamoche and Cunha 2001; Plautz 2005). The arts have also become linked to contemporary ideas about knowledge production. The journal *Leonardo* provides ongoing analysis of the ways art as praxis and artworks are forms of knowing. Historical and critical work looks at interactions between artists and scientists in the past, as in Holton's (2001) analysis of the reliance of visual artist Marcel Duchamp (1887–1968) on the work of mathematician Henri Poincaré (1854–1912).

Information Policy and Change in Social Systems

Freedom of speech versus national security Most of the sources useful in understanding the tension between the constitutional bias toward protection of freedom of speech and the need to protect national security are found in the bibliographic essay accompanying chapter 4, particularly in the section dealing with the constitutional distinction between the communicative space of peace and that of war. Chafee's 1941 book, *Free Speech in the United States*, is a classic presentation of the argument from the free speech side. Redish (1982) examines critiques of the clear and present danger test and concludes that, while the test is not perfect, it is the best means available of evaluating whether to treat advocacy as lawful because it provides a means of incorporating the context within which speech takes place into evaluations. Recent work includes analyses of means of achieving censorship that fall outside the classical definition, including cultural approaches (Post 1998), private sector actions (Soley 2002), the threat of liability charges (McCraw 2000), and use of contractual arrangements for access to the Internet as a means of controlling speech (Braman and Lynch 2003). In the Homeland Security environment interactions between free speech and the dissemination of scientific information have gotten more complex (Salyers 2002), and the academic environment has become more fraught (Strauss 2004). There is increasing interest in economic theories of censorship (Brennan 1992b; Sidak 2004), and empirical work on incidents of censorship continues (e.g., Harer and Harris 1994).

The vote Electronic voting machines present the most deeply contended election issues in the early twenty-first century. The run-up to the current situation took several decades: the first governmental analysis of electronic voting machines was a 1975 report jointly produced by the National Bureau of Standards and the Office of Federal Elections of the Government Accounting Office, and political scientists first evaluated the computational aspects of voting shortly thereafter (Campbell 1977). The presidential election of 2000 was of course a turning point for the turn to electronic voting machines (Hayduk and Mattson 2002; Rakove 2001; Watson 2004).

Yang and Gaines (2004) analyze laws dealing with electronic voting machines, and Coggins (2004) does the same for laws and practices dealing with independent testing of these voting systems. A 2001 report by the Federal Elections Commission provides a history of the development of standards for the design and testing of electronic voting machines. Celeste, Thornburgh, and Lin (2005) have collected papers produced for the National Research Council in the course of its analysis of issues raised by the use of any type of electronic device that plays or could play an important role in any part of the voting system, from voter registration to ballot casting to final certification of election results. A 2001 report from the National Commission on Federal Election Reform detailed the types of technologies and ballot designs used in that election and types of federal iniatives—legislative and otherwise—that might be needed to redress the problems.

Brazil was the first country to hold an all-electronic national election (Riebeek 2002).

Concern over the possibility that the use of computerized voting machines would increase the possibility of fraud also preceded the 2000 election and debates that have followed. In response to the possibility that New York would take up such machines in the early 1990s, for example, Mercuri (1992) synthesized analyses of a wide range of potential means of tampering with computerized votes—as well as the concern that the voting machines of that era presented themselves as mechanical, not electronic, and thus might deceive voters. Since the 2000 election, concern about possible flaws in electronic voting machines have risen. A 2005 Government Accountability Office report documented vulnerabilities in electronic voting machines in use; failures that have already occurred during elections; and problems with implementation of voluntary standards, testing, and federal efforts to improve voting system security. It turns out that the outcome of an election can be changed by manipulating one vote per voting machine through software manipulations (Di Franco et al. 2004). There are usability issues (Herrnson et al. 2005), concerns that the elderly will be put off if asked to use a new voting technology (Roseman and Stephenson 2005), and socioeconomic questions raised by the strong correlation between county income and the take-up of computerized voting (Garner and Spolaore 2005). The nonprofit organization Verified Voting Foundation (www.verifiedvoting.org) provides ongoing news about, results of research on, and details of litigation involving electronic voting.

Miller (2001) presents the counterargument that voting machines could improve the quality of elections by standardizing procedures. Other positive benefits have been discovered. Nichols and Strizek (1995), for example, have found that the use of such equipment reduces ballot roll-off (the practice of voting for those candidates at the top of the ticket), and a study by Tomz and Van Houweling (2003) showed that use of electronic voting machines cuts the black-white gap in invalid ballots by a factor of ten.

The possibility of electronically voting from a distance presents different issues (Birch and Watt 2004). Studies have shown that U.S. citizens have been quite interested in this possibility for a while (Beachboard, McClure, and Bertot 1997), though Carey and Sims (1976) warned long ago that the potential for electronic democracy in this form should not be overstated because the vote itself is only one among many steps in decision-making processes that are also importantly dependent on the quality of public discourse. Differences in electronic voting practices and attitudes across thirteen European countries demonstrate the impact of existing institutional frameworks on Internet voting (Svensson and Leenes 2003). Dyck and Gimpel (2005) have been able to demonstrate, however, that Internet voting does increase the likelihood that those who live at a distance from polling places would vote.

Debate over and experimentation with electronic voting takes place with a long history of struggles over the right to vote in the United States; see Keyssar (2000) and Rogers and Scriabine (1992) for social, cultural, and political dimensions of this history; Rusk (2001) for a legal history; and Zelden (2002) for documentation of battles over voting rights in the courts. Mitchell (1992) and

Lehoucq (2003) explore the history of tampering with ballots, emphasizing the wide range of techniques available and the sensitivity of choices regarding those techniques to political inequality and the relative importance of various political institutions at any given historical conjuncture. Meanwhile, gerrymandering—the redrawing of voting districts in order to favor particular parties or candidates—remains such a problem that Issacharoff (2002) describes the current situation as a morass.

Information Policy and Change in Technological Systems

Direct funding of research For details of federal funding for research across agencies and overviews of what shifts in funding priorities mean for the sciences, see the Web site of the American Association for the Advancement of Science (www.aaas.org). The AAAS journal, *Science*, provides ongoing analysis and discussion of federal funding for research. The Web site for each funding agency also provides details regarding budget figures, funding trends, and research priorities; see, for example, the Web site of the National Science Foundation (www.nsf.gov) and of the National Institutes of Health (www.nih.gov). There is some discussion of increasing the efficiency of government funding of research by coordinating R&D across government departments in a form of "virtual agency" of the government (Castro et al. 2001). Current concerns include the movement of scientists around the globe in response to funding trends (Goth 2005), transformations of public universities as they become ever-more-reliant on outside research funds for survival (Tuunainen 2005), use of research publications as a performance indicator for government funding of science (Druss and Marcus 2005), and exploration of how the postnormal science goal of involving citizens in decisions about research funding might be accomplished (O'Donnell and Entwistle 2004).

Tax credits Patents, discussed earlier, are the oldest technique the U.S. government has used to try to stimulate research and development. The use of tax credits is a relatively recent policy tool that serves the same goal. Fischer and Black (1979) argued for use for tax incentives to stimulate research as a more effective incentive than simply providing research funds. Subsequently, Bozeman and Link (1985) presented arguments in favor; Eisner (1984) offered arguments against (he remained a skeptic—see Eisner [1998]); and Bortnick (1986), of the Congressional Research Service, summarized the pros and cons of this policy tool for the U.S. government. Hines (1993) was able to show that tax incentives did encourage multinationals to stay in the United States, and by 1994 the International Bank for Reconstruction and Development had become a supporter of the use of this policy technique. A longitudinal study of the use of tax incentives for R&D across a number of countries did show that they were successful in increasing the amount of research undertaken; Bloom, Griffith, and Van Reenen (2002) concluded that a 10 percent drop in the cost of R&D stimulates over a 1 percent rise in the level of R&D in the short run and under under a 10 percent rise in R&D in the long run. State-level tax credits for R&D also affect the location of firms within the United States (Wilson 2005). Support for continuation of tax credits for R&D comes from continued evidence that otherwise there is underinvestment in R&D (Hall 2002) and from comparative study of what has worked and what has not across a number of countries (Heath 2002).

Procurement As a subject of scholarly research, government procurement processes are a bit like the field of public relations—enormously influential, often described, but relatively little studied. The U.S. government, however, has long been the largest customer for telecommunications technologies in the United States, and probably in the world (Leeson 1984). There is a Web site devoted to requests for proposals, analysis of procurement trends, and related news in the area of information technology, Government Computer News (at www.gcn.org). Greenstein (1995) compared the results of sole sourcing as opposed to competitive bidding for government mainframe computers, and the authors in Johnston (1990) track changes in information technology procurement practices in the United States over time. In 1986, for example, the OMB published its first five-year plan for acquiring computing and telecommunications equipment in a deliberate effort to spur competition by providing advanced planning to industry.

The nature of procurement processes changed in the last couple of decades of the twentieth century because instead of simply issuing contracts the U.S. government began to bargain with the corporations that serve as vendors, which Lawton (1997) argues is a clear sign of a decline in state autonomy. The proportion of the Department of Defense budget that goes to support R&D is so large that van Nostrand (1994) describes the process of defense procurement as itself a means of producing knowledge. President Nixon tried to use procurement practices as a means of improving the quality of consumer goods when he suggested, in Executive Order 11566 (1970) that all the documents produced by the federal government in the course of procuring consumer products be made public.

Discussions about including trade in services under international trade agreements brought the fact that government procurement practices also function as non-tariff trade barriers. Telecommunications was among the industries in which this was a real problem (Bruce 1983; Cowhey 1990). There is a tension between policies that put export controls in place and yet simultaneously seek access to the markets of other countries (National Academy of Sciences 1987). There are other areas in which procurement practices have surprising effects. It has been difficult for the U.S. government to gather information about tribal cultural practices, for example, because doing so would fall under federal procurement laws; tribes have been resistant to sharing information that would then become the property of the government (Ruppert 1994).

Information Policy and Change in Information Systems

The types of change in access to government information discussed in this section of the text also rely on the references to government information systems cited earlier in these essays.

Direct funding for the arts is only one of the panoply of policy tools governments can use to discourage, encourage, or channel the arts. For an extraordinarily rich analysis of the interplay of the range of policy tools as applied to multiple different art forms under changing political circumstances, see Forgacs's (1990) history of cultural policy in Italy over a hundred-year-period. Bennett (1995) goes so far as to define culture as a field that is "intrinsically governmental," created not by artists, practices, or communities, but as inscribed in government programs. The concept of ongoing government support for the arts is a twentieth-century phenomenon (Slavin 1995) that, in the United States, received a big impetus from a speech by President Kennedy in 1963 stressing the value of the artist's individual vision to the nation. Some funding for the arts comes from other budgets, such as education (Greene 2000).

A 2000 report from the National Endowment for the Arts provides a year-by-year history of its policy developments, funding programs, and funding levels; data since publication of that report can be found on the agency's Web site (www.nea.gov). Most research on this funding, and its effects, is descriptive, as in a study of impressions of government funding from state and jurisdictional art agencies (Mankin et al. 2001), a review of the ways changes in the nature of funding affects the kinds of services offered by nonprofit arts organizations (Hughes and Luksetich 2004), and a discussion of the growth in local government support of arts and culture in municipalities that link such support to other social needs (Gray 2002). Data from social science research about the arts that have policy relevance are available from the Cultural Policy & the Arts National Data Archive (CPANDA) Web site (www.cpanda.org).

Some more theoretically rich, and sometimes critical, analysis of the social processes behind and generated by government funding for the arts has appeared. Howard (2004) argues that the U.S. government used its support for the arts during the Cold War as a means of reinforcing cultural boundaries. Brooks (2001) draws upon survey research to identify predictors of opposition to government support, which include income, political views, gender, and region of residence, but also varies with level of government involved and extent of funding. The political tensions over arts funding that began in the 1980s was inevitable, since the arts professionals who make funding decisions have views that diverge significantly from those of the general population (Lewis and Brooks 2005). Milyo and Oh (2004), on the other hand, link the extent of social capital to public support for arts funding. Heathorn (2005) uses a war memorial as a case through which to explore the tension over whether governments should support artists—rather than the soldiers actually involved—to create a monument important from the perspective of national identity. Demands for the repatriation of cultural property, such as requests for the return of tribal material from museums to the descendants of those who created the objects, demonstrate how linkages between cultural identity and artistic artifacts complicate governmental support for the arts via acquisition (Glass 2004). Use of the methods and materials of science, as in the creation of a transgenic animal as a piece of art by Eduardo Kac, introduces new First Amendment issues that may also have an impact on funding in the future (Nahmod 2001).

References

Abbate, Janet. 1999. *Inventing the Internet*. Cambridge, MA: MIT Press.

Abell, Peter. 1977. The many faces of power and liberty: Revealed preference, autonomy, and teleological explanation. *Sociology* 11(1): 3–24.

Abernathy, Kathleen Q. 2001. Speech to the Wireless Communication Alliance, June 25.

Abler, Ronald. 1977. The telephone and the evolution of the American metropolitan system. In Ithiel de Sola Pool, ed., *Social impact of the telephone*, 318–341. Cambridge, MA: MIT Press.

Abrams, D., R. M. Baecker, and M. Chignell. 1998. Information archiving with bookmarks: Personal Web space construction and organization. In *Proceedings of the CHI '98 Conference*, 41–48. New York: ACM Press.

Abu-Laban, Yasmeen, and Judith A. Garber. 2005. The construction of the geography of immigration as a policy problem. *Urban Affairs Review* 40(4): 520–562.

Acheson, Keith, and Christopher Maule. 1994. International regimes for trade, investment, and labour mobility in the cultural industries. *Canadian Journal of Communication* 19(3–4): 149–169.

Ackerman, Bruce. 1984. *Reconstructing American law*. Cambridge, MA: Harvard University Press.

Ackleson, Jason. 2003a. Directions in border security research. *The Social Science Journal* 40(4): 573–581.

Ackleson, Jason. 2003b. Securing through technology? "Smart borders" after September 11. *Knowledge Technology & Policy* 16(1): 56–75.

Adelman, Howard. 2002. Canadian borders and immigration post 9/11. *International Migration Review* 36(1): 15–29.

Agre, Philip E. 1999. The architecture of identity: Embedding privacy in market institutions. *Information, Communication and Society* 2(1): 1–25.

Agre, Philip, and Marc Rotenberg, eds. 1998. *Technology and privacy: The new landscape*. Cambridge, MA: MIT Press.

Aharoni, Y. 1993. Globalization of professional business services. In Y. Aharoni, ed., *Coalitions and competition: The globalization of business services*, 1–19. New York: Routledge.

Ahlqvist, O. 2005. Using uncertain conceptual spaces to translate between land cover categories. *International Journal of Geographic Information Science* 19(7): 831–857.

Akdeniz, Yaman. 2000. New privacy concerns: ISPs crime prevention and consumers' rights. *International Review of Law, Computers and Technology* 14(1): 55–61.

Alavi, H. 1972. The state in post-colonial societies. *New Left Review* 74.

Aldrich, Richard W. 2000. How do you know you are at war in the information age? *Houston Journal of International Law* 22(2): 223–264.

Aleinikoff, T. Alexander, and Douglas Klusmeyer, eds. 2002. *Citizenship today: Global perspectives and practices*. Washington, DC: Carnegie Endowment for International Peace.

Alford, Robert, and Roger Friedland. 1985. *Powers of theory*. New York: Cambridge University Press.

Allen, David S., and Robert Jensen, eds. 1995. *Freeing the First Amendment: Critical perspectives on freedom of expression*. New York: New York University Press.

Allison, Graham. 1971. *Essence of decision: Explaining the Cuban missile crisis*. Boston: Little, Brown.

Allison, Graham T., Owen R. Coté, Jr., Richard A. Falkenrath, and Steven E. Miller. 1996. *Avoiding nuclear anarchy: Containing the threat of loose Russian nuclear weapons and fissile material*. Cambridge, MA: MIT Press.

Almond, Gabriel A. 1963. Political systems and political change. *American Behavioral Scientist* 6(6): 3–10.

Almond, Gabriel A. 1983. Corporatism, pluralism, and professional memory. *World Politics* 35(2): 245–260.

Almond, Gabriel A., and Sidney Verba. 1963. *The civic culture*. Princeton, NJ: Princeton University Press.

Altbach, Philip G., and Robert Oliver Berdahl. 2005. *American higher education in the twenty-first century: Social, political, and economic challenges*. Baltimore, MD: Johns Hopkins University Press.

Althusser, Louis. 1984. *Essays on ideology*. London: Verso.

Altman, M., K. MacDonald, and M. McDonald. 2005. From crayons to computers: The evolution of computer use in redistricting. *Social Science Computer Review* 23(3): 334–346.

Alvarez, Robert. 1995. The Mexican-U.S. border: The making of an anthropology of borderlands. *Annual Review of Anthropology* 24: 447–470.

Amani, Bita, and Rosemary Coombe. 2005. The Human Genome Diversity Project: The politics of patents at the intersection of race, religion, and research ethics. *Law & Policy* 27(1): 152–188.

American Library Association (ALA). [1973] 1981. *Policy on governmental intimidation.* Available at www.ala.org/ala/oif/statementspols/otherpolicies/governmentalintimidation.pdf. Washington, DC: American Library Association.

Amponsah, Peter Nkrumah. 2004. *Libel law, political criticism, and defamation of public figures: The United States, Europe, and Australia.* New York: LFB Scholarly Publishing LLC.

Amsterdam, Anthony G., and Jerome Bruner. 2000. On categories. In *Minding the law*, 19–53. Cambridge, MA: Harvard University Press.

Andemicael, Berhanykun, and John Mathiason. 2005. *Eliminating weapons of mass destruction: Prospects for effective international verification.* Houndsmills, UK: Palgrave Macmillan.

Anderson, Benedict. 1983. *Imagined communities: Reflections on the origin and spread of nationalism.* New York: Shocken Books.

Anderson, David A. 1975. The selective impact of libel law. *Columbia Journalism Review* 14(1): 38.

Anderson, Margo J. 1988. *The American census: A social history.* New Haven, CT: Yale University Press.

Anderson, Margo J., and Stephen E. Fienberg. 1999. *Who counts? The politics of census-taking in contemporary America.* New York: Russell Sage Foundation.

Anderson, Margo J., and Stephen E. Fienberg. 2001. To sample or not to sample? The 2000 census controversy. *The Journal of Interdisciplinary History* 32(1): 1–37.

Andreas, Peter, and Timothy Snyder. 2002. *The wall around the West: State borders and immigration controls in North America and Europe.* Lanham, MD: Rowman and Littlefield.

Angelova, Galia. 2005. Language technologies meet ontology acquisition. In Dau Fritjhof, Marie-Laure Mugnier, and Gerd Stunne, eds., *Conceptual structures for sharing knowledge*, 367–380. Berlin: Springer.

Antonelli, Cristiano. 1981. *Transborder data flows and international business: A pilot study.* Paris: OECD, Division for Science, Technology and Industry, DSTI/ICCP/81.16.

Antonelli, Cristiano, ed. 1992. *The economics of information networks.* Amsterdam: North-Holland.

Appadurai, Arjun. 1993. Consumption, duration, and history. In D. Palumbio-Liu and H. U. Gumbrecht, eds., *Streams of cultural capital: Transnational cultural studies*, 23–46. Stanford, CA: Stanford University Press.

Archer, Margaret S. 1982. Morphogenesis versus structuration: On combining structure and action. *The British Journal of Sociology* 33(4): 455–483.

Archer, Margaret S. 1988. Towards theoretical unification: Structure, culture and morphogenesis. In *Culture and agency: The place of culture in social theory*, 274–307. New York: Cambridge University Press.

Arenas, Frank B. 2003. Cyberspace jurisdiction and the implications of Sealand. *Iowa Law Review* 88(5): 1165–1204.

Armstrong, Elizabeth. 1990. *Before copyright: The French book-privilege system, 1498–1526.* Cambridge: Cambridge University Press.

Arnold, Gregory T. 1995. Bordering on unreasonableness? The Third Circuit again expands the border search exception in *United States v. Hyde. Villanova Law Review* 40(3): 835–868.

Aron, Raymond. 1965. *Main currents in sociological thought.* New York: Penguin Books.

Arquilla, John, and David Ronfeldt. 1999. *The emergence of noopolitik: Toward an American information strategy.* Santa Monica, CA: Rand Corporation.

Arquilla, John, and David Ronfeldt, eds. 2001. *Networks and netwars: The future of terror, crime, and militancy.* Santa Monica, CA: Rand Corporation.

Arrow, Kenneth. 1957. Statistics and economic policy. *Econometrica* 25(4): 523–531.

Arrow, Kenneth J. 1962. Economic welfare and the allocation of resources for innovation. In Richard R. Nelson, ed., *The rate and direction of innovative activity,* 609–626. Princeton, NJ: Princeton University Press.

Arrow, Kenneth. 1969. Classificatory notes on the production and transmission of technological knowledge. *The American Economic Review* 59(2): 29–35.

Arzberger, P. P. Schroeder, A. Beaulieu, G. C. Bowker, K. Casey, L. Laaksonen, D. Moorman, P. Uhlir, and P. Wouters. 2004. An international framework to promote access to data. *Science* 303: 1777–1778.

Askew, K. M. 2003. As Plato duly warned: Music, politics, and social change in coastal East Africa. *Anthropological Quarterly* 76(4): 609–637.

Association of College and Research Libraries. 2005. *Colleges, code, and copyright: The impact of digital networks and technological controls on copyright and the dissemination of information in higher education.* Chicago: Association of College and Research Libraries.

Atinc, T., A. Behnain, A. Cornford, R. Glasgow, H. Skipper, and A. Yusuf. 1984. International transactions in services and economic development. *Trade and Development* 5: 141–273.

Aufderheide, Patricia. 1987. Universal service: Telephone policy in the public interest. *Journal of Communication* 37(1): 81–96.

Aufderheide, Patricia. 1999. *Communications policy and the public interest: The Telecommunications Act of 1996.* New York: Guilford Press.

Avenhaus, R., and D. M. Kilgour. 2004. Efficient distributions of arms-control inspection effort. *Naval Research Logistics* 51(1): 1–27.

Ayers, Irene Segal. 1999. The "facts" of cultural reality: Redrawing the line between fact and expression in copyright law. *University of Cincinnati Law Review* 67: 563–586.

Bachi, Roberto. 1999. *New methods of geostatistical analysis and graphical presentation: Distributions of populations over territories.* New York: Kluwer Academic and Plenum Publishers.

Bachrach, Peter, and Morton Baratz. 1963. Decisions and non decisions: An analytical framework. *American Political Science Review* 57(3): 632–642.

Badie, Bertrand, and Pierre Birnbaum. 1983. *The sociology of the state*, trans. by A. Goldhamer. Chicago: University of Chicago Press.

Baez, Benjamin. 2002. *Affirmative action, hate speech, and tenure: Narratives about race and law in the academy*. New York: Routledge Palmer.

Bagrow, Leo. 1964. *History of cartography*. Cambridge, MA: Harvard University Press.

Bailey, J. 2000. Some meanings of "the private" in sociological thought. *Sociology* 34(3): 381–401.

Bailey, Mark Warren. 2004. *Guardians of the moral order: The legal philosophy of the Supreme Court, 1860–1910*. DeKalb: Northern Illinois University Press.

Baird, D. G., R. H. Gertner, and R. C. Picker. 1994. *Game theory and the law*. Cambridge, MA: Harvard University Press.

Baker, C. Edwin. 1981. The process of change and the liberty theory of the First Amendment. *Southern California Law Review* 55(2): 293–344.

Baker, Jerill. 1987. Who owns broadcasting: A change of hands. *Channels* (April): 47–52.

Baker, Karen S., Geof Bowker, and Helen Karasti. 2002. Designing an infrastructure for heterogeneity in ecosystem data, collaborators, and organizations. In *Proceedings of the Second National Conference on Digital Government Research*, 141–144. Los Angeles, CA: Digital Government Research Center, University of Southern California.

Baldwin, David A. 1978. Power and social exchange. *American Political Science Review* 72(4): 1229–1247.

Baldwin, David A. 1979a. Interdependence and power: A conceptual analysis. *International Organization* 34(4): 471–506.

Baldwin, David A. 1979b. Power analysis and world politics: New trends versus old tendencies. *World Politics* 31(2): 161–194.

Balkin, Jack M. 2004. Digital speech and democratic culture: A theory of freedom of expression for the information society. *New York University Law Review* 79(1): 1–58.

Ball, Harry V., George Eaton Simpson, and Kyoshi Ikeda. 1962. Law and social change: Sumner considered. *American Journal of Sociology* 67(5): 532–540.

Ball, Terence. 1975. Models of power: Past and present. *Journal of the History of the Behavioral Sciences* 11(3): 211–222.

Ball, Terence. 1978. Power, causation and explanation. *Polity* 8(2): 189–214.

Ballinger, Pamela. 2002. *History in exile: Memory and identity at the borders of the Balkans*. Princeton, NJ: Princeton University Press.

Band, J., and M. Katoh. 1995. *Interfaces on trial: Intellectual property and interoperability in the global software industry*. Boulder, CO: Westview Press.

Banisar, David. 2002. Virtual borders, real laws. *IEEE Spectrum* 39(10): 51–53.

Barabasi, Albert-Laszlo. 2003. *Linked.* New York: Penguin.

Barker, Carol M., and Matthew H. Fox. 1972. *Classified files: The yellowing pages—A report on scholars' access to government documents.* New York: Twentieth Century Fund.

Barlow, J. P. 1996. *A declaration of the independence of cyberspace.* Available at www.eff.org/~barlow/Declaration-Final.html.

Barrera, Eduardo. 1995. State intervention and telecommunications in Mexico. *Journal of Communication* 45(4): 489–501.

Barron, Jerome A., and C. Thomas Dienes. 2003. *Constitutional law*, 6th ed. St. Paul, MN: West Group.

Barrow, Clyde W. 1993. *Critical theories of the state.* Madison: University of Wisconsin Press.

Barth, K. H. 2003. The politics of seismology: Nuclear testing, arms control, and the transformation of a discipline. *Social Studies of Science* 33(5): 743–781.

Barthes, Roland. 1968. *Elements of semiology*, trans. by Annette Lavers and Colin Smith. New York: Hill and Wang.

Bartlett, Thomas. 2005. Harvard proposes overhaul of undergraduate curriculum, with emphasis on science and study abroad. *Chronicle of Higher Education* (April 28). Available at www.chronicle.com/prm/daily/2004/04/2004042801n.htm.

Bass, Kenneth C., III. 1999. The costs of encryption export controls: What about our constitutional values? In Solveig Singleton and Daniel T. Griswold, eds., *Economic casualties: How U.S. foreign policy undermines trade, growth, and liberty*, 113–117. Washington, DC: Cato Institute.

Bastien, D. T., and T. J. Hostager. 1988. Jazz as a process of organizational innovation. *Communication Research* 15(5): 582–602.

Baudrillard, Jean. 1983. *Simulations.* New York: Semiotext(e).

Baumann, S., and O. Hummel. 2005. Enhancing music recommendation algorithms using cultural metadata. *Journal of New Music Research* 34(2): 161–172.

Baumer, David, and J. C. Poindexter. 2002. *Cyberlaw and e-commerce.* Boston: McGraw-Hill/Irwin.

Baym, Nancy K. 1997. Identity, body, and community in on-line life. *Journal of Communication* 47(4): 142–148.

Bazelon, David L. 1979. The First Amendment and the "new media": New directions in regulating telecommunications. *Federal Communications Law Journal* 31(2): 201–213.

Beachboard, John C., Charles R. McClure, and John Carlo Bertot. 1997. A critique of federal telecommunications policy initiatives relating to universal service and open access to the national information infrastructure. *Government Information Quarterly* 15(1): 11–26.

Bean, Frank D., Rodolfo Corona, Rodolfo Tuiran, Karen A. Woodrow-Lafield, and Jennifer van Hook. 2001. Circular, invisible, and ambiguous migrants: Components of difference in estimates of the number of unauthorized Mexican migrants in the United States. *Demography* 38(3): 411–422.

Bean, Richard. 1973. War and the birth of the nation state. *Journal of Economic History* 33(1): 203–221.

Beard, Charles. 1930. *The rise of American civilization*. New York: Macmillan.

Beardsley, Tim. 1995. Environmental secrets: Medea brings intelligence in from the cold. *Scientific American* 273(1): 28–30.

Beaumont, Roger A. 1994. *War, chaos, and history*. New York: Praeger.

Beck, Ulrich. 1992. *Risk society: Towards a new modernity*. Thousand Oaks, CA: Sage.

Becker, Jörg. 1986. New information technologies (NITs) and transnational culture: Is there a European response? In George Muskens and Cees Hamelink, eds., *Global networks and European communities: Applied social and comparative approaches*, 7–25. Tilburg, FRG: Institute for Social Research, Tilburg University.

Beisky, Leah, Reidar Lie, Aaditya Mattoo, Ezekiel J. Emanuel, and Gopal Sreenlvasan. 2004. The General Agreement on Trade in Services: Implications for health policymakers. *Health Affairs* 23(3): 137–146.

Bell, Daniel. 1966. *The reforming of general education: The Columbia College experience in its national setting*. New York: Columbia University Press.

Bell, Daniel. 1973. *The coming of post-industrial society: A venture in social forecasting*. New York: Basic Books.

Bell, Desmond. 1987. Acts of union: Youth sub-culture and ethnic identity amongst Protestants in Northern Ireland. *The British Journal of Sociology* 38(2): 158–183.

Bell, Desmond. 1995. Communications, corporatism, and dependent development in Ireland. *Journal of Communication* 45(4): 70–89.

Bell, H. K. 2001. From herbals to Hotbot: The development of journal indexing. *Learned Publishing* 14(2): 123–130.

Bellamy, Ian. 2005. *Curbing the spread of nuclear weapons*. Manchester, UK: Manchester University Press.

Bellia, Patricia L., Paul Schiff Berman, and David G. Post. 2004. *Cyberlaw: Problems of policy and jurisprudence in the information age*. St. Paul, MN: West Publishing.

Beltran, Cristina. 2004. Patrolling borders: Hybrids, hierarchies and the challenge of mestizaje. *Political Research Quarterly* 57(4): 595–608.

Bendell, Jem, and Xavier Font. 2004. Which tourism rules? Green standards and GATS. *Annals of Tourism Research* 31(1): 139–156.

Bender, Thomas, ed. 2002. *Rethinking American history in a global age*. Berkeley: University of California Press.

Beniger, James R. 1990. Conceptualizing information technology as organization, and vice versa. In Janet Fulk and Charles Steinfield, eds., *Organizations and communication technology*, 29–45. Newbury Park, CA: Sage.

Benkler, Yochai. 2000. Net regulation: Taking stock and looking forward. *University of Colorado Law Review* 71(4): 1203–1262.

Benkler, Yochai. 2003. Freedom in the commons: Towards a political economy of information. *Duke Law Journal* 52(4): 1245–1276.

Bennett, Colin J., and Charles D. Raab. 2003. *The governance of privacy: Policy instruments in global perspective*. Aldershot, UK: Ashgate Publishing.

Bennett, J. A. 1997. Museums and the establishment of the history of science at Oxford and Cambridge. *British Journal for the History of Science* 30(1): 29–46.

Bennett, Tony. 1995. *The birth of the museum: History, theory, politics*. New York: Routledge.

Bennett, W. Lance. 1998. The uncivic culture: Communication, identity, and the rise of lifestyle politics. *PS: Political Science and Politics* 31(4): 741–761.

Benoliel, Daniel. 2004. Technological standards, inc.: Rethinking cyberspace regulatory epistemology. *California Law Review* 92(4): 1071–1116.

Berg, Marc. 1998. The politics of technology: On bringing social theory into technological design. *Science, Technology, & Human Values* 23(4): 456–489.

Bergen, T. 1987. Trade in services: Toward a "development round" of GATT negotiations benefiting both developing and industrialized states. *Harvard International Law Journal* 28(1): 1–30.

Berger, Peter L., and Thomas Luckmann. 1966. *The social construction of reality*. New York: Doubleday.

Berger, Raoul. 1984. Lawyerizing vs. philosophizing: Facts or fancies. *University of Dayton Law Review* 9(2): 171–217.

Berman, P. J., and Anthony G. Oettinger. 1976. *The medium and the telephone: The politics of information resources*. Cambridge, MA: Program on Information Technologies, John F. Kennedy School, Harvard University.

Bernays, Edward. [1928] 2004. *Propaganda*. Brooklyn: Ig Publishing.

Berners-Lee, Tim, James Hendler, and Ora Lassila. 2001. The semantic web. *Scientific American* 284(5) (May 17): 34–43.

Bernhard, Nancy E., ed. 2003. *U.S. television news and Cold War propaganda, 1947–1960*. Cambridge: Cambridge University Press.

Bernier, J. 1988. A Canadian dilemma: Free trade with the United States. *Journal of Cultural Geography* 8(2): 135–142.

Bertsch, Gary K., and Steven Elliott-Gower, eds. 1992. *Export controls in transition: Perspectives, problems, and prospects*. Durham, NC: Duke University Press.

Besterman, Theodore. 1971. *Technology, including patents: A bibliography of bibliographies*. Totowa, NJ: Rowman and Littlefield.

Beville, Hugh M., Jr. 1948. The challenge of the new media: Television, FM, and facsimile. *Journalism Quarterly* 24(1): 3–11.

Bezanson, Randall P., Gilbert Cranberg, and John Soloski. 1987. *Libel law and the press: Myth and reality*. New York: Free Press.

Bhagwati, Jagdish N. 2003. Borders beyond control. *Foreign Affairs* 82(1): 98–105.

Bhagwati, Jagdish N., and John G. Ruggie. 1984. *Power, passions, and purpose: Prospects for North-South negotiations*. Cambridge, MA: MIT Press.

Bhojraj, Sanjeev, Charles M. C. Lee, and Derek Oler. 2003. What's my line? A comparison of industry classification schemes for capital market research. Social Science Research Network. Available at http://ssrn.com/abstract=356840.

Biegel, Stuart. 2001. *Beyond our control: Confronting the limits of our legal system in the age of cyberspace*. Cambridge, MA: MIT Press.

Biesecker, Barbara, Roseann Mandziuk, and Thomas Nakayama. 1998. Propaganda and democracy. *Critical Studies in Mass Communication* 15(4): 450–457.

Bijker, W. E., T. P. Hughes, and T. Pinch. 1987. *The social construction of technological systems*. Cambridge, MA: MIT Press.

Bijker, W. E., and J. Law, eds. 1992. *Shaping technology/building society*. Cambridge, MA: MIT Press.

Billig, Miriam, and Arza Churchman. 2003. Building walls of brick and breaching walls of separation. *Environment & Behavior* 35(2): 277–350.

Bimber, Bruce. 2002. *The Internet and American democracy: Technology in the evolution of political power*. Cambridge: Cambridge University Press.

Bingham, Jonathan B., and Victor C. Johnson. 1979. A rational approach to export controls. *Foreign Affairs* 57(4): 894–920.

Binns, Leonard J. 1993. Inference through secondary path analysis. *Results of the Sixth Working Conference of IFIP Working Group 11.3 on Database Security*, 195–209. Vancouver, British Columbia: Simon Fraser University.

Birch, Sarah, and Bob Watt. 2004. Remote electronic voting: Free, fair and secret? *Political Quarterly* 75(1): 60–72.

Birrell, Augustine. 1899. *Seven lectures on the law and history of copyright in books*. London: Cassell.

Bischof, Henrik. 1989. CoCom politics and the data flow between East and West. In Jörg Becker and Tamas Szecsko, eds., *Europe speaks to Europe: International information flows between Eastern and Western Europe*, 305–308. Oxford: Pergamon Press.

Black, Sharon K. 2002. *Telecommunications law in the Internet age*. San Diego: Academic Press.

Blackman, Colin R. 1998. Convergence between telecommunications and other media: How should regulation adapt? *Telecommunications Policy* 22(3): 163–170.

Blair, Melissa. 2003. Terrorism, America's porous borders, and the role of the Invasion Clause post 9/11/2001. *Marquette Law Review* 87(1): 167–223.

Blanchard, Margaret A. 1986. *Exporting the First Amendment.* New York: Longman.

Blasi, Vincent. 1986. The role of strategic reasoning in constitutional interpretation: In defense of the pathological perspective. *Duke Law Journal* 1986(4): 696–709.

Blasi, Vincent. 2002. Free speech and good character: From Milton to Brandeis to the present. In Lee C. Bollinger and Geoffrey Stone, eds., *Eternally vigilant: Free speech in the modern era*, 60–95. Chicago: University of Chicago Press.

Blau, Peter M. 1981. Diverse views of social structure and their common denominator. In Peter M. Blau and Robert K. Merton, eds., *Continuities in structural inquiry*, 1–23. Beverly Hills, CA: Sage.

Blau, Peter M., and Robert K. Merton, eds. 1981. *Continuities in structural inquiry*. Beverly Hills, CA: Sage.

Blaug, Mark. 1997. *Economic theory in retrospect*, 5th ed. Cambridge: Cambridge University Press.

Bloom, Nick, Rachel Griffith, and John Van Reenen. 2002. Do R&D tax credits work? Evidence from a panel of countries 1979–1997. *Journal of Public Economics* 85(1): 1–31.

Blue, Lily. 2004. Internet and domain name governance: Antitrust litigation and ICANN. *Berkeley Technology Law Journal* 19(1): 387–403.

Blum, H. P. 1989. The concept of termination and the evolution of psychoanalytic thought. *Journal of the American Psychoanalytic Association* 37(2): 275–295.

Blumenthal, Marjory S., and David D. Clark. 2001. Rethinking the design of the Internet: The end-to-end arguments vs. the brave new world. In Benjamin M. Compaine and Shane Greenstein, eds., *Communications policy in transition: The Internet and beyond*, 91–140. Cambridge, MA: MIT Press.

Blumler, Jay G. 1978. Purposes of mass communications research: A transatlantic perspective. *Journalism Quarterly* 55(2): 219–230.

Blumler, Jay G., and Elihu Katz. 1974. *The uses of mass communications: Current perspectives on gratifications research*. Beverly Hills, CA: Sage.

Blumler, Jay G., and Dennis Kavanagh. 1999. The third age of political communication: Influences and features. *Political Communication* 16(3): 209–230.

Boag, Jordana. 2004. The battle of piracy versus privacy: How the Recording Industry Association of America (RIAA) is using the Digital Millennium Copyright Act (DMCA) as its weapon against Internet users' privacy rights. *California Western Law Review* 41(2): 241–276.

Bobrow, Davis B. 1973–1974. Mass communication and the political system. *Public Opinion Quarterly* 37(4): 551–568.

Bodin, Jean. [1576] 1962. *Six books of a commonwealth*, trans. by R. Knolles and ed. by K. D. McRae. Cambridge, MA: Harvard University Press.

Boettinger, Henry M. 1976. *The telephone book*. Croton-on-Hudson, NY: Riverwood Press.

Bohman, James. 1999. Theories, practices, and pluralism: A pragmatic interpretation of critical social science. *Philosophy of the Social Sciences* 29(4): 459–480.

Bohmer, Alois. 1960. *Copyright in the USSR and other European countries or territories under communist government*. South Hackensack, NJ: F. B. Rothman. Published for the Copyright Society of the U.S.A.

Bok, Derek. 2004. *Universities in the marketplace: The commercialization of higher education*. Princeton, NJ: Princeton University Press.

Bollier, David, and Tim Watts. 2002. *Saving the information commons: A public interest agenda in digital media*. Washington, DC: New America Foundation and Public Knowledge.

Bollinger, Lee C. 1977. Freedom of the press and public access: Toward a theory of partial regulation of the mass media. *Michigan Law Review* 75(1): 1–42.

Bollinger, Lee C. 1986. *The tolerant society: Freedom of speech and extremist speech in America*. New York: Oxford University Press.

Bollinger, Lee C., and Geoffrey R. Stone. 2001. Dialogue. In Lee C. Bollinger and Geoffrey R. Stone, eds., *Eternally vigilant: Free speech in the modern era*, 1–31. Chicago: University of Chicago Press.

Bollinger, Lee, and Geoffrey R. Stone, eds. 2003. *Eternally vigilant: Free speech in the modern era*. Chicago: University of Chicago Press.

Bolter, J. David. 1984. *Turing's man: Western culture in the computer age*. Chapel Hill: University of North Carolina Press.

Bonacich, Phillip, and G. William Domhoff. 1981. Latent classes and group membership. *Social Networks* 3(3): 175–196.

Bonatti, Piero, Sabrina de Capitani di Vimercati, and Pierangela Samarati. 2002. An algebra for composing access control policies. *ACM Transactions on Information and System Security* 5(1): 1–35.

Borawski, John, ed. 1986. *Avoiding war in the nuclear age: Confidence-building measures for crisis stability*. Boulder, CO: Westview Press.

Borchers, Patrick J. 2004. Internet libel: The consequences of a non-rule approach to personal jurisdiction. *Northwestern University Law Review* 98(2): 473–492.

Borjas, George J. 1999. *Heaven's door: Immigration policy and the American economy*. Princeton, NJ: Princeton University Press.

Bork, Robert H. 1993. *The antitrust paradox: A policy at war with itself*. New York: Oxford University Press.

Bortnick, Jane. 1986. Support for information technology in science: The federal role. *Government Information Quarterly* 3(3): 233–250.

Bosniak, Linda. 2000. Citizenship denationalized. *Indiana Journal of Global Legal Studies* 7(2): 447–510.

Boudon, Raymond. 1983. Why theories of social change fail: Some methodological thoughts. *Public Opinion Quarterly* 47(2): 143–160.

Boughton, James M. 2004. New light on Harry Dexter White. *Journal of the History of Economic Thought* 26(2): 179–195.

Boulding, Kenneth E. 1966. The economics of knowledge and the knowledge of economics. *American Economic Review* 56(1/2): 1–24.

Boulding, Kenneth E. 1971. National images and international systems. In W. F. Hanrieder, ed., *Comparative foreign policy: Theoretical essays*, 90–107. New York: David McKay.

Bourdieu, Pierre. 1991. *Language and symbolic power*, trans. by G. Raymond and M. Adamson. Cambridge, MA: Harvard University Press.

Bowen, William G., and Derek Bok. 2000. *The shape of the river: Long-term consequences of considering race in college and university admissions*. Princeton, NJ: Princeton University Press.

Bowers, James R. 1993. Looking at OMB's regulatory review through a shared powers perspective. *Presidential Studies Quarterly* 23(2): 331–346.

Bowker, Geoffrey C. 1994. *Science on the run: Information management and industrial geophysics at Schlumberger, 1920–1940*. Cambridge, MA: MIT Press.

Bowker, Geoffrey C., and S. Leigh Star. 1999. *Sorting things out: Classification and its consequences*. Cambridge, MA: MIT Press.

Bowker, R. R. 1912. *Copyright, its history and law*. Boston: Houghton Mifflin.

Bowler, S., T. Donovan, and R. Hanneman. 2003. Art for democracy's sake? Group membership and political engagement in Europe. *Journal of Politics* 65(4): 1111–1129.

Bowles, Samuel, and Herbert Gintis. 1982. The crisis of capital and the crisis of liberal democracy: The case of the United States. *Politics & Society* 11(1): 51–94.

Boyd, Steven R. 1992. *Alternative constitutions for the United States: A documentary history*. Westport, CT: Greenwood Press.

Boyd-Barrett, Oliver. 1980. *The international news agencies*. Thousand Oaks, CA: Sage.

Boyle, James. 1996. *Shamans, software, and spleens: Law and the construction of the information society*. Cambridge, MA: Harvard University Press.

Bozeman, B., and A. Link. 1985. Public support for private R&D: The case of the research tax credit. *Journal of Policy Analysis and Management* 4: 370–382.

Bradshaw, Jeffrey. 1997. *Software agents*. Menlo Park, CA: AAAI Press.

Braithwaite, Nick, ed. 1995. *The international libel handbook*. London: Butterworth-Heinemann.

Braman, Sandra. 1984a. FCC decision-making for the international arena. Unpublished manuscript, University of Minnesota.

Braman, Sandra. 1984b. The location of the Lockiean consciousness in news reports from El Salvador: The public locus of the *New York Times* vs. the individual locus of Joan Didion. Unpublished M.A. thesis, University of Minnesota.

Braman, Sandra. 1988. Information policy and the United States Supreme Court. Unpublished doctoral diss., University of Minnesota.

Braman, Sandra. 1989. Defining information: An approach for policymakers. *Telecommunications Policy* 13(3): 233–242.

Braman, Sandra. 1990. Turning black to white: The CSCE and information policy for the new Europe. Presented to the Second Conference on Europe Speaks to Europe, Moscow, December.

Braman, Sandra. 1991a. Contradictions in Brilliant Eyes. *Gazette: The International Journal of Communication Studies* 47(3): 177–194.

Braman, Sandra. 1991b. The impact of confidence-building measures on information policy. In Kaarle Nordenstreng and Wolfgang Kleinwachter, eds., *Confidence-building in the non-military field*, 47–58. Tampere, Finland: University of Tampere.

Braman, Sandra. 1993. Harmonization of systems: The third stage of the information society. *Journal of Communication* 43(3): 133–140.

Braman, Sandra. 1995a. Horizons of the state: Information policy and power. *Journal of Communication* 45(4): 4–24.

Braman, Sandra. 1995b. Policy for the net and the Internet. *Annual Review of Information Science and Technology* 30: 5–75.

Braman, Sandra. 1999. The information economy: An evolution of approaches. In Stuart Macdonald and J. Nightingale, eds., *Information and organisation*, 109–125. Amsterdam: Elsevier Science.

Braman, Sandra. 2002a. Informational meta-technologies and international relations: The case of biotechnologies. In James Rosenau and J. P. Singh, eds., *Information technologies and global politics: The changing scope of power and governance*, 91–112. Albany: State University of New York Press.

Braman, Sandra. 2002b. Posthuman law: Information policy and the machinic world. *First Monday* 7(12). Available at www.firstmonday.org/issues/issue7_12/braman/index.html.

Braman, Sandra, ed. 2003. *Communication researchers and policy-making*. Cambridge, MA: MIT Press.

Braman, Sandra. 2004a. The emergent global information policy regime. In Sandra Braman, ed., *The emergent global information policy regime*, 12–37. Houndsmills, UK: Palgrave Macmillan.

Braman, Sandra. 2004b. The meta-technologies of information. In Sandra Braman, ed., *Biotechnology and information: The meta-technologies of information*, 3–36. Mahwah, NJ: Lawrence Erlbaum Associates.

Braman, Sandra. 2004c. Where has media policy gone? Defining the field in the twenty-first century. *Communication Law and Policy* 9(2): 153–182.

Braman, Sandra. 2005. The micro- and macroeconomics of information. *Annual Review of Information Science and Technology* 40: 3–52.

Braman, Sandra, and Stephanie Lynch. 2003. Advantage ISP: Terms of service as media law. In Lorrie F. Cranor and Steven S. Wildman, eds., *Rethinking rights and regulations: Institutional responses to new communication technologies*, 250–278. Cambridge, MA: MIT Press.

Brams, Steven J., and Morton D. Davis. 1987. The verification problem in arms control: A game-theoretic analysis. In Claudio Cioffi-Revilla, Richard L. Merritt, and Dina A. Zinnes, eds., *Communication and interaction in global politics*, 141–161. Beverly Hills, CA: Sage.

Branscomb, Anne W., ed. 1986. *Toward a law of global communication networks*. New York: Longman.

Branscomb, Lewis M., ed. 1993. *Empowering technology: Implementing a U.S. policy*. Cambridge, MA: MIT Press.

Brants, Kees. 1989. The social construction of the information revolution. *European Journal of Communication* 4(1): 79–92.

Braudel, Ferdinand. 1977. *Afterthoughts on material civilization and capitalism*, trans. by Patricia M. Ranum. Baltimore, MD: Johns Hopkins University Press.

Brecher, Michael, B. Steinberg, and J. Stein. 1969. A framework for research on foreign policy behavior. *Journal of Conflict Resolution* 13(1): 75–101.

Breckheimer, Peter J., II. 2002. A haven for hate: The foreign and domestic implications of protecting Internet hate speech under the First Amendment. *Southern California Law Review* 75(5): 1493–1528.

Brennan, Timothy J. 1983. Economic efficiency and broadcast content regulation. *Federal Communications Law Journal* 35(2): 117–138.

Brennan, Timothy J. 1990. Vertical integration, monopoly, and the First Amendment. *Journal of Media Economics* 3(1): 57–76.

Brennan, Timothy J. 1992a. Integrating communications theory into media policy: An economic perspective. *Telecommunications Policy* 16(6): 460–474.

Brennan, Timothy J. 1992b. Rational ignorance: The strategic economics of military censorship. *Southern Economic Journal* 58(4): 966–974.

Brennan, Timothy J. 1993. Copyright, property, and the right to deny. *Chicago-Kent Law Review* 68(2): 675–714.

Brennan, Timothy J. 1995. Does the theory behind *U.S. v. AT&T* still apply? *Antitrust Bulletin* 40(3): 455–482.

Brennan, Timothy J., and Molly Macauley. 1997. Technology and coordination: Antitrust implications of remote sensing satellites. *Antitrust Bulletin* 42(2): 477–502.

Brenner, Susan W. 2004. Toward a criminal law for cyberspace: Distributed security. *Boston University Journal of Science and Technology Law* 10(1): 1–109.

Briggs, Asa. 2004. Man-made futures, man-made pasts. In Marita Sturken, Douglas Tomas, and Sandra J. Ball-Rokeach, eds., *Technological visions: The hopes and fears that shape new technologies*, 92–109. Philadelphia: Temple University Press.

Brook, D. 2004. Art history? *History and Theory* 43(1): 1–17.

Brooks, A. C. 2001. Who opposes government arts funding? *Public Choice* 108(3–4): 355–367.

Brooks, John. 1976. *Telephone: The first hundred years*. New York: Harper & Row.

Brooks, Stephen, and Alain-G. Gagnon, eds. 1990. *Social scientists, policy, and the state*. New York: Praeger.

Brown, Bartram S. 2004. Barely borders. *Harvard International Review* 26(1): 52–58.

Brown, Charlie L. 1983. AT&T and the consent decree. *Telecommunications Policy* 7(2): 91–95.

Brown, James Seely, and Paul Duguid. 2002. *The social life of information*. Cambridge, MA: Harvard Business School Press.

Brown, Ralph S., and Robert C. Denicola. 2005. *Cases on copyright, unfair competition, and related topics bearing on the protection of works of authorship*. New York: Foundation Press.

Browne, Mairead. 1997a. The field of information policy, 1: Fundamental concepts. *Journal of the American Society of Information Science* 23(4): 261–275.

Browne, Mairead. 1997b. The field of information policy, 2: Redefining the boundaries and methodologies. *Journal of the American Society of Information Science* 23(5): 339–352.

Brubacher, J. S., and W. Rudy. 1976. *Higher education in transition: A history of American colleges and universities, 1636–1976*. New York: Harper and Row.

Brucan, Silviu. 1980. The state and the world system. *International Social Science Journal* 32(4): 752–769.

Bruce, Julie. 2003. Bioterrorism meets privacy: An analysis of the model state emergency health powers act and the HIPAA privacy rule. *Annals of Health Law* 12(1): 75–120.

Bruce, Robert R. 1983. A strategic perspective on U.S. telecommunications regulation. *InterMedia* 11(4/5): 76–79.

Bruce, Robert R., J. P. Cunard, and Mark D. Director. 1986. *From telecommunications to electronic services: A global spectrum of definitions, boundary lines, and structures*. Boston: Butterworth.

Bruck, Peter, ed. 1988. *A proxy for knowledge: The news media in arms control and verification*. Carleton, Ottawa: Norman Paterson School of International Affairs.

Bruner, Jerome. 1990. *Acts of meaning*. Cambridge, MA: Harvard University Press.

Buckland, Michael, and Ziming Liu. 1998. History of information science. In Trudi Bellardo Hahn and Michael Buckland, eds., *Historical studies in information science*, 272–295. Medford, NJ: Information Today.

Bucy, Erik. 2004. *Living in the information age: A new media reader*. New York: Wadsworth.

Bucy, Erik P., and Paul D'Angelo. 1999. The crisis of political communication: Normative critiques of news and democratic processes. *Communication Yearbook* 22: 301–339.

Bueno de Mesquita, Bruce, and David Lalman. 1988. Empirical support for systemic and dyadic explanations of international conflict. *World Politics* 41(1): 1–20.

Bunker, Matthew D. 1996. First Amendment theory and conceptions of the self. *Communication Law and Policy* 1(2): 241–270.

Bunker, Matthew D. 2001. *Critiquing free speech: First Amendment theory and the challenge of interdisciplinarity*. Mahwah, NJ: Lawrence Erlbaum Associates.

Burchell, Graham, Colin Gordon, and Peter Miller, eds. 1991. *The Foucault effect: Studies in governmentality*. Chicago: University of Chicago Press.

Burkert, Herbert. 1995. Access to information and data protection considerations. In Cecile de Terwangne, Herbert Burkert, Yves Poullet, Florence Berrisch, and J. Michael, eds., *Towards a legal framework for a diffusion policy for data held by the public sector*, 23–54. Deventer, The Netherlands: Kluwer.

Burnham, James B. 1999. Export controls: A national emergency? In Solveig Singleton and Daniel T. Griswold, eds., *Economic casualties: How U.S. foreign policy undermines trade, growth, and liberty*, 31–37. Washington, DC: Cato Institute.

Burns, Arthur. 1960. Progress towards economic stability. *American Economic Review* 50(1): 1–19.

Burns, Tom. 1961. Micropolitics: Mechanisms of institutional change. *Administrative Science Quarterly* 6: 257–281.

Burns, Tom R., and Walter Buckley, eds. 1976. *Power and control: Social structures and their transformation*. London: Sage.

Burrell, Robert, and Allison Coleman. 2005. *Copyright exceptions: The digital impact*. Cambridge: Cambridge University Press.

Burton-Jones, A., V. C. Storey, V. Sugumaran, and P. Ahluwalia. 2005. A semoitic metrics suite for assessing the quality of ontologies. *Data and Knowledge Engineering* 55(1): 84–102.

Bush, George Pollock, and Robert H. Dreyfuss. 1979. *Technology and copyright: Sources and materials*. Mt. Airy, MD: Lomond Books.

Calavita, Kitty. 1984. *U.S. immigration law and the control of labor, 1820–1924*. London: Academic Press.

Calhoun, Craig. 1991. Indirect relationships and imagined communities: Large-scale social integration and the transformation of everyday life. In Pierre Bourdieu and James S. Coleman, eds., *Social theory for a changing society*, 95–120. Boulder, CO: Westview Press.

Campbell, Donald E. 1977. Computational criteria for voting systems. *British Journal of Political Science* 7(1): 85–98.

Canclini, Néstor García. 1988. Culture and power: The state of research. *Media, Culture & Society* 10(4): 467–497.

Caplan, Priscilla. 2003. *Metadata fundamentals for all librarians*. Chicago: American Library Association.

Caporaso, James A. 1986. *Changing international division of labor*. Boulder, CO: Lynne Rienner.

Caporaso, James A. 2000. Transnational markets, thin citizenship, and democratic rights in the European Union: From cradle to grave or from job to job? Presented to the International Studies Association, Los Angeles, March.

Cardozo, Benjamin J. 1921. *The nature of the judicial process*. New Haven, CT: Yale University Press.

Carey, James W. 1980. Changing communications technology and the nature of the audience. Presented to the American Academy of Advertising Conference, Columbia, MO, March 23.

Carey, James W. 1989. *Communication as culture: Essays on media and society*. Boston: Unwin & Hyman.

Carey, James W., and John J. Quirk. 1970. The mythos of the electronic revolution. *The American Scholar* 39(2) (Spring): 219–241.

Carey, James W., and Norman Sims. 1976. The telegraph and the news report. Unpublished paper, University of Illinois, Urbana.

Carlton, Dennis W., and Robert H. Gertner. 2003. Intellectual property, antitrust, and strategic behavior. In Adam B. Jaffe, Josh Lerner, and Scott Stern, eds., *Innovation policy and the economy*, vol. 3, 29–59. Cambridge, MA: MIT Press and NBER.

Carroll, M. 2002. Commitment or abrogation? Avant-garde music and Jean-Paul Sartre's idea of committed art. *Music & Letters* 83(4): 590–606.

Carruthers, D. V. 2001. The politics and ecology of indigenous folk art in Mexico. *Human Organization* 60(4): 356–366.

Carter, Lief H. 1984. *Reason in law*, 2nd ed. Boston: Little, Brown.

Carter, Lief H. 1985. *Contemporary constitutional lawmaking: The Supreme Court and the art of politics*. New York: Pergamon Press.

Carter, Susan B., and Richard C. Sutch. 1995. *Fixing the facts: Editing of the 1880 U.S. Census of Occupations with implications for long-term trends and the sociology of official statistics*. Washington, DC: NBER Working Paper No. H0074.

Carter, T. Barton, Marc A. Franklin, and Jay B. Wright. 2003. *The First Amendment and the fifth estate: Regulation of electronic mass media*, 6th ed. St. Paul, MN: Thompson/West.

Cartwright, Roger I. 2005. *Key concepts in information and communication technology*. Houndsmills, UK: Palgrave Macmillan.

Carty, John J. [1922] 1924. Ideals of the telephone service: A tribute to the memory of Alexander Graham Bell. Presidential address delivered at the Ninth Annual Meeting of the Telephone Pioneers of America, Cleveland, OH, September 1922. Reprinted in *Annual Report of the Smithsonian*, 533–540. Washington, DC: Government Printing Office, Pub. 2724.

Cass, Ronald A. 1987. The perils of positive thinking: Constitutional interpretation and negative First Amendment theory. *UCLA Law Review* 34(5–6): 1405–1491.

Castells, Manuel. 1996. *The rise of the network society*. Malden, MA: Blackwell.

Castells, Manuel. 1997a. *End of millennium*. Malden, MA: Blackwell.

Castells, Manuel. 1997b. *The power of identity*. Malden, MA: Blackwell.

Castro, Miguel, Roger Foster, Kevin Gunn, and Edward B. Roberts. 2001. Managing research and development across government departments: The "virtual agency" concept in the United States. Cambridge, MA: MIT Sloan Working Paper No. 4174-01.

Cate, Fred H. 1994. The national information infrastructure: Policymaking and policymakers. *Stanford Law and Policy Review* 6(1): 43–59.

Cate, Fred H. 1997. *Privacy in the information age*. Washington, DC: Brookings Institution.

Cave, Martin, and Len Waverman. 1998. The future of international settlements. *Telecommunications Policy* 22(11): 883–898.

Cawkell, A. E., ed. 1987. *Evolution of an information society*. London: ASLIB.

Celeste, Richard, Dick Thornburgh, and Herbert Lin, eds. 2005. *Asking the right questions about electronic voting*. Washington, DC: National Research Council.

Cerni, Dorothy M. 1982. *The CCITT: Organization, U.S. participation, and studies toward the ISDN*. Boulder, CO: NTIA.

Cerni, Dorothy M., and Evelyn M. Gray. 1983. *International telecommunications standards: Issues and implications for the '80s*. Boulder, CO: NTIA.

Cerny, Philip G. 1995. Globalization and the changing logic of collective action. *International Organization* 49(4): 595–625.

Ceselli, A., E. Damiani, S. De Capitani Di Vimercati, S. Jajodia, S. Paraboschi, and P. Samarati. 2005. Modeling and assessing inference exposure in encrypted databases. *ACM Transactions on Information and System Security* 8(1): 119–152.

Chafee, Zechariah. 1941. *Free speech in the United States*. Cambridge, MA: Harvard University Press.

Chaffee, Steven H. 1992. Search for change: Survey studies of international media effects. In Felipe Korzenny and Stella Ting-Toomey, eds., *Mass media effects across cultures*, 35–54. Newbury Park, CA: Sage.

Chakravarty, Sumita S. 1994. *National identity in Indian popular cinema, 1947–1987*. Austin: University of Texas Press.

Chandler, Alfred D., Jr. 1979. *The visible hand*. Cambridge, MA: Belknap Press.

Chandler, Alfred D., Jr. 2000. The information age in historical perspective. In Alfred D. Chandler, Jr., and James W. Cortada, eds., *A nation transformed: How informaiton has shaped the United States from colonial times to the present*. New York: Oxford University Press.

Chandler, Alfred D., Jr., and James W. Cortada, eds. 2000. *A nation transformed: How information has shaped the United States from colonial times to the present*. New York: Oxford University Press.

Chase-Dunn, Christopher. 1994. Hegemony and social change. *Mershon International Studies Review* 38(2): 361–376.

Chatterjee, Partha. 1986. *Nationalist thought and the colonial world: A derivative discourse.* Minneapolis: University of Minnesota Press.

Cheh, Mary M. 1982. Government control of private ideas: Striking a balance between scientific freedom and national security. *Jurimetrics Journal* 23(1): 1–32.

Cherry, Barbara A., Steven S. Wildman, and Allen S. Hammond. 1999. *Making universal service policy: Enhancing the process through multidisciplinary evaluation.* Mahwah, NJ: Lawrence Erlbaum Associates.

Chesebro, James W. 1976. Political communication. *Quarterly Journal of Speech* 62(3): 289–300.

Chiron, Stuart Z., and Lise A. Rehberg. 1986. Fostering competition in international telecommunications. *Federal Communications Law Journal* 38(1): 1–57.

Chishti, Muzzaffar A., Doris Meissner, Demetrios G. Papademetriou, Jay Peterzell, Michael J. Wishnie, and Stephen W. Yale-Loehr. 2003. *America's challenge: Domestic security, civil liberties, and national unity after September 11.* Washington, DC: Migration Policy Institute.

Chomsky, Noam, Immanuel Wallerstein, Laura Nader, Richard C. Lewontin, and Richard Ohmann. 1997. *The Cold War and the university: Toward an intellectual history of the postwar years.* New York: New Press.

Choper, Jesse H. 2001. *Constitutional law: Cases, comments, questions*, 9th ed. St. Paul, MN: West Publishing.

Christiansen, Thomas. 2000. Fuzzy politics around fuzzy borders: The European Union's "near abroad." *Cooperation and Conflict* 35(4): 389–415.

Chun, Kyung-Kap. 1986. A critical reassessment of Marxian base-superstructure explanations of the role of education in social change. *Journal of Educational Thought* 20(2): 90–102.

Church, R. L., and M. W. Sedlak. 1976. *Education in the United States: An interpretive history.* New York: Free Press.

Civille, Richard. 1993. A national strategy for civic networking: A vision of change. *Internet Research* 3(4): 2–21.

Claessens, Joris, Claudia Díaz, Caroline Goemans, Jos Dumortier, Bart Preneel, and Joos Vandewalle. 2003. Revocable anonymous access to the Internet? *Internet Research: Electronic Networking Applications and Policy* 13(4): 242–258.

Clanchy, Michael. 1979. *From memory to written record: England, 1066–1307.* Cambridge, MA: Harvard University Press.

Clapp, George Luther. 1917. *Conflict of laws.* Chicago: Blackstone Institute.

Clapp, Verner W. 1968. *Copyright: A librarian's view.* Washington, DC: Copyright Committee, Association of Research Libraries.

Clasby, Alison E. 1989. The McCarran-Walter Act and ideological exclusion: A call for reform. *University of Miami Law Review* 43: 1141–1168.

Clausewitz, Carl von. [1832] 1976. *On war*, trans. by Michael Eliot Howard and Peter Paret. Princeton, NJ: Princeton University Press.

Clavir, Miriam. 2002. Heritage preservation: Museum conservation and First Nations' perspectives. *Ethnologies* 24(2): 33–46.

Cleland v. National College of Business, 435 U.S. 213. 1978.

Clemens, Elisabeth S. 2000. The encounter of civil society and the states: Legislation, law, and association, 1900–1920. Presented to the Social Science History Association, Fort Worth, TX, January.

Cleveland, Harlan. 1985. *The knowledge executive: Leadership in an information society*. New York: W. P. Dutton.

Clifford, James. 1988. *The predicament of culture: Twentieth-century ethnography, literature, and art*. Cambridge, MA: Harvard University Press.

Clift, Steven. 1997–2005. *DoWire.Org: Democracies Online*. Available at www.dowire.org.

Cline, William R., N. Kawanabe, T. Kronso, and T. Williams. 1978. Trade negotiations and the less developed countries. In William R. Cline, ed., *Trade negotiations in the Tokyo Round: A quantitative assessment*, 207–227. Washington, DC: Brookings Institution.

Cloud, Stanley W. 2001. The Pentagon and the press. *Nieman Reports* 55(4): 13–17.

Coase, Ronald J. 1937. The nature of the firm. *Economica* 4: 386–405.

Codding, George Arthur, Jr. 1972. *The International Telecommunications Union: An experiment in international communications*. New York: Arno Press.

Coen, David. 1998. The European business interest and the nation state: Large-firm lobbying in the European Union and member states. *Journal of Public Policy* 18(1): 75–100.

Cogburn, Derrick. 2004. Elite decision-making and epistemic communities: Implications for global economic policy. In Sandra Braman, ed., *The emergent global information policy regime*, 154–178. Houndsmills, UK: Palgrave Macmillan.

Coggins, Carolyn. 2004. Independent testing of voting systems. *Communications of the ACM* 47(10): 34–38.

Cohen, Akiba A., and Itzhak Roeh. 1992. When fiction and news cross over the border: Notes on differential readings and effects. In Felipe Korzenny and E. Stella Ting-Toomey, eds., *Mass media effects across cultures*, 23–34. London: Sage.

Cohen, Bernard S. 1996. *Colonialism and its forms of knowledge: The British in India*. Princeton, NJ: Princeton University Press.

Cohen, Felix S. 1935. Transcendental nonsense and the functional approach. *Columbia Law Review* 35(5): 809–849.

Cohen, Felix S. 1950. Field theory and judicial logic. *Yale Law Journal* 59(2): 238–272.

Cohen, Julie E. 2003. The law and technology of digital rights management. *Berkeley Technology Law Journal* 18(2): 575–617.

Cohen, Paul E. 2002. *Mapping the West: America's westward movement, 1524–1890*. New York: Rizzoli.

Cohen, R. 2002. Local government support of arts and culture. *Journal of Arts Management, Law, and Society* 32(3): 206–221.

Cohen, S. 1999. *Challenging orthodoxies: Toward a new cultural history of education*. New York: Peter Lang.

Cohen, Stephen P., ed. 1990. *Towards a nuclear verification regime in South Asia*. Los Alamos, NM: Study for Los Alamos National Lab, LANL Subcont. #9-XC9-C4353-1.

Cohen, Wesley Marc, and Stephen A. Merrill. 2003. *Patents in the knowledge-based economy*. Washington, DC: National Academies Press.

Cohendet, P., and F. Meyer-Krahmer. 2001. The theoretical and policy implications of knowledge codification. *Research Policy* 30(9): 1563–1591.

Cohendet, P., and W. E. Steinmueller. 2000. The codification of knowledge: A conceptual and empirical exploration. *Industrial and Corporate Change* 9(2): 361–376.

Colas, Dominique. [1991] 1997. *Civial society and fanaticism*, trans. by Amy Jacobs. Stanford, CA: Stanford University Press.

Cole, David. 1999. Hanging with the wrong crowd: Of gangs, terrorists, and the right of association. *Supreme Court Review* (1999): 203–252.

Cole, Rosanne. 1990. Reviving the federal statistical system: A view from industry. *American Economic Association Papers and Proceedings* 80(2): 333–336.

Colles, William Morris, and Harold Hardy. 1906. *Playright and copyright in all countries: Showing how to protect a play or a book throughout the world*. New York and London: Macmillan.

Collins, H. M. 2001. Tacit knowledge, trust and the Q of sapphire. *Social Studies of Science* 31(1): 71–85.

Colloredo-Mansfeld, R. 2002. An ethnography of neoliberalism: Understanding competition in artisan economies. *Current Anthropology* 43(1): 113–137.

Committee on International Security and Arms Control. 2005. *Monitoring nuclear weapons and nuclear-explosive materials*. Washington, DC: National Academies Press.

Congressional Research Service (CRS). 2001. *Terrorism: Automated lookout systems and border security options and issues*. Washington, DC: Government Printing Office, RL31019, June.

Connolly, Kevin J. 2003. *Law of Internet security and privacy*. New York: Aspen Publishers.

Connolly, Thomas A. 1988. Does the Constitution limit on-site inspection? *Arms Control Today* 18(5): 8–12.

Connors, Michael. 1993. *The race to the intelligent state: Towards the global information economy of 2005*. Cambridge, MA: Blackwell Business.

Conrad, Jack G., and Daniel P. Dabney. 2001. Automatic recognition of distinguishing negative indirect history language in judicial opinions. In *Proceedings of the Tenth International Conference on Information and Knowledge Management*, 287–294. New York: Association for Computing Machinery.

Cook, Karen S., and Joseph M. Whitmeyer. 1992. Two approaches to social structure: Exchange theory and network analysis. *Annual Review of Sociology* 18: 109–127.

Cooley, Charles Horton. 1897. The process of social change. *Political Science Quarterly* 12(1): 63–81.

Cooley, Charles Horton. 1902. *Human nature and the social order*. New York: Scribner.

Cooley, George Horton. 1909. *Social organization: A study of the larger mind*. New York: Scribner.

Cooper, Joseph, and William F. West. 1988. Presidential power and Republican government: The theory and practice of OMB review of agency rules. *Journal of Politics* 50(4): 864–895.

Cornug, M. 1983. A history of indexing technology. *The Indexer* 13(3): 15–27.

Corsi, Jerome R. 1984. *Judicial politics: An introduction*. Englewood Cliffs, NJ: Prentice-Hall.

Corson, Dale. 1982. *Scientific communication and national security* ("The Corson Report"). Washington, DC: National Academies Press.

Cortada, James W. 2000. Progenitors of the information age: The development of chips and computers. In Alfred D. Chandler, Jr., and James W. Cortada, eds., *A nation transformed by information*, 177–216. New York: Oxford University Press.

Coulmas, Florian. 1993. *Language and economy*. Cambridge, MA: Blackwell.

Courtney, R. H., Jr. 1988. Another perspective on sensitive but unclassified data. *Computers and Security* 7(1): 19–23.

Couto, Richard A. 1993. Narrative, free space, and political leadership in social movements. *The Journal of Politics* 55(1): 57–79.

Cowhey, Peter F. 1990. The international telecommunications regime: The political roots of regimes for high technology. *International Organization* 44(2): 169–199.

Cox, Adam B. 2004. Citizenship, standing, and immigration law. *California Law Review* 92(2): 374–423.

Coyne, Richard. 1995. *Designing information technology in the postmodern age: From method to metaphor*. Cambridge, MA: MIT Press.

Crandall, Robert W. 1989. Surprises from telephone deregulation and the AT&T divestiture. *American Economic Review* 78(2): 323–327.

Crandall, Robert W., and Leonard Waverman. 2000. *Who pays for universal service? When telephone subsidies become transparent*. Washington, DC: Brookings Institution Press.

Crane, Rhonda J. 1978. Communication standards and the politics of protectionism: The case of colour television systems. *Telecommunications Policy* 2(4): 267–281.

Crawford, Elisabeth. 1992. *Nationalism and internationalism in science, 1880–1939: Four studies of the Nobel population.* Cambridge: Cambridge University Press.

Crawford, Gregory A., and Lisa R. Stimatz. 2000. Rhetoric versus reality: A reexamination of access to U.S. government information during the presidency of Ronald Reagan. *Journal of Government Information* 27(1): 13–27.

Crawford, James. 1997. *Best evidence: Research foundations of the Bilingual Education Act.* Washington, DC: National Clearinghouse for Bilingual Education, George Washington University.

Crawford, James. 2000. *At war with diversity: U.S. language policy in an age of anxiety.* Clevedon, UK: Multilingual Matters.

Creech, Kenneth C. 2003. *Electronic media law and regulation*, 4th ed. Oxford: Boston Focal Press.

Critical Art Ensemble. 1996. *Electronic civil disobedience and other unpopular ideas.* Brooklyn: Autonomedia.

Critical Art Ensemble. 2001. *Digital resistance: Explorations in tactical media.* Brooklyn: Autonomedia.

Crosby, Alfred W. 1994. *Germs, seeds, and animals: Studies in ecological history.* Armonk, NY: M. E. Sharpe.

Cruise O'Brien, Rita. 1977. Specialized information and interdependence: Problems of concentration and access. *Telecommunications Policy* 4(1): 42–48.

Cruise O'Brien, Rita. 1983. *Information, economics and power: The North-South dimension.* London: Hodder and Stoughton.

Cubberly, Ellwood P. 1919. *Public education in the United States: A study and interpretation of American educational history.* Boston: Houghton Mifflin.

Cupitt, Richard T. 2000. *Reluctant champions: U.S. presidential policy and strategic export controls, Truman, Eisenhower, Bush, and Clinton.* New York: Routledge.

Cutrera, Terri A. 1992. Computer networks, libel and the First Amendment. *Computer Law Journal* 11(4): 555–583.

Dahl, Robert Alan. 1956. *Who governs?* New Haven, CT: Yale University Press.

Dahl, Robert Alan. 1967. The concept of power. *Behavioral Science* 2(3): 201–215.

Dahl, Robert Alan. 2003. *How democratic is the American Constitution?*, 2nd ed. New Haven, CT: Yale University Press.

Dahlgren, Peter. 2004. Theory, boundaries, and political communication. *European Journal of Communication* 19(1): 7–18.

Dahlin, Kristina B., and Dean M. Behrens. 2005. When is an invention really radical? Defining and measuring technological radicalness. *Research Policy* 34(5): 717–737.

Dallmeyer, Dorinda G. 1997. *Joining together, standing apart: National identities after NAFTA*. The Hague, The Netherlands: Kluwer Academic.

Damon, L. 1986. Freedom of information versus national sovereignty: The need for a new global forum for the resolution of transborder data flow problems. *Fordham International Law Journal* 10(2): 262–287.

Dandeker, Christopher. 1990. *Surveillance, power and modernity: Bureaucracy and discipline from 1700 to the present day*. New York: St. Martin's Press.

Daniels, Roger. 2004. *Guarding the golden door: American immigration policy and immigrants since 1882*. New York: Hill and Wang.

D'Anieri, Paul, Claire Ernst, and Elizabeth Kier. 1990. New social movements in historical perspective. *Comparative Politics* 22(4): 445–458.

Dauterman, Walter C., Jr. 2002. Foreign actors and local harms—At the crossroads of pornography, hate speech, and freedom of expression, *North Carolina Journal of Law & Technology* 3(4): 175–220.

Davis, Diane E. 1999. The power of distance: Re-theorizing social movements in Latin America. *Theory and Society* 28(4): 585–638.

Davis, Gerald F., Robert L. Kahn, and Mayer N. Zald. 1990. Contracts, treaties, and joint ventures. In Robert L. Kahn and Mayer N. Zald, eds., *Organizations and nation-states: New perspectives on conflict and cooperation*, 19–54. San Francisco: Jossey-Bass.

Davis, Lennard J. 1983. *Factual fictions: The origins of the English novel*. New York: Columbia University Press.

Davis, Richard. 1999. *The web of politics: The Internet's impact on the American political system*. New York: Oxford University Press.

Dawkins, Richard. 1989. *The selfish gene*. Oxford: Oxford University Press.

Dean, Jodi. 2002. *Publicity's secret: How technoculture capitalizes on democracy*. Ithaca, NY: Cornell University Press.

Dearing, Bruce. 1972. General education and radical social change. *Journal of General Education* 24(3): 139–143.

de Avillez Pereira, M., ed. 2000. *Antitrust and new media*. The Hague, The Netherlands: Kluwer Law International.

Dede, Christopher. 1975. The coming emergence of education as a major force for conscious social change. *Journal of Thought* 10(4): 303–309.

De Greene, Kenyon B., ed. 1982. *A systems-based approach to policymaking*. Boston: Kluwer Academic.

Dekker, Jeroen J. H. 1990. The fragile relation between normality and marginality: Marginalization and institutionalization in the history of education. *Paedagogica Historica* 26(2): 13–29.

de Landa, Manuel. 1991. *War in the age of intelligent machines*. New York: Zone.

Delaney, Edward J. 1993. Technology search and firm bounds in biotechnology: New firms as agents of change. *Growth and Change* 24(2): 206–228.

Del Castillo, Adelaida R. 2002. Illegal status and social citizenship: Thoughts on Mexican immigrants in a postnational world. *Aztlán* 27(2): 11–32.

del Fiol, Raul Antonio, and José Eugênio Guisard Farraz. 1985. National telecommunications policy planning in Brazil. *Telecommunications Policy* 9(3): 229–239.

Deleuze, Gilles, and Félix Guattari. 1987. *A thousand plateaus: Capitalism and schizophrenia*. Minneapolis: University of Minnesota Press.

Deller, N., and J. Burroughs. 2003. Arms control abandoned: The case of biological weapons. *World Policy Journal* 20(2): 37–42.

Dellinger, Hampton. 1997. Words are enough: The troublesome use of photographs, maps, and other images in Supreme Court opinions. *Harvard Law Review* 110(8): 1704–1753.

Delta, George B., and Jeffrey H. Matsuura. 2001. *Law of the Internet*. New York: Aspen Publishers.

Demac, Donna A. 1984. *Keeping America uninformed: Government secrecy in the 1980's*. New York: Pilgrim Press.

Demaske, Chris. 2004. Modern power and the First Amendment: Reassessing hate speech. *Communication Law and Policy* 9(3): 273–316.

Demchak, Chris C. 1991. *Military organizations, complex machines: Modernization in the U.S. armed services*. Ithaca, NY: Cornell University Press.

Deng, Fang. 1997. Information gaps and unintended outcomes of social movements: The 1989 Chinese student movement. *American Journal of Sociology* 102(4): 1085–1112.

Dennis, Everette E., and Eli M. Noam. 1989. *The cost of libel: Economic and policy implications*. New York: Columbia University Press.

Dennis v. U.S., 341 U.S. 494. 1951.

Derrida, Jacques. 1976. *Of grammatology*. Baltimore, MD: Johns Hopkins University Press.

Derrida, Jacques. 1992. *The other heading: Reflections on today's Europe*, trans. by Pascale-Anne Brault and Michael B. Naas. Bloomington: Indiana University Press.

Dervin, Brenda, and Kathleen Diana Clark. 1993. Communication and democracy: Mandate for procedural invention. In Slavko Splichal and Janet Wasko, eds., *Communication and democracy*, 103–140. Norwood, NJ: Ablex.

Desrosieres, Alain. 1991. The part in relation to the whole: How to generalize? The prehistory of representative sampling. In Martin Bulmer, Kevin Bales, and Kathryn Kish Sklar, eds., *The social survey in historical perspective, 1880–1940*, 217–244. Cambridge: Cambridge University Press.

Desrosieres, Alain. 1998. *The politics of large numbers: A history of statistical reasoning*, trans. by C. Naish. Cambridge, MA: Harvard University Press.

Dessler, David. 1989. What is at stake in the agent-structure debate? *International Organization* 43(3): 441–474.

de Swaan, Abram. 1997. Widening circles of disidentification: On the psycho- and sociogenesis of the hatred of strangers—Reflections on Rwanda. *Theory, Culture and Society* 14(2): 105–122.

Deutsch, Karl W. 1961. Social mobilization and political development, *American Political Science Review* 55(3): 493–614.

Deutsch, Karl W. 1966. *Nationalism and social communication: An inquiry into the foundations of nationality*, 2nd ed. Cambridge, MA: MIT Press.

DeVorkin, David. 2002. *Beyond earth: Mapping the universe*. Washington, DC: National Geographic.

DeVries, Will Thomas. 2003. Protecting privacy in the digital age. *Berkeley Technology Law Journal* 18(1): 283–311.

Dewdney, Christopher. 1998. *Last flesh: Life in the transhuman era*. San Francisco: HarperSan Francisco.

Dewey, John. [1916] 2004. *Democracy and education*. Mineola, NY: Dover.

Dezalay, Yves. 1989. Putting justice "into play" on the global market: Law, lawyers, accountants and the competition for financial services. *Tidskrift für rattssociologi* 6(1–2): 9–67.

Dezalay, Yves, and Bryan G. Garth. 1996. *Dealing in virtue: International commercial arbitration and the construction of a transnational legal order*. Chicago: University of Chicago Press.

Dharmapala, Dhammika, and Richard H. McAdams. 2005. Words that kill? An economic model of the influence of speech on behavior (with particular reference to hate speech). *The Journal of Legal Studies* 34(1): 93–136.

Diamond v. Chakrabarty, 447 U.S. 303. 1980.

Diamond v. Diehr, 450 U.S. 175. 1981.

Dibbell, Julian. 1993. A rape in cyberspace. *The Village Voice* (December 21): 36–42.

DiChiara, Michael. 1997. A modern day myth: The necessity of English as the official language. *Third World Law Journal* 17(1): 101–131.

Dick, Trevor J. O. 1970. *An economic theory of technological change: The case of patents and the United States railroads, 1871–1950*. New York: Arno Press.

Diderot, Denis. [1751] 1969. *The encyclopedia: Selections*, ed. by Stephen J. Gendzier. New York: Harper & Row.

Diebold, William, Jr. 1987. Balancing the national interest: U.S. national security export controls and global economic competition. *Foreign Affairs* 65(5): 1102–1106.

Di Franco, Anthony, Andrew Petro, Emmett Shear, and Vladmir Vladmirov. 2004. Small vote manipulations can swing elections. *Communications of the ACM* 47(10): 43–45.

DiMaggio, Paul. 1991. Social structure, institutions, and cultural goods: The case of the United States. In Pierre Bourdieu and James Coleman, eds., *Social theory for a changing society*, 133–155. Boulder, CO: Westview Press.

Dingledine, Roger, ed. 2004. *Privacy enhancing technologies*. New York: Springer.

Dinh, Van Tran. 1987. *Communication and diplomacy in a changing world*. Norwood, NJ: Ablex.

Dixon, William J. 1985. Change and persistence in the world system: An analysis of global trade concentration, 1955–1975. *International Studies Quarterly* 29(2): 171–189.

Dizard, Wilson P. 2004. *Inventing public diplomacy: The story of the U.S. Information Agency*. Boulder, CO: Lynne Rienner.

Dodgson, Mark. 1993. *Technological collaboration in industry: Strategy, policy and internationalization in innovation*. New York: Routledge.

Doel, R. E. 2003. Constituting the postwar earth sciences: The military's influence on the environmental sciences in the USA after 1945. *Social Studies of Science* 33(5): 635–666.

Domhoff, G. William. 1975. Social clubs, policy-planning groups and corporations: A network study of ruling-class cohesiveness. *Insurgent Sociologist* 5(3): 173–184.

Dore, Patricia A. 1991. Florida limits policy development through administrative adjudication and requires indexing and availability of agency orders. *Florida State University Law Review* 19(2): 437–455.

Dorros, Irwin. 1982. ISDN: The telecommunications network architecture of the future. *New Jersey Bell Journal* 5(2): 38–45.

Dosi, Giovanni. 1997. Opportunities, incentives and the collective patterns of technological change. *The Economic Journal* 107(444): 1530–1547.

Dosi, Giovanni, Richard Nelson, Christopher Freeman, Luc Soete, and Gerald Silverberg, eds. 1988. *Technical change and economic theory*. London: Pinter Publishers.

Douglas, Susan J. 1989. *Inventing American broadcasting, 1899–1922*. Baltimore, MD: Johns Hopkins University Press.

Dowdall, Harold C. 1923. The word "state." *Law Quarterly Review* 39(1): 98–125.

Drahos, Peter, and Imelda Mayer. 2004. Innovation, competition, standards, and intellectual property: Policy perspectives from economics and law. *Information Economics and Policy* 16(1): 1–11.

Drake, William J., and Kalypso Nicolaides. 1992. Ideas, interests, and institutionalization: Trade in services and the Uruguay Round. *International Organization* 46(1): 37–100.

Drexl, Josef, and Annette Kur. 2005. *Intellectual property and private international law*. Oxford: Hart.

Drone, Eaton S. 1879. *A treatise on the law of property in intellectual productions in Great Britain and the United States*. Boston: Little, Brown.

Dror, Yehezkiel. 1976. Some features of a meta-model for policy studies. In Phillip M. Gregg, ed., *Problems of theory in policy analysis*, 51–61. Lexington, MA: Lexington Books.

Druss, B. G., and S. C. Marcus. 2005. Tracking publication outcomes of National Institutes of Health grants. *American Journal of Medicine* 118(6): 658–663.

Dudley, Leonard M. 1991. *The word and the sword: How techniques of information and violence have shaped our world*. Cambridge, MA: Blackwell.

Dugan, Robert E., Peter Hernon, and Harold C. Relyea. 1998. Public printing reform: The Wendell H. Ford Government Publications Reform Act proposal. *Journal of Academic Librarianship* 24(6): 470–478.

Dunn, Donald A. 1982. Developing information policy. *Telecommunications Policy* 6(1): 21–38.

Dunning, John H. 2000. *Regions, globalization, and the knowledge-based economy*. New York: Oxford University Press.

Durand, Jorge, Douglas S. Massey, and Rene M. Zenteno. 2001. Mexican immigration to the United States: Continuities and changes. *Latin American Research Review* 36(1): 107–127.

Durkheim, Emile. 1986. *Durkheim on politics and the state*, ed. by Anthony Giddens and trans. by W. D. Halls. Cambridge: Polity Press.

Duvall, Raymond, and John Freeman. 1983. The techno-bureaucratic elite and the entrepreneurial state in dependent industrialization. *American Political Science Review* 77(3): 569–587.

Dworkin, Ronald. 1977. *Taking rights seriously*. Cambridge, MA: Harvard University Press.

Dworkin, Ronald. 1986. *Law's empire*. Cambridge, MA: Harvard University Press.

Dyck, J. J., and J. G. Gimpel. 2005. Distance, turnout, and the convenience of voting. *Social Science Quarterly* 86(3): 531–548.

Easton, David. 1953. *The political system: An enquiry into the state of political science*. New York: Knopf.

Easton, David. 1979. *A framework for political analysis*. Chicago: University of Chicago Press.

Easton, David. 1981. The political system besieged by the state. *Political Theory* 3(3): 303–326.

Eberhardt, Charles N. 1986. Integrating the right of association with the Bellotti right to hear—Federal Election Commission v. Massachusetts Citizens for Life, Inc. *Cornell Law Review* 72: 159–194.

Echeverria, John D. and Julie B. Kaplan. 2003. Poisonous procedural "reform": In defense of environmental right-to-know. *Kansas Journal of Law and Public Policy* 12(3): 579–640.

Economic Classification Policy Committee. 1994. *Report No. 1: Economic concepts incorporated into the Standard Industrial Classification of industries of the United States*. Washington, DC: U.S. Department of Commerce, August.

The Economist. 1985. A GATT for services. *The Economist* (October 12): 20.

The Economist. 1992. Blind wisdom. *The Economist* 323(7760) (May 23): 93.

The Economist. 1993. The other hand: Chiral drugs. *The Economist* 329(7840) (December 4): 89.

Edvinsson, Leif, and Freij Ake. 1999. Skandia: Three generations of intellectual capital. In Nicholas Imparato, ed., *Capital for our time: The economic, legal, and management challenges of intellectual capital*, 192–201. Stanford, CA: Hoover Institute Press, Pub. No. 448.

Eggan, Fred. 1963. Cultural drift and social change. *Cultural Anthropology* 4(4): 347–355.

Einhorn, Michael A., 2005. *Media, technology and copyright: Integrating law and economics*. Cheltenham, UK: Edward Elgar.

Einhorn, Michael A., and Bill Rosenblatt. 2005. *Peer-to-peer networking and digital rights management: How market tools can solve copyright problems*. Washington, DC: Cato Institute.

Eisenstadt, Stuart N. 1964. Social change, differentiation and evolution. *American Sociological Review* 29(3): 375–386.

Eisenstadt, Stuart N. 1980. Comparative analysis of state formations in historical contexts. *International Social Science Journal* 32: 624–653.

Eisenstein, Elizabeth. 1979. *The printing press as an agent of change: Communications and cultural transformation in early-modern Europe*. Cambridge: Cambridge University Press.

Eisner, R. 1984. The new incremental tax credit for R&D: Incentive or disincentive? *National Tax Journal* 37: 171–183.

Eisner, Robert. 1998. The R&D tax credit: A flawed tool. In *The selected essays of Robert Eisner*, vol. 2, 380–387. Cheltenham, UK: Edward Elgar.

Ekstrand, Victoria Smith. 2003. Unmasking Jane and John Doe: Online anonymity and the First Amendment. *Communication Law and Policy* 8(4): 405–427.

Electronic Privacy Information Center and Privacy International. 2003. *Privacy & human rights*. Washington, DC: EPIC. Available at www.privacyinternational.org.

Electronic Privacy Information Center. 2005. *The USA PATRIOT Act*. Available at www.epic.org/terrorism/usapatriot/default.html.

Eliade, Mircea. 1954. *Cosmos and history: The myth of the eternal return*, trans. by W. Trask. Princeton, NJ: Princeton University Press.

Elichirigoity, Fernando. 1999. *Planet management: Limits to growth, computer simulation, and the emergence of global spaces*. Evanston, IL: Northwestern University Press.

El-Kholy, O. A. 1980. The winds of change: From an information embargo to a national survey of information needs and resources in Egypt. Presented to the International Association for Mass Communication Research.

Elkin-Koren, Niva. 2001. Let the crawlers crawl on: On virtual gatekeepers and the right to exclude indexing. *University of Dayton Law Review* 26(2): 179–210.

Elkins, David J. 1997. Globalization, telecommunication, and virtual ethnic communities. *International Political Science Review* 18(2): 139–152.

Ellig, Jerry, and Daniel Lin. 2001. A taxonomy of dynamic competition theories. In Jerry Ellig, ed., *Dynamic competition and public policy: Technology, innovation, and antitrust issues*, 16–44. Cambridge: Cambridge University Press.

Ellsberg, Daniel. 2004. Secrecy oaths: A license to lie? *Harvard International Review*. Available at http://hir.harvard.edu/articles/1235/.

Ellul, Jacques. [1954] 1964. *The technological society*, trans. by John Wilkinson. New York: Vintage Books.

Eloff, J. H. P., R. Holbein, and S. Teufel. 1996. Security classification for documents. *Computers & Security* 15(1): 55–71.

Elwell, Christine. 2001. NAFTA effects on water: Testing for NAFTA effects in the Great Lakes basin. *Toledo Journal of Great Lakes' Law, Science & Policy* 3(2): 151–212.

Ely, John Hart. 1978. On discovering fundamental values. *Harvard Law Review* 92(1): 5–55.

Ely, John Hart. 1980. *Democracy and distrust: A theory of judicial review*. Cambridge, MA: Harvard University Press.

Elzinga, Kenneth G. 1989. Unmasking monopoly: Four types of economic evidence. In Robert J. Larner and James W. Meehan, Jr., eds., *Economics and antitrust policy*, 11–38. Westport, CT: Greenwood Press.

Emerson, Thomas I. 1970. *The system of freedom of expression*. New York: Random House.

Emerson, Thomas I. 1977. Colonial intentions and current realities of the First Amendment. *University of Pennsylvania Law Review* 125(4): 737–760.

Engel, Charles, and John R. Rogers. 1996. How wide is the border? *American Economic Review* 86(5): 1112–1125.

Entman, Robert. 1993. Putting the First Amendment in its place: Enhancing American democracy through the press. *The University of Chicago Legal Forum* 1993: 61–82.

Entman, Robert M. 1999. *Residential access to bandwidth: Exploring new paradigms*. A report of the Thirteenth Annual Aspen Institute Conference on Telecommunications Policy. Aspen: Aspen Institute.

Entman, Robert, and Steve Wildman. 1992. Reconciling economic and noneconomic perspectives on media policy: Transcending the "marketplace of ideas." *Journal of Communication* 42(1): 5–19.

Erdur, R. C., O. Dikenelli, I. Seylan, and Ö. Gürcan. 2005. Semantically federating multi-agent organizations. In M.-P. Gleizes, A. Omicini, and F. Zambonelli, eds., *Engineering Societies in the Agents World V*, 74–89. Berlin: Springer.

Ericson, Richard V., Patricia M. Baranek, and Janet B. L. Chan. 1991. *Representing order: Crime, law, and justice in the news media*. Toronto: University of Toronto Press.

Erikson, Erik H. 1968. *Identity: Youth and crisis*. New York: Norton.

Erskine, Toni. 2002. "Citizen of nowhere" or "the point where circles intersect"? Impartialist and embedded cosmopolitanisms. *Review of International Studies* 28(3): 457–478.

Escobar, Edward J. 1999. *Race, police, and the making of a political identity: Mexican Americans and the Los Angeles Police Department, 1900–1945*. Berkeley: University of California Press.

Escolano, Agustin. 1996. Postmodernity or high modernity? Emerging approaches in the new history of education. *Paedagogica Historica* 32(2): 325–341.

Espenshade, Thomas J. 2001. High-end immigrants and the shortage of skilled labor. *Population Research and Policy Review* 20(1–2): 135–141.

Estlund, Cynthia L. 2000. Working together: The workplace, civil society, and the law. *Georgetown Law Journal* 89(1): 1–96.

Eswaran, Mukesh, and Nancy Gallini. 1996. Patent policy and the direction of technological change. *RAND Journal of Economics* 27(4): 722–746.

Etzioni, Amitai. 1968. *The active society*. New York: Free Press.

Evans, Gail E. H. 1992. Storm over Niagara: A catalyst in reshaping government in the United States and Canada during the Progressive Era. *Natural Resources Journal* 32(1): 27–54.

Evans, Peter. 1985. Transnational linkages and the economic role of the state: An analysis of developing and industrialized nations in the post-World War II period. In Peter Evans, Dietrich Rueschemeyer, and Theda Skocpol, eds., *Bringing the state back in*, 192–226. Cambridge: Cambridge University Press.

Evans, Peter, Dietrich Rueschemeyer, and Theda Skocpol, eds. 1985. *Bringing the state back in*. Cambridge: Cambridge University Press.

Evernden, Roger, and Elaine Evernden. 2003. Third-generation information architecture. *Communications of the ACM* 46(3): 95–98.

Ewing, A. 1985. Why freer trade in services is in the interest of developing countries. *Journal of World Trade* 19(2): 147–169.

Fairchild, Amy L. 2003. *Science at the borders: Immigrant medical inspection and the shaping of the modern industrial labor force*. Baltimore, MD: Johns Hopkins University Press.

Falk, B. G. 1988. *Borderline: A bibliography of the United States–Mexico borderlands*. Los Angeles: UCLA.

Fallon, Richard H. 2004. *The dynamic Constitution: An introduction to American constitutional law*. Cambridge: Cambridge University Press.

Farber, Daniel A., and Suzanna Sherry. 2002. *Desperately seeking certainty: The misguided quest for constitutional foundations*. Chicago: University of Chicago Press.

Faulk, John Henry. 1964. *Fear on trial.* New York: Simon and Schuster.

Federal Elections Commission. 2001. *Voting system standards.* Washington, DC: Government Printing Office.

Federal Geographic Data Committee. 2004. *Beyond boundaries: Working together for our common good—the National Spatial Data Infrastructure.* Washington, DC: Federal Geographic Data Committee.

Feeley, M. M., and Samuel Krislov. 1985. *Constitutional law.* Boston: Little, Brown.

Feinberg, Richard A., Lori S. Westgate, and W. Jeffrey Burroughs. 1992. Credit cards and social identity. *Semiotica* 91(1–2): 99–108.

Feketekuty, Geza, and Jonathan Aronson. 1984. Restrictions on trade in communication and information services. *The Information Society* 2(3/4): 217–248.

Feketekuty, Geza, and Katherine Hausar. 1985. The impact of information technology on trade in services. *Transnational Data Report* 8(4): 220–224.

Feldman, Mark B. 1985. The restructuring of national security controls under the 1985 amendments to the Export Administration Act: Multilateral diplomacy and the extraterritorial application of United States law. *Stanford Journal of International Law* 21: 235–279.

Fellman, D. 1963. *The constitutional right of association.* Chicago: University of Chicago Press.

Feng, P. 2000. Rethinking technology, revitalizing ethics: Overcoming barriers to ethical design. *Science and Engineering Ethics* 6(2): 207–220.

Ferguson, Marjorie, ed. 1986. *New communication technologies and the public interest: Comparative perspectives on policy and research.* Beverly Hills, CA: Sage.

Ferguson, Yale H., and Richard W. Mansbach. 1996. *Politics: Authority, identities and change.* Columbia: University of South Carolina Press.

Ferrera, Gerald R., Stephen D. Lichtenstein, Margo E. K. Reder, Robert C. Bird, and William T. Schiano. 2004. *Cyberlaw: Text and cases.* Cincinnati, OH: West/Thomson Learning.

Fessenden, Thomas Green. 1810. *An essay on the law of patents for new inventions.* Boston: D. Mallory.

Feurer, Lewis S., ed. 1959. *Marx and Engels: Basic writings on politics and philosophy.* New York: Doubleday.

Fischer, W. A., and G. Black. 1979. Federal funding of industrial R&D: Stimulus or substitute? *Research Management* 22: 27–30.

Fish, Stanley. 1989. *Doing what comes naturally: Change, rhetoric, and the practice of theory in literary and legal studies.* Durham, NC: Duke University Press.

Fisher, Linda E. 2004. Guilt by expressive association: Political profiling, surveillance and the privacy of groups. *Arizona Law Review* 46(4): 621–676.

Fisher, Louis. 1990. Congressional-executive struggles over information: Secrecy pledges. *Administrative Law Review* 42(1): 89–107.

Fisher, Louis. 2002. Congressional access to information: Using legislative will and leverage. *Duke Law Journal* 52(2): 323–402.

Fiske, John. 1982. *Introduction to communication studies*. New York: Methuen.

Fiss, Owen M. 1979. The forms of justice. *Harvard Law Review* 93(1): 1–58.

Fiss, Owen M. 2003. *The law as it could be*. New York: New York University Press.

Fitzgerald, Scott T., Mack C. Shelley, and Paula W. Dail. 2001. Research on homelessness: Sources and implications of uncertainty. *American Behavioral Scientist* 45(1): 121–148.

Flannery, Peter M. 2003. How to pry with maps: The Fourth Amendment privacy implications of governmental wetland geographic information systems (GIS). *Rutgers Computer and Technology Law Journal* 29(2): 447–473.

Flew, Terry. 1997. Citizenship, Participation and Media Policy Formation. *The Public* 4(4): 87–102.

Flores, Gloria Hernandez, and Colin Lankshear. 2000. Facing NAFTA: Literacy and work in Mexico. *Journal of Adolescent & Adult Literacy* 44(3): 240–245.

Florida, Richard, and Martin Kenney. 1994. The globalization of Japanese R&D: The economic geography of Japanese R&D investment in the United States. *Economic Geography* 70(4): 344–369.

Florini, Ann M. 2000. The politics of transparency. Presented at the International Studies Association, Los Angeles, CA, March.

Folk, George E. 1942. *Patents and industrial progress: A summary, analysis, and evaluation of the record on patents of the Temporary National Economic Committee*. New York: Harper.

Foray, Dominique. 2004. *The economics of knowledge*. Cambridge, MA: MIT Press.

Forden, Geoffrey. 2005. Avoiding enrichment: Using financial tools to prevent another Khan network. *Arms Control Today* 35(5): 14–19.

Forgacs, David. 1990. *Italian culture in the industrial era, 1880–1980*. New York: Manchester University Press.

Forman, Howard I. 1957. *Patents, their ownership and administration by the United States government*. New York: Central Book Co.

Foros, Oystein, Hans Jarle Kind, and Jan Yngve Sand. 2005. Do Internet incumbents choose low interconnection quality? *Information Economics and Policy* 17(2): 149–164.

Fortunati, Leopoldina, James Everett Katz, and Raimonda Riccini. 2003. *Mediating the human body: Technology, communication, and fashion*. Mahwah, NJ: Lawrence Erlbaum Associates.

Foster, Gregory D. 2001. Environmental security: The search for strategic legitimacy. *Armed Forces & Society* 27(3): 373–396.

Foster, Hal. 1993. *Compulsive beauty*. Cambridge, MA: MIT Press.

Foucault, Michel. 1973. *The order of things: An archaeology of the human sciences*. New York: Knopf.

Foucault, Michel. 1976. *The history of sexuality: An introduction*. New York: Knopf.

Foucault, Michel. 1980. *Power/knowledge*, ed. Colin Gordon. New York: Pantheon Books.

Foucault, Michel. 1983. The subject and power. Afterword to Hubert L. Dreyfus and Paul Rabinow, *Michel Foucault: Beyond structuralism and hermeneutics*, 2nd ed. Chicago: University of Chicago Press.

Foucault, Michel. 1984. Space, knowledge, and power. In Paul Rabinow, ed., *The Foucault reader*, 239–256. New York: Pantheon Books.

Foweraker, Joe, and Todd Landman. 1999. Individual rights and social movements: A comparative and statistical inquiry. *British Journal of Political Science* 29(2): 291–322.

Fowler, Mark S., and Daniel L. Brenner. 1982. A marketplace approach to broadcast regulation. *Texas Law Review* 60(207): 207–257.

Fox, Eleanor M., and James T. Halverson, eds. 1991. *Collaborations among competitors: Antitrust policy and economics*. Chicago: American Bar Association.

Fox, Harold G. 1947. *Monopolies and patents: A study of the history and future of the patent monopoly*. Toronto: University of Toronto Press.

Fox, James W., Jr. 2003. Relational contract theory and democratic citizenship. *Case Western Reserve Law Review* 54(1): 1–67.

Fox, M. S., and J. Huang. 2005. Knowledge provenance in enterprise information. *International Journal of Production Research* 43(20): 4471–4492.

Francois, William E. 1994. *Mass media law and regulation*, 6th ed. Prospect Heights, IL: Waveland Press.

Frankel, Boris. 1983. *Beyond the state: Dominant theories and socialist strategies*. London: Macmillan Press.

Frankfurter, Felix. 1939. *Law and politics*. New York: Harcourt, Brace.

Franklin, Marc A. 2000. *Mass media law: Cases and materials*, 3rd ed. New York: Foundation Press.

Frau-Meiggs, Divina A. 2000. A cultural project based on multiple temporary consensus: Identity and community in *Wired*. *New Media and Society* 2(2): 227–244.

Frederick, Howard H. 1989. "Development sabotage communication" in low intensity warfare: Media strategies against democracy in Central America. In Marc Raboy and Peter Bruck, eds., *Communication for and against democracy*, 19–35. Montreal: Black Rose Books.

Freeman, Christopher, and Carlota Perez. 1988. *Structural crises of adjustment, business cycles and investment behaviour*. London: Pinter.

Freire, Paolo. [1970] 2000. *Pedagogy of the oppressed*, trans. by Myra Bergman Ramos. New York: Continuum International Publishing Group.

Freudenburg, William R., and Robert Gramling. 1992. Community impacts of technological change: Toward a longitudinal perspective. *Social Forces* 70(4): 937–955.

Frieden, Rob. 2004. The FCC's name game: How shifting regulatory classifications affect competition. *Berkeley Technology Law Journal* 19(4): 1275–1314.

Frieden, Robert M. 1991. Accounting rates: The business of international telecommunications and the incentive to cheat. *Federal Communications Law Journal* 43(2): 111–139.

Frieden, Rob M. 1983a. The Computer Inquiries: Mapping the communications/information processing terrain. *Federal Communications Law Journal* 33: 55–115.

Frieden, Rob M. 1983b. International telecommunications and the Federal Communication Commission. *Columbia Journal of Transnational Law* 21(3): 423–485.

Frieden, Rob M. 1984. The international application of the Second Computer Inquiry. *Michigan Yearbook of International Legal Studies* 5: 189–218.

Frieden, Rob M. 1993. International toll revenue division—Tackling the inequities and inefficiencies. *Telecommunications Policy* 17(3): 221–233.

Frieden, Rob M. 1997. The impact of call-back and arbitrage on the accounting rate regime. *Telecommunications Policy* 21(9/10): 819–827.

Frieden, Rob M. 1998. Falling through the cracks: International accounting rate reform at the ITU and WTO. *Telecommunications Policy* 22(11): 963–975.

Friedman, B., and Helen Nissenbaum. 1996. Bias in computer systems. *ACM Transactions on Information Systems* 14(3): 330–347.

Friedman, Lawrence M. 1985. *A history of American law*, 2nd ed. New York: Simon and Schuster.

Friedman, Lawrence M. 2004. What, me worry about metadata? *CBA Record* 18: 43ff.

Froomkin, A. Michael. 1996. Flood control on the information ocean: Living with anonymity, digital cash, and distributed databases. *Journal of Law and Commerce* 15(2): 395–508.

Froomkin, A. Michael. 1999. Legal issues in anonymity and pseudonymity. *The Information Society* 15(2): 113–127.

Frye, Rex. 1921. *The income and other federal taxes as affected by patents, trade-marks, copyrights and goodwill.* Chicago: Gunthorp-Warren Print Co.

Fuchs, Stephan, and Peggy S. Plass. 1999. Sociology and social movements. *Contemporary Sociology* 28(3): 271–277.

Fulk, Janet, and Charles Steinfeld, eds. 1990. *Organizations and communication technology*. Newbury Park, CA: Sage.

Gaines, Jane M. 1991. *Contested culture: The image, the voice, and the law.* Chapel Hill: University of North Carolina Press.

Galbi, Douglas A. 1998. Distinctive arrangements for international interconnection? *Telecommunications Policy* 22(11): 945–951.

Galenson, D. W. 2002. Quantifying artistic success: Ranking French painters, and paintings, from Impressionism to Cubism. *Historical Methods* 35(1): 5–19.

Galenson, D. W. 2005. One-hit wonders: Why some of the most important works of modern art are not by important artists. *Historical Methods* 38(3): 101–117.

Gallegos, Gabriela A. 2004. Borders matters: Redefining the national interest in U.S.-Mexico immigration and trade policy. *California Law Review* 92: 1729–1779.

Gamson, William A. 1991. Commitment and agency in social movements. *Sociological Forum* 6(1): 27–50.

Ganley, Oscar H., and Gladys D. Ganley. 1982. *To inform or to control? The new communications networks*. New York: McGraw-Hill.

Gans, G., M. Jarke, G. Lakemeyer, and D. Schmitz. 2005. Deliberation in a metadata-based modeling and simulation environment for inter-organizational networks. *Information Systems* 30(7): 587–607.

Garcia, D. Linda. 2004. Networks and the evolution of property rights in the global, knowledge-based economy. In Sandra Braman, ed., *The emergent global information policy regime*, 130–153. Houndsmills, UK: Palgrave Macmillan.

Garcia, David, and Geert Lovink. 1997. The ABC of tactical media. *nettime*. Available at www.nettime.org/Lists-Archives/nettime-l-9705/msg00096.html.

Garcia-Alonso, Maria del Carmen, and Keith Hartley. 2003. Export controls, market structure and international coordination. In Paul Levine and Ron Smith, eds., *Arms trade, security and conflict*, 37–54. London: Routledge.

Garcia-Barriocanal, E., M. A. Sicilia, and S. Sanchez-Alonso. 2005. Usability evaluation of ontology editors. *Knowledge & Organization* 32(1): 1–9.

Garfield, Eugene. 1957. Breaking the subject index barrier: A citation index for chemical patents. *Journal of the Patent Office Society* 39(8): 583–595.

Garner, P., and E. Spolaore. 2005. Why chads? Determinants of voting equipment use in the United States. *Public Choice* 123(3–4): 363–392.

Garramone, Gina M., and Charles K. Atkin. 1986. Mass communication and political socialization: Specifying the effects. *Public Opinion Quarterly* 50(1): 76–86.

Garvey, John H., and Thomas Alexander Aleinikoff. 1991. *Modern constitutional theory: A reader*. St. Paul, MN: West.

Gassmann, Hans, ed. 1981. *Information, computer and communications policies for the 80's*. Amsterdam: OECD.

Gastil, John. 1992. Undemocratic discourse: A review of theory and research on political discourse. *Discourse and Society* 3(4): 469–500.

Geertz, Clifford. 1957. Ritual and social change: A Javanese example. *American Anthropologist* 59(1): 32–54.

Geertz, Clifford. 1980. Blurred genres: The refiguration of social thought. *American Scholar* 49(2): 165–179.

Geertz, Clifford. 1983. *Local knowledge: Further essays in interpretive anthropology*. New York: Basic Books.

Geller, Henry. 1984. The FCC and Congress. In Harry M. Shooshan, III, ed., *Disconnecting Bell: The impact of the AT&T divestiture*, 83–99. New York: Pergamon Press.

Geller, Henry, and Donna Lampert. 1983. Cable, content regulation and the First Amendment. *Catholic University Law Review* 32(3): 603–631.

Geller, Paul Edward. 2000. Copyright history and the future: What's culture got to do with it? *Journal of the Copyright Society of the USA* 47: 209–264.

Gellner, Ernest. 1983. *Nations and nationalism*. Ithaca, NY: Cornell University Press.

Gemmill, Gary, and Charles Smith. 1985. A dissipative structure model of organization transformation. *Human Relations* 38(8): 751–766.

General Accounting Office (GAO). 1986. *Telephone communications: The FCC's monitoring of residential telephone service*. Washington, DC: Government Printing Office, GAO RCED-86-146.

General Accounting Office (GAO). 1993. *Classified information: Costs of protection are integrated with other security costs*. Washington, DC: Government Printing Office, GAO NSIAD-94-55.

General Accounting Office (GAO). 2002. *Justice plans to improve oversight of agency projects*. Washington, DC: Government Printing Office, GAO-03-135.

General Accounting Office (GAO). 2003. *H-1B foreign workers: Better tracking needed to help determine H-1B program's effects on US workforce*. Washington, DC: Government Printing Office, GAO-03-883.

Gerbner, George, Larry P. Gross, and William H. Melody, eds. 1973. *Communications technology and social policy: Understanding the new "cultural revolution."* New York: Wiley-Interscience.

Gergen, Kenneth J. 1991. *The saturated self: Dilemmas of identity in contemporary life*. New York: Basic Books.

Gergen, Kenneth J., and Keith E. Davis, eds. 1985. *The social construction of the person*. New York: Springer-Verlag.

Gerlach, Michael L. 1992. *Alliance capitalism: The social organization of Japanese business*. Berkeley: University of California Press.

Gershuny, Jonathan, and Ian Miles. 1983. *The new services economy*. London: Frances Pinter.

Gibbon, Edward. [1776] 1960. *The decline and fall of the Roman Empire*. New York: Harcourt, Brace.

Gibbons, Phillip B., Brad Karp, Yan Ke, Suman Nath, and Srinivasan Suman Seshan. 2003. IrisNet: An architecture for a worldwide sensor web. *Pervasive Computing* 2(4): 22–34.

Giddens, Anthony. 1985. *The constitution of society: Outline of the theory of structuration.* Berkeley: University of California Press.

Giddens, Anthony. 1987. *Social theory and modern sociology.* Stanford, CA: Stanford University Press.

Giddens, Anthony, and Held, David, eds. 1990. *Classes, power and conflict: Classical and contemporary debates*, 2nd ed. Berkeley: University of California Press.

Gifreu, Josep. 1986. From communication policy to reconstruction of cultural identity: Prospects for Catalonia. *European Journal of Communication* 1(4): 463–476.

Gilat, David. 1994. *Experimental use and patents.* Munich, Germany: Max Planck Institute for Foreign and International Patent, Copyright and Competition Law.

Gilbertson, Greta, and Audrey Singer. 2003. The emergence of protective citizenship in the USA: Naturalization among Dominican immigrants in the post-1996 welfare reform era. *Ethnic and Racial Studies* 26(1): 25–51.

Gilboa, Eytan. 2000. Mass communication and democracy: A theoretical framework. *Communication Theory* 10(3): 275–309.

Giles, Bob. 2001. Reporting clashes with government policies. *Nieman Reports* 55(4): 3.

Gillam, L., and K. Ahmad. 2005. Machine learning and data mining in pattern recognition. *Lecture Notes in Artificial Intelligence* 3587: 570–579.

Gillmor, Donald M. 1992. *Power, publicity, and the abuse of libel law.* New York: Oxford University Press.

Gillmor, Donald M., Jerome A. Barron, and Todd F. Simon. 1998. *Mass communication law: Cases and comment*, 6th ed. Belmont, CA: Wadsworth.

Gilmore, Debra A. 1988. The antitrust implications of boycotts by health care professionals: Professional standards, professional ethics and the First Amendment. *American Journal of Law & Medicine* 14(2/3): 221–248.

Ginsberg, Morris. 1958. Social change. *British Journal of Sociology* 9(3): 205–229.

Ginsburg, Douglas H., Michael H. Botein, and Mark D. Director. 1998. *Regulation of the electronic mass media: Law and policy for radio, television, cable and the new video technologies*, 2nd ed. St. Paul, MN: West.

Ginsburg, Jane C. 1990. Creation and commercial value: Copyright protection of works of information. *Columbia Law Review* 90: 1865–1938.

Gipe, George A. 1967. *Nearer to the dust: Copyright and the machine.* Baltimore, MD: Williams & Wilkin.

Girasa, Rosario J. 2002. *Cyberlaw: National and international perspectives.* Upper Saddle River, NJ: Prentice Hall.

Giroux, Henry. 1992. *Border crossings: Cultural workers and the politics of education.* New York: Routledge, Chapman & Hall.

Giugni, Marco G. 1998. Was it worth the effort? The outcomes and consequences of social movements. *Annual Review of Sociology* 24: 371–393.

Glaser, Jack, Jay Dixit, and Donald P. Green. 2002. Studying hate crime with the Internet: What makes racists advocate racial violence? *Journal of Social Issues* 58(1): 177–195.

Glass, A. 2004. Return to sender: On the politics of cultural property and the proper address of art. *Journal of Material Culture* 9(2): 115–139.

Godin, Benoît. 2002. The numbers makers: Fifty years of science and technology official statistics. *Minerva* 40(4): 375–397.

Godwin, Mike. 1998. *Cyber-rights: Defending free speech in the digital era*. New York: New York Times Books.

Goff, Patricia. 2000. Invisible borders: Economic liberalization and national identity. *International Studies Quarterly* 44(4): 533–560.

Goguen, J. 2005. Three perspectives on information integration. In Y. Kalfoglou et al., eds., *Semantic interoperability and integration*. Dagstuhl Seminar Proceedings 04391. Leibniz, Germany: Schloss Daghstuhl.

Gold, David A., Clarence Y. H. Lo, and Erik Olin. 1975. Recent developments in Marxist theories of the state. *Monthly Review* 27(5/6): 29–43, 36–51.

Goldberg, David. 1990. A re-examination of the international law of libel in inter-state broadcasting. Presented to the International Association for Mass Communication Research, Bled, Yugoslavia, July.

Goldberg, David, Anthony Prosser, and Stefaan Verhulst. 1998. *Regulating the changing media: A comparative study*. New York: Oxford University Press.

Goldberg, Joseph P., and William T. Moye. 1985. *The first hundred years of the Bureau of Labor Statistics*. Washington, DC: U.S. Department of Labor.

Goldberg, Stephanie B. 1990. Bridging the gap: Law school in the nineties, *ABA Journal* 76 (September): 44–50.

Goldey, Michael J. 1983. Aspects of international voice communications to and from the United States. *Jurimetrics Journal* 24(1): 1–18.

Goldin, Claudia. 1999. *A brief history of education in the United States*. Cambridge, MA: National Bureau of Economic Research (NBER), NBER Historical Paper H0119.

Golding, Peter. 1974. Media role in national development: A critique of a theoretical orthodoxy. *Journal of Communication* 24(3): 39–53.

Goldstein, Judith. 1988. Ideas, institutions, and American trade policy. *International Organization* 42(1): 179–217.

Goodchild, Michael F., and Donald G. Janelle, eds. 2004. *Spatially integrated social science*. New York: Oxford University Press.

Goral, Craig R. 2000. Knowledge management and the FAR: Charting a new course at GSA. *The Public Manager* 29(4): 39–43.

Gordon, Hedy. 1981. The interface of living systems and computers: The legal issues of privacy. *Computer/Law Journal* 2: 877–890.

Gordon, J. W. 1897. *Monopolies by patents and the statutable remedies available to the public.* London: Stevens and Sons.

Gorman, Sean P. 1963. Copyright protection for the collection and representation of facts. *Harvard Law Review* 76: 1569–1605.

Gorman, Sean P., and E. J. Malecki. 2000. The networks of the Internet: An analysis of provider networks in the U.S.A. *Telecommunications Policy* 24: 113–134.

Gotfredson, Garen. 2001. Business-to-business Internet purchasing exchanges: The promises and antitrust risks of a new e-commerce platform. *Minnesota Intellectual Property Review* 2(2): 107–137.

Goth, G. 2005. Following the money: Research funding fluctuates globally. *Software, IEEE* 22(5): 110–112, 114.

Gotlieb, Allan, Charles Dalfen, and Kenneth Katz. 1974. The transborder transfer of information by communications and computer systems: Issues and approaches to guiding principles. *American Journal of International Law* 68(2): 227–257.

Gottardo, David A. 1997. Commercialism and the downfall of Internet self-governance: An application of antitrust law. *John Marshall Journal of Computer & Information Law* 16(1): 125, 129–130.

Gottschalk v. Benson, 409 U.S. 63. 1972.

Gottweis, Herbert. 1995. German politics of genetic engineering and its deconstruction. *Social Studies of Science* 25: 195–235.

Gouldner, Alvin. 1976. *The dialectic of ideology and technology: The origins, grammar, and future of ideology.* New York: Seabury Press.

Government Accountability Office. 2005. *Elections: Federal efforts to improve security and reliability of electronic voting systems are under way, but key activities need to be completed.* Washington, DC: Government Printing Office, GAO-05-956.

Grabher, Gernot, ed. 1993. *The embedded firm: On the socioeconomics of industrial networks.* New York: Routledge.

Graham, Thomas, Jr. 2002. *Three decades of arms control and international law.* Seattle: University of Washington Press.

Grant, August E., and Jennifer Harman Meadows. 2004. *Communication technology update.* Oxford: Focal.

Grattet, Ryken, and Valerie Jenness. 2001. The birth and maturation of hate crime policy in the United States. *American Behavioral Scientist* 45(4): 668–696.

Gray, C. 2002. Local government and the arts. *Local Government Studies* 28(1): 77–90.

Gray, Chris Hables. 1989. The cyborg soldier: The U.S. military and the postmodern warrior. In Les Levidow and Kevin Robins, eds., *Cyborg worlds: The military information society*, 59–72. London: Free Association Books.

Gray, Chris Hables. 2002. *Cyborg citizen*. New York: Routledge.

Gray, Chris Hables, Heidi J. Figueroa-Sarriera, and Steven Mentor, eds. 1995. *The cyborg handbook*. New York: Routledge.

Gray, H. Peter. 1983. A negotiating strategy for trade in services. *Journal of World Trade Law* 17: 377–388.

Green, Andy. 1990. *Education and state formation: The rise of education systems in England, France and the USA*. London: Macmillan.

Green, Andy, and John Preston. 2001. Education and social cohesion: Recentering the debate. *Peabody Journal of Education* 76(3–4): 247–284.

Green, Marci, and Ian Grosvenor. 1997. Making subjects: History-writing, education and race categories. *Paedagogica Historica* 33(3): 883–908.

Greenawalt, Kent. 1992. Fairness in classification. In *Law and objectivity*, 121–140. New York: Oxford University Press.

Greenberg, Dolores. 1990. Energy, power, and perceptions of social change in the early nineteenth century. *American Historical Review* 95(3): 693–714.

Greene, Maxine. 2000. *Releasing the imagination: Essays on education, the arts, and social change*. New York: Jossey-Bass.

Greenfeld, Liah. 1992. *Nationalism: Five roads to modernity*. Cambridge, MA: Harvard University Press.

Greenstein, Ruth. 1982. National security controls on scientific information. *Jurimetrics Journal* 23(1): 50, 76–83.

Greenstein, Shane. 1998a. Access and bundling in high-technology markets: A comment. In Jeffrey A. Eisenach and Thomas M. Lenard, eds., *Competition, innovation and the Microsoft monopoly: Antitrust in the digital marketplace*, 129–136. Boston: Kluwer Academic.

Greenstein, Shane. 1998b. *Universal service in the digital age: The commercialization and geography of U.S. Internet access*. Cambridge, MA: NBER Working Paper No. 6453.

Greenstein, Shane M. 1995. Sole-sourcing versus competitive bidding: U.S. government agencies' procedural choices for mainframe computer procurement. *Journal of Industrial Economics* 43(2): 125–140.

Greenwald, Marilyn S., and Joseph Bernt. 2000. *The big chill: Investigative reporting in the current media environment*. Ames: Iowa State University Press.

Gregory, Robert. 1989. Political rationality or "incrementalism"? Charles E. Lindblom's enduring contribution to public policy-making theory. *Policy and Politics* 17(2): 139–152.

Grieshaber-Otto, Jim, and Matthew Sanger. 2002. *Perilous lessons: The impact of the WTO Services Agreement (GATS) on Canada's public education system*. Ottawa: Canadian Centre for Policy Alternatives.

Griffin, Robert J., ed. 2003. *The faces of anonymity: Anonymous and pseudonymous publication from the sixteenth to the twentieth century*. Houndsmills, UK: Palgrave Macmillan.

Griffiths, Jonathan, and Uma Suthersanen. 2005. *Copyright and free speech: Comparative and international analyses*. Oxford: Oxford University Press.

Griliches, Zvi. 1984. *R&D, patents, and productivity*. Chicago: University of Chicago Press.

Groenendijk, Kees. 2004. Reinstatement of controls at the internal borders of Europe: Why and against whom? *European Law Journal* 10(2): 150–171.

Grossman, George S. 1994. *Legal research: Historical foundations of the electronic age*. New York: Oxford University Press.

Grossman, Joel B. and Richard S. Wells, eds. 1988. *Constitutional law and judicial policy making*, 3rd ed. New York: Longman.

Grubesic, Tony H., and Alan T. Murray. 2005. Geographies of imperfection in telecommunication analysis. *Telecommunications Policy* 29(1): 69–94.

Gurr, Ted Robert. 1973. The revolution, social-change nexus: Some old theories and new hypotheses. *Comparative Politics* 5(3): 359–392.

Guthrie, Kendall K. and William H. Dutton. 1992. The politics of citizen access technology: The development of public information utilities in four cities. *Policy Studies Journal* 20(4): 574–597.

Gutierrez, Hannah M. T. 2003. Guam's future political status: An argument for free association with U.S. citizenship. *Asian-Pacific Law and Policy Journal* 4(1): 122–148.

Guttmann, Amy, ed. 1998. *Freedom of association*. Princeton, NJ: Princeton University Press.

Haas, Ernst B. 1990. *When knowledge is power: Three models of change in international organizations*. Berkeley: University of California Press.

Haas, Leslie, and Jan Robertson. 2004. *The information commons*. Washington, DC: Association of Research Libraries.

Habakkuk, H. J. 1962. *American and British technology in the nineteenth century: The search for labour-saving inventions*. Cambridge: Cambridge University Press.

Habermas, Jürgen. 1968. *Knowledge and human interests*. Boston: Beacon Press.

Hackenberg, Robert A., and Robert R. Alvarez. 2001. Close-ups of postnationalism: Reports from the U.S.-Mexico borderlands. *Human Organization* 60(2): 97–105.

Hacking, Ian. 1984. *The emergence of probability: A philosophical study of early ideas about probability, induction and statistical inference*. Cambridge: Cambridge University Press.

Hacking, Ian. 1990. *Taming of chance*. Cambridge: Cambridge University Press.

Hacking, Ian. 1999. *The social construction of what?* Cambridge, MA: Harvard University Press.

Hadwiger, Don F. 1982. *The politics of agricultural research*. Lincoln: University of Nebraska Press.

Haggard, Stephen. 1988. The institutional foundations of hegemony: Explaining the Reciprocal Trade Agreements Act of 1934. *International Organization* 42(1): 81–119.

Hahn, Robert W., and Anne Layne-Farrar. 2002. The benefits and costs of online privacy legislation. *Administrative Law Review* 54(1): 85–172.

Hahn, Trudi Bellardo, and Michael Buckland. 1998. *Historical studies in information science.* Medford, NJ: Information Today, Inc.

Haight, Timothy, ed. 1979. *Telecommunications policy and the citizen.* New York: Praeger Special Studies.

Haiman, Franklyn S. 1993. *"Speech acts" and the First Amendment.* Carbondale: Southern Illinois University Press.

Haines, Richard C., and Frank E. Joyce. 1987. *Monitoring and management of renewable resources: The use of remote sensing.* Brussels, Belgium: FAST Internal Paper #191, XII-591-87.

Hakansson, Hakan, and Jan Johanson. 1993. The network as a governance structure: Interfirm cooperation beyond markets and hierarchies. In Gernot Grabher, ed., *Rediscovering the social in the economics of interfirm relations,* 35–51. New York: Routledge.

Hall, Bronwyn H. 2002. *The financing of research and development.* Cambridge, MA: NBER Working Paper No. W8773.

Halsing, David. 2004. *A cost-benefit analysis of the national map.* Reston, VA: U.S. Department of the Interior, U.S. Geological Survey.

Halstuk, Martin E. 2002. Policy of secrecy—Pattern of deception: What Federalist leaders thought about a public right to know, 1794–98. *Communication Law and Policy* 7(1): 51–76.

Hamelink, Cees J. 1979. Informatics: Third World call for new order. *Journal of Communication* 29(3): 144–148.

Hamelink, Cees J. 1989. The relationship between cultural identity and modes of communication. *Communication Yearbook* 12: 417–426.

Hammond, Allen S., IV. 2005. Universal service: Problems, solutions, and responsive policies. *Federal Communications Law Journal* 57(2): 187–200.

Hanley, Sheena, and Ulf Fredriksson. 2003. Effects of the General Agreement on Trade in Services on the education systems in Europe. *Education Review* 16(2): 97–103.

Hansen, Allen C. 1989. *USIA: Public diplomacy in the computer age.* New York: Praeger.

Hansen, Niles. 1977. Border regions: A critique of spatial theory and a European case study. *Annals of Regional Science* 11(1): 1–14.

Hanson, Gordon H., Raymond Robertson, and Antonio Spilimbergo. 2002. Does border enforcement protect U.S. workers from illegal immigration? *Review of Economics and Statistics* 84(1): 73–93.

Haraway, Donna J. 1991. *Simians, cyborgs, and women: The reinvention of nature.* New York: Routledge.

Harchaoui, Tarek M. 2004. The role of industrial classification in micro-macro integration: The case of the banking business in the 1997 North American Industrial Classification System. *Review of Income and Wealth* 50(2): 203–212.

Hardt, Hanno. 1979. *Social theories of the press: Early German and American perspectives*. Beverly Hills, CA: Sage.

Harer, John B., and Steven R. Harris. 1994. *Censorship of expression in the 1980s: A statistical survey*. Westport, CT: Greenwood Press.

Harlan, Leigh M. 2004. When privacy fails: Invoking a property paradigm to mandate the destruction of DNA samples. *Duke Law Journal* 53(3): 967–1066.

Harley, John Brian, and David Woodward, eds. 1987. *The history of cartography*. Chicago: University of Chicago Press.

Harrison, David Lombard. 2004. The USA PATRIOT Act: A new way of thinking, an old way of reacting, higher education responds. *North Carolina Journal of Law & Technology* 5(2): 177–212.

Hart, Kenya. 2003. Defending against a "death by English": English-only, Spanish-only, and a gringa's suggestions for community support of language rights. *La Raza Law Journal* 14(2): 177–224.

Hart, Mitchell Bryan. 2000. *Social science and the politics of modern Jewish identity*. Stanford, CA: Stanford University Press.

Harty, Maura. 2005. U.S. visa policy: Securing borders and opening doors. *Washington Quarterly* 28(2): 23–35.

Hasian, Marouf, and Edward Panetta. 1994. Richard Posner's redefinition of the marketplace of ideas: A law and economics adaptation of the First Amendment. *Free Speech Yearbook* 32: 33–50.

Hawkins, Richard. 1999. The rise of consortia in the information and communication technology industries: Emerging implications for policy. *Telecommunications Policy* 23(2): 159–173.

Hay, George, John C. Hilki, and Phillip B. Nelson. 1991. After the Herfindahls are counted: Assessment of entry and efficiencies in merger enforcement by the Department of Justice. In Eleanor M. Fox and James T. Halverson, eds., *Collaborations among competitors*, 597–624. Chicago: American Bar Association.

Hayashi, Koichiro. 1992. From network externalities to interconnection: The changing nature of networks and economy. In Cristiano Antonelli, ed., *The economics of information networks*, 192–215. Amsterdam: North-Holland.

Hayduk, Ronald, and Kevin Mattson, eds. 2002. *Democracy's moment: Reforming the American political system for the 21st century*. Lanham, MD: Rowman and Littlefield.

Hayek, Fritz A. 1945. The use of knowledge in society. *American Economic Review* 35: 519–530.

Hayles, N. Katherine. 1999. *How we became posthuman*. Chicago: University of Chicago Press.

Hazard, William R., and Victor G. Rosenblum. 1976. Education, the law, and social change. *Education and Urban Society* 8(3): 259–266.

Hazlett, Thomas W. 1990. The rationality of U.S. regulation of the broadcast spectrum. *The Journal of Law & Economics* 33(1): 133–175.

Headrick, Daniel R. 1990. *The invisible weapon: Telecommunications and international relations, 1851–1945*. New York: Oxford University Press.

Headrick, Daniel R. 2000. *When information came of age: Technologies of knowledge in the age of reason and revolution, 1700–1850*. Oxford: Oxford University Press.

Heald, Paul J. 2005. A transaction costs theory of patent law. *Ohio State Law Journal* 66: 473–509.

Healey, Patsy. 1993. Planning through debate: The communicative turn in planning theory. In Frank Fischer and John Forester, eds., *The argumentative turn in policy analysis and planning*, 233–253. Durham, NC: Duke University Press.

Health, Belinda L. 2002. The importance of research and development tax incentives in the world market. *Journal of International Law* 11: 351–368.

Heater, Derek Benjamin. 2004. *A brief history of citizenship*. New York: New York University Press.

Heathorn, S. 2005. A "matter for artists, and not for soldiers"? The cultural politics of the Earl Haig National Memorial, 1928–1937. *Journal of British Studies* 44(3): 536–561.

Hecht, Michael L. 1993. A research odyssey: Toward the development of a commumication theory of identity. *Communication Monographs* 60(1): 76–82.

Hechter, Michael, and William Brustein. 1980. Regional modes of production and patterns of state formation in Western Europe. *American Journal of Sociology* 85(5): 1061–1093.

Heisenberg, Dorothee, and Marie-Hélène Fandel. 2004. Projecting EU regimes abroad: The EU Data Protection Directive as global standard. In Sandra Braman, ed., *The emergent global information policy regime*, 109–219. Houndsmills, UK: Palgrave Macmillan.

Held, David. 1980. *Introduction to critical theory: Horkheimer to Habermas*. Berkeley: University of California Press.

Held, David. 1989. *Political theory and the modern state: Essays on state, power, and democracy*. Stanford, CA: Stanford University Press.

Helewitz, Jeffrey A. 2003. *Cyberlaw: Legal principles of emerging technologies*. Englewood Cliffs, NJ: Prentice Hall.

Helgerson, Richard. 1992. *Forms of nationhood: The Elizabethan writing of England*. Chicago: University of Chicago Press.

Helleiner, Eric. 2000. The technology of money matters: "Industrial money" and the rise of territorial currencies. Presented to the International Studies Association, Los Angeles, CA, March.

Helleiner, Eric. 2001. Financial globalization and social response? In K. Thomas and T. Sinclair, eds., *Structure and agency in international capital mobility*, 168–186. London: Palgrave.

Hellmann, John. 1981. *Fables of fact: The new journalism as new fiction*. Urbana: University of Illinois Press.

Hemmer, Joseph J. 2000. *Communication law: The Supreme Court and the First Amendment*. Lanham, MD: Austin & Winfield.

Henry, Mark, and Leslie Armstrong, eds. 2004. *Mapping the future of America's national parks: Stewardship through geographic information systems*. Redlands, CA: ESRI Press.

Henry, Nicholas. 1978. *Copyright, Congress, and technology: The public record*. Phoenix, AZ: Oryx Press.

Hensley, Thomas R., ed. 2001. *The boundaries of freedom of expression and order in American democracy*. Kent, OH: Kent State University Press.

Hernon, Peter, and Charles R. McClure. 1988. *Public access to government information: Issues, trends, and strategies*, 2nd ed. Norwood, NJ: Ablex.

Hernon, Peter, Charles R. McClure, and Harold C. Relyea, eds. 1996. *Federal information policies in the 1990s*. Norwood, NJ: Ablex.

Herrnson, Paul S., Benjamin Bederson, Lee Bongshin, Peter L. Francia, Robert M. Sherman, Frederick G. Conrad, Michael Traugott, and Richard G. Niemi. 2005. Early appraisals of electronic voting. *Social Science Computer Review* 23(3): 274–292.

Herz, John H. 1957. Rise and demise of the territorial state. *World Politics* 9(4): 473–493.

Herzog, David. 2003. *Mapping the news: Case studies in GIS and journalism*. Redlands, CA: ESRI Press.

Hester, Al. 1974. The news from Latin America via a world news agency. *Gazette* 20(1): 82–98.

Hettling, J. K. 2003. The use of remote sensing satellites for verification in international law. *Space Policy* 19(1): 33–39.

Heyman, Josiah McC. 1999. Why interdiction? Immigration control at the United States-Mexico border. *Regional Studies* 33(7): 619–630.

Hibbert, Michelle. 2001. DNA databanks: Law enforcement's greatest surveillance tool? *Wake Forest Law Review* 34: 767–826.

Higgs, Edward. 2001. The rise of the information state: The development of central state surveillance of the citizen in England, 1500–2000. *The Journal of Historical Sociology* 14(2): 175–197.

Hill, J. S. 2005. Analog people for digital dreams: Staffing and educational considerations for cataloging and metadata professionals. *Library Resources & Technical Services* 49(1): 14–18.

Hill, Kevin, and John E. Hughes. 1998. *Cyberpolitics: Citizen activism in the age of the Internet*. Lanham, MD: Rowman and Littlefield.

Hill, Stephen. 1988. Technology and organization culture: The human imperative in integrating new technology into organization design. *Technology in Society* 10: 233–253.

Hilpert, Ulrich. 1992. *Archipelago Europe: Islands of innovation.* Brussels, Belgium: Commission of the European Commission.

Hines, J. R., Jr. 1993. *No place like home: Tax incentives and the location of R&D by American multinationals.* Cambridge, MA: National Bureau of Economic Research.

Hinke, T. H., H. S. Delugach, and R. P. Wolf. 1997. Protecting databases from inference attacks. *Computers and Security* 16(8): 687–708.

Hitchings, S. 2003. Policy assessment of the impacts of remote-sensing technology. *Space Policy* 19(2): 119–125.

Hobart, Michael E., and Zachary S. Schiffman. 1998. *Information ages: Literacy, numeracy, and the computer revolution.* Baltimore, MD: Johns Hopkins University Press.

Hobbes, Thomas. [1651] 1991. *Leviathan*, ed. by Richard Tuck. Cambridge: Cambridge University Press.

Hobsbawm, Eric. 1991. *Nations and nationalism since 1780*, 2nd ed. New York: Cambridge University Press.

Hobsbawm, Eric J., and Terence Ranger, eds. 1983. *The invention of tradition.* Cambridge: Cambridge University Press.

Hoelscher, Christoph, and Hans-Michael Wolffgang. 1998. The Wassenaar Arrangement between international trade, non-proliferation, and export controls. *Journal of World Trade* 32(1): 45–63.

Hoff, Joan. 1996. Researchers' nightmare: Studying the Nixon presidency. *Presidential Studies Quarterly* 26(1): 259–276.

Hoffman, David. 2002. Beyond public diplomacy. *Foreign Affairs* 81(2): 83–95.

Hoffman, Donna L., Thomas P. Novak, and Marcos A. Peralta. 1999. Information privacy in the market space: Implications for the commercial uses of anonymity on the Web. *The Information Society* 15(2): 129–139.

Hoffman, Sandra A. 1986. Farmland and open space preservation in Michigan: An empirical analysis. *University of Michigan Journal of Law Reform* 19(4): 1107–1197.

Hofstadter, Richard. 1991. What happened to the antitrust movement? In E. Thomas Sullivan, ed., *The political economy of the Sullivan Act: The first one hundred years*, 20–31. New York: Oxford University Press.

Hollifield, C. Ann, Joseph F. Donnermeyer, Gwen H. Wolford, and Robert Agunga. 2000. *Telecommunications Policy* 24: 761–779.

Hollowell, John. 1977. *Fact and fiction: The new journalism and the nonfiction novel.* Chapel Hill: University of North Carolina Press.

Holmes, Oliver Wendell. 1897. The path of the law. *Harvard Law Review* 10(8): 457–478.

Holsinger, Ralph L., and Jon Dilts. 1997. *Media law*, 4th ed. New York: McGraw-Hill.

Holt, Charles A., and David T. Scheffman. 1989. Strategic business behavior and antitrust. In Robert J. Larner and James W. Meehan, Jr., eds., *Economics and antitrust policy*, 39–82. Westport, CT: Greenwood Press.

Holton, G. 2001. Henri Poincare, Marcel Duchamp and innovation in science and art. *Leonardo* 34(2): 127–134.

Holum, John. 2005. Looking back: Arms control reorganization, then and now. *Arms Control Today* 35(5): 41–44.

Holzer, Rachel S. 2005. National security versus defense counsel's "need to know": An objective standard for resolving the tension. *Fordham Law Review* 73: 1941–1985.

Hookway, Brandon. 1999. *Pandemonium: The rise of predatory locales in the postwar world*. Princeton, NJ: Princeton Architectural Press.

Hooper, Michael. 1976. The structure and measurement of social identity. *Public Opinion Quarterly* 40(2): 154–164.

Hooper-Greenhill, E. 1992. *Museums and the shaping of knowledge*. New York and London: Routledge.

Hopkins, W. Wat. 1989. *Actual malice: Twenty-five years after Times v. Sullivan*. New York: Praeger.

Hopkins, W. Wat, ed. 2004. *Communication and the law*. Northport, AL: Vision Press.

Hoppe, Robert. 1993. Political judgment and the policy cycle: The case of ethnicity policy arguments in the Netherlands. In Frank Fischer and John Forester, eds., *The argumentative turn in policy analysis and planning*, 77–100. Durham, NC: Duke University Press.

Hopwood, Anthony G., and Peter Miller, eds. 1994. *Accounting as social and institutional practice*. Cambridge: Cambridge University Press.

Horowitz, Donald L. 1983. Decreeing organizational change: Judicial supervision of public institutions. *Duke Law Journal* 1983(6): 1265–1307.

Horwitz, Milton J. 1992. *The transformation of American law, 1870–1960: The crisis of legal orthodoxy*. New York: Oxford University Press.

Horwitz, Robert Britt. 1986. For whom the Bell tolls: Causes and consequences of the AT&T divestiture. *Critical Studies in Mass Communication* 3(2): 119–154.

Horwitz, Robert Britt. 1989. *The irony of regulatory reform: The deregulation of American telecommunications*. New York: Oxford University Press.

Horwitz, Robert Britt. 1991. *The irony of regulatory reform: The deregulation of American telecommunications*. Oxford: Oxford University Press.

House, Floyd N. 1928. Social change and social science. *Social Forces* 7(1): 11–17.

Hovencamp, Herbert. 1994. *Federal antitrust policy: The law of competition and its practice*. St. Paul, MN: West.

Howard, D. B. 2004. Between avant-garde and kitsch: Pragmatic liberalism, public arts funding, and the Cold War in the United States. In Cornelis A. van

Minnen and Silvia L. Hilton, eds., *Frontiers and boundaries in U.S. history*, 197–206. Amsterdam: VU University Press.

Howard, Philip. 2005. Deep democracy, thin citizenship: The impact of digital media in political campaign strategy. *The Annals of the American Academy of Political and Social Science* 597(1): 153–170.

Howard, V. A. 2001. Funding the arts: An investment in global citizenship? *Journal of Aesthetic Education* 35(4): 83–95.

Howells, J. 1987. *Technological innovation, industrial organisation and location of services in the European community: Regional development prospects and the role of information services.* Brussels, Belgium: EC FAST XII-260-87 #142.

Huang, Yasheng. 1994. Information, bureaucracy, and economic reform in China and the Soviet Union. *World Politics* 47(1): 102–134.

Huber, Peter. 1987. *The geodesic network: 1987 report on competition in the telephone industry.* Washington, DC: U.S. Department of Justice, Antitrust Division.

Hudec, Robert. 1987. *Developing countries in the GATT legal system.* London: Trade Policy Research Centre.

Huffman, Lisa, and Woody Talcove. 1995. Information infrastructure: Challenge and opportunity. *Public Management* 77(5): 9–14.

Hughes, P., and W. Luksetich. 2004. Nonprofit arts organizations: Do funding sources influence spending patterns? *Nonprofit and Voluntary Sector Quarterly* 33(2): 203–220.

Hume, David. [1741] 1975. *Enquiries concerning human understanding and concerning the principles of morals.* Oxford: Clarendon Press.

Hunt, Alan, and Gary Wickham. 1994. *Foucault and law: Towards a sociology of law as governance.* London: Pluto Press.

Hunter, Richard S. 2002. *World without secrets: Business, crime, and privacy in the age of ubiquitous computing.* New York: Wiley & Sons.

Huse, Charles C. 2005. Database protection in theory and practice: Three recent cases. *Berkeley Technology Law Journal* 20: 23–45.

Hutchins, Robert. 1936. *The higher learning in America.* New Haven, CT: Yale University Press.

Hveem, Helge. 1987. Small countries under great pressure: The politics of national vulnerability under international restructuring. *Cooperation and Conflict* 22(2): 193–208.

Hyde, Alan. 2003. *Working in Silicon Valley: Economic and legal analysis of a high-velocity labor market.* London: M. E. Sharpe.

Hyde, Lewis. 1983. *The gift: Imagination and the erotic life of property.* New York: Vintage Books.

Içduygu, Ahmet, and Özlem Kaygusuz. 2004. The politics of citizenship by drawing borders: Foreign policy and the construction of national citizenship identity in Turkey. *Middle Eastern Studies* 40(6): 26–51.

IEEE Computer Society Staff. 2003. *1st IEEE Annual Conference on Pervasive Computing and Communications*. Fort Worth, TX: IEEE.

Ikenberry, G. John. 1988. An institutional approach to American foreign policy. *International Organization* 42(1): 219–243.

In re Appalat, 33 F.3d 1526 (Fed. Cir. 1994) (en banc).

INS v. AP, 248 U.S. 215. 1918.

International News Service v. Associated Press, 248 U.S. 215. 1918.

International Statistical Programs Center. 1977. *Mapping for census and surveys*. Washington, DC: U.S. Department of Commerce, Census Bureau.

Introna, L., and Helen Nissenbaum. 2000. Shaping the Web: Why the politics of search engines matter. *The Information Society* 16(3): 1–17.

Irwin, Manley R., and John D. Ela. 1981. U.S. telecommunications regulation: Will technology decide? *Telecommunications Policy* 5(1): 24–32.

Irwin, Manley Rutherford. 1984. *Telecommunications America: Markets without boundaries*. Westport, CT: Quorum Books.

Isin, Engin F., and Bryan Turner, eds. 2003. *Handbook of citizenship studies*. Thousand Oaks, CA: Sage.

Issacharoff, S. 2002. Gerrymandering and political cartels. *Harvard Law Review* 116(2): 593–648.

Ito, Youichi. 1991. *Johoka* as a driving force of social change. *Keio Communication Review* 12: 33–58.

Ivers, Gregg, and Kevin T. McGuire, eds. 2004. *Creating constitutional change: Clashes over power and liberty in the Supreme Court*. Charlottesville: University of Virginia Press.

Jackson, John H. 1984. Perspectives on the jurisprudence of international trade: Costs and benefits of legal procedures in the United States. *Michigan Law Review* 82(5/6): 1570–1583.

Jackson, John H. 1988. *International competition in services: A constitutional framework*. Washington, DC: American Enterprise Institute.

Jackson, Robert H. 1990. *Quasi-states: Sovereignty, international relations, and the Third World*. Cambridge: Cambridge University Press.

Jacobsohn, Gary Jeffrey. 2004. The permeability of constitutional borders. *Texas Law Review* 82(7): 1763–1819.

Jacobson, David, and Galya Benarieh Ruffer. 2003. Courts across borders: The implications of judicial agency for human rights and democracy. *Human Rights Quarterly* 25(1): 74–93.

Jacobson, Jacqueline M. 2001. English-only rules and the effect of the business necessity defense on the small business employer. *The Journal of Small and Emerging Business Law* 5(2): 265–284.

Jaeger, David A., Sarah E. Turner, Susanna Loeb, and John Bound. 1998. *Coding geographic areas across census years: Creating consistent definitions of metropolitan areas*. Washington, DC: NBER Working Paper No. W6772.

Jaffe, Adam B., and Manuel Trajtenberg. 2002. *Patents, citations, and innovations: A window on the knowledge economy.* Cambridge, MA: MIT Press.

Jakubowicz, Karol. 1995. Media within and without the state: Press freedom in Eastern Europe. *Journal of Communication* 45(4): 125–139.

Janes, Allene Rosalind. 1978. *Dextran bibliography: Extensive coverage of research literature (exclusive of clinical) and patents, 1861–1976.* Washington, DC: Science and Education Administration, U.S. Department of Agriculture.

Jasper, James M. 1998. The emotions of protest: Affective and reactive emotions in and around social movements. *Sociological Forum* 13(3): 397–424.

Jasper, Margaret C. 1996. *The law of libel & slander.* Dobbs Ferry, NY: Oceana Publications.

Jayakar, Krishna P., and Harmeet Sawhney. 2004. Universal service: Beyond established practice to possibility space. *Telecommunications Policy* 28(3–4): 339–357.

Jeltema, Laura A. 2004. Legislators in the classroom: Why state legislatures cannot decide higher education curricula. *American University Law Review* 54(1): 215–255.

Jenkins, J. Craig. 1983. Resource mobilization theory and the study of social movements. *Annual Review of Sociology* 9: 527–553.

Jenness, Valerie, and Ryken Grattet. 2001. *Making hate a crime: From social movement to law enforcement.* New York: Russell Sage Foundation.

Jensen, Klaus Bruhn. 1990. The politics of polysemy: Television news, everyday consciousness and political action. *Media, Culture & Society* 12(1): 57–77.

Jensen, Robert, and David Allen, eds. 1995. *Freeing the First Amendment.* New York: New York University Press.

Jessop, Bob. 1977. Recent theories of the capitalist state. *Cambridge Journal of Economics* 1(4): 353–373.

Jimenez, Maria. 2000. The U.S.-Mexico border: A strategy of low-intensity conflict. *Social Justice* 27(4): 32–36.

John, Richard E. 1995. *Spreading the news: The American postal system from Franklin to Morse.* Cambridge, MA: Harvard University Press.

Johnson, Deborah G., and Keith Miller. 1998. Anonymity, pseudonymity, or inescapable identity on the net. In *Proceedings of Shaping policy in the information age*, 37–38. Washington, DC: Association of Computing Machinery.

Johnson, Elizabeth. 1986. Telecommunication market structure in the USA: The effects of deregulation and divestiture. *Telecommunications Policy* 10(1): 57–67.

Johnson, H. Thomas. 1991. Managing by remote control: Recent management accounting practice in historical perspective. In Peter Temin, ed., *Inside the business enterprise: Historical perspectives on the use of information*, 41–66. Chicago: University of Chicago Press.

Johnson-Cartee, Karen S., and Gary Copeland. 2003. *Strategic political communication: Rethinking social influence, persuasion, and propaganda*. Lanham, MD: Rowman and Littlefield.

Johnson-Freese, Joan. 2000. Alice in licenseland: U.S. satellite export controls since 1990. *Space Policy* 16(3): 195–203.

Johnston, Wesley J., ed. 1990. *Purchasing in the 1990s: The evolution of procurement in the telecommunications industry*. Greenwich, CT: JAI Press.

Jones, Bryan D. 1998. Policy punctuations: U.S. budget authority, 1947–1995. *Journal of Politics* 60(1): 1–33.

Jones, William K. 2003. *Insult to injury: Libel, slander, and invasion of privacy*. Boulder: University Press of Colorado.

Jonscher, Charles. 1982. The economic causes of information growth. *Inter-Media* 10(6): 34–37.

Jonsson, Christer, and Richard T. B. Langhorne, eds. 2004. *Diplomacy*. Thousand Oaks, CA: Sage.

Jordan, Sandra D. 1991. Classified information and conflicts in independent counsel prosecution: Balancing the scales of justice after Iran-Contra. *Columbia Law Review* 91(7): 1651–1698.

Jorde, Thomas M., and David J. Teece. 1991. Innovation and cooperation: Implications for competition and antitrust. In Eleanor M. Fox and James T. Halverson, eds., *Collaborations among competitors: Antitrust policy and economics*, 887–910. Chicago: American Bar Association.

Jowett, Garth S. 1987. Propaganda and communication: The re-emergence of a research tradition. *Journal of Communication* 37(1): 97–114.

Jussawalla, Meheroo, and Chee-Wah Cheah. 1983. Emerging economic constraints on transborder data flow. *Telecommunications Policy* 7(4): 285–296.

Kahin, Brian. 1991. Information policy and the Internet: Toward a public information infrastructure in the United States. *Government Publication Review* 18(5): 451–472.

Kahin, Brian. 1992. *Building information infrastructure*. New York: McGraw-Hill.

Kahin, Brian. 1995. Institutional and policy issues in the development of the digital library. *Journal of Electronic Publishing* 2(1). Available at www.press.umich.edu/jep/works/Kahin.dl.html.

Kahin, Brian. 2003. Information process patents in the U.S. and Europe: Policy avoidance and policy divergence. *First Monday* 8(3). Available at www.firstmonday.org/issues/issue8_3/kahin/index.html.

Kahin, Brian. 2004. Codification in context. In Sandra Braman, ed., *The emergent global information policy regime*, 39–61. Houndsmills, UK: Palgrave Macmillan.

Kahin, Brian, and Charles Nesson, eds. 1997. *Borders in cyberspace: Information policy and the global information infrastructure*. Cambridge, MA: MIT Press.

Kahle, Kathleen M., and Ralph A. Walkling. 1996. The impact of industry classifications on financial research. *Journal of Financial and Quantitative Analysis* 31(3): 309–320.

Kain, Robert J. P., and Elizabeth Baigent. 1992. *The cadastral map in the service of the state: A history of property mapping.* Chicago: University of Chicago Press.

Kairys, David. 1982. Legal reasoning. In David Kairys, ed., *The politics of law: A progressive critique*, 11–17. New York: Pantheon.

Kaiser, Frederick M. 1989. The amount of classified information: Causes, consequences, and correctives of a growing concern. *Government Information Quarterly* 6(3): 247–266.

Kaiser, Frederick M. 2003. Access to classified information: Seeking security clearances for state and local officials and personnel. *Government Information Quarterly* 20(3): 213–233.

Kalinowski, M. B. 2004. Nuclear arms races and arms control at the beginning of the 21st century. *Security Dialogue* 35(2): 217–225.

Kamalipour, Yahya R., and Nancy Snow, eds. 2004. *War, media, and propaganda: A global perspective.* Lanham, MD: Rowman & Littlefield.

Kamenshine, Robert D. 1985. Embargoes on exports of ideas and information: First Amendment issues. *William & Mary Law Review* 26(5): 863–896.

Kamoche, K., and M. P. E. Cunha. 2001. Minimal structures: From jazz improvisation to product innovation. *Organization Studies* 22(5): 733–764.

Kanter, Rosabeth Moss. 1991. The future of bureaucracy and hierarchy in organizational theory: A report from the field. In Pierre Bourdieu and James S. Coleman, eds., *Social theory for a changing society*, 63–86. Boulder, CO: Westview Press.

Kaplin, William A., and Barbara A. Lee. 1995. *Law of higher education: A comprehensive guide to legal implications of administrative decision making*, 3rd ed. San Francisco: Jossey-Bass.

Kargman, Steven T. 1986. OMB intervention in agency rulemaking: The case for broadened record review. *Yale Law Journal* 95(8): 1789–1810.

Karpf, Jorgen. 1989. Competition between types of regulation: The impact of computerization on the law. *Jurimatics* 12.

Kase, Francis Joseph. 1967. *Copyright thought in continental Europe: Its development, legal theories, and philosophy.* South Hackensack, NJ: F. B. Rothman.

Kaserman, David L., John W. Mayo, and Joseph E. Flynn. 1990. Cross-subsidization in telecommunications: Beyond the universal service fairy tale. *Journal of Regulatory Economics* 2(3): 231–249.

Katsh, M. E. 1989. *The electronic media and the transformation of the law.* New York: Oxford University Press.

Kay, John, and Paul Willman. 1993. Managing technological innovation: Architecture, trust and organizational relationships in the firm. In Peter Swann, ed.,

New technologies and the firm: Innovation and competition, 19–35. London: Routledge.

Kaysen, Carl, and Donald F. Turner. 1991. Antitrust policy: An economic and legal analysis. In E. Thomas Sullivan, ed., *The political economy of the Sherman Act: The first one hundred years*, 181–192. New York: Oxford University Press.

Keane, John. 1991. *Media and democracy*. Malden, MA: Blackwell.

Keegan, John. 1987. *The mask of command*. New York: Elizabeth Sifton Books/ Viking.

Keegan, John. 1993. *A history of warfare*. London: Hutchinson.

Keel, B. A. 2004. Protecting America's secrets while maintaining academic freedom. *Academic Medicine* 79(4): 333–342.

Keet, C. Maria. 2005. Data integration in the life sciences. *Lecture Notes in Computer Science* 3615: 46–62.

Keller, Bruce P., and Stacy A. Snowman. 1995. *Conducting intellectual property audits*. New York: Practicing Law Institute.

Kellogg, M. K., J. Thorne, and Peter W. Huber. 1992. *Federal telecommunications law*. Boston: Little, Brown.

Keohane, Robert O., and Joseph S. Nye, Jr. 1977. *Power and interdependence: World politics in transition*. Boston: Little, Brown.

Kerr, Clark, M. L. Gade, and M. Kawaoka. 1994. *Higher education cannot escape history: Issues for the twenty-first century*. Albany: State University of New York Press.

Kersch, Kenneth Ira. 2004. *Constructing civil liberties: Discontinuities in the development of American constitutional law*. Cambridge: Cambridge University Press.

Kettinger, William J. 1994. National infrastructure diffusion and the U.S. information superhighway. *Information & Management* 27(6): 357–368.

Keynes, John Maynard. 1936. *The general theory of employment, interest and money*. New York: Harcourt, Brace.

Keyssar, Alexander. 2000. *The right to vote: The contested history of democracy in the United States*. New York: Basic Books.

Khalilzad, Zalmay M., and John P. White. 1999. *Strategic appraisal: The changing role of information in warfare*. Santa Monica, CA: Rand Corporation.

Khan, B. Zorina. 2005. *The democratization of invention: Patents and copyrights in American economic development, 1790–1920*. New York: Cambridge University Press.

Kielbowicz, Richard B. 1986. Origins of the second-class mail category and the business of policy-making, 1863–1879. *Journalism Monographs* 96.

Kielbowicz, Richard B. 1989. *News in the mail: The press, Post Office, and public information, 1700–1860s*. New York: Greenwood Press.

Kikuchi, Toru. 2003. On the interconnection of networks and gains from trade in business services. *Journal of Economic Research* 8(2): 179–186.

Kim, Jae-Young. 1998. Universal service and Internet commercialization: Chasing two rabbits at the same time. *Telecommunications Policy* 22(4–5): 281–288.

Kim, Keechang. 2001. *Aliens in medieval law: The origins of modern citizenship*. New York: Cambridge University Press.

Kim, Sangbae, and Jeffrey Hart. 1998. The global political economy of Wintelism: A new mode of power and governance in the global computer industry. In James P. Rosenau and J. P. Singh, eds., *Information technologies and global politics: The changing scope of power and governance*, 153–168. Albany: State University of New York Press.

Kirschbaum, Leo. 1946. Author's copyright in England before 1640. *Papers of the Bibliographic Society of America* 40(1): 43–80.

Kittross, John M., ed. 1980. *Administration of American telecommunications policy*. New York: Arno Press.

Kitzinger, Jenny, and Jacquie Reilly. 1997. The rise and fall of risk reporting: Media coverage of human genetics research, "false memory syndrome" and "mad cow disease." *European Journal of Communication* 12(3): 319–350.

Klanderman, Bert, and Dirk Oegema. 1987. Potentials, networks, motivations, and barriers: Steps towards participation in social movements. *American Sociological Review* 52(4): 519–531.

Klapp, Orrin E. 1976. Identity as playback. *Communication* 2(2): 159–172.

Klein, Hans. 2004. Private governance for global communications: Technology, contracts, and the Internet. In Sandra Braman, ed., *The emergent global information policy regime*, 179–202. Houndsmills, UK: Palgrave Macmillan.

Klein, Richard, and Lawrence Russ. 2001. *Art at the edge of the law*. Ridgefield, CT: Aldrich Museum of Contemporary Art.

Kleindienst v. Mandel, 408 U.S. 758. 1972.

Klensin, J. C. 1995. When the metadata exceed the data: Data management with uncertain data. *Statistics and Computing* 5(1): 73–84.

Kliebard, Herbert M. 1995. Why history of education? *Journal of Educational Research* 88(4): 194–199.

Kline, S. J., and N. Rosenberg. 1986. An overview of innovation. In R. Landau and N. Rosenberg, eds., *The positive sum game*. Washington, DC: National Academies Press.

Klinenberg, Eric. 2005. Convergence: News production in a digital age. *The Annals of the American Academy of Political and Social Science* 597(1): 48–64.

Kling, Rob, and W. Scacchi. 1982. The web of computing: Computing technology as social organization. *Advances in Computers* 21(1): 3–78.

Kloppenburg, Jack Ralph, Jr. 1988. *First the seed: The political economy of plant biotechnology, 1492–2000*. Cambridge: Cambridge University Press.

Kloppenburg, Jack Ralph, Jr., and Daniel Lee Kleiman. 1987. Seed wars: Common heritage, private property, and political strategy. *Socialist Review* 17(5): 9–41.

Knight, G. N. 1968. Book indexing in Great Britain: A brief history. *The Indexer* 6(1): 14–18.

Knowles, Anne Kelly, ed. 2002. *Past time, past place: GIS for history*. Redlands, CA: ESRI Press.

Kolankiewicz, George. 1996. Social capital and social change. *British Journal of Sociology* 47(3): 427–441.

Kolly, Faye M. 2004. The right of association: Enforcing international labor rights of undocumented workers via the Alien Tort Claims Act. *Saint Louis University Public Law Review* 23: 669–695.

Kondratiev, Nikolai D. 1998. *The works of Nikolai D. Kondratiev*, ed. by Natalia Makasheva and Warren J. Samuels. London: Pickering & Chatto.

Korpi, Walter, and Joakim Palme. 2003. New politics and class politics in the context of austerity and globalization: Welfare state regress in 18 countries, 1975–1995. *American Political Science Review* 97(3): 425–446.

Kors, Alan Charles, and Harvey A. Silverglate. 1999. *The shadow university: The betrayal of liberty on America's campuses*. New York: HarperCollins.

Kort, John R. 2001. The North American Industry Classification System in BEA's economic accounts. *Survey of Current Business* 81(5): 7–23.

Kraidy, Marwan. 2005. *Hybridity, or, the cultural logic of globalization*. Philadelphia, PA: Temple University Press.

Kranich, Nancy C. 2004. *The information commons: A public policy report*. New York: Free Expression Policy Project, Brennan Center for Justice at NYU School of Law.

Krasner, Stephen. 1976. State power and the structure of international trade. *World Politics* 28(3): 317–347.

Krasner, Stephen D. 1990. Global communications and national power: Life on the Pareto frontier. *World Politics* 43(3): 336–366.

Kraus, Sidney. 1973. Mass communication and political socialization: A reassessment of two decades of research. *Quarterly Journal of Speech* 59(4): 390–400.

Krehbiel, Carl C. 1989. *Confidence- and security-building measures in Europe: The Stockholm conference*. New York: Praeger.

Kremic, Tibor. 2001. *Why the lack of academic literature on export controls?* Cleveland, OH: Glenn Research Center, NASA/TM-2001-210982.

Krepon, Michael. 2004. Cornerstones of security: Arms control treaties in the nuclear era. *International History Review* 26(2): 434–436.

Krepon, Michael, and Mary Umberger, eds. 1988. *Verification and compliance: A problem-solving approach*. Cambridge, MA: Ballinger.

Kriegman, Daniel, and Charles Knight. 1988. Social evolution, psychoanalysis, and human nature. *Social Policy* 19(2): 49–55.

Krimsky, Sheldon. 1991. *Biotechnics & society: The rise of industrial genetics*. New York: Praeger.

Krippendorff, Klaus. [1984] 1996. Information, information society and some Marxian propositions. In Hartmut B. Mokros, ed., *Between communication and information, 5: Interaction and identity*, 487–521. New Brunswick, NJ: Transaction Publishers.

Krislov, Marvin. 2004. Affirmative action in higher education: The value, the method, and the future. *University of Cincinnati Law Review* 72(3): 899–908.

Kroker, Arthur. 1992. *The possessed individual: Technology and the French postmodern*. New York: St. Martin's Press.

Krommenacker, Raymond J. 1986. The impact of information technology on trade interdependence. *Journal of World Trade Law* 20(4): 381–400.

Kruger, Loren. 1992. *The national stage: Theatre and cultural legitimation in England, France, and America*. Chicago: University of Chicago Press.

Krusten, Maarja. 1996. Watergate's last victim. *Presidential Studies Quarterly* 26(1): 277–281.

Ku, Raymond. 2000. Antitrust immunity, the First Amendment and settlements: Defining the boundaries of the right to petition. *Indiana Law Review* 33(2): 385–434.

Kumar, Sapna. 2003. Website libel and the single publication rule. *University of Chicago Law Review* 70(2): 639–688.

Kurzweil, Ray. 1999. *The age of spiritual machines: When computers exceed human intelligence*. New York: Viking Press.

Kysar, Douglas A. 2002. Kids and cul-de-sacs: Census 2000 and the reproduction of consumer culture. *Cornell Law Review* 87(3): 853–899.

Kyvig, David E. 1996. *Explicit and authentic acts: Amending the U.S. Constitution, 1776–1995*. Lawrence: University Press of Kansas.

Lacan, Jacques. 1988. *The seminar of Jacques Lacan*, ed. by Jacques-Alain Miller. New York: W. W. Norton.

Lagemann, Ellen C. 1997. Contested terrain: A history of education research in the United States, 1890–1990. *Educational Researcher* 26(9): 5–17.

Lagemann, Ellen Condiffe. 2002. *An elusive science: The troubling history of education research*. Chicago: University of Chicago Press.

Lagerquist, Peter. 2004. Fencing the last sky: Excavating Palestine after Israel's "separation wall." *Journal of Palestine Studies* 33(2): 5–36.

Lahav, Gallya, and Johan P. Olsen. 2004. *Immigration and politics in the new Europe: Reinventing borders*. Cambridge: Cambridge University Press.

Lambe, Jennifer L. 2002. Dimensions of censorship: Reconceptualizing public willingness to censor. *Communication Law and Policy* 7(2): 187–235.

Lamberton, Donald M., ed. 1971. *Economics of information and knowledge*. Harmondsworth, UK: Penguin Books.

Lamberton, Donald M. 1984. The emergence of information economics. In Meheroo Jussawalla and Helene Ebenfield, eds., *Communication and information economics: New perspectives*, 7–22. Vol. 5 of Information Research and Resource Reports. Amsterdam: North-Holland.

Lamberton, Donald M. 1992. Information economics: "Threatened wreckage" or new paradigm? In Ulf Himmelstrand, ed., *Interfaces in Economic and Social Analysis*, 113–123. London: Routledge.

Lambright, William H. 1976. *Governing science and technology*. New York: Oxford University Press.

Lamoreaux, Naomi R., Daniel M. G. Raff, and Peter Temin. 2002. *Beyond markets and hierarchies: Toward a new synthesis of American business history*. Cambridge, MA: NBER Working Paper No. 9029, July.

Lan, Yi-Chen. 2005. *Global information society: Operating information systems in a dynamic global business environment*. Hershey, PA: Idea Group Publishing.

Land, Kenneth C. 1980. Modeling macro social change. *Sociological Methodology* 11: 219–278.

Landau, E. B., and T. Malz. 2003. Assessing regional security dialogue through the agent/structure lens. *Journal of Strategic Studies* 26(3): 155–179.

Landreth, Harry, and David C. Colander. 2001. *History of economic thought*, 4th ed. New York: Houghton Mifflin.

Lane, Ruth. 1990. Concrete theory: An emerging method. *American Political Science review* 84(3): 927–940.

Lapid, Yosef. 1995. Revisiting the "national": Toward an identity agenda in neorealism? In Yosef Lapid and Friedrich Kratochwil, eds., *The return of culture andidentity in international relations theory*, 105–126. Boulder, CO: Lynne Rienner.

LaRue, Lewis H. 1995. *Constitutional law as fiction: Narrative in the rhetoric of authority*. University Park: Pennsylvania State University Press.

Laslett, Barbara. 1990. Unfeeling knowledge: Emotion and objectivity in the history of sociology. *Sociological Forum* 5(3): 413–433.

Lasswell, Harold D. 1953. Nations and classes: The symbols of identification. In Bernard Berelson and Morris Janowitz, eds., *Reader in public opinion and communication*, 2nd ed. New York: Free Press.

Lasswell, Harold D., and Abraham Kaplan. 1950. *Power and society*. New Haven, CT: Yale University Press.

Latour, Bruno, Stephen Woolgar, and Jonas Salk. 1986. *Laboratory life: The construction of scientific facts*. London: Sage.

Laurence, William. 1951. *The hell bomb*. New York: Alfred A. Knopf.

Lawrence, John Shelton, and Bernard Timberg. 1980. *Fair use and free inquiry: Copyright law and the new media*. Norwood, NJ: Ablex Publishing Corp.

Lawson, Gary, and Guy Seidman. 2004. *The constitution of empire: Territorial expansion and American legal history*. New Haven, CT: Yale University Press.

Lawton, Thomas C. 1997. *Technology and the new diplomacy*. Aldershot, UK: Avebury Publishing.

Layne, Sara Shatford. 1994. Some issues in the indexing of images. *Journal of the American Society for Information Science* 45(8): 583–588.

Lazarsfeld, Paul F., Bernard Berelson, and Hazel Gaudet. 1984. *The people's voice: How the voter makes up his mind in a presidential campaign*. New York: Columbia University Press.

Lazerson, Marvin, and W. Norton Grubb. 1974. *American education and vocationalism: A documentary history 1870–1970*. New York: Teachers College Press, Columbia University.

Lazinger, Susan S., and Helen R. Tibbo. 2001. *Digital preservation and metadata: History, theory, practice*. Englewood, CO: Libraries Unlimited.

Lear, Rick S. 2003. Your social security number or your life: Disclosure of personal identification information by military personnel and the compromise of privacy and national security. *Boston University International Law Journal* 21(1): 1–28.

Leary, Mark R., and June Price Tangney. 2003. *Handbook of self and identity*. New York: Guilford Press.

Leca, Jean. 1992. Questions on citizenship. In Chantal Mouffe, ed., *Dimensions of radical democracy: Pluralism, citizenship, community*, 17–32. New York and London: Routledge.

LeDuc, Don R. 1987. *Beyond broadcasting: Patterns in policy and law*. White Plains, NY: Longman.

Lee, A. D. 1993. *Information and frontiers: Roman foreign relations in late antiquity*. Cambridge: Cambridge University Press.

Lee, Edward. 2003. The public's domain: The evolution of legal restraints on the government's power to control public access through secrecy or intellectual property. *Hastings Law Journal* 55: 91–208.

Lee, Hyung K. 2005. Mapping the law or legalizing maps: The implications of the emerging rule on map evidence in international law. *Pacific Rim Law & Policy Journal* 14(1): 159–188.

Lee, J. O., M. C. Ko, W. Paik, H. S. Jeon, J. Kim, H. K. Kang, and J. Kim. 2004. The roles of ontology and metadata registry for interoperable databases. *Distributed Computing and Internet Technology, Proceedings* 3347: 217–226.

Lee, Yong-Ho, Im-Yeong Lee, and Hyung-Woo Lee. 2003. New identity escrow scheme for anonymity authentication. *Lecture Notes in Computer Science* 2551: 382–394.

Leeson, Kenneth W. 1984. *International communication: A blueprint for policy*. Amsterdam: North-Holland.

Leets, Laura, and Howard Giles. 1997. Words as weapons—When do they wound? Investigations of harmful speech. *Human Communication Research* 24(2): 260–301.

Lehoucq, F. 2003. Electoral fraud: Causes, types, and consequences. *Annual Review of Political Science* 6: 233–256.

Leifer, Richard. 1989. Understanding organizational transformation using a dissipative structure model. *Human Relations* 42(10): 899–916.

Leipnik, Mark R., and Donald P. Albert, eds. 2003. *GIS in law enforcement: Implementation issues and case studies*. London: Taylor & Francis.

Leitner, P. M., and R. J. Stupak. 1997. Ethics, national security and bureaucratic realities: North, Knight, and designated liars. *American Review of Public Administration* 27(1): 61–75.

LeMay, Michael C., and Elliott Robert Barkan. 1999. *U.S. immigration and naturalization laws and issues: A documentary history*. Westport, CT: Greenwood Press.

Lemley, Mark A. 1996. Antitrust and the Internet standardization problem. *Connecticut Law Review* 28(4): 1041–1094.

Lemley, Mark A., Peter S. Menell, Robert P. Merges, and Pamela Samuelson. 2003. *Software and Internet law*, 2nd ed. New York: Aspen Publishers.

Lenski, Gerhard. 1976. History and social change. *American Journal of Sociology* 82(3): 548–564.

Leong, Wai-Teng. 1989. The culture of the state: National tourism and the state manufacture of cultures. In Peter Bruck and Marc Raboy, eds., *Communication for and against democracy*, 75–94. Montreal: Black Rose Books.

Lerner, Daniel. 1954. *The passing of traditional society*. Glencoe, IL: Free Press.

Lessig, Lawrence. 1999. *Code and other laws of cyberspace*. New York: Basic Books.

Lessig, Lawrence. 2001. *The future of ideas: The fate of the commons in a connected world*. New York: Random House.

Levi, Michael A., and Michael E. O'Hanlon. 2005. *The future of arms control*. Washington, DC: Brookings Institution Press.

Levine, Paul, Fotis Mouzakis, and Ron Smith. 2003. Arms export controls and emerging domestic producers. In Paul Levine and Ron Smith, eds., *Arms trade, security and conflict*, 55–77. London: Routledge.

Levine, Paul, and Ron Smith. 2000. Arms export controls and proliferation. *Journal of Conflict Resolution* 44(6): 885–896.

Levinson, Sanford. 1995. *Responding to imperfection: The theory and practice of constitutional amendment*. Princeton, NJ: Princeton University Press.

Lévi-Strauss, Claude. 1963. *Structural anthropology*, trans. by Claire Jacobson and Brooke Grundfest Schoepf. New York: Basic Books.

Levy, J. S. 1983. Misperception and the causes of war: Theoretical linkages and analytical problems. *World Politics* 36(1): 76–99.

Levy, Stephen. 2004. *Crypto: How the code rebels beat the government—Saving privacy in the digital age*. Collingdale, PA: DIANE Publishing Company.

Lewis, Anthony. 1991. *Make no law: The Sullivan case and the First Amendment*. New York: Random House.

Lewis, G. B., and Brooks, A. C. 2005. A question of morality: Artists' values and public funding for the arts. *Public Administration Review* 65(1): 8–17.

Lewis, Phillip V. 1987. *Organizational communication: The essence of effective management*, 3rd ed. New York: Wiley & Sons.

Lewis, Tracy R., and David E. M. Sappington. 1991. Technological change and the boundaries of the firm. *American Economic Review* 81(4): 887–900.

Leydesdorff, Loet. 2004. The university-industry knowledge relationship: Analyzing patents and the science base of technologies. *Journal of the American Society of Information Science and Technology* 55(11): 991–1001.

Library of Congress, Legislative Reference Service. 1958. *Economic aspects of patents and the American patent system: A bibliography*. Washington, DC: Government Printing Office.

Lievrouw, Leah, ed. 1994. Information resources and democracy. Special issue of the *Journal of the American Society for Information Science and Technology* 45(6).

Lilly, Martha S., and Ronald O. Reed. 1999. Accounting for intellectual capital. *Journal of Applied Business Research* 15(4): 47–54.

Lin, Shin-Jeng. 2002. Design space of personalized indexing: Enhancing successive Web searches for transmuting information problems. In *Proceedings of the Eighth Americas Conference on Information Systems*, 1092–1101. Atlanta, GA: Association for Information Systems.

Lindblom, Charles E. 1995. The science of "muddling through." In Stella Theodoulou and Matthew Can, eds., *Public policy: The essential readings*, 113–127. Englewood Cliffs, NJ: Prentice Hall.

Ling, Yeh Ling. 2004. Mexican immigration and its potential impact on the political future of the United States. *Journal of Social, Political & Economic Studies* 29(4): 409–432.

Linklater, Andrew. 2002. Cosmopolitan political communities in international relations. *International Relations* 16(1): 135–150.

Lipschultz, Jeremy Harris. 2000. *Free expression in the age of the Internet: Social and legal boundaries*. Boulder, CO: Westview Press.

Lipsky, Abbott B., Jr. 1976. Reconciling *Red Lion* and *Tornillo*: A consistent theory of media regulation. *Stanford Law Review* 28: 563–588.

Lipson, Michael. 1999. The reincarnation of CoCom: Explaining post-Cold War export controls. *Nonproliferation Review* 6(2): 33–51.

Litfin, Karen T. 1997. The status of the statistical state: Satellites and the changing global knowledge structure. Presented at the International Studies Association, Toronto, March.

Little, Iain, and Julian Wright. 2000. Peering and settlement in the Internet: An economic analysis. *Journal of Regulatory Economics* 18(2): 151–173.

Lively, Donald E. 1992. *Foreshadows of the law: Supreme Court dissents and constitutional development*. Westport, CT: Praeger.

Lloyd, R. 2002. Neo-bohemia: Art and neighborhood redevelopment in Chicago. *Journal of Urban Affairs* 24(5): 517–532.

Loader, Brian, and William Dutton, eds. 2002. *The digital academe: New media in higher education and learning*. New York: Routledge.

Locke, John. [1690] 1979. *An essay concerning human understanding*, ed. by Peter H. Nidditch. Oxford: Clarendon Press.

Loescher, Gil, and John A. Scanlan. 1986. *Calculated kindness: Refugees and America's half-open door, 1945 to the present*. New York: Free Press.

Lohmann, Susanne. 1994. The dynamics of informational cascades: The Monday demonstrations in Leipzig, East Germany, 1989–1991. *World Politics* 47: 42–101.

Long, D. E. 1997. Hidden persuaders: Medical indexing and the gendered professionalism of American medicine, 1880–1932. *Osiris* 12: 100–120.

Loo, Chalsa M. 1985. The "biliterate" ballot controversy: Language acquisition and cultural shift among immigrants. *International Migration Review* 19(3): 493–515.

Lopatka, John E., and William H. Page. 1999. Antitrust on Internet time: Microsoft and the law and economics of exclusion. *Supreme Court Economic Review* 7: 157–231.

Lott, Juanita Tamayo. 1998. *Asian Americans: From racial category to multiple identities*. Walnut Creek, CA: AltaMira Press.

Lowell, B. Lindsay, ed. 1999. *Foreign temporary workers in America: Policies that benefit the U.S. economy*. New York: Quorum Press.

Lowell, Lindsay. 2000. The demand and new legislation for skilled temporary workers (H-1Bs) in the United States. *People and Place* 8(4): 29–36.

Lowell, B. Lindsay. 2001. Skilled temporary and permanent immigrants in the United States. *Population Research and Policy Review* 20(1–2): 33–58.

Lucas, Christopher J. 1994. *American higher education: A history*. New York: St. Martin's Griffin.

Lugmayr, Artur, Samuli Niiranen, and Seppo Kalli. 2004. *Digital interactive TV and metadata: Future broadcast multimedia*. Berlin: Springer.

Luhmann, Niklas. 1985. *A sociological theory of law*. London: Routledge & Kegan Paul.

Luhmann, Niklas. 1992. Autopoiesis: What is communication? *Communication Theory* 2(3): 251–259.

Luke, Timothy W. 1989. *Screens of power: Ideology, domination, and resistance in informational society*. Urbana: University of Illinois Press.

Lukes, Stephen. 1974. *Power: A radical view*. London: Macmillan.

Lukes, Stephen. 1986. *Power*. Oxford: Blackwell.

Lull, James. 1997. Hybrids, fronts, borders: The challenge of cultural analysis in Mexico. *Cultural Studies* 1(3): 405–418.

Lundvall, Bengt-Ake. 1993. Explaining interfirm cooperation and innovation: Limits of the transaction-cost aproach. In Gernot Grabher, ed., *The embedded firm: The socioeconomics of industrial networks*, 52–64. New York: Routledge.

Lynch, William T., and Ellsworth R. Fuhrman. 1991. Recovering and expanding the normative: Marx and the new sociology of scientific knowledge. *Science, Technology, & Human Values* 16(2): 233–248.

Lyotard, Jean-François. 1984. *The postmodern condition: A report on knowledge*. Minneapolis: University of Minnesota Press.

Lyotard, Jean-François. 1991. *The inhuman: Reflections on time*. Stanford, CA: Stanford University Press.

MacArthur, John R. 2004. *Second front: Censorship and propaganda in the 1991 Gulf War*. Berkeley: University of California Press.

MacBride, Sean. 1980. *Many voices, one world: The MacBride Commission Report*. Paris: UNESCO.

Macdonald, Stuart. 1989. Out of control? US export controls and technological information. In Jörg Becker and Tamas Szecsko, eds., *Europe speaks to Europe: International information flows between Eastern and Western Europe*, 309–338. Oxford: Pergamon Press.

Macdonald, Stuart. 1990. *Technology and the tyranny of export controls: Whisper who dares*. New York: St. Martin's Press.

Machiavelli, Niccolò. [1515] 1985. *The Prince*, trans. by Harvey Claflin Mansfield. Chicago: University of Chicago Press.

Machlup, Fritz. 1958. *An economic review of the patent system*. Washington, DC: Government Printing Office.

Machlup, Fritz. 1962. *The production and distribution of knowledge in the United States*. Princeton, NJ: Princeton University Press.

Machlup, Fritz. 1980. *Knowledge: Its creation, distribution, and economic significance*. Vol. I: Knowledge and knowledge production. Princeton, NJ: Princeton University Press.

Machlup, Fritz. 1983. The economics of information: A new classification. *InterMedia* 11(2): 28–37.

Machlup, Fritz, and Una Mansfield, eds. 1983. *The study of information: Interdisciplinary messages*. New York: Wiley & Sons.

MacIver, Robert. 1926. *The modern state*. London: Oxford University Press.

MacKay, Donald M. 1983. The wider scope of information theory. In Fritz Machlup and Una Mansfield, eds., *The study of information: Interdisciplinary messages*, 485–492. New York: Wiley & Sons.

MacKenzie, Donald. 1978. Statistical theory and social interests: A case study. *Social Studies of Science* 8(1): 35–83.

MacKenzie, Donald, and Graham Spinardi. 1995. Tacit knowledge, weapons design, and the uninvention of nuclear weapons. *The American Journal of Sociology* 101(1): 44–99.

MacLeod, W. C. 1924. *The origins of the state.* Indianapolis, IN: Bobbs-Merrill.

Magat, Wesley A., and W. Kip Viscusi. 1992. *Informational approaches to regulation.* Cambridge, MA: MIT Press.

Maggs, Peter B., John T. Soma, and James A. Sprowl. 2000. *Internet and computer law.* St. Paul, MN: West Publishing.

Mains, Susan P. 2004. Cultural geography in a new millennium: Translation, borders, and resistance. *Journal of Cultural Geography* 22(1): 151–154.

Malinowski, Bronislaw. 1944. *A scientific theory of culture and other essays.* Chapel Hlil: University of North Carolina Press.

Malki, Riad. 2002. The depths of the Wall. *Palestine-Israel Journal of Politics, Economics & Culture* 9(3): 45–51.

Mamiya, Christin J. 1991. *Pop art and consumer culture: American supermarket.* Austin: University of Texas Press.

Manheim, Jerol B. 1994. *Strategic public diplomacy and American foreign policy: The evolution of influence.* New York: Oxford University Press.

Mankin, L. D., S. Cohn, R. W. Perr, and N. J. Cayer. 2001. The national government and the arts: Impressions from the state and jurisdictional art agencies. *Journal of Arts Management, Law, and Society* 31(3): 184–197.

Mann, Michael. 1984. The autonomous power of the state: Its origins, mechanisms and results. *Archives Europiennes de Sociologie* 25: 185–213.

Mann, Michael. 1986. *The sources of social power.* Cambridge: Cambridge University Press.

Mansell, Robin, and Brian S. Collins. 2005. *Trust and crime in information societies.* Cheltenham, UK: Edward Elgar.

Mansell, Robin, and Roger Silverstone, eds. 1997. *Communication by design: The politics of information and communication technologies*, 2nd ed. New York: Oxford University Press.

Mansell, Robin, and Ute Wehn. 1998. *Knowledge societies: Information technology for sustainable development.* New York: Oxford University Press and United Nations Commission on Science and Technology for Development.

Mansfield, Edwin. 1988. Intellectual property rights, technological changes, and economic growth. In Charles E. Walker and Mark A. Bloomfield, eds., *Intellectual property rights and capital formation in the next decade*, 3–26. Boston: University Press of America.

Manzione, J. 2000. Amusing and amazing and practical and military: The legacy of scientific internationalism in American foreign policy, 1945–1963. *Diplomatic History* 24(1): 21–55.

Marcella, Albert J., Jr., and Carol Stucki. 2003. *Privacy handbook: Guidelines, exposures, policy implementation, and international issues.* New York: Wiley & Sons.

March, James G. 1955. An introduction to the theory and measurement of influence. *American Political Science Review* 49(2): 431–451.

March, James G. 1966. The power of power. In David Easton, ed., *Varieties of political theory*, 39–70. Englewood Cliffs, NJ: Prentice Hall.

March, James G. 1987. Ambiguity and accounting: The elusive link between information and decision making. *Accounting, Organizations and Society* 12(2): 153–168.

Marchand, de Montigny. 1981. The impact of information technology on international relations. *InterMedia* 9(6): 12–15.

Marchand, Donald A. 1979. Privacy, confidentiality and computers: National and international implications of US information policy. *Telecommunications Policy* 3(3): 192–208.

Marcus, George E., ed. 1994. *Perilous states: Conversations on culture, politics, and nation*. Chicago: University of Chicago Press.

Mariotti, Renato. 2005. Cyberspace in three dimensions. *Syracuse Law Review* 55(2): 251–300.

Marlin-Bennett, Renee. 2004. *Knowledge power: Intellectual property, information, and privacy*. Boulder, CO: Lynne Rienner.

Marsh, David, ed. 1998. *Comparing policy networks*. Milton Keynes, UK: Open University Press.

Marshall, T. H. [1950] 2003. *Class, citizenship, and social development*. Chicago: University of Chicago Press.

Martin, Shannon, Bil F. Chamberlin, and Irina Dmitrieva. 2001. State laws requiring World Wide Web dissemination of information: A review of state government mandates for documents online. *Information & Communications Technology Law* 10(2): 167–179.

Martin-Barbero, Jesus. 1988. Communication from culture: The crisis of the national and the emergence of the popular. *Media, Culture and Society* 10(4): 447–465.

Martin-Barbero, Jesus. 1993. *Communication, culture and hegemony: From the media to mediations*. Thousand Oaks, CA: Sage.

Martine, Brian J. 1992. *Indeterminacy and intelligibility*. Albany: State University of New York Press.

Marvin, Carolyn. 1988. *When old technologies were new*. New York: Oxford University Press.

Marx, Anthony W. 1996. Race-making and the nation-state. *World Politics* 48(2): 180–208.

Marx, Gary T. 1999. What's in a name? Some reflections on the sociology of anonymity. *The Information Society* 15(2): 99–112.

Marx, Karl. 1904. Preface to *A contribution to the critique of political economy*. Chicago: Charles H. Kerr.

Massey, Dorreen, Paul Quintas, and David Wield. 1992. *High-tech fantasies: Science parks in society, science and space*. New York: Routledge.

Masuda, Yoneji. 1981. *The information society as post-industrial society*. Washington, DC: World Future Society.

Mathiasen, David G. 1988. The evolution of the Office of Management and Budget under President Reagan. *Public Budgeting and Finance* 8(3): 3–14.

Mattei, Ugo. 1998. *Comparative law and economics*. Ann Arbor: University of Michigan Press.

Mattelart, Michele, and Armand Mattelart. 1990. *The carnival of images: Brazilian television fiction*, trans. David A. Buxton. New York: Bergin & Garvey.

Matthews, Jessica. 1997. Power shift: The rise of global civil society. *Foreign Affairs* 76(1) (Jan.–Feb.): 50–66.

Maule, William R. 1994. Current information infrastructure policy in the United States. *Knowledge and Policy* 7(2): 17–30.

Maurseth, Per Botolf. 2005. Lovely but dangerous: The impact of patent citations on patent renewal. *Economics of Innovation and New Technology* 14(5): 351–374.

Maxwell, Richard. 1996. Out of kindness and into difference: The value of global market research. *Media, Culture and Society* 18: 105–126.

Maynard, Emerson P., Jr. 1977. Nomenclature, cross-indexing, and research: Beginnings in the United States. *New York State Journal of Medicine* 77(5): 810–814.

Mazzoleni, Roberto. 2005. University patents, R&D competition, and social welfare. *Economics of Innovation and New Technology* 14(6): 499–515.

McCalips, Rosanna. 2002. What recent court cases indicate about English-only rules in the workplace: A critical look at the need for a Supreme Court ruling on the issue. *University of Pennsylvania Journal of Labor & Employment Law* 4(2): 417–438.

McChesney, Robert W. 1993. *Telecommunications, mass media, and democracy: The battle for the control of U.S. broadcasting, 1928–1935*. New York: Oxford University Press.

McClellan, Grant S. 1981. *Immigrants, refugees, and U.S. policy*. New York: H. W. Wilson.

McClure, Charles R., Anne P. Bishop, Philip Doty, and Howard Rosenbaum. 1991. *The National Research and Education Network (NREN): Research and policy perspectives*. Norwood, NJ: Ablex.

McClure, Kirstie. 1992. On the subject of rights: Pluralism, plurality and the political. In Chantal Mouffe, ed., *Dimensions of radical democracy: Pluralism, citizenship, community*, 108–127. London: Verso.

McCraw, Robin R. 2000. Rice v. Paladin: Freedom of speech takes a hit with "deep pocket" censorship. *Northern Kentucky University Law Review* 27(1): 128–162.

McCurdy, Howard E. 1993. *Inside NASA: High technology and organizational change in the US space program*. Baltimore, MD: Johns Hopkins University Press.

McDermott, Patrice and Gary D. Bass. 1996. Federal statistical policy: An interview. *Government Information Insider* 5(2): 2–9.

McDowell, Stephen D. 1995. The return of the license Raj: Indian software export policies. *Journal of Communication* 45(4): 25–51.

McDowell, Stephen D. 2000. Globalization, local governance, and the United States Telecommunications Act of 1996. In James O. Wheeler, Yuko Aoyama, and Barney Wharf, eds., *Cities in the telecommunications age: The fracturing of geographies*, 112–129. New York: Routledge.

McGarity, Thomas O. 1991. *Reinventing rationality: The role of regulatory analysis in the federal bureaucracy*. New York: Cambridge University Press.

McGarty, Terrence P. 1991. Alternative networking architectures: Pricing, policy, and competition. In Brian Kahin, ed., *Building information infrastructure*, 218–270. New York: McGraw-Hill Primis.

McGrath, John. 2004. *Loving big brother: Performance, privacy and surveillance space*. New York: Routledge.

McGraw, Kathleen M., and Milton Lodge. 1996. Political information processing: A review essay. *Political Communication* 13(1): 131–138.

McGuire, Robert A. 2003. *To form a more perfect union: A new economic interpretation of the United States Constitution*. Oxford: Oxford University Press.

McKibben, Bill. 1996. Some versions of pastoral. *New York Review of Books* (July 11): 42–45.

McLeod, Jack M., Gerald M. Kosicki, and Dianne M. Ricinski. 1988. Political communication research: An assessment of the field. *Mass Comm Review* 15(1): 8–15, 30.

McLuhan, Marshall. 1964. *Understanding media*. New York: McGraw-Hill.

McNelis, D. N., and G. E. Schweitzer. 2001. Environmental security: An evolving concept. *Environmental Science & Technology* 35(5): 108–114.

Mead, George Herbert. 1934. *Mind, self and society*. Chicago: University of Chicago Press.

Mead, Margaret. 1940. Social change and cultural surrogates. *Journal of Educational Sociology* 14(2): 92–109.

Meadow, Robert G. 1985. Political communication research in the 1980s. *Journal of Communication* 35(1): 157–173.

Meiklejohn, Alexander. 1961. The First Amendment is an absolute. *Supreme Court Review* 1961: 245–266.

Melody, William H. 2000. Telecom myths: The international revenue settlement subsidy. *Telecommunications Policy* 24(1): 51–61.

Melucci, Alberto. 1996. *Challenging codes: Collective action in the information age*. Cambridge: Cambridge University Press.

Mencken, Henry L. 1921. *The American language: An inquiry into the development of English in the United States*. New York: Knopf.

Mendelsohn, L. D. 1992. Technology-transfer policy: Its role as a scientific and technical-information policy and its impact on technological growth. *Journal of the American Society for Information Science* 43(1): 80–88.

Mercuri, Rebecca. 1992. Voting-machine risks. *Communications of the ACM* 35(11): 138.

Merelman, Richard M. 1988. Cultural displays: An illustration from American immigration. *Qualitative Sociology* 11(4): 335–354.

Merelman, Richard M. 1998. The mundane experience of political culture. *Political Communication* 15(4): 515–535.

Merino, B. D. 1998. Critical theory and accounting history: Challenges and opportunities. *Critical Perspectives in Accounting* 9(6): 603–616.

Merton, Robert K. 1949. *Social theory and social structure.* New York: Free Press.

Merton, Robert K. 1955. A paradigm for the study of the sociology of knowledge. In Paul F. Lazarsfeld and Morris Rosenberg, eds., *The language of social research: A reader in the methodology of social research*, 498–510. Glencoe, IL: Free Press.

Merton, Robert K. 1981. Remarks on theoretical pluralism. In Peter M. Blau and Robert K. Merton, eds., *Continuities in structural inquiry*, i–vii. London: Sage.

Mertz, Henriette. 1950. *Copyright bibliography for checking purposes.* Washington, DC: Copyright Office, Library of Congress.

Meyer, David J. 1984. *Paine, Webber, Jackson and Curtis, Inc. v. Merrill Lynch, Pierce, Fenner & Smith*: Methods of doing business held patentable because implemented on a computer. *Computer/Law Journal* 5: 101–124.

Meyer, David S., Nancy Whittier, and Belinda Robnett, eds. 2002. *Social movements: Identity, culture, and the state.* Oxford: Oxford University Press.

Meyers, Deborah Waller. 2003. Does "smarter" lead to safer? An assessment of the border accords with Canada and Mexico. *International Migration* 41(4): 5–44.

Meyers, Eytan. 2004. *International immigration policy: Theoretical and comparative analysis.* Houndsmills, UK: Palgrave Macmillan.

Meyers, Tedson J. 1984. International information networks. *Jurimetrics Journal* 24(27): 171–178.

Meyler, Bernadette. 2001. The gestation of birthright citizenship, 1868–1898: States' rights, the law of nations, and mutual consent. *Georgetown Immigration Law Journal* 15(1): 519–562.

Micarelli, William F. 1998. Evolution of the US economic census: The nineteenth and twentieth centuries. *Government Information Quarterly* 15(3): 335–378.

Michaels, Eric. 1994. *Bad aboriginal art: Tradition, media, and technological horizon.* Minneapolis: University of Minnesota Press.

Michalec, Mitchell J. 2002/2003. The Classified Information Protection Act: Killing the messenger or killing the message? *Cleveland State Law Review* 50: 455–486.

Michener, W. K., J. W. Brunt, J. J. Helly, T. B. Kirchner, and S. G. Stafford. 1997. Nongeospatial metadata for the ecological sciences. *Ecological Applications* 7(1): 330–342.

Middleton, Kent R., Robert Trager, and Bill F. Chamberlin. 2005. *The law of public communication*. Boston: Pearson/Allyn & Bacon.

Mill, John Stuart. 1963. *The collected works of John Stuart Mill*. Toronto, ON: University of Toronto Press.

Miller, Arthur S. 1968. *The Supreme Court and American capitalism*. New York: Free Press.

Miller, Arthur S., and R. F. Howell. 1960. The myth of neutrality in constitutional adjudication. *The University of Chicago Law Review* 27(4): 661–695.

Miller, Clark A. 2001. Making democracy count. *Social Studies of Science* 31(3): 454–459.

Miller, John. 1998. Settling accounts with a secret police: The German law on the Stasi records. *Europe-Asia Studies* 50(2): 305–330.

Miller, Peter, and Michael Power. 1995. Calculating corporate failure. In Yves Dezalay and David Sugarman, eds., *Professional competition and professional power*, 51–76. London: Taylor & Francis.

Millon, David. 1991. The Sherman Act and the balance of power. In E. Thomas Sullivan, ed., *The political economy of the Sherman Act: The first one hundred years*, 85–115. New York: Oxford University Press.

Mills, C. Wright. 1956. *The power elite*. New York: Oxford University Press.

Milne, C. 1998. Stages of universal service policy. *Telecommunications Policy* 22(9): 775–780.

Milyo, Jeffrey, and Oh, Hye-Jin. 2004. Social capital and support for public funding of the arts. Presented to the Cultural Policy Workshop at the University of Chicago, January 20.

Minkoff, Debra C. 1997. The sequencing of social movements. *American Sociological Review* 62(5): 779–799.

Minow, Newton. 1991. *How vast the wasteland now?* New York: Gannett Foundation Media Center.

Mirabito, Michael, and Barbara L. Morgenstern. 2004. *The new communications technologies: Applications, policy, and impact*. Amsterdam: Elsevier.

Mitchell, Jack. 1992. *How to get elected: An anecdotal history of mudslinging, red-baiting, vote-stealing, and dirty tricks in American politics*. New York: St. Martin's Press.

Mitchell, Kevin. 2001. Antitrust analysis: A roadmap for election reform under the First Amendment. *CommLaw Conspectus* 10(1): 157–174.

Mizzaro, Stefano. 1997. Relevance: The whole history. *Journal of the American Society of Information Science* 48(9): 810–832.

Mody, Bella. 1995. State consolidation through liberalization of telecommunication services in India. *Journal of Communication* 45(4): 107–112.

Mohr, Lawrence B. 1971. Organizational technology and organizational structure. *Administrative Science Quarterly* 16: 444–459.

Mokros, Hartmut B., ed. 2003. *Identity matters: Communication-based explorations and explanations.* Cresskill, NJ: Hampton Press.

Mokyr, Joel. 1990. *Lever of riches: Technological creativity and economic progress.* Oxford: Oxford University Press.

Mokyr, Joel. 2002. *The gifts of Athena: Historical origins of the knowledge economy.* Princeton, NJ: Princeton University Press.

Monge, Peter R., and Noshir S. Contractor. 2003. *Theories of communication networks.* New York: Oxford University Press.

Monk, Peter. 1992. Innovation in the information economy. In Cristiano Antonelli, ed., *The economics of information networks*, 35–50. Amsterdam: North-Holland.

Monroe, Paul. 1918. *A brief course in the history of education.* London: MacMillan.

Montesquieu, Charles de Secondat. [1748] 1949. *On the spirit of laws.* New York: Hafner Publishing.

Moore, David W. 1987. Political campaigns and the knowledge-gap hypothesis. *Public Opinion Quarterly* 51(2): 186–200.

Moore, Nick. 1997. Neo-liberal or dirigiste? Policies for an information society. *Political Quarterly* 68(3): 276–284.

Moore, Roy L. 1999. *Mass communication law and ethics*, 2nd ed. Mahwah, NJ: Lawrence Erlbaum Associates.

Moore, Wilbert E. 1964. Predicting discontinuities in social change. *American Sociological Review* 29(3): 331–338.

Morgan, Gareth. 1986. Toward self-organization: Organizations as brains. In *Images of organizations*, 77–109. Beverly Hills, CA: Sage.

Morgenthau, Hans J. 1954. *Politics among nations: The struggle for power and peace.* New York: Knopf.

Morin, Arthur L. 1994. Regulating the flow of data: OMB and the control of government information. *Public Administration Review* 54(5): 434–443.

Morrison, Alan B. 1986. OMB interference with agency rulemaking: The wrong way to write a regulation. *Harvard Law Review* 99(5): 1059–1074.

Mortensen, Jorgen. 2000. Intellectual capital: Economic theory and analysis. In Pierre Buigues, Alexis Jacquemin, and Jean-Francois Marchipont, eds., *Competitiveness and the value of intangible assets*, 3–16. Brussels: Centre for European Policy Studies.

Mörth, Ulrika, and Bengt Sundelius. 1993. Dealing with a high technology vulnerability trap: The USA, Sweden, and industry. *Cooperation and Conflict* 28(3): 303–328.

Moschella, James M. 1995. Osorio v Immigration and Naturalization Service: The Second Circuit and "well-founded fear of persecution on account of political opinion." *Brooklyn Journal of International Law* 21: 471–504.

Mosco, Vincent. 1989. Critical thinking about the military information society: How Star Wars is working. In Marc Raboy and Peter A. Bruck, eds., *Communication for and against democracy*, 37–57. Montreal: Black Rose Books.

Mosco, Vincent. 1990. Toward a transnational world information order: The Canada-U.S. Free Trade Agreement. *Canadian Journal of Communication* 15(2): 46–63.

Mossman, Elliot. D. 1993. Research, ethics and the marketplace: The case of the Russian archives. *Slavic Review* 52(1): 87–89.

Mossoff, Adam. 2003. *Rethinking the development of patents: An intellectual history, 1550–1800.* East Lansing: Michigan State University-DCL College of Law.

Mouffe, Chantal. 1992. Democratic politics today. In Chantal Mouffe, ed., *Dimensions of radical democracy: Pluralism, citizenship, community*, 1 16. London: Verso.

Mouffe, Chantal. 1993. *The return of the political.* London: Verso.

Mouritzen, Hans. 1988. *Finlandization: Towards a general theory of adaptive politics.* Aldershot, UK: Avesbury.

Mowlana, Hamid and Laurie Wilson. 1990. *The passing of modernity: Communication and the transformation of society.* White Plains, NY: Longman.

Moynihan, D. P. 2004. Building secure elections: E-voting, security, and systems theory. *Public Administration Review* 64(5): 515–528.

Moynihan, Daniel P. 1997. *Report of the Commission on Protecting and Reducing Government Secrecy: Pursuant to Public Law 236, 103rd Congress.* Washington, DC: Government Printing Office.

Moynihan, Daniel P. 1998. *Secrecy: The American experience.* New Haven, CT: Yale University Press.

Mueller, Milton. 1989. *The telephone war: Interconnection, competition, and monopoly in the making of universal telephone service: 1894–1920.* Unpublished diss., University of Pennsylvania.

Mueller, Milton. 1995. Why communications policy is passing mass communication by: Political economy as the missing link. *Critical Studies in Mass Communication* 13(3): 457–472.

Mueller, Milton. 1996. *Universal service.* Cambridge, MA: MIT Press.

Mueller, Milton. 2002. *Ruling the root.* Cambridge, MA: MIT Press.

Mueller, Milton, and Dale Thompson. 2003. ICANN and INTELSAT: Global communication technologies and their incorporation into international regimes. In Sandra Braman, ed., *The emergent global information policy regime*, 62–85. Houndsmills, UK: Palgrave Macmillan.

Mueller, Milton L., and Jorge Reina Schement. 1996. Universal service from the bottom up: A study of telephone penetration in Camden, New Jersey. *The Information Society* 12: 273–292.

Müller, Jan-Werner, ed. 2002. *Memory and power in post-war Europe: Studies in the presence of the past*. Cambridge: Cambridge University Press.

Murdock, Graham, and Peter Golding. 1989. Information poverty and political inequality: Citizenship in the age of privatized communications. *Journal of Communication* 39(3): 180–195.

Murphy, Paul L. 1992. *The shaping of the First Amendment, 1791 to the present*. New York: Oxford University Press.

Murphy, Walter F. 1964. *Elements of judicial strategy*. Chicago: University of Chicago Press.

Murray, R. 1971. The new internationalization of capital and the nation-state. *New Left Review* 67: 84–112.

Musen, M. A. 1992. Dimensions of knowledge sharing and reuse. *Computers and Biomedical Research* 25: 435–467.

Myers, Gary. 1994. Antitrust and First Amendment implications of professional real estate investors. *Washington & Lee Law Review* 51(4): 1199–1256.

Nadel, Mark S. 1983. A unified theory of the First Amendment: Divorcing the medium from the message. *Fordham Urban Law Journal* 11(2): 163–224.

Nagel, Robert F. 1989. *Constitutional cultures: The mentality and consequences of judicial review*. Berkeley: University of California Press.

Nahmod, Sheldon. 2001. The GFP (green) bunny: Reflections on the intersection of art, science, and the First Amendment. *Suffolk University Law Review* 34: 473–484.

Napoli, Philip M. 2001. *Foundations of communications policy: Principles and process in the regulation of electronic media*. Cresskill, NJ: Hampton Press.

Nardi, Bonnie and Vicki O'Day. 2000. *Information ecologies: Using technology with heart*. Cambridge, MA: MIT Press.

Nasri, William Z. 1976. *Crisis in copyright*. New York: Dekker.

National Academy of Sciences, Committee on Science, Engineering, and Public Policy. 1987. *Balancing the national interest: U.S. national security export controls and global economic competition*. Washington, DC: National Academies Press.

National Academy of Sciences, Committee on Science, Engineering, and Public Policy. 1989. *Information Technology and the Conduct of Research*. Washington, DC: National Academies Press.

National Academy of Sciences, Committee on Science, Engineering, and Public Policy. 1991. *Finding common ground: U.S. export controls in a changed global environment*. Washington, DC: National Academies Press.

National Commission on Federal Election Reform. 2001. *To assure pride and confidence in the elecctoral process*. Washington, DC: Federal Election Reform Network.

National Committee of the United States of America on International Intellectual Cooperation. 1938. *Comparative study of copyright protection in Latin America, 1938*. N.p. Washington, DC: Committee for the Study of Copyright, Subcommittee of the American National Committee on International Intellectual Cooperation.

National Endowment for the Arts. 2000. *The National Endowment for the Arts 1965–2000: A brief chronology of federal support for the arts*. Washington, DC: Government Printing Office.

National Information Standards Organization (NISO). 2004. *Understanding metadata*. Bethesda, MD: NISO Press.

National Research Council. 1962. *The role of patents in research*. Washington, DC: National Academy of Sciences.

National Research Council. 1995. *Modernizing the U.S. census*. Washington, DC: National Academies Press.

National Research Council. 2003. *Weaving a national map: Review of the US Geological Survey concept of the national map*. Washington, DC: National Academies Press.

National Telecommunications and Information Administration (NTIA). 1991. *Telecommunications in the age of information*. Washington, DC: U.S. Department of Commerce, NTIA Special Pub. 91-26.

Naughton, Edward J. 1992. Is cyberspace a public forum? Computer bulletin boards, free speech, and state action. *Georgetown Law Journal* 81(2): 409–441.

Neely, Richard. 1981. *How courts govern America*. New Haven, CT: Yale University Press.

Negash, G. 2004. Art invoked: A mode of understanding and shaping the political. *International Political Science Review* 25(2): 185–201.

Nelkin, D., and L. Andrews. 1999. DNA identification and surveillance creep. *Sociology of Health & Illness* 21(5): 689–706.

Nelson, Anna Kasten, ed. 1978. *The records of federal officials: A selection of materials from the National Study Commission on Records and Documents of Federal Officials*. New York: Garland.

Nelson, Richard R. 1987. *Understanding technical change as an evolutionary process*. Amsterdam: North-Holland.

Nelson, Richard R., and Sidney G. Winter. 2000. In search of a useful theory of innovation. In C. Edquist and M. D. McKelvey, eds., *Systems of innovation: Growth, competitiveness and employment*, 81–121. Cheltenham, UK: Elgar Reference Collection.

Ness, Susan. 1998. Remarks before the Policy Summit of the Information Technology Association of America, Washington, DC, March 30.

Neu, Werner, Karl-Heinz Neumann, and Thomas Schnöring. 1987. Trade patterns, industry structure and industrial policy in telecommunications. *Telecommunications Policy* 11(1): 31–44.

Neuborne, Burt, and Steven R. Shapiro. 1985. The nylon curtain: America's national border and the free flow of ideas. *William & Mary Law Review* 26(3): 719–777.

New York Times v. U.S., 403 U.S. 713. 1971.

Newman, A. 2004. Arms control, proliferation and terrorism: The Bush administration's post–September 11 security strategy. *Journal of Strategic Studies* 27(1): 59–88.

Newman, R. 1995. The effectiveness of an unpublished rule. *Annual Survey of American Law* 1995: 1–35.

Newmann, William. 2001. Causes of change in national security processes: Carter, Reagan, Bush decision making on arms control. *Presidential Studies Quarterly* 31(1): 69–103.

Nichols, Stephen M., and Gregory A. Strizek. 1995. Electronic voting machines and ballot roll-off. *American Politics Quarterly* 23(3): 300–319.

Nicholson, Michael. 1987. Misperceptions and satisficing in international conflict. In Claudio Cioffi-Revilla, Richard L. Merritt, and Dina A. Zinnes, eds., *Communication and interaction in global politics*, 117–139. Beverly Hills, CA: Sage.

Nickles, David Paull. 2003. *Under the wire: How the telegraph changed diplomacy*. Cambridge, MA: Harvard University Press.

Nicoll, Chris, Corien Prins, and Miriam J. M. van Dellen. 2003. *Digital anonymity and the law: Tensions and dimensions*. The Hague, The Netherlands: T. M. C. Asser Press.

Nimmer, Melville B. 1963. *Nimmer on copyright: A treatise on the law of literary, musical and artistic property, and the protection of ideas*. Albany, NY: M. Bender.

Nissel, Muriel. 1995. Social trends and social change. *Journal of the Royal Statistical Society* 158(3): 491–504.

Nissen, Hans J., Peter Damerow, and Robert K. Englund. 1994. *Archaic bookkeeping: Writing and techniques of economic administration in the ancient Near East*, trans. by Paul Larsen. Chicago: University of Chicago Press.

Noam, Eli M. 1982. The choice of government level in regulation. *Kyklos* 35(2): 278–291.

Noam, Eli M. 1983. Federal and state roles in telecommunications: The effects of deregulation. *Vanderbilt Law Review* 36(4): 949–983.

Noam, Eli M. 1987. The public telecommunications network: A concept in transition. *Journal of Communication* 37(1): 30–48.

Noam, Eli M. 1989. Network pluralism and regulatory pluralism. In P. Newberg, ed., *New directions in telecommunications policy*, vol. 1, 66–91. Durham, NC: Duke University Press.

Noam, Eli M. 1990. The historic evolution of the network system: Past change, present impact, and future policy. In Sylvie Schaff, ed., *Legal and economic aspects of telecommunications*, 461–477. Amsterdam: Elsevier.

Noam, Eli M. 1992. A theory for the instability of public telecommunications system. In Cristiano Antonelli, ed., *The economics of information networks*, 107–128. Amsterdam: Elsevier.

Noam, Eli M. 1993. Reconnecting communication studies with communications policy. *Journal of Communication* 43(3): 199–206.

Noam, Eli M. 1994. Beyond liberalization: From the network of networks to the system of systems. *Telecommunications Policy* 18(4): 286–294.

Noam, Eli. 2000. The next stage in the digital economy: Nano-transactions and nano-regulation. Presented to the Telecommunications Policy Research Conference, Alexandria, VA, September.

Noam, Eli M. 2001. *Interconnecting the network of networks*. Cambridge, MA: MIT Press.

Nobles, Melissa. 2000. History counts: A comparative analysis of racial/color categorization in U.S. and Brazilian censuses. *American Journal of Public Health* 90(11): 1738–1746.

Noelle-Neumann, Elisabeth. 1984. *The spiral of silence: Public opinion—Our social skin*. Chicago: University of Chicago Press.

Nora, Simon, and Alain Minc. 1980. *The computerization of society*. Cambridge, MA: MIT Press.

Norberg, Arthur L., and Judy E. O'Neill. 1996. *Transforming computer technology: Information processing for the Pentagon, 1962–1986*. Baltimore, MD: Johns Hopkins University Press.

Nordenstreng, Kaarle, and Herbert J. Schiller. 1979. *National sovereignty and international communication*. Norwood, NJ: Albex.

Nordenstreng, Kaarle, and Tapio Varis. 1973. The nonhomogeneity of the national state and the international flow of communication. In George Gerbner, Larry Gross and William Melody, eds., *Communication technology and social policy: Understanding the new "cultural revolution,"* 393–412. New York: Wiley & Sons.

Norman, D. A., and S. W. Draper. 1986. *User-centered system design: New perspectives on human-computer interaction*. Mahwah, NJ: Lawrence Erlbaum Associates.

Norris, Pippa, W. Lance Bennett, and Robert M. Entman. 2001. *Digital divide: Civic engagement, information poverty, and the Internet worldwide*. Cambridge: Cambridge University Press.

North, Douglass C. 1979. A framework for analyzing the state in economic history. *Explorations in Economic History* 16(3): 249–259.

North, Douglass C. 1984. Government and the cost of exchange in history. *Journal of Economic History* 44(2): 255–264.

North, Douglass C., and Joel Mokyr, eds. 2005. *Understanding the process of economic change*. Princeton, NJ: Princeton University Press.

Note. 2005. Secret evidence in the war on terror. *Harvard Law Review* 118(6): 1962–1984.

Novak, Marcus. 1997. Transmitting architecture: The transphysical city. In Arthur Kroker and Marilouise Kroker, eds., *Digital delirium*, 260–271. New York: St. Martin's Press.

Nowotny, Helga. 1983. Marienthal and after: Local historicity and the road to policy relevance. *Knowledge: Creation, Diffusion, Utilization* 5(2): 169–192.

Nowotny, Helga. 1990. *In search of usable knowldge: Utilization concepts and the application of knowledge*. Boulder, CO: Westview Press.

Nunberg, Geoffrey. 1997. Lingo jingo: English-only and the new nativism. *The American Prospect* 33(July–August): 40–47.

Nusbaumer, Jacques. 1987. *The services economy: Lever to growth*. Boston, MA: Kluwer Academic.

Nye, Joseph. 1990. The changing nature of world power. *Political Science Quarterly* 105(2): 177–192.

Nye, Joseph. (2004). *Soft power: The means to success in world politics*. New York: Perseus Publishing.

Oakes, Angela D. 2001. The impact of state English-only laws on environmental justice and the Title VI remedy. *Land Resources & Environmental Law* 21(2A): 397–414.

Oakley, Robert L. 1990. *Copyright and preservation: A serious problem in need of a thoughtful solution*. Washington, DC: Commission on Preservation and Access.

Ochel, Wolfgang, and Manfred Wegner. 1987. *Service economies in Europe: Opportunities for growth*. Boulder, CO: Westview Press.

O'Connor, Kathleen M. 1988. OMB involvement in FDA drug regulations: Regulating the regulators. *Catholic University Law Review* 38(1): 175–212.

O'Donnell, Guillermo. 1980. Comparative historical formations of the state apparatus and socio-economic change in the Third World. *International Social Science Journal* 32: 717–729.

O'Donnell, Máire, and Vikki Entwistle. 2004. Consumer involvement in research projects: The activities of research funders. *Health Policy* 69(2): 229–238.

Oettinger, Anthony G. 1980. Information resources: Knowledge and power in the twenty-first century. *Science* 209(4452) (July 4): 191–198.

Oettinger, Anthony G., Paul J. Berman, and William H. Read. 1977. *High and low politics of information resources for the 80s*. New York: Ballinger.

Office of the Federal Register. 1994. *Guide to record retention requirements in the Code of Federal Regulations*. Washington, DC: National Archives and Records Administration.

O'Harrow, Robert, Jr. 2005. *No place to hide: Behind the scenes of our emerging surveillance society*. New York: Free Press.

Olick, Jeffrey K., and Joyce Robbins. 1998. Social memory studies: From "collective memory" to the historical sociology of mnemonic practices. *Annual Review of Sociology* 24(1): 105–141.

Olivas, Michael A. 1997. *The law and higher education: Cases and materials on colleges in court*, 3rd ed. Durham, NC: Carolina Academic Press.

Olivas, Michael A. 2003. *Law and higher education 2003*. Durham, NC: Carolina Academic Press.

Ollmann, Bertell. 1976. The state as a value relation. In *Alienation: Marx's conception of man in capitalist society*, 215–221. Cambridge: Cambridge University Press.

Olsen, Marvin E., and Martin N. Marger, eds. 1993. *Power in modern societies*. Boulder, CO: Westview Press.

Olson, Charles. 1965. *Proprioception*. San Francisco: Four Seasons Foundation, Writing 6.

Ordover, Janusz A., and Robert D. Willig. 1998. Access and bundling in high-technology markets. In Jeffrey A. Eisenach and Thomas M. Lenard, eds., *Competition, innovation and the Microsoft monopoly: Antitrust in the digital marketplace*, 103–128. Boston: Kluwer Academic.

Oreskes, Naomi. 2003. A context of motivation: U.S. navy oceanographic research and the discovery of sea-floor hydrothermal vents. *Social Studies of Science* 33(5): 697–742.

Ottolia, Andrea, and Dan Wielsch. 2003/2004. Mapping the information environment: Legal aspects of modularization and digitalization. *Yale Journal of Law & Technology* 6: 174–276.

Overbeck, Wayne. 2004. *Major principles of media law*. Belmont, CA: Thompson Wadsworth.

Owen, Bruce M. 1970. Public policy and emerging technology in the media. *Public Policy* 18(3): 539–552.

Owen, Bruce M. 1975. *Economics and freedom of expression: Media structure and the First Amendment*. Cambridge, MA: Ballinger.

Owen, Bruce M., and Ronald Braeutigam. 1978. *The regulation game: Strategic use of the administrative process*. Cambridge, MA: Ballinger.

Owen, Bruce M., and Steven S. Wildman. 1992. *Video economics*. Cambridge, MA: Harvard University Press.

Pal, Leslie A. 1990. Knowledge, power, and policy: Reflections on Foucault. In Stephen Brooks and Alain G. Gagnon, eds., *Social scientists, policy, and the state*, 139–158. New York: Praeger.

Palmer, Laura R. 2001. A very clear and present danger: Hate speech, media reform, and post-conflict democratization in Kosovo. *Yale Journal of International Law* 26(1): 179–218.

Palumbio-Liu, David. 1997. Unhabituated habituses. In David Palumbio-Liu and Hans Ulrich Gumbrecht, eds., *Streams of cultural capital*, 1–22. Stanford, CA: Stanford University Press.

Pang, Laikwan. 2005. *Cultural control and globalization in Asia: Copyright, piracy, and cinema*. New York and London: Routledge.

Panitch, Leo. 1980. Recent theorizations of corporatism: Reflections on a growth industry. *British Journal of Sociology* 31: 159–187.

Panofsky, W. K. H. 2000. National security and scientific communication. *Proceedings of the National Academy of Sciences* 97(10): 5034–5036.

Papa, Michael J., Arvind Singhal, Sweety Law, Saumya Pant, Suruchi Sood, Everett M. Rogers, and Corinne L. Shefner-Rogers. 2000. Entertainment-education and social change: An analysis of parasocial interaction, social learning, collective efficacy, and paradoxical communication. *Journal of Communication* 50(4): 31–55.

Parker, Elizabeth Rindskopf, and Leslie Gielow Jacobs. 2003. Government controls of information and scientific inquiry. *Biosecurity and Bioterrorism: Biodefense Strategy, Practice, and Science* 1(2): 83–95.

Parry-Giles, Shawn J. 1993. The rhetorical tension between propaganda and democracy: Blending competing conceptions of ideology and theory. *Communication Studies* 44(2): 117–131.

Parry-Giles, Trevor. 1988. Stemming the red tide: Free speech and immigration policy in the case of Margaret Randall. *Western Journal of Speech Communication* 52(2): 167–183.

Parsons, Talcott. 1951. *The social system.* Glencoe, IL: The Free Press.

Parsons, Talcott. 1963. On the concept of political power. *Proceedings of the American Philosophical Society* 103(3): 232–262.

Passavant, Paul. 2002. *No escape: Freedom of speech and the paradox of rights.* New York: New York University Press.

Patterson, Thomas E. 1985. *Toward new research on communication technologies and the democratic process.* Aspen, CO: Aspen Institute.

Paulin, Tom. 1992. *Minotaur: Poetry and the nation state.* Cambridge, MA: Harvard University Press.

Peach, M. 2004. Henrich Mann's novels and essays: The artist as political educator. *German Studies Review* 27(1): 165–166.

Pearce, Robert D., and Satwinder Singh. 1992. *Globalizing research and development.* New York: St. Martin's Press.

Pearton, Maurice. 1984. *Diplomacy, war and technology since 1830.* Lawrence, KS: University Press of Kansas.

Peha, Jon M. 1999. Tradable universal service obligations. *Telecommunications Policy* 23(5): 363–374.

Pelton, Joseph N. 1994. The public versus private objectives for the US national information infrastructure initiative. *Telematics and Informatics* 11(3): 179–191.

Pember, Don R., and Clay Calvert. 2005/2006. *Mass media law.* New York: McGraw-Hill.

Penn, Ira A. 1997. Information management legislation in the last quarter of the 20th century: A records management disaster. *Records Management Quarterly* 31(1): 3–9.

Pepper, Robert and Stuart N. Brotman. 1987. Restricted monopolies or regulated competitors? The case of the Bell Operating Companies. *Journal of Communication* 37(1): 64–72.

Peritz, Rudolph J. R. 1990. A counter-history of antitrust law. *Duke Law Journal* (April): 263–320.

Perks, Robert. 2002. *Rewriting the rules: The Bush administration's assault on the environment.* Washington, DC: Natural Resources Defense Council.

Peters, John Durham. 1986. Institutional sources of intellectual poverty in communication research. *Communication Research* 13(4): 527–559.

Peters, John Durham. 1988. *Information*: Notes toward a critical history. *Journal of Communication Inquiry* 12(2): 9–23.

Peters, John Durham. 1999. *Speaking into the air: A history of the idea of communication.* Chicago: University of Chicago Press.

Peters, John Durham. 2004. The marketplace of ideas: A history of the concept. In Andrew Calabrese and Colin Sparks, eds., *Toward a political economy of culture: Capitalism and communication in the twenty-first century*, 65–82. Boulder, CO: Rowman and Littlefield.

Petersmann, Ernst, and Meinhard Hilf, eds. 1988. *The new GATT round of multilateral trade negotiations: Legal and economic problems.* Deventer, The Netherlands: Kluwer.

Petersmann, Ernst-Ulrich. 1988. Trade policy as a constitutional problem: On the "domestic policy functions" of international trade rules. In Heinz Hauser, ed., *Protectionism and structural adjustment*, 243–277. Grusch, Switzerland: Verlag.

Petersmann, Ernst-Ulrich. 1991. *Constitutional functions and constitutional problems of international economic law.* Fribourg, Switzerland: University Press.

Peterson, P. G. 2002. *Public diplomacy: A strategy for reform.* Washington, DC: Council on Foreign Relations.

Pew, Richard W. 2003. Evolution of human-computer interaction: From memex to bluetooth and beyond. In Julie A. Jacko and Andrew Sears, eds., *The human-computer interaction handbook: Fundamentals, evolving technologies and emerging applications*, 1–18. Mahwah, NJ: Lawrence Erlbaum Associates.

Pichardo, Nelson A. 1997. New social movements: A critical review. *Annual Review of Sociology* 23: 411–430.

Pickles, John. 2004. *A history of spaces: Cartographic reason, mapping, and the geo-coded world.* London: Routledge.

Pierce, Kenneth J. 1984. Public cryptography, arms export controls, and the First Amendment: A need for legislation. *Cornell International Law Journal* 17(1): 197–236.

Pieterse, Jan Nederveen. 1997. Multiculturalism and museums: Discourse about others in the age of globalization. *Theory, Culture & Society* 14(4): 123–146.

Piore, Michael J., and Charles F. Sabel. 1986. *The second industrial divide: Possibilities for prosperity.* New York: Basic Books.

Pipe, G. Russell. 1979. Transborder data flows: The international legal framework. *Computer/Law Journal* 3(4): 551–562.

Pitofsky, Robert. 1991. New definitions of relevant market and the assault on antitrust. In Eleanor M. Fox and James T. Halverson, eds., *Collaborations among competitors: Antitrust policy and economics*, 553–596. Chicago: American Bar Association.

Plautz, D. 2005. New ideas emerge when collaboration occurs. *Leonardo* 38(4): 302–309.

Ploman, Edward N. 1982a. *International law governing communications and information: A collection of basic documents*. Westport, CT: Greenwood Press.

Ploman, Edward W. 1982b. Transborder data flows: The international legal framework. *Computer/Law Journal* 3: 551–562.

Podolny, Joel, and Karen Page. 1998. Network forms of organization. *Annual Review of Sociology* 24: 57–76.

Podolny, Joel M., and Toby E. Stuart. 1995. A role-based ecology of technological change. *American Journal of Sociology* 100(5): 1224–1260.

Pogorel, Gerard. 1992. Network dynamics and societal interactions. In Cristiano Antonelli, ed., *The economics of information networks*, 363–366. Amsterdam: North-Holland.

Pool, Ithiel de Sola. 1983. *Technologies of freedom*. Cambridge, MA: Belknap Press.

Popkewitz, Thomas S. 1991. *A political sociology of educational reform: Power/knowledge in teaching, teacher education, and research*. New York: Teachers College Press, Columbia University.

Porat, Marc Uri. 1977. *The information economy: Definition and measurement*. Washington, DC: Office of Telecommunications, U.S. Department of Commerce, OT Special Publication 77-12(1).

Porter, Bruce D. 1994. *War and the rise of the state: The military foundations of modern politics*. New York: Free Press.

Poskanzer, Steven G. 2001. *Higher education law: The faculty*. Baltimore, MD: Johns Hopkins University Press.

Posner, Richard A. 1984. An economic theory of privacy. In Ferdinand David Schoeman, ed., *Philosophical dimensions of privacy*, 333–345. Cambridge: Cambridge University Press.

Posner, Richard A. 2002. *Antitrust law*. Chicago: University of Chicago Press.

Posner, Richard A. 2003. The speech market and the legacy of *Schenck*. In Lee Bollinger and Geoffrey Stone, eds., *Eternally vigilant: Free speech in the modern era*, 120–151. Chicago: University of Chicago Press.

Post, Robert C. 1998. *Censorship and silencing: Practices of cultural regulation*. Los Angeles, CA: Getty Research Institute.

Post, Robert C. 2000. Reconciling theory and doctrine in First Amendment jurisprudence. *California Law Review* 88(6): 2353–2375.

Potok, Nancy Fagenson. 2000. Behind the scenes of Census 2000. *The Public Manager* 29(4): 3–5.

Potter, William C. 1980. Issue area and foreign policy analysis. *International Organization* 34(3): 405–427.

Poulantzas, Nicos. 1974. Internationalization of capitalist relations and the nation-state. *Economy & Society* 3(2): 145–179.

Powell, Joan, ed. 2001. *Education for action: Undergraduate and graduate programs that focus on social change*, 4th ed. Oakland, CA: Institute for Food and Development Policy.

Prelas, Mark Antonio, and Michael S. Peck. 2005. *Nonproliferation issues for weapons of mass destruction*. Boca Raton, FL: Taylor & Francis.

Premfors, Rune. 1991. Knowledge, power, and democracy: Lindblom, critical theory and postmodernism. *Knowledge and Policy* 92(5): 77–94.

Presidential Information Technology Advisory Council (PITAC). 2005. *Computational science: Ensuring America's competitiveness*. Washington, DC: PITAC.

Pressman, Rebecca R. 2002. *Classification, description and comparison of state laws related to the Internet*. Unpublished diss., Florida State University.

Preston, Paschal. 2001. *Rethinking communications technology, information, and social change*. London: Sage.

Previts, Gary John, and Barbara Dubis Merino. 1998. *A history of accountancy in the United States: The cultural significance of accounting*. Columbus: Ohio State University Press.

Pribis, William B. 1994. Telephone company entry into the cable television market: The clash between the First Amendment and the laws and procedures of antitrust enforcement. *Suffolk University Law Review* 28(3): 715–746.

Price, Monroe, and Mark Thompson, eds. 2002. *Forging peace: Intervention, human rights and the management of media space*. Bloomington: Indiana University Press.

Prindle, Edwin J. 1908. *Patents as a factor in manufacturing*. New York: Engineering Magazine.

Proimos, C. V. 2002. The politics of mimesis in the Platonic dialogues: A comment on Plato's art theory from the vantage point of the "statesman." *International Studies in Philosophy* 34(2): 83–93.

Project Gutenberg. Available at www.gutenberg.org.

Prosser, William. 1971. *Handbook of the law of torts*, 4th ed. St. Paul, MN: West Publishing.

Prosser, William. 1984. Privacy: A legal analysis. In Ferdinand David Schoeman, ed., *Philosophical dimensions of privacy*, 104–155. Cambridge: Cambridge University Press.

Public Citizen v. Carlin, 184 F.3d 900. 1999.

Puckett, Christopher J. 2004. Is the experiment over? The OMB's decision to change the game through a shortening of the forecast. *Georgetown Journal on Poverty Law & Policy* 11(1): 169–190.

Pugh, Derek S., David J. Hickson, Christopher R. Hinings, and Christopher Turner. 1968. Dimensions of organization structure. *Administrative Science Quarterly* 13(1): 65–105.

Pulliam, John D., and James J. Van Patten. 1987. *History of education in America*. Columbus, OH: Merrill.

Putnam, George Haven. 1891. *The question of copyright*. New York: G. P. Putnam's Sons.

Pye, Lucian W. 1956. Communication patterns and the problems of representative government in non-Western societies. *Public Opinion Quarterly* 20(1): 249–257.

Qvortrup, Lars. 1988. The challenges of telematics: Social experiments, social informatics, and orgware architecture. In George Muskens and Jacob Gruppelaar, eds., *Global telecommunication networks: Strategic considerations*, 159–170. Dordrecht, The Netherlands: Kluwer Academic.

Rabban, David M. 1997. *Free speech in its forgotten years*. New York: Cambridge University Press.

Rabkin, Jeremy. 1983. The judiciary in an administrative state. *Public Interest* 71: 62–84.

Race, Katherine L. 2003. The future of digital movie distribution on the Internet: Antitrust concerns with the movielink and movies.com proposals. *Rutgers Computer and Technology Law Journal* 29(1): 89–137.

Radcliffe-Brown, A. R. 1952. *Structures and function in primitive societies*. Glencoe, IL: Free Press.

Radin, Margaret J., John Rothchild, and Gregory Silverman. 2002. *Internet commerce: The emerging legal framework*. New York: Foundation Press.

Rakove, Jack N. 2001. *The unfinished election of 2000*. New York: Basic Books.

Ransom, Harry Huntt. 1956. *The first copyright statute: An essay on an act for the encouragement of learning*. Austin: University of Texas Press.

Rantanen, Terhi, and Oliver Boyd-Barrett. 1999. *The globalization of news*. Thousand Oaks, CA: Sage.

Rasmussen, M. B. 2004. The Situationist International, Surrealism, and the difficult fusion of art and politics. *Oxford Art Journal* 27(3): 365–387.

Ravault, Rene J. 1981. Information flow: Which way is the wrong way? *Journal of Communication* 31(4): 129–134.

Reber, A. S. 1997. *Implicit learning and tacit knowledge: An essay on the cognitive unconscious*. New York and Oxford: Oxford University Press.

Redish, Martin. 1982. Advocacy of unlawful conduct and the First Amendment: In defense of clear and present danger. *California Law Review* 70(3): 1159–1200.

Reed, Chris. 2004. *Internet law: Text and materials*. Cambridge: Cambridge University Press.

Rehnquist, William H. 1976. The First Amendment: Freedom, philosophy, and the law. *Gonzaga Law Review* 12(1): 1–18.

Rehnquist, William H. 1998. *All the laws but one: Civil liberties in wartime.* New York: Vintage.

Relyea, Harold. 1994. *Silencing science: National security controls and scientific communication.* Norwood, NJ: Ablex.

Relyea, Harold. 1996. Dissemination of government information. *Bowker Annual* 41: 220–235.

Renaud, Jean-Luc. 1987. The ITU and development assistance. *Telecommunications Policy* 11(2): 179–192.

Reporters Committee for Freedom of the Press. 2004. *Homefront confidential: How the war on terrorism affects access to information and the public's right to know*, 5th ed. Arlington, VA: Reporters Committee for Freedom of the Press. Available at www.rcfp.org/homefrontconfidential/.

Rheingold, Howard. 1991. *Virtual reality.* New York: Simon & Schuster.

Rheingold, Howard. 2002. *Smart mobs.* Cambridge, MA: Perseus Publications.

Rice, Don. 1979. *Animals, a picture sourcebook: Over 700 copyright-free illustrations for direct copying and reference.* New York: Van Nostrand Reinhold.

Rice, Ron. 1987. Computer-mediated communication and organizational innovation. *Journal of Communication* 37(4): 65–94.

Ricento, Thomas. 2005. *Introduction to language policy: Theory and methods.* London: Blackwell.

Richards, Thomas. 1993. *The imperial archive: Knowledge and the fantasy of empire.* New York: Verso.

Riebeek, Holli. 2002. Brazil holds all-electronic national election. *IEEE Spectrum* 39(11): 25–27.

Rindskopf, Elizabeth R., and Marshall L. Brown, Jr. 1985. Embargoes on exports of ideas and information: First Amendment issues—Scientific and technological information and the exigencies of our period. *William & Mary Law Review* 26(5): 909–924.

Ringer, Fritz. 1990. The intellectual field, intellectual history, and the sociology of knowledge. *Theory and Society* 19(3): 269–294.

Rivette, Kevin G., and David Kline. 2000. *Rembrandts in the attic: Unlocking the hidden value of patents.* Cambridge, MA: Harvard Business School Press.

Roach, Colleen. 1987. The US position on the New World Information and Communication Order. *Journal of Communication* 37(4): 36–51.

Roberts, Helene E. 2001. A picture is worth a thousand words: Art indexing in electronic databases. *Journal of the American Society of Information Science* 52(11): 911–916.

Roberts, Michael M. 1992. The university role in the United States National Research and Education Network. *Computer Networks and ISDN Systems* 25(4–5): 512–517.

Robertson, Margaret. 2001. Abridging the freedom of non-English speech: English-only legislation and the free speech rights of government employees. *Brigham Young University Law Review* 2001(4): 1641–1696.

Robinson, Glen O., ed. 1978. *Communications for tomorrow: Policy perspectives for the 1980s*. New York: Praeger.

Roeh, Itzahak, and Akiba Cohen. 1992. One of the bloodiest days: A comparative analysis of open and closed television news. *Journal of Communication* 42(2): 42–56.

Rogers, Donald Wayne, and Christine Brendel Scriabine. 1992. *Voting and the spirit of American democracy: Essays on the history of voting and voting rights in America*. Urbana: University of Illinois Press.

Rogers, Walter F. d. 1914. *The law of patents as illustrated by leading cases*. Indianapolis, IN: Bobbs-Merrill.

Rohracher, H., ed. 2005. *User involvement in innovation processes: Strategies and limitations from a socio-technical perspective*. Vienna, Austria: Profil-Verlag.

Roland, Alex. 1992. Theories and models of technological change: Semantics and substance. *Science, Technology, & Human Values* 17(1): 79–100.

Romero, Victor C. 2001. Restricting hate speech against "private figures": Lessons in power-based censorship from defamation law. *Columbia Human Rights Law Review* 33(1): 1–40.

Rose, M. 1993. *Authors and owners: The invention of copyright*. Cambridge, MA: Harvard University Press.

Rosecrance, Richard. 1986. *The rise of the trading state: Commerce and conquest in the modern world*. New York: Basic Books.

Rosecrance, Richard. 1996. The rise of the virtual state. *Foreign Affairs* 75(4): 45–61.

Roseman, G. H., and E. F. Stephenson. 2005. The effect of voting technology on voter turnout: Do computers scare the elderly? *Public Choice* 123(1–2): 39–47.

Rosen, Jeffrey. 2004. The naked crowd: Balancing privacy and security in an age of terror. *Arizona Law Review* 46(4): 607–619.

Rosenau, James N. 1970. *The adaptation of national societies: A theory of political system behavior and transformation*. New York: McCaleb-Seller Publishing.

Rosenau, James N. 1984. A pre-theory revisited? World politics in an era of cascading interdependence. *International Studies Quarterly* 28(3): 245–306.

Rosenau, James N. 1990. *Turbulence in world politics: A theory of change and continuity*. Princeton, NJ: Princeton University Press.

Rosenau, James N., and Mary Durfee. 1995. *Thinking theory thoroughly: Coherent approaches to an incoherent world*. Boulder, CO: Westview Press.

Rosenberg, Norman L. 1986. *Protecting the best men: An interpretive history of the law of libel*. Chapel Hill: University of North Carolina Press.

Rosenfeld, Louis, and Peter Morville. 2002. *Information architecture for the World Wide Web*, 2nd ed. Sebastopol, CA: O'Reilly & Associates.

Rosenfeld, Michel. 1994. Modern constitutionalism as interplay between identity and diversity. In Michel Rosenfeld, ed., *Constitutionalism, identity, difference, and legitimacy: Theoretical perspectives*, 3–38. Durham, NC: Duke University Press.

Rosenour, Jonathan. 1997. *Cyberlaw: The law of the Internet*. New York: Springer-Verlag.

Rosenthal, Naomi, Meryl Fingrudt, Michele Ethier, Roberta Karant, and David McDonald. 1985. Social movements and network analysis: A case study of nineteenth-century women's reform in New York state. *American Journal of Sociology* 90(5): 1022–1054.

Rosenzweig, Paul S. 1985. Functional equivalents of the border, sovereignty, and the Fourth Amendment. *University of Chicago Law Review* 52(4): 1119–1145.

Rosler, M. 2004. Out of the Vox: Art's activist potential—the return of political art. *Artforum International* 43(1): 218–219.

Ross, Susan Dente, and R. Kenton Bird. 2004. The ad that changed libel law: Judicial realism and social activism in New York Times Co. v. Sullivan. *Communication Law and Policy* 9(4): 489–523.

Rosston, Gregory L., and Bradley S. Wimmer. 2000. The "state" of universal service. *Information Economics and Policy* 12(3): 261–283.

Rostow, Walter W. 1994. The five stages of growth: A summary. In Rajani Kanth, ed., *Paradigms in economic development: Classic perspectives, critiques, and reflections*, 99–106. Armonk, NY: M. E. Sharpe.

Rotenberg, Marc. 2003. *The privacy law sourcebook 2003: United States law, international law, and recent developments*. Washington, DC: Electronic Privacy and Information Center (EPIC).

Rothenberg, Jeff. 1995. Ensuring the longevity of digital documents. *Scientific American* 272(1): 42–47.

Rothschild, Lincoln. 1957. *Economic problems of the professional fine artist*. New York: Artists Equity Association.

Rotunda, Ronald D., and John E. Nowak. 1999. *Treatise on constitutional law: Substance and procedure*, 3rd ed. St. Paul, MN: West Group.

Rowland, Diane. 2003. Privacy, freedom of expression and cyberSLAPPs: Fostering anonymity on the Internet? *International Review of Law, Computers & Technology* 17(3): 303–312.

Rowland, Willard D., Jr. 1982. The process of reification: Recent trends in communications legislation and policy-making. *Journal of Communication* 32(4): 114–136.

Rozenberg, Joshua. 2004. *Privacy and the press*. New York: Oxford University Press.

Rubinyi, Robert M. 1990. Computers and community: The organizational impact. *Journal of Communication* 39(3): 110–123.

Rudney, Robert, and T. J. Anthony. 1996. Beyond CoCom: A comparative study of five national export control systems and their implications for a multilateral nonproliferation regime. *Comparative Strategy* 15(1): 41–57.

Rudy, Willis. 1991. *Total war and twentieth-century higher learning: Universities of the western world in the First and Second World Wars*. Cranbury, NJ: Fairleigh Dickinson University Press.

Ruggles, Myles A. 1994. *The audience reflected in the medium of law: A critique of the political economy of speech rights in the United States*. Norwood, NJ: Ablex.

Rules, Charles F., and David L. Meyer. 1991. An antitrust enforcement policy to maximize the economic wealth of all consumers. In Thomas E. Sullivan, ed., *The political economy of the Sherman Act: The first one hundred years*, 210–226. New York: Oxford University Press.

Ruppert, David. 1994. Buying secrets: Federal government procurement of intellectual cultural property. In Tom Greaves, ed., *Intellectual property rights for indigenous peoples: A sourcebook*, 111–128. Oklahoma City, OK: Society for Applied Anthropology.

Rury, John L. 2002. Democracy's high school? Social change and American secondary education in the post-Conant era. *American Educational Research Journal* 29(2): 307–336.

Rushton, M. 2003. Transaction cost politics and the National Endowment for the Arts. *Poetics* 31(2): 133–150.

Rusk, Jerrold G. 2001. *A statistical history of the American electorate*. Washington, DC: Congressional Quarterly Press.

Russell, Bertrand. 1938. *Power: A new social analysis*. London: Allen and Unwin.

Russell, Donald J., and Sheri Lynn Wolson. 2002. Dual antitrust review of telecommunications mergers by the Department of Justice and the Federal Communications Commission. *George Mason Law Review* 11(1): 143–156.

Russell, Stuart J., and Peter Norvig. 1995. *Artificial intelligence: A modern approach*. Englewood Cliffs, NJ: Prentice-Hall.

Rustad, Michael L. 2004. Punitive damages in cyberspace: Where in the world is the consumer? *Chapman Law Review* 7(1): 39–105.

Rutkowski, Anthony M. 1981. *United States policy making for the public international forums on communication*. New York: Communications Media Center, New York Law School.

Rutkowski, Anthony M. 1983. The integrated services digital network: Issues and options for the future. *Jurimetrics Journal* 24(1): 19–42.

Ryan, Bryce. 1965. The resuscitation of social change. *Social Forces* 44(1): 1–7.

Ryan, K. 1992. Law and the creation of deviance: The case of the drug courier profile. Presented at the Law and Society Association, Philadelphia, May.

Sabel, Charles. 1991. Moebius-strip organizations and open labor markets: Some consequences of the reintegration of conception and execution in a volatile economy. In Pierre Bourdieu and James S. Coleman, eds., *Social theory for a changing society*, 23–54. Boulder, CO: Westview Press.

Sabety, Ted. 2005. Nanotechnology innovation and the patent thicket: Which IP policies promote growth? *Albany Law Journal of Science & Technology* 15: 477–516.

Sadiq, Kamal. 2005. When states prefer non-citizens over citizens: Conflict over illegal immigration into Malaysia. *International Studies Quarterly* 49(1): 101–123.

Sagasti, F. R. 1992. Knowledge and development in Latin America: Science, technology and production five centuries after the encounter with Europe. *International Social Science Journal* 13(4): 579–591.

Salgado, Richard P. 1998. Government secrets, fair trials, and the Classified Information Procedures Act. *Yale Law Journal* 98: 427–446.

Salyers, Abigail A. 2002. Microbes and the law: From censorship to forensics. *University of Illinois Journal of Law and Policy* 2002(2): 413–419.

Samorski, Jan H. 2001. *Issues in cyberspace: Communication, technology, law and society on the Internet frontier*. Boston: Allyn & Bacon.

Samuelson, Pamela. 1989. Information as property: Do *Ruckelshaus* and *Carpenter* signal a changing direction in intellectual property law? *Catholic University Law Review* 38: 365–400.

Samuelson, Pamela. 1995. Counterpoint: An entirely new legal regime is needed. *The Computer Lawyer* 12(2): 11–17.

Samuelson, Pamela. 2003. Mapping the digital public domain: Threats and opportunities. *Law and Contemporary Problems* 66(1): 147–171.

Santos, Bonaventura de Sousa. 1980. Law and community: The changing nature of state power in late capitalism. *International Journal of the Sociology of Law* 8: 379–397.

Sarnoff, David. 1915–1916. The vision of David Sarnoff: Memorandum to E. J. Nally. In Elmer R. Buchers, *Radio and David Sarnoff*, unpublished manuscript.

Saunders, D. 1992. *Authorship and copyright*. New York: Routledge.

Saussure, Ferdinand de. [1913] 1959. *Course in general linguistics*. New York: Philosophical Library.

Sauvant, Karl. 1986. *Trade and foreign direct investment in data services*. Boulder, CO: Westview Press.

Sawhney, Harmeet, ed. 2000. *Manifold facets of universal service*. Special issue of *The Information Society* 16(2): 91–164.

Scanlan, John A. 1988. Aliens in the marketplace of ideas: The government, the academy, and the McCarran-Walter Act. *Texas Law Review* 66: 1481–1546.

Scazzieri, Roberto. 1993. *A theory of production: Tasks, processes, and technical practices*. Oxford: Clarendon Press.

Schabas, William A. 2000. Hate speech in Rwanda: The road to genocide. *McGill Law Journal* 46(1): 141–172.

Schauer, Frederick. 1982. *Free speech: A philosophical enquiry*. New York: Cambridge University Press.

Schement, Jorge R. 1995. Beyond universal service: Characteristics of Americans without telephones, 1980–1993. *Telecommunications Policy* 19(6): 477–485.

Schement, Jorge Reina, Joan Parker, and Cynthia Shelton. 1985. *Bibliography of information societies*. Los Angeles: University of California-Los Angeles Graduate School of Library and Information Science Report.

Schenck v. U.S., 249 U.S. 47. 1919.

Scherer, Frederick M. 1992. *International high-technology competition*. Cambridge, MA: Harvard University Press.

Scheufele, Dietram A., Matthew C. Nisbet, Dominique Brossard, and Erik C. Nisbet. 2004. Social structure and citizenship: Examining the impacts of social setting, network homogeneity, and informational values on political participation. *Political Communication* 21(3): 315–338.

Schiff, Eric. 1971. *Industrialization without national patents: The Netherlands, 1869–1912; Switzerland, 1850–1907*. Princeton, NJ: Princeton University Press.

Schildkraut, Deborah. 2005. *Press ONE for English: Language policy, public opinion, and American identity*. Princeton, NJ: Princeton University Press.

Schlachter, Eric. 1993. Cyberspace, the free market and the free marketplace of ideas: Recognizing legal differences in computer bulletin board functions. *Hastings Communications and Entertainment Law Journal* 16(1): 87–150.

Schlesinger, Peter. 1991. Media, the political order and national identity. *Media, Culture and Society* 13(3): 297–308.

Schmeckebier, Laurence F. 1941. *Congressional apportionment*. Washington, DC: Brookings Institution.

Schmitter, Phillipe C. 1985. Neo-corporatism and the state. In W. Grant, ed., *The political economy of corporatism*, 32–62. New York: St. Martin's Press.

Schoeman, Frederick. 1984. Privacy: Philosophical dimensions of the literature. In Frederick Schoeman, ed., *Philosophical dimensions of privacy*, 1–33. Cambridge: Cambridge University Press.

Schrag, Philip G. 1989. *Listening for the Bomb: A study in nuclear arms and verification*. Boulder, CO: Westview Press.

Schrag, Philip G. 1994. Working papers as federal records: The need for new legislation to preserve the history of national policy. *Administrative Law Review* 46(2): 95–140.

Schudson, Michael. 1992. *Watergate in American memory: How we remember, forget, and reconstruct the past*. New York: Basic Books.

Schudson, Michael. 1998. *The good citizen: A history of American civic life*. Cambridge, MA: Harvard University Press.

Schumpeter, Joseph A. [1911] 1949. *The theory of economic development: An inquiry into profits, capital, credit, interest, and the business cycle*, trans. by Redvers Opie. Cambridge, MA: Harvard University Press.

Schwab, J. D. 1990. National security restraints of the federal government on academic freedom and scientific communication in the United States. *Government Publications Review* 17(1): 17–48.

Schwartz, Joseph. 2001. *Cassandra's daughter: A history of psychoanalysis*. New York: Penguin Books.

Schwartz, Thomas A. 1990. A bibliographic analysis of First Amendment scholarship in US Supreme Court opinions, 1964–1986. Presented to the Association for Education in Journalism and Mass Communication, August, Chicago.

Schweber, Libby. 2001. Manipulation and population statistics in nineteenth-century France and England. *Social Research* 68(2): 547–583.

Scott, W. R. 1994. The legalistic organization. In S. B. Sitkin and R. J. Bies, *The legalistic organization*, 1–9. Newbury Park, CA: Sage.

Sedjo, Roger A., and R. David Simpson. 1995. Property rights contracting and the commercialization of biodiversity. In Terry L. Anderson and Peter J. Hill, eds., *Wildlife in the marketplace*, 167–178. Lanham, MD: Rowman & Littlefield.

The Sedona Conference. 2005. *The Sedona principles: Best practices, recommendations & principles for addressing electronic document production*. Sedona, AZ: The Sedona Conference.

Self, Glen D., and Donna K. Love. 1991. Policy issues arising out of EDS' research. Presented to the 19th Telecommunications Policy Research Conference, Solomons, MD, September.

Selkowitz, Ira C. 1983. A well-kept secret: Informal adjudication in the Copyright Office—A Freedom of Information Act violation? *Administrative Law Review* 35: 133–145.

Seller, Maxine Schwartz. 1991. Boundaries, bridges, and the history of education. *History of Education Quarterly* 31(2): 195–206.

Seltzer, Leon E. 1978. *Exemptions and fair use in copyright: The exclusive rights tensions in the 1976 Copyright Act*. Cambridge, MA: Harvard University Press.

Seltzer, William, and Margo Anderson. 2001. The dark side of numbers: The role of population data systems in human rights abuses. *Social Research* 68(2): 481–514.

Selznick, Philip. 1957. *Leadership in administration: A sociological interpretation*. Berkeley: University of California Press.

Servaes, Jan. 1989. Cultural identity and modes of communication. *Communication Yearbook* 12: 383–416.

Shadlen, Kenneth C. 2004. Patents and pills, power and procedure: The North-South politics of public health in the WTO. *Studies in Comparative International Development* 39(3): 76–108.

Shamir, Jacob, and Michal Shamir. 2000. *The anatomy of public opinion*. Ann Arbor: University of Michigan Press.

Shane, Peter M. 2004. *Democracy online: The prospects for political renewal through the Internet*. New York: Routledge.

Shane, R. R. 2004. Personal and political: The dynamics of East German art in the painting of Willi Sitte. *Art Criticism* 19(2): 121–142.

Shannon, Claude E. 1948. A mathematical theory of communication. *Bell System Technical Journal* 27(10): 379–423, 625–656.

Shannon, Claude E., and Warren Weaver. 1949. *The mathematical theory of communication*. Urbana: University of Illinois Press.

Shapin, Steven. 1995. Here and everywhere: Sociology of scientific knowledge. *Annual Review of Sociology* 21: 289–321.

Shapiro, Carl. 2003. Antitrust limits to patent settlements. *RAND Journal of Economics* 34(2): 391–413.

Shapiro, Carl, and Hal Varian. 1999. *Information rules: A strategic guide to the information economy*. Cambridge, MA: Harvard Business School Press.

Shapiro, Steven R. 1987. Ideological exclusions: Closing the border to political dissidents. *Harvard Law Review* 100(4): 930–945.

Shattuck, John. 1986. Federal restrictions on the free flow of academic information and ideas. *Government Information Quarterly* 3(1): 5–29.

Shea, Timothy J. 1990. CIPA under siege: The use and abuse of classified information in criminal trials. *American Criminal Law Review* 27(4): 657–716.

Shelanski, Howard A., and J. Gregory Sidak. 2001. Antitrust divestiture in network industries. *University of Chicago Law Review* 68(1): 1–100.

Shell, Marc. 1993. *Children of the earth: Literature, politics and nationhood*. New York: Oxford University Press.

Shelp, Ronald K. 1986/1987. Trade in services. *Foreign Policy* 65(1): 64–84.

Shelton, Michael, Derek R. Lane, and Enid S. Waldhart. 1999. A review and assessment of national educational trends in communication instruction. *Communication Education* 48(3): 228–237.

Shields, Peter. 1995. Beyond individualism and the ecology of games: Structures, institutions, and communication policy. *Communication Theory* 5(4): 366–378.

Shiffrin, Steven. 1978. Defamatory non-media speech and First Amendment methodology. *UCLA Law Review* 25(5): 915–963.

Shooshan, Harry M., III, ed. 1984. *Disconnecting Bell: The impact of the AT&T divestiture*. New York: Pergamon Press.

Shultz, George, and Thomas L. Whisler, eds. 1960. *Management organization and the computer*. Chicago: Graduate School of Business, University of Chicago.

Shupsky, Donald S. 1995. Structuring records management under the legal department. *Records Management Quarterly* 29(3): 33–35.

Sidak, J. Gregory. 2004. An economic theory of censorship. *Supreme Court Economic Review* 11: 81–126.

Sieber, Renée E. 2003. Public participation geographic information systems across borders. *Canadian Geographer* 47(1): 50–62.

Siff, Alan. 1984. ISDNs: Shaping the new networks that might reshape FCC policies. *Federal Communications Law Journal* 37(1): 171–201.

Signitzer, Benno. 1992. Public relations and public diplomacy: Conceptual convergence. *Public Relations Review* 18(2): 137–148.

Silberman, Bernard S. 1993. *Cages of reason: The rise of the rational state in France, Japan, the United States, and Great Britain.* Chicago: University of Chicago Press.

Silberman, Steve. 2002. The fully immersive mind of Oliver Sacks. *Wired* 10(4) (April): 94ff.

Silver, Mike, and Diana Balmori, eds. 2003. *Mapping in the age of digital media: The Yale symposium.* Chichester, UK: Wiley-Academy.

Simmer, Maria A. 2004. Knowledge management in electronic government. *Lecture Notes in Computer Science* 3035.

Simon, Alan M., and Spencer Weber Waller. 1986. A theory of economic sovereignty: An alternative to extraterritorial jurisdictional disputes. *Stanford Journal of International Law* 22: 337–361.

Simon, Herbert. 1947. *Administrative behavior: A study of decision-making processes in administrative organization.* New York: Macmillan.

Simon, Herbert A. 1953. Notes on the observation and measurement of political power. *Journal of Politics* 15(4): 500–516.

Simon, Herbert A. 1979. Information processing models of cognition. *Annual Review of Psychology* 30: 363–396.

Simpson, B. 2004. After the reforms: How have public science research organizations changed? *R&D Management* 34(3): 253–266.

Skelton, Raleigh A. 1972. *Maps: A historical survey of their study and collection.* Chicago: University of Chicago Press.

Sklair, Leslie. 1989. *Assembling for development.* London: Unwin Hyman.

Skocpol, Theda. 1979. *States and social revolutions.* Cambridge: Cambridge University Press.

Skocpol, Theda. 1980. Political response to capitalist crisis: Neo-Marxist theories of the state and the case of the New Deal. *Politics & Society* 10(2): 155–201.

Skocpol, Theda. 1985. Bringing the state back in: Strategies of analysis in current research. In Peter Evans, Dietrich Rueschemeyer, and Theda Skocpol, eds., *Bringing the state back in*, 3–37. New York: Cambridge University Press.

Skocpol, Theda. 1992. *Protecting soldiers and mothers: The political origins of social policy in the United States.* Cambridge, MA: Belknap Press.

Skocpol, Theda, and Kenneth Finegold. 1982. State capacity and economic intervention in the Early New Deal. *Political Science Quarterly* 97(2): 255–278.

Skowronek, Stephen. 1982. *Building a new American state: The expansion of national administrative capacities, 1877–1920.* Cambridge: Cambridge University Press.

Skupsky, Donald S. 1995. Legal and operational definitions of a record. *Records Management Quarterly* 29(1): 39–43.

Slaton, Christa Daryl. 1992. *Televote: Expanding citizen participation in the quantum age.* New York: Praeger.

Slavin, Ruth. 1995. Public art and cultural authority. In Larry P. Gross, ed., *On the margins of art worlds*, 39–66. Boulder, CO: Westview Press.

Slobogin, Christopher. 2002. Public privacy: Camera surveillance of public places and the right to anonymity. *Mississippi Law Journal* 72(1): 213–316.

Smith, James P., and Barry Edmonston. 1997. *The new Americans: Economic, demographic, and fiscal effects of immigration.* Washington, DC: National Academy Press.

Smith, Jeffrey A. 1999. *War and press freedom: The problem of prerogative power.* Oxford: Oxford University Press.

Smith, Martin J. 1993. *Pressure power & policy: State autonomy and policy networks in Britain and the United States.* Pittsburgh, PA: University of Pittsburgh Press.

Smith, Patrick J. 2000. Do lines matter? Cascading concepts of Cascadia: Comparative Canada-U.S./European institutional policy lessons. Presented to Rethinking the Line: The Canada-U.S. Border, Vancouver, October.

Smith, Robert Ellis. 2004. *Ben Franklin's Web site: Privacy and curiosity from Plymouth Rock to the Internet.* Providence, RI: Privacy Journal.

Smith, Woodruff D. 1991. *Politics and the sciences of culture in Germany, 1840–1920.* New York: Oxford University Press.

Smolla, Rodney A. 1986. *Suing the press.* New York: Oxford University Press.

Smythe, Dallas W. 1977. Communications: Blindspot of western Marxism. *Canadian Journal of Political and Social Theory* 1(3): 1–27.

Smythe, Dallas W. 1981. *Dependency road: Communications, capitalism, consciousness, and Canada.* Norwood, NJ: Ablex.

Snethen, John D. 2000. The evolution of sovereignty and citizenship in Western Europe: Implications for migration and globalization. *Indiana Journal of Global Legal Studies* 8(1): 223–250.

Snow, David A., Louis A. Zurcher, Jr., and Sheldon Ekland-Olson. 1980. Social networks and social movements: A microstructural approach to differential recruitment. *American Sociological Review* 45(5): 787–801.

Snow, Marcellus. 1986. *Marketplace for telecommunications: Regulation and deregulation in industrialized democracies.* New York: Longman.

Snyder, Kelley Brooke. 2002. A clash of values: Classified information in immigration proceedings. *Virginia Law Review* 88: 447–484.

Solberg, Thorvald. 1900. *Copyright enactments, 1873–1900.* Washington, DC: Government Printing Office for the Library of Congress.

Soley, Lawrence. 2002. *Free speech and private censorship inc.: The corporate threat to free speech in the United States.* New York: Monthly Review Press.

Solove, Daniel J. 2004. *The digital person: Technology and privacy in the information age.* New York: New York University Press.

Solove, Daniel J., and Marc Rotenberg. 2003. *Information privacy law.* New York: Aspen Publishers.

Solow, Robert M. 2004. *Structural reform and economic policy.* Houndsmills, UK: Palgrave Macmillan.

Soma, John T., and Kevin B. Davis. 2000. Network effects in technology markets: Applying the lessons of Intel and Microsoft to future clashes between antitrust and intellectual property. *Journal of Intellectual Property Law* 8(1): 1–51.

Soma, John T., Rodney D. Peterson, Gary Alexander, and Curt W. Petty. 1983. The communications regulatory environment in the 1980s. *Computer Law Journal* 4: 1–54.

Soma, John T., and Eric K. Weingarten. 2000. Multinational economic network effects and the need for an international antitrust response from the World Trade Organization: A case study in broadcast-media and news corporations. *University of Pennsylvania Journal of International Economic Law* 21(1): 41–130.

Somers, Margaret. 1995. Narrating and naturalizing civil society and citizenship theory. *Sociological Theory* 13(2): 229–273.

Sonntag, Selma K. 2003. *The local politics of global English: Case studies in linguistic globalization.* Lexington, MA: Lexington Books.

Sorana, Valter. 2000. Auctions for universal service subsidies. *Journal of Regulatory Economics* 18(1): 33–58.

Sparks, Colin. 1995. The survival of the state in British broadcasting. *Journal of Communication* 45(4): 140–160.

Spero, Joan. 1981. *The politics of international economic relations*, 2nd ed. New York: St. Martin's Press.

Spero, Joan. 1982. Information and telecommunications is a trade issue. *Inter-Media* 10(2): 9–11.

Splichal, Sigman L. 1996. The evolution of computer/privacy concerns: Access to government information held in the balance. *Communication Law & Policy* 1(2): 203–239.

Spolsky, Bernard. 2003. *Language policy.* New York: Cambridge University Press.

Sprehe, J. Timothy. 1995. Does the U.S. government need an A-130 for STI? *Government Information Quarterly* 12(2): 213–224.

Spring, Joel. 1998. *Education and the rise of the global economy.* Mahwah, NJ: Lawrence Erlbaum Associates.

Springer, Randel S. 1989. Gatekeeping and the *Federal Register*: An analysis of the publication requirement of Section 552(a)(1)(D) of the Administrative Procedure Act. *Administrative Law Review* 41(4): 533–548.

Sproule, J. Michael. 1987. Propaganda studies in American social science: The rise and fall of the critical paradigm. *Quarterly Journal of Speech* 73(1): 60–78.

Stajano, Frank. 2002. *Security for ubiquitous computing*. New York: Wiley & Sons.

Stanton, Cathy. 2002. Historians and the Web. *The Public Historian* 24(1): 119–125.

Star, S. Leigh. 1987. The structure of ill-structured solutions: Boundary objects and heterogeneous distributed problem solving. In Michael N. Huhns, ed., *Distributed artificial intelligence: Research notes in artificial intelligence*, 37–54. London: Pitman.

Star, S. Leigh, and Karen Ruhleder. 1996. Steps toward an ecology of infrastructure: Design and access for large information spaces. *Information Systems Research* 7(1): 111–134.

Starr, Harvey, and G. Dale Thomas. 2005. The nature of borders and international conflict: Revisiting hypotheses on territory. *International Studies Quarterly* 49(1): 123–141.

State Street Bank v. Signature, 927 F. Supp. 502 (D. Mass.). 1996.

Steele, Jane. 1998. Information and citizenship in Europe. In Brian D. Loader, ed., *Cyberspace divide: Equality, agency and policy in the information society*, 161–182. New York: Routledge.

Steinmueller, W. Edward. 1992. The economnics of production and distribution of user-specific information via digital networks. In Cristiano Antonelli, ed., *The economics of information networks*, 173–194. Amsterdam: North-Holland.

Stephen, Leslie. 1907. *English literature and society in the eighteenth century*. New York: G. P. Putnam's Sons.

Stern, J. 2002. Dreaded risks and the control of biological weapons. *International Security* 27(3): 89–123.

Stern, Jill A., Erwin G. Krasnow, and R. Michael Senkowski. 1983. The new video marketplace and the search for a coherent regulatory philosophy. *Catholic University Law Review* 32(3): 529–602.

Sternberg, Ernest. 1992. *Photonic technology and industrial policy: US responses to technological change*. Albany: State University of New York Press.

Stevens, Anne H. 2001. The philosophy of general education and its contradictions: The influence of Hutchins. *The Journal of General Education* 50(3): 165–191.

Stevens, Richard G. 1997. *The American Constitution and its provenance*. Lanham, MD: Rowman & Littlefield.

Stevenson, Robert L. 1994. *Global communication in the twenty-first century*. New York: Longman.

Stewart, Robert Keith. 1990. *Access and efficiency in Reagan-era information policy: A case study of the attempt to privatize the National Technical Information Service*. Unpublished diss., University of Washington, Diss. Ab. 9104302.

Stewart, Thomas A. 1994. Your company's most valuable asset: Intellectual capital. *Fortune* (October 3): 68–74.

Stigler, George J. 1991. The origin of the Sherman Act. In E. Thomas Sullivan, ed., *The political economy of the Sullivan Act: The first one hundred years*, 32–38. New York: Oxford University Press.

Stigler, George J., and Robert A. Sherwin. 1985. The extent of the market. *Journal of Law and Economics* 28(3): 555–585.

Stille, Alexander. 2002. *The future of the past.* New York: Farrar, Straus and Giroux.

Stilling, Erik A. 1995. The history of Spanish-language television in the United States and the rise of Mexican international syndication strategies in the Americas. *Howard Journal of Communication* 6(4): 231–249.

Stilling, Erik A. 1997. The electronic melting pot hypothesis: The cultivation of acculturation among Hispanics through television. *Howard Journal of Communication* 8(1): 77–100.

Stinchcombe, Arthur L. 1990. *Information and organization.* Berkeley: University of California Press.

Stockholm International Peace Research Institute. 2005. *SIPRI yearbook 2005: Armaments, disarmament and international security.* Oxford: Oxford University Press.

Stoddard, Ellwyn R. 1975. The status of borderland studies: Sociology and anthropology. *Social Science Journal* 12(3)/13(1): 29–54.

Stoddard, Ellwyn R. 1986. Border studies as an emergent field of scientific inquiry: Scholarly contribution of U.S.-Mexico borderlands studies. *Journal of Borderlands Studies* 1(1): 1–33.

Stoddard, Ellwyn R. 1991. Frontiers, borders and border segmentation: Toward a conceptual clarification. *Journal of Borderlands Studies* 6(1): 1–22.

Stohr, Greg. 2004. *A black and white case: How affirmative action survived its greatest legal challenge.* Princeton, NJ: Bloomberg Press.

Stokes, Simon. 2005. *Digital copyright: Law and practice.* Portland, OR: Hart.

Stone, Allucquère Rosanne. 1992. Virtual systems. In Jonathan Crary and Sanford Kwinter, eds., *Incorporations*, 608–626. New York: Zone.

Stone, Allucquère Rosanne. 1995. *The war of desire and technology at the close of the mechanical age.* Cambridge, MA: MIT Press.

Stone, Geoffrey R., Cass R. Sunstein, and Louis Michael Weidman. 2005. *Constitutional law*, 5th ed. New York: Aspen Publishers.

Stoner, James Reist, Jr. 1992. *Common law and liberal theory: Coke, Hobbes, and the origins of American constitutionalism.* Lawrence: University Press of Kansas.

Storey, J. Douglas. 1993. Mythology, narrative, and discourse in Javanese *Wayang*: Towards cross-level theories for the new development paradigm. *Asian Journal of Communication* 3(2): 30–53.

Straits, Bruce C. 1991. Bringing strong ties back in: Interpersonal gateways to political information and influence. *Public Opinion Quarterly* 55(3): 432–448.

Strange, Susan. 1982. *Cave! Hic dragones*: A critique of regime analysis. *International Organization* 36(2): 479–495.

Strange, Susan. 1996. *The retreat of the state: The diffusion of power in the world economy*. London: Cambridge University Press.

Straus, Richard, ed. 1982. *Communications and international trade: A symposium*. Washington, DC: U.S. National Committee of the International Institute of Communication.

Strauss, Jeffrey S. 2004. Dangerous thoughts? Academic freedom, free speech, and censorship revisited in a post-September 11th America. *Washington University Journal of Law & Policy* 15: 343–369.

Street, John. 2002. Bob, Bono and Tony: The popular artist as politician. *Media Culture & Society* 24(3): 433–441.

Streeter, Tom. 1990. Beyond freedom of speech and the public interest: The relevance of critical legal studies to communications policy. *Journal of Communication* 40(2): 43–63.

Streeter, Tom. 1996. *Selling the air: A critique of the policy of commercial broadcasting in the United States*. Chicago: University of Chicago Press.

Stumpf, S., and J. McDonnell. 2004. An investigation into sharing metadata: "I'm not thinking what you are thinking." *Journal of Universal Computer Science* 10(6): 740–748.

Subramanian, S. V., Craig Duncan, and Kelvyn Jones. 2001. Multilevel perspectives on modeling census data. *Environment & Planning A* 33(3): 399–418.

Sugarman, David. 1995. Who colonized whom? Historical reflections on the intersection between law, lawyers and accountants in England. In Yves Dezalay and David Sugarman, eds., *Professional competition and professional power: Lawyers, accountants and the social construction of markets*, 226–237. New York: Routledge.

Sullivan, E. Thomas. 1991. *Political economy of the Sherman Act: The first one hundred years*. Oxford: Oxford University Press.

Sumner, William Graham. 1907. *Folkways: A study of the sociological importance of usages, manners, customs, mores, and morals*. Boston: Ginn.

Sun Tzu. [6th c. BC] 1963. *The art of war*, trans. by Samuel B. Griffith. New York: Oxford University Press.

Sunstein, Cass R. 1995. Incompletely theorized agreements. *Harvard Law Review* 108: 17–33.

Sunstein, Cass R., Geoffrey R. Stone, and Richard A. Epstein. 1992. *The bill of rights and the modern state*. Chicago: University of Chicago Press.

Susskind, Richard E. 1996. *The future of law: Facing the challenges of information technology*. New York: Oxford University Press.

Sussman, Gerald. 1995. Transnational communications and the dependent-integrated state. *Journal of Communication* 45(4): 89–107.

Sussman, Leonard R. 1989. *Power, the press, and the technology of freedom: The coming age of ISDN*. New York: Freedom House.

Suter, Sonia M. 2004. Disentangling privacy from property: Toward a deeper understanding of genetic privacy. *George Washington Law Review* 72(4): 737–814.

Sveiby, Karl Erik. 2000. Measuring intangibles and intellectual capital. In Daryl Morey, Mark Maybury, and Bhavani Turaisingham, eds., *Knowledge management: Classic and contemporary works*, 337–353. Cambridge, MA: MIT Press.

Svensson, Jorgen, and Ronald Leenes. 2003. E-voting in Europe: Divergent democratic practice. *Information Polity* 8(1/2): 3–15.

Swann, Peter. 1993. *New technologies and the firm: Innovation and competition*. New York: Routledge.

Swann, Peter, and Jas Gill. 1993. *Corporate vision and rapid technological change: The evolution of market structure*. New York: Taylor and Francis.

Swanson, David L. 1978. Political communication: A revisionist view emerges. *Quarterly Journal of Speech* 64(2): 211–222.

Swanson, Guy E. 1971. An organizational analysis of collectivities. *American Sociological Review* 36(4): 607–624.

Swartz, L. L. 2003. NEPA in an age of terrorism. *Environmental Practice* 5(4): 346–348.

Swidler, Ann, and Jorge Arditi. 1994. The new sociology of knowledge. *Annual Review of Sociology* 20: 305–329.

Swire, Peter P. 1997. The uses and limits of financial cryptography: A law professor's perspective. In *Proceedings of Financial Cryptography '97*, 239–258. London: Springer-Verlag.

Takeyama, Lisa, and Wendy J. Gordon. 2005. *Developments in the economics of copyright: Research and analysis*. Northampton, MA: Edward Elgar.

Tambini, Damian. 2001. Post-national citizenship. *Ethnic and Racial Studies* 24(2): 195–217.

Tangas, Jim, and Angel J. Calderon. 2004. The General Agreement on Trade in Services and educational services: An Australian perspective. *Journal of Higher Education Policy & Management* 26(1): 123–129.

Tarrow, Sidney. 2002. Transnational politics: Contention and institutions in international politics. *Annual Review of Political Science* 4: 1–20.

Taylor, Arlene G. 2004. *The organization of information*, 2nd ed. Westport, CT: Libraries Unlimited.

Taylor, Bob Pepperman. 2004. *Citizenship and democratic doubt: The legacy of Progressive thought*. Lawrence: University Press of Kansas.

Taylor, Philip M. 2003. *Munitions of the mind: A history of propaganda*. Manchester, UK: Manchester University Press.

Teeter, Dwight, and Bill Loving. 2004. *Law of mass communications*, 11th ed. St. Paul, MN: Foundation Press.

Tehranian, Majid. 1977. Global communication and international relations: Changing paradigms and policies. *International Journal of Peace Studies* 2(1): 39–64.

Teich, Al, Mark S. Frankel, Rob Kling, and Ya-Ching Lee. 1999. Anonymous communication policies for the Internet: Results and recommendations of the AAAS conference. *The Information Society* 15(2): 71–77.

Temin, Peter, ed. 1991. *Inside the business enterprise: Historical perspectives on the use of information*. Chicago: University of Chicago Press.

Temin, Peter, ed. 1992. *Inside the business enterprise: Historical perspectives on the use of information*. Chicago: University of Chicago Press.

Tengelin, V. 1981. The vulnerability of the computerised society. In Hans-Peter Gassmann, ed., *Information, computer and communications policies for the 80's*, 205–213. Amsterdam: North-Holland/OECD.

Teske, Paul. 1995. *American regulatory federalism and telecommunications infrastructure*. Mahwah, NJ: Lawrence Erlbaum Associates.

Thant, U. 1964. *The role of patents in the transfer of technology to developing countries*. New York: United Nations.

Thelen, David, and Frederick E. Hoxie. 1994. *Discovering America: Essays on the search for an identity*. Champaign: University of Illinois Press.

Theoharis, Athan G. 1998. *A culture of secrecy: The government versus the people's right to know*. Lawrence: University Press of Kansas.

Thiemie, Michael T. 2000. Two workhorse IT systems of Census 2000. *The Public Manager* 29(4): 14–18.

Thomas, George M., and John W. Meyer. 1984. The expansion of the state. *Annual Review of Sociology* 10: 461–482.

Thomas, Laurence E. 1998. *Information warfare*. Carlisle Barracks, PA: U.S. Army War College.

Thomas, Randall S. 1996. Improving shareholder monitoring of corporate management by expanding statutory access to information. *Arizona Law Review* 38(1): 331–372.

Thorbecke, Erik. 1991. *The anatomy of agricultural product markets and transactions in developing countries*. Washington, DC: Institute for Policy Reform.

Thrower, Norman Joseph William. 1972. *Maps and man: An examination of cartography in relation to culture and civilization*. Englewood Cliffs, NJ: Prentice-Hall.

Tilly, Charles. 1983. Speaking your mind without elections, surveys, or social movements. *The Public Opinion Quarterly* 47(4): 461–478.

Tilly, Charles. 1985. War making and state making as organized crime. In Peter Evans, Dietrich Rueschemeyer, and Theda Skocpol, eds., *Bringing the state back in*, 169–191. New York: Cambridge University Press.

Timofeeva, Yulia A. 2003. Hate speech online: Restricted or protected? Comparison of regulations in the United States and Germany. *Florida State University Journal of Transnational Law & Policy* 12(2): 253–286.

Tocqueville, Alexis de. [1835] 2000. *Democracy in America*, trans. and ed. by Harvey C. Mansfield and Delba Winthrop. Chicago: University of Chicago Press.

Tokaji, Daniel P. 2005. The paperless chase: Electronic voting and democratic values. *Fordham Law Review* 73(4): 1711–1836.

Tomkin, Shelley Lynne. 1998. *Inside OMB: Politics and process in the president's budget office*. Armonk, NY: M. E. Sharpe.

Tomz, Michael, and Robert P. Van Houweling. 2003. How does voting equipment affect the racial gap in voided ballots? *American Journal of Political Science* 47(1): 46–60.

Torbert, William S. 1908. *Digest and trade-mark cases decided by the Court of Appeals of the District of Columbia on appeal from the commissioner of patents and of copyright cases on appeal from the Supreme Court of the District of Columbia*. Washington, DC: J. Byrne.

Toro, Luis Angel. 1995. "A people distinct from others": Race and identity in federal Indian law and the Hispanic classification in OMB Directive No. 15. *Texas Tech Law Review* 26(4): 1219–1274.

Toulmin, Harry Aubrey. 1939. *Patents and the public interest*. New York: Harper & Bros.

Traber, Michael, ed. 1986. *The myth of the information revolution: Social and ethical implications of communication technology*. Beverly Hills, CA: Sage.

Trager, Robert, and Donna L. Dickerson. 1999. *Freedom of expression in the 21st century*. Thousand Oaks, CA: Pine Forge Press.

Trauth, Eileen M. 1986. An integrative approach to information policy research. *Telecommunications Policy* 10(1): 41–50.

Tremblay, Karine. 2005. Academic mobility and immigration. *Journal of Studies in International Education* 9(3): 196–228.

Tribe, Laurence M. 1973. *Channeling technology through law*. Chicago: Bracton Press.

Tribe, Laurence M. 1985a. Constitutional calculus: Equal justice or economic efficiency? *Harvard Law Review* 98(3): 592–621.

Tribe, Laurence M. 1985b. *Constitutional choices*. Cambridge, MA: Harvard University Press.

Tribe, Laurence H. 1991. The Constitution in cyberspace: Law and liberty beyond the electronic frontier. *The Humanist* 51(5): 15–21.

Triplett, Jack. 1993. Economic concepts for economic classifications. *Survey of Current Business* 73(11): 45–50.

Trolley, Jacqueline, and Jill O'Neill. 2001. The history of citation indexing: From computer printout to web of science. In M. E. Bowden, T. B. Hahn, and R. V. Williams, eds., *Proceedings of the Conference on the History and Heritage of Science Information Systems*, 124–126. Medford, NJ: American Society of Information Science and the Chemical Heritage Foundation.

Tsesis, Alexander. 2002. *Destructive messages: How hate speech paves the way for harmful social movements*. New York: New York University Press.

Tsipis, Kosta, David W. Hafemeister, and Penny Janeway, eds. 1986. *Arms control verification: The technologies that made it possible.* McLean, VA: Pergamon-Brasssey's International Defense Publishers.

Tuchman, Gaye. 1978. *Making news: A study in the construction of reality.* New York: Free Press.

Tufte, Edward R. 1983. *The visual display of quantitative information.* Cheshire, CT: Graphics Press.

Tufte, Edward R. 1990. *Envisioning information.* Cheshire, CT: Graphics Press.

Tugendhat, Michael, and Iain Christie. 2004. *The law of privacy and the media.* New York: Oxford University Press.

Tumin, Melvin M., and Robert Rotberg. 1957. Leaders, the led, and the law: A case study in social change. *Public Opinion Quarterly* 21(3): 355–370.

Tunstall, Jeremy. 1986. *Communication deregulation: The unleashing of America's communications industry.* New York: Basil Blackwell.

Turkle, Sherry. 1995. *Life on the screen: Identity in the age of the Internet.* Cambridge, MA: MIT Press.

Turner, Bryan. 1992. Outline of a theory of citizenship. In Chantal Mouffe, ed., *Dimensions of radical democracy: Pluralism, citizenship, community*, 33–62. London: Verso.

Turner, Kenneth J., Evan H. Magill, and David J. Marples. 2004. *Service provision: Technologies for next generation communications.* New York: Wiley & Sons.

Turner, Ralph H. 1969. The theme of contemporary social movements. *British Journal of Sociology* 20(4): 390–405.

Turnlin, Karen C. 2004. Suspect first: How terrorism policy is reshaping immigration policy. *California Law Review* 92(4): 1176–1240.

Tushnet, Mark. 2003. *The new constitutional order.* Princeton, NJ: Princeton University Press.

Tushnet, Mark. 2005. *A Court divided: The Rehnquist Court and the future of constitutional law.* New York: Norton.

Tuunainen, Juha. 2005. Hybrid practices? Contributions to the debate on the mutation of science and university. *High Education* 50(2): 275–298.

Twynholm, Susi Clare. 2003. *Metadata and Web GIS supporting government initiatives within local authorities.* Newcastle-upon-Tyne: University of Newcastle-upon-Tyne.

Tyndall, Andrew. 1999. Seeing past the wall: Network coverage of Central and Eastern Europe since 1989. *Media Studies Journal* 13(3): 182–188.

Uncapher, Willard. 1991. Trouble in cyberspace: Civil liberties at peril in the information age. *The Humanist* 51(5): 5–14.

UNESCO. 1955. *Trade barriers to knowledge.* Paris: UNESCO.

Unger, Roberto Mangabeira. 1975. *Knowledge and politics.* New York: Free Press.

Urry, John. 1987. Some social and spatial aspects of services. *Environment and Planning D: Society and Space* 5(1): 5–26.

United Nations Centre on Transnational Corporations. 1991. *Creating a favourable legal/economic environment for foreign investment*. New York: United Nations.

U.S. Census Bureau. 2002. *Mapping census 2002: The geography of U.S. diversity*. Washington, DC: U.S. Department of Commerce, Economics and Statistics Administration, Census Bureau.

U.S. Congress, Office of Technology Assessment. 1988. *Science, technology, and the First Amendment*. Washington, DC: Government Printing Office, OTA-CIT-369.

Use of the Carterfone Device in Message Toll Telephone Service, 133 FCC2d 420. 1968.

U.S. Federal Elections Commission. 2001. *Voting systems performance and test standards: An overview*. Washington, DC: Federal Elections Commission.

U.S. Government Accountability Office. 2005. *Federal efforts to improve security and reliability of electronic voting systems are under way, but key activities need to be completed*. Washington, DC: Government Accountability Office, GAO-05-956.

U.S. House of Representatives, Committee on Post Office and Civil Service, Subcommittee on Civil Service. 1989. *Office of Management and Budget Censorship of Federal Employees: Hearing, May 17, 1989*. Washington, DC: Government Printing Office.

U.S. National Bureau of Standards and the Office of the Federal Elections. 1975. *Effective use of computing technology in vote tallying*. Washington, DC: General Accounting Office.

U.S. Office of Personnel Management. 2004. *Citizenship laws of the world*. Washington, DC: Office of Personnel Management.

U.S. Panel on the Impact of National Security Controls on International Technology Transfer, Committee on Science, Engineering, and Public Policy. 1987. *Balancing the national interest: US national security export controls and global economic competition*. Washington, DC: National Academies of Science.

U.S. Patent and Trademark Office. 1946. *The classification of patents*. Washington, DC: Government Printing Office.

U.S. v. Microsoft, 87 F. Supp. 2d 30 (D.D.C.). 2000.

U.S. v. Progressive, 467 F. Supp. 990. 1979.

Vaara, Eero, Janne Tienari, and Risto Saentti. 2003. The international match: Metaphors as vehicles of social identity-building in cross-border mergers. *Human Relations* 56(4): 419–451.

Valetti, Tommaso M., Hoernig Steffen, and Pedro P. Barros. 2002. Universal service and entry: The role of uniform pricing and coverage constraints. *Journal of Regulatory Economics* 21(2): 169–190.

Valk, Barbara G. 1988. *Borderline: A bibliography of the United States-Mexico borderlands*. Los Angeles: UCLA Latin American Studies Program.

van Alstyne, William W. 1995, 1996 supplement. *First Amendment: Cases and materials*. Westbury, NY: The Foundation Press.

Van Creveld, Martin. 1991. *Technology and war: From 2000 BC to the present*, rev. ed. New York: Free Press.

Van den Bulck, Hilde, and Luc Van Poecke. 1996. National language, identity formation and broadcasting: Flanders, the Netherlands and German-speaking Switzerland. *European Journal of Communication* 12(4): 435–458.

van Dijk, Jan A. G. M. 2005. *The deepening divide: Inequality in the information society*. London: Sage.

Van Nostrand, A. D. 1994. A genre map of R&D knowledge production for the U.S. Department of Defense. In Aviva Freedman and Peter Medway, eds., *Genre and the new rhetoric*, 133–145. London: Taylor & Francis.

Vasquez, John A. 1987. The steps to war: Toward a scientific explanation of correlates of war findings. *World Politics* 40(1): 108–145.

Vemeri, Carolyn M. 1999. Can occupational labor shortages be identified using available data? *Monthly Labor Review* 1999(March): 15–21.

Venator Santiago, Charles R. 2001. Race, space, and the Puerto Rican citizenship. *Denver University Law Review* 78(4): 1017–1048.

Verified Voting Foundation. Available at www.verifiedvoting.org.

Vernon, Raymond. 1962. *The international patent system and foreign policy*. Washington, DC: Government Printing Office.

Vernon, Raymond. 1966. International investment and international trade in the product cycle. *The Quarterly Journal of Economics* 80(2): 190–207.

Vernon, Raymond. 1968. Economic sovereignty at bay. *Foreign Affairs* 47(1): 119–120.

Veyne, Paul. 1992. *Bread and circuses: Historical sociology and political pluralism*. New York: Penguin.

Vigoda-Gadot, Eran. 2004. *Citizenship and management in public administration: Integrating behavioral theories and managerial thinking*. Northhampton, MA: Edward Elgar.

Virilio, Paul. 1986. *Speed and politics: An essay on dromology*. New York: Columbia University Press.

Volokh, Eugene. 2003. *The First Amendment: Problems, cases and policy arguments*. New York: Foundation Press.

Volpp, Leti. 2001. "Obnoxious to their very nature": Asian Americans and constitutional citizenship. *Asian Law Journal* 7: 71–88.

von Hippel, Eric. 1988. *The sources of innovation*. New York: Oxford University Press.

von Kries, W. 2002. The demise of the ABM Treaty and the militarization of outer space. *Space Policy* 18(3): 175–178.

Wagner, Peter, Carol H. Weiss, Björn Wittrock, and Hellmut Wollmann, eds. 1991. *Social sciences and modern states: National experiences and theoretical crossroads*. Cambridge: Cambridge University Press.

Waisbrod, Silvio. 1998. When the cart of media is before the horse of identity: Critique of technology-centered views on globalization. *Communication Research* 25(4): 377–398.

Waldman, Marc, Aviel D. Rubin, and Lorrie Faith Cranor. 2000. Publius: A robust, tamper-evident and censorship-resistant Web publishing system. In *Proceedings of the 9th USENIX Security Symposium*, 59–72, August.

Walker, Samuel. 1994. *Hate speech: The history of an American controversy*. Lincoln: University of Nebraska Press.

Wallace, L. 2005. Metadata for information management and retrieval. *Journal of the Society of Archivists* 26(1): 169–171.

Wallerstein, Immanuel. 1980. The states in the institutional vortex of the capitalist world-economy. *International Social Science Research Journal* 32: 743–751.

Wallerstein, Immanuel. 1984. *The politics of the world-economy: The states, the movements, and the civilizations*. Cambridge: Cambridge University Press.

Wallerstein, Immanuel. 1990. Culture as the ideological battleground of the modern world-system. In Mike Featherstone, ed., *Global culture: Nationalism, globalization and modernity*, 31–55. London: Sage.

Wallerstein, Immanuel. 2004. *Open the social sciences: Report of the Gulbenkian Commission on the restructuring of the social sciences*. Stanford, CA: Stanford University Press.

Wallerstein, Immanuel, and Paul Starf. 1971. *The university crisis reader*. New York: Random House.

Wallerstein, Mitchel B. 1991. Controlling dual-use technologies in the new world order. *Issues in Science and Technology* 7(4): 70–77.

Wallerstein, Mitchel B., S. B. Gould, R. Mason, J. C. Derian, H. G. Seipel, K. Ikeda, and C. Herz. 1987. A delicate balance: Scientific communication vs. national security. *Issues in Science and Technology* 4(1): 42–55.

Wallerstein, Robert S. 1988. One psychoanalysis or many? *International Journal of Psychoanalysis* 69(1): 5–21.

Walter, Priscilla A., and Eric H. Sussman. 1993. Protecting commercially developed information on the NREN. *Computer Lawyer* 10(4): 1–11.

Wang, Paul P., and Shi-Kuo Chang, eds. 1980. *Fuzzy sets: Theory and applications to policy analysis and information systems*. New York: Plenum Press.

Wark, Wesley K. 1992. In never-never land? The British archives on intelligence. *The Historical Journal* 35(1): 195–203.

Warner, Harry P. 1953. *Radio and television rights*. Albany, NY: M. Bender.

Warren, Samuel, and Louis D. Brandeis. 1890. The right to privacy. *Harvard Law Review* 4(5): 193–220.

Warschauer, Mark. 2003. *Technology and social inclusion: Rethinking the digital divide*. Cambridge, MA: MIT Press.

Wartenburg, Thomas. 1990. *The forms of power: From domination to transformation*. Philadelphia, PA: Temple University Press.

Watson, Robert P. 2004. *Counting votes: Lessons from the 2000 presidential election in Florida*. Gainesville: University of Florida Press.

Watts, Duncan. 2004. *Small worlds: The dynamics of networks between order and randomness*. Princeton, NJ: Princeton University Press.

Watts, Julie R. 2001. The H-1B visa: Free market solutions for business and labor. *Population Research and Policy Review* 20(1–2): 143–156.

Weare, Christopher. 2002. The Internet and democracy: The causal links between technology and politics. *International Journal of Public Administration* 25(6): 659–692.

Webb, Eugene. 1993. *The self between: From Freud to the new social psychology of France*. Seattle: University of Washington Press.

Weber, Cynthia. 1995. *Simulating sovereignty: Intervention, the state and symbolic exchange*. New York: Cambridge University Press.

Weber, Max. 1946. *From Max Weber: Essays in sociology*, ed. and trans. by C. Wright Mills. New York: Oxford University Press.

Weber, Max. [1947] 1964. *The theory of economic and social organization*, trans. and with an introduction by Talcott Parsons. New York: Free Press.

Weber, Max. 1948. The nation. In *From Max Weber: Essays in sociology*, trans. and ed. by Hans H. Gerth and C. Wright Mills, 171–179. London: Routledge.

Weber, Max. 1964. *The theory of social and economic organization*, trans. by A. M. Henderson and Talcott Parsons, ed. and with an introduction by Talcott Parsons. London: Collier-Macmillan.

Weber, Max. 1968. *Max Weber on charisma and institution building: Selected papers*, ed. by Stuart N. Eisenstadt. Chicago: University of Chicago Press.

Webster, Frank, and Kevin Robins. 1986. *Information technology: A Luddite analysis*. Norwood, NJ: Ablex.

Wei, Shang-Jin. 1996. *Intra-national versus international trade: How stubborn are nations in global integration?* Cambridge, MA: NBER Working Paper No. 5531.

Weibel, Peter. 1996. The world as interface: Toward the construction of context-controlled event worlds. In Timothy Druckrey, ed., *Electronic culture: Technology and visual representation*, 338–351. New York: Aperture.

Weibel, Stuart. 1999. The state of the Dublin Core Metadata Initiative. *D-Lib Magazine* 5(4). Available at www.dlib.org/dlib/april99/04weibel.html.

Weibel, Stuart L., and Traugott Koch. 2000. The Dublin Core Metadata Initiative: Mission, current activities, and future directions. *D-Lib Magazine* 6(12). Available at www.dlib.org/dlib/december00/weibel/12weibel.html.

Weick, Karl E. 1977. Organizational design: Organizations as self-designing systems. *Organizational Dynamics* 6(2): 31–46.

Weingarten, Fred W. 1994. Public interest and the NII. *Communications of the ACM* 37(3): 17–19.

Weiser, Mark. 1991. The computer for the twenty-first century. *Scientific American* 265(3): 94–104.

Weiser, Mark. 1993. Some computer science issues in ubiquitous computing. *Communications of the ACM* 36(7): 75–84.

Wells, Miriam J. 2004. The grassroots reconfiguration of U.S. immigration policy. *International Migration Review* 38(4): 1308–1348.

Welsh, Peter C. 1965. *United States patents, 1790–1870: New uses for old ideas.* Washington, DC: Smithsonian Institution.

Wendt, Alexander. 1987. The agent-structure problem in international relations theory. *International Organization* 41(3): 335–370.

Westerfield, H. Bradford, ed. 1995. *Inside CIA's private world: Declassified articles from the agency's internal journal, 1955–1992.* New Haven, CT: Yale University Press.

Westin, Alan F. 1966. *Privacy in American community life.* Delhi: State University of New York at Delhi Press.

Westin, Alan F., ed. 1971. *Information technology in a democracy.* Cambridge, MA: Harvard University Press.

Westin, Alan F. 1977. *Computers, health records, and citizen rights.* Princeton, NJ: Petrocelli Books.

Westin, Alan F., and Michael A. Baker. 1972. *Databanks in a free society: Computers, record keeping and privacy.* New York: Quadrangle Books.

Westwick, P. J. 2000. Secret science: A classified community in the national laboratories. *Minerva* 39(4): 363–391.

Wheeler, B. R. 2002. Modernist reenchantments II: From aestheticized politics to the artwork. *German Quarterly* 75(2): 113–126.

Whetten, David A., and Paul C. Godfrey. 1998. *Identity in organizations: Building theory through conversations.* Thousand Oaks, CA: Sage.

Whichard, Obie G., and Maria Borga. 2002. Selected issues in the measurement of US international services. *Survey of Current Business* 82(6): 36–56.

White-Smith Music Publishing Company v. Apollo, 209 US 1 (1908).

White, Stuart. 1997. Freedom of association and the right to exclude. *Journal of Political Philosophy* 5(4): 373–391.

Whittier, Nancy. 1997. Political generations, micro-cohorts, and the transformation of social movements. *American Sociological Review* 62(5): 760–778.

Wiegele, Thomas C. 1991. *Biotechnology and international relations: The political dimensions.* Gainesville: University of Florida Press.

Wiener, Norbert. 1960, May. Some moral and technical consequences of automation. *Science* 131: 459–467.

Wildavsky, Aaron. 1987. Choosing preferences by constructing institutions: A cultural theory of preference formation. *American Political Science Review* 8(10): 3–21.

Wilensky, Harold. 1975. *The welfare state and equality*. Berkeley: University of California Press.

Wiley, Richard E. 1984. The end of monopoly: Regulatory change and the promotion of competition. In Harry M. Shooshan III, ed., *Disconnecting Bell: The impact of the AT&T divestiture*, 23–46. New York: Pergamon Press.

Wilford, John Noble. 2000. *The mapmakers*, 2nd ed. New York: Knopf.

Williams, C. 2005. Diplomatic attitudes: From Mabillon to metadata. *Journal of the Society of Archivists* 26(1): 1–24.

Williamson, Oliver E. 1981. The modern corporation: Origins, evolution, attributes. *Journal of Economic Literature* 19(4): 1537–1568.

Wills, Garry. 1978. *Inventing America: Jefferson's Declaration of Independence*. Garden City, NJ: Doubleday.

Wilson, Daniel J. 2005. *Beggar thy neighbor? The in-state vs. out-of-state impact of state R&D tax credits*. San Francisco: Federal Reserve Bank of San Francisco, Working Papers in Applied Economic Theory and Econometrics, 2005-08.

Wilson, Woodrow. [1887] 1955. The study of public administration. Originally published in *Political Science Quarterly* (June 1887); reprinted in 1955. Washington, DC: Public Affairs Press.

Wimmer, Maria A., ed. 2004. *Proceedings of Knowledge Management in Electronic Government*. New York: Springer-Verlag.

Winner, Langdon. 1995. Citizen virtues in a technological order. In Andrew Feenberg and Alastair Hannay, eds., *Technology and the politics of knowledge*, 65–84. Bloomington: Indiana University Press.

Wise, Carol, ed. 1998. *The post-NAFTA political economy: Mexico and the western hemisphere*. State College: Pennsylvania State University Press.

Witt, Elder, ed. 1984. *A different justice: Reagan and the Supreme Court*. Washington, DC: Congressional Quarterly.

Wittrock, Björn. 1991. Social knowledge and public policy: Eight models of interaction. In Peter Wagner, Carol Hirschhorn Weiss, Björn Wittrock, and Hellmut Wollman, eds., *Social sciences and modern states: National experiences and theoretical crossroads*, 333–354. Cambridge: Cambridge University Press.

Wittrock, Björn, and Peter Wagner. 1990. Social science and state developments: The structuration of discourse in the social sciences. In Stephen Brooks and Alain-G. Gagnon, eds., *Social scientists, policy, and the state*, 113–138. New York: Praeger.

Wolfe, Christopher. 1981. A theory of U.S. constitutional history. *Journal of Politics* 42(2): 292–316.

Wolfson, Ouri, Bo Xu, Liqin Jiang, and Sam Chamberlain. 1998. Moving objects databases: Issues and solutions. *Proceedings of the 10th International Conference on Scientific and Statistical Database Management*, 111–122. Washington, DC: IEEE Computer Society.

Wollard, C. C., and J. J. Herrero. 2004. An information system to exploit the use of metadata with film and television post-production. *SMPTE Motion Imaging Journal* 114(1): 44–52.

Woollard, Christopher C., and Juan J. Herrero. 2005. An information system to exploit the use of metadata within film and television production. *SMPTE Motion Imaging Journal* 114(1): 44–52.

Wood, Andrew F., and Matthew J. Smith. 2005. *Online communication: Linking technology, identity, and culture*. Mahwah, NJ: Lawrence Erlbaum Associates.

Wood, Laurence I. 1942. *Patents and antitrust law*. New York: Commerce Clearing House.

Woolgar, Steven. 1991. The turn to technology in social studies of science. *Science, Technology & Human Values* 16(1): 20–51.

Wright, Gavin. 1997. Towards a more historical approach to technological change. *The Economic Journal* 107(444): 1560–1566.

Wright, John K., Lloyd A. Jones, Leonard Stone, and T. W. Birch. 1938. *Notes on statistical mapping: With special reference to the mapping of population phenomena*. New York: American Geographical Society/Population Association of America.

Wright, R. George. 2000. Hermeneutics and critique in legal practice: Traces of violence—Gadamer, Habermas, and the hate speech problem. *Chicago-Kent Law Review* 76(2): 991–1014.

Wright, Sue, ed. 2004. *Language policy and language planning: From nationalism to globalisation*. Houndsmills, UK: Palgrave Macmillan.

Wriston, Walter B. 1992. *The twilight of sovereignty*. New York: Charles Scribner's Sons.

Wrong, Dennis H. 1995. *Power, its forms, bases and uses*, 2nd ed. New Brunswick, NJ: Transaction Publishers.

Wuthnow, Robert. 1980. The world-economy and the institutionalization of science in seventeenth-century Europe. In Albert Bergesen, ed., *Studies of the modern world-system*, 25–55. New York: Academic Press.

Wuthnow, Robert. 1987. *Meaning and moral order: Explorations in cultural analysis*. Berkeley: University of California Press.

Xavier, Patrick. 2003. Should broadband be part of universal service obligations? *Info* 5(1): 8–25.

Yang, Elizabeth M., and Kristi Gaines. 2004. Voting technology and the law: From chads to fads and somewhere in between. *Social Education* 68(6): 401–407.

Yates, Francis A. 1966. *The art of memory*. Chicago: University of Chicago Press.

Yates, JoAnne. 1991. Investing in information: Supply and demand forces in the use of information in American firms, 1850–1920. In Peter Temin, ed., *Inside the business enterprise: Historical perspectives on the use of information*, 117–154. Chicago: University of Chicago Press.

Yeatman, Anna. 1994. *Postmodern revisionings of the political.* New York: Routledge.

Yuan, Jing-Dong. 1995. The politics of the strategic triangle: The U.S., COCOM, and export controls in China, 1979–1989. *Journal of Northeast Asian Studies* 14(1): 47–80.

Yuan, Yu, Janet Fulk, Michelle Shumate, Peter R. Monge, J. Alison Bryant, and Matthew Matsaganis. 2005. Individual participation in organizational information commons: The impact of team level social influence and technology-specific competence. *Human Communication Research* 31(2): 212–240.

Zander, Ivo, and Orjan Solvell. 2000. Cross-border innovation in the multinational corporation. *International Studies of Management & Organization* 30(2): 44–67.

Zaretsky, Eli. 2004. *Secrets of the soul: A social and cultural history of psychoanalysis.* New York: Knopf.

Zavodny, Madeline. 2003. The H-1B program and its effects on information technology workers. *Federal Reserve Bank of Atlanta Economic Review* 88(3): 33–43.

Zaye, D. F., W. V. Metanomski, and A. J. Beach. 1985. A history of general subject indexing at Chemical Abstracts Service. *Journal of Chemical Information and Computer Science* 25(4): 392–399.

Zelden, Charles L. 2002. *Voting rights on trial: A handbook with caess, laws, and documents.* Santa Barbara, CA: ABC-CLIO.

Zelezny, John D. 2004. *Communications law: Liberties, restraints, and the modern media*, 4th ed. New York: Wadsworth.

Zelizer, Barbie. 1992. *Covering the body: The Kennedy assassination, the media, and the shaping of collective memory.* Chicago: University of Chicago Press.

Zenger, John Peter, and Vincent Buranelli. 1957. *The trial of Peter Zenger.* New York: New York University Press.

Zerbe, Noah. 2005. Biodiversity, ownership, and indigenous knowledge: Exploring legal frameworks for community, farmers, and intellectual property rights in Africa. *Ecological Economics* 53(4): 493–506.

Zhang, J., and A. Dimitroff. 2004. Internet search engines' response to metadata Dublin Core implementation. *Journal of Information Science* 30(4): 310–320.

Zhao, Dingxin. 1998. Ecologies of social movements: Student mobilization during the 1989 prodemocracy movement in Beijing. *American Journal of Sociology* 103(6): 1493–1529.

Zittrain, Jonathan. 2005. *Technological complements to copyright.* New York: Foundation Press.

Zolberg, Aristide. 1980. Strategic interactions and the formation of modern states: France and England. *International Social Science Journal* 32: 687–716.

Zúñiga, Gloria L. 2001. Ontology: Its transformation from philosophy to information systems. *Proceedings of the International Conference on Formal Ontology in Information Systems* 2001: 187–197.

Zurkowski, Paul G. 1989. *The republic of information: The emerging Soviet information industry*. Chevy Chase, MD: Ventures in Information.

Zwick, Detlev, and Nikhilesh Dholakia. 2004. Whose identity is it anyway? Consumer representation in the age of database marketing. *Journal of Macromarketing* 24(1): 31–43.

Index

Printed in the United States
by Baker & Taylor Publisher Services